SAP® Netweaver AS ABAP System Administration

Frank Föse, Sigrid Hagemann, Liane Will

# SAP® NetWeaver AS ABAP System Administration

SAP system administration fundamentals

Bonn • Boston

**ISBN 978-1-59229-174-8**



1st Edition 2009

German Edition first published 2008 by Galileo Press, Bonn, Germany.

Galileo Press is named after the Italian physicist, mathematician and philosopher Galileo Galilei (1564–1642). He is known as one of the founders of modern science and an advocate of our contemporary, heliocentric worldview. His words *Eppur si muove* (And yet it moves) have become legendary. The Galileo Press logo depicts Jupiter orbited by the four Galilean moons, which were discovered by Galileo in 1610.

**Editor** Mirja Werner
**English Edition Editor** Jutta VanStean
**Translation** Lemoine International, Inc., Salt Lake City UT
**Copy Editor** Julie McNamee
**Cover Design** Tyler Creative
**Layout Design** Vera Brauner
**Production** Iris Warkus
**Typesetting** Publishers' Design and Production Services, Inc.
**Printed and bound in** Canada

# Contents at a Glance

# Contents

# Foreword

An important priority of SAP AG is to enable you to operate SAP software solutions in your enterprise successfully and at the lowest cost possible. You can achieve this "lowest cost of ownership" by implementing the software efficiently and quickly and by making your production operations optimized and secure. SAP Active Global Support provides you with powerful, targeted support in this regard within the framework of SAP's defined standards for end-to-end solution operations. Throughout the entire lifecycle of a solution, SAP provides customers with the services they require, first-class support, the appropriate infrastructure, and the relevant know-how. This strategy is supported by the powerful Premium Support program.

The main focus of this book is on communicating knowledge. It provides you with a detailed overview of the technical aspects and concepts for the management of SAP software solutions.

Regardless of whether you are just getting started in SAP system management or you want further qualification, you will benefit from the authors' practical experience and the first-hand information they provide. Also, with this book, SAP wants to help you independently prepare for the examination to become a Certified Technical Consultant. However, note that books are not a substitute for your own experience with the various SAP solutions. Another benefit of this book is that the authors give you recommendations for your daily work with the software.

The innovations of SAP solutions are a constant source of new challenges — and their solutions — for system managers, too. This has an effect on the requirements of customers' in-house support organizations and external support organizations. The skills and know-how of these organizations can significantly contribute to averting difficulties with using the software, which is why communicating troubleshooting skills is one of the main aims of this book. Even in these Internet-dominated times, books are still an ideal medium for imparting knowledge in a compact format. Their content is also an enhancement to the new service and support platform, the SAP Solution Manager and the new services that SAP offers.

**Gerhard Oswald**
Member of the Board of SAP AG

**Uwe Hommel**
Executive Vice President of SAP AG
SAP Active Global Support

*I certainly cannot say whether it would be better if things were different; but what I can say is that things must be different if they are to be good.*
*—Georg Christoph Lichtenberg (1742-1799),*
*German aphorist and physicist*

# Acknowledgments

It is finally done: the third edition of this book is finished and ready for printing. Behind me lie several months of research, testing, and discussion, but it has been worth it. And I mean "worth it" in many senses. For one thing, I have been able to play a leading role in creating a book on a topic — system administration — that I became properly familiar with only after many years of training. In a personal sense, too, writing this book has been a rewarding challenge. To write a book means spending weeks and months on one single topic and resisting the inner demon that is always ready to distract one with lots of other "interesting" things — not an easy task. Luckily, our editors, Mirja Werner and Florian Zimniak, are intimately acquainted with these phenomena, and always gave us good advice and the push we needed to keep on the right track. For this, we thank them.

I also hope that this book will prove worthwhile for you, the reader. Whether you are taking your first steps in system administration, or you are an old hand who has already handled more than one worst-case scenario, my co-authors and I would be very pleased if you find yourself saying "Oh, so that's how that works" from time to time as you read through this book.

When it comes to SAP NetWeaver AS ABAP, you will doubtless encounter much material that you are already familiar with. Nonetheless, there are still many other exciting new additions for you to discover and, eventually, use.

All of the information, statements, menu paths, and screenshots in this book are based on SAP NetWeaver AS ABAP, Basis Releases 7.00 and 7.10. New releases are certain to be different from these, so be sure to take this into account in your work.

When it comes to thanks, I would particularly like to express my gratitude to my co-authors Liane Will, who was always ready to listen to my queries and provided me with extremely helpful feedback, and Sigrid Hagemann.

I would also like to thank my manager Stefan Schnadt, who gave me the freedom I needed to bring this project to completion.

Nor would I wish to forget the many colleagues who provided me with valuable tips and helped me to keep the goal of this book in sight. Lastly, I want to thank my wife for her understanding. Although I was physically present at home, she still spent many weekends alone while I was, yet again, busy working on this book.

As for you, the reader, I hope that you embrace the challenges that the new functionalities of SAP NetWeaver AS ABAP present to you, and that you benefit greatly from the exciting new possibilities!

**Kind regards,**
**Frank Föse**

# Introduction

With more than 121,000 installations in more than 120 countries, SAP's market penetration is unparalleled in the business world, and SAP software has become the de facto standard among business applications.

SAP's Basis technology has played a significant role in this development, and this technology is now also used in other components in the SAP solution range. *SAP NetWeaver Application Server ABAP* and *SAP NetWeaver Application Server* Java serve as the technological foundation of the SAP platform.

For simplicity, in this book, we often use the term *SAP system* in the context of administrative activities, even though a similar or identical version of the underlying technology can also be used in an SAP NetWeaver BI or SAP CRM system.

**Goal of This Book**

This book is not intended to replace the documentation that comes with the SAP system, and it doesn't provide complete functional descriptions of tools. Rather, it presents a holistic view of practical processes and approaches in the context of a description of the concepts to help you understand the subject matter.

We also touch on the administrative peculiarities that arise from the addition of a Java-based environment to SAP NetWeaver (SAP NetWeaver AS Java).

**Content**

**Chapter 1**, *Architecture of SAP NetWeaver Application Server ABAP*, deals with the basics of the SAP architecture. It looks at the technical implementation of the client/server architecture in SAP applications and introduces you to the main terminology of the SAP world.

In **Chapter 2**, *Process Concept of SAP NetWeaver Application Server ABAP*, you'll become familiar with the various concepts behind the SAP process types. We also deal with background processing, such as the posting concept and the lock concept in SAP NetWeaver.

After you' have become familiar with the basic concepts in the first two chapters, **Chapter 3**, *Getting Started*, explains the underlying administrative tasks and the tools you need to perform them. One of the most important tasks of an SAP system administrator is *Setting Up the System Landscape*, which is the subject of **Chapter 4**.

The client concept in SAP is one of the key pillars of the application. In **Chapter 5**, *Client Administration*, we look at client maintenance from the Basis administration viewpoint, in particular the various copy and transport options and the changeability settings.

Both **Chapter 4**, *Setting Up the System Landscape*, and **Chapter 6**, *Software Logistics*, describe the architecture and usage of the Transport Management System (TMS). Whereas the structure of a system landscape and the central administration of the transport settings are the subjects of Chapter 4, Chapter 6 deals with transports in software logistics. The TMS is required to process these transports. This chapter also deals with importing support packages and add-ons. This use of the Change and Transport System (CMS) applies in every installation.

**Chapter 7**, *Maintaining Instances*, deals with the administration and maintenance of SAP NetWeaver parameters. You can adapt the SAP system to changing user requirements by defining operation modes. This chapter also explains how load balancing between instances for dialog users and load balancing for RFCs are handled.

**Chapter 8**, *SAP Users and Authorizations*, looks at the subject of defining SAP users, and the authorization concept in SAP NetWeaver. Besides the basic principles, such as authorization objects, individual authorizations, and roles, this chapter also deals with concepts such as central user administration and cooperation with directory services.

The subject of **Chapter 9**, *System Monitoring*, is the monitoring and analysis tools used by system administrators. This chapter also goes into greater detail on how tools that you are already familiar with are used. Lastly, it deals with monitoring the integrated ITS and ICM.

**Chapter 10**, *Tools for Creating and Analyzing ABAP Programs*, takes a detailed look at the new functions of established developer tools, such as the ABAP Editor and the ABAP Debugger, and describes how you can use these tools. It also presents additional tools that you can use to analyze applications from different viewpoints, such as performance.

**Chapter 11**, *Monitoring Architecture*, introduces you to the structure, configuration, and usage options of the monitoring architecture, which is an important component of the Computing Center Management System (CCMS) in all SAP Basis systems.

As data quantities increase so does administration work. However, because a lot of data becomes obsolete and, after a certain time period, no longer needs to be accessed directly, *Data Archiving* as described in **Chapter 12** can be used to move data from the SAP database to an external storage location.

In **Chapter 13**, *Data Distribution and Transfer*, we first describe the important communication method known as Remote Function Call (RFC), which is also used as a basic technique for implementing distributed business processes (Application Link Enabling [ALE]). Also, this chapter describes the basics of the batch input procedure, which is a method of quickly transferring data to an SAP system.

**Chapter 14**, *Installation Concepts*, describes the procedure for installing an SAP NetWeaver system. This chapter deals with preparatory and post-processing tasks, the `SAPinst` installation tool, and troubleshooting.

Finally, **Chapter 15**, *Service and Support*, deals with the SAP Support services that are available to you as a customer. It also explains how you can connect your systems to the support systems of SAP AG to use the services you require.

**Notes on the Text**

You can access most of the actions referred to in this book by means of menu paths or by entering transaction codes. This type of action is indicated in the text as an expression, for example, Event Maintenance (SM62). The "Transactions and Menu Paths" section of every chapter explains the expressions used in that chapter. For example:

**Event Maintenance:** SAP Menu • Tools • CCMS • Jobs • Maintain Event (SM62).

Also, the "Tools" and "SAP Notes" sections contain additional sources of information. These are located in the SAP Service Marketplace at *http://service.sap.com*.

If there are differences between the system attributes on the various operating system platforms, all of the UNIX derivatives for which the component in question is released are always grouped together under the term *UNIX*, and likewise, *Windows NT* indicates all of the current releases of a Microsoft operating system that are used for SAP solutions. For a complete release matrix of the permitted combinations of operating system, database, and SAP component, see the SAP Service Marketplace under the quick link */pam* (Product Availability Matrix).

*SAP's Basis technology, for a long time known only as "R/3 Basis," has proven itself as a platform, thanks to its high-performance architecture. Consequently, SAP NetWeaver Application Server (AS) ABAP is not just the Basis component of ECC 6.0; it also fulfills this role for SAP components that have a similar structure, for example, SAP SCM, SAP SRM, or SAP CRM.*

# 1 Architecture of SAP NetWeaver Application Server ABAP

The underlying technology for SAP components is predicated on the multitier client/server architecture. In the following sections, you'll learn how this concept provides a reliable, flexible, and scalable basis for operating complex systems.

First, we'll consider the areas an SAP system administrator needs to influence to ensure that the application runs smoothly. The following sections cover different aspects of system administration, the basis of which is established by the architecture.

## 1.1 Components of SAP NetWeaver AS ABAP

SAP NetWeaver Application Server (also known as SAP NetWeaver AS and previously SAP Web AS up to Release 6.40) represents the underlying technological basis for each SAP component. SAP NetWeaver AS supports applications developed in the established and stable programming language ABAP as well as applications developed in Java. Therefore, SAP NetWeaver AS is no longer only the technical basis for SAP applications; it can also be used as the development platform for non-SAP applications.

Depending on the demands to be placed on SAP NetWeaver AS, you can install it on different instances. Figure 1.1 provides an overview of the different installation options available.

This book concentrates on the administration tasks concerning SAP NetWeaver AS ABAP. For clarity, we won't discuss similar administration activities for AS Java, because they are beyond the scope of this book.

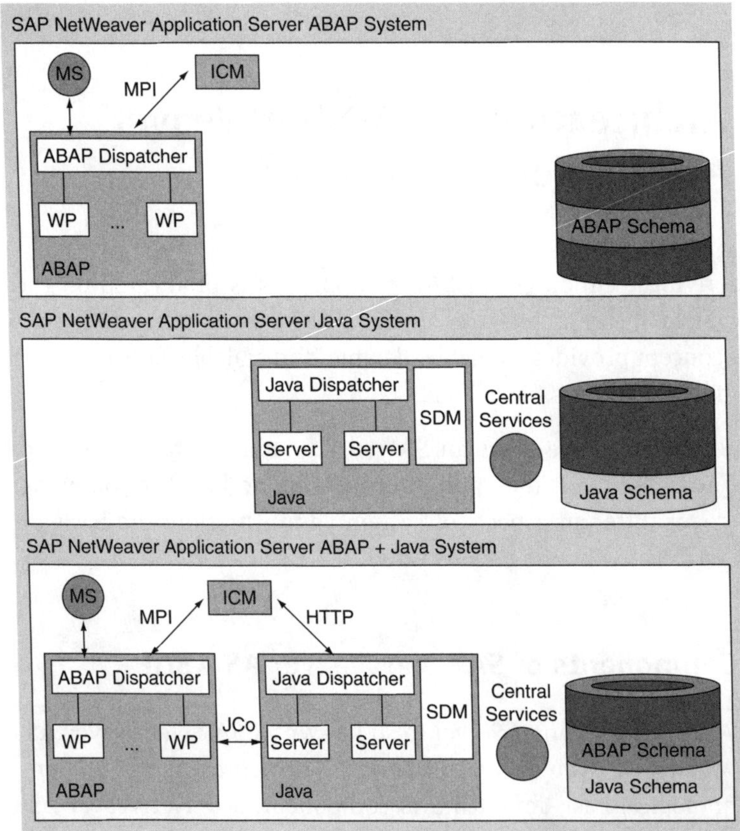


**Figure 1.1** Installation Options for SAP NetWeaver AS

**Installation options**

Three installation options are available:

- **SAP NetWeaver AS ABAP**
  This provides a complete infrastructure in which ABAP-based applications can be developed and used.

- **SAP NetWeaver AS Java**
  This provides a complete infrastructure in which J2EE-based applications can be developed and used.
- **SAP NetWeaver AS ABAP + Java (Double Stack)**
  This provides a complete infrastructure in which ABAP-based and J2EE-based applications can be developed and used. This installation focuses on seamless Java/ABAP integration.

One of the key characteristics of SAP NetWeaver AS is the fact that ABAP tables, programs, and application data are saved in the ABAP schema of the database, whereas Java data is saved in the Java schema. Therefore, the ABAP runtime environment can access the ABAP schema of the database, and the Java runtime environment can access the Java schema. The *SAP Java Connector* (JCo) facilitates integration between the ABAP and Java environments.

## 1.2 Client/Server Architecture in SAP NetWeaver

From a software perspective, we distinguish between the following layers in a three-tier client/server architecture:

- Presentation
- Application
- Database

Hardware implementation can move between the following two extremes: "all components on one host" and "one host for each instance in a layer." When determining the best variant, you must consider the planned system usage alongside the requirements for availability and performance (see Figure 1.2).

Operating all three layers of the client/server architecture on one host is only suitable for demonstration or test purposes.

Two-level configuration

Smaller SAP systems are frequently operated in one central configuration with a separate presentation layer (see Figure 1.2). The database and application run together on one server, and PCs or other workstations are used for the frontend systems. This two-level configuration is frequently used for development or test systems, but also for smaller productive systems.

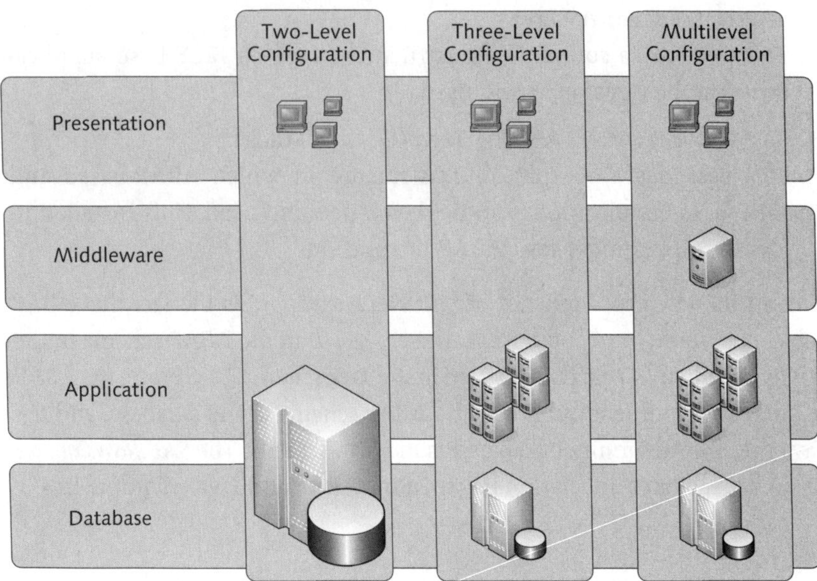


**Figure 1.2** Configuration Variants

**Three-level configuration**

If a two-level configuration no longer satisfies user requirements, then the database server and application server are separated. The SAP software architecture allows the application layer to be distributed across several *instances*, which can also be operated on separate hosts. This results in a highly scalable SAP NetWeaver AS (*horizontal scalability*) whose boundaries are currently set by the database server. Although some database manufacturers also offer concepts here for distributing the database instance across several physical hardware nodes, this is currently not possible for other database systems. Therefore, the database instance represents the smallest, nondivisible component. In benchmarks, several thousand SAP users could be simulated concurrently in three-tier configurations. From a system administration perspective, however, the administration effort increases with each additional host.

A general decision concerning the hardware architecture should be made in the early phases of implementing an SAP system. Afterwards, the system administrator makes optimal adjustments to the system so that it meets the requirements of SAP users but still remains within the initial specifications. If, while using the SAP system productively for the first time, the architecture chosen at the outset is found to be inadequate and can't be adjusted sufficiently, this results in higher costs and an additional organizational effort.

The software implementation discussed next is the basis for the hardware variants described previously.

**Multilevel configuration**

For certain application scenarios, it's possible and sometimes also necessary to insert another layer (known as *middleware*) between the presentation layer and the application layer. For example, in certain CRM scenarios, middleware is required to control the exchange of data between a mobile frontend (e.g., a PDA) and the CRM system.

**Presentation**

The presentation layer is important because it's the main tool of standard SAP users who use the business functions. From an SAP perspective, the presentation layer conceals the SAP GUI (*SAP Graphical User Interface*). The SAP GUI accepts user input and communicates with the application layer in which the requests are processed. Conversely, it accepts the data from the application layer and converts it to a user-friendly format. A SAP GUI is used to execute most SAP sessions. The technical implementation of the SAP GUI itself is a process that is executed at the operating system level on the frontend.

You can also use a browser to display the user interface. To do this, the screens must be converted into a browser-compatible format in the ITS (*Internet Transaction Server*), which has been an integral part of the system since SAP Web AS 6.40.

As system landscapes become more and more complex, it can quickly become unmanageable to display different development, test, and production systems in the SAP GUI. As a result, the functionalities of SAP NetWeaver Portal are frequently used because, apart from its numerous additional functions, the portal also uses a Web user interface to access the different functions of the SAP systems connected to it. Consequently, the system is more transparent and user friendly.

**Application layer**

The application layer in SAP NetWeaver AS transfers the user requirements from the presentation layer and then performs the actual calculations, analyses, and so on. The database layer requests the necessary data. New, incoming data is processed and forwarded to the database.

The application layer is the distributing center of an SAP system. Therefore, the application layer is one of the main areas that an SAP system administrator must influence. The tools for SAP system administration are almost fully integrated into SAP.

Since SAP Web AS Release 6.40, the application layer also contains an integrated ITS that is used to display the user interface through a browser.

Instance

An SAP instance is a group of processes with appropriate, shared memory areas that are controlled by a dispatcher process and access the same database. The application layer of an SAP system may comprise one or more instances. The terms *application server* and *instance* are used synonymously. One of the tasks of the system administrator is to also configure the number and type of instance processes to achieve the highest possible performance using the least possible resources.

Database

An RDBMS (*Relational Database Management System*) is used in the database layer. The SQL interface is used to exchange data between the application processes and the RDBMS. In almost all cases, SAP system data is held in one database on one host. However, you also have the option of using parallel databases or implementing one database for several SAP systems.

The following general database administration tasks also form part of SAP system administration:

- Software installation and maintenance
- Configuration
- Flow control and optimization
- Memory space administration
- Database backups and data recovery in the event of an error
- Dataset reorganization

The SAP software delivery comprises not only the tools already integrated into the software but also special tools for use on the database server.

If the database and application layer are distributed across at least two hosts, this is known as a *distributed system*.

SID

The SID (*System Identifier*) is the name of your SAP system. You determine the SID when you install an SAP system. You can choose almost any SID apart from the following: ADD, ALL, AND, ANY, ASC, COM, DBA, END, EPS, FOR, GID, IBM, INT, KEY, LOG, MON, NIX, NOT, OFF, OMS, RAW, ROW, SAP, SET, SGA, SHG, SID, SQL, SYS, TMP, UID, USR, and VAR.

Note the SIDs permitted for each installation, which are listed in the installation manual available for each release. The SID should satisfy the following requirements:

- Must be unique within your entire system landscape
- Must have exactly three alphanumeric characters
- Must use a letter as the first character
- Must use only capital letters

Generally, the abbreviation "SID" (*System Identifier*) is used as a placeholder for SAP system names. Sometimes "SAPSID" (*SAP System Identifier*) is also used. In contrast, "DBSID" (Database Identifier) also exists. Both identifiers can differ within an installed SAP system. However, for the sake of clarity and ease of administration, we recommend that you use identical values for SAPSID and DBSID when you install an SAP system.

One exception is the installation of an MCOD system (*Multiple Components in one Database*). Here, several systems use exactly the same database simultaneously, which inevitably results in different SAPSIDs and DBSIDs.

Network

The network technologies commonly used today are deployed between the layers distributed across different hosts and, if necessary, within the layers. They are also used to connect the SAP system to the outside world. TCP/IP is used as the transport protocol. The volume of data transferred between the frontend in a presentation layer and an application server for each dialog step is so low that a WAN connection can be used without any difficulty between the presentation hosts and the application servers. However, you can't use it for communication between the database server and the application server.

The SNA protocol (*Systems Network Architecture*) LU6.2 from IBM can be used to connect an SAP system to the mainframe world.

## 1.3 Access over the Internet

**Internet Communication Framework**

To enable you to use the Internet to communicate directly with SAP NetWeaver AS (HTTP, HTTPS, or SMTP — all of which are known as HTTP requests), NetWeaver AS provides the *Internet Communication Framework* (ICF), which is an integral part of the SAP NetWeaver AS kernel. The ICF provides the following functions:

- Incoming HTTP *requests* from a client (e.g., a browser) are received and processed.
- The ICF forwards the request to one or more ABAP programs, which are used to gather and provide the data required.
- The ICF then returns the data (as a *response*) to the client requesting the data (e.g., the browser) for further processing (e.g., to display the data).

Therefore, the ICF provides the infrastructure for using an SAP work process to process HTTP requests (both as a server role and client role). In its server role, the ICF server provides special services that can be called by an HTTP request. This service contains one or more HTTP request handlers, which are responsible for executing the ABAP functions (see Figure 1.3).

If, however, the ICF works in its client role, a corresponding request is created and forwarded via the ICF to a Web server outside the system for further processing. This may be another SAP system or any Web server that provides the requested service.

In SAP, the corresponding ICF services are implemented for many standard services. However, you can define separate request handlers and services any time and, therefore, use the ICF for your own applications.

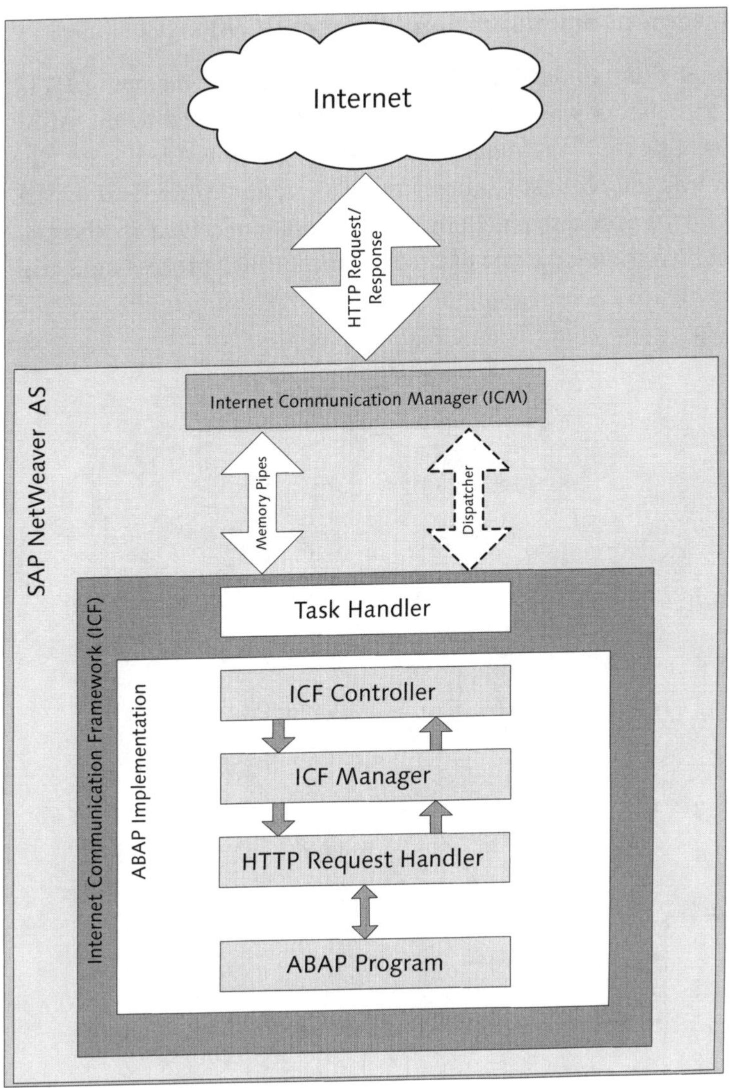


**Figure 1.3** Simplified ICF Architecture

Since SAP Web AS Release 6.40, the *Internet Transaction Server* (ITS) is represented as an ICF service. Here, it's known as an *integrated ITS*. Previously, the ITS was implemented as a standalone software component known as the *external ITS*. Its usage and functions are described in more detail in Section 1.3.2, "Integrated Internet Transaction Server (ITS)."

**Internet Transaction Server**

### 1.3.1 Internet Communication Manager (ICM)

The Internet Communication Manager (ICM) accepts incoming HTTP requests and checks whether these should be transferred to the ABAP stack or Java stack. If the request is transferred to the ABAP stack, the ICM forwards the request to the Internet Communication Framework (ICF) for further processing. Here, the request is received by the task handler, which is already part of the ICF, and further processing is triggered (see Figure 1.4).

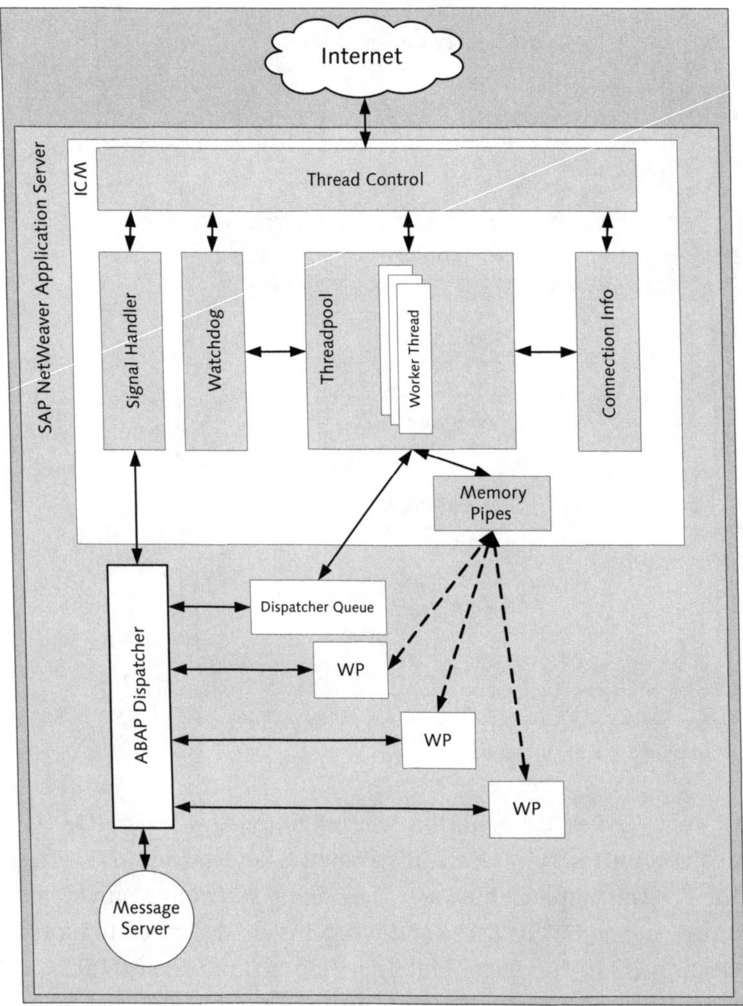


**Figure 1.4** Simplified Inner Structure of the ICM

The ICM is implemented as a standalone process (icman) in the operating system. The dispatcher of an instance (see Section 1.5) starts and monitors this process. The profile parameter of the instance profile (see Section 7.1, "Profile Maintenance") can be used to control whether the ICM process is activated at all. If it is, the profile parameter can also control the configuration used.

Figure 1.4 describes the inner structure of the ICM process. Threads are used to parallelize the load incurred. Threads

The following threads are used:

- **Thread Control**
  This thread accepts the incoming TCP/IP requests and creates (or wakes) a worker thread from the thread pool to process the request.
- **Worker Thread**
  This thread handles connection requests and responses. A worker thread contains an I/O handler for the network input and output as well as various plug-ins for the different supported protocols.
- **Watchdog**
  A worker thread generally waits for a response (irrespective of whether it's a client or server thread). If a timeout occurs, the watchdog assumes the task of waiting for the response. Therefore, the worker thread can be used again for other requests.
- **Signal Handler**
  The signal handler processes signals sent by the operating system or another process (e.g., the ABAP Dispatcher).
- **Connection Info**
  This thread contains a table with information about each network connection that exists.
- **Memory Pipes**
  These memory-based communication objects are used to transfer data between the ICM and the ABAP work processes.

**Important ICM Profile Parameters**

- `exe/icman`: Name and path of the ICM executable.
- `rdisp/start_icman`: Determines whether the ICM process of the instance should be started.

Provided that you have activated the ICM and connected your SAP system through a browser, you can perform a simple test to determine whether the connection is technically correct. The ICF provides a ping service, which you can use to check the connection between a browser and your SAP system.

Ping service

First, you must activate the ping service by calling Transaction SICF in your system. On the next selection screen, enter the value "SERVICE" in the **Hierarchy Type** field and display the relevant hierarchy tree (**Execute** button or the [F8] function key). On the left side of the screen, scroll down the hierarchy until you reach **default_host/sap/bc** (see Figure 1.5).

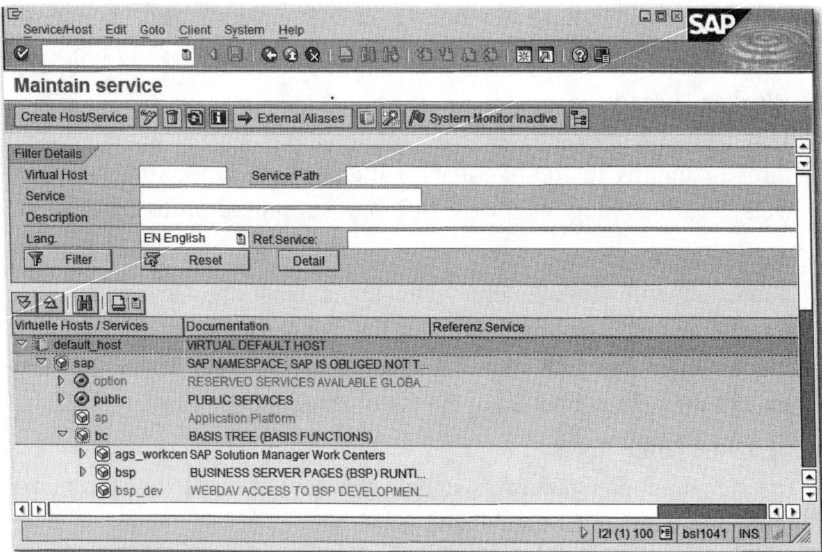


**Figure 1.5** ICF Service Tree

Under the **default_host/sap/bc** node, locate the **ping** service. This is generally colored gray (inactive). Right-click the **ping** service, and select **Activate service** from the context menu. Select **Yes** to confirm the prompt asking you if you really want to activate this service. The service is now colored black to indicate that it has been activated.

Now open a browser, and enter the following URL:

*http://<server>:<HTTP port>/sap/bc/ping*

If you don't know which server name and port to use, choose the **Information about the Port and Host** button on the display screen of the service tree or use the key combination [CTRL] + [SHIFT] + [F12]; the server and port to be used is displayed for each supported protocol.

You're then prompted to specify a valid SAP user (who should have sufficient authorization). Figure 1.6 shows the screen output for a successful test where Internet Explorer was used as a browser.

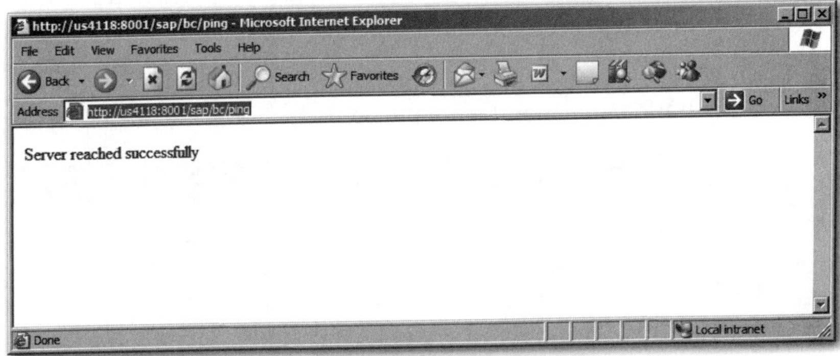


**Figure 1.6** Successful Test

This simple test proves that the ICM process can accept HTTP requests from a browser and correctly forward these to the relevant ICF service for further processing, thus ensuring that the infrastructure has been set up correctly and works properly.

### 1.3.2 Integrated Internet Transaction Server (ITS)

Tasks

The ITS fulfills the following tasks:

- Automatic conversion of SAP screens for use with the SAP GUI for HTML
- Provision of a web display for business processes through screen-based Internet application components (IACs) using predefined HTML displays for selected transactions

As mentioned earlier, the ITS has been an integral part of the kernel since SAP Web AS Release 6.40 and is represented as an ICF service. For this reason, this ITS variant is also known as an *internal ITS*.

The browser uses the ICM to communicate directly with the internal ITS. Therefore, you no longer require an additional Web server for publishing templates and MIME files. These files are now stored in the database of NetWeaver AS. This has several advantages, for example:

Advantages

- You no longer require a separate Web server and ITS server. The overall cost (TCO, *Total Cost of Ownership*) is reduced as a result of a lower administration and maintenance effort.
- For the first time, the ITS is available on all platforms released for SAP NetWeaver AS, which significantly enhances the platform matrix.
- The administrator no longer requires any special administration tools for configuration and monitoring purposes.

**Important Parameters for the Integrated ITS**

- `itsp/enable`: This activates (1) or deactivates (0) the integrated ITS.
- `em/global_area_MB`: Specific memory area used extensively by the internal ITS. For information about the correct ITS configuration, see SAP Note 742048.

### 1.3.3 Standalone Internet Transaction Server

SAP ITS 6.20 was the last available release of the standalone Internet Transaction Server (also known as the *external ITS*). You can no longer use this release to connect to SAP NetWeaver 2004s (7.00)-based systems (and higher). If you use SAP NetWeaver 7.0 (NetWeaver 2004s), you must use the integrated ITS to operate all ITS-based applications. For this reason, you may have to migrate some existing ITS applications because the integrated ITS no longer supports ITS FlowLogic, for example.

Because the external ITS will no longer be used in the near future, we won't discuss its architecture or functions here.

**Important SAP Notes for the ITS**

- 709038 – SAP Integrated ITS
- 197745 – Maintenance strategy for ITS
- 325616 – Platform matrix for ITS

## 1.4 Presentation Layer

The SAP presentation layer represents the user interface. From the user profile, the SAP system administrator, and the business economist through to the executive board, many different demands are placed on the user interface, for example:

- User-friendly, ergonomic design
- Personalization options
- Easy to manage
- Flexible, location-independent access
- Multilingual capability
- Portability between different hardware systems and operating systems that have the same scope of functions and layout

The SAP GUI fulfills these requirements on a different technical basis.

SAP GUI

The SAP GUI implements a single system/single task work environment. This means that the SAP GUI software must be installed for each system on which it's to be used and, after you start it, the SAP GUI then runs as a single task on this host. When a SAP GUI is executed, the user specifies the SAP system that he wants to access as a parameter. On Windows operating systems, a corresponding program icon can be defined for this program call. The SAP GUI is mouse controlled or menu controlled. To fulfill their work tasks, users navigate through the menus and, therefore, work sequentially. If work steps are to be executed in parallel, users can start another SAP GUI or a new window (*session*) for a SAP GUI that is already active. In terms of its technical processes, a new session corresponds, for the most part, to another SAP GUI.

SAPLOGON

Generally, the user wants to access more than one SAP system without having to save a desktop icon for each system. The `SAPLOGON` program makes it possible to define all required SAP GUI connections either indirectly by using an easily replaceable configuration file or directly by adjusting `SAPLOGON`. If you want to start a SAP GUI connection, you just select the relevant system entry from the list of all known connections.

The SAP GUI interface is based on the guidelines for the Windows style guides. Furthermore, it comprises the findings summarized in the standards EG 90/270 and ISO 9241 concerning the ergonomic usability of interfaces.

SAP GUI variants

Different SAP GUI implementations (see Figure 1.7) are provided to support different frontend hardware:

- **SAP GUI for the Windows Environment**
  The following platforms are supported:
  - Windows 98, Windows NT4, Windows 2000, and Windows XP
  - Older versions of Windows through a terminal server

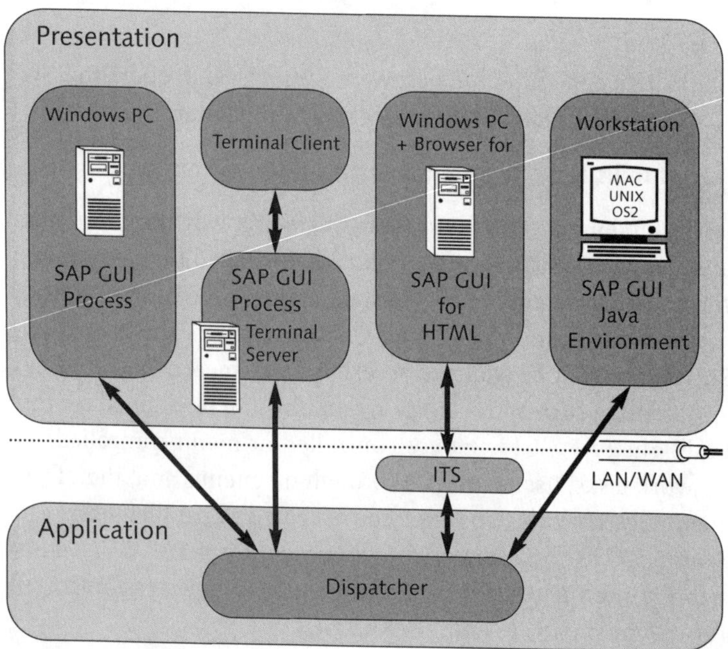


**Figure 1.7** Frontend Variants

- **SAP GUI for the Java Environment**
  The following platforms are supported:
  - Windows 98, Windows NT4, and Windows XP
  - MacOS 9
  - MacOS X

  - Linux, HP-UX, Solaris, AIX, and Tru64
  - OS/2
- **SAP GUI for the HTML Environment**
  The frontends only require a web browser. If you want to convert the display to HTML, you must use an ITS (see Section 1.3.2).

The frontend software is always downward-compatible, which means that you can always use the current version. At the very least, the SAP GUI release must correspond to the Basis release of the SAP system.

An SAP GUI window is divided into different areas. Each window has a title bar that contains the name of the window. In Figure 1.8, the window name is **Simple Job Selection**.

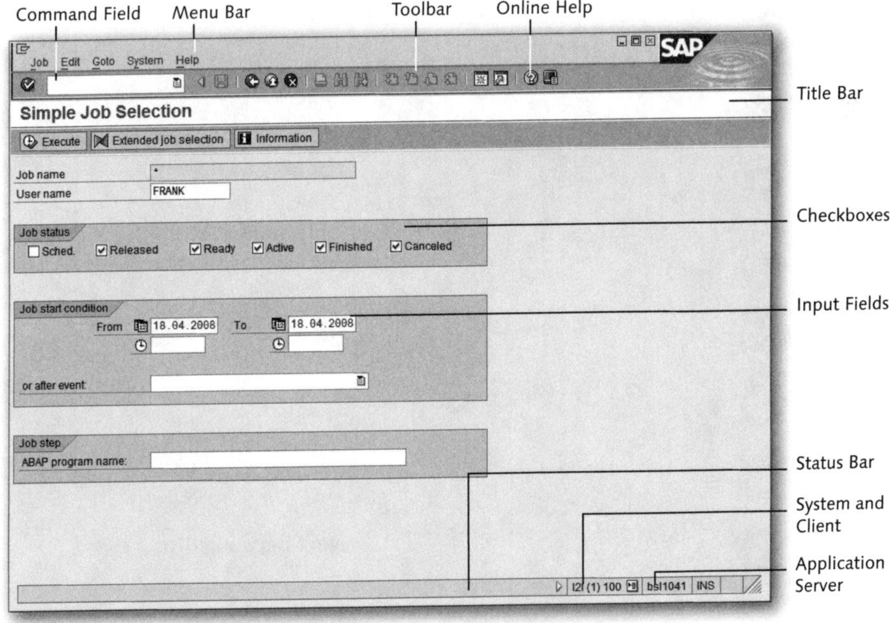


**Figure 1.8** Layout of the SAP GUI

Menu bar

The menu bar is at the top of the screen. Within the SAP GUI, users can use the functions concealed behind the rightmost menu bar icon to adjust the color, font, and font size. The **System** and **Help** menu options are integrated into each menu bar by default. The **System** menu option contains important functions such as creating or deleting a session, editing lists, accessing utilities, and checking system status. The SAP documentation and a context-sensitive help function are available any time under the **Help** menu option.

Standard toolbar

Standardized icons can be used to execute frequently used functions. Table 1.1 contains the most important icons and their meanings. Context-dependent buttons may be available in addition to these icons.

| Icon | Function Key | Meaning |
|---|---|---|
| | Ctrl + S | Save |
| | F3 | Back |
| | Shift + F3 | Exit |
| | F12 | Cancel |
| | Enter | Confirm |
| | Ctrl + P | Print |
| | Ctrl + F | Find |
| | Ctrl + PgUp | First page in a list |
| | PgUp | Previous page in a list |
| | PgDn | Next page in a list |
| | Ctrl + PgDn | Last page in a list |
| | F1 | Help |
| | F8 | Refresh |

**Table 1.1** Important Icons in SAP systems

| Icon | Function Key | Meaning |
|---|---|---|
|  | | Copy |
|  | | Create |
| | | Delete |
|  | | Display |
|  | | Generate |
|  | | Change |
|  | | Check |
|  | | Execute |
|  | | Sort in ascending order |
|  | | Sort in descending order |

**Table 1.1** Important Icons in SAP systems (cont.)

List of favorites and user menu

After you log on to the system, your personal list of favorites and your user menu are expanded, so that you can select a function. The user menu is configured within the role definitions for SAP users and reflects the selection of transactions that you require for your daily work.

To display the entire set of transactions accessible from the menu paths, select **Menu • SAP Menu** to reconfigure the display. The list of favorites doesn't change. In addition to frequently used transactions, you can also store references to web pages and documents in the list of favorites.

Transaction code

A field in which you enter commands (known as the *command field*) is integrated into the standard toolbar. Because the functions offered by SAP are very complex, the SAP menu tree also appears to be very complex and not always strictly hierarchical. Therefore, all workflows within

SAP are assigned a short description known as a *transaction code*. You can enter this transaction code as a direct command, which causes the system to jump directly to the selected function without having to navigate through the menus. You can precede the transaction code with `/n` or `/o`. When you use `/n`, the current work step is canceled, and the action assigned to the transaction code is executed in the current window. On the other hand, when you use `/o`, the new action is executed in a new window (session). Even though this procedure may initially appear to be rather outdated, in practice, it has proven to be very popular, especially among experienced SAP users.

**Status bar**

The lower bar in a SAP GUI window is known as the *status bar*. In addition to important information about the SAP system to which the user has logged on, the status bar also contains workflow information, messages, or error messages.

The actual work area for the SAP user lies between the upper area and the lower bar in the SAP GUI window. The user's work task determines the layout of the work area and its functions.

**Multilingual capability**

The multilingual capability of the SAP GUI is achieved by saving all of the text elements in the display separately. Users can select the language when they log on to the SAP system, or they can permanently set the language in the SAP system. However, they must ensure that the language they select has been previously installed, which means that the text elements for this language have been imported into the SAP database. Each system contains the default languages German and English. Currently, more than 20 different languages can be installed in the system. Unicode is supported as of Basis Release 6.10.

## 1.5 Application Layer

This section focuses on the structure of the application layer. We'll describe the SAP processes in this layer and how they interact as well as the interfaces for the presentation layer and database layer. You will also learn about the processes and settings that you can and must influence as the SAP system administrator.

All of the SAP processes in the application layer form one logical unit. The application layer of an SAP system provides the following services:

Services

- Dialog service (D)
- Update (Update, V)
- V2 update (Update2, V2)
- Lock management (Enqueue, E)
- Background processing (Batch, B)
- Message server (M)
- Gateway (G)
- Spool service (S)

The services can be distributed, according to different criteria, across individual instances (see Section 1.1, "Components of SAP NetWeaver AS ABAP"). Profiles are used to define the number and type of processes for each instance; they are analyzed when you start an application server.

In addition to the name of the associated SAP system, an instance name also contains the letters of the services offered. If a central SAP system has exactly one instance that offers all services, its name is <SID>_DVEBMGS<instance no.> _<host name> where <SID> denotes a three-digit system name that is unique to the system landscape, and <instance no.> is the last two digits of the TCP/IP port used for the network connection. However, this is only a naming convention and is not subject to any technical checks. When a dialog server is installed, the instance is generally installed with the name <SID>_D<instance no.>_<host name>, even if the instance offers other services. The instance number can be any number between 00 and 97; the numbers 98 and 99 are reserved for special purposes.

Message server

Within the application layer, there is exactly one message server on exactly one instance. This process handles communication between the different instances of an SAP system. It checks and, if required, assigns available process resources to the application layer. The instance on which the message server runs is generally known as the *central instance*

(CI) of the SAP system. It has special tasks, which we'll discuss in the following paragraphs. All other instances are called *dialog instances* even if they offer additional services.

**Dispatcher and work processes**

Each of the following services are performed by *work processes*: dialog service, lock management, update service, background service, and output service. Each instance has exactly one dispatcher process, which coordinates the work processes. It recognizes the communication requirements of the work processes and forwards them accordingly. The work processes and dispatcher are always the same program, which is started with the relevant parameters, depending on the function. For each specific instance, the administrator must configure the type and number of processes implemented by a server, depending on the application's requirements and hardware options. The dispatcher starts and manages these processes. If the dispatcher fails, then the entire instance fails. The dispatcher works in the interface between the presentation layer and the application layer. The dispatcher accepts all requests from the presentation layer, that is, the SAP GUI (see Figure 1.9), and assigns them to a work process available in this instance.

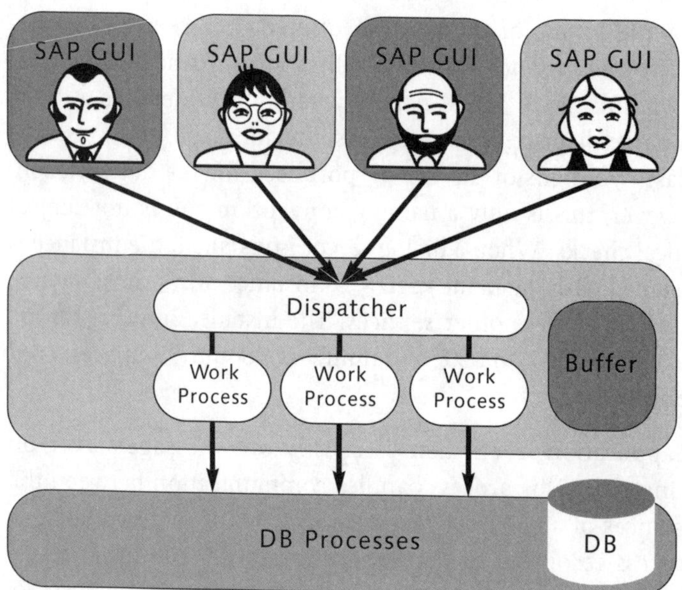


**Figure 1.9** Role of the Dispatcher of an SAP Instance

If you take a closer look at the structure of a work process, you distinguish between the *task handler*, *screen processor*, *ABAP processor*, and the *SQL interface*, all of which work together when you use special main memory areas. The task handler coordinates the activities within the work process. Depending on the upcoming task, the screen processor, the ABAP processor (programs in SAP's own programming language ABAP) or the SQL interface processes the data if the data is to be modified or exchanged with the database.

Dialog service

The work processes are differentiated according to their work tasks. Dialog processes execute the requirements of current user sessions. Each SAP instance must provide at least two dialog processes, so that essential, internal SAP processes can also be handled. The dispatcher doesn't permanently assign a dialog process to exactly one user and, therefore, one SAP GUI (the one currently being used by the user); in fact, the dispatcher of the instance instructs the dialog process that has just become available to execute the requirements. The user data required to execute these requirements (e.g., authorizations) is stored as the user context in all of the main memory areas made available for the work processes. The user's dialog steps correspond to the screen changes. Generally, a user only uses a dialog process while a dialog step is being processed, which allows several users to use a dialog process.

Background service

Work tasks that should be executed in the background are known as *batch work processes* or *background processes*. Background services are particularly useful for tedious work tasks that don't require users to enter data in dialog mode. The user can define the programs to be executed as substeps of a job and schedule these for a certain time or as event-driven jobs. The background service must be supported by at least one instance with at least one corresponding work process.

Update service

The update service makes asynchronous changes to the database. This service is used if changes to the dataset aren't extremely time critical, that is, if they don't require immediate, synchronous execution. An SAP user can't influence when the update service is used or even if it's used at all. This decision is already made when the business application is developed. This is the case, for example, when creating requests. You want to create the individual requests in dialog mode as quickly as possible. The actual update occurs with a delay in the background without the user having to wait for the process to conclude. Within the entire system, at least one update task must be provided on an instance.

V2 update service

For performance reasons, the update service has been further divided. The less critical parts of the update have a separate V2 update service that can execute part of the updates collectively. You don't necessarily have to configure a V2 update task. If there is no V2 update process, its task will continue to be assumed by the update process.

Output service

Output requests are transferred to the output service (also known as the *spool service*), which is initially stored temporarily in *TemSe* objects (*temporary sequential* objects) until it's actually output. The SAP system administrator must decide whether the TemSe objects should be held within the database and, therefore, use the RDBMS security mechanisms or in the file system and, therefore, be managed by the operating system.

At least one spool process must be available within the system. Each instance can offer any number of spool processes.

The spool processes coordinate all output processes such as output and fax requests. Depending on the configuration, the output requests can be transferred directly to the output medium or processed using the operating system's own spool system. The output is monitored in each case. Possible execution messages are provided in SAP's own system logs.

Enqueue service

Lock management plays an important role for services. Like the message server, lock management is a system-wide service; that is, only one instance can offer this service across the entire system. Generally, the service is implemented by exactly one process. If there is a heavy load on the system, several enqueue processes are possible, but these must be on the same instance because the locks are retained in the main memory of the host (in the shared memory). Therefore, the term "enqueue server" is used for the instance that offers the service and also as a synonym for the actual service.

SAP transaction

If possible, the enqueue server and message server should be operated on the same instance because they work closely together. The enqueue server manages the logical SAP transaction locks. An SAP transaction comprises a sequence of consistent, functional, logically related business steps. Furthermore, it generally comprises several screen changes (dialog steps), which can be processed by different processes. From a database perspective, a screen change is already a database transaction that is completed after the dialog step. Only this transaction can coordinate the RDBMS with its own lock management. From an SAP perspective, however, an entire SAP transaction must be fully executed or must be able to be fully rolled back. As a result, *logical units of work* (LUWs) have been implemented in the SAP system. SAP supports the ACID principle for these LUWs, which are defined for transactions within the RDBMS. Therefore, the following rules apply for an LUW:

- **Atomic**
  LUWs form one unit. Either the entire unit is executed, or none of its LUWs are executed.
- **Consistent**
  An LUW transforms a consistent database status into a new, consistent status, that is, a logically correct status is achieved after an LUW is completed.
- **Isolated**
  The LUWs are independent of each other; they can run in parallel. If several LUWs try to process the same sources, they can only be processed sequentially.
- **Durable**
  The outcome of successfully completed LUWs is permanent. The outcome is not affected, for example, by system errors that occur.

The enqueue server is required to fulfill these requirements. Lock requests are transferred from an SAP transaction to the message server, which is executed by the enqueue server. Therefore, in an effort to conserve the additional network load, it makes sense to provide the enqueue and message server on the same instance. The enqueue server manages these locks in a separate main memory area; therefore, if the enqueue server fails, all SAP locks are lost, which results in an automatic rollback of all affected LUWs. Furthermore, if the enqueue server fails, the dispatcher of the corresponding instance immediately tries to start a new enqueue work process.

Gateway service

Moreover, each SAP instance requires a gateway service to implement work tasks that, in the broadest sense, extend beyond the local instance. These include the following:

- Communication between different SAP systems
- RFC (Remote Function Call)
- CPI-C (Common Programming Interface for Communications)
- Connection to external systems such as MAPI servers, EDI systems, external fax machines, and telex services

Exactly one gateway process exists for each instance. It's automatically activated (without having to be specially configured by the administrator) when you start an instance.

Table 1.2 shows the rules for the number of SAP processes in the application layer.

| Service | Across the SAP System | For Each Instance |
|---|---|---|
| Dialog | >=2 | >=2 |
| Update | >=1 | >=0 |
| Enqueue | 1 | 0 or 1 |
| Batch | >=1 | >=0 |
| Message | 1 | 0 or 1 |
| Gateway | >=1 | 1 |
| Spool | >=1 | >=0 |

**Table 1.2** Table 1.2 Rules for the Type and Number of Processes in the Application Layer

The message server is informed at all times about the instances and services currently available and their locations and serves as the cross-system control unit. If the message server fails, the SAP system no longer works. The dispatcher is the controlling unit within an instance. If it fails, the affected instance can't work. If, on the other hand, work processes fail, the dispatcher can start new work processes accordingly. Any work process can assume any task. The dispatcher determines tasks for work processes in accordance with the specifications made by the SAP administrator. To fulfill these tasks, the administrator must be aware of the SAP system requirements, all of which should be clarified during the technical implementation of the SAP system. In the latter phases, you can enhance the system or fine-tune the system configuration previously defined. One of an SAP system administrator's main responsibilities is to customize the application layer. The administrator must make decisions concerning the type and number of instances and their processes, the size of the main memory areas for each instance, and other properties and settings.

The configuration options for an SAP system, in particular, the application layer, are very complex. For central systems, that is, where the application layer only comprises one instance, the administrator must configure the number of processes and the size of their main memory areas. Main memory areas are used, for example, to buffer frequently used table contents, factory calendars, ABAP runtime objects, and also the user context. For distributed systems, that is, several instances within one SAP system, the administrator can define instances that, in extreme cases, only offer one service (e.g., an update server, batch server, or spool server). Performance or administration is generally the motive behind such decisions. We'll discuss this in further detail in Chapter 2, Process Concept of SAP NetWeaver Application Server ABAP.

## 1.6 Database Layer

The database layer of an SAP system is implemented by a central RDBMS. This section explores the SAP database layer in further detail. Here, you will learn how the RDBMS is used for SAP purposes and which administration tasks are involved.

**Native and Open SQL**

Figure 1.10 represents the interfaces between the RDBMS and the work processes. The application layer and the database layer only use SQL to communicate with each other. Despite the SQL standard, each RDBMS that can be used with an SAP system offers its own SQL dialect, which goes beyond the SQL standard. To be as independent as possible of such manufacturer-specific and release-specific enhancements and adjustments, the SAP work processes generally only use the Open SQL interface. ABAP Open SQL corresponds to the entry level after the SQL2 standard. If required, this Open SQL is then converted (within the database interface integrated into the work processes) into the *native SQL* of the RDBMS used in each case. Within ABAP programs, however, you also have the option to use the special language scope of SQL for the RDBMS used. Because these applications are manufacturer-specific, the modules in question are encapsulated within the SAP applications. Usage of these types of applications is reduced to the bare minimum. Authorized areas of use include specific applications such as database monitors. Within the ABAP programs, the following statements are used to encapsulate native SQL statements:

```
EXEC SQL.
  <Native SQL statement>
ENDEXEC.
```

Table types

Data is retained in RDBMS tables. Therefore, all application data has a 1:1 mapping to *transparent tables*. In theory, other SQL or manufacturer-specific tools could be used to access this data. The pure administration data in the SAP system is also stored in other table types. From the perspective of the RDBMS, this of course once again concerns a table. However, SAP sometimes groups together several small tables into one table in the RDBMS. From an SAP perspective, this table repository is known as a *table pool*. The tables contained in this repository are only visible to SAP. The main advantage associated with table pools is the reduction in the total number of tables from an RDBMS perspective. Within the table pool, the individual tables are identified by their unique names and their own record keys.

Pool table

A table within a table pool is known as a *pool table*. Due to the structure and storage type of pool tables, it's considerably more complicated to access the data without using SAP tools. The ATAB table is an example of a typical table pool. It contains several SAP control tables. The control tables are very small, and their contents are relatively consistent, thus making it both possible and useful to buffer the entire table pool.

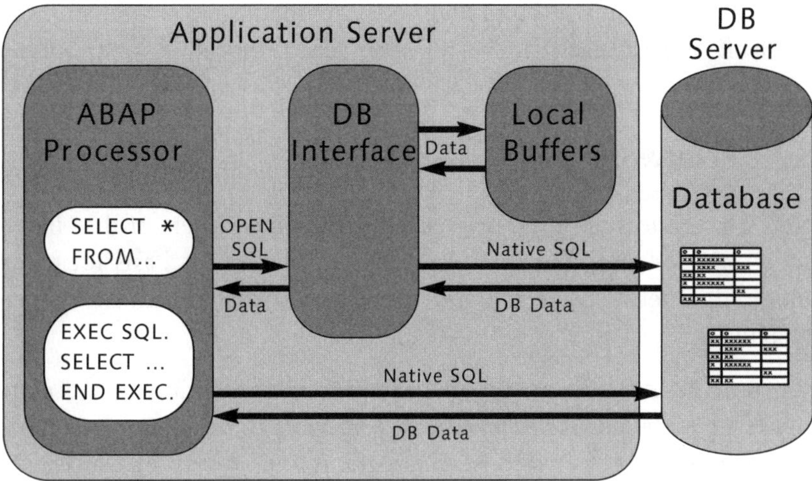


**Figure 1.10** Database Interface

The situation is similar for *table clusters* and their logical *cluster tables*. Furthermore, cluster tables don't exist as standalone tables in RDBMS. Several cluster tables are grouped together to form one table cluster (known as a *cluster*). Here, several rows in the cluster table are generally grouped together under one shared key to form one data record in a cluster. Unlike the table pool in which one data record in the pool table is assigned to one data record, here one data record in the cluster is formed from several data records in the cluster table. The data records are simply strung together and assigned a cluster key. This technology is frequently used in the documentation environment.

**Cluster tables**

Both the database and the RDBMS play a central role in the operation of an SAP system. All data entered by the user (including the SAP administration data) is managed here. Therefore, it's important to manage this data (in particular, to perform a data backup). These activities are also part of SAP system administration. In larger systems, database administration alone often forms a complete area of responsibility for one person or even a group of persons. However, this area of responsibility is characterized by many RDBMS-specific properties. This book only deals with those procedures that are generally applicable. For additional questions, please refer to those books in this series that provide information about the special features of RDBMS administration.

Each of the currently released RDBMS/operating system combinations is available on SAP Service Marketplace under the quicklink */pam*.

## 1.7 Network

Network services are used between the individual layers of the client/server architecture. The TCP/IP protocol is always the basis for communication between the components of an SAP system and with other systems.

CPI-C

SAP provides different services that simplify communication. SAP's own CPI-C interface (*Common Programming Interface Communication*) is used for communication between ABAP programs, thus ensuring a consistent, standardized communication interface. CPI-C corresponds to the SAA standard first defined by IBM in 1987, which comprises the following:

1. Communication setup
2. Communication control
3. Data exchange
4. Communication close

The SAP Gateway is responsible for implementing CPI-C requests. The CPI-C interface is always used if communication is between different SAP systems, or if non-SAP programs are executed. The message server itself processes short messages.

SAP Gateway

When larger volumes of data are exchanged, the SAP Gateway, which specifically assumes this responsibility, is used on the basis of TCP/IP or LU6.2. The CPI-C language is available as an integrated part of SAP's own programming language (ABAP) within starter sets and additional data conversion functions. To prevent users from having to write their own CPI-C communication routines, SAP provides the RFC (*Remote Function Call*) interface. RFC contains a separate protocol for executing both internal and external function modules, which are managed in SAP's own function library. A special *Destination* parameter can be used to execute a function module on any target host within the same SAP system or on other SAP or R/2 systems. RFC supports both asynchronous and synchronous communication (see Chapter 13, Data Distribution and Transfer).

One disadvantage associated with synchronous communication is that a remote program can only be called if the partner is active. If the receiver is very slow, the sender may also experience delays. If the receiver suddenly fails, a data recovery may be necessary for both systems.

Asynchronous communication, on the other hand, can ensure that transactions are consistent. For this, the RFC has the addition `IN BACKGROUND TASK`. If processing is to be manually triggered in a target system, or if the target host is temporarily unable to fulfill the necessary requirements, the data is initially placed in a queue. The Q-API (*Queue Application Programming Interface*) is the management mechanism deployed here.

OLE (*Object Linking and Embedding*) resides above RFC. OLE is used to connect PC programs to the SAP system. The SAP GUI and PC software handle OLE commands within ABAP programs as RFCs. This makes it possible for data to be exchanged with MS Word or MS Excel. **OLE**

From an administrator perspective, the technical prerequisites, that is, stable network connections, must be fulfilled. At the same time, security precautions such as establishing firewalls are necessary. In practice, however, a technical service assumes responsibility for these tasks. In larger systems, we recommend that you entrust these tasks to a network administrator who defines and controls the necessary SAP connections.

## 1.8 Operating System

Now that you have closely examined the structure of the individual layers of the SAP client/server architecture and the network technology between the layers, we'll discuss how the SAP system is embedded into each operating system. Of particular interest is the interaction between the SAP kernel and the operating system on the corresponding application servers.

As is usually the case with PCs, the software SAP GUI and the associated components are installed in any directory on the frontend or installed remotely and then manually or automatically maintained with every new SAP release. In the database layer, embedding of the operating system strictly depends on the RDBMS and is not generally accepted. Because the main responsibility of the SAP system administrator is to customize the SAP application layer, that is, the SAP kernel, this section will mainly focus on this aspect.

### 1.8.1 Directory Structure

Similar to the way in which the individual SAP processes of the instances belonging to an SAP system form one unit, the SAP directory tree also comprises the branches of the instances involved, irrespective of whether the various instances are housed on Windows NT or UNIX systems. Figure 1.11 shows the generally accepted structure of the directory tree.

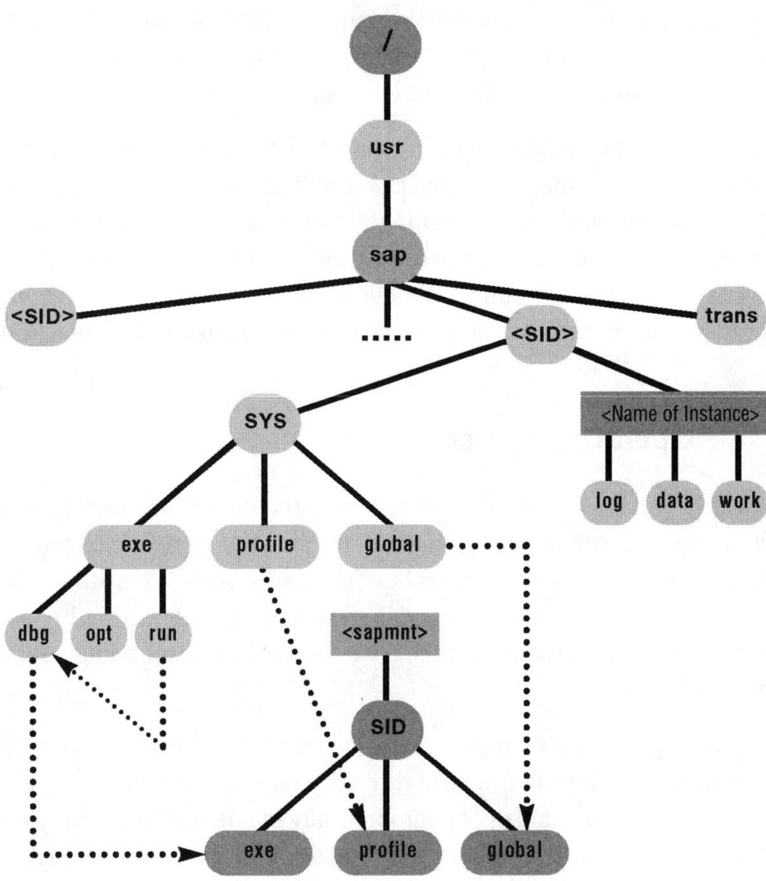


**Figure 1.11** Directory Tree

<SID> refers to the unique SAP system name, which usually corresponds to the database name. SIDs always comprise three letters, digits, or a combination of both. Below this, the directory tree is divided into the *SYS* directories and also the directory of the instance name, for example, DVEBMGS00 for a central instance with the number 00. For Windows NT, the two Windows NT shares, *sapmnt* and *saploc*, are also saved to this *\usr\sap* root directory. For UNIX, links must be used to facilitate this for the */sapmnt* directory. The *SYS* directory itself comprises the following directories: SID

- **Profile**
  Profile of the instance.
- **Global**
  Data and logs that are relevant across the SAP system.
- **Exe**
  Executable programs.

The *exe* directory is divided into the *dbg*, *opt*, and *run* directories. It contains the executable programs for the SAP runtime environment whereby each of the programs in the *run* subdirectory is executed. For historical reasons, a link is used to map the *run* directory in UNIX systems to the *dbg* directory. In addition to the optimized SAP programs, this directory also contains debuggable programs identifiable by the extension *dbg*.

In earlier SAP releases, the *opt* directory in UNIX systems contained the optimized SAP kernel, and the debuggable SAP kernel was available in the *dbg* directory. If problems occur, the link that generally maps the *run* directory to the *opt* directory can be converted to the debuggable and, therefore, slower SAP kernel.

From a logical perspective, the */usr/sap/<SID>* node contains a directory that comprises the *log*, *data*, and *work* directories for each instance of the SAP system. In turn, the *log* directory contains the system log for each SAP instance. Trace and error information concerning the SAP processes of an instance are stored in the *work* directory. The *data* directory contains files arising from the memory management of the SAP processes. Physically, these directories are localized on each application server of the instance. NFS mount is used to display them on the central instance in a logical manner. Furthermore, the respective */usr/sap/<SID>/SYS* directory trees are connected to the directory tree of the central instance.

### 1.8.2 User

Special SAP users are required at the operating system level. The necessary work environment, which comprises authorizations, default settings, and, depending on the RDBMS, the associated database users, is created when the SAP system is installed.

UNIX On UNIX platforms, the following operating system users must be created for an SAP system: <sid>adm and <RDBMS><sid>. Here, <sid> denotes the system ID of the SAP system in lowercase letters, and <RDBMS> stands for the three-letter abbreviation for the database description:

- sqd (MaxDB)
- Edb2 (DB2)
- inf (Informix)
- ora (Oracle)

Essentially, these users differ in their areas of responsibility and, therefore, also in their authorizations at the operating system level. The operating system user <sid>adm is broadly used for SAP administration purposes. Because the administration tasks in the RDBMS environment belong to the area of responsibility of <RDBMS><sid>, the users overlap considerably with each other.

Windows In Windows systems, the user <sid>adm performs all of the tasks described here. Background services are operated under the user ID SAPService<SID>.

Furthermore, a special SAP system user is available in the database, but the characteristics of this user may differ, depending on the database system used. All of the database tables in the SAP system belong to this user. Any other database users who may exist don't have any access rights to these tables.

## 1.9 Tips

- **Menu Paths**
  If you're looking for a menu path for a transaction, you can use Transaction search_sap_menu for the standard menu or search_user_menu for entries in your user menu.
- **Transactions**
  If you're using a keyword or wildcards to search for a transaction, you can use the *data browser* Transaction (SE16) for the TSTCT table.

## 1.10 Transactions and Menu Paths

**Data Browser:** SAP Menu • Tools • ABAP Workbench • Overview • Data Browser (SE16)

## 1.11 Additional Documentation

Quick Links

You can find additional documentation in the SAP Service Marketplace, as follows:

- SAP Service Marketplace, alias *netweaver*
- SAP Service Marketplace, alias *platforms*
- SAP Service Marketplace, alias *sapgui*
- SAP Service Marketplace, alias *pam*

### SAP Notes

Table 1.3 provides an overview of important SAP Notes in the SAP Service Marketplace. Some basic questions about the SAP architecture are asked in the next section.

| Content | Note |
|---|---|
| ITS maintenance strategy | 197746 |
| SAP GUI resources | 26417 |
| SAP GUI maintenance strategy | 147519 |
| SAP GUI restrictions for Java | 454939 |

**Table 1.3** SAP Notes Concerning the SAP NetWeaver Architecture

## 1.12 Questions

1. **Which services are provided by the application layer?**
   a. Communication service
   b. Dialog service
   c. Spool service
   d. Update service
   e. Message service
   f. Transport service
   g. Gateway service
   h. Network service
   i. Enqueue service
   j. Background service
   k. Change service
2. **Which of the following recommendations is correct?**
   a. The dispatcher and dialog processes shouldn't run together in one instance.
   b. The enqueue server and message server work closely together and, therefore, should be operated in one instance.
   c. The background service and update work closely together and, therefore, should never be operated on different instances.

3. **What is the purpose of the gateway service?**
   a. Communication between SAP processes
   b. Communication between SAP systems and instances of another SAP system
   c. Communication with the spooler of the operating system
   d. Connection of external programs such as MAPI, EDI, and telex services
   e. Communication with SAP systems
4. **How many message servers are active in an SAP system?**
   a. 0
   b. 1
   c. 2
5. **How many update tasks can be active for each instance?**
   a. 1
   b. 2
   c. The SAP system automatically regulates the number, according to requirements.
   d. Any number, depending on the resources available. The administrator must define the number in advance.

*In this chapter, we discuss the different process types that are available with SAP NetWeaver AS ABAP. We explain the properties of the process types and introduce the concepts related to the individual processes.*

# 2 Process Concept of SAP NetWeaver Application Server ABAP

The following section introduces the basic process types of SAP NetWeaver AS ABAP and its architecture. You learn why there are different process types and which tasks they perform in particular. Each subsection of this chapter describes a specific process type. You'll find tips and frequently asked questions at the end of each section. As the conclusion to this comprehensive chapter, you will also be given a brief insight into the functions of the virtual machine container (VMC), although this itself is not an independent process type.

## 2.1 Dialog Processing

Dialog processing mainly takes place within dialog work processes. These normally constitute the largest portion of work processes in an OLTP system. At least two dialog work processes in addition to the dispatcher process are required for an independent instance.

Although all of the processes described in the following sections perform specific tasks such as background processing, printing, or updating, dialog work processes deal with the basic load of all pending tasks. All requests made by a user online to SAP NetWeaver are processed by a dialog work process. Depending on the request, a suitable specific process such as the update process may also be included, if necessary. The following components are involved in processing a dialog request (see Figure 2.1):

Components involved in dialog requests

- The dispatcher work process (central control process)
- Possibly the dispatcher queue (dispatcher process queue)
- A dialog work process
- Components in the shared memory of the application server (e.g., buffers)

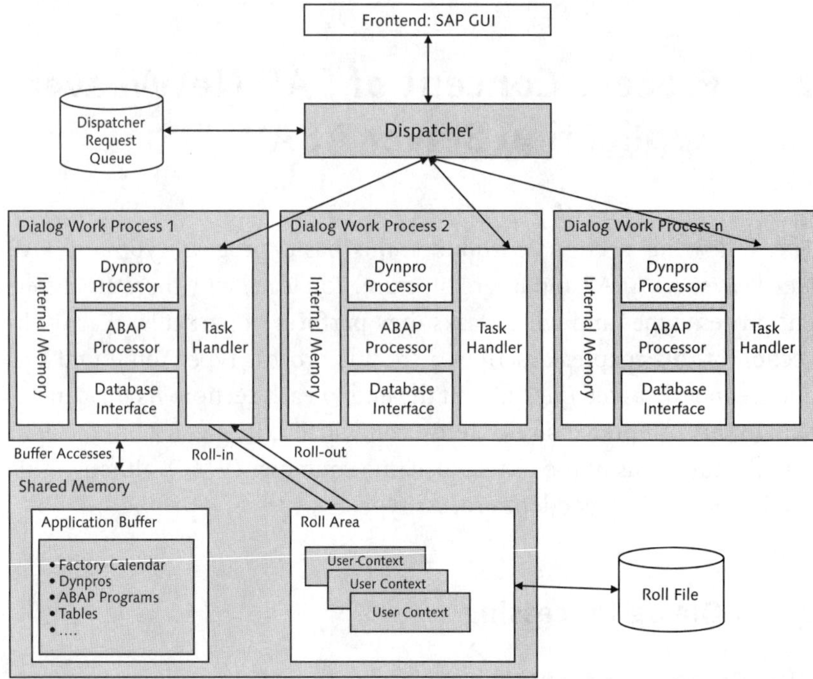


**Figure 2.1** Components Involved in a Dialog Step

If the dispatcher forwards a dialog request to a dialog work process, the task handler takes over the request in the dialog process. It decides whether the screen or ABAP processor should be activated and whether a database query may have to be executed using the database interface. The task handler also looks after the roll-in and roll-out of the user context. The user context contains authorizations and variable values, for example.

Heap memory and cross-process memory

The work process also has access to different memory areas. We differentiate between memory areas that are exclusively available for the dialog work process (*heap memory*) and memory areas that can be shared by all work processes (*cross-process memory*). Mode-specific data that is kept longer than for the duration of a process step is stored in the exclusively used memory. This data is automatically made available for the process at the beginning of a dialog step (rolled in) and saved for the process at the end of the dialog step (rolled out). This is data that characterizes the user (user context), such as authorizations, administration information and other data for the ABAP and dialog processor, which was collected in the dialog steps of the current transaction that were already carried out.

The shared user area contains various SAP buffers such as the factory calendar and screen, program, and table buffers.

## 2.2 Background Processing

In addition to the dialog mode, reports can also be processed in the background in an SAP system. This is particularly interesting for long-running programs that don't require any interactive input. This chapter focuses on the management of background jobs. We'll show you how to schedule time-driven and event-driven background jobs and how to analyze flow traces.

### 2.2.1 Concepts

In principle, you can also run all programs, which don't require any explicit user dialog, in the background. This is particularly useful if the process to be performed is time-consuming and requires a lot of system resources and should therefore be carried out at a time when there is a minimal workload on the system. Performing the process online would block a dialog process for the entire duration and thereby indirectly impede other dialog users.

To prevent users from executing long-running reports interactively, you can define a runtime limit for the dialog steps. The default limit is 600 seconds. The processing terminates after this period has elapsed. You can set this limit in the system profile using the `rdisp/max_wprun_time` parameter. Background processing is not restricted in this way.

The automation of routine tasks for periodic completion is another obvious option you can use. The SAP system provides the background service with its background work processes (also simply *background* or *batch processes*) for background processing. Unlike dialog processing, in which the dispatcher assigns the next available dialog process to each LUW (Logical Unit of Work – see Section 1.5, Application Layer), background processing consists of a fixed connection with exactly one background process during the entire execution. The system administrator or the user schedules the start time of the background job. The user can choose between time control and event control.

**Time-driven job scheduler**

The time-driven approach involves defining a start time when you schedule the job. Each instance of the SAP system, on which background work processes are configured, has an active *time-driven job scheduler* that checks, at defined intervals, whether there are background jobs waiting to be processed. The descriptions of pending jobs are held in central database tables. The time-driven job scheduler is an ABAP program that is interpreted and processed within a selected dialog process. The scheduler automatically selects the specific dialog process when the SAP system is started. The time interval, after which the time-driven job scheduler becomes active, is configured to 60 seconds by default. The administrator can change this time interval as required in the instance profile using the `rdisp/btctime` parameter. The time interval between two job scheduler runs can cause delays when you start a job. You would therefore reduce the time interval if the delays were too great for your own requirements. However, if a possible delay when starting a job is not a crucial factor, you can increase the time interval. Nevertheless, the associated reduction in the frequency of runs of the time-driven job scheduler has hardly any effect on the system load.

**Event-driven job scheduler**

In contrast to the time-driven job scheduler, the *event-driven job scheduler* reacts to events. After an event is triggered (as discussed later), the event-driven job scheduler initiates the start of background jobs that are to start running when the event occurs. The event-driven job scheduler is also processed by a dialog work process; you use the `rdisp/btcname = <host name>` parameter in the standard profile of the SAP system (*DEFAULT.PFL*).

**Parameters for Dialog or Background Processing**

- `rdisp/max_wprun_time`: Time in seconds, after which a dialog step terminates because the runtime has been exceeded.
- `rdisp/btctime`: Time interval of the background job scheduler.
- `rdisp/btcnam`: Instance for background processing.

System events

The events to which you want the job schedulers to react must first be defined as *events* in the SAP system. A number of events are already delivered by default with the SAP system. You can display an overview of these events in Event Maintenance (SM62). The events already included in the SAP system delivery are also called *system events*. They are frequently used for internal SAP control but can also be used by users for their own purposes.

User events

Users can also use the same menu path to define their own events called *user events*. The event definition is initially nothing more than an entry in a table.

Triggers

You can trigger an event in various ways:

- Manually for test purposes using the context menu for an event in Event Maintenance (SM62) (right-click **Trigger• Event**)
- By using the BP_EVENT_RAISE function module from an ABAP program within the SAP system
- Using the `sapevt` external program

sapevt

You can use `sapevt` to trigger an event in an SAP system from an external program. `sapevt` is available for executable programs in the SAP standard directory (see Chapter 1, Architecture of SAP NetWeaver Application Server ABAP). You can use it as follows:

```
sapevt <EventID> [-p <parameter>] [-t]
pf=<profile>|name=<SAP system name> nr=<SAP system number>
```

The `-t` option initiates the writing of a *dev_evt* log file in the `sapevt` call directory. The `-p` option can transfer a parameter that determines an SAP module (e.g., Financials, FI). This means that an event can be assigned to an application area. This assignment is merely descriptive in nature.

For example, the

```
sapevt SAP_TRIGGER_RDDIMPDP name=QO1 nr=00
```

call triggers the `SAP_TRIGGER_RDDIMPDP` event in the QO1 SAP system.

tp Event control is used within the SAP system when transporting objects between SAP systems, for example. Transports performed using the `tp` transport control program are processed in several phases. Beyond the actual data import, you also often have to generate or activate the individual objects. The `tp` program therefore triggers the `SAP_TRIGGER_RDDIMPDP` event after the data import has been completed. In an SAP system, the `RDDIMPDP` job is always scheduled based on this event. When the `SAP_TRIGGER_RDDIMPDP` event is triggered, the `RDDIMPDP` job is executed automatically in the background.

Using this technology gives you greater flexibility. You can't always predict when actions will be completed, therefore, it's almost impossible to establish dependencies between background jobs. Event control creates new possibilities in this case.

### 2.2.2 Defining Background Jobs

You use the Job Definition (SM36) to set up background jobs (see Figure 2.2).

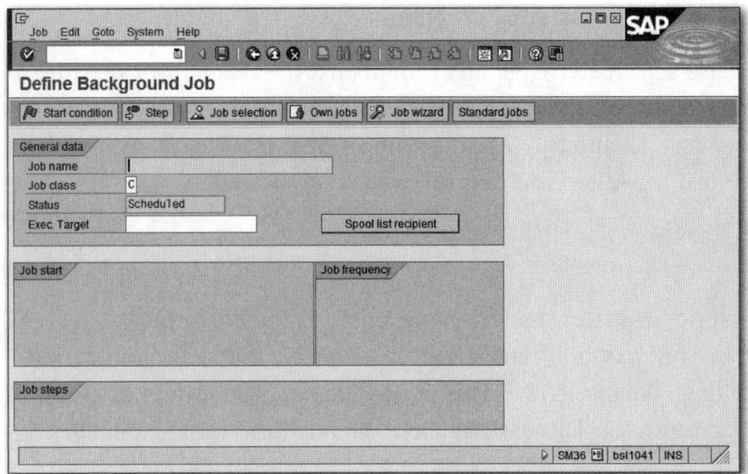


**Figure 2.2** Job Definition

Planning background jobs is also often integrated directly into the applications, for example, when you copy clients or perform a user master comparison. Depending on the application, the appearance of the screen templates for entering the job data may differ, or the application may predefine certain job properties already. However, the basic principles and options of background processing described in this chapter remain valid and can be applied to these specific cases.

Three important aspects are involved in defining background jobs:

- General information such as job name, job class, and target host
- Information about the start time or about assigning a triggering event
- List of processing steps

General information

The general information is the starting point for defining a background job (refer to Figure 2.2). The job name you select should be as descriptive as possible because all logs and overviews that you'll subsequently have to analyze are based on this job name. From a technical point of view, the name is irrelevant; it doesn't need to be unique either.

Job class

The priority when executing a job is initially controlled by assigning the job to a job class. We differentiate between the following job classes:

- **A Highest priority**
  Time-critical jobs that ensure the functional efficiency of the SAP NetWeaver system.
- **B Medium priority**
  Periodic jobs that ensure the functional efficiency of the SAP NetWeaver system.
- **C Normal priority**
  The usual job class for SAP users.

System resources are assigned using these job classes. If a very high number of Class C jobs are frequently waiting to be processed, which means that Class A and B jobs also have to wait for background processes to be released, the system administrator can use Operation Mode Maintenance (RZ04) to keep an *n* number of background processes available for processing Class A jobs. This configuration ensures that *n* background processes are always available for executing Class A jobs. Class B and C jobs must wait with the processing until at least *n+1* processes are available. The configuration is described in Section 7.1, Profile Maintenance, in Chapter 7 as part of the topic on maintaining operation modes.

**Target servers**

In a distributed SAP system, you can assign the execution of a job to any SAP instance with a background service. In the context of background processing, this instance is referred to as a *target server*. If you don't explicitly specify a target server, the first available background process will be selected when you execute the job.

The priorities for processing a request on a defined background server are as follows:

1. Job class A, target server specified
2. Job class A, no target server specified
3. Job class B, target server specified
4. Job class B, no target server specified
5. Job class C, target server specified
6. Job class C, no target server specified

If the pending jobs have equal priority based on the criteria mentioned previously, the queue time is used.

If you have defined a target server, this information is binding. If the target server is not available when you want the job to start, a background work process of another instance won't take over the processing. The job remains in the queue until the defined target server resumes the work, or the processing is explicitly moved to another server.

The output generated by an ABAP program is stored as a spool request in the SAP spool system. You can use *spool list recipients* to send the output to a user, which means that different people can manage a background job and analyze its results, for example. Because the output can be extensive, you should use this option with caution. For performance reasons, the length of an output list sent through SAPoffice is restricted to 1,000 lines. You specify the information about the print parameters themselves in the step definition.

Start time

In another step, you must select the parameters that determine the start time. To do this, you select the **Start Date** button from the initial screen for the job definition. You can define the start date using time data or as event-driven (see Figure 2.3).

The time data and the time zone used are based on the system time. In addition to specifying the start time directly, time-driven scheduling of jobs also enables you to schedule jobs periodically, as it can be useful for regular evaluations or maintenance jobs described later. You can select the time intervals here as you wish: in cycles of minutes, or hourly, daily, weekly, and so on. You can use the **Restrictions** function to define differences in the normal period, which is convenient for taking into account public holidays in the valid factory calendar. For time-sensitive jobs, you can define a time after the elapse of which, these jobs must not be started any more.

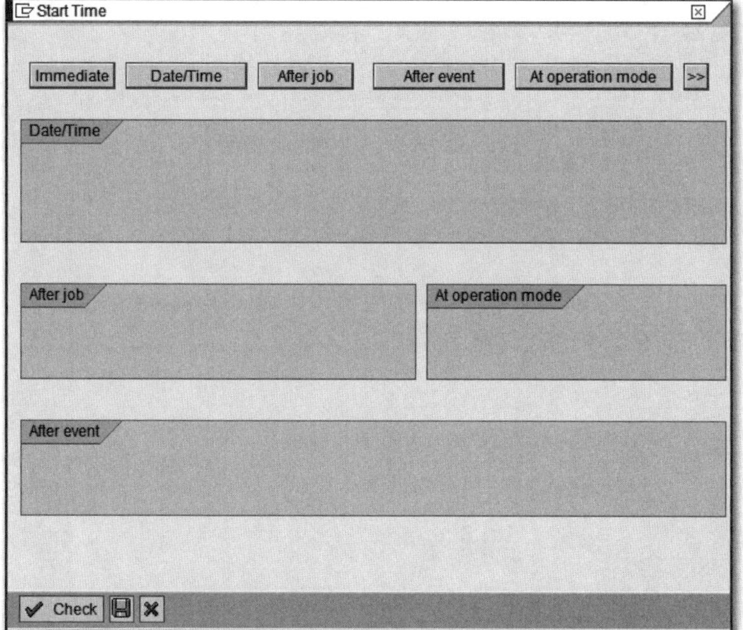


**Figure 2.3** Defining a Start Date and Time

Start event

Instead of time-based control, you can also specify a defined event as the trigger. In particular, operation mode switching and the end of a job are also defined as events to ensure that a background job can also be started as a follow-on job. You can use the **Start status dependent** option to ensure that the job starts, provided the preceding job has been completed successfully. If the preceding job is canceled, the status of the dependent follow-on job is also set to *Canceled*, and the job is not executed.

If jobs with the **After job**, **After event**, or **At operation mode** start date can't be started because no background work processes are available when the expected event occurs, they are earmarked to start at the earliest possible date and then also started using the time-driven job scheduler (see Figure 2.4).

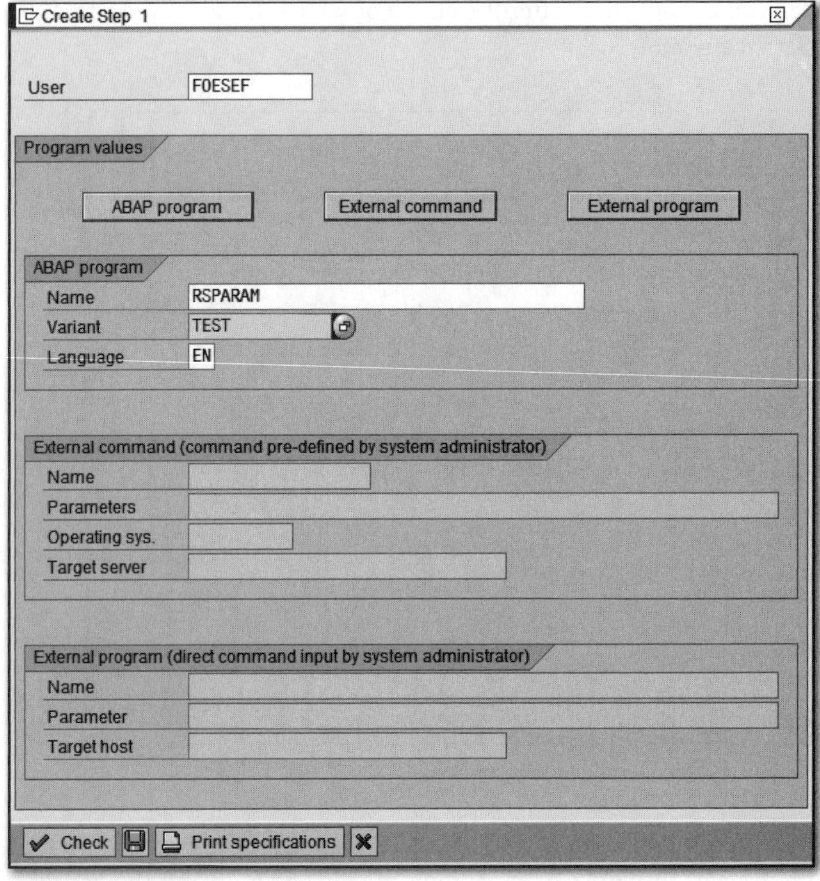


**Figure 2.4** Defining a Processing Step

ABAP program

As already mentioned, you can also run all dialog-free ABAP programs in the background. To do this, select the **ABAP Program** function. Enter the name of the ABAP program to be run and, if necessary, specify a language in which any log is to be generated. Many ABAP programs are controlled using variables. One example is the RSPARAM program. This program generates a list of all set instance parameters. A user can restrict the namespace of the instance parameters to be displayed before he runs the program. To run these types of programs in the background, you must create program *variants*. These variants represent a fixed allocation of values for program variables that is saved under a variant name. You define a variant in the ABAP Editor (SE38) by selecting **Goto• Variants**. You enter a variant name and the required parameter values here. You can then schedule the background execution of an ABAP program variant defined in this way.

Figure 2.4 shows the scheduling of the RSPARAM ABAP program, for which a "TEST" variant was previously created to generate a list of all currently defined instance parameters. The list here is to be generated in English. You can configure the print output of this list using the **Print specifications** function.

External programs

SAP users with administrator authorization can use the **External program** option to run any programs from the SAP system at the operating system level. Parameters can be transferred; the name of the target host must be specified in this case. To execute the program, the SAPXPG routine is started on the target host, and the calling SAP system then communicates with this routine by RFC, using the ID of the specific SAPCPIC SAP user.

External commands

To enable you to use the SAP internal authorization mechanism and also use external programs to a limited degree, *external commands* are preconfigured extensibly. An external command consists of a logical name and an assigned external program with a possible allocation of parameters that can vary greatly, depending on the selected operating system. Before you use external commands in background processing, you must first define these using Create External OS Commands (SM49).

When you define a work step within a background job, the external command to be executed is determined using the name and the relevant operating system, for example, UNIX. You can also allow users to add other parameters to the ones predefined. As with external programs, you must always specify the target host.

If you use external commands or external programs in the step list of a background job, for better integration, you can use the **Control flags** option in the step definition to define whether the data output and the error messages of the operating system program should be included in the step's job log and whether a synchronous or an asynchronous execution is required.

When you have entered the general information, start time, and individual work steps of the background job, its definition is complete. Lastly, you must save the information you entered.

Job wizard

You can also query all described entries step-by-step using the *job wizard*. You can call the job wizard directly from the Job Definition (SM36).

API

To schedule background jobs, SAP also provides an interface (*Application Programming Interface*, API), in addition to the menu-driven method just described, which users can use in their own ABAP programs.

### 2.2.3 Analysis

You analyze and monitor background jobs using Simple Job Selection (SM37) or Extended job selection (SM37C). You can filter jobs according to different criteria such as scheduling user, time period, job period, event, and status. You use the authorization concept to restrict the selection criteria. If you have administrator authorization for background processing, you can display the jobs in all clients in the extended job selection; otherwise, you can only display the jobs in the logon client.

A list of all background jobs is created based on the criteria you select.

Statuses

The statuses of a job are described as follows:

- **Scheduled**
  The step definitions of the job have been saved; a start time has not yet been defined.

- **Released**
  The job has been scheduled, and a start time has been explicitly set, or the job is waiting for an event.
- **Ready**
  The start time was reached, or the expected event has occurred; the job is waiting for system resources for the execution.
- **Active**
  The job is currently being processed.
- **Finished**
  The job was successfully completed.
- **Canceled**
  The processing had to be canceled due to a problem. The job could not be successfully completed.

You can double-click a selected job to display the execution details in its job log. In addition to the start and end times, the log contains valuable information about the causes of any canceled jobs.

All essential operations for background jobs are integrated into the job overview. These include the following:

- Display scheduling data.
- Cancel jobs with the *Active* status.
- Delete jobs with the *Scheduled*, *Released*, *Finished*, or *Canceled* status.
- Undo the release of one or more jobs; the job status changes to *Scheduled*.
- Compare several jobs. Specifying the general job information, step definition, and start conditions.
- Move to another server.
- Interrupt an active job when problems are suspected (long-running programs). This enables you to pause a job that is currently executing an ABAP program and analyze it using the ABAP debugger. The program will continue running again after you exit the debugger.
- Check the status of *active jobs*.

- Copy scheduled, released, or finished jobs; the new job gets the *Scheduled*status.

In addition to this list overview, you can also use a graphical display, which not only enables you to display jobs but also to change and release jobs and check active jobs. You can access the graphical monitor from the Job Monitor (RZ01) path (see Figure 2.5). The statuses of the jobs are displayed in color for a better overview.

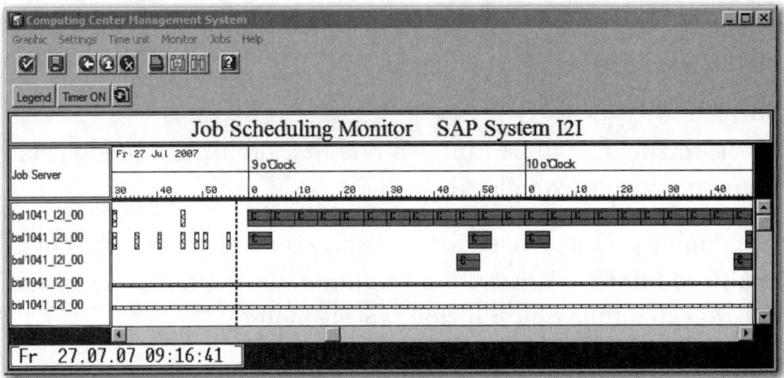


**Figure 2.5** Job Scheduling Monitor

You can also select **Own Jobs (SMX)** or **Job Definition (SM36) • Own Jobs** to display an overview of your own background jobs.

### 2.2.4 Analysis Functions

Because, unlike dialog work, a user will often not immediately notice problems in his background processing, other analysis functions are available within the CCMS.

Runtime analysis

Information about the planned and actual start time and runtime of a background job are integrated into the **Simple Job Selection (SM37)**. Major differences between the planned and actual start times indicate a bottleneck in the available background processes. This means that a long period of time elapsed after the job was released before a background process could be made available for the processing. If performance bottlenecks can be ruled out when scheduled background jobs are executed, the administrator should check the resources in this case and increase the number of background processes, if necessary (`rdisp/wp_no_btc` parameter in the instance profiles, or using profile maintenance, see Section 7.1, Profile Maintenance, in Chapter 7).

**Zombies**

When you start an SAP system, it checks to see whether there are still jobs with the*Ready* or *Active* statuses, which are not possible in this situation. They are then set to the *Scheduled* or *Canceled* status. This type of *zombie* can occur if you shut down an application server before the job finishes and the status could be changed in the database.

**Status check**

To check whether the displayed job status matches the actual status or whether there is an inconsistency, you can select the critical jobs in the Simple Job Selection (SM37) and select **Job • Check Status** to find any possible discrepancies. If necessary, you can reset the status of the jobs to *Scheduled* or cancel the actual jobs.

**Background processing alerts**

Some parameters from the background processing were integrated into the CCMS monitoring architecture. The *Background processing* monitor provides information about the average utilization of the background work processes, the server-specific length and average length of the wait queue for jobs that are ready to be started but can't be processed due to the lack of a background server, and the number of canceled jobs (see Figure 2.6).

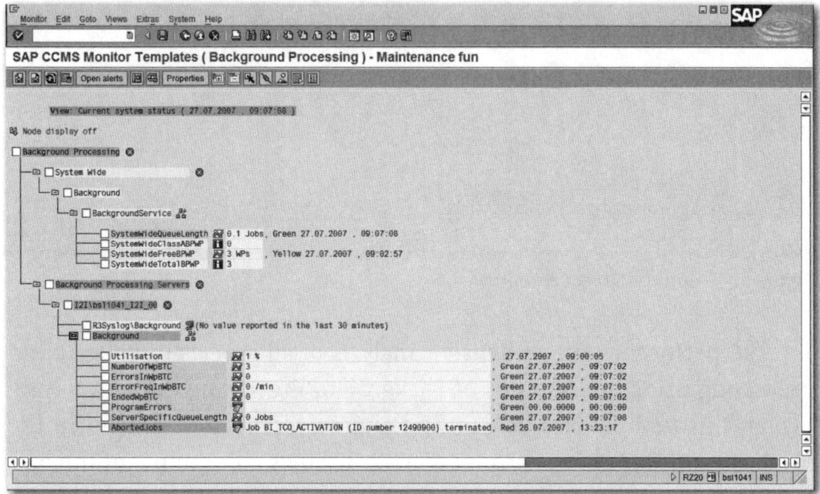


**Figure 2.6** Alert Monitoring in CCMS

Control object list

You can use the Background Control Object Monitor (SM61) to check that the controller is working correctly in background processing. This monitor enables you to check important components of background processing — such as time-driven and event-driven job schedulers, zombie cleanups, the start of external programs, and switching of operation modes — and use additional trace outputs to analyze them.

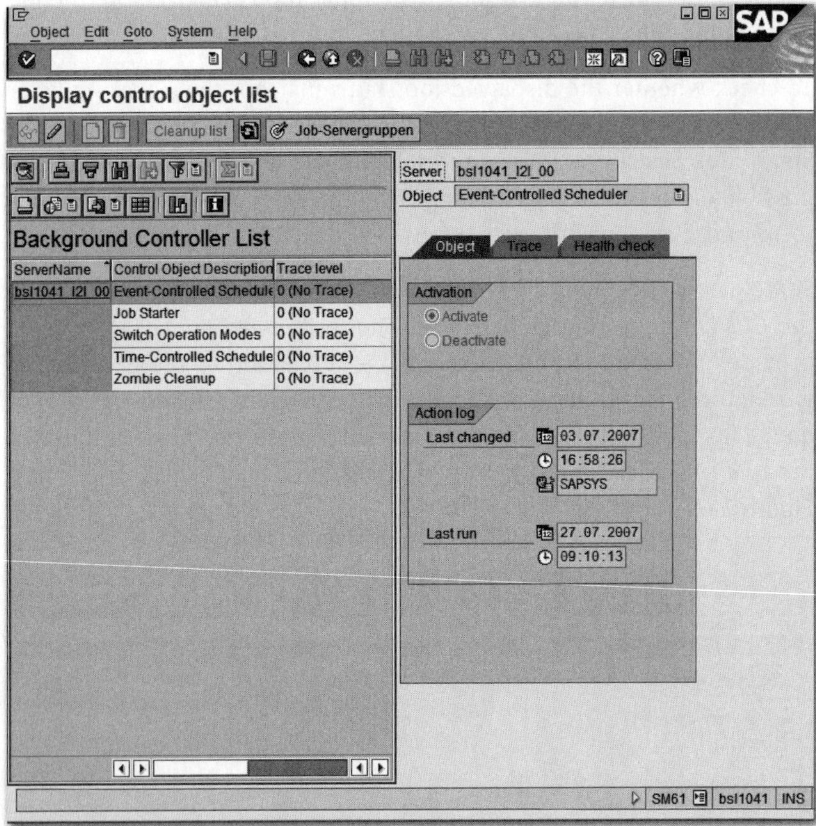


**Figure 2.7** Control Object Monitor

Analysis tool – background processing

You can perform a comprehensive analysis of all aspects of background processing using the Analysis of Background Processing (SM65). In particular, this tool enables you to find and correct inconsistencies in the database tables for job control. Figure 2.8 shows an example of the output from this tool.

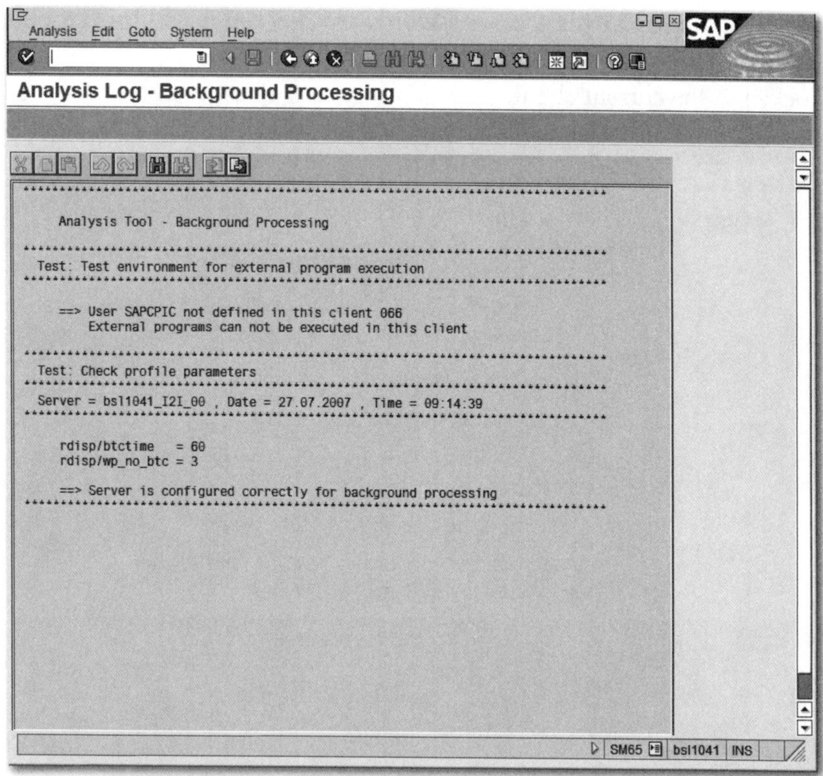
Analysis Edit Goto System Help
Analysis Log - Background Processing
Analysis Tool - Background Processing
Test: Test environment for external program execution
==> User SAPCPIC not defined in this client 066
External programs can not be executed in this client
Test: Check profile parameters
Server = bsl1041_I2I_00 , Date = 27.07.2007 , Time = 09:14:39
rdisp/btctime = 60
rdisp/wp_no_btc = 3
==> Server is configured correctly for background processing
SM65 bsl1041 INS

**Figure 2.8** Analysis Log

### 2.2.5 Authorizations

Authorizations control which actions a user is allowed to perform in background processing. Table 2.1 provides an overview of the most important authorizations in this area. All users are allowed to schedule, cancel, delete, and check the status of their own jobs without special authorization. However, special authorization is required to do the following:

- Manipulate a job that was scheduled by another user.
- Display the job log.
- Display a spool request generated by a background job.
- Release a job for execution.
- Use an external command.

Unlike dialog processing, no passwords are checked in the background operation. The SAP users involved simply have to be created and not locked in the current client.

| Authorization | Description |
|---|---|
| S_BTCH_ADM | Batch administration. |
| S_BTCH_JOB | Operations with client-dependent background jobs.<br>Possible values:<br>DELE – Deletes jobs of other users.<br>LIST – Displays spool lists of other users.<br>PROT – Displays logs of other users.<br>RELE – Schedules own jobs and releases them for execution.<br>SHOW – Shows job details of other users.<br>You can use the Job Group field to restrict the authorization to selected job names. |
| S_BTCH_NAM | Uses an explicit background user. |
| S_DEVELOP | Interrupts jobs. |
| S_LOG_COM | Executes external commands.<br>Required parameters:<br>COMMAND – Name of logical command.<br>OPSYSTEM – Operating system.<br>HOST – Name of target system. |
| S_RZL_ADM | CCMS system administration. |
| S_ADMI_FCD | System authorization for special functions. |

**Table 2.1** Authorizations for Background Processing

### 2.2.6 Maintenance Jobs

The system administrator is responsible for performing certain jobs at regular intervals to ensure the functional efficiency of his SAP system. For example, maintenance jobs delete tables that are no longer required or collect statistical data for analyzing the performance of the system. Table 2.2 provides an overview of the most important programs. Other jobs may be required, depending on the applications used or on your own applications.

| Recommended Job Name/Description | ABAP | Variant | Interval |
|---|---|---|---|
| SAP_COLLECTOR_FOR_PERFMONITOR<br>▶ Collects general statistical data for analyzing the performance of the SAP system.<br>▶ Cross-client.<br>▶ Schedules in client 000 as DDIC. | RSCOLL00 | No | Hourly |
| SAP_COLLECTOR_FOR_JOBSTATISTIC<br>▶ Collects statistical data for evaluating the average runtime of periodically executed jobs.<br>▶ Cross-client. | RSBPCOLL | No | Daily |
| SAP_REORG_JOBS<br>▶ Deletes all logs of successfully executed jobs. System administrator can use variants to define how many days must elapse before a log is to be deleted.<br>▶ Cross-client. | RSBTCDEL | Yes | Daily |
| SAP_REORG_JOBSTATISTIC<br>▶ Cleans up the runtime statistics of background jobs.<br>▶ All objects older than the specified date are deleted.<br>▶ Cross-client. | RSBPSTDE | Yes | Monthly |

**Table 2.2** Important Maintenance Jobs

| Recommended Job Name/Description | ABAP | Variant | Interval |
|---|---|---|---|
| SAP_REORG_BATCHINPUT<br>▶ Deletes processed batch input sessions and their logs as well as logs that no longer have any sessions.<br>▶ Client-specific. | RSBDCREO | Yes | Daily, but at times when there is no batch input activity |
| SAP_REORG_SPOOL<br>▶ Deletes obsolete spool objects.<br>▶ Client-specific. | RSPO0041/ RSPO1041 | Yes | Daily |
| ▶ No standard name.<br>▶ Deletes spool lists that remain from canceled background programs.<br>▶ Consistency check of spool tables.<br>▶ Cross-client. | RSPO0043 / RSPO1043 | Yes | Daily |
| SAP_REORG_ABAPDUMPS<br>▶ Deletes runtime error entries (short dumps).<br>▶ Cross-client. | RSSNAPDL | Yes | Daily |
| SAP_REORG_PRIPARAMS<br>▶ Reorganizes print parameters.<br>▶ Cross-client. | RSBTCPRIDEL | No | Monthly |
| SAP_CCMS_MONI_BATCH_DP<br>▶ System monitoring.<br>▶ Client-specific.<br>▶ No standard name.<br>▶ Implements transport requests. | RSAL_BATCH_TOOL_DISPATCHING<br>RDDIMPDP | No | Hourly<br>Event-driven |

**Table 2.2** Important Maintenance Jobs (Cont.)

| Recommended Job Name/Description | ABAP | Variant | Interval |
|---|---|---|---|
| EU_PUT<br>▸ Administration job for updating object lists and navigation indexes.<br>▸ Cross-client. | SAPRSLOG | | Daily |
| EU_REORG<br>▸ Administration job for updating object lists after a transport.<br>▸ Cross-client. | SAPRSEUT | | Daily |

**Table 2.2** Important Maintenance Jobs (Cont.)

For more information about the properties and parameters of these jobs, refer to the documentation of each individual program. You use the ABAP Editor (SE38) for this purpose. Enter the program name and select **Documentation • Display**.

You can schedule all of the preceding jobs individually or automatically with standard parameter settings by choosing **Job Definition (SM36) • Standard Jobs**.

In addition to the maintenance jobs related to the Basis component, application-specific reorganizations can also improve the performance of the system. One important example is the SBAL_DELETE report for deleting the application log.

### 2.2.7 External Interface

SAP-BC-XBP

You can use the SAP-BC-XBP interface to integrate SAP background jobs with external job management systems. The supported functions are listed here:

- Defining jobs
- Changing, editing, and deleting jobs
- Starting jobs

- Canceling active jobs
- Accessing job information (status, log files, etc.)

This interface is also used by the new *SAP Central Process Scheduling by Redwood* (SAP CPS) tool described in the following section.

### 2.2.8 SAP Central Process Scheduling by Redwood

In cooperation with the software manufacturer, Redwood, SAP provides (with SAP NetWeaver 2004 SP12) SAP Central Process Scheduling by Redwood as an external job scheduling tool that enables you to execute and monitor time-driven processes in the complex SAP Central Process Scheduling by Redwood system landscape.

This enabled SAP to react to new requirements, some examples of which are as follows:

- Using SAP NetWeaver as the integration platform, a cross-component tool that supports both AS ABAP and AS Java is required for automating processes.
- More and more business processes run on a time-driven or event-driven basis.
- The conventional tool for planning background jobs in the SAP environment, Transaction SM36 (Job Definition), has its limitations (e.g., defining job chains across systems) and can therefore no longer completely meet today's requirements.

In contrast, the external SAP Central Process Scheduling tool offers several new functions that facilitate the administration of company-critical business processes centrally and across systems in SAP and non-SAP environments. Realtime-driven and event-driven functions form the basis for this.

SAP CPS is available in two versions: basic and full.

**Basic version** The basic version of SAP CPS is available at no extra cost to all SAP customers with an SAP NetWeaver license. SAP CPS provides the central administration point for defining, controlling, and monitoring jobs of an ABAP system landscape.

However, you can't use it to schedule and manage processes from third-party applications, operating system commands, and database jobs.

**Full version**

The full version can be licensed separately and provides additional options beyond the functions mentioned previously, such as scheduling and managing background jobs for many non-SAP systems, starting activities at the operating system level, a wide range of options for the load distribution of background jobs, and many more.

Table 2.3 shows an overview of the range of functions in the basic and full versions.

| Function | Basic Version | Full Version |
|---|---|---|
| Schedules ABAP programs as a job (also in older SAP releases up to 3.1) | Yes | Yes |
| Schedules event-driven jobs within SAP systems | Yes | Yes |
| Defines, manages, and controls jobs from a central administration interface | Yes | Yes |
| Uses calendars | Yes | Yes |
| Uses alarms | Yes | Yes |
| Models complex jobs with a graphical user interface | Yes | Yes |
| Generates reports and forecasts | Yes | Yes |
| Monitors job logs and spool lists from a central administration console | Yes | Yes |
| Uses predefined job chains | Yes | Yes |
| Executes and manages jobs in non-SAP systems | No | Yes |
| Starts activities at the operating system level | No | Yes |
| Configures several process servers for load distribution and system stability | No | Yes |
| Creates, plans, and executes database jobs, for example, backups | No | Yes |
| Supports adaptive computing environments | No | Yes |

**Table 2.3** Range of Functions in Versions

SAP CPS is currently available as a standalone solution (see Figure 2.9).

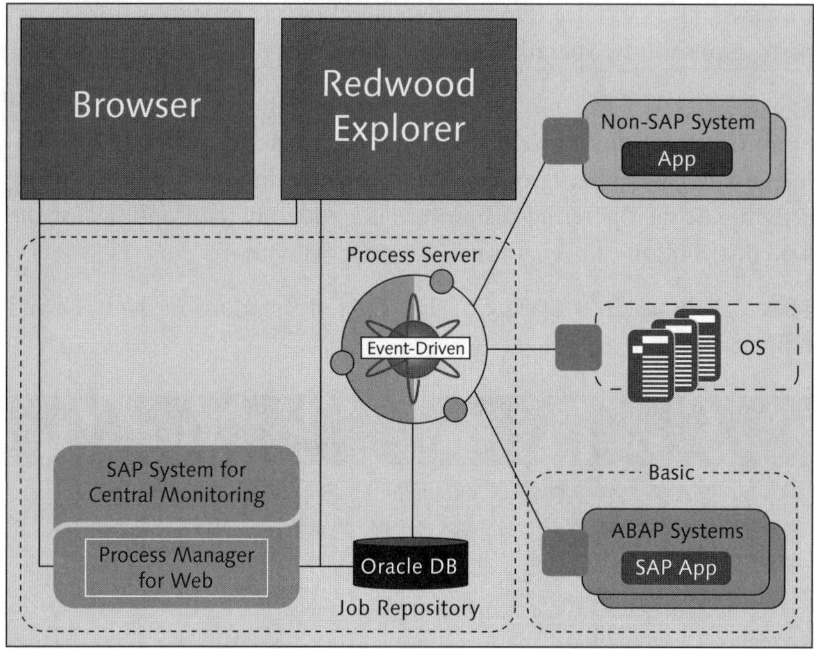


**Figure 2.9** CPS Architecture

For the CPS architecture, a standalone solution means the following:

- The core element, the process server, is installed separately.
- The process server requires a separate Oracle database for saving the job repository; an Oracle runtime license is required for this.
- An existing Oracle database, for example, for an SAP NetWeaver system, can be used as the database for the job Repository; no additional Oracle license fees are incurred in this case.
- An alternative database system is not supported.
- The process server can be installed on all operating systems supported by SAP.
- The Redwood Explorer is used as the user interface; it connects to the process server via HTTP or OracleNet.
- The process manager for the Web should be deployed in an SAP NetWeaver AS Java for maintenance reasons. The Redwood Explorer

or any browser can connect to the process server by HTTP, albeit with restricted functions.

**Integrated version**

One approach is to change the architecture of SAP CPS to an extent that it no longer is a standalone solution but instead is fully integrated into SAP NetWeaver (see Figure 2.10). This solution has been available since March, 2008.

In the integrated version of SAP CPS, the job Repository moves from the previous standalone Oracle database to the database of the SAP NetWeaver system. The biggest advantage here is that you now no longer have to save the job Repository exclusively in an Oracle database. You can use all operating systems and database combinations supported by SAP NetWeaver. The process server is deployed as a service in an SAP NetWeaver AS Java. There will no longer be an independent user interface; a browser-based user interface integrated into SAP NetWeaver AS Java will be provided instead.

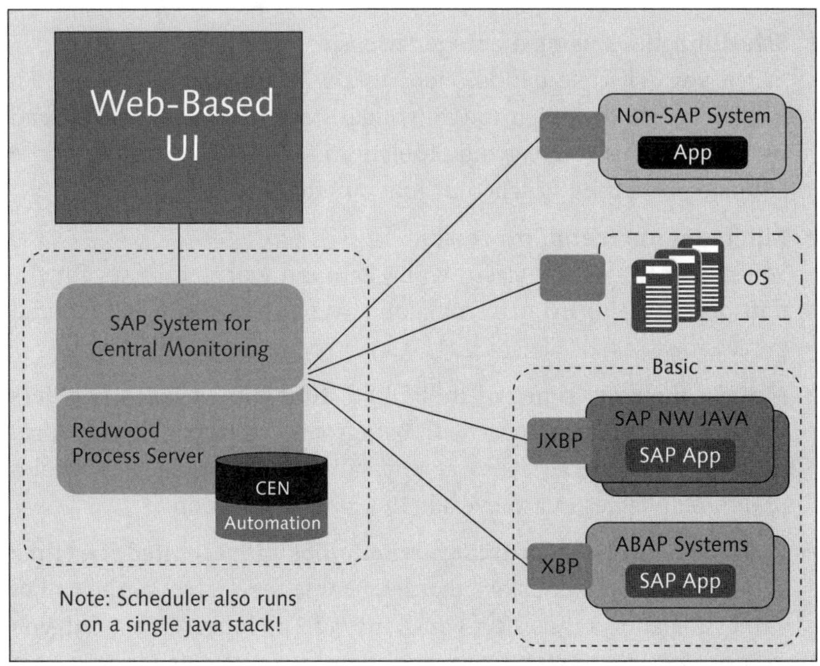


**Figure 2.10** CPS Architecture of Integrated Version

### 2.2.9 Tips

- **Defining jobs, specifying a target host**
  If you often use job definitions where you specify a target server, you must make sure to modify the job definitions when there are configuration changes. For example, this applies when:
  - You move an application server to other hardware (server name changes).
  - You change the distribution of work processes when defining an operation mode.
- **Deleting jobs with the Scheduled status that are no longer current**
  When you display the current job queue in the Simple Job Selection (SM37), the checkbox for the *Scheduled* job status is not selected by default, which means that the administrator may not notice jobs with this status that are no longer required. Users also often overlook the **Or after event** checkbox, which means that event-triggered jobs won't be displayed.
- **Scheduling jobs using a non-generic user**
  When you schedule periodic jobs that will run over a long period, it makes sense to assign the individual steps to generic background users. This helps you to avoid problems that occur when users, whose accounts were used to schedule jobs, are deleted.
- **Minimum number of processes**
  You must configure at least two background work processes for the transport system, even if you don't want to use any background processing.
- **Moving the start times of individual, time-driven job schedulers**
  If you use several instances with background work processes, it may be useful to set the `rdisp/btctime` parameters in the instance profiles to different values to achieve a better load distribution.
- **Problems with self-scheduling periodic jobs with a limited start time**
  When you use periodic jobs that reschedule themselves at the end of a run and define a time after which they can no longer be started, you may not be able to start these jobs anymore following a long system shutdown. You must monitor these jobs manually.

### 2.2.10 Transactions and Menu Paths

**ABAP Editor:** SAP Menu • Tools • ABAP Workbench • ABAP Editor (SE38)

**Analyzing background processing:** SAP Menu • Tools • CCMS • Jobs • Check Environment (SM65)

**Creating external operating system commands:** SAP Menu • Tools • CCMS • Configuration • External Commands (SM69)

**Maintaining operation modes:** SAP Menu • Tools • CCMS • Configuration • Operation Modes/Instances(RZ04)

**Own Jobs:** System • Own Jobs (SMX)

**Simple job selection:** SAP Menu • Tools • CCMS • Jobs • Maintenance (SM37)

**Extended job selection:** SAP Menu • Tools • CCMS • Jobs • Maintenance • Extended Job Selection (SM37C)

**Triggering events:** SAP Menu • Tools • CCMS • Jobs • Trigger Event (SM64)

**Maintaining events:** SAP Menu • Tools • CCMS • Jobs • Maintain Event (SM62)

**External operating system commands:** SAP Menu • Tools • CCMS • Jobs • External Commands (SM49)

**Background control object monitor:** SAP Menu • Tools • CCMS • Jobs • Background Objects (SM61)

**Job definition:** SAP Menu • Tools • CCMS • Jobs • Definition (SM36)

**Job monitor:** SAP Menu • Tools • CCMS • Control/Monitoring • Job Scheduling Monitor (RZ01)

**Performance analysis:** SAP Menu • Tools • CCMS • Jobs • Performance Analysis (SM39)

### 2.2.11 Questions

1. **Which transaction can you use to analyze job logs?**
   a. SE38
   b. SM37
   c. S000
2. **Which external programs can you use to trigger events in the SAP system?**
   a. `sapevt`
   b. `sapxpg`
   c. `sapstart`
   d. `spmon`
3. **What does the Ready status mean for a background job?**
   a. The job scheduling was completed and saved.
   b. The job was run and is ready for printing the log.
   c. The job is waiting for system resources so that it can begin running.

## 2.3 Updating

Each change by an SAP transaction ultimately results in an update on the database. The term *update* means the implementation of changes in the database within the SAP environment. The SAP update system usually performs an update asynchronously when you enter or change data. This system ensures that the changes within an SAP LUW are consistent. Special features for monitoring and troubleshooting an update are explained next.

The update system is a central component of the SAP NetWeaver AS ABAP. However, it's not an independent system but is instead always to be considered in connection with other services of the SAP system such as dialog, background, and, in particular, enqueue services. The update works closely with these services.

SAP LUW

In the SAP system, a business process is mapped to an SAP LUW that can consist of several screen changes. This dialog or background processing causes a data change that must only be implemented completely on the database (in other words, with all changes from the LUW) or not at all. The SAP update system therefore ensures that changes are first written to the database when the SAP LUW is completed, and that no data whatsoever is changed if the SAP transaction terminates. In most cases, the update is implemented *asynchronously* at the end of an LUW. This significantly improves the performance for the dialog user, who can already continue working in the next LUW, while the update system is still implementing the change on the database.

As long as the update has not been implemented, the objects to be changed remain locked; depending on the type of lock, other users can't access these objects, or at least not in change mode. Updating problems impair the functions of the entire system and, consequently, the highest priority is to solve the problems. The following sections describe the basic concepts of updating and explain how to use the update monitoring tools integrated into the SAP NetWeaver AS ABAP.

### 2.3.1 Concepts of Updating

Updating system

You need a special update system to map the SAP LUW to database transactions. Logical SAP units of work are converted into independent SAP LUWs that can in turn consist of several database transactions. This is only possible with a separate update system because each SAP LUW would otherwise have to be mapped to exactly one database transaction. You can use this update system to manage the data entry and updating separately and bundle update processes.

If a user enters data, for example, this is first received by the dialog process. However, the required changes in the database are not performed by the dialog process itself, but by update work processes specifically provided for this purpose; the changes are therefore made asynchronously (see Figure 2.11).

During the dialog processing of the SAP LUW, the changes to be made are saved in the update request as modules that are defined by function modules and associated data. At the end of the dialog part of an SAP transaction, the update request is completed, the update header (see Figure 2.12) is written, and the update task that performs the changes on the database according to the update request is called. The lock entries from the dialog or background processing are inherited by the update task, which only unlocks the objects after the update has been completed successfully.

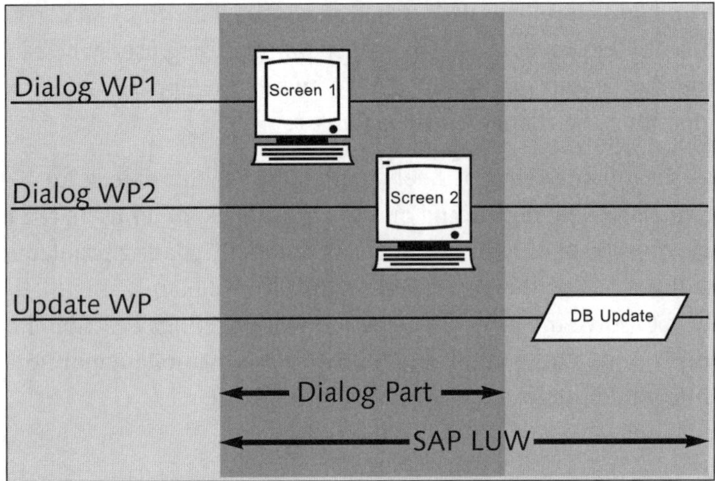


**Figure 2.11** Asynchronous Update

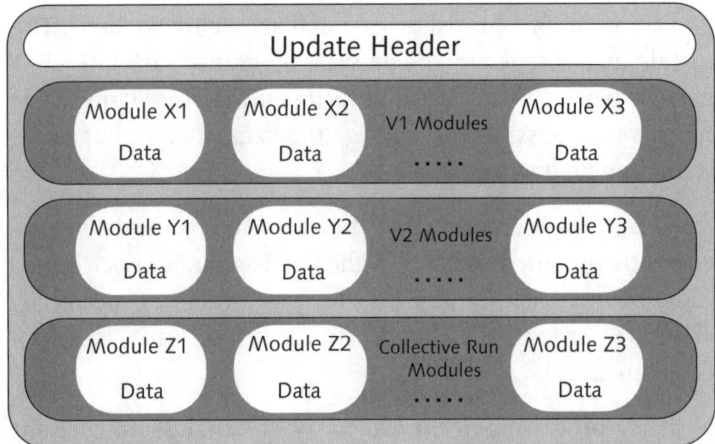


**Figure 2.12** Update Request

This increases the performance for the user, compared to a synchronous data change, that is, an immediate change by the dialog process itself. While the user is quickly entering, changing, or deleting data, he doesn't have to wait for the changes to be updated in the database. This is done asynchronously by the update work processes. The asynchronous update method particularly improves the performance of the system where comprehensive data changes are made in dialog mode, for example, order entry. In addition, the concept of the asynchronous update increases the scalability of SAP NetWeaver AS ABAP. However, the user doesn't normally have any influence over whether his database changes are made asynchronously or synchronously. This depends on the relevant implementation in the ABAP program used.

**Update request**

The data changes to be made for an SAP LUW are saved in an *update request* (also known as an *update record*). The update request consists of an update header and one or more V1, V2, and collective run modules (see Figure 2.12).

**Update tables**

Information about update requests is saved in *update tables*:

- **VBHDR**
  Update headers.
- **VBMOD**
  Update modules.
- **VBDATA**
  Data transferred to modules.
- **VBERROR**
  Error information when an update is canceled.

Because these tables permanently change, database statistics must not be generated for them. The processing of the update tables is designed in such a way that these tables are relatively small. For performance reasons, it's therefore important to monitor the update and cleanup canceled updates.

### Update mode and update modules

Update mode

There are three different update types in ABAP programming:

- Local update
- Asynchronous update
- Synchronous update

The program design already controls which mode is used, and this can't be altered by the administrator or user.

Local update

The local update bypasses the methods described previously and makes the change on the database directly from the relevant work process. These updates are not visible in the update monitoring and can't be administrated.

Asynchronous update

The asynchronous update is the most frequently used update mode and offers dialog users the best possible performance. To ensure that the system will work correctly, you must monitor the update system with the update requests.

Synchronous update

The synchronous update works with the same methods as the asynchronous update. After the update request has been transferred to the update task, the calling program nevertheless waits until the update work process returns the status of the update. Synchronous updates are identified accordingly in the information column (see Table 2.4) in update management.

V1 and V2 updates

We differentiate between V1 and V2 update modules within an update. There are also collective runs called *V3 updates* for frequently used function modules. V1 updates contain critical changes with control functions. They relate to business processes such as changes to material stock, for example. These objects must always be changed as quickly as possible. In contrast, V2 updates are mostly used for statistical purposes and are therefore subordinate. You therefore need to treat V1 updates with higher priority than V2 updates.

Each update module corresponds to one update function module. The allocation as to whether this is a V1, V2, or V3 update is a property of the function module and can't be altered by the administrator.

At the system level, the processing of the V1 and V2 modules can be distributed to separate update work processes of the UPD and UPD2 classes. You define the number of V1 and V2 update processes using profile parameters. You can check this distribution of work processes in the Process Overview (SM50). If UPD2 work processes were not configured for a system, the V2 update is performed in the UPD work process.

You can only perform V2 updates after V1 updates. When processing a V1 component, the system also automatically tries to process the V2 components from this update request.

**Collective run modules**

Updates for collective run modules(V3) are performed asynchronously using a batch job (report `RSM13005`), rather than in an update process. All function module calls collected are first aggregated; if the same entry is repeatedly modified, the resulting value is calculated first and only this value is written to the database once. Otherwise, you manage and handle the function modules identically to the V2 update modules, whichmeans that the update requests remain in the update tables until they are processed by the collective run.

Either the ABAP programming or application customizing will already specify whether V3 modules will be used for a collective run (one example is the delta extraction in logistics in Transaction LBWE). If the application specifies that V3 modules will be used, the SAP administrator will be responsible for scheduling and monitoring a regular collective run.

From the system administrator's point of view, it's not of major importance which processes a user carries out, that is, which transactions generate update records. On the contrary, it's not important to the user how an update process is performed within the SAP system. What matters to the user is throughput and results. The system administrator's task is to guarantee the throughput and results. The following sections explain the tools and methods available for this purpose.

### 2.3.2 Configuration of the Update System

By default, update requestsare evenly distributed from the SAP system to all update work processes; *update dispatching* takes place with load balancing.

The number of V1 and V2 update processes is defined by the `rdisp/wp_no_vb` and `rdisp/wp_no_vb2` parameters in the instance profile. The number of update records to be processed is the crucial factor for the number and distribution of update processes. The upper limit here is set by the hardware performance and therefore the resources available for the SAP system. This consequently means that you need to monitor the work of the update processes. As a guideline for the initial settings, you specify approximately one update work process (UPD) for every four dialog processes. Because the V2 update is not time-critical, a UPD2 work process is normally sufficient for each system.

**Parameters for Configuring the Update System**

- `rdisp/wp_no_vb`: Number of UPD work processes.
- `rdisp/wp_no_vb2`: Number of UPD2 work processes.

Multiplexing

In rare cases, it can be useful to deactivate the automatic dispatching (i.e., the automatic distribution of pending update requests on the available update processes) and instead carry out multiplexing using server groups that have to be configured manually (similar to installations with several database instances). However, this is a special case that we can't discuss in detail here.

The Update Program Administration (SM14) provides a good overview of the profile parameters for controlling the update task, as well as a brief description of each parameter. We explain some of the most important configuration parameters in detail in the following list:

**Configuration Parameters for the Update**

- **`rdisp/vbmail`**
  You can configure the SAP system so that a message is automatically sent to the relevant user if an error occurs with his update request. You can do this using the `rdisp/vbmail` = 1 setting. The 0 value, in contrast, deactivates the option for messages to be sent to the user if an update terminates. This parameter is set to 1 by default during installation.

**Configuration Parameters for the Update**

- `rdisp/vbdelete`
  This parameter specifies a period in days, whereby date requests that are incomplete after this period has elapsed are deleted when you restart the SAP system or an instance. This parameter is set to 50 days by default when the SAP system is delivered. The business environment will determine whether update requests are allowed to be deleted automatically; this will also probably have to be agreed upon by the auditors. Set the value of this parameter to 0 if you never want incomplete update requests to be deleted.
- `rdisp/vbreorg`
  This parameter controls whether you want incomplete update requests to be deleted when you restart the SAP system or an instance. The 0 value suppresses the reorganization of update requests, whereas 1 activates it. You can also delete incomplete update requests using Update Program Administration (SM14), Administration of Update Requests (SM13), or the `RSM13002` report. Incomplete update requests are caused by the user explicitly triggering terminations (rollbacks), whereby part of the update request was nevertheless already written by the database before a termination.
- `rdisp/vb_stop_active`
  This parameter determines whether the update can be deactivated. You can either deactivate the update manually using the 1 value, or it can be deactivated automatically if serious database problems occur. If the 0 value is set, you can't deactivate the update.

### 2.3.3 Monitoring and Troubleshooting an Update

The canceled update already causes the entire system to shut down after a short time because the objects to be changed remain locked, and the update tables permanently increase. No regular maintenance measures are normally required for updating an SAP system. However, if database-related problems occur, you must clean up these exceptional situations as quickly as possible.

**Causes of errors**

Possible causes of incorrect updates or even of an entire update system breaking down include database problems or lock conflicts in the application.

There are basically two different issues:

- System-wide difficulties that may be caused by database problems often result in the update being deactivated. For example, a possible cause would be reaching the maximum size of a table in an Oracle system. If an update is stopped, you should first refer to the SAP system log (see Chapter 15) and the database log files to find general system problems. After you have solved the problem, you must start the update again manually.
- The second category of update problems is more isolated and local. This type of problem is often caused by programming errors in customer-specific objects, whereby the developer and user department must consult with each other to solve the problem. Together, they must decide what should be done with the canceled update records. In the overview of the Update Records (SM13), you can use the Update Records menu option to delete, repeat, update, or reset individual records or all records. Repeat means that the update is continued, whereas update means that the status of the update records is still initial (*init* status). If a repeat update or new update is not successful, you must delete or reset the records in question and process them again.

#### Monitoring an update

Initially select either Update Requests (SM13) administration (see Figure 2.13) or Update Program Administration (SM14) (see Figure 2.14) to monitor the update generally and for detailed troubleshooting.

The most important information is the current status of the update. In extreme error situations, the update is deactivated automatically. Each user who wants to update data then receives the information in the status bar that the update has been stopped and is prompted to wait. The current mode remains blocked until the update runs again.

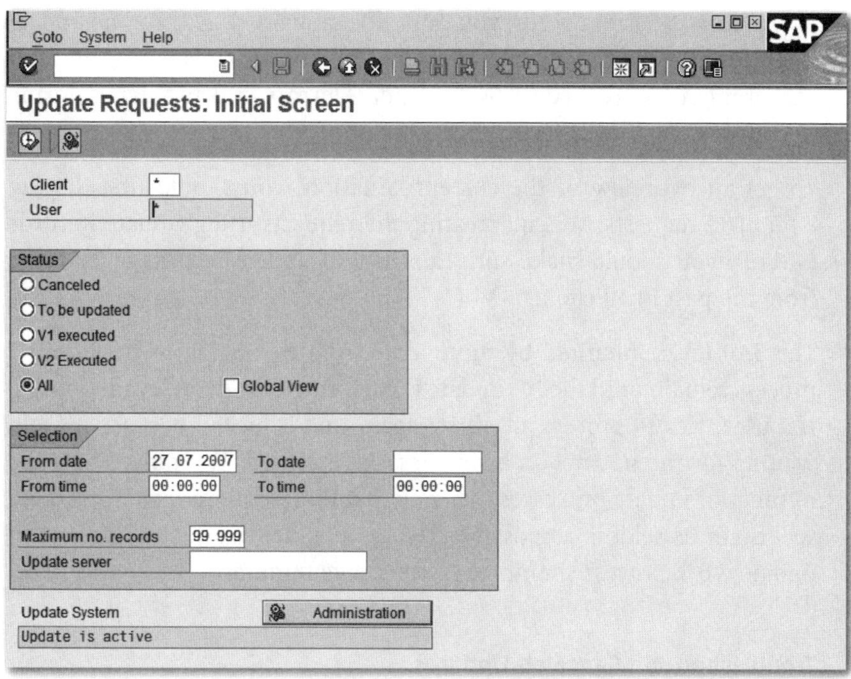


**Figure 2.13** Update Requests (SM13)

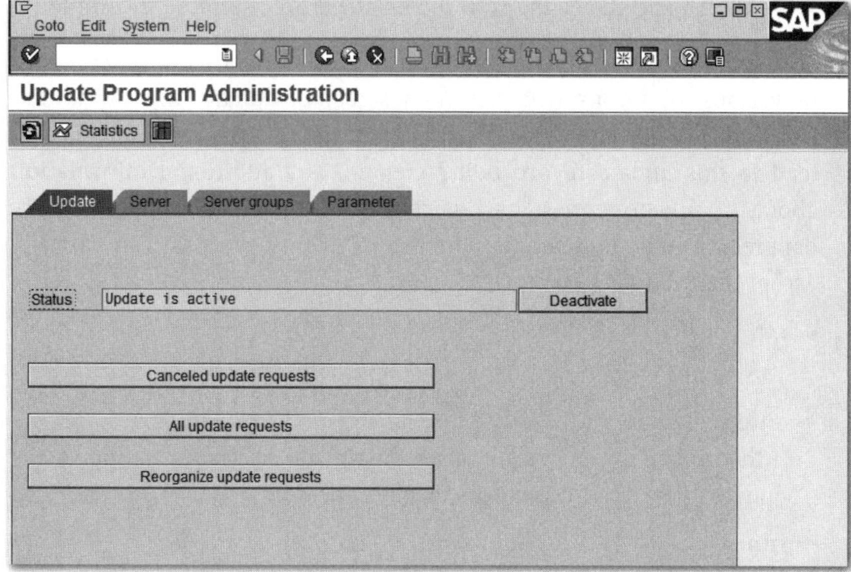


**Figure 2.14** Update Program Administration (SM14)

If system-wide errors occur, you can also manually deactivate the update in Update Program Administration (SM14) and reactivate it again after the problems have been solved. Update errors and problems during updating are recorded in the SAP system log.

To get an overview of the current situation, you should first display all update requests. When accessing the requests using Update Records (SM13), you should make sure to select all update records of all users from the past in all clients.

Locks

The SAP locks inherited by the update from the dialog or background process remain until the V1 update is performed for the relevant objects. If a user tries to process an object again that is locked because it's still waiting for the update, an error message is issued. You must select the number of update processes in a way that these types of error messages will occur as seldom as possible. As a guideline, the queue time on an update work process should not exceed five minutes.

### Troubleshooting Canceled Updates

Canceled updates are particularly critical. When updates are canceled, the required operations for updating a data record can't be performed successfully, and the changes in the database are therefore incomplete.

To analyze canceled updates, you can select the update processes, based on various conditions, from the initial screen of Update Program Administration (SM14). The client, user, entry time, and transaction code that lead to this update record being created, any additional information about the update request, and its current status are displayed for every data record to be updated (update record). Update records can basically accept the following statuses:

Update record statuses

- **init**
  The record is waiting for the update.
- **auto**
  If the update is active again after the update server was stopped, the update of the record is automatically repeated.
- **run**
  The record is currently in process.

- **err**
  An error occurred, which caused the update to cancel.
- **V1**
  The V1 modules of the request were carried out incorrectly; the request is now waiting for the V2 update.
- **V2**
  The request is waiting for a collective run (V3 update).

The information column contains additional information about the type of update generation or current status. Table 2.4 shows the possible icons and their descriptions.

| Icon | Short Text from Update Records (SM 13) | Description |
|---|---|---|
| | Synchronous update | Update request with synchronous update. |
| | No restart possible | Update request in V1 module canceled; update can't be repeated. |
| | Update request with enqueues | SAP locks exist for this request. |
| | Enqueues released | The SAP locks for this request are already released. |
| | External commit | Update request was created by an external system. |
| | Created by the batch input | Update request was created by batch input session. Request update can't be repeated. |

**Table 2.4** Table 2.4 Description of Information Icons

Troubleshooting

You must analyze the cause of cancellations in detail in each case. In addition to solving the cause of an error, you must also decide what to do with the canceled update requests. Business aspects are the crucial factors here, which means that you can only carry out the analysis in close cooperation with the user department as follows:

1. In the Update Records (SM13) management, select the **Canceled** status, corresponding client, user, and relevant period.
2. Select **Execute**.

3. A list of all canceled updates is displayed. The client, user, timestamp, transaction code that created the update, and status are displayed for each record.
4. Analyze the cancellation of the update together with the responsible user department.
5. You can select individual update records for this and test them by selecting **Update Records • Test**. You can also carry out an update in debugging mode by selecting **Update Records • Debugging**. However, use this function carefully because it places considerable strain on a system's resources.
6. If this doesn't achieve any results, check the update header of the data record. The update header contains all of the update record's management data. Select **Goto• Update Header** here.

   From the overview of the canceled **update records**, you can select **Update Modules** to find out which function modules (update modules) should be executed for updating a record. This overview reflects the structure of an update request from Figure 2.12.
7. Select **Goto• Display Data** to check the actual data of an update record.
8. Analyze the System Log (SM21) of the SAP system for error messages that were issued when the update canceled.

**Note**

During normal operation of the SAP system, you have to monitor three essential points concerning the update:

- Is the update active?
- Are there update cancellations?
- How big is the queue for the pending requests to be updated?

Monitoring update activities is one of the system administrator's daily tasks.

### 2.3.4 Tips

- **Overview of all open updates**
  When you access Transaction SM13, you should enter "*" as the user and client for an initial overview and select a date before the installation date. Otherwise, you'll only receive a list of your own update records from the current date for the default settings in the current client.
- **Deleting lock entries**
  The update request inherits the SAP locks during the update. If lock entries are simply deleted, the corresponding objects can be processed further by other users, and a clear decision can no longer be made about how the relevant update request must be processed. Lock entries and update records must therefore always be processed together when there is manual intervention.

### 2.3.5 Transactions and Menu Paths

**Lock Entries**: SAP Menu • Tools• Administration • Monitor • Lock Entries (SM12)

**System Log**: SAP Menu • Tools • Administration • Monitor • System Log (SM21)

**Update Program Administration:** Can't be accessed from the standard SAP menu (SM14)

**Update Records**: SAP Menu • Tools • Administration • Monitor • Update (SM13)

### 2.3.6 Additional Documentation

SAP Notes

Table 2.5 provides an overview of important SAP Notes in relation to the update system.

| Contents | SAP Note |
|---|---|
| V3 Update, Questions and Answers | 396647 |
| Update Groups (for Deactivated Dispatching) | 109515 |

**Table 2.5** Notes for the Update System

### 2.3.7 Questions

1. **The update was deactivated because of a tablespace overflow. Which actions are required after you extend the tablespace?**
   a. No actions are required; the update is automatically activated again.
   b. The update must be activated.
   c. All update records must be manually updated again.
2. **What status does an update record have when it's waiting to be updated?**
   a. Active
   b. Released
   c. init
   d. Start
3. **Which SAP profile parameters can you use to control whether an SAP user is sent a message when his update is canceled?**
   a. `rdisp/vbmail`
   b. A message is always sent to the user.
   c. `rdisp/rbdelete`

## 2.4 Lock Management

SAP NetWeaver AS ABAP has an independent lock mechanism that is used to synchronize database access and at the same time ensure that two transactions can change the same data in the database in parallel.

Lock object and lock entry

Locks are defined as a *lock object* in the SAP system's ABAP dictionary. A *lock entry* is a specific characteristic of a lock object. A specific data object (e.g., exactly one table row) is locked by a lock entry. The program automatically sets lock entries and also deletes them again. As administrator, you therefore have no power over when a lock entry is created or deleted again. Nevertheless, it's extremely important that you understand the SAP lock mechanism because you may have to delete orphaned lock entries. The lock mechanism works closely with the update mechanism (see Section 2.3).

### 2.4.1 Types of Locks

You can create different types of locks from any ABAP program. Table 2.6 provides an overview.

| Type of Lock | Lock Mode | Description |
| --- | --- | --- |
| Shared lock | **S** (Shared) | Several users (transactions) can access locked data at the same time in display mode. Requests for other shared locks are accepted, even if these come from different users. An exclusive lock on an object that already has a shared lock is refused. |
| Exclusive lock | **E** (Exclusive) | An exclusive lock protects the locked object against all types of locks from other transactions. Only the same lock owner can set (cumulate) the lock again. |
| Exclusive but not cumulative | **X** (eXclusive noncumulative) | Although the same transaction can be requested and successively processed several times from the same transaction, an exclusive but not cumulative lock can only be called once from the same transaction. All other lock requests are rejected. |
| Optimistic lock | **O** (Optimistic) | Optimistic locks initially behave like shared locks, however, they can be converted into exclusive locks. |

**Table 2.6** Types of Locks

The programmer determines which of the possible lock types are used in a program. Naturally, several SAP locks can be set and also deleted again during the course of an SAP transaction. Several database locks can occur within an SAP lock, however, they have a considerably shorter lifetime than SAP locks. An SAP lock can be held over several database LUWs.

A lock can be transferred to the update during the course of an SAP transaction. Locks that were transferred to the update are saved in a backup file in addition to the lock table to ensure that they won't be lost if the enqueue server fails. The backup indicator is then set in lock management.

### 2.4.2 Lock Owners

**Dialog owner and update owner**

A lock entry can basically have one or two owners. When you begin a transaction, two owners, the *dialog owner* and *update owner,* are created. Both owners can request locks.

The programmer can define the lock owner when a lock is requested. The _SCOPE parameter is used for this purpose, which the programmer must set using an ENQUEUE function module each time a lock is requested. Table 2.7 shows possible characteristics of the parameter.

| Value | Description |
|---|---|
| _SCOPE = 1 | The lock only belongs to the dialog owner (E_1) and therefore only exists in the dialog transaction. The lock is removed by calling DEQUEUE or by ending the transaction, not by COMMIT WORK or ROLLBACK WORK. |
| _SCOPE = 2 | The lock only belongs to the update owner (E_2) and is therefore inherited by the update when CALL FUNCTION '...' IN UPDATE TASK and COMMIT WORK are called. The lock is removed when the update transaction is completed. Before the lock is transferred to the update, it can be removed using ROLLBACK WORK. COMMIT WORK has no effect, provided CALL FUNCTION '...' IN UPDATE TASK was not called. |
| _SCOPE = 3 | The lock belongs to both owners (E_1 and E_2) and therefore combines both behavioral patterns. This lock is removed when the last of the two owners releases it. |

**Table 2.7** _SCOPE Parameters

**Example**

Figure 2.15 shows the locks during an SAP LUW in conjunction with the _SCOPE parameter. The figure displays how long the SAP locks are active for (these are not the actual database locks).

The lock is held until either the corresponding DEQUEUE function module is called, or (as shown in Figure 2.15) the transaction is ended using an implicit DEQUEUE_ALL.

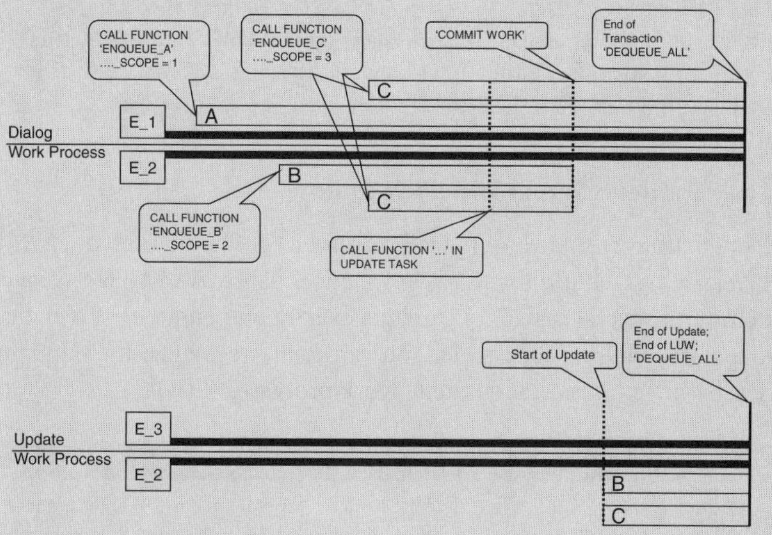


**Figure 2.15** Example of a Lock

In this example, lock object A (that the programmer previously created in the ABAP dictionary) is therefore locked by the CALL FUNCTION 'ENQUEUE_A' function call during the course of the transaction. Setting the _SCOPE parameter to 1 means that lock A is not forwarded to the update task (it only belongs to the E_1 dialog owner) and will be removed when DEQUEUE_A is called or, at the latest, at the end of the dialog transaction.

Lock B, lock E_2 belonging to the update owner (_SCOPE is set to 2) and lock C belonging to the two owners (_SCOPE is set to 3) are requested later. An update request is generated by calling CALL FUNCTION '...' IN UPDATE TASK. COMMIT WORK calls the update task, which inherits the locks and update owner of locks B and C. These locks are released at the end of the update. However, lock C belonging to the dialog owner may exist for longer (depending on the transaction programming).

**Example**

Dialog locks A and C are held until the end of the dialog transaction.

If _SCOPE is set to 2 for a lock and `COMMIT WORK` is called before `CALL FUNCTION '...' IN UPDATE TASK`, the lock remains as a dialog lock until this time (displayed in black in the Transaction SM12 overview) becaue it could not yet be transferred to an update work process.

The lock will only be transferred to the update process when `CALL FUNCTION '...' IN UPDATE TASK` and `COMMIT WORK` are called at a later stage. In the detail view of **Lock Management (SM12) • Details**, it's subsequently identified with the backup indicator as a lock that belongs to an update request and is displayed in blue.

### 2.4.3 Enqueue Server and Lock Table

The enqueue server (also called a lock server ) is the instance of an SAP NetWeaver installation that manages the lock table. An SAP NetWeaver system with several instances contains exactly one enqueue server that manages exactly one lock table. You can easily recognize the enqueue server by the existence of enqueue work processes (ENQ).

**Caution**

An enqueue work process is only absolutely necessary if an SAP NetWeaver installation consists of several instances (distributed installation). If the installation is simply a central installation, you don't necessarily need an enqueue work process.

However, to avoid errors, if you want to add applications servers to this central instance again at a later stage, we recommend that you always configure an enqueue work process.

Lock collision

Lock requests from programs of different instances are forwarded by the dispatcher there to the message server. This in turn forwards the lock request to the lock server's dispatcher. There, the dispatcher transfers the lock request to the enqueue work process. This work process checks the lock table to see whether a lock collision might occur; that is, that the requested lock was already set by another process. The enqueue server rejects the lock in this case; otherwise, it accepts the requested lock and enters the lock entry in the lock table (see Figure 2.16).

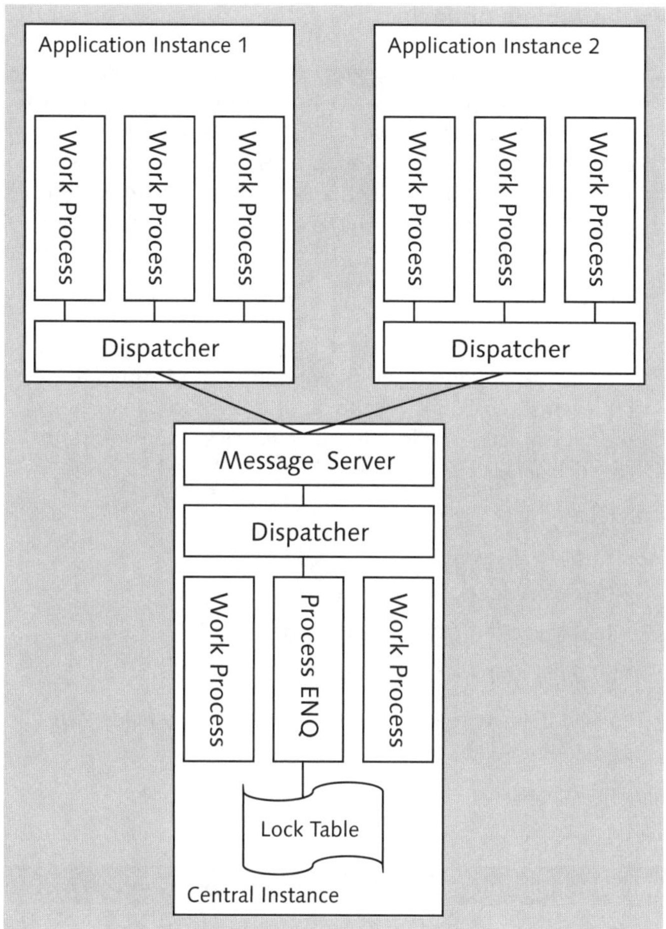


**Figure 2.16** Functional Principle of Enqueue Server

**Lock table**

The lock table is a table in the main memory of the lock server that contains the list of current locks. When the lock server receives a lock request, it first searches the lock table to check whether the requested lock may collide with an existing lock entry. If this is not the case, the requested lock is saved in the lock table as a lock entry.

> **Note**
>
> Locks in the lock table are not set at the database layer.

Table 2.8 shows the content of the lock table.

| Field | Description |
|---|---|
| **Owner_1** | *Owner ID* and *Cumulation Counter* of owner_1: The ID contains the host name, work process and a timestamp, and is also used to identify the SAP LUW. The cumulation counter specifies how often the owner has already set this elementary lock. |
| **Owner_2** | The same applies for owner_2 as for owner_1. |
| **Backup ID** | Backup ID (index used to save the lock entry in the backup file) and backup indicator (0 represents no backup or 1 represents a backup). When you set the backup indicator, the system saves the lock on the hard disk when you start the lock server. |
| **Lock mode** | S (Shared lock).<br>O (Optimistic lock).<br>E (Exclusive lock).<br>X (eXclusive but not cumulative lock). |
| **Name** | Name of database table where fields are to be locked. |
| **Argument** | Locked fields in the database table (linked key fields; can also contain wildcards). |

**Table 2.8** Content of Lock Table

**Important Parameters for the Lock Table**

- `enque/table_size`
  Size of the lock table held by the enqueue server in the main memory.
- `rdisp/wp_no_enq`
  Number of enqueue work processes that are to run on this instance.
- `enque/backup_file`
  Complete path to the backup file.
- `rdisp/enqname`
  Name of application server that provides the enqueue service, in other words, on which the enqueue server runs.

When you start the lock server, locks are lost if you did not save them in the backup file on the hard disk. The locks that the update task inherited after `CALL FUNCTION ... IN UPDATE TASK` was called with `COMMIT WORK` are saved on the hard disk. The locks are saved on the hard disk at the time when the update request is valid, that is, in the `COMMIT WORK`. Each time you restart the enqueue server, the lock entries saved on the hard disk are reloaded into the lock table.

**Performance**

You can increase the throughput of the lock server by making several CPUs available. The load on the message server process, dispatcher process, and enqueue process of the lock server is distributed almost equally when a lock request is being processed, which means that up to three processors can be occupied simultaneously. For up to three processors, the scaling of the processing duration of a lock request is almost linear with the number of CPUs; however, this is only the case if there are also sufficient lock requests available for processing to ensure that the message server, dispatcher, and enqueue work process are occupied continuously and simultaneously.

The message server process and dispatcher process here create the performance bottleneck because the lock requests that may arrive cumulatively in parallel in both of these processes are serialized and forwarded to the ENQ work process for processing.

**Standalone enqueue servers**

If you need to further increase the throughput of lock operations, or operate the lock processing in a high-availability environment, we recommend that you use a standalone enqueue server. You can use this as of Kernel Release 6.40, and it's available for downloading from the SAP Service Marketplace.

The standalone enqueue server was implemented in a multithreaded architecture and therefore enables lock requests to be processed in parallel. The load that the enqueue server's dispatcher must process serially in the scenario described previously can be distributed to several threads with the standalone enqueue server. This means that the throughput of lock requests to be processed can be increased.

**Caution**

If you're operating SAP NetWeaver AS ABAP on only one instance (classic ABAP central system), and you don't necessarily have to guarantee the high availability of the enqueue server, we recommend that you do *not* use a standalone enqueue server because the work processes of the central instance can directly access the lock table in the main memory.

The enqueue clients (SAP application servers) and enqueue server no longer communicate through the dispatchers involved (see Figure 2.16) and the message server; instead, they communicate directly. In other words, the work process has a TCP connection to the enqueue server (see Figure 2.17).

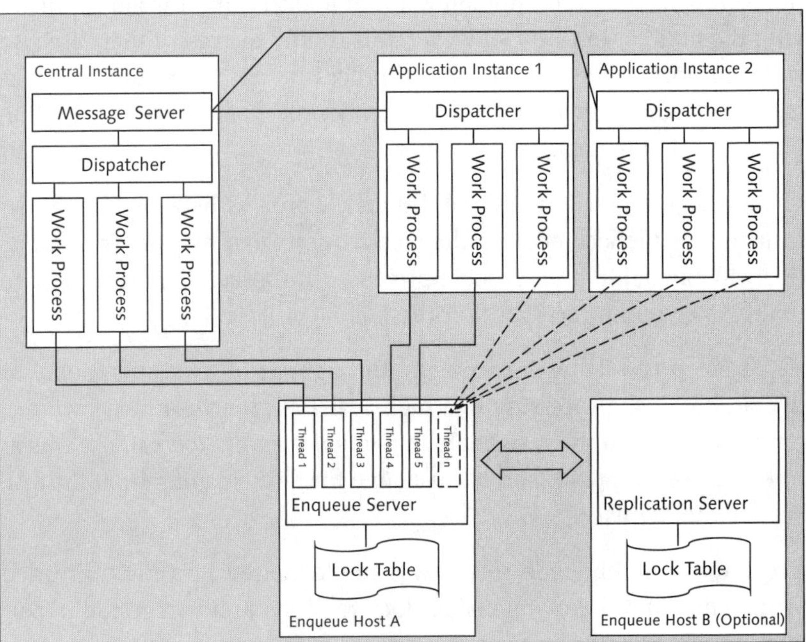


**Figure 2.17** Functional Principle of the Standalone Enqueue Server

**High availability**

As already mentioned, not only can you increase the throughput of processed lock requests using a standalone enqueue server, you can also integrate the enqueue server into a high-availability solution. The high-availability enqueue server consists of the standalone enqueue server (enqueue host A in Figure 2.17) and an enqueue replication server (enqueue host B in Figure 2.17) that you start on a different host and contains a replica of the lock table (*replication table*).

### 2.4.4 Managing Lock Entries

SAP NetWeaver AS ABAP provides Lock Management (SM12) as a tool for monitoring the system in terms of the lock logic.

The access point is always a selection screen, which you can use to restrict the lock entries to be displayed, for example, for only a user, client, and so on. After you make your selection, you receive the list of lock entries (see Figure 2.18). The following information is displayed:

- The **Client** column contains the client where a lock entry was created.
- The **User** column contains the user who set the lock (i.e., the user who executed the ABAP program that created the lock).
- The **Time** column shows when the LUW, where the lock entry was created, began.
- The **Lock mode** column indicates the type of lock object.
- The **Table name** column shows the table where rows are locked.
- The **Lock Argument** column contains the argument (key field) of the lock entry.

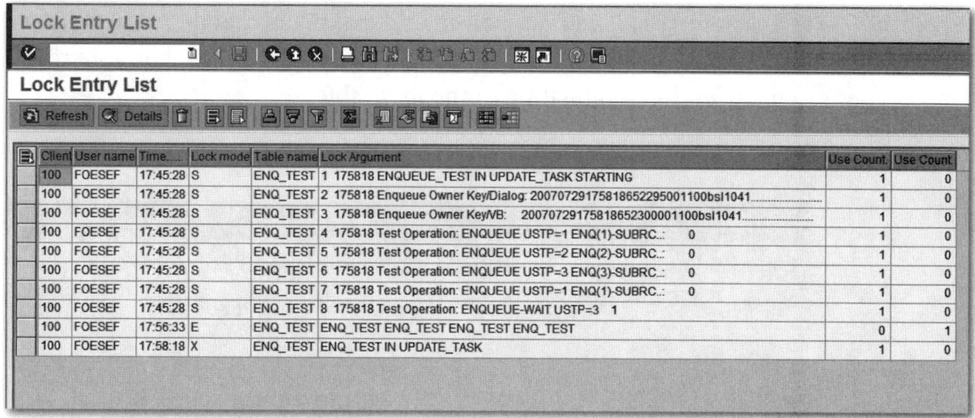


| Client | User name | Time..... | Lock mode | Table name | Lock Argument | Use Count. | Use Count |
|---|---|---|---|---|---|---|---|
| 100 | FOESEF | 17:45:28 | S | ENQ_TEST | 1 175818 ENQUEUE_TEST IN UPDATE_TASK STARTING | 1 | 0 |
| 100 | FOESEF | 17:45:28 | S | ENQ_TEST | 2 175818 Enqueue Owner Key/Dialog: 20070729175818652295001100bsl1041.................... | 1 | 0 |
| 100 | FOESEF | 17:45:28 | S | ENQ_TEST | 3 175818 Enqueue Owner Key/VB: 20070729175818652300001100bsl1041.................... | 1 | 0 |
| 100 | FOESEF | 17:45:28 | S | ENQ_TEST | 4 175818 Test Operation: ENQUEUE USTP=1 ENQ(1)-SUBRC..: 0 | 1 | 0 |
| 100 | FOESEF | 17:45:28 | S | ENQ_TEST | 5 175818 Test Operation: ENQUEUE USTP=2 ENQ(2)-SUBRC..: 0 | 1 | 0 |
| 100 | FOESEF | 17:45:28 | S | ENQ_TEST | 6 175818 Test Operation: ENQUEUE USTP=3 ENQ(3)-SUBRC..: 0 | 1 | 0 |
| 100 | FOESEF | 17:45:28 | S | ENQ_TEST | 7 175818 Test Operation: ENQUEUE USTP=1 ENQ(1)-SUBRC..: 0 | 1 | 0 |
| 100 | FOESEF | 17:45:28 | S | ENQ_TEST | 8 175818 Test Operation: ENQUEUE-WAIT USTP=3 1 | 1 | 0 |
| 100 | FOESEF | 17:56:33 | E | ENQ_TEST | ENQ_TEST ENQ_TEST ENQ_TEST ENQ_TEST | 0 | 1 |
| 100 | FOESEF | 17:58:18 | X | ENQ_TEST | ENQ_TEST IN UPDATE_TASK | 1 | 0 |

**Figure 2.18** Overview of Lock Entries

The entries in this list correspond to the entries in the lock table. The lock entries can have different colors:

- Blue means that update task has already inherited the lock, and the backup indicator has therefore been set. This type of lock is also saved in the lock table again when you restart the enqueue server.
- Black means that the lock (still) belongs to the dialog owner. The backup indicator is not set.

By double-clicking an entry, you can display detailed information about each lock entry, including the host name and number of the SAP system where a lock was created.

You can also delete individual lock entries from here, if required. However, you should only do this in exceptional cases because database inconsistencies may occur if you inadvertently delete lock entries.

Monitoring

After you call Lock Management (SM12), you can test the lock processing by selecting the **Extras • Diagnosis** or **Extras • Diagnosis in update** menu options. You can also display the lock statistics by selecting **Extras • Statistics**. The `Peak Util` of the lock table is important for monitoring the lock mechanism. This should never overflow. There is a risk of an overflow if the `Peak Util` value in the **Owner Names**, **Granule Arguments**, or **Granule Entries** rows is the same as, or has almost reached, the maximum number of possible entries. If you encounter this type of situation, you can increase the size of the lock table (`enque/table_size` parameter). However, you should make sure that there are no other causes for the lock table overflowing. A slow update can therefore result in many entries cumulating in the lock table.

Table 2.9 shows an example of lock statistics.

| Statistics | Description |
|---|---|
| Enqueue Requests ....... 164733 | Number of lock requests |
| Rejects.................... 234 | Rejected lock requests |
| Errors....................... 0 | Errors |
| Dequeue Requests....... 135472 | Release requests (`DEQUEUE`) |
| Errors....................... 0 | Release errors |

**Table 2.9** Example of Lock Statistics

| Statistics | Description |
|---|---|
| DequeueAll Requests. . . . . 106014 | Release of all locks for an LUW |
| CleanUp Requests . . . . . . . . . . . . 0 | Release of all locks for a server (when server stopped) |
| Backup Requests . . . . . . . . . . . . 27 | Number of requests inherited by the update |
| Reporting Requests . . . . . . . . 4748 | Requests to read lock entries (e.g., SM12) |
| Compress Requests . . . . . . . . . . . 0 | Internal use |
| Verify Requests . . . . . . . . . . . . . . 0 | Internal use |
| Writes to File. . . . . . . . . . . . . 3659 | Write accesses to file |
| Backup . . . . . . . . . . . . . . . . . . . 56 | Write accesses to backup file |
| Owner Names . . . . . . . . . . . . 3603 | Maximum number of owner names that can be stored in the lock table |
| Peak Util . . . . . . . . . . . . . . . . . . . 6 | Maximum number of owners stored simultaneously in the lock table |
| Actual Util . . . . . . . . . . . . . . . . . . 0 | Current number of owners in the lock table |
| Granule Arguments . . . . . . . . 3603<br>Peak Uti. . . . . . . . . . . . . . . . . . 493<br>Actual Util . . . . . . . . . . . . . . . . . . 0 | Similar to `Peak Util` of the lock table, elementary locks - affecting arguments |
| Granule Entries . . . . . . . . . . . 3603<br>Peak Util . . . . . . . . . . . . . . . . . 494<br>Actual Util . . . . . . . . . . . . . . . . . . 0 | Similar to `Peak Util` of the lock table, elementary locks - affecting names |
| Update Queue Peak. . . . . . . . . . . 1 | Maximum number of cumulated update requests (high water mark) |
| Actual Util . . . . . . . . . . . . . . . . . . 0 | Current outstanding update requests |
| Total lock time . . . . . . . . . . . . . . .42.663468s total | Total time required for lock operations |
| Total Lock Wait Time . . . . . . . . . . . . . . .0.434615s total | Total wait time of all work processes when accessing the lock table |
| Total lock time in server . . . . . . . . . . . . . . .0.000000s total | Total time required by all processes in the enqueue server for lock operations |

**Table 2.9** Example of Lock Statistics (Cont.)

### 2.4.5 Useful SAP Notes

Table 2.10 provides an overview of important SAP Notes concerning lock management.

| Contents | SAP Note |
|---|---|
| Analyzing Enqueue Errors with Enqueue Logging | 125041 |
| Enqueue Log, Sequence of Operations Not Guaranteed | 597024 |
| Better Options for Enqueue Logging | 658495 |
| Analyzing Lock Table Overflows | 746138 |

**Table 2.10** SAP Notes About Lock Management

### 2.4.6 Questions

1. **Where is the lock table stored?**
   a. In the database
   b. In the enqueue server's main memory
   c. In each application server's main memory
2. **Are the locks in the lock table also set on the database?**
   a. No
   b. Yes
   c. Only if the locks are unique table locks
3. **Can you avoid the ENQ work process in a central system?**
   a. Never; it's absolutely essential.
   b. Yes, because the work processes of a central instance communicate directly with the lock table; however, we don't recommend this approach.
4. **Can the lock table already contain lock entries directly after you start the system?**
   a. Yes, the locks inherited by the update task and saved in a backup file are reloaded into the lock table directly after you start the system.

b. No, this is not possible because you did not execute any transactions in the system.

5. **Is there only a lock table on the enqueue server if there is also an ENQ work process?**

   a. Yes, because the ENQ work process creates the lock table.

   b. This depends on the operating system you're using.

   c. No, there is always a lock table, completely irrespective of whether an ENQ work process exists.

## 2.5 Output Processing

When working with an SAP system, users create a large number of output requests of varying importance, for example, invoices, documents, master data sheets, or logs. The integrated spool system backs up essential Basis functions of the SAP system. The system administrator, together with the operating system administrator, must configure and administrate the spool landscape, and monitor and ensure that the system is working correctly.

Print outputs created in the SAP system are converted into a device-specific data stream within the system and output using a host spool system. To facilitate this procedure, the device properties must be declared in the SAP system. In addition to defining the output devices at the operating system level, a specification therefore also needs to be made in the SAP system.

### 2.5.1 Basic Principles

**Spool and output requests**

The output request is processed by the dialog or background work process. Based on the information provided by the user (see Figure 2.19) about the format type and spool control, this active work process first creates a *spool request*; the raw data to be output is stored in the *TemSe* (short for *temporary sequential objects*) in the database or at the file system level. The description of the request itself is stored in the SAP database. If the spool request is then to be printed, the spool work process assigned to the required output device formats the data in a printable format and forwards it to the operating system spooler responsible for the output device. The spool work process therefore creates an *output request*.

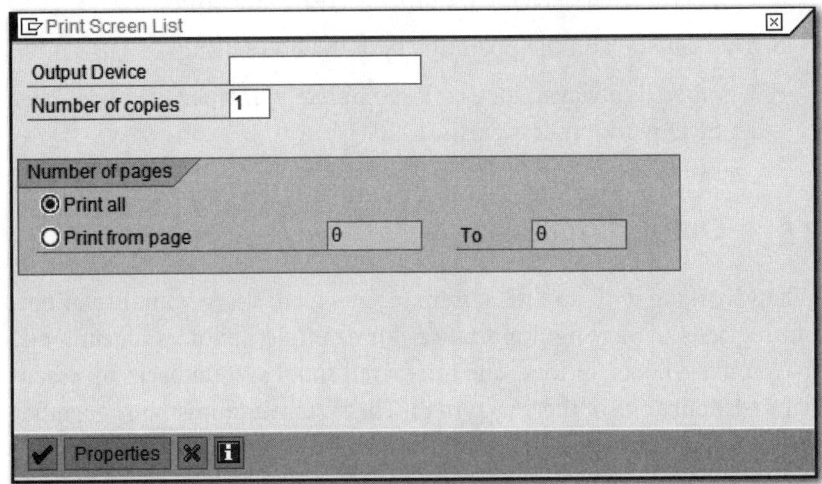


**Figure 2.19** Output Requirement

Each output occurs in the following two steps (see Figure 2.20):

1. A spool request is created containing the request information such as author, number of copies, date of request in the database, and device-independent print data in the TemSe
2. An output request is created and processed from the spool request when the output device is defined and ready for receiving data

This separation in spool and output request means that the output can be displayed before it's actually printed out, and, if necessary, several output requests with different parameter settings can be created from a spool request, without the application having to create a new spool request.

If the host spool print manager can't access an output device at the operating system level, data can't be printed from the SAP system.

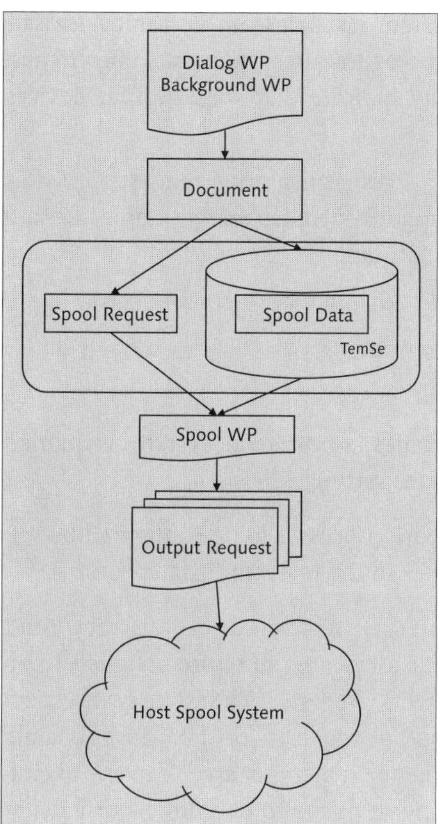


**Figure 2.20** Data Flow of Print Output

### 2.5.2 Configuring the Spool Work Processes

The output management system formats, coordinates, performs, and monitors the output requests. Spool work processes are used here.

Theoretically, you can use any number of spool work processes for each instance of an SAP system. Depending on the specific requirements of your spool environment, for an optimum configuration, you must evaluate the following criteria:

- A sufficient number of spool work processes must be configured to ensure that all requests accrued can also be processed in an acceptable time during peak load.

- Because all servers that SAP system instances run on can't necessarily access all used printers in the operating system, in some circumstances, an instance failure may indicate that some output devices can't be accessed.
- In addition to their actual task, formatting print requests and forwarding the requests to a host spool system, spool work processes are also responsible for administration tasks:
  - Reorganizing the spool system (deleting obsolete requests)
  - Redirecting requests if a server fails
  - Finding unprocessed requests

  In addition, the status of the queues in host spool systems is queried at regular intervals in the standard setting:

You define the number of spool work processes to be configured by setting the `rdisp/wp_no_spo` parameter in the relevant instance profile.

**Request management**

The spool work processes of an instance form one unit; they can't be addressed separately. An output device is therefore assigned to an instance, not to a dedicated spool work process. Each instance with spool services manages the incoming output requests for them in a separate spool request queue as objects in the main memory area. If overload situations occur, causing the spool request queue to overflow, a dispatcher queue is used as a collecting tank for incoming requests to ensure that no spool requests are lost. If space is available again in the spool request queue, the spool work processes transfer requests from the dispatcher queue into the separate spool request queue again. The processing of the spool requests only continues when the dispatcher queue is empty or the spool request queue is full.

**Sequential processing**

The configured spool work processes deal with requests within an instance independently of each other or possibly also in parallel. Several spool work processes within an instance won't guarantee that the print requests will be processed in the sequence in which they were submitted; queue-jumping may occur. However, you can use a special option when defining the devices, which enables individual output devices to be processed sequentially, if required. In this case, a spool work process always completes all requests for this device in the spool queue in each case before it accepts other requests again. Nevertheless, this limits the full parallelism between several spool work processes. Therefore, you should only use this option if really necessary.

### 2.5.3 Configuring Spool Servers

A *real spool server* is an SAP application server with at least one spool work process. Each output request is processed on such a spool server using one of the spool work processes configured on this instance. Each output device is assigned a spool server that processes the requests for this device.

You can define a logical spool architecture for the following purposes:

- Balancing the load between spool servers
- Providing an alternative if a spool server fails
- Option to transport a defined printer landscape simply

**Logical servers**

A logical server means a hierarchy of one or more logical servers and exactly one real spool server where the output requests are ultimately processed. You can use logical servers in place of a real spool server when setting up a logical spool architecture. When defining a logical server, you can also assign an alternative spool server in addition to the spool server that the logical server is to map. This alternative spool server can take over the tasks if the actual spool server fails, or it can be used to distribute the load based on the corresponding setting.

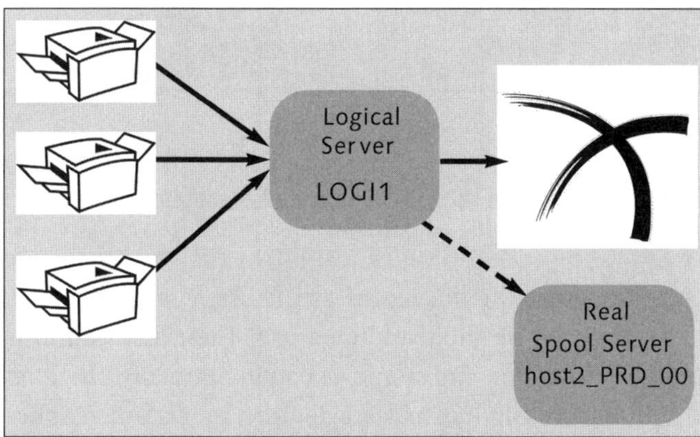


**Figure 2.21** Failure Scenario with a Logical Server

Figure 2.21 illustrates how a failure scenario is implemented by defining a logical server with alternative servers. The logical server, LOGI1, is assigned to the printers; LOGI1 is a mapping on the real spool server, host1_PRD_00. The real spool server, host2_PRD_00, is specified as an alternative server. If the host1_PRD_00 spool server fails, all print requests defined for the devices assigned to the logical LOGI1 server are processed by the alternative host2_PRD_00 server.

If a load distribution is also allowed in the LOGI1 definition, the system always determines the more suitable spool server and distributes the requests to host1_PRD_00 and host2_PRD_00 (see Figure 2.22).

If the printers are assigned directly to the host1_PRD_00 spool server, pending output requests won't be processed if this server fails.

The load for a spool server is determined based on the number of spool work processes for this instance, requests to be processed, and pages to be output.

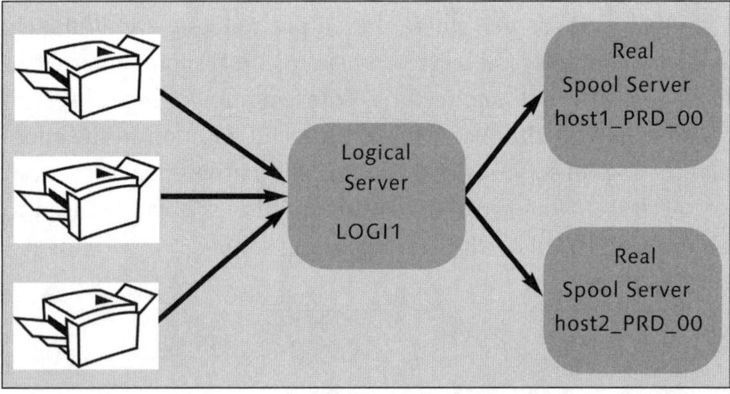


**Figure 2.22** Load Distribution

By using logical servers, you can therefore define the output device landscape flexibly.

**Classification** To make it easier to organize the output infrastructure, you should classify the spool servers based on their intended use. The classification is reflected in the device definition and supports you in optimally planning the landscape. When you assign an output device to a classified spool server, the consistency of the classification is checked, and a warning is issued if there are inconsistencies.

You can use the following variants for classifying real and logical spool servers:

- Production printing, for example, documents, disposal documents
- Mass printing, for example, cost center lists
- Desktop printing, for example, SAPoffice documents
- Test servers or test printing
- Production printing and mass printing
- Production printing and desktop printing
- Production printing, mass printing, and desktop printing
- Production printing and test printing
- Unclassified

Spool administration

You can access the SAP spool system administration from the Spool Administration (SPAD) transaction. Three different views are available here for basic, extended, and full administration (see Figure 2.23).

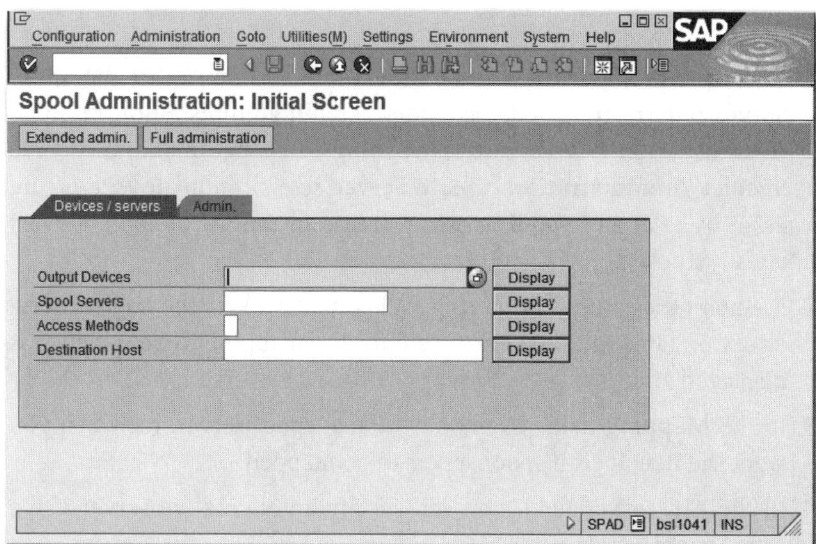


Figure 2.23 Spool Administration

The differences in the views can be summarized as follows:

- **Basic administration**
  - Devices and servers (displaying and editing output devices, displaying and editing spool servers, displaying access methods and distributing devices to same, displaying destination hosts and distributing devices to same)
  - Management (settings, deleting obsolete spool requests, consistency checks on spool databases, overviews of print requests)
- **Extended administration**
  - Additional output management systems (displaying and editing real OMSs, displaying and editing logical OMSs)
- **Full administration**
  - Additional device types (device types, print controls, format types, page formats, cover sheet texts)
  - Additional character sets (character sets, SAP characters, character set manufacturers)

Defining spool servers

After you configure the spool work processes at the profile level, you then define the logical and real spool servers. Proceed as follows to do this:

1. Select the **Configuration • Spool Server** menu entries or the **Spool Server** button from basic, extended, or full administration in Spool Administration (SPAD). After switching to change mode, go to the **Spooler Administration: Create Server** screen template (see Figure 2.24) by selecting **Spool Server • Create** in the list of spool servers already known.
2. Maintain the server's properties. When you activate the **Logical server** option, an additional entry field for the mapping to be specified is displayed after you press **Enter**.
3. In the **Mapping** field, you enter the real spool server, to which you want the new logical spool server to be mapped.
4. In the **Alt. server** field, you can specify an alternative server if the actual spool server fails.

5. You can enable a load-controlled assignment of spool servers or alternative servers by activating the **Allow load balancing** option.

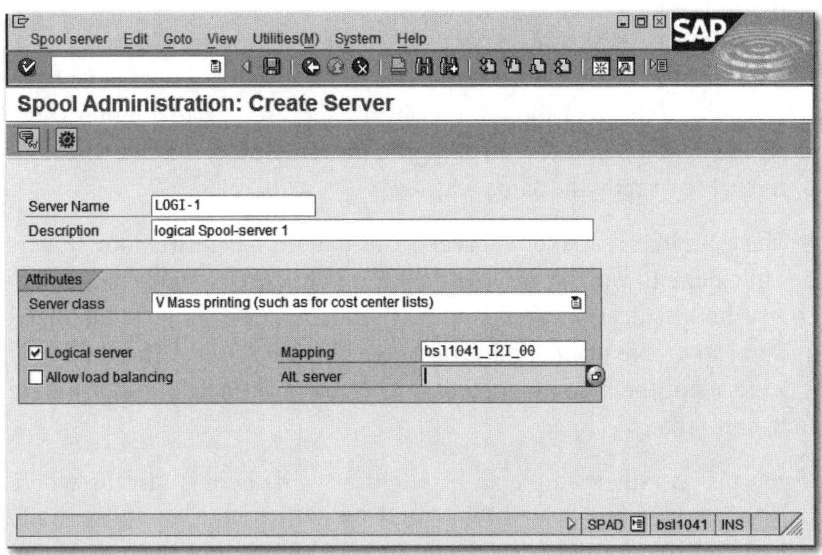

**Figure 2.24** Defining a Logical Server

Mapping relationships

Because, in addition to a real spool server, you can also specify an extra logical spool server as the mapping and alternative server of a logical spool server, this can sometimes result in relatively complex spool landscapes. To avoid losing track here, you can display different graphical displays of dependencies. For example, you can get descriptions of mapping relationships via horizontally connected logical or real spool servers, and of alternative relationships via vertically connected logical or real spool servers, by selecting the **Spool Administration (SPAD) • Spool Servers • View • Mapping Relationships** menu options.

The following options are also areas of use for a logical spool architecture:

- **Grouping**
  By assigning printers to logical spool servers, you can group them according to local and network printers. You assign the groups to different logical servers for structuring purposes, although these servers refer to the same real spool server. By modifying the mappings on

real spool servers, you can then simply assign these groups to different spool servers, if required.

- **Redirecting**
  If you can't access a real spool server for a certain time due to maintenance work, you can in turn redirect all devices, which have been assigned to this real spool server by a logical server, to another spool server by changing the mapping definition. You can undo this redirecting in exactly the same way.

Because, unlike real spool servers, the name of logical spool servers doesn't depend on the instance name of the SAP system and can of course be identical on all systems, it's useful to define a standardized and transportable print architecture using logical servers. You then only have to adapt the mapping definitions to the physical conditions on the transport targets.

If you plan a rather simple and straightforward spool landscape where only a low number of possible spool servers is configured, naturally the mentioned properties of a logical spool architecture may barely be used.

From a technical perspective, you don't need to map a logical structure.

### 2.5.4 Configuring the Landscape of Output Devices

Because the SAP spool system manages its output devices itself, the printer, fax and archiving devices must also be defined within the SAP spool system, except at the operating system level. Configuring a device within the SAP spool system means that an SAP device type is assigned to it, and a connection is defined. This indirectly determines how the spool request data contained in the TemSe must be formatted based on the specific device so that the required output request can be created for the device.

Classification

To ensure optimum printer throughput, you should plan your printer landscape carefully, particularly if different printing tasks such as time-critical printing, mass printing, or a quick output on the frontend printer occur and have to be coordinated. The starting point for configuring the landscape should therefore be to classify the output devices according to the following technical criteria:

- **Production printing**
  For performance reasons, you should operate devices that are used for time-critical outputs, such as the printing of shipping documents, in a local access method if possible (discussed after this list).
- **Mass printing**
  You classify printers where you want to print comprehensive documents as mass printers. To avoid creating a bottleneck when processing long lists, use a separate spool server for mass printing. You can select any access method you want for mass printing.
- **Desktop printing**
  Work center printers are situated locally on a user's work center and enable the user to print relatively small amounts without taking up too much time.
- **Test printing**
  A separate class of printers can be provided for new printers or changes in the output configuration.

**Access methods**

In the broadest sense, the *access method* to be assigned to an output device describes the method or protocol used to transfer the data for the output request from the spool server to the host printer. The data can be transferred from the spool work process of the assigned spool server directly to a host spool system, output management system, network printer, relevant print system for the frontend PC, or to the `SAPLPD/SAPSprint` communication program. `SAPLPD/SAPSprint` is a communication program between a spool work process and a Windows print manager. You start `SAPLPD/SAP Sprint` on the Windows host. `SAPLPD` is replaced by `SAPSprint` (see Section 2.5.5, SAPSprint Service).

**Local access methods**

When the spool server transfers the data directly to the spooler or print manager of the host, this is a *local access method*. It doesn't matter here whether the host spool system subsequently outputs the data on a local or remote printer. Local access is normally the quickest and most reliable method. The following local access methods are available:

- **Access Method L: Local printing using commands**
  The spool service stores the data to be printed in the form of a file on the host. The data is printed from there using the corresponding host spool command. By default, this is the `lp` or `lpr` command on UNIX systems and `print` in a Windows NT environment. The output status is also determined using a stored operating system command. If the device needs commands that differ from the default commands for printing and querying purposes, you can define *command sets*. To do this, you select **Output Controller (SP01) • Output Devices** to select the required printer and **Edit • Command Set** to assign an existing command set ID to the device, or you enter a letter in the **Command Set ID** field and then double-click to define a new command set by specifying the print command to be used and the command for querying statuses. This new command set can then be used by all devices created with access method L. The default settings for print and status query commands are stored in the `rspo/host_spool/print` and `rspo/host_spool/query` instance parameters. For example, the print command for Windows systems is

  ```
  rspo/host_spool/print = print /d:&P &F,
  ```

  where `/d` is the printer port option, `&P` is used as the macro for the port to be used (LPT1, COM1, and so on), and `&F` refers to the file to be printed (see Figure 2.25).

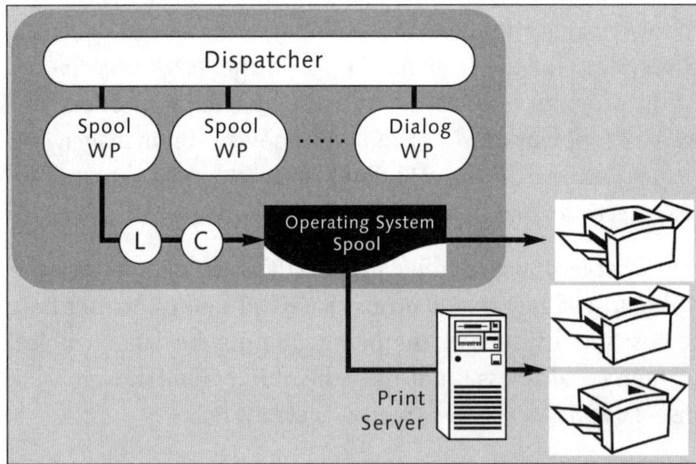


**Figure 2.25** Local Coupling

- **Access method C: Direct operating system call**
  Unlike access method L, data is transferred directly to the system's print manger using the print API, without being buffered in the host's file system. You can only use this access method for Windows systems.
- **Access method E: External output management system**
  If you also want to make a device used by an external output management system (OMS) available for printing from an SAP system, you can assign the local access method E to the device after installing the OMS and defining the OMS properties in the SAP system. Like access method L, the spool server responsible stores the data in the file system. The data obtains a local installation of the OMS from there.
- **Access method P: Pool printer**
  You use access method P to logically group several printers, preferably of the same device category, to a pool printer. You can specify output requests as follows:
  - In parallel on all output devices for the pool
  - Alternately on different devices for the pool

  All pool devices are created in a SAP spool system with a separate access method and can therefore also be addressed separately using their printer names.

Remote access methods

In contrast to the local access methods described, with *remote access methods*, the spool work process transfers the data through the network to the spooler or print manager of the printer host (see Figure 2.26). These access methods can therefore react sensitively to network problems. If problems occur in establishing a connection, the active spool work process must wait — in a worst-case scenario, until a timeout is reported. If possible, you should therefore use local access methods for production printing or very large-scale printing. If the receiving printer server doesn't have sufficient memory capacity for the incoming request, the spool service can only send the data at the speed that the printer can output it. You have two options for remote coupling:

- **Access method S: Printing using SAP protocol**
  You use this access method for printers that act as work center printers on a Windows system. The data is compressed and sent through

the network to the SAPLPD/SAPSprint communication program that is started automatically, if required.

- **Access method U: Printing using Berkeley protocol**
  You use access method U as a protocol for the spool system of UNIX systems. Unlike access method S, the data is not compressed. Although you can use it on Windows systems together with the SAPLPD communication program, access method S is more suitable in this case. You also use access method U to connect network printers with their own operating system spooler.

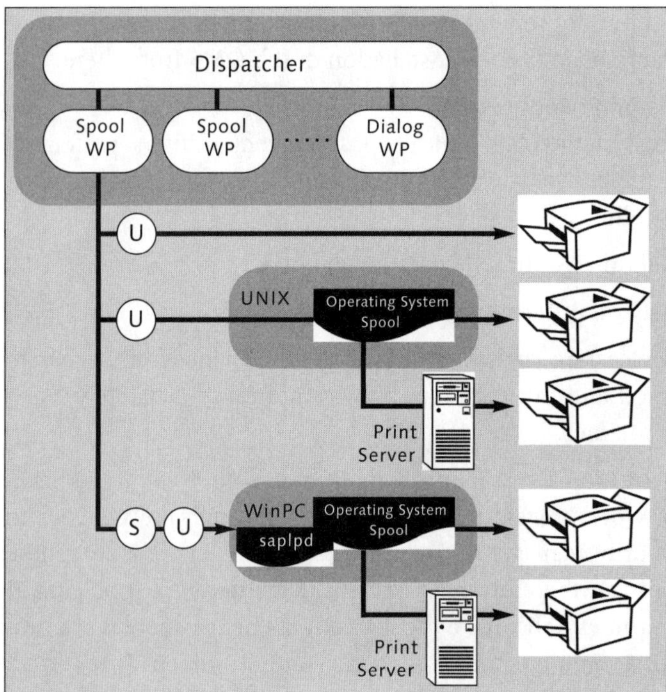


**Figure 2.26** Remote Coupling

Frontend printing

Normally, all printers that you want to print to from the SAP system must be created in the SAP system as output devices. To reduce the considerable administrative effort associated with this, you can use frontend printing. This means that a user logged to the SAP system through the SAP GUI can use the printers that are set up on his frontend PC. The following access methods are available for frontend printing:

- **Access method F: Frontend printing**
  You can use access method F to direct your output to printers that can be accessed from your frontend PC but are not necessarily defined in the SAP system. This access method is therefore not allowed for printing immediately from background jobs. Frontend printing is also processed by a spool work process. You can use the `rdisp/wp_no_spo_Fro_max` instance parameter to restrict the number of spool work processes available for frontend printing to avoid hindering regular print requests. When you print immediately with access method F, the output for Windows frontends is transferred to `SAPLPD/SAPSprint`, which is started automatically, if required. It sends the request to the defined `__DEFAULT` default printer. If a default printer is not defined for the UNIX system, you must specify a host printer in the device definition for frontend printing.
- **Access method G: Frontend printing with control technology**
  Unlike conventional frontend printing with access method F, frontend printing with control technology and access method G, available as of SAP Web AS 6.20, offer the following benefits:
  - Simplified configuration and more stable execution, mainly when printing using the Windows Terminal Server because the new type of frontend printing no longer requires `SAPLPD` as a separate process. The `LP_CMD` environment variable in terminal server environments is also no longer required.
  - Printer selection in the SAP system is not displayed anymore; instead, you can call a Windows printer selection screen directly from the control (discussed next). The restriction about the length of print names therefore doesn't apply.
  - You can perform frontend printing with the SAP GUI for Java on non-Windows platforms

Controls

Technically, the new frontend printing is based on *controls* already in use for a long time in the SAP GUI. Controls are DLLs that run in the process context of the SAP GUI. The new print control receives the print data and forwards it to the relevant print system of the operating system. When you use SAP GUI for Windows, you can also use the SAPWIN device type to use any printer with a Windows driver.

When printing with SAP GUI for Java on other platforms, you must use a corresponding device type such as PostScript, for example.

Exotic access methods

In addition to the local and remote access methods described, there are other connection options that don't apply to printers as output devices:

- **Access method I: Connection using ArchiveLink**
  You use this access method when using SAP ArchiveLink. The spool system is only used as a buffer here for the documents to be archived. SAP ArchiveLink takes over the further processing.

Defining output devices

Proceed as follows to define the output devices and assign the required spool server:

1. Select the **Configuration • Output Devices** menu entries or the **Output Devices** button from basic, extended, or full administration in Spool Administration (SPAD). After switching to change mode, go to the **Spooler Administration: Create Output Device** screen template (see Figure 2.27) by selecting **Output Device • Create**.
2. First assign a name to your new **Output Device**. If you leave this field blank, the system will determine the **Short name**.
3. Select the relevant SAP device type for the printers to be accessed, and assign the device to the required logical or real **Spool Server**. A suitable device type is normally already defined in the SAP system because device types represent model families, not models. If required, you can also download other device types from the SAP *sapserv[x]* service hosts, use the compatibility mode of many models, or, by specifying the *SWIN* device type in Windows environments, implement the formatting using the print manager and Windows driver instead of the SAP spool work process. You can also define your own device types, although that is a major task.
4. We differentiate the following in terms of device class
   - Standard printer
   - Archiving device
   - Telefax
   - Telex
   - Pool printer

- Logical output device
- Job ticket

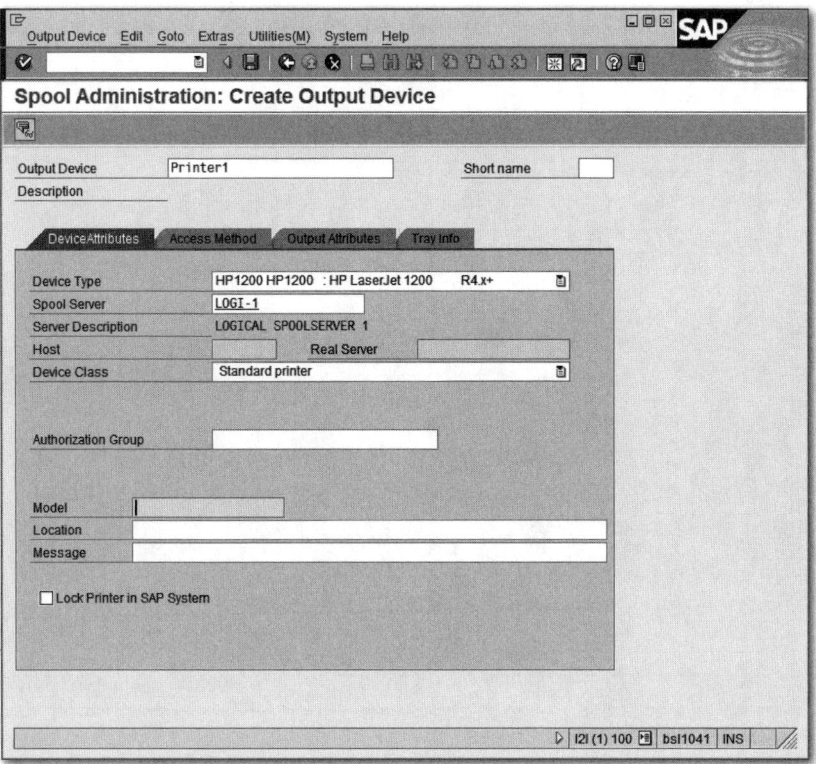


**Figure 2.27** Device Attributes

5. The **Authorization Group** combines a group of output devices that you can specify in an authorization definition instead of a single device.
6. You can use the **Model**, **Location**, and **Message** fields for explanatory texts. The content of the message field, or if this is empty, standard information, is displayed in the overview list of all defined output devices. You can lock the printer in the SAP system for the purpose of maintenance work.

**Host Spool Access Method** defines the communication between spool servers and host spoolers (see Figure 2.28).

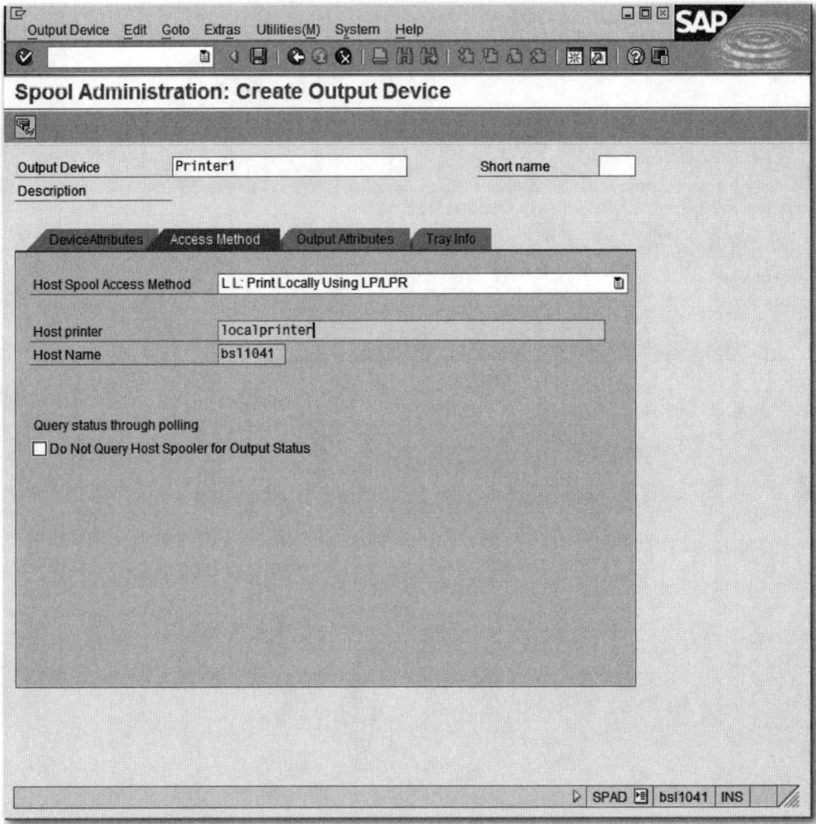


**Figure 2.28** Host Spool Access Method

**Host printer** is the name the device is known under at the operating system level, for example, *\\host\printername or _DEFAULT*. In the case of a local coupling, the host on which the spool servers and host spoolers are running is displayed here. Where you have a remote access method, you must explicitly specify the **destination host** that receives the data.

To trace the status of the print request from the SAP system after it has already been transferred to the host spool system, the active spool work process can explicitly query the host spooler. To avoid this for performance reasons, you can activate the **Do Not Query Host Spooler for Output Status** indicator. This explicit querying option is not possible for frontend printing. Here, and when the host spool status query is deactivated, a request in the spool system is considered to be complete when it's transferred to the host spool process.

You can select **Monitor using monitoring architecture** for important output devices (see Figure 2.29).

**Process requests sequentially** ensures that requests for a device are processed in the order they were assigned. Setting devices takes priority over defining the load balance of the spool server.

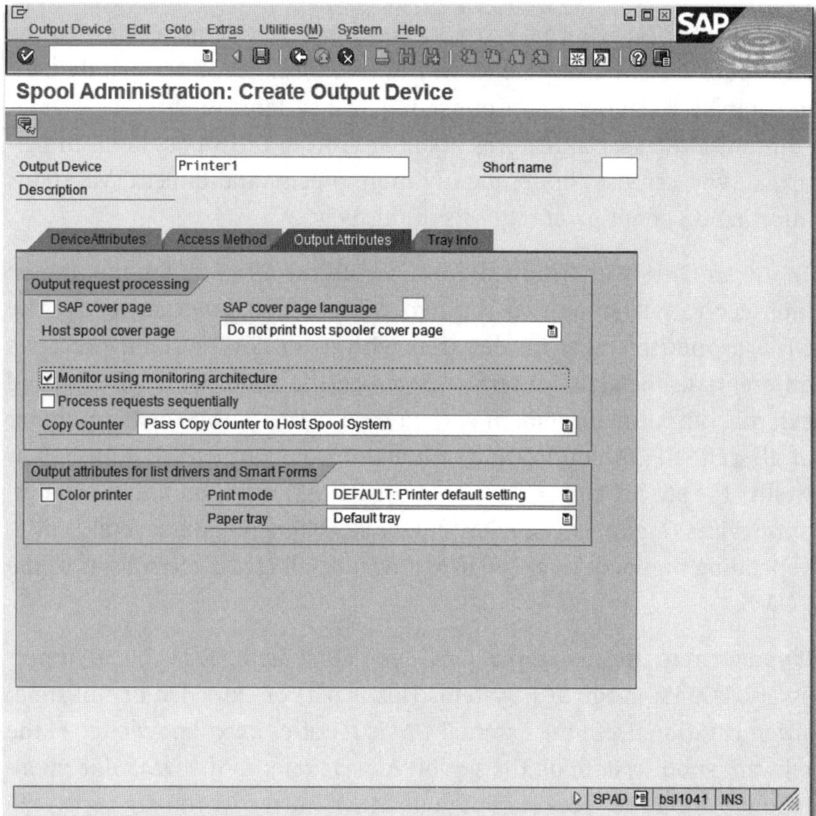


**Figure 2.29** Output Attributes

You can use the **Tray Info** tab to access the output device's individual paper trays directly.

You classify a device by selecting **Edit • Classify**.

You can explicitly define where you want the data to be printed to be buffered for each device: according to the system settings, in the database or in the file system. To do this, you select the **Edit • Data Storage** menu options.

If required, you can assign the device definitions made individually or completely to a transport request and transport them to other SAP systems.

Output management systems

You can connect external output management systems (OMSs) to the SAP spool system using the XOM-API interface. OMSs are mainly used in complex IT landscapes. Connecting SAP systems to an OMS enables you to use the special features of an OMS from the SAP system. In particular, you can use the frequently more precise and direct OMS status information about print requests in this way.

ROMS and LOMS

To use an OMS with SAP, SAP must certify the OMS on the mentioned interface to guarantee that the two will work together correctly. The OMS properties must be declared within the SAP system; here, we differentiate the actual interface between the spool work process and external output management system (real OMS, ROMS) as the number of all defined communication commands and property definitions as well as the special characteristics of the ROMS, based on individual output devices (logical OMS, LOMS). One ROMS may have several LOMS, depending on the device scenario; however, all LOMS are subsets of the ROMS.

Defining external OMSs

If you want to use an external OMS, you must define ROMS, and, if necessary, LOMS, in the SAP system. This is part of extended or full spool administration. Defining external OMSs requires exact knowledge of the relevant spool system on the server. Always refer to the OMS documentation to enter the properties of your ROMS correctly. You can access the ROMS administration by selecting **Spool Administration (SPAD) • Configuration • Output Management Systems**, or by clicking the **Output Management Systems** button.

### 2.5.5 SAPSprint Service

`SAPSprint` is a communication program for printing output with a Microsoft Windows operating system. `SAPSprint` replaces `SAPLPD` as a print server implementation. You only require the service for remote printing with Microsoft Windows. The host spool system (Microsoft Windows spooler) and spool system (application server with a spool work process) in this case are located on different hosts. The SAP spool system therefore needs an external process for transferring the output requests from the SAP spool server to the Microsoft Windows spooler. This transfer process is provided by the `SAPSprint` service.

`SAPSprint` consists of a `xSprint.exe` program that contains the implementation of the Windows service and the recipient for print data from the SAP system. The SAPWIN data stream is processed in the `sapwin.dll` component. The `sapwin.dll` component is also used for the new frontend printing (see access method G).

**Function**

`SAPSprint` retains the range of functions from `SAPLPD` as a communication program:

- You can use `SAPSprint` in all Windows systems.
- `SAPSprint`, like the line printer daemon, accepts lpd print data and forwards this to the host spooler.
- `SAPSprint` also interprets the special SWIN/SAPWIN data stream and converts it into GDI calls for Microsoft Windows. The printer drivers that accompany Windows and/or the printers are used here. `sapwin.dll` contains the SAPWIN interpreter.

`SAPSprint` is implemented as a Windows service with several threads and has the following additional functions:

- **Avoiding errors**
  If an error occurs when you're printing to a device, you can continue your printing on other devices defined in the system. However, SAPlpd blocks all output devices until the error has been corrected manually.

- **Error autorecovery**
  You can configure SAPSprint in such a way that this service restarts automatically following an error. SAPSprint is therefore more robust than SAPLPD.
- **Logging and storing print files**
  You can configure SAPSprint in such a way that information about print requests are logged, and print files are stored after printing.
- **Administration using command lines**
  SAPSprint doesn't have a graphical user interface. You can use a command line to set the different configuration options for SAPSprint. In contrast, SAPLPD was directly managed by accessing the Windows Registry Editor.

### 2.5.6 Analysis and Troubleshooting

When errors occur, it's important to have tools for analysis and troubleshooting purposes. These tools are described in the following section. SAP also provides usage statistics that enable you to obtain an overview of the processed spool and output requests.

#### Usage Statistics

You basically have two options to trace the productive operation of the SAP spool:

- TheOutput Controller (SP01)
- The **Administration • Requests Overview** function from Spool Administration (SPAD) for statistical purposes

You can use the Output Controller (SP01) to display all spool and output requests, selected according to many different criteria such as user, date, output device, or request number (see Figure 2.30). Authorizations will determine whether a user is allowed to display other users' requests. The actions allowed for pending spool requests are also controlled. Spool requests can bc issued again, for example, or redirected to a different printer. You can also display the content.

Each user can also display his own spool requests by selecting the **System • Own Spool Requests** menu options. Overview

The possible statuses of a spool or output requestare summarized in Table 2.11.

Problems or errors in the Output Controller are indicated by missing or corrupt outputs. In these cases, the administrator with the required authorization can display the output log, which contains information about the cause of the error.

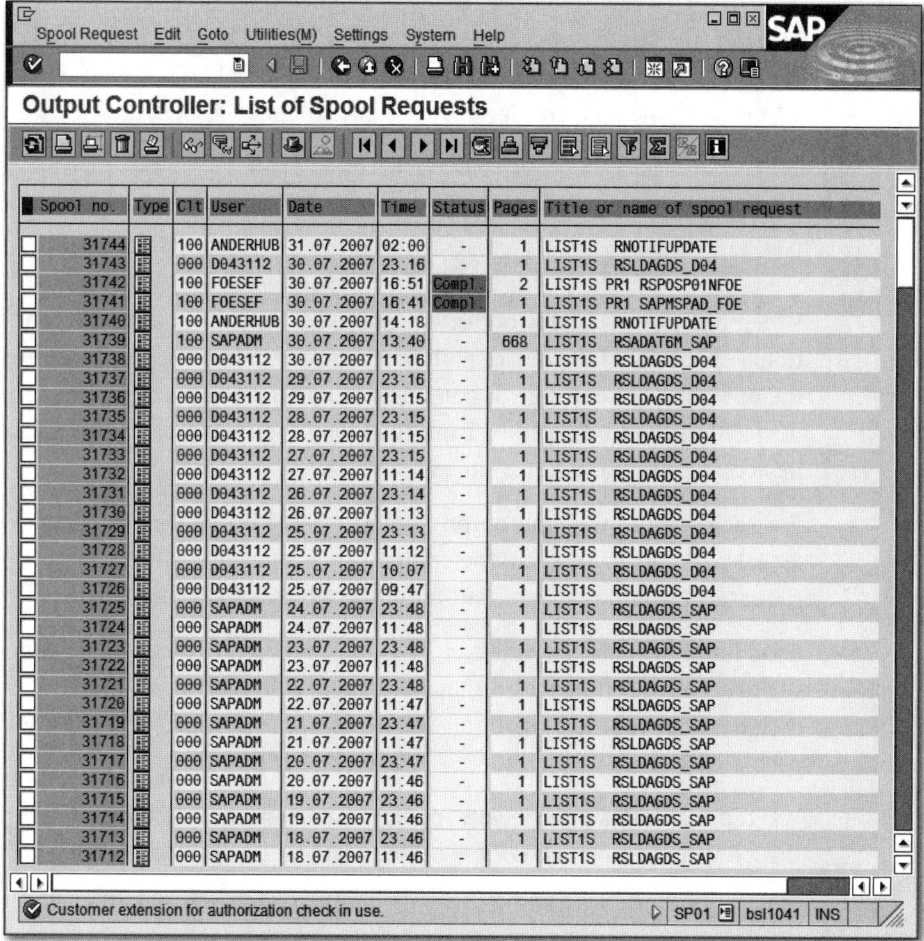


**Figure 2.30** Overview – Spool Requests

| Code | Status |
|---|---|
| – | There is no output request. |
| + | The spool request is being created. |
| waiting | The output request has not yet been processed. |
| Proc. | The request is in process. |
| Print. | The host spooler is printing the request. |
| Compl. | The request has been printed or transferred to the host spooler. |
| <F5> | Several output requests with different statuses have been generated for the spool request. |
| Problem | Despite a minor problem, the request was printed, although it's probably incorrect. |
| Error | The spool request could not be printed. |
| Archive | The request was processed and is waiting to be archived. |
| Time | A specific time was defined for printing the request. |

**Table 2.11** Statuses of Spool and Output Requests

When printing problems occur, you should always first check the functional efficiency of the device at the operating system level. You must use the operating system-specific commands for this, such as `lpr` or `print`. A device that can't be accessed from the operating system level can't also be accessed from the SAP system.

For each of the spool and output requests listed in the Output Controller (SP01), you can display the content, selected settings for generating requests, output log (for output requests only), and statistical data.

In addition to containing the configuration functions of the spool system, the overview of output requests within Spool Administration (SPAD) also includes statistical information such as the number of print requests for each device, each destination host, or each user (see Table 2.11).

You can access this overview in Spool Administration (SPAD) by selecting the **Administration• Overview of Requests** menu options.

This information is useful for assessing the overall configuration of the landscape of the output requests. The load should be distributed as evenly as possible across the different SAP instances.

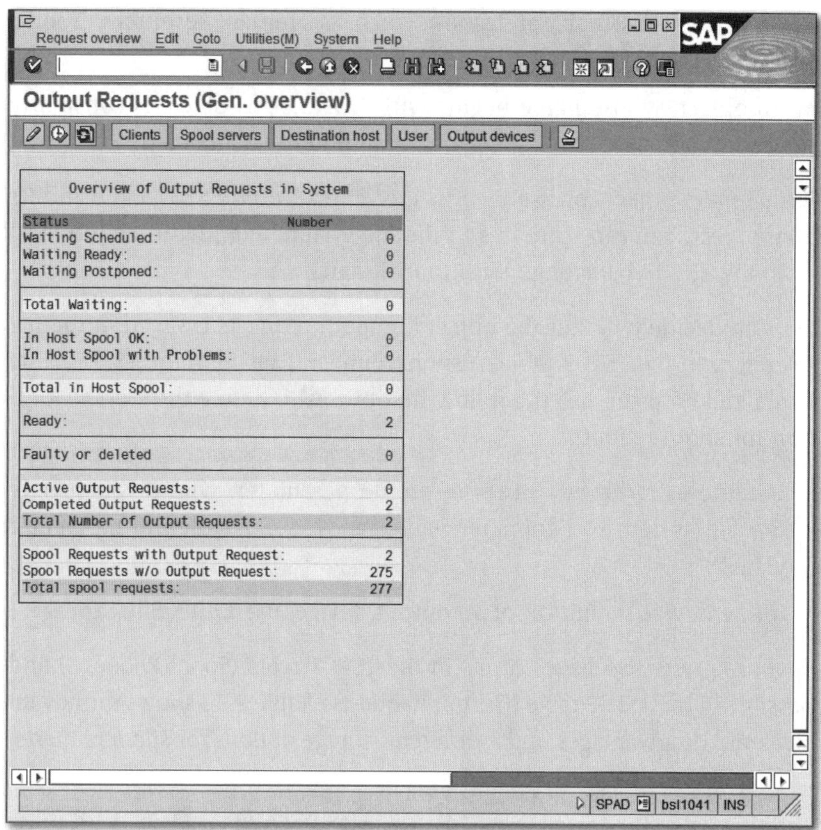


**Figure 2.31** Complete Overview of Output Requests

### Administration Tasks

Installation check

Immediately after you install a new system, or following major changes in the spool landscape, it's useful to get an overview of the configuration using the *installation check*. This check ignores spool data (spool and output requests, TemSe). You access the installation check using Spool Administration (SPAD) and the **Configuration • Check Installation** menu path.

TemSe

Spool request data is stored unformatted in temporary sequential objects (*TemSe*). The following are some of the TemSe objects available:

- Spool requests (TemSe name: spool...).
- Job logs (TemSe name: JOBLG...).

- Objects from other applications such as Human Resources (TemSe name: HR...).
- An object, whose name begins with KONS. This object is constantly used by the `RSPO1043` report and should never be deleted.

Each TemSe object consists of a header entry in the TST01 table and its own object. You can store this in the file system (e.g., with the job logs) or in the TST03 table (e.g., with the HR data).

You can decide whether the object for spool requests is saved in the file system or in the TST03 table. A spool request is saved in the TST03 table by default. You can use the following options to define the storage location for spool requests:

- Use the `rspo/store_location` profile parameter, where you specify the file system (`G` parameter value) and TST03 table (`db` parameter value).
- In the device definition of an output device, use **Edit • File Storage**.

Spool requests also have entries in the TSP01 table (Spool Requests) and possibly in the TSP02 table (Output Requests). Table 2.12 shows the advantages and disadvantages of the different storage options for spool requests.

| Storage Method | Advantages | Disadvantages |
|---|---|---|
| File system | ▸ Fast.<br>▸ Better performance. | ▸ TemSe data must be backed up and restored separately from the database using operating system tools.<br>▸ If problems occur, it may be difficult to restore consistency between the data in the files and the TemSe object administration in the database. |
| Database | ▸ Regular backup.<br>▸ Restored using database tools.<br>▸ Consistency is guaranteed. | ▸ Slower than file system storage.<br>▸ Increased database load. |

**Table 2.12** Advantages and Disadvantages of Different Storage Options

TemSe administration

You can use TemSe Administration (SP12) or **Spool Administration (SPAD) • Environment • TemSe Administration** to obtain statistical information about fill levels and TemSe content. By selecting **TemSe Data Storage • Memory Allocation**, you'll receive a detailed list of all data for each user and client contained in the TemSe data storage as well as information about their memory allocation. In terms of retaining data in the SAP database, the size of the TemSe data storage is restricted by the size of the corresponding database segments. If the data is retained as a file at the operating system level, the maximum size of the file system therefore constitutes the upper limit. For performance reasons, keep the TemSe data storage as small as possible.

**Caution**

The TemSe can't manage objects that require more than 2GB of memory space, regardless of whether the objects are stored in the database or file system. You must therefore split spool requests that are over 2GB in size into several small requests.

Reorganizing the spool system

As administrator, you must ensure that spool requests that are no longer required are removed from the TemSe. You should schedule the RSPO1041 report regularly for this purpose (see Table 2.2). One essential selection criterion is the age of the spool request, depending on its status and/or obsolescence. A spool request is considered obsolete when it has exceeded its deletion date. The default setting for the spool retention period is eight days. You can also automate the deletion of obsolete spool requests from the Spool Administration (SPAD) menu by selecting **Administration • Clean Up Spool**.

The previously mentioned report only deletes spool data from the TemSe. To clean up the other data types in the TemSe, for background processing logs, use the RSBTCDEL report to be scheduled regularly (refer to Table 2.2).

Consistency check

To react quickly enough to potential problems, you should schedule regular consistency checks of the spool system and TemSe data storage:

- **Consistency check of spool system**
  You should schedule the RSPO1043 report daily (see Table 2.2).
- **Consistency check of TemSe data storage**
  You can start this check in dialog mode from the **TemSe Administra-**

**tion (SP12) • TemSe Data Storage • Consistency Check** menu options, or schedule it regularly using the `RSTS0020` report.

The following procedure has proven useful for checking the consistency of the TemSE data storage:

1. Execute the `RSTS0020` report in the background.

   You'll receive a list of inconsistencies as the result.

2. Execute the report at least once again at an interval of approximately 30 minutes.

   You must determine the exact interval based on the length of the running jobs.

3. Compare the results.

   Temporary inconsistencies

   The first time you run the report, an entry may contain an inconsistency that is no longer there the second time you run the report. This is a temporary inconsistency.

   Temporary inconsistencies are not real inconsistencies and must not be deleted. They occur when a user writes data into the TemSe during the consistency check, for example. You must perform a check several times to ensure that an inconsistency is not just temporary.

   Inconsistencies that appear in several logs are real and should be deleted. However, you can't delete inconsistencies in the background in the TemSe.

4. To delete inconsistencies, start the `RSTS0030` report in the foreground for the subareas of the TemSe where the consistency check found inconsistent objects.

5. Select the check for TST01 and TST03 here.

6. As soon as the report has created the object list, either delete all inconsistencies or the selected inconsistencies.

   The names here can only be specified generically with placeholders and not as an area with an upper and a lower limit.

### 2.5.7 Authorizations

As is the case with all SAP tasks, restrictions on activities are also controlled in this area using separate authorizations. We differentiate between the following authorization areas:

- Authorizations for devices: S_SPO_DEV
- Authorizations for selections: S_ADMI_FCD
- Authorizations for operations in spool requests: S_SPO_ACT
- Authorizations for managing the TemSe: T_TMS_ACT
- Authorizations for restricting the maximum number of pages allowed to be printed: S_SPO_PAGE

Device authorizations

Device authorizations are used to define the requests a user can generate for output devices. The real or generic name of one or more output devices or an authorization group is assigned to the authorization object. It's an advantage at this point if certain naming conventions were implemented when the output devices were being defined. If a group assignment is already reflected in the first character of the printer name, for example, "D*" for all desktop printers, you can easily define the authorizations for certain output groups.

Selection authorizations

The S_ADMI_FCD authorization object controls which output requests a user can display. Each user can basically call information about his own spool requests by selecting **System • Own Spool Requests**. The Output Controller (SP01) is generally used to display spool requests.

Action authorizations

The S_SPO_ACT authorization object controls which actions a user is allowed to execute for his displayable spool requests. Table 2.13 shows the available authorization values.

| Authorization Value | Description |
| --- | --- |
| BASE | Authorization to display all spool requests |
| ATTR | Changes the attributes of requests |
| AUTH | Changes the authorization value |
| DISP | Displays the content of a spool request |
| DELE | Deletes spool requests |
| PRNT | First output |
| REDI | Redirects the spool request to another device |
| REPR | Authorization for repeating a request output |

**Table 2.13** Authorization Values and Their Significance for S_SPO_ACT Object

### 2.5.8 Tips

- **Maximum number of spool requests**
  The maximum number of spool requests that can be managed in the system is 32,000. With some effort, you can increase this number to 2 billion.
- **Priorities**
  A priority as a number between 0 and 9 (0 being the highest priority) can be specified for each spool request. The default setting is 5. This value is forwarded to the host spooler but is not evaluated by the SAP spool system itself.
- **Restricting printers being displayed on clients**
  If you want printers that have been set up across the system to be accessed from defined clients only, you can implement this restriction using the **Spool Administration (SPAD) • Configuration • Output Devices** menu options, select the device, and then select **Extras • Display Client Field**.
- **Network Load**
  To minimize the load on the network, you should use access method S instead of U if possible because data is transferred uncompressed for access method U. Because the administration overload for many small print requests has a major effect on the network load, as few large print requests as possible should be submitted.
- **Printing non-Latin-1 code pages on standard printers**
  If an output device is connected through access method S, the data is formatted in the server. The device itself is sent a graphic that can be printed out without the printer supporting the required font.

### 2.5.9 Transactions and Menu Paths

**Output Controller**: SAP Menu • Administration • Spool • Output Controller (SP01)

**Spool Administration**: SAP Menu • Administration • Spool • Spool Administration (SPAD)

**TemSe administration**: SAP Menu • Administration • Spool • TemSe Administration (SP12)

### 2.5.10 Questions

1. **Which types of access methods are there?**
   a. Local access methods
   b. Remote access methods
   c. Special access methods
   d. Access methods with formatting
   e. Access methods without formatting
   f. Internal access methods
   g. External access methods
2. **For which authorizations does SAP provide authorization objects?**
   a. Device authorizations
   b. Display authorizations for spool requests
   c. TemSe administration authorization
   d. Authorizations for operations with spool requests
3. **Which of the following statements is correct?**
   An output request
   a. is generated by the spool work process from a spool request.
   b. can be printed out several times.
   c. can be output on any printer.
4. **Which access methods are recommended for mass printing?**
   a. Local access method L for transferring data to the host spooler using the corresponding command interface
   b. Local access method C for directly transferring data to the print manager of the host spooler using the corresponding command interface
   c. Local access method F for frontend printing
   d. Remote access method S for the work center printer via SAPLPD
   e. Remote access method U based on the Berkeley protocol

5. **What is a dedicated spool server?**

   A dedicated spool server is

   a. a selected application server of the SAP system used for managing spools centrally.

   b. the application server assigned to an output device defined in the SAP system. The spool service of the dedicated spool server takes over the formatting and management of the spool requests sent to this device.

   c. the frontend host (desktop) that is currently managing a frontend printing action.

   d. the application server of the SAP system explicitly assigned to a user as a spool server for his spool requests.

## 2.6 SAP Virtual Machine Container (VMC)

SAP VMC technology represents a new, significant step in the work process architecture of SAP NetWeaver. Although SAP VMC is a Java technology, in this chapter, we nevertheless want to briefly explain the architecture and administration options because the ABAP and Java worlds merge together here.

With the Virtual Machine Container technology (also called the VM Container or VMC technology), SAP has created a technological basis that enables Java applications to be executed in a similarly robust way as software developed in ABAP. The objective is to isolate individual users from each other as strictly as possible to avoid any unwanted adverse effects. To provide an optimum runtime environment for selected scenarios with particularly high demands on a narrow ABAP-Java coupling, a Java VM can also run integrated in the ABAP work process as of SAP NetWeaver 7.0 (SAP NetWeaver 2004s).

VM Container technology enables a Java VM to be integrated into the ABAP work process.

Architecture

You generally execute Java applications on the J2EE engine. Executing an application on the Java VM integrated into the ABAP work process is only intended for components developed by SAP. The VMC is solely used as a runtime environment for selected SAP Java components (e.g., for the Internet Pricing Configurator). SAP NetWeaver Application Server Java (J2EE Engine) provides you with a J2EE-compliant runtime and development environment.

VM Container technology in connection with a Java VM integrated into the ABAP work process offers the following advantages:

- **Reliability and supportability as in the ABAP environment**
  Integrating the Java VM into the ABAP work process enables you to strictly isolate active user sessions, which guarantees a high degree of robustness and supportability.

  A work process only processes one user query at a time, which means that if an entire Java VM crashes, only the current active user will be affected.
- **Close ABAP-Java communication (In process)**
  Because ABAP and the Java VM run in the same work process, you can implement a quicker and more efficient communication path between both languages to ensure that the security and speed of the communication increases significantly.
- **Managing resources and sharing**
  When a request is being processed, a Java VM works exclusively for one user. A pool of VMs are dynamically assigned to the work processes. These VMs can access shared data in the shared memory:
  - Java shared closures.
  - Java objects can be moved and shared across process boundaries. This enables you to implement an efficient session failover. At the same time, shared closures enable you to reduce the memory consumption of the overall system through cross-process caching.
  - Shared class pool.
  - Like ABAP PXA, the ABAP program buffer, Java classes only have to be loaded into the memory once and can be used by all processes on the system. This reduces the memory consumption and start time of other processes.
- **High supportability**
  SAP kernel technology is reusable, so the CCMS can be used for monitoring purposes. Likewise, the known SAP statistics are used.

- **Debugging**
  Each individual user can dynamically switch back and forth between normal operation and debugging.

**Components involved**

The components and resources involved when a user is processing a Java request are as follows:

- The work processes map a free Java VM from the VM pool (*attach*) and put this back into the pool at the end of the request processing (*detach*).
- The user contexts are located in the shared memory.
- The Java VMs use a user context and process the request (exactly as occurs with ABAP requests).

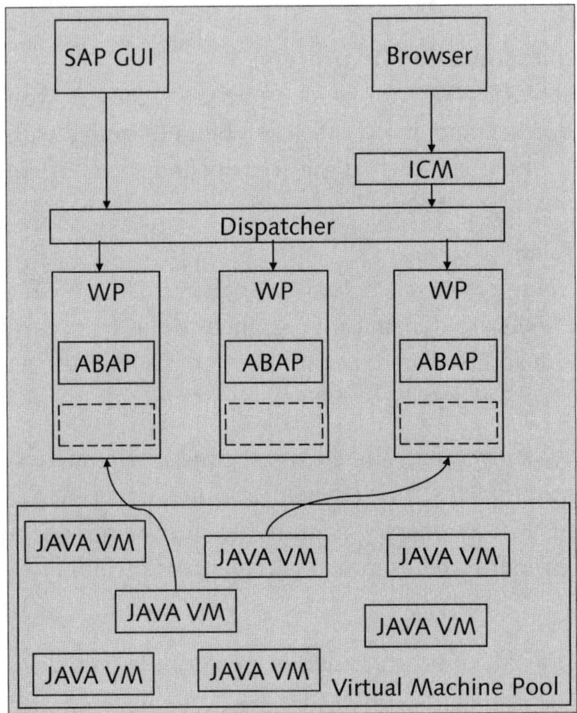


**Figure 2.32** SAP VMC Architecture

In terms of isolation, it would make sense to start a Java VM for each user. Due to the high memory requirement and the time needed to start a Java VM, there is a VM pool from which you can attach VMs to work processes, as required. This pool must contain more VMs than the number of configured work processes because a VM may also remain firmly assigned to a user in certain cases if it doesn't urgently need the work process (e.g., it's waiting for an I/O operation to complete, debugging).

Shared memory

Shared memory contains data that is shared among all VMs. It contains the following:

- *Shared classes*, which are loaded Java classes that were initially loaded by one of the VMs and are subsequently available to all VMs *(engine shared data*, similar to ABAP PXA). Shared classes contain the byte code of classes, their constant pool, and the generated native code.
- Configuration data required by all VMs.

Activation and administration

To start running the VM Container in your system, proceed as described in SAP Note 854170. The following important profile parameters affect the VMC configuration:

**VMC Profile Parameters**

- vmcj/enable
- vmcj/option/maxJavaHeap

Note that you may have to adjust the memory parameterization of your instance. Therefore, to activate the VMC, make absolutely sure to proceed as described in the previously mentioned Note.

After you have activated the VM Container component, SAP NetWeaver provides some basic tools for the administration of the VM Container:

- The VM Overview (SM52) provides an overview of the configured Java VMs and their category as well as their memory consumption. You can also actively control the VM Container and VMs.
- VMC System Administration (SM53) provides information about the status of the Java runtime environment and the option to implement urgent corrections for Java functions.

You can also use the profile parameter settings to change the configuration.

*This chapter introduces you to the administration tasks and handling processes initially performed in a system. The tools described here are essential for the work of a system administrator.*

# 3 Getting Started

First, we'll show you how to start and subsequently stop your SAP NetWeaver system. Then you'll learn how to obtain analysis information in the event of an error. Finally, we'll discuss those fundamental activities that you, as an administrator, need to fully understand.

## 3.1 Starting SAP NetWeaver AS ABAP and Java

The operating system user <sid>adm is responsible for starting an SAP NetWeaver AS, a process that comprises several steps. First, a special program called `saposcol` (*SAP Operating System Collector*) is started if it's not already active. The task of this program is to gather statistical information about the load on the host and its operating system. Only one `saposcol` runs for each SAP server even if several SAP systems or instances run on one machine. After `saposcol` is activated, the startup process for SAP NetWeaver AS begins. Because the database is an essential element of the SAP system, it must be operational first. This occurs automatically for each database system when the central instance of SAP NetWeaver AS is activated. Additional instances can't be started until the message server and enqueue server are active. After that, the process associated with starting the SAP system ends. The frontends required to access SAP NetWeaver AS can be started separately at any time. Therefore, this activity isn't part of the SAP startup process. Usually, the individual steps associated with starting an SAP system are automatically implemented at once; the operating system determines the procedure and the resources available.

Windows

In Windows environments, management of all accessible SAP NetWeaver AS systems is integrated into the *Microsoft Management Console* (MMC) as a snap-in. The MMC is implemented in a tree structure. The SAP NetWeaver snap-in comprises an SAP system root node under which different SAP systems (with their SIDs and their associated instances) are represented as subnodes. Detailed information about the processes, the current status, and open alerts, as well as additional data if expert mode is active, is displayed for the instances. By selecting an SID and choosing **Start** from the context menu, the entire SAP system is started with all of its associated instances (database, central instance, and dialog instances). Individual instances (e.g., a dialog instance) can be started separately by selecting the relevant instance and choosing the **Start** option from the context menu.

UNIX

On UNIX platforms, shell scripts are used to start SAP systems. The alias `startsap`, which references the shell script actually being executed (`startsap_<hostname>_<instance number>`) in its home directory, is available to the SAP administrator <sid>adm.

The startup process is almost identical to the process on Windows. Calling `startsap [ALL]` triggers the following sequence of events:

1. The `saposcol` collector starts.
2. The RDBMS with the SAP database starts.
3. The SAP system starts.

The preceding components start if they aren't already active. `startsap` also provides the following options:

- **`startsap DB`**
  This option only executes the script until the database starts.
- **`startsap R3`**
  This option requires the database to be already active. This is similar to `startsap J2EE` because `J2EE` is simply a synonym for the `R3` parameter.

Additional instances

The tools used to start the central instance are also used to start additional instances in a distributed SAP installation. Of course, the message server and RDBMS don't start here; the tools are configured accordingly.

If there are no active SAP instances on the database server, RDBMS-specific tools or `startsap db` can be used to activate the database.

Double-stack installations

This procedure is identical to the process for starting pure ABAP and Java instances. If your installation is an *add-in installation*, that is, the ABAP stack and Java stack are installed together in one system (also known as a *double-stack installation*), then the ABAP stack and Java stack are also started together. However, this requires the parameter `rdisp/j2ee_start` to be set to the value 1 in the relevant instance profile. In a double-stack installation, you can't start the J2EE instance without the ABAP instance. However, the reverse scenario is conceivable if, for example, the profile parameter `rdisp/j2ee_start` is set to the value 0.

## 3.2 Stopping SAP NetWeaver AS ABAP and Java

The process of stopping an SAP NetWeaver AS occurs in the reverse sequence of the startup process. Therefore, the AS dialog instances are stopped first, then the central instance of a system, and, lastly, the database. Unlike the startup process of an SAP NetWeaver AS system, the database isn't automatically stopped when you stop the central instance. You must use the relevant database tools to manually stop the database.

In Windows systems, you use the SAP NetWeaver AS snap-in for the MMC to stop SAP instances. You must explicitly stop the database; the procedure here depends on the database system used.

UNIX

In UNIX systems, you use the `stopsap` shell script, which can be applied as follows:

- **`stopsap [ALL]`**
  To stop the SAP system and the database.
- **`stopsap R3`**
  To shut down the instance of the SAP system. This is similar to `startsap J2EE` because `J2EE` is simply a synonym for the `R3` parameter.
- **`stopsap DB`**
  To stop the database if the SAP system has already been shut down.

## 3.3 Logging the Startup Process

The startup process is used to define logs in text format at the file system level in the home directory of the <sid>adm user. If startup problems occur, these logs may provide valuable information, such as error messages or problem descriptions. The logs are evaluated manually; in a Windows environment, the context menu of the instance can be used to view the logs from the MMC (Microsoft Management Console). Listing 3.1 shows you the content of the *sapstart.log* file in the directory */usr/sap/SLO/DVEBMGS01/work*:

```
SAP-R/3-Startup Program Rel 700 V1.8 (2003/04/24)

Starting at 2007/04/17 16:53:38
Startup Profile: „/usr/sap/SLO/SYS/profile/START_DVEBMGS01_
us4118"

Setup Environment Variables

(16595) SETENV LD_LIBRARY_PATH=/usr/sap/SLO/DVEBMGS01/exe:/
usr/sap/SLO/DVEBMGS01/exe:/usr/dt/lib:/usr/openwin/lib:/opt/
SUNWspro/lib:/opt/SUNWmotif/lib:/usr/sap/SLO/SYS/exe/run:/
sapdb/programs/lib
(16595) SETENV SHLIB_PATH=/usr/sap/SLO/DVEBMGS01/exe:
(16595) SETENV LIBPATH=/usr/sap/SLO/DVEBMGS01/exe:

Update local Kernel Files

(16595) Local: /usr/sap/SLO/SYS/exe/run/sapcpe name=SLO
(16595) system(/usr/sap/SLO/SYS/exe/run/
sapcpe name=SLO) returns 255
(16595) Return-Code 255 in Local-Kernel-Update. See sapcpe.log.

Execute Pre-Startup Commands

(16595) Local: /usr/sap/SLO/SYS/exe/run/sapcpe pf=/usr/sap/SLO/
SYS/profile/SLO_DVEBMGS01_us4118
(16595) system(/usr/sap/SLO/SYS/exe/run/sapcpe pf=/usr/sap/SLO/
SYS/profile/SLO_DVEBMGS01_us4118) returns 1
(16595) Local: /usr/sap/SLO/DVEBMGS01/exe/sapmscsa pf=/usr/sap/
SLO/SYS/profile/SLO_DVEBMGS01_us4118 -n
```

```
(16595) Local: rm -f ms.sapSLO_DVEBMGS01
(16595) Local: ln -s -f /usr/sap/SLO/DVEBMGS01/exe/msg_
server ms.sapSLO_DVEBMGS01
(16595) Local: rm -f dw.sapSLO_DVEBMGS01
(16595) Local: ln -s -f /usr/sap/SLO/DVEBMGS01/exe/
disp+work dw.sapSLO_DVEBMGS01
(16595) Local: rm -f co.sapSLO_DVEBMGS01
(16595) Local: ln -s -f /usr/sap/SLO/DVEBMGS01/exe/rslgcoll co.
sapSLO_DVEBMGS01
(16595) Local: rm -f se.sapSLO_DVEBMGS01
(16595) Local: ln -s -f /usr/sap/SLO/DVEBMGS01/exe/rslgsend se.
sapSLO_DVEBMGS01
(16595) Local: rm -f ig.sapSLO_DVEBMGS01
(16595) Local: ln -s -f /usr/sap/SLO/DVEBMGS01/exe/igswd_mt ig.
sapSLO_DVEBMGS01

Starting Programs

(16634) Starting: local ms.sapSLO_DVEBMGS01 pf=/usr/sap/SLO/
SYS/profile/SLO_DVEBMGS01_us4118
(16634) New Child Process created.
(16634) Starting local Command:
 Command:  ms.sapSLO_DVEBMGS01
           pf=/usr/sap/SLO/SYS/profile/SLO_DVEBMGS01_us4118
(16635) Starting: local dw.sapSLO_DVEBMGS01 pf=/usr/sap/SLO/
SYS/profile/SLO_DVEBMGS01_us4118
(16635) New Child Process created.
(16635) Starting local Command:
 Command:  dw.sapSLO_DVEBMGS01
           pf=/usr/sap/SLO/SYS/profile/SLO_DVEBMGS01_us4118
(16636) Starting: local co.sapSLO_DVEBMGS01 pf=/usr/sap/SLO/
SYS/profile/SLO_DVEBMGS01_us4118 -F
(16636) New Child Process created.
(16636) Starting local Command:
Command:  co.sapSLO_DVEBMGS01
          pf=/usr/sap/SLO/SYS/profile/SLO_DVEBMGS01_us4118
          -F
16637) Starting: local se.sapSLO_DVEBMGS01 pf=/usr/sap/SLO/SYS/
profile/SLO_DVEBMGS01_us4118 -F
16637) New Child Process created.
16637) Starting local Command:
```

```
Command:   se.sapSLO_DVEBMGS01
           pf=/usr/sap/SLO/SYS/profile/SLO_DVEBMGS01_us4118
           -F
16638) Starting: local ig.sapSLO_DVEBMGS01 -mode=profile pf=/
usr/sap/SLO/SYS/profile/SLO_DVEBMGS01_us4118
16595) Waiting for Child Processes to terminate.
16638) New Child Process created.
16638) Starting local Command:
Command:   ig.sapSLO_DVEBMGS01
           -mode=profile
            pf=/usr/sap/SLO/SYS/profile/SLO_DVEBMGS01_us4118
```

**Listing 3.1** sapstart.log

In addition to the values of some environment variables, you can also see which programs are executed at system startup. These include the following:

- Message server
- Dispatcher
- Sys Log Daemons
- IGS watchdog

The characteristics of an SAP instance, for example, the type and number of processes, SAP-specific main memory sizes, and additional options are controlled using a profile, which is generally the case with many software products. SAP systems use three profiles:

- **System profile:** DEFAULT.PFL
- **Start profile:** START_<instance><instance_number>_<host_name>
- **Instance profile:** <SID>_<instance><instance_number>_<host_name>

Each of these profiles is already defined in a profile directory that is defined when the SAP system is installed. All instances of an SAP system can use share or mount technology to read the profile directory.

DEFAULT.PFL

The SAP system contains only one DEFAULT.PFL profile, which contains the system-wide settings. These include, for example, the system name, the database host, and also the name of the enqueue server. Each SAP instance reads this profile before it's started in an SAP system; the profile contains important system-wide information.

**Start profile of the instance**

The profiles `START_<instance><instance_number>_<host_name>` and `<SID>_<instance><instance_number>_<host_name>` are instance-specific. When the instances are installed, they are assigned predefined names determined by the processes active in the instance. In the case of the central instance (see Section 1.2, Client/Server Architecture in SAP NetWeaver), the name `DVEBMGS` indicates that the following processes are started:

- **D**ialog
- Update task (denoted by the letter **V**)
- **E**nqueue
- **B**atch
- **M**essage
- **G**ateway
- **S**pool

However, during installation, all other instances are automatically assigned the letter "D" even if they are mainly used in background processing or as spool servers.

**Example**

Take a look at the profile `START_DVEBMGS01_us4118` as an example (see Listing 3.2). The first segment of the profile name indicates that this concerns the start profile of an instance. An underscore then separates the profile type from the instance name. `DVEBMGS` represents the services active in this instance, and it's also the name of the instance. It's a central instance because there is a message service. `01` represent the last two digits of the TCP/IP port used by the dispatcher on the host. Another underscore then separates the instance name from the name of the host (`us4118`) on which the instance is running. The start profile of an instance determines how, where, and the name under which the individual SAP services or processes are to be started. In the following excerpt, for example, the message server and the dispatcher are started in the instance `DVEBMGS01_us4118` (see Listing 3.2).

```
Directory:  /usr/sap/SLO/SYS/profile
Name:       START_DVEBMGS01_us4118

#.******************************************************
#.*
#.*       Start profile START_DVEBMGS01_US4118
#.*
#.*       Version                     = 000002
#.*       Generated by user = SAP*
#.*       Generated on = 31.03.2006 , 13:34:15
#.*
#.******************************************************
SAPSYSTEMNAME = SLO
SAPSYSTEM = 01
INSTANCE_NAME = DVEBMGS01
DIR_CT_RUN = $(DIR_EXE_ROOT)/run
DIR_EXECUTABLE = $(DIR_INSTANCE)/exe
DIR_PROFILE = $(DIR_INSTALL)/profile
_PF = $(DIR_PROFILE)/SLO_DVEBMGS01_us4118
SETENV_00 = LD_LIBRARY_PATH=$(DIR_LIBRARY):%(LD_LIBRARY_PATH)
SETENV_01 = SHLIB_PATH=$(DIR_LIBRARY):%(SHLIB_PATH)
SETENV_02 = LIBPATH=$(DIR_LIBRARY):%(LIBPATH)
#
# Copy SAP Executables
#
Execute_00 = immediate $(DIR_CT_RUN)/sapcpe$(FT_EXE) pf=$(_PF)
#
# Start SCSA administration
#
Execute_01 = local $(DIR_EXECUTABLE)/sapmscsa pf=$(_PF) -n
#
# Start SAP messaging service
#
_MS = ms.sap$(SAPSYSTEMNAME)_$(INSTANCE_NAME)
Execute_02 = local rm -f $(_MS)
Execute_03 = local ln -s -f $(DIR_EXECUTABLE)/msg_server$(FT_E
......
```

**Listing 3.2** Start Profile

The operations listed with `Execute_<no.>` are in preparation for executing the actual commands. These are started with `Start_Program_<no.>`.

Specifying the keyword `local` or the server name (in the same place) defines the host on which the command should run.

**Instance profile**

The runtime environment of the instance is configured in the instance profile. This configuration is mainly concerned with defining the resources used, describing the services provided by the instance, and specifying the location of other services (e.g., the database). The instance profile has the following naming convention:

`<SID>_<instance><instance_number>_<host_name>`

**Example**

Our example shows the profile `SLO_DVEBMGS01_US4118` (see Listing 3.3), which determines how many work processes of a certain type are to be started. The next excerpt from this profile, for example, shows seven dialog processes (parameter `rdisp/wp_no_dia=8`). An important part of this instance profile is the definition of the size of the main memory areas used in the SAP system. However, the instance profile is also responsible for settings such as the logon parameters and the size of the logs.

```
Directory:  /usr/sap/SLO/SYS/profile

Name:       SLO_DVEBMGS01_us4118


#.*******************************************************

#.*

#.*      Instance profile SLO_DVEBMGS01_US4118

#.*

#.*      Version                 = 000010

#.*      Generated by user = SAPADM

#.*      Generated on = 04.01.2007 , 11:25:26

#.*

#.*******************************************************

SAPSYSTEMNAME = SLO

SAPSYSTEM = 01
```

```
INSTANCE_NAME = DVEBMGS01
DIR_CT_RUN = $(DIR_EXE_ROOT)/run
DIR_EXECUTABLE = $(DIR_INSTANCE)/exe
jstartup/trimming_properties = off
jstartup/protocol = on
jstartup/vm/home = /usr/j2se
jstartup/max_caches = 500
jstartup/release = 700
jstartup/instance_properties = $(jstartup/j2ee_proper
ties):$(jstartup/sdm_properties)
j2ee/dbdriver = /sapdb/programs/runtime/jar/sapdbc.jar
PHYS_MEMSIZE = 512
exe/saposcol = $(DIR_CT_RUN)/saposcol
#old_value: 4
rdisp/wp_no_dia = 8
rdisp/wp_no_btc = 1
exe/icmbnd = $(DIR_CT_RUN)/icmbnd
rdisp/j2ee_start_control = 1
rdisp/j2ee_start = 1
rdisp/j2ee_libpath = $(DIR_EXECUTABLE)
exe/j2ee = $(DIR_EXECUTABLE)/jcontrol$(FT_EXE)
rdisp/j2ee_timeout = 600
rdisp/frfc_fallback = on
icm/HTTP/j2ee_0 = PREFIX=/,HOST=localhost,CONN=0-500,PORT=5$$00
icm/server_port_0 = PROT=HTTP,PORT=80$$
....
```

**Listing 3.3** Instance Profile

When an SAP system is installed, the necessary profiles are created with default values that are based on the user's specifications. During productive operation, it's frequently necessary (especially at the start) to adjust the settings to the actual requirements. In Chapter 7, Section 7.1, Profile Maintenance, provides more detailed information about this as well as the parameters available. Here, we assume that the profiles already exist.

Profile evaluation

For most system parameters, default values are already determined in the source code of the SAP kernel. However, the special characteristics of the system environment used (e.g., the host name, system name, and resource distribution) must be specified in the profiles. The profiles are read when an instance is started. Therefore, if you change an instance profile, you must restart the instance for these changes to take effect; if you change the system profile, then you must restart all of the instances.

Values defined in the system profile `DEFAULT.PFL` overwrite the default settings in the source code. For this instance, the values specified in the instance profiles overwrite the parameters set in `DEFAULT.PFL` (see Figure 3.1).

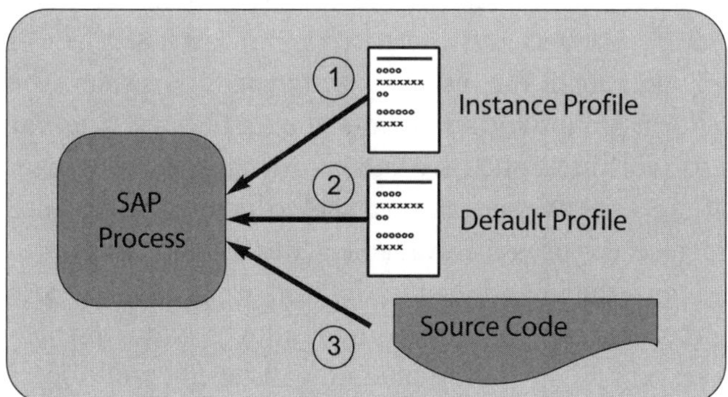


**Figure 3.1** Evaluation Hierarchy of Parameter Definitions

## 3.4 SAP GUI — The Graphical User Interface

SAPLOGON

To establish a frontend PC connection to an SAP instance, both the host name and instance number must be transferred to the instance. For frontend PCs, icons can be created on the desktop to correspond with each of these SAP GUI calls to the instances of possible SAP systems. However, because this would quickly become unmanageable due to the number of similar icons, it's more effective to use the SAPLOGON program. SAPLOGON allows you to define all possible connections under a name of your choice. The user then selects the relevant connection from the list of these names, which generates the corresponding SAP GUI call. The data is entered once and saved to the following files:

- *saplogon.ini*
- *sapmsg.ini*
- *saproute.ini*

You can transfer these files to other frontend hosts, which considerably reduces the time and effort required to manually enter possible connections. It's even better to use load distribution across all instances of an SAP system. For this purpose, only the respective message server of each available SAP system is entered in the file *sapmsg.ini* as follows:

```
<SID>=<Host name of message server>
```

**Load distribution**

The TCP/IP port for communication between the frontend and the message server is stored in the *services* file (UNIX: */etc/services*, Windows: *%SYSTEMROOT%\system32\drivers\etc\services*). The message server contains all information about the instances within an SAP system. The administrator can form groups within the total number of instances, for example, for certain work areas such as Materials Management or Financial Accounting. The SAPLOGON user can then select the relevant instance group. The message server uses the available statistical information to select the instance with the lowest load in the instance group. The SAP GUI is started for this instance. This procedure is known as *load distribution based on logon groups*. Chapter 7, Maintaining Instances, will discuss this in further detail.

In Figure 3.2, our sample system SLO on host us4118 with instance number 01 is added to the SAPLOGON entries. Similarly, the following command line can be used to directly call the SAP GUI connected to the SLO:

```
sapgui /H/us4118/S/sapdp01
```

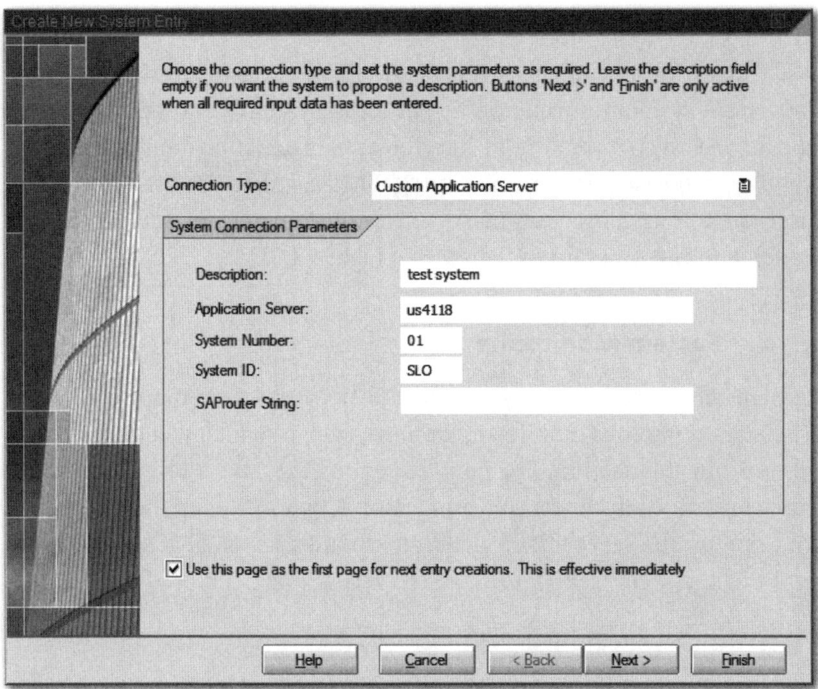


**Figure 3.2** Adding a New Entry to SAPLOGON

SAPLOGONPAD

Similar to SAPLOGON, you can also use SAPLOGONPAD to log on to an SAP NetWeaver AS system. However, SAPLOGONPAD doesn't allow the user to create, modify, or delete system entries. From an administration perspective, we recommend that SAPLOGONPAD is used on the frontend PCs of all users. Even at the early stage of installing the SAP GUI software, you can decide whether SAPLOGON (*saplogon.exe*) or only SAPLOGONPAD (*saplgpad.exe*) should be installed.

## 3.5 General Administration Tasks

As soon as SAP NetWeaver AS is started, and you can access the system via a frontend, you can execute all of the administration tasks within the system. Before we discuss this in detail in the following chapters, we'll first introduce you to some of the basic functions of SAP NetWeaver AS.

### 3.5.1 Status

Each menu option in the SAP system allows you to display the most important system information by choosing **System • Status**. In addition to the SAP system data (e.g., the release, installation number, license validity, database server name, and RDBMS used), it also lists the current user name, the transaction that is currently active (using the transaction code), and the program executed (see Figure 3.3).

### 3.5.2 System Monitoring

System monitoring is a key responsibility of the system administrator. There are numerous monitoring options, each of which will be discussed in detail in this section. For now, it's enough to take a brief look at the overview of all instances and processes active in the application layer. You can use the **server list** function to obtain a list of all active instances and their services (see Figure 3.4). To access this overview, call Transaction SM51.

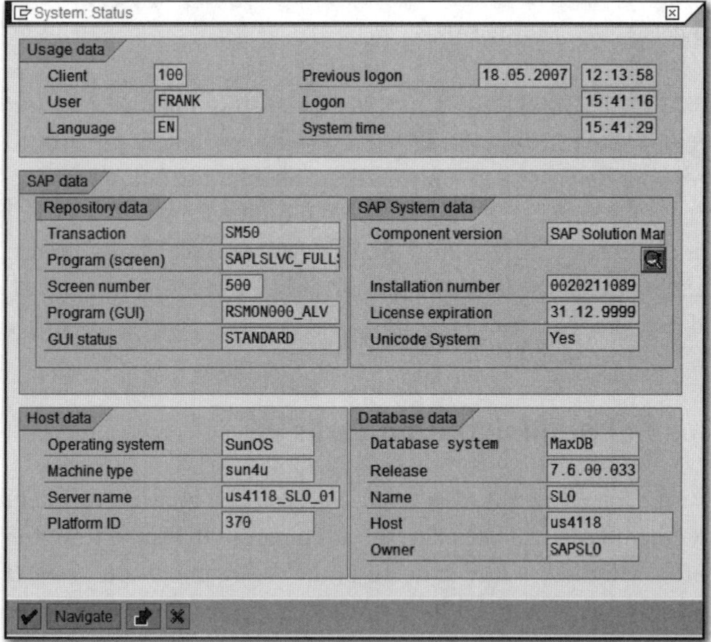


**Figure 3.3** System Status

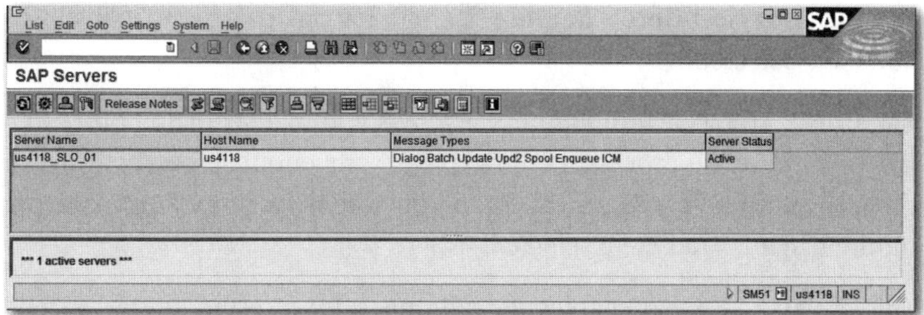


**Figure 3.4** List of All Instances and Their Services

After you select an instance, you can branch to a number of overviews including the following:

Overviews

- **Goto • Processes**
  Process overview (see Figure 3.5).
- **Goto • Users**
  User currently logged on.
- **Goto • System Log**
  System log (see Section 3.5.3, System Log).
- **Goto • Server • Information • Release Information**
  Description of SAP kernel data (version, patch number, generation date, database library, supported environment).

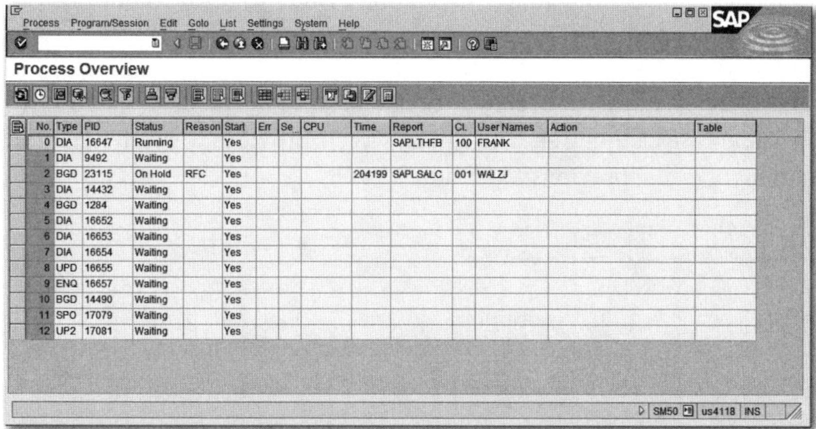


**Figure 3.5** Process Overview of an Instance

You can also select **Goto • Remote Login** to log on directly to the instance you have selected.

Process overview

The **Process overview** in Figure 3.5 shows you that six dialog processes (DIA), two update processes (UPD/UPD2), one enqueue process (ENQ), three background processes (BTC), and one spool process (SPO) are active on the instance you have selected.

The Process overview enables the administrator to estimate the current activities and the resulting load on an instance. It plays a central role in system monitoring. In addition to the many display options, which will be discussed later, the system administrator can terminate work processes in an emergency (**Process • Kill with Core** or **• without Core**). In the case of *Kill with Core*, a memory extract is created as a core file at the operating system level. This file isn't created if the process is terminated *without Core*. This doesn't impact seriously on the functional efficiency of the instance. Open transactions are rolled back. The dispatcher of the instance sees that a work process has terminated and immediately tries to start a new work process of this type. The dispatcher and the message server processes aren't displayed in the Process overview. The User Overview (SM04) provides similar options, but the display is sorted by user.

dpmon

At the operating system level, a tool with a similar scope of functions is available to the administrator (operating system user <sid>adm):

```
dpmon  pf=<instance_profile>
```

This delivers a process overview of the instance in character-based form as shown in Listing 3.4. The initial screen provides a short statistical summary of the previous I/O load.

```
Dispatcher Queue Statistics
===========================

+------+-------+-------+-------+---------+---------+
|  Typ |    now |    high |     max | writes   |   reads   |
+------+-------+-------+-------+---------+---------+
| NOWP |      0 |      18 |   2000 | 2349360 | 2349360 |
+------+-------+-------+-------+---------+---------+
|  DIA |      0 |      49 |   2000 | 1428784 | 1428784 |
+------+-------+-------+-------+---------+---------+
```

```
| UPD |       0 |       2 |    2000 |     7587 |     7587 |
+-----+---------+---------+---------+----------+----------+
| ENQ |       0 |       0 |    2000 |        0 |        0 |
+-----+---------+---------+---------+----------+----------+
| BTC |       0 |       3 |    2000 |    15464 |    15464 |
+-----+---------+---------+---------+----------+----------+
| SPO |       0 |       1 |    2000 |    25638 |    25638 |
+-----+---------+---------+---------+----------+----------+
| UP2 |       0 |       1 |    2000 |      612 |      612 |
+-----+---------+---------+---------+----------+----------+
max_rq_id                 9351
wake_evt_udp_now          0
wake events               total3102978,  udp2954229
(95%),  shm148749 (  4%)
since last update         total     0,  udp     0 (  0%),
shm     0 (  0%)
    q - quit
    m - menue
```

**Listing 3.4** Output from dpmon

The user can use the abbreviation m to choose from the following monitors provided:

```
Dispatcher Monitor Menu
------------------------
d - dispatcher queue statistic
p - work-process-admin-table
l - work-process-admin-table (long)
t - trace level/components for wp
w - wp_ca blocks
a - appc_ca blocks
m - mbuf status
v - tm_ad dump
q - quit
```

Option l essentially corresponds to the Process overview within the SAP system. Listing 3.5 was obtained from a UNIX system. When this snapshot was taken, dialog processes 0, 2, and 3, as well as all four background work processes, were active. Similar to the Process overview of the SAP system, you can also use dpmon to terminate processes.

```
Workprocess Table (long)
========================
No Ty.      Pid Status  Cause Start Err Sem CPU    Time
 Program    Cl  User     Action             Table
------------------------------------------------------- 0  DIA
28577 Run          yes     0   0  37
 SAPLEDI1 001  SCHAAK   Insert             EDI40
1  DIA   28578 Wait          yes     0   0   0
2  DIA   28579 Run           yes     0   0   9
         001  SCHAAK   Sequential Read     DD01L
3  DIA   28580 Run           yes     0   0  33
 SAPLEDIN 001  SCHAAK
4  DIA   28581 Run           yes     0   0   8
         001  SCHAAK
5  DIA   28582 Wait          yes     0   0   0
6  DIA   28583 Wait          yes     0   0   0
7  DIA   28584 Wait          yes     0   0   0
.......
20 DIA   28597 Wait          yes     0   0   0
21 UPD   28598 Wait          yes     0   0   0
22 UPD   28599 Wait          yes     0   0   0
23 UPD   28600 Wait          yes     0   0   0
24 ENQ   28601 Wait          yes     0   0   0
25 BTC    7176 Run           yes     0   0 158
/SAPAPO/  001  SCHAAK                      DB-PROC "S
26 BTC    6590 Run           yes     0   0 439
/SAPAPO/  001  SCHAAK   Direct Read        /SAPAPO/MA
27 BTC   10238 Run           yes     0   0   7
         001  SCHAAK   Delete              RSDELPART
28 BTC    6823 Run           yes     0   0  17
         001  SCHAAK                       DB-PROC "S
29 SPO   28606 Wait          yes     0   0   0
30 SPO    28607 Wait         yes     0   0   0
31 BTC    28608 Wait         yes     0   0   0
32 UP2    28609 Wait         yes     0   0   0
    s - stop workprocess
    k - kill workprocess (with core)
    r - enable restart flag (only possible in wp-status
        "ended")
    q – quit
    m – menue
```

**Listing 3.5** Process List

OS-specific tools

The user can also use other operating system-specific tools to obtain information about SAP processes. In Windows systems, this is primarily the *Task Manager*. The MMC also provides some monitoring options. However, it's not possible to prepare large volumes of information in a manner that is as comprehensive and as specific as the SAP system because only the SAP system itself has extensive information about its own processes.

`ps -ef` was used to create the following excerpt (see Listing 3.6) in a UNIX environment on a distributed instance with the RDBMS Oracle. For the sake of clarity, the overview was manually restricted to SAP and Oracle processes and sorted accordingly. The `saposcol` program is the first process in the overview. The subsequent `sapstart` processes were activated after the `startsap` shell script was executed. They are used to start the individual SAP processes on central instance `01` and dialog instance `64`. A process that gathers data and writes it to the central system log of an SAP system is started under the abbreviation `co.sap<SID>_<instance>`. The equivalent of this is the process `se.sap<SID>_<instance>`, which acts as a sender of system log information. The start script activates the processes directly; you'll be aware of this because the process number (**PID** column) of the `sapstart` program corresponds with the parent process number (**PPID** column) of the other processes. The abbreviation `ms` denotes the message server. All of the work processes of an instance are executed under the abbreviation `dw`. This abbreviation stands for `disp+work`, that is, the dispatcher and work processes. You identify the dispatcher behind the work processes from the fact that the parent process number corresponds to the process number of the start script because only the start script activates the dispatcher directly. The dispatcher starts all other work processes. As a result, its parent process number corresponds to the process number of the dispatcher. In Listing 3.6, both the message server and the dispatcher are highlighted in bold.

```
   UID      PID   PPID COMMAND
  root    29710      1 saposcol
orahuy    13047      1 /oracle/HUY/817_64/bin/tnslsnr
huyadm    19080      1 /usr/sap/HUY/SYS/exe/run/sapstart
     pf=/usr/sap/HUY/SYS/profile/START_DVEBMGS01_us7400
huyadm    24273      1 /usr/sap/HUY/SYS/exe/run/sapstart
     pf=/usr/sap/HUY/SYS/profile/START_D64_us7400
```

```
huyadm   19113  19080co.sapHUY_DVEBMGS01
     pf=/usr/sap/HUY/SYS/profile/HUY_DVEBMGS01_us7400
huyadm   19114  19080se.sapHUY_DVEBMGS01
     pf=/usr/sap/HUY/SYS/profile/HUY_DVEBMGS01_us7400
huyadm   19111  19080ms.sapHUY_DVEBMGS01
     pf=/usr/sap/HUY/SYS/profile/HUY_DVEBMGS01_us7400
huyadm   19112  19080dw.sapHUY_DVEBMGS01
     pf=/usr/sap/HUY/SYS/profile/HUY_DVEBMGS01_us7400
huyadm    5063  19112dw.sapHUY_DVEBMGS01
     pf=/usr/sap/HUY/SYS/profile/HUY_DVEBMGS01_us7400
huyadm   19117  19112dw.sapHUY_DVEBMGS01
     pf=/usr/sap/HUY/SYS/profile/HUY_DVEBMGS01_us7400
huyadm   19120  19112dw.sapHUY_DVEBMGS01
     pf=/usr/sap/HUY/SYS/profile/HUY_DVEBMGS01_us7400
huyadm   19121  19112dw.sapHUY_DVEBMGS01
     pf=/usr/sap/HUY/SYS/profile/HUY_DVEBMGS01_us7400
huyadm   19128  19112dw.sapHUY_DVEBMGS01
     pf=/usr/sap/HUY/SYS/profile/HUY_DVEBMGS01_us7400
huyadm   19131  19112dw.sapHUY_DVEBMGS01
     pf=/usr/sap/HUY/SYS/profile/HUY_DVEBMGS01_us7400
huyadm   19191  19112dw.sapHUY_DVEBMGS01
     pf=/usr/sap/HUY/SYS/profile/HUY_DVEBMGS01_us7400
.......
huyadm   24290  24273dw.sapHUY_D64
     pf=/usr/sap/HUY/SYS/profile/HUY_D64_us7400
huyadm   24292  24290dw.sapHUY_D64
     pf=/usr/sap/HUY/SYS/profile/HUY_D64_us7400
huyadm   24293  24290dw.sapHUY_D64
     pf=/usr/sap/HUY/SYS/profile/HUY_D64_us7400
huyadm   24294  24290dw.sapHUY_D64
     pf=/usr/sap/HUY/SYS/profile/HUY_D64_us7400
huyadm   24295  24290dw.sapHUY_D64
     pf=/usr/sap/HUY/SYS/profile/HUY_D64_us7400
huyadm   24296  24290dw.sapHUY_D64
     pf=/usr/sap/HUY/SYS/profile/HUY_D64_us7400
huyadm   19115  19112gwrd
     pf=/usr/sap/HUY/SYS/profile/HUY_DVEBMGS01_us7400
huyadm   24291  24290gwrd
     pf=/usr/sap/HUY/SYS/profile/HUY_D64_us7400
orahuy    5067      1    oracleHUY
orahuy    7305      1    oracleHUY
orahuy    7307      1    oracleHUY
.......
```

```
orahuy    7237    1    ora_arc0_HUY
orahuy    7231    1    ora_ckpt_HUY
orahuy    7227    1    ora_dbw0_HUY
orahuy    7229    1    ora_lgwr_HUY
orahuy    7225    1    ora_pmon_HUY
orahuy    7235    1    ora_reco_HUY
orahuy    7233    1    ora_smon_HUY
```

**Listing 3.6** Process Overview with Operating System Tools

Gateway processes have the ID `gwrd`. The dispatcher of each instance also starts these processes. The abbreviations for the processes (as they appear at the operating system level) are defined in the start profile (refer to Listing 3.2). You can't determine further information in this way (e.g., the current task of a process within SAP). This can only be achieved using SAP tools.

### 3.5.3 System Log

All important events in a productive operation are logged in the system log of an SAP system or instance. Therefore, one of the permanent responsibilities of the system administrator is to monitor the system log. To read the messages contained in the system log, call Transaction SM21 in SAP NetWeaver AS ABAP. If an error occurs in SAP NetWeaver AS ABAP, the system log is the starting point for more accurate analysis and, therefore, has already been mentioned in this chapter. Section 9.3 in Chapter 9 provides detailed information about using this log.

### 3.5.4 System Messages

The system administrator can send messages to all or a chosen number of SAP users if, for example, imminent maintenance work may restrict system operation. This basic function is available to you under Create System Messages (SM02). All users of the entire SAP system, a specific instance, or a client can receive system messages. You can also restrict the validity period of a message, which means that users receive the message only if they are working in the system or instance during the specified period. A system message is transferred with the next dialog step of a user, and a new window opens to display the relevant message. It's particularly useful to send system messages if a special instance needs to be stopped. In this case, we recommend that you always notify users in good time (see Figure 3.6).

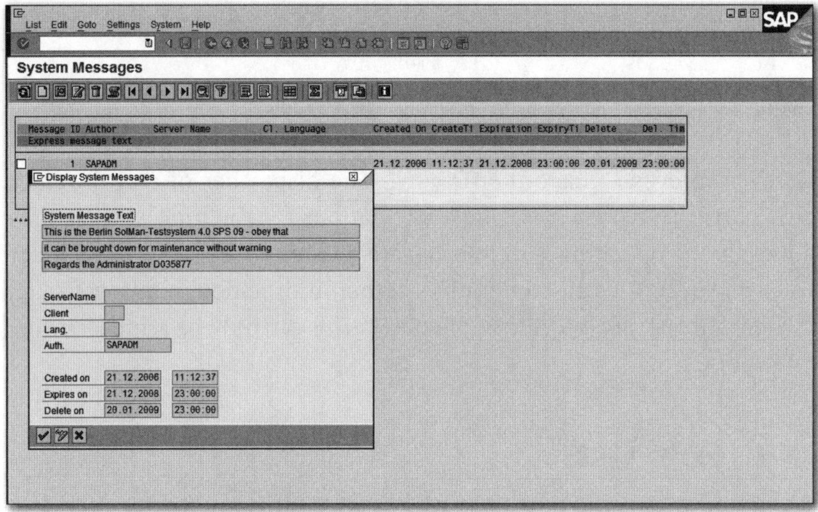


**Figure 3.6** System Messages

### 3.5.5 Lists

Any display that doesn't require interactive user input is known as a *list*. Lists can be printed, transferred from the SAP system, and stored in local files on the frontend PC or sent to other SAP users. Each time you display a list, you can also access the relevant functions under **System • List**. You can also trigger these actions by entering the relevant information in the command field:

Actions

- `%sc` enables you to search for character strings in the list and their subsequent positioning. You can use `%sc+` to continue to search for the same pattern.
- `%pc` enables you to save a list to a local file on the frontend PC.
- `%sl` enables you to save a list in Office.

In system administration, list displays are used, for example, for statistics, logs, and analyses. As system administrator, you'll frequently analyze lists, so you must be proficient in working with them.

### 3.5.6 Table Maintenance

You can use the table maintenance integrated into the SAP system to adjust some SAP administration tables. For example, Table T000 contains a list of all clients in an SAP system. If you want to create an additional client, you must first add a new entry to this table. Table maintenance is used for this purpose. SAP NetWeaver AS provides the following tools for table maintenance:

- **Data Browser (SE16) Within the ABAP Workbench**
  The option of using the data browser to maintain a table must be embedded in the table properties. Up to R/3 4.6C, you set the **Table maintenance allowed** indicator in the **ABAP Dictionary (SE11): Initial Screen • Change • Properties**; in the application server, you can choose between the following three variants in the **Initial Screen** of the **ABAP Dictionary** under **Change • Delivery and Maintenance**:
  - **Display/maintenance allowed with restrictions**
  - **Display/maintenance allowed**
  - **Display/maintenance not allowed**
- **Extended Table Maintenance (SM30)**
  You can access extended table maintenance from any SAP window under **System • Services • Table Maintenance • Extended Table Maintenance** or by calling Transaction SM30.
- **Special Object-Dependent Transactions**
  Examples include Client Maintenance (SCC4) or Transaction Maintenance (SM01), which can be used to add entries to the TSTC table.

**Extended table maintenance**

Extended table maintenance fully replaces the standard table maintenance used in earlier SAP releases. You can only use extended table maintenance if a corresponding maintenance interface has been generated for the table in question. In each case, the table maintenance layout depends on the interface created for this special table. A table maintenance interface is already delivered by default for all tables delivered by SAP that may have to be adjusted (including Table T000).

To add a new entry to Table T000, follow these steps (see Figure 3.7):

1. Call Table Maintenance (SM30).
2. Specify the table to be changed (here: T000).
3. Select **Maintain**.
4. Select **New Entries**.

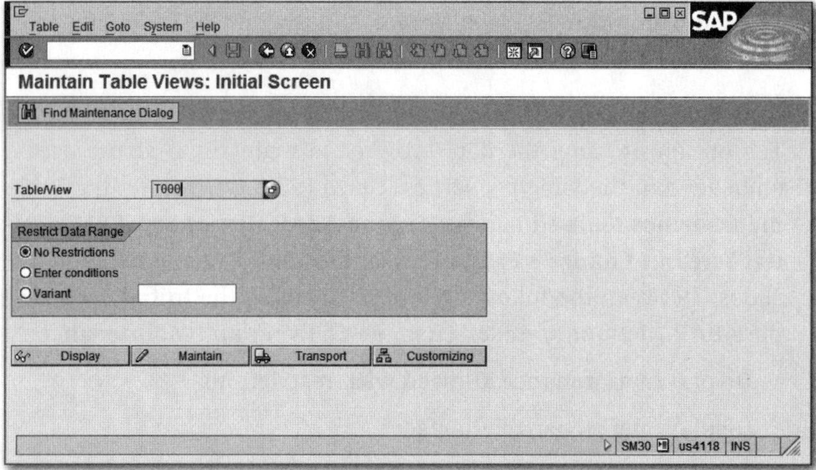


**Figure 3.7** Table Maintenance

When you select **Customizing** (see Figure 3.7), an overview of the activities in which it's necessary to maintain the selected table is displayed within the implementation guide. You can navigate directly to these activities.

On the other hand, table maintenance within the ABAP Workbench doesn't depend on the table contents and meaning. It's primarily used to display the table contents.

Log

SAP tools can be used to log changes to the table contents. Here, the relevant option in the dictionary of SAP NetWeaver AS ABAP must be activated for this table, and the `rec/client` profile parameter must be used to activate table logging for the relevant client.

## 3.6 Tips

- **Startup Problems**
  If the system fails to start, you should first use the database tools to try to start the database. You'll then be better able to isolate the source of the problem. Only when you have successfully identified the problem should you use MMC or a script to start SAP NetWeaver AS.

  In addition to the previously mentioned special log files in the home directory of the user <sid>adm, you should also consult the developer traces (see Section 9.5, Trace Files, in Chapter 9) and the **Application** area of the event viewer in the case of Windows systems.

  In particular, it may be helpful to look at the profile files after you have modified the parameters.
- **Communication Problems after Adding a New Application Server**
  If you add a new application server to an existing system landscape, we recommend that you check that the entries in the *services* file (see Section 3.4) on all servers involved and presentation hosts are complete.
- **Analyzing Problems Without Accessing the SAP System**
  Routines (e.g., `dpmon`) at the operating system level are especially helpful if you are unable to log on to the SAP system even though it's running and, therefore, are unable to access the internal analysis options.

## 3.7 Transactions and Menu Paths

**ABAP Dictionary:** Initial Screen: SAP Menu • Tools • ABAP Workbench • Development • Dictionary (SE11)

**User Overview:** SAP Menu • Tools • Administration • Monitor • System Monitoring • User Overview (SM04)

**Data Browser:** SAP Menu • Tools • ABAP Workbench • Overview • Data Browser (SE16)

**Client Maintenance:** SAP Menu • Tools • Administration • Administration • Client Administration • Client Maintenance (SCC4)

**Process Overview:** SAP Menu • Tools • Administration • Monitor • System Monitoring • Process Overview (SM50)

**Server List:** SAP Menu • Tools • Administration • Monitor • System Monitoring • Server (SM51)

**System Log:** SAP Menu • Tools • Administration • Monitor • System Log (SM21)

**Creating System Messages:** SAP Menu • Tools • Administration • Administration • System Messages (SM02)

**Table Maintenance:** System • Services • Table Maintenance • Extended Table Maintenance (SM31)

**Transaction Maintenance:** SAP Menu • Tools • ABAP Workbench • Development • Other Tools • Transactions (SE93)

## 3.8 Additional Documentation

SAP Notes

Table 3.1 provides an overview of important SAP Notes concerning SAP GUI.

| Content | Note |
|---|---|
| Hardware and Software Requirements for SAP GUI for Windows | 26417 |
| Information About Supported Frontend PC Platforms | 66971 |
| Release and Maintenance Strategy for SAP GUI | 147519 |

**Table 3.1** SAP Notes Concerning SAP GUI

Table 3.2 provides an overview of important SAP Notes concerning general administration.

| Content | Note |
|---|---|
| Table Maintenance in R/3 | 28504 |
| Using the Dispatcher Monitor `dpmon` | 42074 |
| Test Tool for Message Server `lgtst` | 64015 |
| Using the SAP Gateway Monitor `gwmon` | 64016 |

**Table 3.2** SAP Notes Concerning General Administration

## 3.9 Questions

1. **Which profile is used to configure the SAP system?**
   a. SAP profile
   b. Instance profile
   c. Application server profile
   d. `DEFAULT.PFL`
   e. Start profile
   f. Stop profile
2. **You are unable to start your SAP system. Where do you find information about the cause of the problem?**
   a. *startdb.log*
   b. *startsap_<host_name>_<instance_number>.log*
   c. *startsap.log*
   d. Developer traces
   e. System log
   f. SQL trace
3. **Which of the following statements is correct?**
   a. The `SAPLOGON` program allows you to define receipts for different SAP systems.
   b. When you use the `SAPLOGON` program, you no longer have to use the SAP GUI.
   c. The names entered in `SAPLOGON` must be identical to the SID of the SAP system.

*One of the most important responsibilities of the system administrator is to operate a reliable, high-performance production system. This includes preventing problems that result from insufficiently tested modifications, and distributing resources effectively. All of this can be supported by a carefully considered system landscape structure as well as regulated processes for new developments and modified system settings.*

# 4 Setting Up the System Landscape

Initializing the *Change and Transport System* (*CTS*) is a particularly important post-installation step for a newly installed SAP system. You should never work with the system until the CTS has been initialized. In particular, you should not make any business settings in *Customizing*. In this chapter, we'll introduce the components of CTS and explain how to set up a transport landscape.

Components of CTS

The CTS comprises the following three blocks (see also Figure 4.1):

- Transport Organizer (and Transport Organizer – extended view)
- Transport Management System
- Transport tools

The Transport Organizer is one of the most important tools for project team members who work with Customizing and development, as well as system administrators who are responsible for transports. Chapter 6, Software Logistics, contains information about the characteristics and options associated with the Transport Organizer.

Transports

The Transport Management System forms the basis for the system landscape's regulated distribution of new system settings, developments, and modifications (grouped together into *transports*). The system administrator is responsible for the technical implementation of a transport landscape that best represents the applications' requirements. Following the initial configuration, the system administrator uses the Transport Management System to schedule, execute, and monitor all import activities.

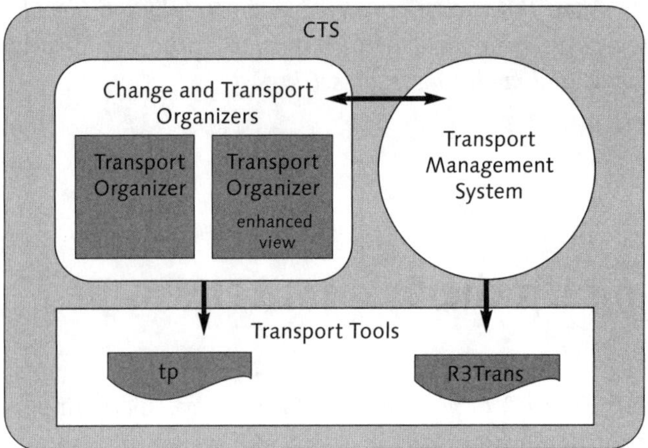


**Figure 4.1** Components of the Change and Transport System

The `tp` and `R3trans` programs at the operating system level export transport requests into files at the operating system level and import them into the target system. For this purpose, a transport directory in which all of the transport system's files are stored is already created when the system is installed.

## 4.1 Tasks of a System Landscape

**Separate systems**

Each SAP system that you install contains all of the resources necessary to cover the entire range of SAP functions. In addition to the business applications, the following areas are supported: software development, software administration, quality assurance for self-developed SAP components, and special system settings. To satisfy the different requirements associated with these usage options and to ensure risk-free operation of the production environment, we recommend that you use separate SAP systems for these purposes. A single system can only be justified for training or demonstration purposes.

This is due to the very different requirements of, for example, a production system and a test system:

- Any modification to the repository affects the entire runtime environment of the SAP system and, therefore, also affects production.
- Developers can use reports to access all of the production data.
- Development activities impact negatively on system performance. If, for example, programs are processed in debugging mode for test purposes, a dialog work process can be permanently assigned to the user during this time. This dialog work process then works for this user only. Furthermore, training courses held concurrently in one SAP system impact negatively on the performance of the production activities.

Consequently, the development activities in a single system configuration should be defined after the system goes live.

Therefore, it is advisable to distribute the tasks across different systems and to only transfer modifications from the test system to the production system after you have ensured that all functions are working properly. This process is known as *transporting* modifications. The Change and Transport System (CTS, see Figure 4.1) manages all system enhancements and developments as well as any transports between systems.

**Two-system landscape**

SAP AG always recommends that you install a system landscape with at least two systems. The development and test activities take place in one system and productive operation takes place in another system.

In a two-system landscape, the development and test system (in the sense of a transport system) is used as an integration system, and the production system is used as a consolidation system.

If the developments are satisfactory, the changes are transported from the integration system into a subsequent system (the consolidation system). However, the production system has already implemented the consolidation system in a two-system landscape (see Figure 4.2), so the transports can't be tested as such in this scenario. For complex developments in which dependencies will be considered, it isn't possible to fully test the transports in a two-system landscape.

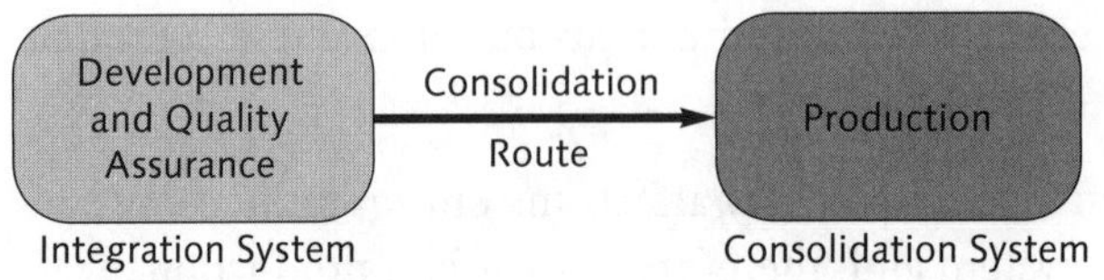


**Figure 4.2** Two-System Landscape

Furthermore, it isn't possible to test the intermediate statuses of an ABAP program while it is undergoing further development.

Three-system landscape

Only the recommended three-system system landscape adequately covers these requirements (see Figure 4.3). From a technical perspective, we distinguish between the following:

- **Integration System**
  For development and customer-specific system settings (Customizing).
- **Consolidation System**
  For testing and verifying the developments and the customer-specific system settings already made in a similar production environment.
- **Delivery System**
  As a standalone production system.

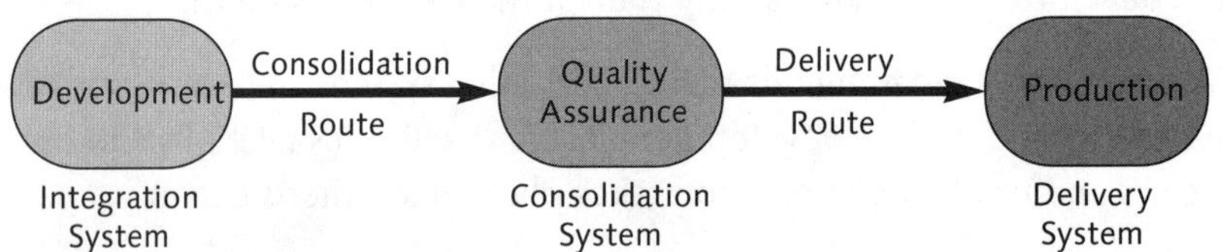


**Figure 4.3** Three-System Landscape

The following three system roles are kept strictly separate: development, quality assurance, and production. Developments can be initially tested in a separate system before they are used in a production system. To benefit from these advantages, the technical system settings and the organizational approach must support strict compliance with this role model.

Basic rules

Operation of a three-system landscape must comply with the following basic rules:

- All Customizing and development activities take place in the integration system. Test datasets verify the basic, correct functions and their characteristics.
- For quality assurance purposes, the developments (whose functions have already undergone basic testing) and the system settings are transported to the dedicated consolidation system and tested there in a similar production environment. If an error is detected, this is corrected in the integration system, and the modified version of the development or system setting is transported to the consolidation system again so that it can undergo a retest.
- Only verified changes are transported from the consolidation system and integrated into the production system. No changes are made in the production system itself.

You can technically support compliance with these basic rules. The necessary resources include the settings for the system change option (see Section 4.2, Initializing the Transport System), the settings for the client change option (see Chapter 7, Maintaining Instances), and the definition of transport routes between the systems in your landscape (see Section 4.3, Configuring the Transport Management System).

When choosing a system landscape, the cost-benefit ratio in view of the requirements plays an important role. In addition to the advantages associated with a three-system landscape, you must also consider that themore complex the system landscape, the higher the hardware costs, and the greater the administration effort. Therefore, it is essential to strike a balance between the requirements and the associated time and effort.

**Multisystem landscapes**

There are certainly constellations in which it makes sense for a system landscape to comprise more than three systems. For example, it may be advisable to use several production systems in different locations, for example, to separate the different subsidiaries of a company. In these system landscapes, a distinction is still made among integration, consolidation, and delivery systems because the technical functions remain identical. In such landscapes, several systems in a class exist in parallel to each other. Here, it is no longer possible to accurately determine the role of each system; in some cases, the systems have to play two roles.

Figure 4.4 shows an example of a multisystem landscape. Here, the starting point is a central integration system that is used, for example, for development tasks of an international nature. A downstream consolidation system is responsible for quality assurance of these developments. This is then connected to standalone system landscapes for country-specific developments.

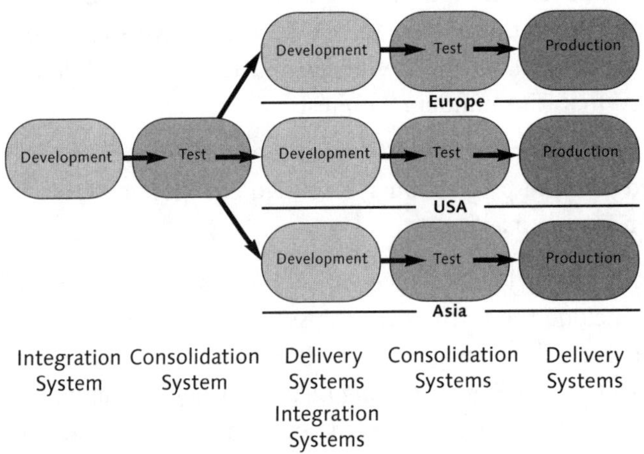


**Figure 4.4** Multisystem Landscape

## 4.2 Initializing the Transport System

**System change option**

After you install an SAP NetWeaver system, you must define the global and object class-specific *system change option* for each SAP system in the landscape. The SAP objects considered here include cross-client data such as programs, screens, menus, tables, or structures as well as client-independent customizing. The system change option is defined manually in each SAP system. Essentially, you must first consider whether it should even be possible to modify all of the objects in an SAP system. The *change option* allows customers to create and further develop their own new objects as well as customize objects delivered by SAP. This data must be stored as nonmodifiable data in a production system. The type and scope of the developments (e.g., whether or not SAP's own objects are modified) determine which modifications are permitted in a development system.

To set the system change option, select **Transport Organizer Tools (SE03) • Administration • Set System Change Option**. First, you use the **Global Settings** to define whether or not changes should be permitted. The repository objects are grouped into software components and assigned a namespace. The system in which an object has been created is known as the *original system* of this object. You can use these settings to fine-tune the change settings. You can only change an object if the following are true:

1. The global system change option has the value "modifiable."
2. The software component of the object has the value "modifiable."
3. The object namespace has the value "modifiable."

Table 4.1 illustrates this relationship.

| | | Software Component | | |
|---|---|---|---|---|
| | | Modifiable | Restricted Modifiability | Not Modifiable |
| Namespace | Modifiable | Existing objects can be repaired;<br>New objects have the System ID as the original system. | Existing objects can be repaired;<br>New objects have "SAP" as the original system. | – |
| | Not modifiable | – | – | – |

**Table 4.1** System Change Option at the Namespace and Software Component Level

Software component

A *software component* describes a set of logically related objects that are delivered and processed together. Objects are assigned to a *namespace*; the namespace prefix then precedes the object name. *Name ranges* are subsets of a namespace.

The most important software components within an SAP system are as follows:

- **Customer Developments (HOME)**
  This covers all transportable customer developments and all of the tools available in the SAP system.
- **Local Developments (No Automatic Transport, LOCAL)**
  This covers all nontransportable (local) customer-specific developments.
- **Cross-Application Components (SAP_ABAP)**
  The ABAP Workbench (Development Workbench) tools can be used to modify all application components delivered by SAP.
- **SAP Application Platform (SAP_APPL)**
  This contains the Logistics and Accounting components.
- **SAP Basis Component (SAP_BASIS)**
  All available tools can be used to modify the Basis components. All components of the Development Workbench and ABAP Query as well as the use of the Function Builder are permitted.
- **Human Resources (SAP_HR)**
  This covers the components delivered by SAP for the HR (Human Resources) component.

In addition to the namespaces listed here, your system may also have additional namespaces such as SAP Solution Tools Plug-in (ST-PI) or similar, depending on the additional software installed.

Namespaces

The following is a list of the most important namespaces and name ranges:

- **Customer Name Range**
  This covers all objects whose names do not have a prefix and start with the letters Y or Z.
- **General SAP Name Range**
  This covers all objects whose names do not have a prefix and do not start with the letters Y or Z.
- **ABAP and GUI Tools, Prefix/1BCABA/**
  This only permits SAP object processing with the ABAP Editor, Screen Painter, and Menu Painter. However, you aren't permitted to modify functions.

- **Development Workbench, Prefix/1BCDWB/**
  This covers SAP object processing and all Development Workbench tools, that is, the ABAP Editor, Screen Painter, and Menu Painter as well as changes to repository objects. However, you aren't permitted to modify functions.
- **Enqueue Function Groups, Prefix/1BCDBWEN/**
  This covers SAP functions used for lock management by SAP.

Your system may also have additional namespaces here, depending on the SAP software used or the add-ons installed.

If you want to set the change option for your system so that only customer objects can be modified, set the HOME and LOCAL software components and the customer name range to "modifiable."

**Initializing the CTS**

If you have recently used `R3setup` or `SAPinst` to install your SAP system from a CD-ROM, you do not have to initialize the CTS. However, if the system has been created as a copy of an existing system, you must perform the Post-Installation Actions (SE06) (see Figure 4.5) to regenerate the basic settings of the Change and Transport System. Furthermore, you must close all external requests and tasks in the system.

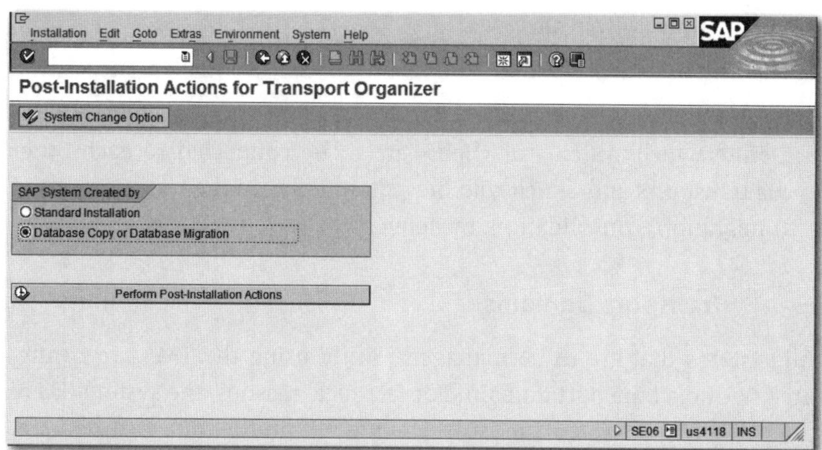


**Figure 4.5** Post-Installation Actions

For this, select the **Database Copy or Database Migration** setting on the **Post-Installation Actions (SE06)** screen and perform the post-installation actions. You can select **Extras • Display Log** to analyze a log of the actions performed.

## 4.3 Configuring the Transport Management System

The Transport Management System (TMS) provides a central administration view of the settings and transports in an SAP system landscape. For this purpose, SAP systems whose transport attributes should be jointly managed centrally can be grouped together into *transport domains*. In most cases, systems are grouped into transport domains between which data is to be transported. From an administration perspective, however, several such system chains can be managed jointly within a transport domain.

**Mapping the system environment within transport management**

To map the required system environment within transport management, you must complete the following basic steps:

1. Decide which systems should be grouped together into a transport domain for central management of the transport attributes. Virtual placeholder systems can be configured for systems that physically do not yet exist at the time when transport landscapes are being modeled and mapped within the TMS.
2. Determine which system you want to use to implement central management.
3. Define which systems or clients are to be connected to each other via transports and which role they should play in the transport group (integration, consolidation, or delivery).

### 4.3.1 Transport Domains

**Transport Domain Controller (TDC)**

All systems that are to be managed jointly using the TMS are configured within a transport domain. For technical reasons, the system IDs of the participating systems must be unique within the transport domain. The *Transport Domain Controller* (TDC) is an explicitly specified transport domain system that manages all TMS settings. To ensure a consistent view of all systems in the domain, the TMS reference configuration is in the TDC; a copy of the configuration is available to all members of the transport domain. Therefore, the Transport Domain Controller makes all of the required settings such as defining the transport routes (see Section 4.3.2).

RFC connections are used for communication between the TDC and the other SAP systems in the domain (see Section 13.1, RFC Connections, in Chapter 13). The necessary RFC connections are automatically created when the TMS is configured.

Within the landscape, an SAP system with high availability and good security mechanisms should be selected as the Transport Domain Controller. Furthermore, the SAP system should have the latest release version, if possible. Therefore, production systems and quality assurance systems are most suitable as development systems. In an SAP system, the load caused by the Transport Management System is low and doesn't impact negatively on performance.

If necessary, another system in the domain can subsequently assume the tasks of the Transport Domain Controller. This option is often used when restructuring a system landscape whereby the development system is initially installed and can then assume the role of the TDC until the production system is configured.

**Creating a transport domain**

When creating a transport domain and domain controller, proceed as follows:

1. The Transport Management System (STMS) is used to configure the domain in client 000 of the SAP system, which is initially regarded as the Transport Domain Controller.
2. If the TMS should not be defined yet, this is indicated here, and a domain name is proposed in the next step. The default name is DOMAIN_<SID> where <SID> denotes the system ID of the system used for the configuration.
3. Select **New Domain**, and enter a domain name and description. The name must not contain any blank characters. After you have chosen a domain name, you can only change it if the TMS is fully reconfigured.
4. Save your entries.

The system used to create the transport domain is defined as the domain controller. Therefore, all other configuration work must be carried out in client 000 of this system.

The domain and its controller are defined in this way. You can check the definition made by choosing **Transport Management System (STMS) • Overview • Systems**. When you define the Transport Domain Controller and, later, when you integrate additional systems into the domain, some actions are automatically performed in the background in preparation for subsequent TMS functions:

- The configuration data is saved in the database and, to some extent, stored in the *DOMAIN.CFG* file in the *bin* subdirectory of the transport directory at the operating system level.
- In the SAP system, the special user TMSADM is created with *communication* as its type. This user only has the authorizations required for the TMS tasks.
- All of the necessary RFC connections to the other systems in the domain are created.

Integrating additional systems

To integrate additional SAP systems into the domain, you must proceed with the following two steps:

1. Call the Transport Management System (STMS) in client 000 of the system that is to be added to the transport domain. The Transport Management System automatically recognizes that the current system doesn't belong to any domain. If the transport directory of the transport domain that already exists is used (see Section 4.4, Transport Control Program `tp`), the *DOMAIN.CFG* configuration file is analyzed, and the domain in this file is proposed. You can overwrite this proposal if you want to select another domain or create a new domain. Accept the domain proposed, or enter the domain you require. After you select Save, the new system is added to this domain.
2. In the second step, the TDC must now confirm that the new system has been added, so that it can be fully integrated into the domain. For this purpose, restart the Transport Management System (SMTS) in client 000 of the TDC, and select **Overview • Systems**. The new system appears in this list with the status *System waiting to be added to the domain*. Select the system, and then select **SAP System • Accept** to add it to the domain.

This configuration change is now complete in the TDC and must be transferred to all systems in the domain to ensure that the TMS configuration view is consistent. Changes are either distributed immediately after the action or they are collected for subsequent distribution. You initiate configuration distribution in client 000 of the Transport Domain Controller by choosing **Transport Management System (STMS) • Overview • Systems • Extras • Distribute and Activate Configuration**.

If errors occur during the configuration, the relevant detailed information is displayed on the screen. Furthermore, a history of all errors, including information about possible causes and solutions is available in the alert monitor of the TMS. You access the alert monitor in the Transport Management System by choosing **Monitor • TMS Alerts • TMS Alert Viewer**. The functions of the Transport Management System are also fully integrated into CCMS Alert Monitoring (see Section 11.1, Alert Monitor, in Chapter 11); you can access this monitor directly, or you can access it from the Transport Management System by choosing **Monitor • TMS Alerts • CCMS Alert Monitor**.

Backup domain controller

The Transport Domain Controller must always be available for configuration changes such as integrating an additional system. To safeguard against a TDC failure, you can introduce the concept of a *Backup Domain Controller* (BDC), which will allow the system to remain operational in the event of a TDC failure. When you use a BDC, the TDC functions can also be transferred to another system in the same domain. Here, this system is first defined as a Backup Domain Controller as follows: **Transport Management System (STMS) • Overview • Systems**, select a system, **SAP System • Change**, and enter the system ID in the **Backup** field on the **Communication** tab. If you want the Backup Domain Controller to assume the tasks of the Transport Domain Controller, you must activate it in the system list by choosing **Extras • Activate Backup Domain Controller**. This is the only configuration activity that isn't performed in the TDC.

You can delete the entire TMS configuration from the System overview by choosing **Extras • Delete TMS Configuration**; you can also delete a single system from the System overview in the TDC by choosing **SAP System • Delete**. After you do this, some settings still exist, but they are inactive and must be overwritten in the event of a new TMS configuration.

Virtual systems

If you want to model a transport landscape in which some of the systems involved do not yet physically exist or aren't yet accessible, you can define virtual systems as placeholders. The transports being accumulated for these systems are gathered and can be imported immediately whenever a virtual system is replaced with a real system. Virtual systems are created under **Transport Management System (STMS) • Overview • Systems • SAP System • Create • Virtual System** by specifying a *communication system*. The communication system is required to provide the necessary RFC connection. If the real system is available, you must delete the virtual placeholder from the configuration and integrate the system into the domain in the usual manner. Note that the SID of the new system must correspond with the SID of the virtual system so that the defined settings can be used.

External systems

In addition to virtual system definitions, *external system* entries are also possible. External systems represent a special type of virtual system that also doesn't physically exist in the transport domain. External system entries are necessary if the following are true:

- Data is to be transferred between different transport domains, that is, to a system in another transport domain.
- Transport data is to be exported from or imported to a removable disk.

The main difference between a virtual system and an external system is the transport directory used. Virtual systems use the standard transport directory of the communication system; for external systems, you can use any other directory. Similar to a virtual system, an external system is created under **Transport Management System (STMS) • Overview • Systems • SAP System • Create • External System**. The SAP system from which the external SAP system is to be managed is known as the *communication system*. When you create the external system, the Transport Domain Controller is proposed here. You must also make known the transport directory used; all of the data required for transports from or to the external systems is stored here along with the logs.

In Figure 4.6, the external system QAS in DOMAIN_A is used as a placeholder for the real system QAS in DOMAIN_B and the external system DEV in DOMAIN_B is used as a placeholder for the real system DEV in DOMAIN_A. Data is exchanged using the *trans_ext* directory, which must be accessible from both communication systems assigned to the external systems.

Domain link

The *domain link* is another method for connecting transport domains. A direct link can be used to connect two domains whose TDCs are at least Basis Release 4.6C. Here, you select **Transport Management System (STMS) • Overview • Systems • SAP System • Create • Domain Link** to request a connection to the TDC of a remote domain that is still accessible through a network connection. The TDC in the remote domain must confirm the connection — all of the necessary RFC connections are then defined and the systems in the remote domain can be contacted.

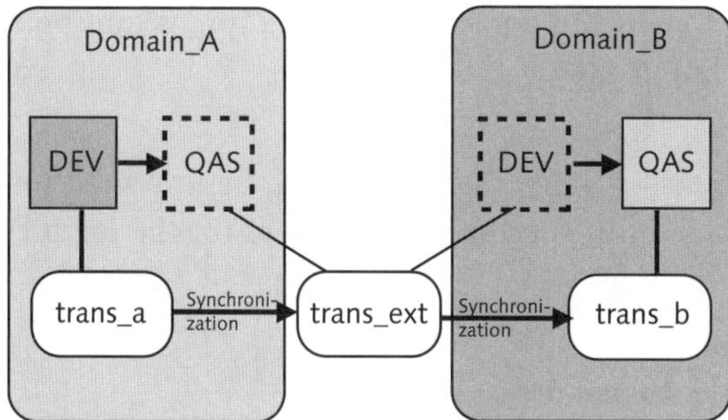


**Figure 4.6** External System as a Placeholder

The central transport directory, which was already created during installation, is used by default to store all of the necessary transport data and logs. Figure 4.7 shows the structure of the directory tree.

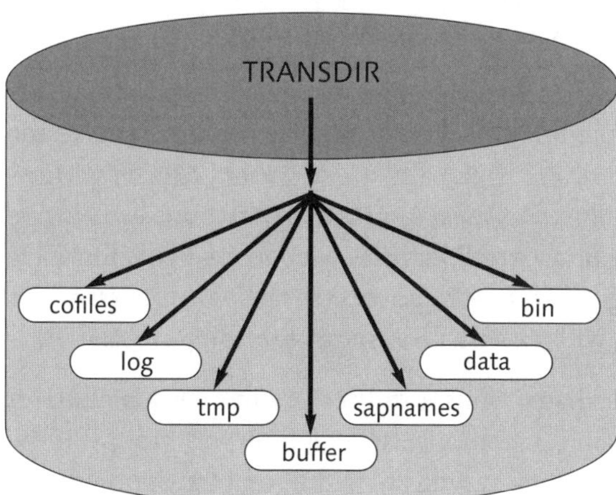


**Figure 4.7** Transport Directory

Subdirectories

The subdirectories contain the following:

- **bin**
  The *TP_<domain>.PFL* configuration file of the `tp` transport program (see Section 4.4) and the *DOMAIN.CFG* configuration file of the domain
- **data**
  The data files of the transport requests.
- **sapnames**
  A log file for each CTS user; the transport activities for its transport requests are retained in this file.
- **buffer**
  An import buffer for each system. The requests to be imported for this system, including all of the necessary work steps for the import, are listed in the buffers.
- **tmp**
  Temporary log files and semaphores.
- **log**
  General and request-specific log files.
- **cofiles**
  The control files of the transport requests. The object classes, the required import steps, and the return values are recorded here. Of particular interest is the import status of the relevant transport request in the different systems within the transport group.

Not every SAP system needs to have its own local directory tree. It is more advisable to use the relevant operating system tools to make the transport directory tree available globally (*share*, *mount*, *NFS link*). However, systems that are subject to special security restrictions can also be assigned their own local transport directories with access rights that have been reduced accordingly. Figure 4.8 shows the transport processes in a three-system landscape with a shared transport directory (TRANSDIR).

Transport group

SAP systems that have a shared transport directory tree form a *transport group*. A transport domain can comprise several transport groups. If the exporting system and importing system are in different transport groups, the import queues must be synchronized before the import, and the data files and control files required for the import must be transferred to the transport directory of the target system. This transfer is called from the TMS.

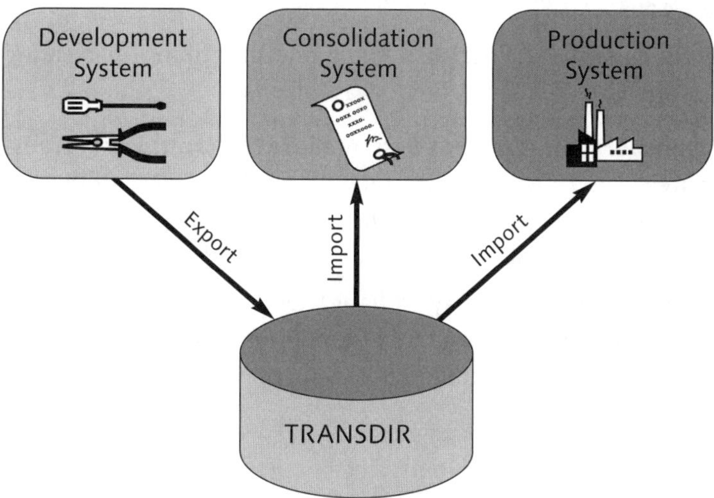


**Figure 4.8** Three-System Landscape with a Shared Transport Directory

### 4.3.2 Transport Routes

After the SAP systems available in the landscape are made known throughout the system, the last step is to define the transport routes between the systems. Here, we assume that the purpose of the configuration is already known and will, therefore, proceed with showing you how to make the necessary settings for a three-system landscape.

Editors

System table entries organize control of the transport routes and the role of each system. The *hierarchical list editor* or the *graphical editor* is used to create the table entries when the transport routes are being configured. In particular, information about the role of each system (integration, consolidation, or delivery system) is required here. Due to the central configuration of the Transport Management System, this information must only be entered once; it is then distributed to all systems involved.

Therefore, the following descriptions for defining the transport routes require the user to log on to the SAP system of the TDC with sufficient administration permissions in client 000.

To simplify transport route configuration, you should select one of the predefined standard configurations (one-system, two-system, or three-system landscape) and enhance it as required.

**List editor**

When you use the hierarchical list editor, the procedure for creating transport routes between the systems is as follows:

1. Select **Transport Management System (STMS) • Overview • Transport Routes** to access the hierarchical link tree. Initially, all of the systems are only defined as single systems, and their configuration status is only available in display mode.
2. Select **Configuration • Display • Change** to switch to change mode, and then select **Configuration • Standard Configuration** to select the basic model you require from the following options:
   - Single system
   - Development and production system
   - Three-system group

   Each system is assigned a role within this constellation (see Figure 4.9).

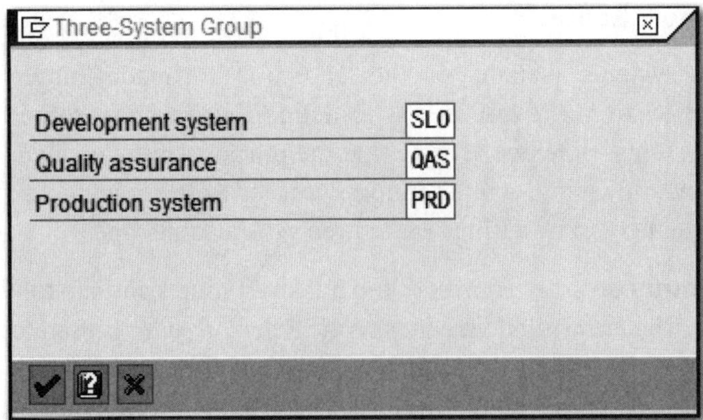


**Figure 4.9** System Assignment

3. Save your entries. The systems are linked automatically, and the necessary table entries are created automatically. To save the new settings, select **Configuration • Check • Transport Routes**.
4. You then distribute these new settings by choosing **Configuration • Distribute and Activate**.

Integrated version management

*Integrated version management* is used to log configuration changes and to restore an older version. The configuration defined and saved is numbered automatically, and the version number is displayed in the screen title (see Figure 4.10). If you subsequently modify the system landscape configuration, a new version number is assigned each time you select Save. A new version must also be activated. Here, you should check whether the required change needs to be reconciled with the system settings and the requests that have already been partly transported.

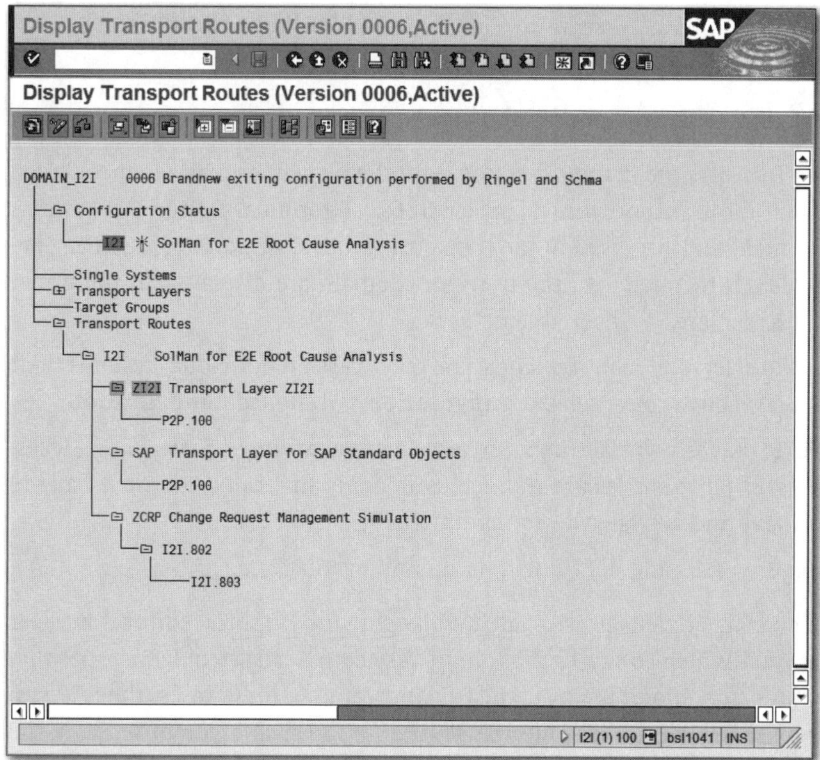


**Figure 4.10** List Editor

Transport layer

Figure 4.10 also shows that a *transport layer* called Z<integration system> is generated between the integration system and the consolidation system. A transport layer always describes the transport route that data should follow from a development system. This route is also known as the *consolidation route*. The transport route from a consolidation system or delivery system to another delivery system is also known as the *delivery route*. Therefore, a delivery route can only exist in a system landscape that comprises at least three systems. A delivery route always requires an upstream consolidation route.

In addition to the transport layer between the integration system and the consolidation system, an "SAP" transport layer is also generated automatically in the systems. This transport layer ensures that any changes made to the objects delivered by SAP AG can be imported into the systems.

Depending on the development project, it may make sense or you may even be forced to create several consolidation routes for different transport layers.

Graphical editor

We'll now use the graphical editor to make the same configurations:.

1. To access the graphical editor from the display or maintenance screen of the transport routes, select **Goto • Graphical Editor.** All systems that aren't yet used in the transport route definition but are nevertheless integrated into the transport domain are displayed in the upper screen area as insertable objects.
2. To select the required landscape and to assign individual systems their respective roles, select **Configuration • Standard Configuration**.
3. To save your settings, select **Configuration • Save**. The necessary table entries are then generated automatically. You now have to save and activate the configuration.

Figures 4.10 and 4.11 illustrate the same situation.

The main advantage associated with using the graphical editor is its clear layout, which comes to the fore in very complex system landscapes that don't correspond to any standard landscape. In these cases, the SAP systems available are initially transferred, at the click of a mouse, from the area containing the insertable objects to the display area.

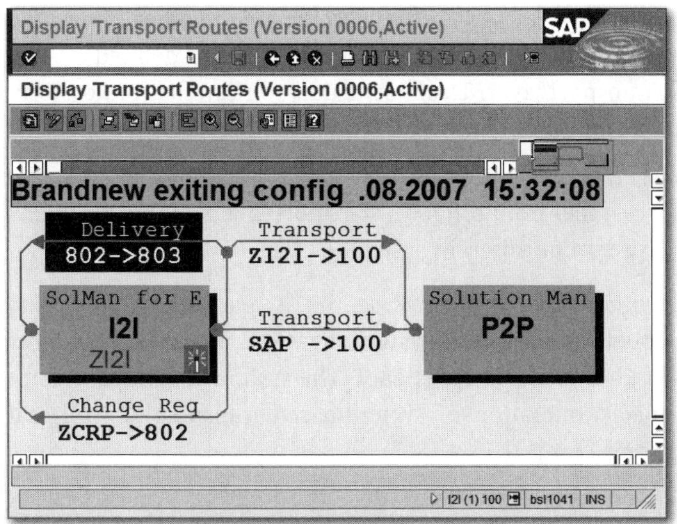


**Figure 4.11** Graphical Editor

You then select **Edit • Transport Route • Add Transport Route** to define the transport routes between the systems. If you define any incorrect transport routes, you can remove them by choosing **Delete** in the same menu path. When you trigger this function, the mouse pointer in the display area changes to a pencil, which you can then use to draw a connecting line between the required systems. For each transport route drawn in this way, you must determine whether it is a consolidation route, that is, a transport from the integration system to the consolidation system with a corresponding transport layer, or a delivery route.

The display area now contains a flowchart of the development data in the system landscape.

### 4.3.3 Extended Transport Control

**Client-based procedure**

In extended transport control, you can select a client-based procedure instead of a system-based procedure:

- When defining a consolidation route or delivery route, the target client or a group of target clients (*target group*) is specified instead of the target system.

- The standard transport layer used to specify, among other things, the transport target from the customizing settings, can be defined as a client-specific transport layer. This means that you can forward customizing requests from different clients into different transport targets.
- Defining target groups under an informative name enables requests to be sent in parallel from different transport layers to several clients in the same system or different systems.

To activate extended transport control, set the `CTC` parameter to the value 1 under **Transport Management System (STMS) • Overview • Systems • SAP System • Change • Transport Tool**. The system landscape doesn't support the mixed operation of system-based transport control and extended transport control.

### 4.3.4 QA Approval Procedure

To provide technical support to the basic rules described in Section 4.3, Configuring the Transport Management System, you can implement a QA approval procedure in a transport landscape with at least three systems as well as one consolidation route and one delivery route.

Requests in a QA system can only be released for import into the production system after they have completed a defined number of approval steps.

Under **Transport Management System (STMS) • Overview • Transport Routes**, select the consolidation system that you want to configure as a QA system. To expand the system attributes for the system that you have selected, select **Edit • System • Change**. You can define the approval procedure after you have set a confirmation in the **Quality Assurance** field.

System attributes

On the System Attributes screen (see Figure 4.12), you can choose from the following variants:

- Queue-controlled mass transports
- Queue-controlled single transports
- Workflow-controlled transports

The queue-controlled mass transport is the default setting.

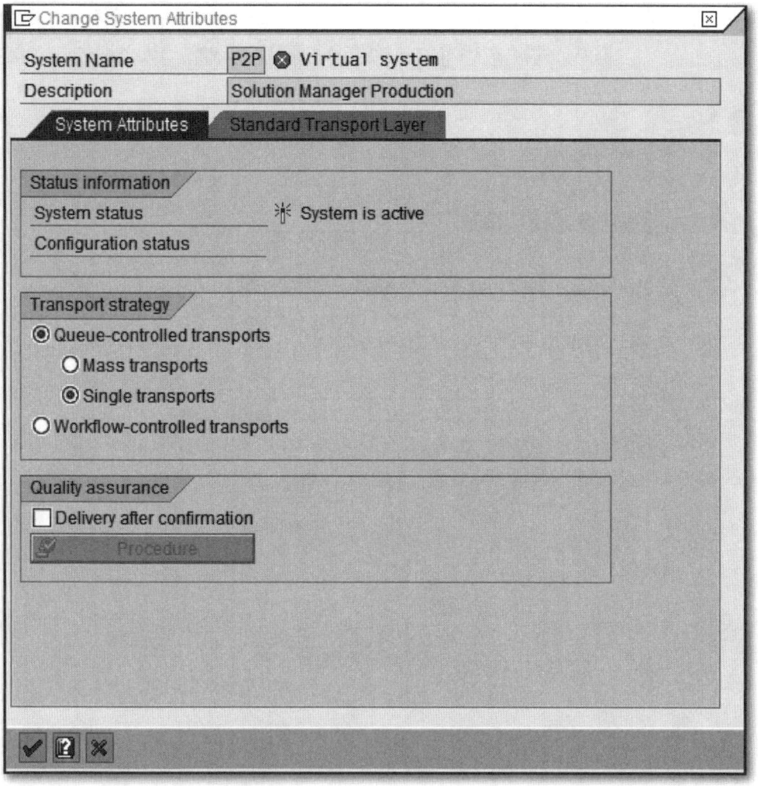

**Figure 4.12** System Attributes

## 4.4 Transport Control Program tp

The `tp` program is used at the operating system level to actually control and execute the transports between the systems. By using tools such as the `R3trans` transport program at the operating system level and other integrated tools, `tp` triggers both the export of data from an SAP system and the import of data into other systems. To enable `tp` to provide all of the necessary system landscape information, a *TP_<domain>.PFL* configuration file is stored in the *bin* subdirectory of the transport directory when transport management is initialized. Default values are already predefined for all parameter values. Parameters can be adjusted and enhanced by making the necessary changes under **Transport Management System (STMS) • Overview • Systems • SAP System • Change • Transport Tool**.

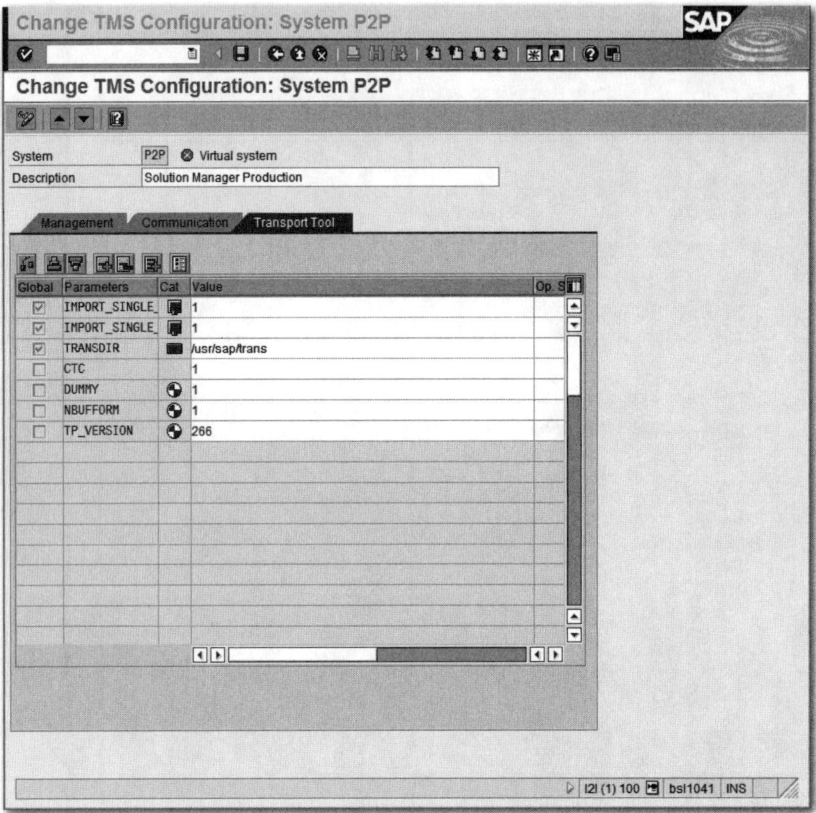


**Figure 4.13** Maintenance of `tp` Parameters

Note that unreliable or unknown parameter values don't trigger an error message. Instead, they are simply ignored. To display the actual current values, select **Goto • TP Parameters** in the screen shown in Figure 4.13.

Logs

All actions executed by `tp` are logged in the *log* subdirectory of the transport directory. By default, the *ALOG* file contains all entries for which `tp` transport requests are used. The *SLOG* file, on the other hand, logs the start time, the work steps, their duration, and the end time for each transport. If you want to deviate from this standard file name, you must define the following two `tp` parameters: `alllog` and `syslog`. For example, the parameter

```
alllog = ALOG$(syear).$(yweek)
```

defines that a new log file of the form *ALOG<YY>.<WW>* is written for each year and each week of the year.

Furthermore, a *ULOG<year>_<number>* log file is maintained whereby each `tp` call performed is recorded with its parameters, and the associated operating system user. *<year>* denotes the last two numbers of the year, and *<number>* denotes the current quarter.

## 4.5 Tips

- A virtual consolidation system doesn't support extended transport control.
- Even though a virtual system can be created as a consolidation system in a configuration with extended transport control, a transport request can't be released for this system.

## 4.6 Transactions and Menu Paths

**Transport Management System**: SAP Menu • Tools • Administration • Transports • Transport Management System (STMS)

**Transport Organizer Tools**: No standard menu entry (SE03)

## 4.7 Additional Documentation

SAP Service Marketplace, alias *swchangemanagement* Quick Links

### SAP Notes

Table 4.2 provides an overview of important SAP Notes concerning the structure of transport landscapes.

| Content | Note |
|---|---|
| System Change Option and Client Control | 40672 |
| R3trans: Logging Table Changes | 163694 |

**Table 4.2** SAP Notes Concerning the Transport Management System

## 4.8 Questions

1. **Which of the following statements applies to TMS configuration?**
   a. A transport domain can contain several transport groups.
   b. All systems that access a shared transport directory */usr/sap/trans* are assigned to a transport group.
   c. In a system, only one transport layer can be defined at a specific point in time.
   d. The transport layer indirectly determines the route to the target system.
2. **Which statement is applicable?**

In a multisystem landscape, the transport:

   a. Is only controlled by the system into which data is to be imported or from which data is to be exported.
   b. Is controlled centrally by the domain controller of the transport domain.
   c. Is only controlled at the operating system level when you use the `tp` program.
   d. Is verified in a transport domain by each SAP system in the domain.
3. **Which of the following transport routes do we distinguish between?**
   a. Direct transport route
   b. Indirect transport route
   c. Consolidation route
   d. Delivery route
   e. Alternative route

4. **Which program at the operating system level is responsible for executing transports?**

   a. `R3load`

   b. `SAPinst`

   c. `tp`

   d. `dpmon`

   e. `sapdba`

*Clients have played a role in many of the previous chapters of this book. In this chapter, we'll look at clients and their administration in more detail. Important aspects with respect to this include copying clients within an SAP NetWeaver AS system and the transmission of clients to another system.*

# 5 Client Administration

**Client**

A client is an independent unit from the point of view of business accounting, which means that a separate financial statement can be made for each client. Nearly all of the technical settings of SAP NetWeaver AS are client-independent.

Data is called client-independent or cross-client data if it's valid throughout the system. This primarily includes the SAP Repository. The Repository contains things such as ABAP programs, function modules, and the objects in the ABAP Data Dictionary. Changes to the configuration in this area thus have system-wide effects.

Other data, on the other hand, is client-specific, meaning that it's only visible from a single client account. Within client-specific data, we distinguish between *Customizing*, *application*, and *user* data. Customizing includes specific functional settings to fulfill business requirements. Initially (after system installation), these settings are company-neutral. During the process of Customizing, functionality will be adapted to company-specific business requirements. However, Customizing can also handle system-wide settings such as the choice of factory calendar, ArchiveLink configuration, and so forth. There are close relationships between the client-specific data groups. Application and user data is primarily influenced by the client-specific Customizing settings made. Application data is therefore usually consistent only in its associated Customizing environment. Figure 5.1 illustrates the interplay of the different data classes.

Thus, clients within an SAP system are suitable, for instance, for the implementation of relatively independent plant sections but less so for the implementation of business processes of completely independent companies.

Data classes

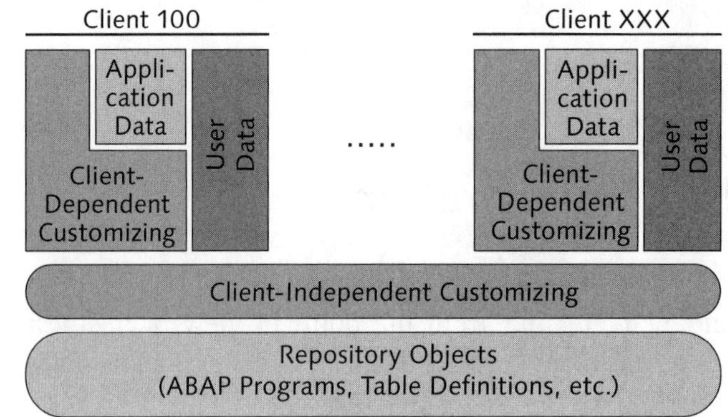


**Figure 5.1** Data Classes in SAP NetWeaver AS

Technical implementation

From a technical point of view, each client is identified by a three-digit number. This number is used as a key in tables containing application data. Such tables are called client-dependent, which means that the first column of such a table is always the column MANDT. This is also the first field in the so-called primary key of the table. A user only has access to the data associated to the client that was chosen during login. Besides the client-dependent tables, there are also client-independent tables. The data stored in those tables is equally valid for all clients. Consequently, the first column MANDT is omitted. The content of these tables has system-wide effects.

## 5.1 Default Clients and Users

Default clients

During installation of an SAP system, the following preconfigured clients are created:

- **Reference client 000**
  For administrative purposes as a template for additional clients.
- **Client 001**
  For production preparation and as a template for additional clients.

- **Client 066**
  For the remote services of SAP.

Clients 000 and 001 initially have identical content in the delivery state. Neither of these clients should be used for actual production operations. Client 000 already includes preconfiguration and sample entries and is supplied with the current sample Customizing through release upgrades, support packages, and so on. If languages in addition to German and English are imported, the language-dependent Customizing, such as units of measure, is also available only in client 000. Thus, client 000 more or less represents an "original client," which is used as a template. As a result, it's not suitable for use as a production client. All these specific settings must be transferred into other clients.

Default users

In clients 000 and 001, there are two default users defined. Because there are default names and default passwords for these users that may be known to third parties, you must protect them from unauthorized access. Note that no special users are created in client 066. The following list describes the two special users of the SAP system:

SAP*

- **SAP system super-user, SAP***
  SAP* is the only user in the SAP system for which no user master record is needed because this user is defined in the system code. SAP* has the password PASS by default, along with unrestricted access authorizations to the system. When you install the SAP system, a user master record is automatically created in client 000 and 001 for SAP*, with the initial password 06071992. This deactivates the special properties of SAP*, so that only the authorizations specified in the user master record and the password are valid. For protection from unauthorized access, you should always change the initial password; in addition, for security reasons, it's recommended that SAP* be deactivated, and a custom super user defined.

DDIC

- **DDIC user, responsible for the maintenance of the ABAP Dictionary and software logistics**
  When you install the SAP system, a user master record is automatically created in client 000 and 001 for DDIC. The default password for this user is 19920706. For the user DDIC, certain authorizations are predefined in the system code, so that it can log in as the only user

during installation of a maintenance level in the SAP system, for instance. To protect the DDIC user from unauthorized access, you must change its initial password in clients 000 and 001.

EarlyWatch

The user EarlyWatch is delivered in client 066 and is protected with the password SUPPORT. The EarlyWatch experts at SAP work with this user, so the user should not be deleted. You should change its password, however. The EarlyWatch user should only be used for EarlyWatch functions (monitoring and performance).

**Special Features Protecting the SAP* User**

During installation of an SAP NetWeaver AS, a user master record is created for SAP*, but this user master record isn't necessarily required because SAP* is programmed in the system code. Even if you delete the user master record for the SAP* user, you can still log in to the system with that user and a special initial password, PASS. The SAP* user then has the following properties:

- The user has all authorizations because no authorization checking is performed.
- The standard password PASS can't be changed.

If you want to deactivate the special properties of SAP*, you must set the profile parameter `login/no_automatic_user_sapstar` (see Section 7.1, Profile Maintenance, in Chapter 7) to a value greater than zero. If that parameter is set, SAP* has no special features. If the user master record SAP* doesn't exist, then SAP* can no longer be used to log in.

You should set the parameter in the global system profile `DEFAULT.PFL` so that it will affect all instances of the SAP system. Even with the parameter set, make sure that a user master record is present for SAP*; otherwise, logging in with SAP*, password PASS, and unrestricted privileges will be possible after you set the parameter back to 0.

We recommend deactivating the SAP* user by following these steps:

- In all new clients and in client 066, create a user master record for SAP*.
- Assign a new password for SAP* in clients 000 and 001.
- Delete all profiles from the SAP* profile list to deactivate all authorizations.
- Assign SAP* to the user group SUPER to prevent the user master record from accidental deletion and changes.

If you want to replace SAP* with a new super user, you must assign the `SAP_ALL` profile to another user. This profile contains all authorizations, including the new authorizations in profile `SAP_NEW`.

**Special Features Protecting the SAP* User**

The SAP_NEW profile guarantees upward compatibility of authorizations when a new release level or an update introduced authorization checks for functions that have previously been unprotected.

**Note**

User group SUPER has a special status in the predefined user profiles. The users in group SUPER can only be maintained and deleted by newly defined super users if the following are true:

- They use the predefined profiles.
- SAP recommendations for user and authorization maintenance are followed.

## 5.2 Creating New Clients

To work in production with an SAP NetWeaver AS, you must create your own clients in which the company-specific settings can be made. An existing client is copied to do this, generally client 000, or an already-configured client is transferred from another SAP system. Clients can be copied directly within a system or between systems, or transported to a remote system with a special transport request. Creating your own client is among the first steps in customizing a system and is therefore one of the basic functions within the IMG. SAP recommends creating a client in a development system exclusively for Customizing purposes. After completion of the Customizing in this system, all of the settings can be copied into the clients of the downstream SAP systems, particularly the later production system. This allows the settings to be tested first in the consolidation system. It also preserves the uniformity of settings of SAP systems in the landscape, which is of enormous importance for later testing environments.

**Copying a client**

The copying of a client, however, can only be considered during the initialization of the new client. If additional changes are made to the source client after the copy process is complete, which must also be made in the target client, you must use the Change and Transport System (CTS). The creation and copying of clients is a typical task in the implementation phase of an SAP system when implementing the system landscape. Figure 5.2 shows the procedures involved in order of execution for a three-system landscape. After copying a client, there is always a test phase, during which additional maintenance tasks or corrections to the new client may be necessary.

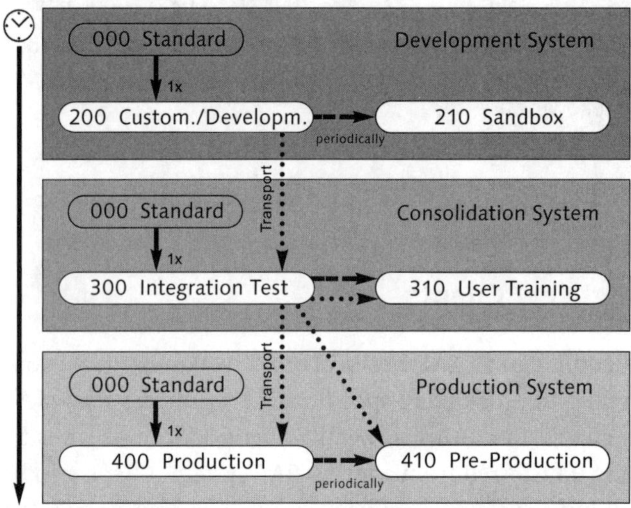


**Figure 5.2** Sample Structure of a Three-System Landscape

The creation of a new client is carried out in two steps:

1. Make the new client known to the SAP Web AS ABAP, and define some important basic settings.
2. Populate the client with data and post-processing. Only after this is a client ready to function.

Role

When planning an SAP system landscape, it should be taken into consideration right from the start how the different activities will be distributed across systems and clients. When creating a client, this is reflected in the role assigned to it. This role already expresses the purpose of the client and what properties describe it. The following roles are possible:

- Production client
- Test client

- Customizing client
- Demo client
- Training/education client
- SAP reference client

Besides documentation, the classification of clients also serves to protect the production clients in a system using multiple other (test) clients. For instance, a client marked as production can't be overwritten by a local or remote client copy. Customizing activities called directly from the application as ongoing settings (e.g., currency exchange rates, posting periods) can be directly performed in production clients, even if customizing isn't permitted according to the client settings.

In the context of system measurement, a system is considered production when at least one of its clients is classified as production.

The client classification can be changed at any time to reflect its actual use.

**Changeability**

One of the basic properties of a client is the determination of whether its data and objects may be changed, which must be considered in combination with the system changeability defined for the SAP system. The defined SAP system changeability controls whether the objects in the Repository and the cross-client Customizing are changeable or not; it has no influence on client-dependent Customizing changes.

In training, demo, or test clients in a system, it's not always desirable for all client-dependent Customizing changes to be automatically recorded, and possibly even accidentally transported into a downstream system.In the context of client control, therefore, you can determine the settings for change and transport of client-dependent and cross-client Customizing objects.

**Client-dependent objects**

The following options are available for fine-tuning clients regarding maintenance and transport of client-specific objects:

- Changes without automatic recording
- Automatic recording of changes
- No changes allowed

- Changes without automatic recording, no transports allowed

For clients in which Customizing should be performed, all changes must be recorded for later transport to other systems (option **Automatic recording of changes**). If changes are allowed but shouldn't be recorded, then a client setting can be used to determine whether manual transport of the changes should be possible. For a production client, it's recommended to set a client block or at least to store all changes automatically.

Client-independent objects

The control for maintaining client-independent objects (the Repository and client-independent Customizing) is defined separately:

- Changes to Repository and cross-client Customizing allowed
- No changes to cross-client Customizing objects
- No changes to Repository objects
- No changes to Repository or cross-client Customizing objects

In addition to setting options regarding system changeability (see Section 5.1, Default Clients and Users), which regulate the changeability in systems based on objects, you can also use these settings to define a client, preferably in the development system, as the only client in the system landscape in which cross-client Customizing and Repository changes are allowed. Unintended side effects can be avoided in this manner.

Protection levels

To avoid, for instance, accidentally or intentionally overwriting a production or Customizing client with a copy, clients can be protected with another setting. The following options are available:

- **Protection level 0**
  No restrictions.
- **Protection level 1**
  No overwriting.
- **Protection level 2**
  No overwriting, no external access.

A client in protection level 1 or 2 can no longer act as the target client of a client copy operation. Protection level 2 also prevents comparative external access to the client. SAP provides a special comparison tool for clients. For instance, it allows you to check whether the Customizing settings of two clients are identical or what differences there are between them. This information can be important for testing, where the testing environment must be identical to the production environment. Protection level 2 prevents the use of the Customizing Cross-System Viewer (SCU0) on the clients involved. This form of data protection prevents revelation of the Customizing settings of a client and unauthorized access to the client data it contains.

If necessary, you can restrict the use of the new client to the following areas:

- **Starting of CATT/eCATT processes**
  CATT stands for *Computer-Aided Test Tool*, whereas eCATT stands for *extended CATT*. This flag can be used to control whether it's permitted to start the following in this client:
  - CATT test cases
  - eCATT test scripts
  - eCATT test configurations

  Under some circumstances, allowing CATT/eCATT processes can mean a massive database change, which at least in production clients isn't permitted.
- **Protection against SAP upgrade**
  This setting is only possible for clients classified as test or SAP reference. In an upgrade of the SAP release, a marked client isn't supplied with changes; after the upgrade, the client can't be used. This functionality is only provided for exceptional cases, for instance, to have a basis for comparison after an upgrade is performed.

The properties described previously must be set during preparation of a new client before it can be populated with data. To do this, proceed as follows:

1. Select **Client Maintenance (SCC4)**. This takes you to an overview of all of the clients available in the system (see Figure 5.3).

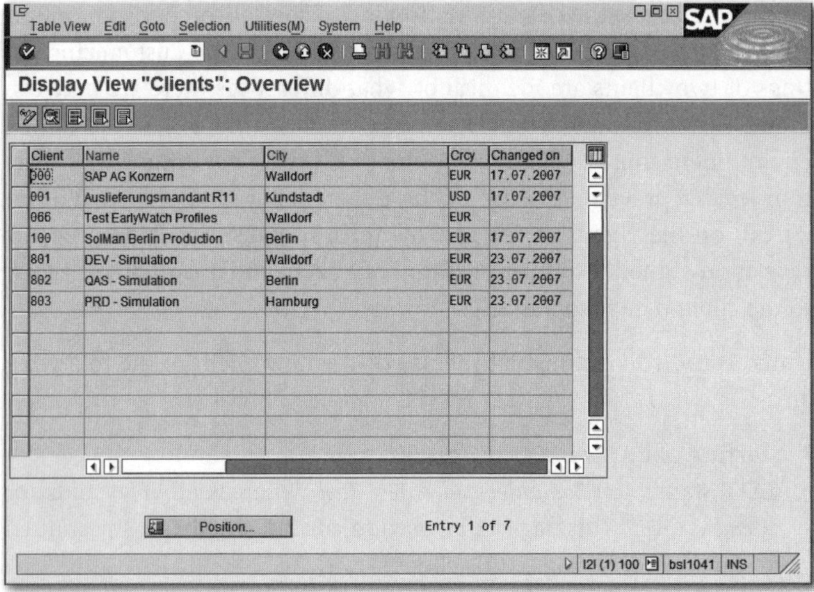


**Figure 5.3** Initial Screen for Client Maintenance

2. First create a new entry here, and define the properties of the new client in the maintenance screen for technical properties (see Figure 5.4).
3. Assign the client a role.
4. Select the changeability of the client.
5. Define the scope of possible changes to cross-client objects in these clients.
6. If necessary, protect future clients from copying from and comparison with other clients.

With that, all settings are complete for the new client. The work steps described initially cause no more than one entry in Table T000, which describes the properties of the new client. The new client receives no client-specific data and, in particular, no user data. The only thing hard-coded in the SAP system is the user SAP* with password PASS.

To make the client ready for use, you must copy the necessary data in the second step.

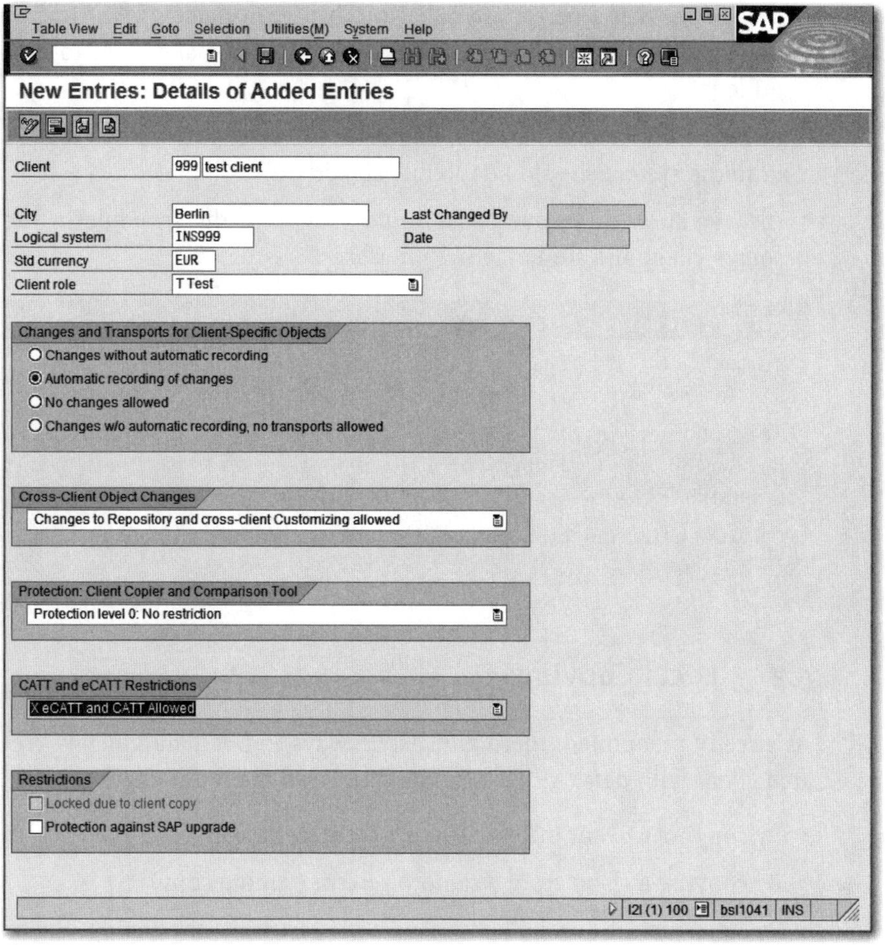

**Figure 5.4** Detail Maintenance

**Preparatory tasks**

Client copies, whether in the ongoing implementation project or during production system operation, present some risk that can be minimized by proper preparation:

- As a system administrator, you must make sure that certain client copies are announced in a timely manner via a system message, so that the users in your system can adjust their activity. A reminder on the day before the copy is often helpful.

- Make sure that a current data backup has been made at the time of the copy. Depending on the RDBMS used, it may make sense to turn off logging.
- Immediately before the copy, any warned users who are still logged in to the system should be forcibly signed off.
- Also be sure to remove background jobs from the schedule in the source client and stop external interfaces.

**Warning**

You can use the Mass Changes (SU10) function to block users in the source client for the client copy during the copy process!

Use this transaction with great care because incorrect selection of users will block all users (including yours)! This can make even an experienced administrator sweat.

At least one user should still be available with authorization to unblock other users.

## 5.3 Local Copying

As already mentioned, there are several ways to populate a newly created client with data. A client can be created in the following ways:

- By copying a client into the same system (local copy)
- By copying a client from a remote system (remote copy)
- By transmission through a transport request from another system to the target client (client transport)

Which of these methods you should use depends on the particular system landscape and the type of data to be copied. The work steps involved are quite similar. To avoid inconsistencies during the copy process, no work may be performed in either the target or the source client.

Copy profiles

Depending on the data structures in the SAP database, certain data types may be selected for the copy process. SAP provides so-called copy profiles for this purpose. Figure 5.5 shows the profiles currently available for copying clients.

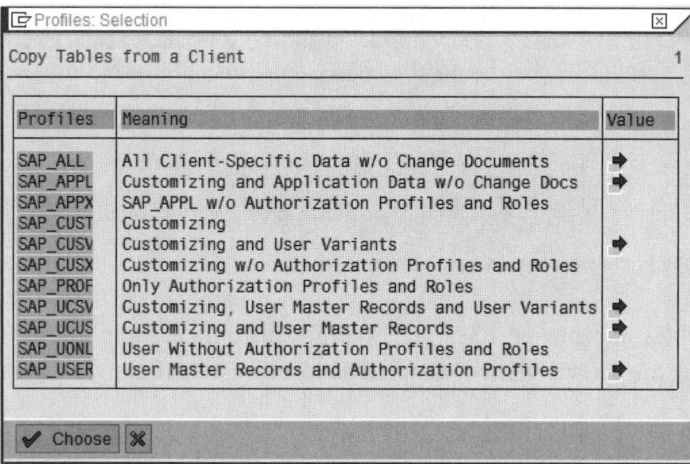


**Figure 5.5** Copy Profiles

You can't create your own profiles, and the existing ones can't be changed. However, you can copy user master data and other application data from different clients and store the resulting source combinations for reuse as variants. One component of the combination is always the source client of the user master data. It's not possible to mix application data from different clients in this way. The meanings of the copy profiles are shown in Table 5.1.

| Profile Name | Meaning |
|---|---|
| SAP_ALL | All of the data for a client (exception: change documents and local data) are copied to the target client. |
| SAP_APPL | Like SAP_ALL but without user master data. |
| SAP_APPX | Like SAP_APPL, without the authorization profiles or roles. |
| SAP_CUST | The client-dependent Customizing (including authorization profiles) is copied to the target client. The application data is deleted, but user data is retained. |
| SAP_CUSV | Like SAP_CUST, but variants are also copied. |
| SAP_CUSX | Customizing without authorization profiles or roles. |
| SAP_PROF | Only authorization profiles and roles. |

**Table 5.1** Copy Profiles for Local Copies

| Profile Name | Meaning |
|---|---|
| SAP_UONL | Users only, without authorization profiles or roles. |
| SAP_UCUS | Like SAP_CUST, but user master data is also copied. |
| SAP_UCSV | Like SAP_UCUS, but variants are also copied. |
| SAP_USER | Users, roles, and authorization profiles are copied. |

**Table 5.1** Copy Profiles for Local Copies (Cont.)

For all profiles except SAP_USER, all existing Customizing and application data in the target client is deleted before the actual copy process begins.

Change documents are not copied in a client copy. If they are needed in the target client, however, assuming the source and target clients have the same names, they can be copied later via a transport request.

The user master records created in the target client are only overwritten when a copy profile with user master data is selected.

**Procedure for a local copy**

First, let's examine the procedure for creating a local client copy, assuming that the target client has already been prepared as described previously:

1. Log in to the newly defined client as user SAP* with password PASS.
2. Confirm that no users are logged in to the source or target client, and send a system message about the impending client copy.
3. Select **Local Client Copy (SCCL)**.

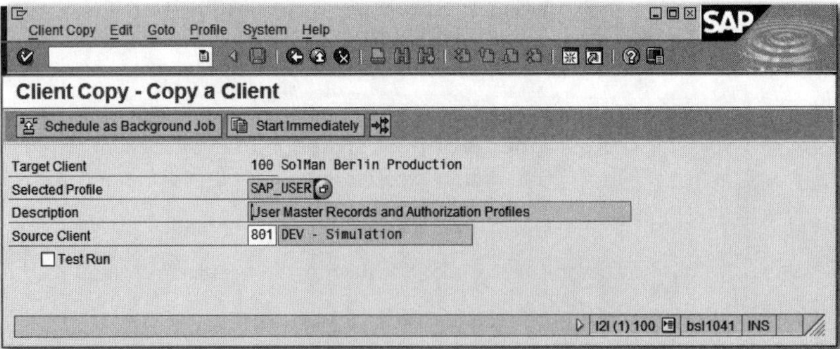


**Figure 5.6** Local Client Copy

4. Use the profile to select the data to be copied from the source client. If you have any doubt about the type of data selection in the profiles available, you can use the menu item **Profile Display** to clarify the content to be copied by each profile.
5. Perform the copy of a client in the background using **Schedule as background job** (see Figure 5.6).
6. Using Log Analysis Client Copy (SCC3), you can monitor the current status of the copy at any point and analyze the logs of completed copy runs. The system then creates detailed logs of the copy process (see Figure 5.7).

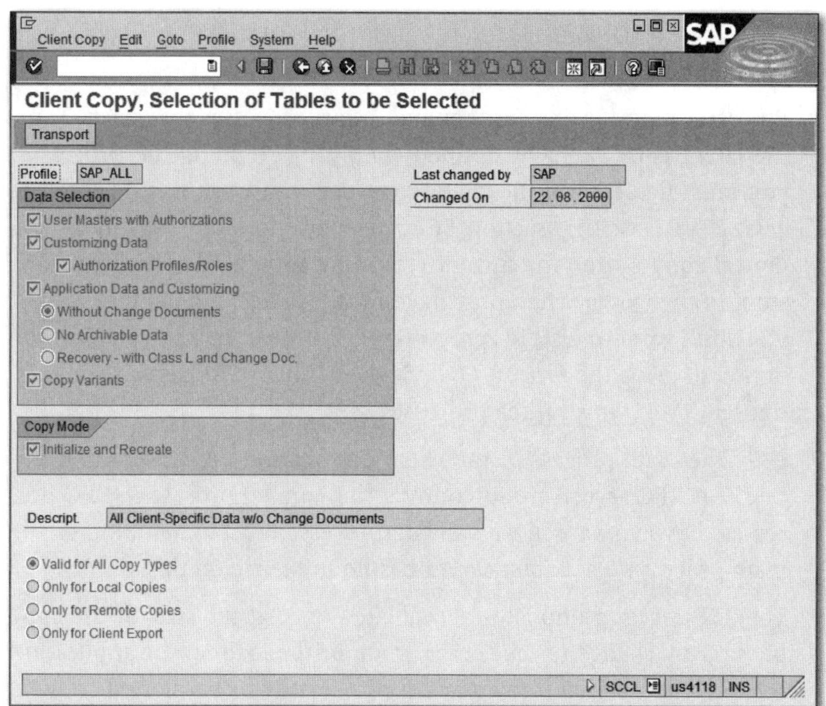


**Figure 5.7** Detailed Description of the SAP_ALL Profile

Using parallel processes

For remote copies, local copies, and client solutions, you can use parallel processes to make better use of the capabilities of your database. The tasks to be carried out are not processed by a single process in this case, but by processes working in parallel, leading to a significant performance boost.

To select the maximum number of processes to be used and the associated RFC server group, a **Parameters** button is available for parallel processes in the respective transactions. If you have not yet created an RFC server group, you can go from there to **RFC Server Group Maintenance (RZ12)** (see Section 5.5, Client Transport).

The following conditions should be noted when using parallel processes:

- A good rule of thumb is to have two processes for each database CPU available. Any number of application servers can be used.
- Parallel processes are only used during the actual copy phase but not during the analysis and post-processing phases.
- Under certain circumstances, resource administration may only assign the client copy a limited number of processes.
- Processes monitor one another and restart processes that crash. Thus, the client copy can't be stopped simply by stopping the processes; you must first inform the client copy that you want to stop the process. If you use Transaction SCC3 to view the copy log, there is a **Cancel copy** button for currently running copies. The processes then stop on their own when they have finished their momentary task. If you don't want to wait for processes to stop themselves, you have the option of using the Process Overview (SM50) or SAP Server Administration (SM51) to stop the processes.
- Only the main process of the client copy can use a background process. An RFC server group controls the parallel processes. RFC processes, however, are always dialog processes. The scheduling of the main process on a certain server has no influence on this.
- The RFC server group is only evaluated once at the start of the copy phase. Any change to the server group or the load on the application servers will only have an effect on a later copy or a restarted copy.

You can also theoretically carry out the copy of a client in the foreground by selecting **Start immediately**, but then the copy process will automatically be handled by the current instance. In the background, on the other hand, any instance within the SAP NetWeaver AS that provides the background service can be selected. Depending on the amount of data to be copied and the performance of the hardware, the process may take several hours. If the copy process were to run in the foreground, then the dialog process would be blocked during that time. Moreover, the processing time is limited by the dialog work process by the `rdisp/max_wp_runtime` instance parameter. If a transaction exceeds that time, it's stopped and rolled back. For background execution, you can schedule the copy process to start at any time. Using **Schedule as background job**, you can then enter the required data at the starting time during background execution.

Restart

If the copy process is stopped due to any problems, it can be continued to its end using the **Restart mode** option provided. In that case, the copy process is started at the point of interruption and need not be started from the beginning.

Test run

Using the **Test run** option, you can initially run the entire process as a test. The **Resource check** and **Simulation** options are available in this context. In the resource check, the system checks whether there is sufficient database space for the copy on the target system, whereas in simulation, the table structures are checked to determine whether they are identical in the source and target systems.

During the copy run, you can view the logs from any other client account to gain insight into the progress of the operation. For an active copy run, the monitor can also be enabled, which shows a graphical presentation of the progress of the procedure based on the number of tables still to be copied.

Listing 5.1 shows the summarized file log of a local client copy carried out in the background. This is a test system that was copied from Client 001 to the newly created client 100.

```
Log file:          /usr/sap/trans/log/CC000004.SLO

         Client copy on 02.05.2006 17:01:03
         SYSID...............................SLO
         Target client.......................100
         SAP Release.........................700
           Basis Support Package..............SAPKB70007
         Host................................us4118
```

```
Start in background..................X
User.................................SAP*
Parameter
Source client........................001
Copy profile:........................SAP_APPL
Table selection
Customizing data.....................X
with application data................X
Initialize and create................X
Change documents not copied
Tables selected            :           15,007
Data copied, in kbytes     :          364,007
Data deleted, in kbytes    :            8,940
Program ended successfully.
Run time in seconds        :            3,104
Processing ended           : 17:52:21
```

**Listing 5.1** Log of a Local Client Copy Executed in the Background

## 5.4 Remote Copy

As you already know, in a multisystem landscape every SAP system has special and clearly defined tasks. For instance, Customizing, quality assurance, and production should be performed in separate systems. However, for the settings made in the SAP systems to be truly identical, the copying of clients between systems is a useful feature. One way to implement this data transfer is remote copy.

**Note**

A client can only be copied between systems if both SAP systems are at the same release level and the repositories have not diverged due to patches or transports.

The interface between the SAP systems is an RFC connection. As a result, an RFC connection must be defined from the target system for the source clients of the source systems. The data transfer over the RFC interface is slower than for a local copy or client transport between systems. This, together with the significant quantity of data to be copied to the remote system, results in a correspondingly long runtime. A remote copy procedure is, in any case, slower than a local copy, if only because of the network connection used. During that time, neither the source client nor the target client may be used. From a practical standpoint, the copy process should also run in the background for this method to avoid blocking on a dialog process. Its long running time also means that the process easily exceeds the runtime defined for dialog processes within the SAP system. If the process is interrupted, this method also allows a restart at the point of interruption if the copy run is activated with the corresponding restart option. However, even when processing in the background, the reading RFC process on the source system occupies a dialog work process during the time it takes to read a table. Depending on the size of the largest table, the maximum dialog time in the source system may still need to be increased.

**Procedure for remote copy**

The procedures for a local copy process and for copying clients from another SAP system differ only in that for the latter, the use of an RFC connection is necessary. Proceed as follows:

1. In the target system, create the new client as described in Section 5.2, Creating New Clients.
2. Log in to the target system in the target client with user SAP* and password "PASS".
3. For the scheduled copy run, you must define the RFC connection between the SAP systems for the source client, if this hasn't yet been done. To do this, proceed as described in Section 13.1 in Chapter 13.
4. Here, too, during the copy run, the source client on the source system should be protected from any changes. Confirm that no users are logged in to the source or target client, and send a system message about the impending client copy.
5. Then you can start the copy process in the target system. By selecting **Remote Client Copy (SCC9)**, you reach the corresponding client copier (see Figure 5.8).

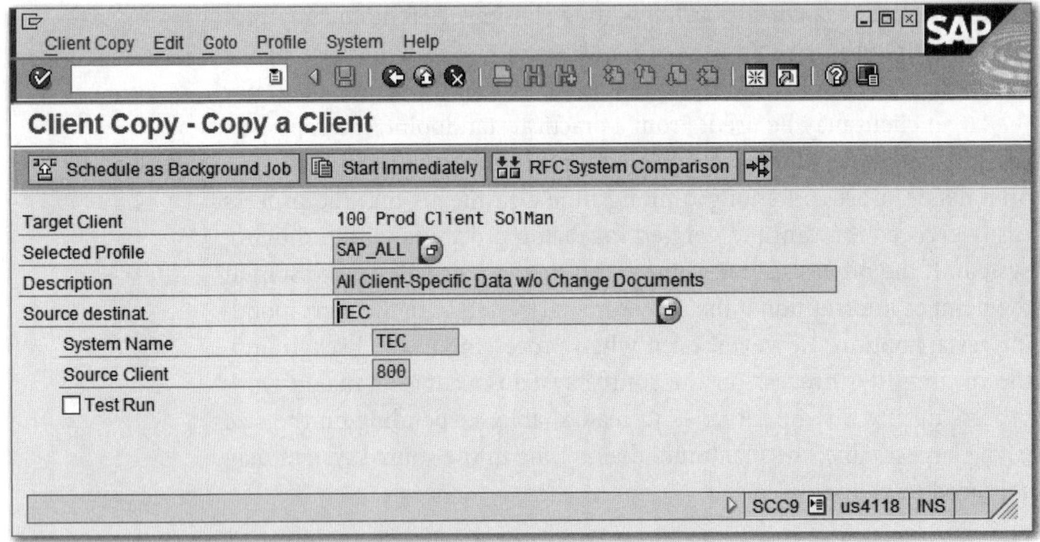


**Figure 5.8** Remote Client Copy

6. Use the profile again to select the data to be transmitted.
7. Select the RFC connection. The selection of the RFC connection automatically determines the source system and client.
8. Prior to the actual copy run, you should test the RFC connection using **RFC system check**. In addition to the connection test, the version of the two SAP systems involved are also checked for matching, and their dictionaries are checked for compatibility.
9. Start the copy run in the background. Here, too, you can parallelize the processing. The settings for this can be found in the **Goto • Parallel processes** menu or by using the corresponding button.
10. Check the status of the copy process from the target system.

A remote copy run is no different from a local copy run, either in its execution alternatives (foreground or background) or in the associated options, and here, too, for the reasons already mentioned, processing in the background is preferable to processing in the foreground. Again, you can perform a test run before starting the actual copy process. No later than the start of the process, all work in the source and target clients must be stopped. If the copy process is interrupted, a restart is possible for a remote copy as well.

**Note**

For a remote client copy, only table data is moved, not table definitions. If client-dependent custom tables have been created in the source client, they are not automatically transmitted to the target client; this would result in an error. The structure of all of the tables to be copied is examined. If a copy would result in a loss of data — for instance, because tables are missing in the target system or the field structure of tables in source and target systems are not the same — the copy is stopped, and all differences are recorded in the log. To generate dictionary compatibility, you must transport the missing table structures from the server system to the target system before the client copy. Here, any program changes associated with the new tables must be taken into consideration.

Copy profiles

For remote client copies, the same copy profiles are available as are used for local copies. In SAP NetWeaver, these are extended with additional profiles with which cross-client Customizing can also be transferred in the context of a client copy (see Table 5.2).

| Profile Name | Meaning |
| --- | --- |
| SAP_RECO | Recovery (only if source client = target client) |
| SAP_RMBC | Like SAP_UCSV, with cross-client Customizing |
| SAP_RMPA | Like SAP_ALL, with cross-client Customizing |
| SAP_RMPC | Like SAP_CUSV, with cross-client Customizing |

**Table 5.2** Additional Copy Profiles for Remote Client Copies

## 5.5 Client Transport

In a *client transport*, the data to be copied isn't transmitted directly to the remote target system. Instead, the transport control tool `tp` is first used to create data and control files for the data to be exported from a client and store them in the global transport directory. The import of this data into the target system can then take place at some later time. A client transport can also be used to transport client-dependent data to a system outside the system landscape using an external data medium, or to create a backup copy of the client.

**Note**

The minimum prerequisite for this method is again the fact that the source and target systems must have the same SAP release. Just as for a remote copy, for client transport, the dictionaries of the two systems must also be compatible. If the target system is already known and an RFC connection is possible, these conditions can be checked directly with **RFC System Check**, just as for a remote copy.

**Copying client data**

The procedure for copying client data using a client export differs in a few ways from the procedure for a local or remote copy:

1. The first step is again the creation of the target client in the target system. In contrast with local and remote copies, however, this step can only be done after the transport request is created in the source system.
2. Then log in to the source system in the source client with a transport-authorized user (not SAP* or DDIC).
3. Be sure that except for you, nobody is logged in to the source client, and inform the other system users with a system message that the client export is beginning.
4. Start the client export.
5. Just as for local and remote copies, you also select the data to be copied using the data profile (see Figure 5.9). It's also possible to export client-independent settings. Profiles are also available for this:
   - `SAP_EXBC`
   - Like `SAP_UCSV`, with cross-client Customizing
   - `SAP_EXPA`
   - Like `SAP_ALL`, with cross-client Customizing
   - `SAP_EXPC`
   - Like `SAP_CUSV`, with cross-client Customizing
6. As the target system, you can specify any system described in the definition of the system landscape, including virtual and external systems. However, the system only provides SAP systems for selection that have the same release as the source system. With this method, you can also execute either online or in the background, with the same advantages and disadvantages already explained.

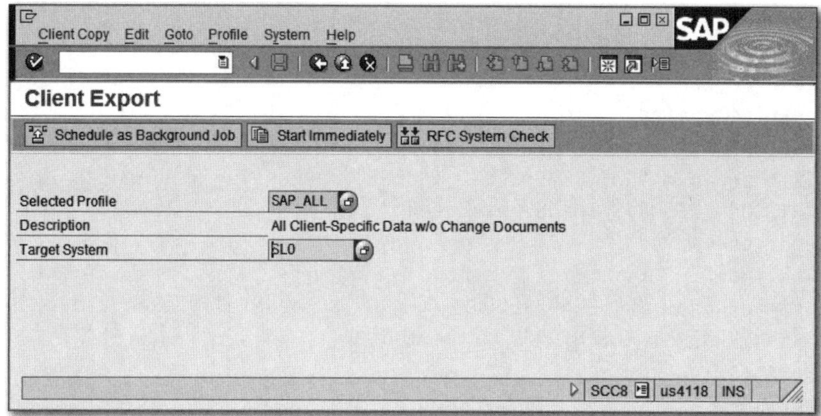


**Figure 5.9** Client Export

7. Confirm the selection made; you are informed which transport requests have been created for this task.
8. Check the logs generated for the export run.

For this type of copying of data from a client, logs are also created. Listing 5.2 shows the copy log for a client export with profile SAP_CUST.

**Log**

```
Client export from „03.10.2002" „15:56:14"
System ID........................... „KLU"
R/3 Release......................... „46C" Host..............
.................. „SLUQAS"
User................................ SHAGEM
Parameter
Source client....................... "600"
Copy profile:......................."SAP_CUST"
Table selection
Customizing data ...................."X"
with application data............... " "
Initialize and recreate......... "X"
With cross-client tables............." "
"ADDR_CLIENTCOPY_SELECT_TABLES" executed "        25"("
0") entries copied
Runtime "                0" seconds
Exit program "ADDR_CLIENTCOPY_SELECT_TABLES" successfully
executed
"RKC_CC_EXCLUDE_TABLES" executed "        0"("        0")
entries copied
```

```
Runtime "            10" seconds
Exit program "RKC_CC_EXCLUDE_TABLES" successfully executed
"RKE_CC_EXCLUDE_TABLES" executed "        4"("        0")
entries copied
Runtime "            12" seconds
Exit program "RKE_CC_EXCLUDE_TABLES" successfully executed
"RV_COND_RECORDS_TRANS" executed "        4"("    1.046")
entries copied
Runtime "            11" seconds
Exit program "RV_COND_RECORDS_TRANS" successfully executed
"SCCB_VARIANT_CLIENTCOPY" executed "        4"("    5.573")
entries copied
Runtime "           121" seconds
Exit program "SCCB_VARIANT_CLIENTCOPY" successfully executed
"CLIENTCOPY_SELECT_TEXTID_STD" executed. "             1"
entries found
Runtime "             0" seconds
Exit program "CLIENTCOPY_SELECT_TEXTID_STD" successfully
executed
"CLIENTTRA_SELECT_TEXTID_FORM" executed. "             6"
entries found
Runtime "             0" seconds
Exit program "CLIENTTRA_SELECT_TEXTID_FORM" successfully
executed
"CLIENTTRA_SELECT_TEXTID_STYL" executed. "             0"
entries found
Runtime "             0" seconds
Exit program "CLIENTTRA_SELECT_TEXTID_STYL" successfully
executed
Command file for "tp" is written under: "KLUKT00116"
For client transport, "        12.508" entries entered in
command file
Command file for "RSTXR3TR" is written under: "KLUKX00116"
For client transport, "             7" entries entered in
command file
Selected objects          : "        30.961"
Program ran successfully
Runtime (seconds)         : "           352"
```

**Listing 5.2** Copy Log for a Client Export

Important parts of the log content, besides any errors that occurred, are the names of the transport requests created for the client export. In addition to the option already mentioned of using **Log Analysis • Client Copy (SCC3)** to be informed of the status and progress of a client copy, in this case, the Client Transports function of the Transport Organizer (Expanded View) (SE01) must be used for evaluating the results. The log from the client copier only describes the setup of the command files for the transport program tp, which handles the actual export of the client. The logs from the export run can be viewed using the Transport Organizer. Listing 5.3 shows an example.

```
Directory  \\SLUQAS\sapmnt\trans\log
Name: KLUEX00116.KLU1
ETP199X######################################
1 ETP183 EXPORT PREPARATION
1 ETP101 transport order      : "KLUKX00116"
1 ETP102 system               : "KLU"
1 ETP108 tp path              : "tp"
1 ETP109 version and release : "305.12.42" "46D"
1 ETP198
2 EPU230X Execution of the export pre-processing methods for
request "KLUKX00116"
4 EPU111    on the application server: "SLUQAS"
4 EPU138    in client             : "000"
.........
2 EPU232 End:  Adapting the object directory for the objects of
the request "KLUKX00116"
1 ETP183 EXPORT PREPARATION
1 ETP110 end date and time   : "20021003160206"
1 ETP111 exit code            : "0"1
ETP199X######################################
1 ETP150 MAIN EXPORT
1 ETP101 transport order      : "KLUKX00116"
1 ETP102 system               : "KLU"
1 ETP108 tp path              : "tp"
1 ETP109 version and release : "305.12.42" "46D"
4 ETW000 R3trans.exe version 6.05 (release 46D - 18.10.01 - 11:
30:00).                                                  =======
========================================
4 ETW000 control file: \\SLUQAS\sapmnt\trans\tmp\KLUKKX00116.
KLU
4 ETW000 > #pid 4380 on SLUQAS (APServiceKLU)
4 ETW000 > export
```

```
4 ETW000 > file='\\SLUQAS\sapmnt\trans\data\RX00116.KLU'
4 ETW000 > client=600
4 ETW000 > buffersync=yes
4 ETW000 >
4 ETW000 > use comm 'KLUKX00116'
4 ETW000 R3trans was called as follows: R3trans.exe -u 1 -w \\
SLUQAS\sapmnt\trans\tmp\KLUEX00116.KLU \\SLUQAS\sapmnt\trans\
tmp\KLUKKX00116.KL
4 ETW000 date&time   : 03.10.2002 - 16:02:14
4 ETW000 active unconditional modes: 1
4 ETW000 Connected to DBMS = MSSQL     SERVER = 'SLUQAS\KLU'
DBNAME = 'KLU'     SYSTEM = 'KLU'.
4 ETW000  trace at level 1 opened for a given file pointer
4 ETW000 ================== STEP 1 =====================
4 ETW000 date&time   : 03.10.2002 - 16:02:14
4 ETW000 function    : EXPORT
4 ETW000 data file   : \\SLUQAS\sapmnt\trans\data\RX00116.KLU
4 ETW000 buffersync  : YES
4 ETW000 client      : 600
4 ETW000 Language    :
ABCDEFGHIJKLMNOPQRSTUVWXYZ0123456789abcdefghijklmnopqrstuvwxyz
4 ETW000 Compression : L
4 ETW000 l.s.m.      : VECTOR
4 ETW000 commit      : 100000
4 ETW000 table cache : dynamic
4 ETW000
3WETW129 transport request "KLUKX00116" has trstatus "D".
3 ETW673XUse Commandfile "KLUKX00116"
4 ETW000       /* Mandantenexport Texte */
4 ETW000       trfunction: 'M' (client transport)
4 ETW000       trstatus  : 'D'
4 ETW000       tarsystem : PLU.600
4 ETW000       user      : SHAGEM
4 ETW000       date      : 03.10.2002 - 16:01:52
4 ETW000   1 entry from E070 exported (KLUKX00116).
4 ETW000   7 entries from E071 exported (KLUKX00116
*).
.........
4 ETW000 Disconnected from database.
4 ETW000 End of Transport (0004).
4 ETW000 date&time: 03.10.2002 - 16:02:16
4 ETW000 1 warning occured.
1 ETP150 MAIN EXPORT
```

```
1 ETP110 end date and time    : "20021003160216"
1 ETP111 exit code            : "4"
1 ETP199 ##########################################
```

**Listing 5.3** Client Export Log from tp

**Note**

If there are restrictions on file sizes in the operating system used with the SAP system, for instance 2GB, then the data files created for the transport request can't grow past that limit. This would lead to a crash.

The data files created during the client export form the basis for the import of the data into another SAP system. Table 5.3 describes the fields created in the transport directory during a complete client export.

| Subdirectory | File Name | Meaning |
|---|---|---|
| *\data* | *RO<request number>.<SID>* | Client-independent data |
| *\data* | *RT<request number>.<SID>* | Client-dependent data |
| *\data* | *RX<request number>.<SID>* | Text and forms |
| *\cofiles* | *KO<request number>.<SID>* | Client-independent metainformation |
| *\cofiles* | *KT<request number>.<SID>* | Client-dependent metainformation |
| *\cofiles* | *KX<request number>.<SID>* | Metainformation for text and forms |

**Table 5.3** Files Important for the Import

Only those files are created for which data is present in the system, and which should be exported according to the copy profile. For instance, if no client-independent data is exported for a client export, as is the case in our example when using the profile `SAP_CUST`, then the associated data file is omitted. In our example, therefore, no file RO0116.PLU would be created.

**Procedure for import**

Follow these steps to import the data into another SAP system:

1. If the exported client is going to be loaded into a system not connected by a shared transport domain, then manual actions are necessary at the operating system level. First, the files needed are copied into the corresponding subdirectory of the local transport directory on the target system.
2. At the operating system level, in the subdirectory *bin* of the local transport directory on the target system, the commands

   ```
   tp addtobuffer <request> <target system>
   ```

   and

   ```
   tp import <target system> client <target client>
   ```

   are executed for the transport request for the client-independent data and then for the transport request with the client-specific data. These actions generally take considerable time, similar to the execution of an export. The transport request for text and forms is imported and generated by the post-processing described in step 4.
3. After the actual import through the transport management system, or manually with `tp`, then you must adapt the SAP runtime environment to the current state of the data by calling Post-Client Import Methods (SCC7), preferably using the user SAP* or DDIC to avoid authorization problems. The import post-processing must always be carried out. Even during import post-processing, no users may work in the target client.
4. You can use the Transport Management System (STMS) to find the import logs (see Figure 5.10), even if the import was started directly with **tp**. In the Client Copy Log Analysis (SCC3), all post-processing performed is listed.

This concludes the client import. In practice, client import is quite doable, particularly when client-independent data is included. Client-independent data influences the entire SAP system, so the imported data necessarily affects all of the clients in the target system. In the worst case, other clients could be rendered inoperable by the import of client-independent data from another SAP NetWeaver AS. If client-independent data isn't accepted from the source system, however, the functionality of the imported clients may suffer if there are significant differences between the source and target systems. During client export and import, the differences between the source and target systems must be considered with particular care.

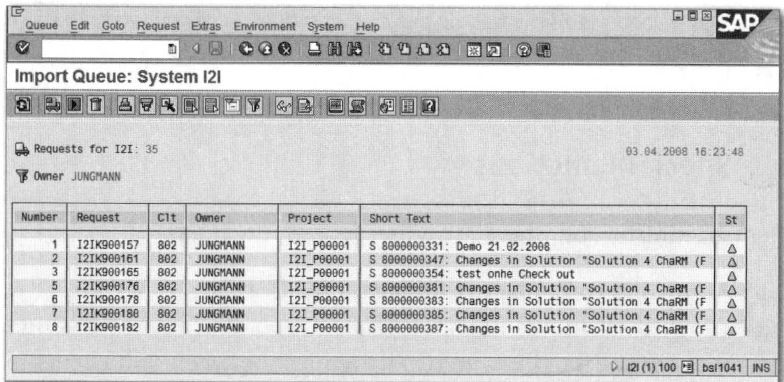


**Figure 5.10** Import Through the Transport Management System

**Post-processing**

After a client copy is complete, some attention must be paid to the post-processing required:

- If the client settings for the copy were initially set to a transitional value, otherwise the copy would have been impossible, these settings must now be given their final values.
- If you turned off logging in the database during the client copy, then for production operation, you must reactivate it after a new full backup.
- The client-specific background jobs must be scheduled.
- If logical systems are used (see Section 13.2, Application Link Enabling, in Chapter 13), then the names of the logical systems must be adjusted in the non-production systems after the client copy using Convert Logical System Names (BDLS).
- When using SAP Business Workflow, the default workbench must be maintained.
- The connection of interfaces for client-specific settings must be checked and maintained as needed.
- If the database in use works with a cost-based optimizer, then after the client copy, the statistics must be regenerated.

**Summary**

Copying clients isn't suitable for merging data from different clients or moving a differential set of data from one client to another. Copying clients should be seen as the first step in the development of the system landscape. After the copy process is complete, the data in the clients must be maintained with CTS and transported as needed.

## 5.6 Special Functions

In client administration, there are a few special functions:

- **Copy According to Transport Request (SCC1)**
  With a copy according to transport request, you can copy the Customizing changes collected in a transport request between two clients in a system. Along with the object list in the request itself, the object lists of unreleased tasks in the request can also be copied. The request itself need not be released. Entries in the target client are overwritten or deleted according to the key entries in the transport request.
- **Delete Client (SCC5)**
  Now and then, a client must be deleted entirely, for instance, in SAP systems originating as a copy of another system. This function isn't at all trivial. There are nearly as many changes to the database as for the copy of a client. Depending on the RDMBS in use, the drive space no longer required after the client is deleted may not be released until a reorganization is performed.
- **Client Comparison**
  To compare the Customizing settings of two clients in the same system or between SAP systems, SAP NetWeaver AS provides various functions that all require RFC communication between the two clients. The Customizing Cross-System Viewer (SCU0) can be used to compare complex Customizing environments under the control of different criteria. The client setting **Protection level 2: no overwriting, no external access** prevents the use of the Customizing Cross-System Viewer. Any two tables can be compared using Table Comparison (SCMP).

## 5.7 Tips

Due to the quantities of data moved during the copying of clients, the copy process must be considered critical. Probably the most common error is underestimating the data growth during the copy. If the database turns out to be too small, then not only the copy process will crash, but under some circumstances, any further work with the system may also be impossible until it's expanded. Thus, perform a test run to determine the data volume to be added. Test whether there is sufficient space in the database!

Client size

- The results of the test run, particularly the determination of the resource consumption to be expected, are based on estimates. To get a more exact picture of the size of a client, SAP NetWeaver AS provides the reports RSTABLESIZE (see Figures 5.11 and 5.12) and RSSPACECHECK (see Figure 5.13), which can be used for a more exact analysis at the table level.

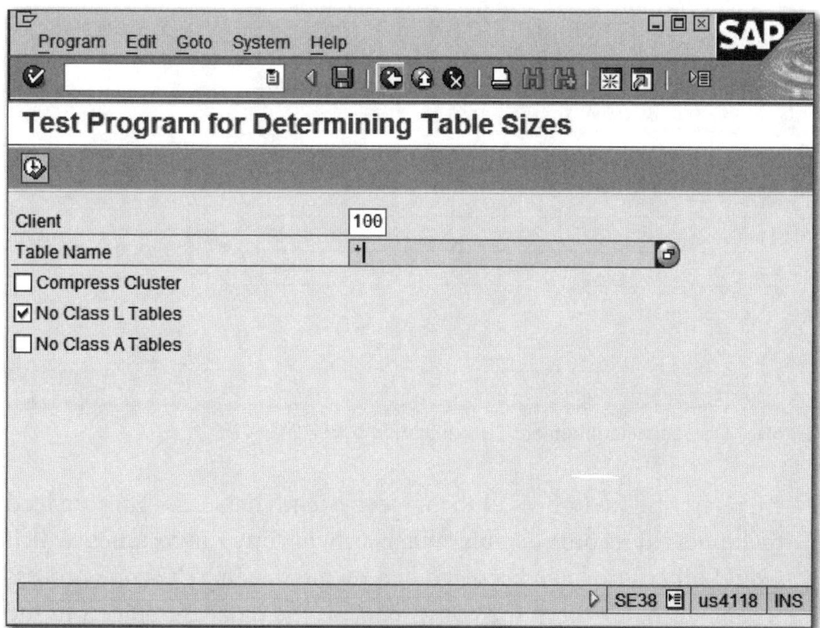


**Figure 5.11** Size Determination Using RSTABLESIZE

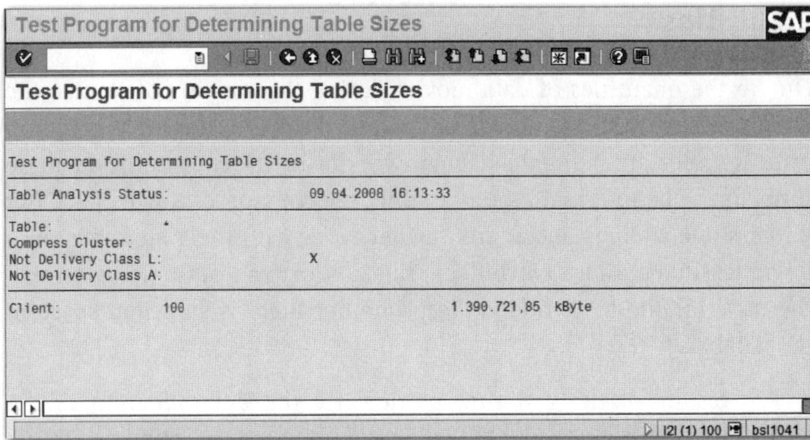


**Figure 5.12** Results of the Size Determination

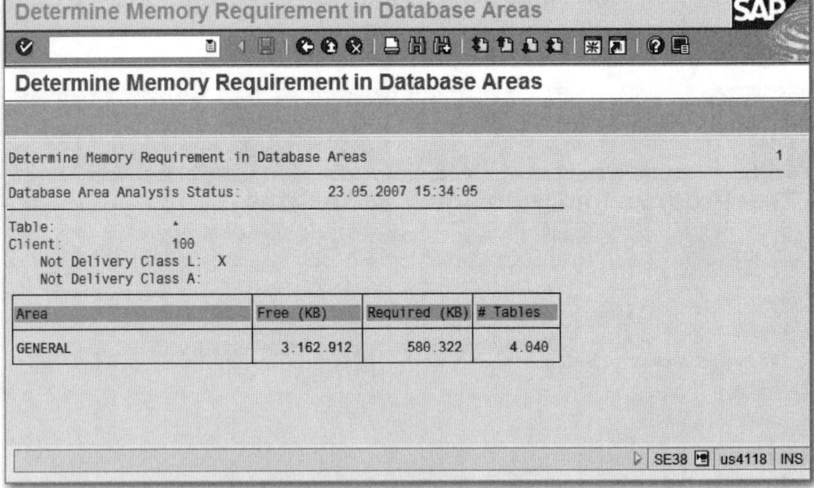


**Figure 5.13** Space Requirement Determination by RSSPACECHECK

Indices

- There are still no indices in the target system's database. This can lead to duplicated records in tables when a client copy run resumes, which would otherwise have been avoided by the system. The copy process would crash. So check the consistency of the database objects in the target system, particularly the indices, using Database Performance: Tables and Indices (DB02).

- If the client is very large, and client-independent data must also be copied, then the possibility of the homogeneous database copy should be considered. However, the RDBMS and operating system of the source and target systems must match, although a remote client copy or client transport between different system configurations is possible.

Database copy

- By parallelizing a client copy or deletion run, you can achieve significantly faster throughput. According to the definition of RFC server groups (see Section 5.5, Client Transport), you can active a server group during local or remote client copies and during client deletion from the start transaction using **Goto • Parallel Processes**. During the actual copy phase, parallel processes will be used. Note that only the main process runs in the background when correspondingly configured; all other parallel processes occupy dialog work processes. The serial scheduling of individual client copies with parallel processes is cheaper than parallel scheduling of several client copies (with different source clients) that don't use parallel processes. Simultaneous copying from the same client isn't possible.

Tuning

- If you want to overwrite an existing client with a new copy, it makes sense to delete the client first and then to start the copy, even though a copy implicitly deletes all data. Particularly when deleting large tables, especially when using Oracle, the rollback segments can overflow. In a deletion run, this problem can be solved better; besides, in case of a crash, at least part of the data has already been deleted.

Copying over

- When stopping and restarting a client export, be sure that all of the associated `tp` runs have stopped before you restart the export. Otherwise, there is a risk that inconsistent transport files will be generated, which can't then be imported.

Restarting a client export

- For extremely large tables, you can get a performance advantage by deleting the secondary indices before performing the client copy and then recreating them, to avoid having to change the index after every record copied. The report RSCCEXPT can be used to set tuning parameters for a client copy. Be careful with these options, however: Note especially that the settings must be reset after the end of the client copy.

Copying large tables

## 5.8 Transactions and Menu Paths

**Customizing Cross-System Viewer:** SAP Menu • Tools • AcceleratedSAP • Customizing • Customizing Cross-System Viewer (SCU0)

**Database Performance: Tables and Indices:** SAP Menu • Tools • Administration • Monitor • Performance • Database • Tables/Indexes (DB02)

**Copy According to Transport Request:** SAP Menu • Tools • Administration • Administration • Client Administration • Special Functions • Copy Transport Request (SCC1)

**Local Client Copy:** SAP Menu • Tools • Administration • Administration • Client Administration • Special Functions • Local Copy (SCCL)

**Client Export:** SAP Menu • Tools • Administration • Administration • Client Administration • Client Transport • Client Export (SCC8)

**Transport Management System:** SAP Menu • Tools • Administration • Transport • Transport Management System (STMS)

**Client Maintenance:** SAP Menu • Tools • Administration • Administration • Client Administration • Client Maintenance (SCC4)

**Post-Client Import Methods:** SAP Menu • Tools • Administration • Administration • Client Administration • Client Transport • Post-Client Import Methods (SCC7)

**Client Copy Log Analysis:** SAP Menu • Tools • Administration • Administration • Client Administration • Copy Logs (SCC3)

**Remote Client Copy:** SAP Menu • Tools • Administration • Administration • Client Administration • Client Copy • Remote Copy (SCC9)

**Table Comparison:** SAP Menu •·Tools •·Administration •·Administration •·Client Administration • Customizing Objects • Object Comparison (SCMP)

**Transport Organizer (Extended View):** SAP Menu • Tools • Administration • Transport • Transport Organizer (SE01)

**Conversion of Logical System Names:** Not accessible through the standard SAP menu (BDLS)

## 5.9 Additional Documentation

SAP Notes

Table 5.4 gives an overview of the important SAP Notes related to SAP client maintenance.

| Contents | SAP Note |
|---|---|
| Client Capability in R/3 | 31557 |
| Copying Large Productive Clients (Web AS 6.10 and Up) | 489690 |
| Size of a Client | 118823 |
| Parallel Processes (Web AS 6.10 and Up) | 541311 |

**Table 5.4** SAP Notes Concerning Client Maintenance

## 5.10 Questions

1. **Which of the following statements on the client concept in SAP NetWeaver AS are correct?**
   a. Customizing settings are always client-independent.
   b. A client is a unit within an SAP system that is independent in terms of business accounting.
   c. Each client has its own application data.
   d. Each client has its own technical data independent of the other clients.
   e. Each client has its own application tables.
2. **Which methods of copying clients are offered by SAP NetWeaver AS?**
   a. Local copy
   b. Remote copy
   c. Data exchange procedures
   d. Client export
   e. Data backup

3. **Which data can be transmitted in a remote client copy?**

   a. Client-dependent application data

   b. Client-dependent table definitions

   c. Client-independent data

   d. All data in the SAP system

*This chapter introduces the topic of software logistics, that is, the tools and methods for maintaining SAP software, distributing objects, and managing change in the system landscape.*

# 6 Software Logistics

After the installation and initial configuration of your SAP software landscape, you must continually adapt it to changing requirements (such as further development of functionality, changes to company organization, or the business processes being modeled) or to the integration of quality improvements to SAP components provided by SAP.

The functions of software logistics standardize and automate the distribution and maintenance of software in complex software landscapes. The goal of software logistics is the consistent, solution-independent change management of software, allowing flexible reaction to changed requirements. The central objects of software logistics are *change requests* and *transport requests*.

In this chapter, we'll first provide a brief overview of how a transport request arises and what the concept entails. Then, we'll describe the functionality of the Transport Organizer and how to work with it. The Transport Organizer is used for the actual distribution of changes into downstream receiving systems.

## 6.1 Implementation Guide

**Customizing**

SAP software provides standard solutions for nearly all of the areas of business processes for a company. The term *standard solution*, however, doesn't at all mean that its features are rigid and inflexible. Rather, within the SAP system, there are often multiple variants and kinds of processes integrated. Thus, it's a significant implementation task to adapt the SAP system to special customer requirements using corresponding parameters and settings. This process is called *Customizing*. During Customizing, variants are selected from those available that cover existing requirements, and they are extended with customer-specific data. In close connection with Customizing is the *Implementation Guide* (IMG). The IMG isn't only the basis and prerequisite for pure application Customizing, but it's also used for all activities connected with basic administration, so that a detailed knowledge of the options and use of the IMG is also an advantage for the Basis administrator.

SAP reference IMG

The SAP standard package includes the SAP reference IMG, a complete implementation guide for all solution components in the SAP system in question. The outline of the implementation guide matches the hierarchy of application components of your SAP system. The SAP reference IMG contains all of the work steps needed for implementation, with the associated documentation.

In the following examples, we refer to an SAP ERP system. You can find the IMG at **Implementation Guide (SPRO) • SAP Reference IMG** (see Figure 6.1).

One of the first tasks in a company wanting to introduce SAP ERP is to select the application areas relevant for the concrete case. To structure the entire process of Customizing, project groups in the company create individual Customizing projects taking various criteria into consideration. Possible selection criteria include the following:

- Restriction on countries
- Restriction on components
- Restriction on a manual selection of individual tasks

Project IMGs

Based on the SAP reference IMG, *project IMGs* can be created for these subtasks. The processing of all of the activities described in the project IMG is called the *project*: the terms "project" and "project IMG" are used synonymously in the system. When implementing individual projects, the user is largely supported by SAP ERP. For instance, there are functions integrated for project administration, such as time planning, status maintenance, and documentation.

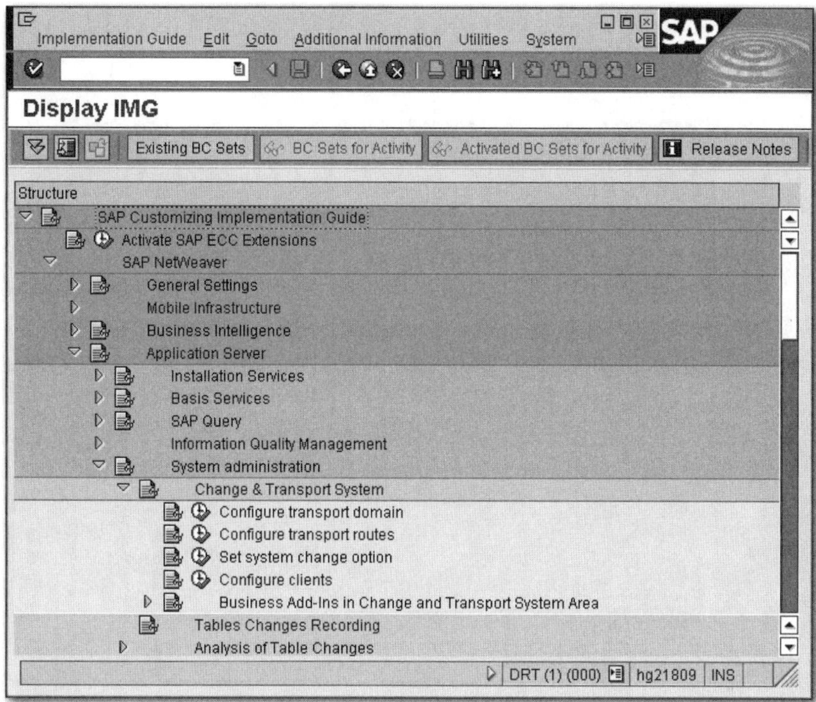


**Figure 6.1** Excerpt from the SAP Reference IMG (Basis Area)

Project IMGs

As an example project, let's consider the configuration of Basis Customizing (see Figure 6.2). Using **Project Administration (SPRO_ADMIN)**, new project IMGs can be created and existing projects changed or deleted.

1. To create a new project, select **Project Administration (SPRO_ADMIN)**.
2. Give the project a descriptive name so you can identify it later.
3. Select the countries and components relevant for the subproject, or make a manual selection from the SAP reference IMG.
4. Save your settings and generate your project IMG.

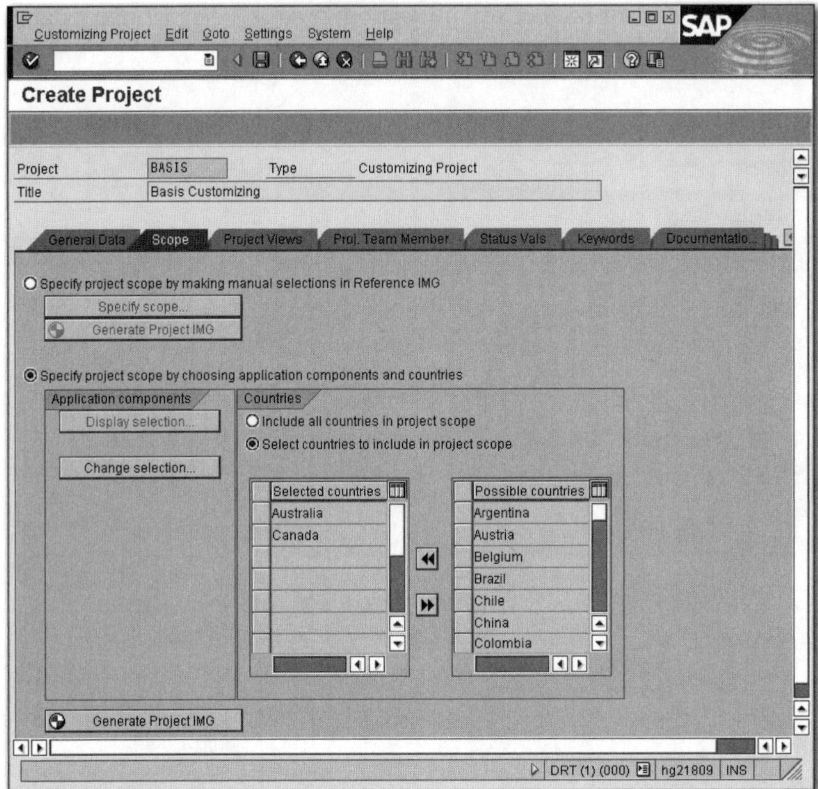


**Figure 6.2** Creating a Project IMG

Views

In addition, the activities of each project can be assigned *views*, which further structure the Customizing projects. The definition of a view filters the activities of a project already created. By explicitly assigning project team members, it's possible to add just those activities to the worklist of an employee for which that person is actually responsible. This assignment is particularly practical for the following:

- The creation of implementation projects
- During release upgrades
- When integrating legal changes

The following criteria apply to the creation of views (see also Figure 6.3):

- **Activity necessity**
All of the attributes listed in the SAP reference IMG have attributes assigned that classify the performance of the activity as "must" (no complete SAP preconfiguration possible), "can" (SAP preconfiguration should be checked and possibly adjusted), or as "not necessary" (SAP preconfiguration maps an SAP standard system). In addition, the activities are classified as "critical" or "not critical."
- **Manual selection in project IMG**
From the partial tree of available actions defined for the project in Customizing, an additional limiting selection can be made.
- **Release Customizing**
Based on release-specific attributes for the IMG entries, activities can be filtered out that can be performed to ensure the functionality used in the old release after an upgrade (*upgrade Customizing*) or to implement additional functionality of the new release (*delta Customizing*).
- **Legal changes**
If you want to load legal changes into your system, create a project view from all of the Customizing activities affected by these changes. This selection is also made based on release-specific attributes (law keys).
- **Selection by transport requests**
Using this option, you can summarize the transport requests in a table, which enables the customizing of IMG activities. The project view generated after having selected and saved the requests now contains all of the IMG activities included in the selected transport requests.

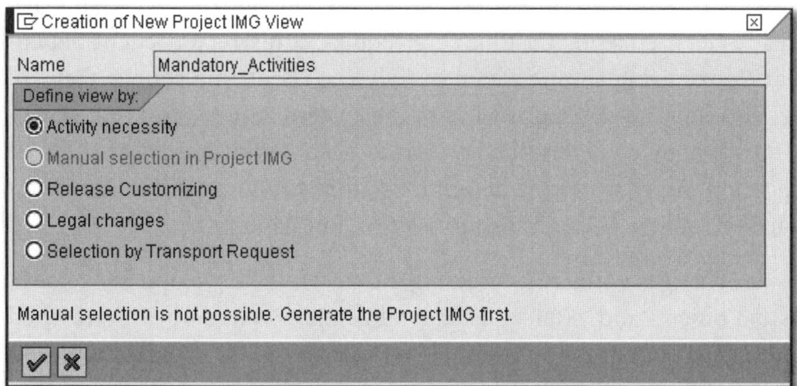


**Figure 6.3** Creating a View of a Project

Assignment of change requests

If you have activated the CTS functionality in IMG project administration for your project on the **Transport Requests** tab, you can assign change requests to a CTS project during creation. The requests grouped in this way can then be imported via the Transport Management System by project.

## 6.2 Processing Objects

The user can make different adaptations within the SAP system. First, when introducing SAP ERP, Customizing settings are absolutely necessary because Customizing primarily addresses business processes. Therefore, Customizing generally is client-specific. Secondly, any specific processes must be extended, existing functionality modified, and client-independent settings configured. These changes affect the runtime environment and are therefore client-independent. These changed or newly created objects are transferred to downstream systems through transports. Depending on the type, objects are grouped in different requests for transport.

### 6.2.1 Change Requests

Customizing requests

If the client has been defined with automatic saving of changes (see Section 5.2, Creating New Clients, in Chapter 5), then a task and a customizing request is always created when a user makes Customizing changes in an SAP system. The user can also control explicitly the assignment of tasks to customizing requests when the customizing requests have already been created. Customizing requests thus record client-dependent Customizing settings from exactly *one* client (the source client of the request). The transportability of the customizing request into downstream systems is determined from the client-specific settings, and the suggested target system is determined from the transport route definition (see Section 4.3.2, Transport Routes, in Chapter 4).

Workbench requests

Besides changes within Customizing, however, the development of new, custom objects and extensions or modifications to the objects provided by SAP (*SAP-delivered objects*) might be necessary. Such changes, however, are client-independent, so they have system-wide effects. Analogous to the processes in Customizing, this change data is recorded immediately, but this time in a task assigned to a *workbench request*. Workbench requests thus contain Repository objects and client-independent Customizing. For workbench requests, there can also be mixtures: They can also contain additional client-dependent Customizing. However, this applies only with the limitation that all of the client-dependent objects included must originate in exactly one client (namely the source client for the request). For workbench requests the transportability to downstream systems is also determined from the settings for transport routes in the Transport Management System (see Section 4.3.2 in Chapter 4).

**Local change request**

Besides transportable changes, local changes are also possible. For this type of change, there are tasks available in *local change requests*. A transport to other systems isn't possible. In particular, local change requests are also created when the transport route configuration has not yet been created or is incorrect. If the change requests have not yet been released, they can be converted into transportable change requests by subsequent assignment of a target system. A local change request becomes a transportable request when an SID is entered in the request header as the transport target.

By assigning a task in a change request related to a development, security measures are taken regarding access by other users. For users other than the owner of the task and the change request, the affected object is locked, unless the responsible developer explicitly transfers the rights to the task to another user. After a development project is concluded, first the tasks and then the change request are released. Only after release of the change request is the object freely accessible for changes again. Through this mechanism, simultaneous changes by multiple users of the same object are prevented.

**Request number**

Each task and each request has a unique code made up of the three-character SAP system name, the letter K, and a sequential six-digit number, for example, EA1K905975. Every change request has exactly one owner, the project head, who is responsible for the administration of the request. The owner can be changed if necessary. A change request can also be made up of multiple tasks, each of which is in turn assigned to one user. A change request can be seen as a project within which different users must handle separate tasks (see Figure 6.4). A task can also be transferred to another user if needed.

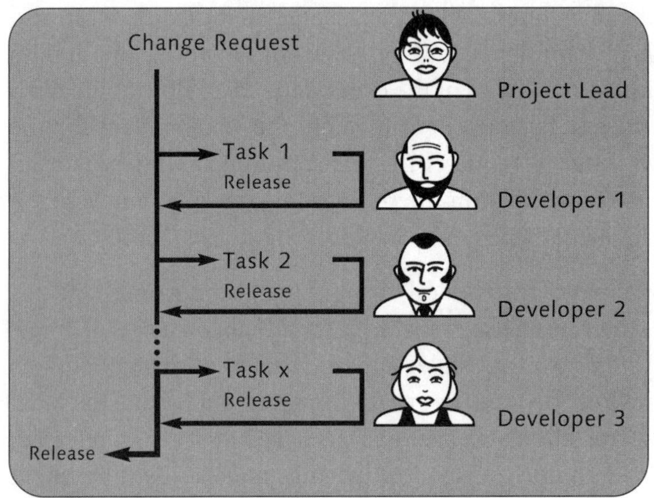


**Figure 6.4** Project Management

**Releasing tasks and requests**

If all tasks in a change request are completed and released, then the project can also be completed, and the change request itself released. If this isn't a local change request, then the release is automatically associated with the preparation of the transport. The current status of the objects included in the request at the point of release is exported into files at the operating system level; the request is marked in each target system as an import.

The import must be started explicitly (see also Section 6.3, Importing Transport Requests); at the time of import, the objects will have the statuses contained in the request at the time of export. This also applies when the objects have been changed again in the source system during the time between release and import into the target system.

### 6.2.2 Processing Requests with the Transport Organizer

Up to and including SAP R/3 Basis Release 4.6B, Customizing and workbench requests were managed with separate tools, the Customizing Organizer and the Workbench Organizer. As of SAP R/3 Release 4.6C, the Transport Organizer (TO) is available for processing all change requests and the tasks they contain. The management of change requests with the Transport Organizer can best be clarified by a practical example.

**Example**

In the area of archiving, verifiable archive files should be generated. For this purpose, a change in the object-independent customizing of data archiving must be performed using the IMG. This is a typical change from the area of Customizing.

**Generating a customizing request**

There are two basic procedures for the generation of a customizing request:

1. You first perform the change and allow the SAP system to generate the customizing request and task for this change.
2. You first generate a customizing request with the Transport Organizer with a task included. Then the change is made and is explicitly assigned to the previously generated task.

The selection of procedure depends primarily on the user concept. By assigning authorizations, users can be forbidden from creating their own change requests. This task can be reserved for a selected group of users. This procedure has the advantage that you retain control of customizing requests and their assignment. It's also possible to revoke the authorization from a developer for the creation of change requests of any kind. Thus, the user can only make changes when an authorized person, normally the project leader, has previously generated and assigned corresponding change requests. This allows development in the SAP system to be coordinated far better (see Figure 6.4).

**Unclassified tasks**

Using the Transport Organizer, *unclassified tasks* can also be created. Unclassified tasks are only assigned a type with the assignment of a change.

In terms of our example, you might proceed according to the second procedure as follows:

1. Call the Transport Organizer (SE09) (see Figure 6.5).
2. Use **Request/Task • Create**, or first select **Display** and then **Request/ Task • Create**.

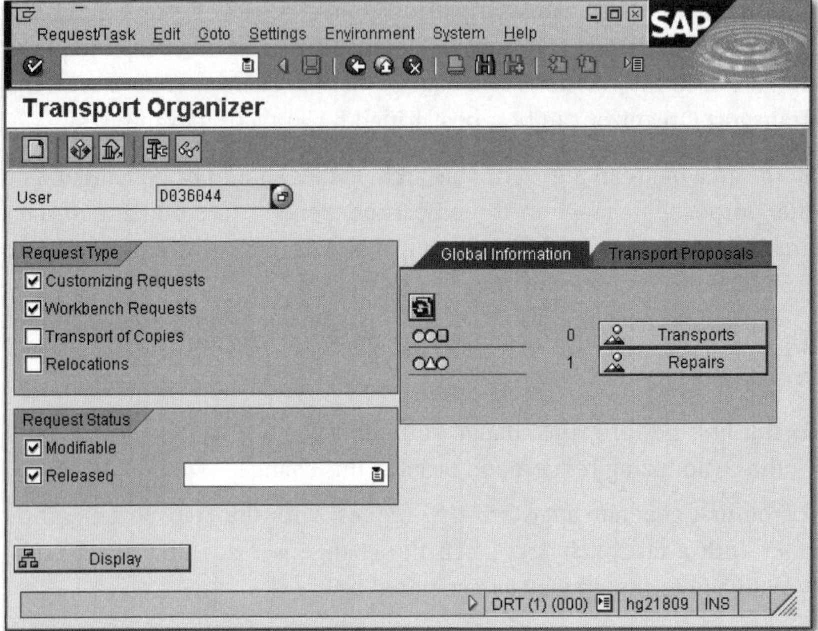


**Figure 6.5** Transport Organizer—Initial Screen

3. From the types of change requests offered, select **Customizing Request**.
4. You are asked, besides a comment specifying the content more specifically, to name additional people involved in the request. For each of these people, a task is created in this customizing request.
5. Save your entries. The customizing request is now generated.

Figure 6.6 shows the screen for the input of data needed for such a change request. In the field **Source client**, the client assigned to the customizing request is displayed. The **Target** field contains the name of the SAP system in whose transport queue the customizing request is entered upon release. In our case, the field is blank; an assignment can be carried out later.

Figure 6.7 shows the hierarchical display mode of the Transport Organizer. Here, you see customizing request DRTK923687 created in client 100 with owner D036044. Task DRTK923688 was assigned to this request. If needed, you can change the owner of a request and/or the task via **Owner**. Additional tasks for a request can be added by selecting the request and then selecting **Request/Task • Create**.

Create Request

| | | | |
|---|---|---|---|
| Request | | Customizing request | |
| Short description | Modify archiving parameters | | |
| Project | | | |
| Owner | D036044 | Source client | 100 |
| Status | New | Target | |
| Last changed | 02.09.2007 16:30:12 | | |

Tasks

| User |
|---|
| D036044 |

**Figure 6.6** Details for the Customizing Request Created

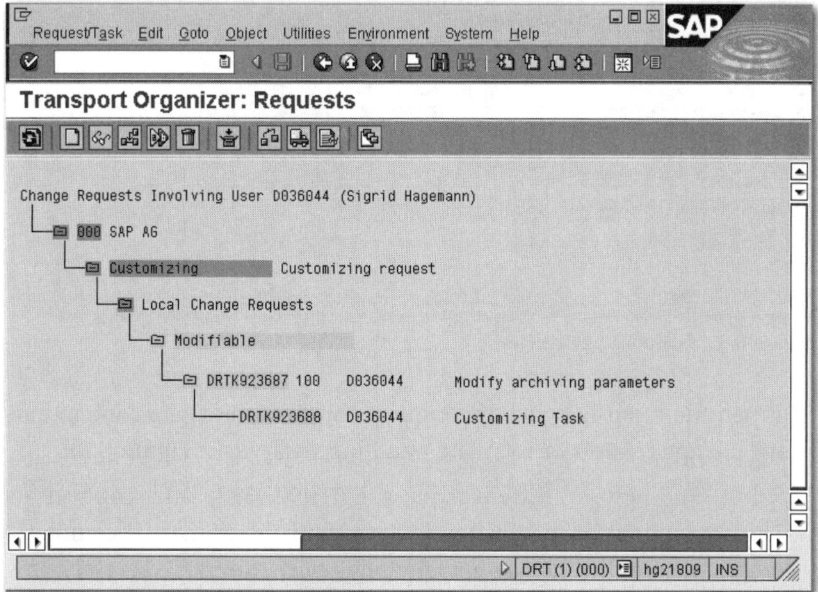


**Figure 6.7** Display of All Change Requests

**Assignment to a customizing request**

Let's now look at how a Customizing change is assigned to a request.

In our example, we want to make a change to archiving settings. To do this, follow these steps:

1. Starting from **Implementation Guide (SPRO) • SAP Reference IMG**, navigate through the IMG structure through **SAP Customizing Implementation Guide • SAP NetWeaver • Application Server • System Administration • Data Archiving** until you get to **Cross-Object Customizing**, and select a verification of the archive contents at all possible times (see Figure 6.8).

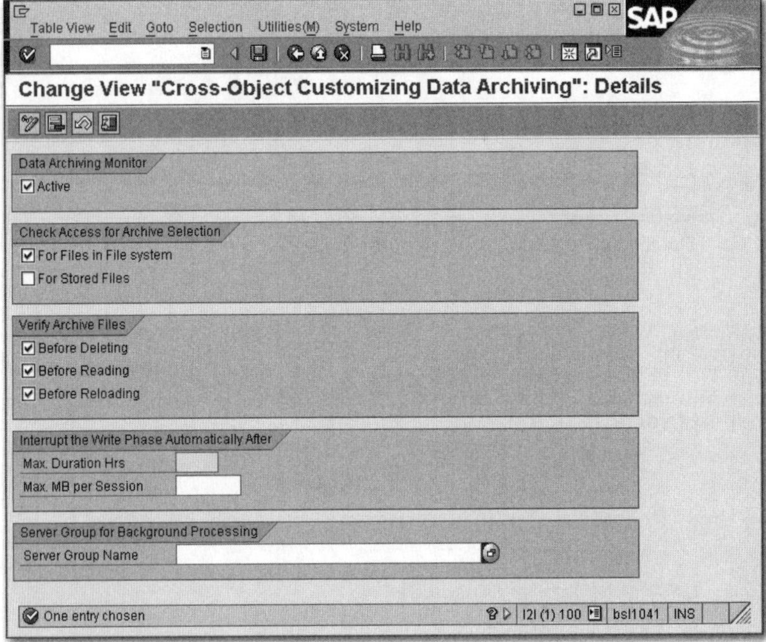


**Figure 6.8** Customizing Change

2. When the input is saved, the request appears to assign a corresponding change request or to create one if necessary (see Figure 6.9).
3. Select the newly created request DRTK923687, and confirm it. The assignment of the change to a customizing request is complete. Only now are the changes actually physically stored. Conversely, this also means that changes to objects can only be made permanent if they are logged in change requests.

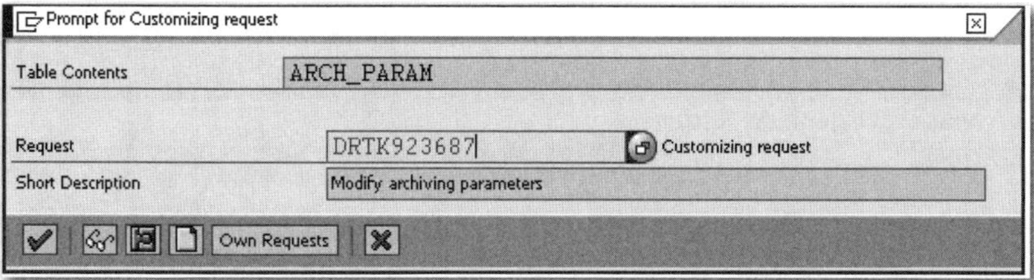


**Figure 6.9** Assignment of a Change Request

**Releasing the customizing request**

In our example, the Customizing process is now complete. The customizing request can be concluded, that is, released. To release a request, the person responsible for maintenance of the customizing request proceeds as follows:

1. In the Transport Organizer (SE09), select the desired category of request and their status, if you want to limit the number of requests displayed to just the truly necessary ones. Select **Display**.
2. All tasks in the customizing request must be closed, that is, they must all be released by their owners. If this isn't the case, as in our example, select the task in question, here task DRTK923688, and execute **Request/Task • Release.**
3. You are asked to document the content of the changes made.
4. Activate and save your documentation in the final form, and then leave the screen. All of the changes contained in the task are passed to the assigned customizing request. By opening the tree, you can get more details about the objects included (see Figure 6.10). In our case, the changes involved the object `ARCH_PARAM`.
5. After all of the tasks are released, then the actual customizing request can be released in the same way. Select the customizing request in question, execute **Request/Task • Release** again, and document the changes in the request.

This causes the customizing request to be exported during release. A customizing request can also be released to a workbench request, which, in turn, is only released and transported at a later point in time. This has the advantage that multiple customizing requests are collected and can be exported as a group at a later date.

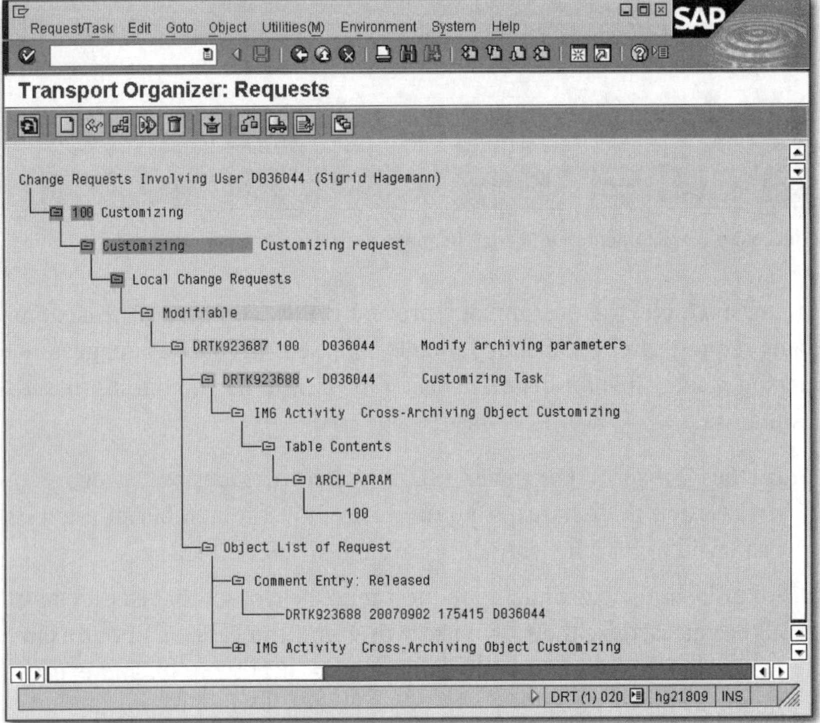


**Figure 6.10** Released Task DRTK923688

Developments and modifications

Besides the tasks described in the Customizing of an SAP solution, you can also adapt the objects of the solution using the ABAP Workbench, or even develop your own. In the ABAP Workbench, the development has the following tools available:

- **Package Builder**
  For the administration of packages and the migration of existing development classes.
- **Object Navigator/ABAP Development Workbench**
  For hierarchical display of different development object lists and navigation in browsers, such as the Repository Browser and the Repository infosystem, the MIME Repository, the tag browser, and the test repository for the development of tables, structures, indices, domains, match codes, and so on.

- **Web Dynpro Explorer**
  For the development of web applications in the ABAP environment.
- **Class Builder**
  To edit global ABAP classes and interfaces.
- **ABAP Editor and Function Builder**
  To edit programs and functions.
- **Screen Painter**
  To develop screen forms.
- **Menu Painter**
  To create menu trees.
- **Test Tools in ABAP Development**
  For debugging for runtime analysis and for the creation and evaluation of a performance trace.

All of these tools are used for developing new functionality or changing existing functionality in the SAP system. The further development of SAP functionality may not often be part of the direct task scope of the SAP administrator, but due to the administrator's system-wide administrative tasks, such as the performance of necessary release upgrades and even the entry of error corrections, the system administrator will often be involved. An example should clarify the most important processes. Administrative tasks are in the focus. Details on the new ABAP Editor (integrated into the frontend as of SAP GUI 6.40) as well as the extended options of the ABAP Debugger as of NetWeaver 7.0 can be found in Sections 10.1 and 10.2 of Chapter 10.

Developer registration

Every user who wants to develop new objects in an SAP system or make changes to the objects provided by SAP must first be registered as a developer for the SAP system in question (see Figure 6.11). The keys needed can be generated using the SAP Support Portal (see Chapter 15, Service and Support).

This gives both the administrator and SAP an overview of how much custom development is taking place in an SAP system. In a later procedure, then, it must be determined again whether a change to an SAP-delivered object or the development of a newly created object should take place.

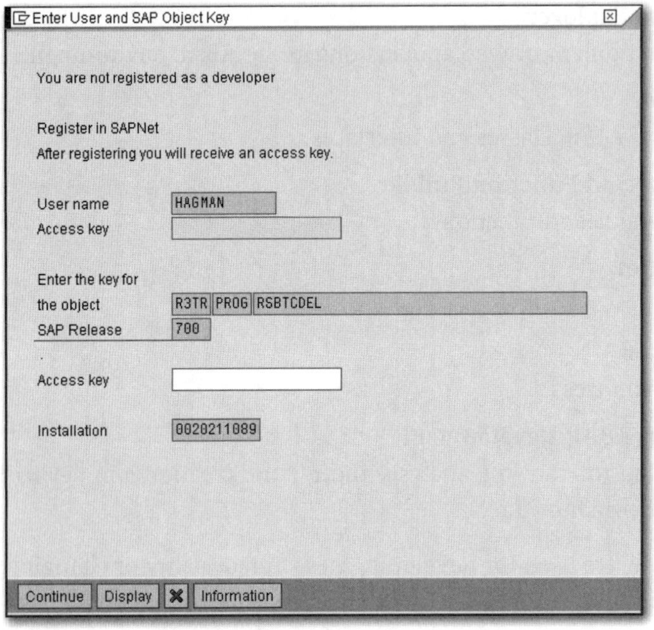

Figure 6.11 Developer Registration

**Changing SAP-delivered objects**

Changes to SAP-delivered objects must also be registered. Just as for developer registration, the access key is obtained from the SAP Support Portal. Enter the information about the desired object (see Figure 6.12), and copy the generated access key into the query form.

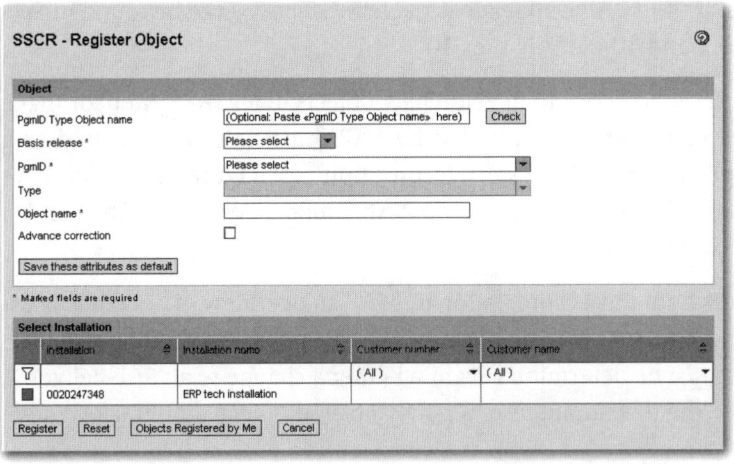

Figure 6.12 Requesting an Object Key Through the SAP Support Portal

Only now can the SAP-delivered object be edited. These security measures were taken to log changes to SAP-delivered objects to better track customer-specific adaptations in case of problems.

**New development**

New development in a system landscape must be carefully planned to avoid conflict situations with SAP-delivered and also customer-specific objects. Basically, new development should only be performed in a two-system landscape or, even better, in a three-system landscape. A mixture of development and production work must always be avoided. Let's assume that the system landscape is already completely configured, and thus the transport routes between the systems have been determined.

**Packages**

*Packages* are used as tools for technical modularizing, encapsulating, and decoupling units of the SAP system and represent a further development of the development classes familiar from older releases (prior to SAP Web AS 6.10) with new additional semantics.

In a package, objects are grouped together that should be developed, maintained, and transported together. So before new objects can be created, such a package must be created in the integration system in which the development is performed. Packages are themselves objects and can therefore also be transported.

To be sure that all of the objects in a package are transported following the same transport route, the package is assigned a transport layer (see Section 4.3.2, Transport Routes, in Chapter 4). The package $TMP plays a special role. This package is used for all local (temporary), that is, not transportable, objects.

**Customer namespace**

For the creation of objects, which include packages, SAP provides a separate *customer namespace*. This ensures that there will be no name conflicts between SAP and customer objects and, for instance, customer objects can be unambiguously identified during upgrades. To form the names of packages and objects from the workbench, the following rules apply:

- All customers have the namespace starting with Y or Z.
- For particularly extensive custom development, customers can request their own namespace. These namespaces are implemented with a prefix of at least 5 characters and no more than 10, enclosed in slashes,

which is placed before the customer object name. An SAP license key protects these namespaces from unauthorized use. Customer internal namespaces are reserved for complex customer-specific development projects or development by SAP partners. To request a customer namespace through SAP Support Portal, you'll need a valid development license.

**Object catalog** For every object in the SAP system, there is an object catalog entry (see Figure 6.13) that contains all the important information about the object. Besides the package of an object and the associated transport layer, the original system of the object is also particularly important for the system group.

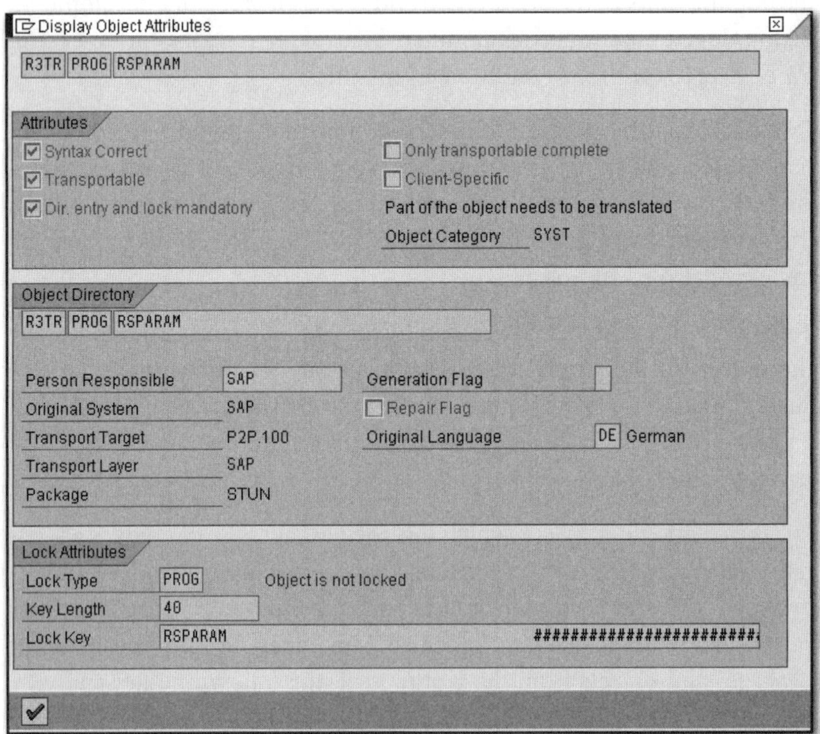


**Figure 6.13** Object Catalog Entry for Program RSPARAM

Original

For every object there is exactly one system in which the original of this object is maintained. With this assignment, different protective mechanisms are associated. If we look at the situation in the system landscape, for a correctly used development and transport strategy, the objects in the integration system are the originals. This is where they are developed. Changes to the originals are called *corrections*. To test and later for productive use, copies are transported to the downstream systems. If changes to the copies of the objects are required in these systems, on the other hand, we speak of *repair*. These changes can, after all, be overwritten by a new transport from the integration system, if they are not also made to the original in the integration system.

Release and export

The release and transport of development or of changes to client-independent objects take place via workbench requests, analogous to the release and transport of customizing requests.

**Note**

Note that for the release of a local change request, no data is written at the operating system level.

### 6.2.3 Transport Logs

Action log

All transports (both exports and imports) take place in several steps; each step is logged. Finally, a return code is passed back, allowing conclusions about the general process. It's absolutely recommended that the export logs be evaluated and any errors that occurred corrected. Otherwise, incomplete data can be expected during a later import in the target system. To view the logs, in the display of all transport requests in the Transport Organizer (SE09), first select the desired transport request. **Goto • Action Log** displays all of the actions that have been carried out so far relative to the transport request. Figure 6.14 shows this for request IE4K903522. The log files are stored in the *actlog* subdirectory of the transport directory (see Section 4.4 in Chapter 4) if this directory is created manually.

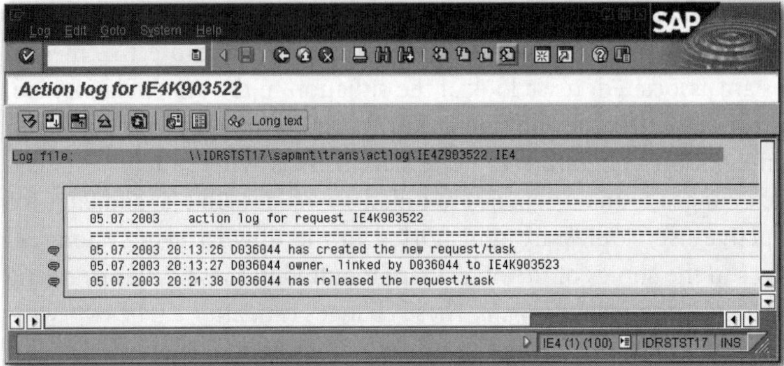


**Figure 6.14** Action Log for Request IE4K9003522

Transport logs

Besides the action log, for each transport, there are separate log files stored in the *log* subdirectory. The log file name is built using the following system:

```
<SID of the source system><Step><Number of the transport
request>.<SID of the source or target system>
```

`<Step>` denotes the step performed, using the following naming conventions:

- A: Activation of the repository
- C: Transport of C source code
- D: Import of application-defined objects
- E: Main export
- G: Generation of programs and screens
- H: Repository import
- I: Main import
- L: Import of the command file
- M: Activation of the enqueue components
- P: Test import
- R: Version comparison during release upgrades
- T: Import of table entries
- V: Setting of the version ID for imported objects
- X: Export of application-defined objects

The logs are stored in human-readable form in the operating system and can therefore be evaluated using operating system tools. The usual, and more convenient, way to view these logs is accessed from the Transport Organizer (SE09) by selecting the request to be analyzed using **Goto • Transport Logs**. First, the steps are displayed in compressed form, and then they can be resolved into four layers. Our concrete case is only an export; thus, one log file, *IE4E903233.IE4* in our example below, is created. The content of this file corresponds to the highest resolution level of the log view from the SAP system. Listing 6.1 represents an excerpt from that log file. Particularly important information for the evaluation is printed in bold.

```
Name: IE4E903233.IE4
1 ETP199X######################################
1 ETP182 CHECK WRITEABILITY OF BUFFERS
1 ETP101 transport order     : „IE4K903522“
1 ETP102 system              : „IE4“
1 ETP108 tp path             : „tp“
1 ETP109 version and release : „305.12.57“ „46D“
1 ETP198
4 ETP201 Check target systems buffer: \\psasb009\sapmnt\trans\
buffer\DUM
3 ETP203 Buffer "\\psasb009\sapmnt\trans\buffer\DUM" is
writeable
...
1 ETP182 CHECK WRITEABILITY OF BUFFERS
1 ETP110 end date and time   : "20030223133946"
1 ETP111 exit code           : "0"
1 ETP199X######################################
1 ETP150 MAIN EXPORT
1 ETP101 transport order     : "IE4K903522"
1 ETP102 system              : "IE4"
1 ETP108 tp path             : "tp"
1 ETP109 version and release : "305.12.57" "46D"
1 ETP198
4 ETW000 R3trans.exe version 6.05 (release 46D - 17.07.02 -
14:00:00).
4 ETW000 control file: \\psasb009\sapmnt\trans\tmp\IE4KK903522.
IE4
4 ETW000 > #pid 811 on psasb009 (APServiceIE4)
4 ETW000 > export
4 ETW000 > file='\\psasb009\sapmnt\trans\data\R903522.IE4'
4 ETW000 > client=100
```

```
4 ETW000 > buffersync=yes
4 ETW000 >
4 ETW000 > use comm 'IE4K903522'
4 ETW000 R3trans was called as follows: R3trans.exe -w \\
psasb009\sapmnt\trans\tmp\IE4E903522.IE4 \\psasb009\sapmnt\
trans\tmp\IE4KK903522.IE4
4 ETW000 date&time   : 23.02.2003 - 13:40:08
4 ETW000 Connected to DBMS = ORACLE --- dbs_ora_tnsname = 'IE4'
--- SYSTEM = 'IE4'.
4 ETW000  trace at level 1 opened for a given file pointer
4 ETW000 ================== STEP 1 =====================
4 ETW000 date&time   : 23.02.2003 - 13:40:15
4 ETW000 function    : EXPORT
4 ETW000 data file   : \\psasb009\sapmnt\trans\data\R903522.IE4
4 ETW000 buffersync  : YES
4 ETW000 client      : 100
4 ETW000 Language    :
ABCDEFGHIJKLMNOPQRSTUVWXYZ0123456789abcdefghijklmnopqrstuvwxyz
4 ETW000 Compression : L
4 ETW000 l.s.m.      : VECTOR
4 ETW000 commit      : 100000
4 ETW000 table cache : dynamic
4 ETW000
3 ETW673XUse Commandfile "IE4K903522"
4 ETW000       /* Conversion of archiving parameters */
4 ETW000       trfunction: 'W' (customizing transport)
4 ETW000       trstatus  : 'O'
4 ETW000       tarsystem : /TEST/
4 ETW000       user      : D036044
4 ETW000       date      : 23.02.2003 - 13:39:51
4 ETW000   1 entry from E070 exported (IE4K903522).
...
4 ETW000   1 entry from E07T exported (IE4K903522).
4 ETW000  [developertrace,0] Sun Feb 23 13:40:18 2003
2201862  2.201862
4 ETW000  [developertrace,0] dbrclu3.c : info : my major
identification is 387318425, minor one 262100.
4 ETW000 DOCUTD TA T IE4K903522 exported
...
3 ETW678Xstart export of "R3TRTABUARCH_PARAM" ...
4 ETW000   1 entry from ARCH_PARAM exported (100).
4 ETW679 end export of "R3TRTABUARCH_PARAM".
4 ETW000 IE4K903522 touched.
```

```
4 ETW000 IE4K903522 released.
4 ETW000 1776 bytes written.
4 ETW000 Transport overhead 56.6 %.
4 ETW000 Data compressed to 13.1 %.
4 ETW000 Duration: 3 sec (592 bytes/sec).
4 ETW000   0 tables in P-buffer synchronized.
4 ETW000   0 tables in R-buffer synchronized.
4 ETW690 "512" "512"
4 ETW000 COMMIT (1776).
4 ETW000
4 ETW000 Summary:
4 ETW000
4 ETW000   1 COMML exported
4 ETW000   1 COMMT exported
4 ETW000   1 DOCUT exported
4 ETW000 Totally 4 Objects exported
4 ETW000 Totally 1 tabentry exported
4 ETW000
4 ETW000  [developertrace,0] Disconnecting from ALL
connections:
...
4 ETW000 End of Transport (0000).
4 ETW000 date&time: 23.02.2003 - 13:40:19
1 ETP150 MAIN EXPORT
1 ETP110 end date and time   : "20030223134033"
1 ETP111 exit code           : "0"
1 ETP199 ##################################################
```

**Listing 6.1** Excerpt from an Export Log

For the administrator, the return code has real significance. For a return code of "0", as in our example, the execution was free of errors. Warnings are marked with a "W" in the associated log line. In that case, "4" is returned as the return code. Severe errors, which presumably mean an incomplete transport, are marked in the appropriate log line with an additional "E." The return code in this case is equal to or greater than "8." In the log files, hints are given about the cause of the error. The cause must be corrected and the export then repeated. Possible causes may be problems in the database. An interrupted transport request would appear in the Transport Organizer with status *Export not completed.*

Cofile and data file

Besides the log file, a *data file* and a so-called *cofile* are written during the export with metainformation about the objects included in the request. Data file and cofile are the actual data to be transported. They include all of the data required for the import. Cofiles are always stored in the *cofiles* directory, and data files are stored in the *data* subdirectory of the transport directory tree. The name of the files is built as follows:

```
<File type><Number of the transport request>.<SID of the source
sys>
```

The file type "K" is used for cofiles, and "R" and "D" for data files. In our example, the cofile is *K903522.IE4*, and the data file is *R903522.IE4*.

Transports of copies and object moves.

The Transport Organizer (SE09), besides the functions described for the administration of change requests during the customizing and development process, also provides tools for the reorganization of your development landscape.

For various reasons, it can be necessary to transport objects specifically into a different system. Depending on requirements, the objects can retain their original system, or the original system can be converted to the new system. Possible scenarios include the following:

- Simple copy of objects into another system that can be freely selected.
- Relocation of objects without switching the packages for temporary displacement of development projects in another system. The original system of the objects is changed on the new system.
- Relocation of objects with switching the packages for the permanent move of development projects to another system. The original system of the objects is changed to the new system; when selecting a suitable package with assigned transport layer, the transport properties need not be adjusted.
- Relocation of entire packages for the final displacement of an entire package to the other system. The original system of the objects is changed on the new system, and the transport layer adapted.

The applicable object lists, except for moves of entire packages, must be manually constructed.

Requests for the transport of copies and relocations of originals can also be created from the Transport Organizer.

### 6.2.4 Transport Organizer (Extended View)

In addition to the possibility of administration of customizing and workbench requests, transport of copies, and moves of objects already familiar from the Transport Organizer, the extended view of the Transport Organizer (SE01) offers additional transport options. These additional procedures share the fact that they follow no predefined transport routes. The following are provided:

- **Single display**
  For individual transport requests and tasks, you can display the action and transport logs.
- **Creation of object lists**
  Object lists are a collection of objects that can be grouped into transport requests as templates. Object lists can be automatically generated, for instance, across all objects in a development class or other shared features of objects. The manual entry of object lists is also possible. The object list created can be stored under any name (the first three characters of the name, however, may not be "SAP", and the fourth may not be "K").

  Object lists have an entry in the object catalog and are therefore assigned to a package. They have the same transport properties as all objects in the package.
- **Functions for evaluation of client transports**
  In addition to the possibilities in client administration (see Section 5.5, Client Transport, in Chapter 5), you can obtain an overview here of the client transports performed.
- **Administration of deliveries from SAP or their partners to customers**
  Corrections and preliminary patches provided by SAP and their partners are governed by a special administration because they naturally contain SAP-delivered objects. Transport requests of this type can already be recognized by their name, which consists of SAPK <number>.

### 6.2.5 Transport Tools

In the Transport Organizer Tools (SE03), you can find an entire collection of practical tools for working with the Change and Transport System. Based on authorizations, tools are also provided that come with some risk.

All functions are described by selecting **Tool • Documentation**; selecting **Tool • Execute** or double-clicking starts the functions (see Figure 6.15).

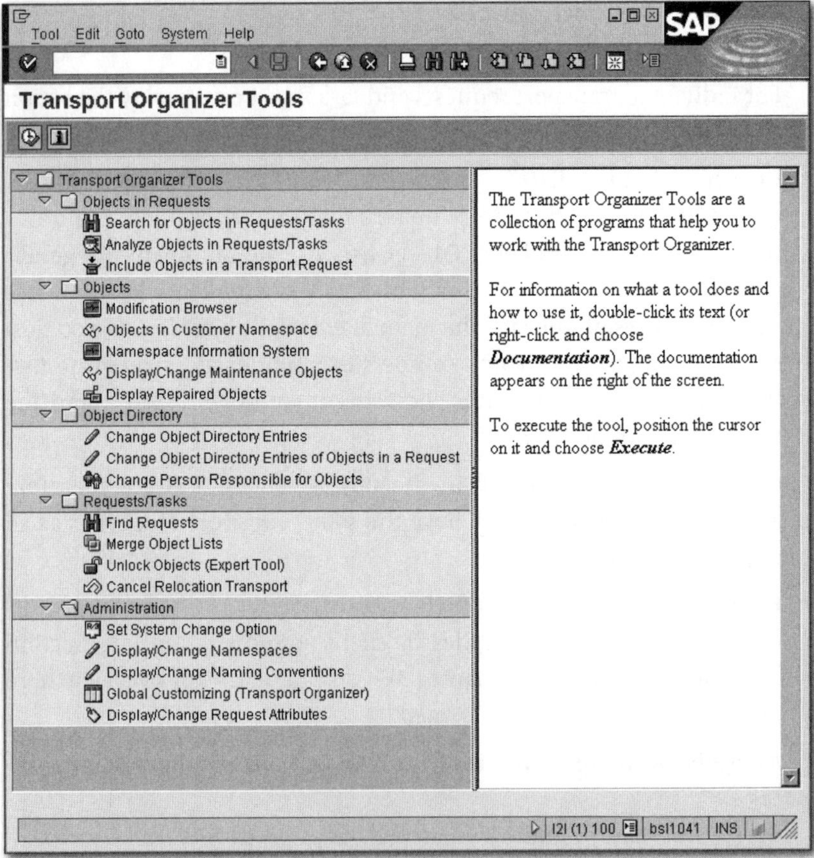


**Figure 6.15** Tools for the CTS

Attributes

With these tools, you can display or change the attributes of transport requests under **Administration • Display/Change Request Attributes**, for instance; you can also determine which attributes are required, for instance, whether the project assignment of a transport request may be the prerequisite for release of the request.

## 6.3 Importing Transport Requests

Upon release of a change request in a fully configured transport landscape, not only are the data to be transported exported but also the new request is placed on the import queue of the target system or systems.

Queues

Using **Transport Management System (STMS) • Overview • Imports** from any participating system, you can administrate and analyze the import queues of all of the systems in a transport domain (see Section 4.3.1, Transport Domains, in Chapter 4) — and, of course, you can also start imports.

In Figure 6.16, there are no requests for the quality assurance system, and 12 requests for the production system for the next import in the queue. You can get more detailed information about the type and number of waiting requests by selecting the desired system. Figure 6.17 shows the import queue for our example DRP. Using that display, the administrator is capable of coordinating all of the waiting imports. In the following paragraphs, we describe the most important work steps in normal operations.

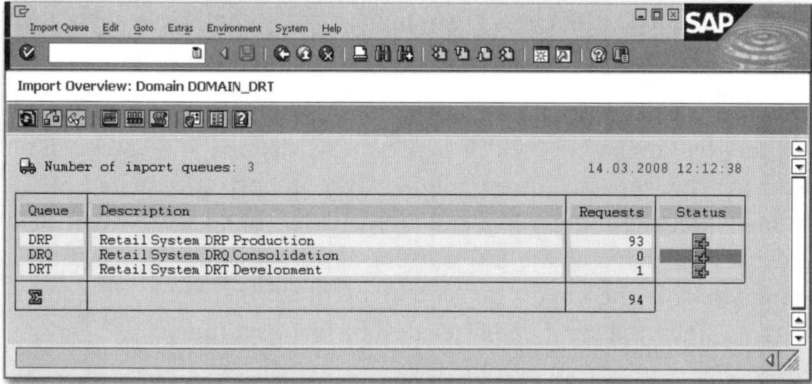


**Figure 6.16** Import Overview of a Three-System Landscape

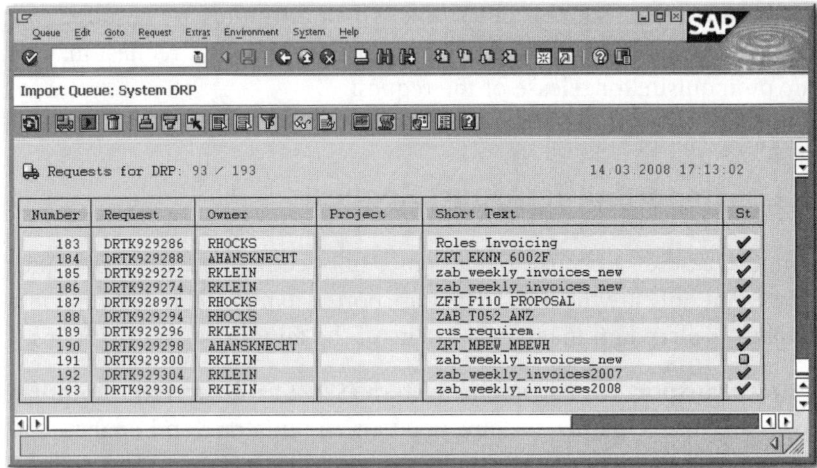


| Number | Request | Owner | Project | Short Text | St |
|---|---|---|---|---|---|
| 183 | DRTK929286 | RHOCKS | | Roles Invoicing | ✔ |
| 184 | DRTK929288 | AHANSKNECHT | | ZRT_EKNN_6002F | ✔ |
| 185 | DRTK929272 | RKLEIN | | zab_weekly_invoices_new | ✔ |
| 186 | DRTK929274 | RKLEIN | | zab_weekly_invoices_new | ✔ |
| 187 | DRTK928971 | RHOCKS | | ZFI_F110_PROPOSAL | ✔ |
| 188 | DRTK929294 | RHOCKS | | ZAB_T052_ANZ | ✔ |
| 189 | DRTK929296 | RKLEIN | | cus_requirem. | ✔ |
| 190 | DRTK929298 | AHANSKNECHT | | ZRT_MBEW_MBEWH | ✔ |
| 191 | DRTK929300 | RKLEIN | | zab_weekly_invoices_new | ☐ |
| 192 | DRTK929304 | RKLEIN | | zab_weekly_invoices2007 | ✔ |
| 193 | DRTK929306 | RKLEIN | | zab_weekly_invoices2008 | ✔ |

**Figure 6.17** Import Queue in the DRP System

**Order in the import queue**

The order of requests in the import queue results from the time of export of the request from the source systems. The order of performance of the exports is also the order in which the requests are imported using queue import. Released transport requests from the same transport group (see Section 4.3.1, Transport Domains, in Chapter 4) are automatically checked into the import queue of the target system. If the target system is assigned to a different transport group — that is, if it uses a different transport directory — then the administrator must first use **Extras • Additional Requests • Search in External Groups** to find the other requests pending. The same is true if transport domains are connected via domain links. If requests are found for the system in question, then they are accepted in the import queue of the selected system.

**Opening and closing the import queue**

The import of completed development tasks must be performed according to a fixed schedule, which is previously defined and agreed upon with the developers. Correspondingly, the imports are carried out at defined intervals of time. To avoid inconsistencies and achieve a defined intermediate stage of the SAP system, it's a good idea to use an *end marker* to close the import queue temporarily at that time. All requests arriving afterward are then preselected for the next import.

An end marker can be inserted into an import queue using **Queue • Close**. Using **Queue • Move end marker**, the end marker can be set before or after a given entry. You can open a closed import queue using **Queue • Open**.

Importing

Import into a system can be started for any subset of the waiting requests. You can group individual requests using **Edit • Mark • Mark Request** or **Edit • Mark • Mark Block**, process the entire queue up to the end marker (**Queue • Start Import**), or import selected individual transports (**Request • Import**). You can configure whether previously imported single requests should remain on the queue.

Statuses and logs

You can follow the progress of the import process using the Import Monitor (**Goto • Import Monitor**). The log of the executing program `tp` is available under **Goto • TP System Log**.

Transport requests in the import queue can also be deleted using the **Delete** function under the **Request** menu item, or they can be forwarded to a different SAP system. Analogous to the Transport Organizer, the content, logs, and size of selected transport requests can also be displayed.

RDDIMPDP

The actual work of the import is carried out at the operating system level by the programs `tp` and `R3trans` (implicitly called by `tp`), and by `RDDIMPDP` of the SAP system level. `RDDIMPDP` must be scheduled in client 000 of the target system, and `RDDIMPDP_CLIENT_<client number>` must be scheduled in all clients that will be receiving transports. The `RDDIMPDP*` programs are scheduled for background processing on an event-controlled basis (see Section 2.2, Background Processing, in Chapter 2) and wait for a message from `tp` that a transport has arrived. Thus, every import also requires one free batch process. If a transport seems to be hanging for no reason, a glance at report `RDDIMPDP` is often of great help.

## 6.4 Manual Operation of the Transport Control Program tp

As complex and user-friendly as the Transport Management System is, in exceptional cases, you can't avoid processing imports manually at the operating system level using `tp`. Let's briefly discuss the possible `tp` calls.

The transport control program `tp` is controlled using the parameter file *TP_<domain>.PFL* in the *bin* subdirectory of the transport directory. Before using `tp` for the first time, it makes sense to test first whether a connection to the desired target system is even possible. To do this, use the command

```
tp connect <target system> pf=<full path of parameter file>
```

The clause `pf=...` allows the use of any parameter file.

**Adding a request**

The addition of a request to the import queue of an SAP system is carried out with the command

```
tp addtobuffer <request> <target system> pf=<full path of
parameter file>
```

For the successful execution of this command, it's assumed that the data file of the request is in the *data* subdirectory and the associated cofile is present in the *cofiles* subdirectory of the transport directory.The import of a single selected order is carried out using

```
tp import <request> <target system> pf=<full path of parameter file>
```

The entire import queue is imported in the current order with the clause `all`.

```
tp import all <target system> pf=<full path of parameter file>
```

The specification of a special client can be done with the clause

```
client=<number of the client>
```

If no client is specified, then the data is copied into the client with the same number as the client from which the data was exported. If the client you're importing into doesn't exist in the target system, then the import stops with an error message.

**Deleting obsolete requests**

Over a longer development period, numerous old transport requests can pile up in the transport directory. It would be rather tedious to determine the status for each individual request in the Transport Organizer to delete old requests manually. With the command

```
tp check all
```

obsolete transport requests can be found, and then

```
tp clearold all
```

can be used to delete them. The retention time for data files, cofiles, and log files can be controlled using the `tp` parameters `datalifetime`, `olddatalifetime`, `cofilelifetime`, and `logfilelifetime`. Data files older than `datalifetime` are first moved into the directory *olddata*, and then on the next call, if `olddatalifetime` has been exceeded, they are finally deleted.

## 6.5 Installing Support Packages and Industry Solutions

The support packages for the correction of errors in the different software components (see Section 4.1, Tasks of a System Landscape, in Chapter 4), as well as the industry solutions and plug-ins for communication with other SAP systems such as SAP NetWeaver BI are also loaded using transports in the CTS.

The loading in either case takes place in client 000; in all other clients, only a display function is available.

The prerequisite for the installation of support packages or add-ons is a current version of the installation tools. The first step in the processing of support packages or add-ons is to update these tools, which are also integrated into the Support Package Manager (SPAM).

### 6.5.1 Installing Support Packages

For each of the available software components of SAP, support packages are regularly supplied with error corrections and performance improvements. Depending on the product and basis release, there are different package types for your installation. The *Component Packages* (COP) SAP_BASIS (Basis Support Package) and SAP_ABA (Application Interface SP) exist in every system.

Process

The core installation consists of the following steps:

1. Load the packages.
2. Update the installation tools.

3. Define a queue.
4. Install the queue.
5. Confirm.

You start the installation process from the Support Package Manager (SPAM) (see Figure 6.18).

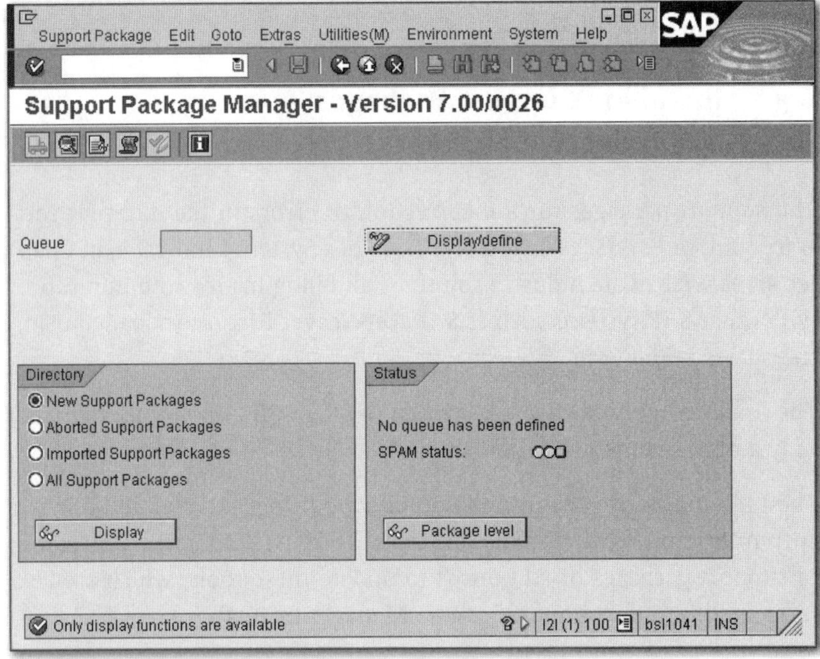


**Figure 6.18** Support Package Manager

First, you must transfer the support packages needed to your system. After downloading the packages using the Maintenance Optimizer in your Solution Manager system (for systems based on SAP NetWeaver 7.0 or later) from the */swcd* area in the SAP Support Portal, there are two different processes available for the transfer process:

- Copying the package from the SAP Support Portal to the transport directory. There, the packages must then be decompressed. Next, the loading of the packages is carried out using menu item **Support Package • Load Packages • From Application Server**.

- Copying of the packages from the SAP Support Portal to the local frontend and then loading them with menu item **Support Package • Load Packages • From Frontend**.

Support package collections

In addition, about four times a year, all of the support packages available up to that point are provided on CD/DVD in the form of support package collections. The latest version of the Support Package Manager must be loaded in the same way. In a first step, then, this version can be installed via menu item **Support Package • Load SPAM/SAINT Update**.

The support packages don't need to be loaded individually; a system-supported queue can be defined that is then loaded by the Support Package Manager. This simplifies loading significantly, ensuring that dependencies between packages for different software components are taken into consideration.

Possible variants for the composition of the queue include the following:

- **Definition of a support package queue for a specific software component**
  Select the desired components from the list of installed software components; the system lists the maximum possible queue that can be manually adapted.
- **Definition of a support package queue for multiple software components**
  Select the highest support package you want to load for each component from the selection list. The system calculates the maximum possible queue from those selections, based on the selected target support packages for the desired components.

The queue must have no gaps for any component, that is, you can't leave any individual support packages out. Because there may be conflicts in the queue definition, you must always check the current SAP Notes to see which packages may be installed together in one queue.

In the next step, this queue can be installed. For loading through the Support Package Manager, the familiar software logistics mechanisms of that tool are used internally, meaning that from a technical standpoint, transport requests (which are also visible in the Transport Management System) are loaded with the `tp` command. If problems occur, in addition to the logs from the Support Packages, the logs of the transport system are available for analysis.

**Conflicts** When loading support packages, conflicts can arise when Data Dictionary objects are loaded that have been modified in your system. In that case, you are asked to perform a Data Dictionary comparison (due to the transaction used, this is often simply called an *SPDD adjustment*). This is generally performed by the development department that also created the modifications. Analogously, after the load, the loaded Repository objects may need to be matched against Repository modifications (the *SPAU adjustment*).

After installation is complete, you still have to confirm the status. Only after that confirmation can other support packages be loaded.

### 6.5.2 Installing Add-ons

Add-ons are loaded using the SAP Add-on Installation Tool (SAINT). In the context of this transaction, an add-on is anything that doesn't belong to the SAP standard of the given release. This includes, for instance, industry solutions, plug-ins, and even SAP Preconfigured Systems (PCS, SAP Best Practices). With the Add-on Installation Tool, both the installation and the upgrade of such add-ons can be handled. From the initial screen (see Figure 6.19), the packages needed, analogous to the support packages, must first be loaded from the Installation Package menu, either from the frontend or from the application server.

After loading, the Add-on Installation Tool creates a queue that you can install with the **Continue** button.

The loading takes place analogously to the support packages; in the same way, a modification adjustment may be necessary. After the installation, the logs must be checked in menu item **Goto • Import Logs** and then the installation is confirmed in the last screen (screen 4/4) of the installation tool. Only after confirmation can additional add-ons or support packages be installed.

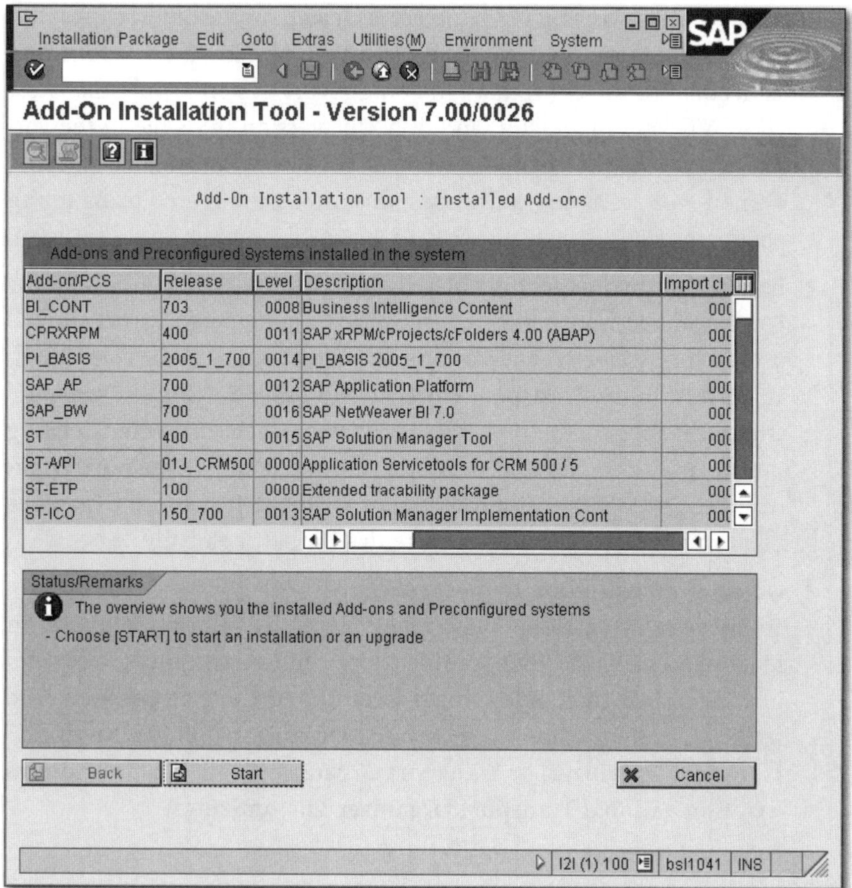


**Figure 6.19** Add-on Installation Tool

## 6.6 Tips

- **Deactivating mass import**
  By setting the `tp` parameter `NO_IMPORT_ALL` to 1, you can prevent all of the pending imports from being processed at once. For a transport strategy with single requests, this is the standard parameterization.
- **Versioning**
  Generally, versioning is only done on the source system of a transport request, meaning that during storage of a change in a transport

request, a new version of the object is created. In the object history, all of the old versions are visible, and they can be compared or retrieved as needed. In the consolidation and delivery systems, only the latest version is kept by default, and only this version is visible in the version history. If the change history of versioning is used for tracking even in more complex landscapes, this can be configured using the `tp` parameter `VERS_AT_IMP`.

- **Popup about transport problems on login**
  For automatic notification of transports ending with errors, for all users or only selected ones, a corresponding popup can be configured. To do this, in the **Transport Organizer (SE09) • Settings • Transport Organizer**, set the setting **Display transport errors when logging into SAP system** for the personal settings. Using **Transport Organizer Tools (SE03) • Administration • Global Transport Organizer Customizing**, you can also activate this property globally.
- **Object verification on request release**
  To prevent syntactically incorrect objects from being released in requests, a global or user-specific check can be carried out. Requests in which erroneous objects have been found can't be released. The settings are then made via **Transport Organizer (SE09) • Settings • Transport Organizer**, or **Transport Organizer Tools (SE03) • Administration • Global Transport Organizer Customizing.**
- **Downloading support package stacks**
  To support the actual support package loading behavior of many customers, support package stacks have been available for a while. These stacks include the best combination of support package and patch levels of individual components available at the time of release.

## 6.7 Transactions and Menu Paths

**Add-on Installation Tool:** No standard menu entry (SAINT)

**Implementation Guide:** SAP Menu • Tools • Customizing • IMG • Project Processing (SPRO)

**Project Administration:** SAP Menu • Tools • Customizing • IMG • Project Administration (SPRO_ADMIN)

**Support Package Manager:** SAP Menu • Tools • ABAP Workbench • Tools • Maintenance • Support Package Manager (SPAM)

**Transport Management System**: SAP menu • Tools • Administration • Transports • Transport Management System (STMS)

**Transport Organizer:** SAP Menu • Tools • Administration • Transports • Transport Organizer (SE09)

**Transport Organizer extended:** SAP menu • Tools • Customizing • IMG • Transport Organizer (extended view) (SE01)

**Transport Organizer Tools:** no standard menu entry (SE03)

## 6.8 Additional Documentation

### Quick links

- SAP Support Portal, alias *spmanager*
- SAP Support Portal, alias *patches*
- SAP Support Portal, alias *swdc*
- SAP Support Portal, alias *ocs*
- SAP Support Portal, alias *ocs-schedules*
- SAP Support Portal, alias *solman-mopz*
- SAP Support Portal, alias *namespaces*

### SAP Notes

Table 6.1 provides an overview of the important Notes from the SAP Support Portal on software logistics.

| Content | SAP Note |
|---|---|
| Transport System FAQ | 556734 |
| OCS FAQ: Recommendations in Error Situations | 556972 |
| SAP R/3 Support Package Collections on CD/DVD | 63974 |
| Inactive Import of Reports | 361735 |
| Maintenance Optimizer: Collective Note | 1024932 |
| Solution Manager Maintenance Optimizer: BC Set | 990534 |

**Table 6.1** Important SAP Notes Concerning Software Logistics

## 6.9 Questions

1. **Which statement is correct?**
   a. The transport system for an SAP system is equivalent to the copying of clients.
   b. The transport system for an SAP system is used for the exchange of development and Customizing data between different SAP systems.
   c. The transport system for an SAP system is used for data exchange between different clients on a single SAP system.
2. **Which statement is correct?**
   A development class is
   a. a defined group of developers.
   b. client-independent.
   c. assigned to the object when changing an SAP original object.
   d. assigned to a transport layer.
3. **Which statement is correct?**
   Modifications to SAP-delivered objects
   a. must be registered in the OSS.
   b. are not allowed.
   c. are urgently recommended for the implementation of company-specific processes.

4. **Which statement is correct?**

   A Repository object in an SAP system

   a. is automatically blocked when a developer makes changes to the object. When the changes are saved, the block is automatically removed.

   b. can only be changed when a corresponding change request is assigned. Thus, the object is automatically locked against changes from all other users until the assigned task and the change request are released by the developer.

   c. can only be changed when a corresponding change request is assigned. Changes to the object can then only be made by the users involved in the change request.

*In the previous chapters, instance parameters have continually been mentioned that significantly influence the configuration of SAP NetWeaver AS and the processing of user requests. In comparison with the manual adaptation of profiles, the profile administration and parameter maintenance integrated into SAP NetWeaver AS is much more convenient and secure.*

# 7 Maintaining Instances

In this chapter, we describe how to work with integrated profile administration and parameter maintenance, as well as possible variants (operation modes) of instances and how they can be changed on a scheduled basis.

## 7.1 Profile Maintenance

The configuration definitions for an SAP NetWeaver AS ABAP are stored in initialization files at the operating system level, either system-wide or on an instance-specific basis. These so-called *profiles* are generated by `R3setup` (up through SAP R/3 Release 4.6C) or `SAPinst` (as of Web Application Server 6.10) during installation and prepopulated with default values. During the usage phase of an SAP system, new conditions, such as an increase in numbers of users, release upgrades, introduction of additional components, or hardware upgrades, result in the need to adjust the parameterization of the system.

Manual changes

System settings can be optimized by making manual changes to the profile files, which can be edited using an editor. However, in this case, the entries are neither syntactically nor semantically checked. If parameters cannot be interpreted when an instance is started, they are ignored. If the same profile value is defined multiple times in a profile, the last setting read is valid.

Advantages

For these reasons, profile administration within the SAP system has the following significant advantages for the user:

- **Centrality**
  The profiles for all instances can be administered and maintained centrally.
- **Version management**
  Every saved change to a profile is stored as a version in the database. The versions are numbered sequentially.
- **Consistency checks**
  After changes are made, the consistency of the profile is checked, meaning that the logical connections and basic rules for the parameter settings are checked.
- **Comparison between active and saved profile in the database**
  Deviations between the currently configured profile and the version stored in the database can be analyzed. This allows you to determine whether a profile maintained in the SAP system has been manually modified.
- **Immediate activation of parameter changes**
  Some parameters can be activated immediately, without restarting the SAP system.

At the same time, profile administration within the SAP NetWeaver AS is a prerequisite for the use of system monitoring tools such as the Control Panel and the use of mode.

Using Profile Maintenance (RZ10) within SAP NetWeaver AS, both the default profile `DEFAULT.PFL` of the system and also the start profiles `Start_<instance name>_<host_name>` and the instance profile `<SID>_<instance name>_<host_name>` for all instances can be maintained centrally. The meaning and content of these profiles were already explained in Chapter 3, Getting Started. To edit the profiles with SAP tools, they must first be imported from the file system into the database. The installation programs only create the profile files in the file system but not in the database. Proceed as follows for the import:

1. Select **Profile Maintenance (RZ10)**. This takes you to the **Edit Profiles** screen (see Figure 7.1). Step 1
2. Select **Tools • Import Profiles • Of Active Servers**. The central directory structure of the entire SAP system allows the profiles of all instances to be imported and saved in the database. Listing 7.1 shows the log of the import for the central system IE4. During the import, a consistency check is performed for all of the parameters received. The file name without the path specification is used as the logical profile name for the imported profiles. Step 2

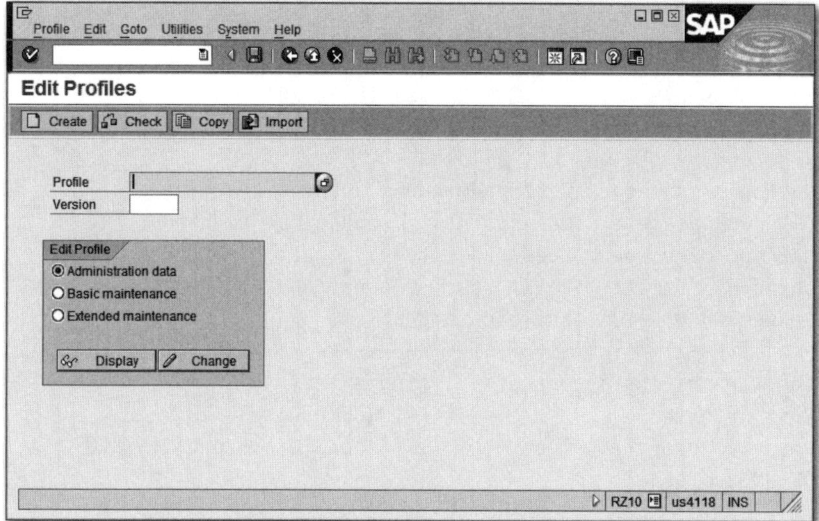


**Figure 7.1** Initial Screen for Profile Maintenance

```
-----------------------------------------------------------
Importing the initial and instance profiles of all active
servers
-----------------------------------
The following default profile is imported:
-----------------------------------------------------------
us4118_SLO_01:/usr/sap/SLO/SYS/profile/DEFAULT.PFL
-----------------------------------------------------------
The following instance profiles will be imported:
-----------------------------------------------------------
us4118_SLO_01:/usr/sap/SLO/SYS/profile/SLO_DVEBMGS01_us4118
----------------------------------------------------------
```

```
The following starting profiles will be imported:
------------------------------------------------------------
us4118_SLO_01:/usr/sap/SLO/SYS/profile/START_DVEBMGS01_us4118
------------------------------------------------------------
Log of the import of profiles
------------------------------------------------------------
Import of profiles completed without errors.
------------------------------------------------------------
Overall test for instance profiles and a default profile
------------------------------------------------------------
Protocol for the default profile, individual test
Profile name                : DEFAULT
Physical profile name       : /usr/sap/SLO/SYS/profile/DEFAULT.
PFL
Test on server              : us4118_SLO_01
------------------------------------------------------------
j2ee/dbname changes not allowed
Unknown parameter j2ee/dbadminurl , cannot be checked
Unknown parameter j2ee/scs/host , cannot be checked
Unknown parameter j2ee/scs/system , cannot be checked
Unknown parameter j2ee/ms/port , cannot be checked
Change to DIR_PUT can lead to problems
------------------------------------------------------------
Log for the instance profile, single test
Profile name               : SLO_DVEBMGS01_US4118
Physical profile name      : /usr/sap/SLO/SYS/profile/SLO_
DVEBMGS01_us4118
------------------------------------------------------------
Unknown parameter jstartup/trimming_properties , cannot be
checked
Unknown parameter jstartup/protocol , cannot be checked
Unknown parameter jstartup/vm/home , cannot be checked
Unknown parameter jstartup/max_caches , cannot be checked
Unknown parameter jstartup/release , cannot be checked
Unknown parameter jstartup/instance_properties , cannot be
checked
Unknown parameter j2ee/dbdriver , cannot be checked
Unknown parameter rdisp/frfc_fallback , cannot be checked
Unknown parameter dbs/ada/schema , cannot be checked
Unknown parameter j2ee/instance_id , cannot be checked
------------------------------------------------------------
Log for the instance profile, total check
Profile name               : SLO_DVEBMGS01_US4118
```

```
Physical profile name       : /usr/sap/SLO/SYS/profile/SLO_
DVEBMGS01_us4118
Log for overall test
----------------------------------------------------------------
No errors found
----------------------------------------------------------------
Overall test of start profiles
----------------------------------------------------------------
Log for the start profile, single test
Profile name                : START_DVEBMGS01_US4118
Physical profile name       : /usr/sap/SLO/SYS/profile/START_
DVEBMGS01_us4118
----------------------------------------------------------------
No errors found
----------------------------------------------------------------
Log for the start profile, overall test
Profile name                : START_DVEBMGS01_US4118
Physical profile name       : /usr/sap/SLO/SYS/profile/START_
DVEBMGS01_us4118
Log for the start profile list
---------------------------------------------------------------
No errors found
---------------------------------------------------------------
```

**Listing 7.1** Log of the Profile Import with Subsequent Consistency Check

The log in Listing 7.1 shows the individual phases of the consistency check associated with the import. The log starts with the import of the default, instance, and start profiles. Because this is a central SAP NetWeaver AS, only one start profile and one instance profile are present. Then the parameters of each profile are checked in their mutual relationships. In this log, no problems were diagnosed. After the single test, for each profile class, there is a system-wide overall test. This checks whether the basic rules of configuration of an SAP NetWeaver AS have been fulfilled. In the example listing, this test also completed with no errors found.

**Profiles: importing**

The imported profiles are the basis for changes to the parameters they contain. Individual profiles can also be loaded into the database by giving the desired profile name and the corresponding file using **Import** (refer to Figure 7.1). This is particularly necessary when an existing SAP

NetWeaver AS system is extended with additional instances. Copies of existing profiles can be stored in the database under different logical names (administrative names). The physical arrangement of the profile is retained. The administrative name of the profile in the database is arbitrary. The advantage of separating an arbitrary administrative name and the actual profile name at the file level lies in the administration of the files. This allows different variations on the same type of profile, each of which serves a different purpose, to be saved under different administrative names. In the following, let's look at an example of an instance profile that can be activated with the SNC option for encrypted data transfer enabled or disabled. The procedure is as follows:

1. In **Profile Maintenance (RZ10)**, select the **Copy** function. A window opens asking for the source and target. As source, any information you may have given when starting profile maintenance is provided as a suggestion, but that data can be changed.
2. Now enter the desired target name. As target, you can retain the same profile name if you want to generate another version of the existing profile, or you give a new name (see Figure 7.2).

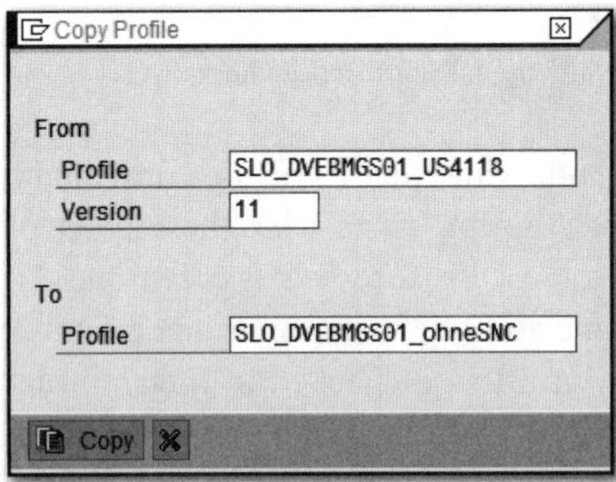


**Figure 7.2** Copy of a Profile

3. Select **Copy**. Version 1 of the new profile is generated. If you've used the same name, then only a new version of the existing profile is generated.

   The editing of profiles is carried out in three phases:

   - **Management data**
     Besides the most informative comments possible, the management

data includes the type of profile (instance profile, default profile, or start profile), the time of activation, and the name of the user who performed the activation. The associated operating system file and the application server are also included which should be used to check the operating system-specific entries in the profile. Figure 7.3 shows this for profile SLO_DVEBMGS01_OHNESNC created from a copy of instance profile SLO_DVEBMGS01_US4118.

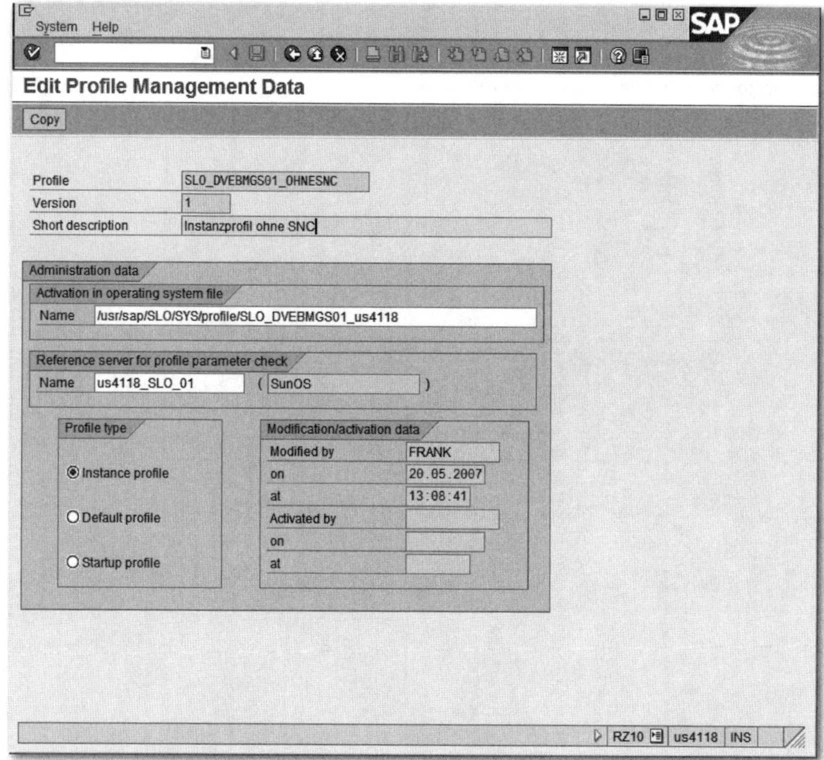


Figure 7.3 Changing Management Data in a Profile

- **Basic maintenance**

  Basic maintenance includes maintaining the most important parameters of each profile. Due to the different meanings and content of the profiles, the appearance of basic profile maintenance depends on the profile type. Basic maintenance only allows the adaptation of the most important parameters and supports the user by the use of logical names. Besides the work process and buffer values shown in Figure 7.4, for an instance profile, these include the directories to be used, the languages used, and other information about storage management. For the settings made, in basic maintenance mode, the initial or maximum swap requirements of the instance are displayed for an instance profile. Note that for performance reasons, the initial value should not be more than 150% of the total main memory of the machine.

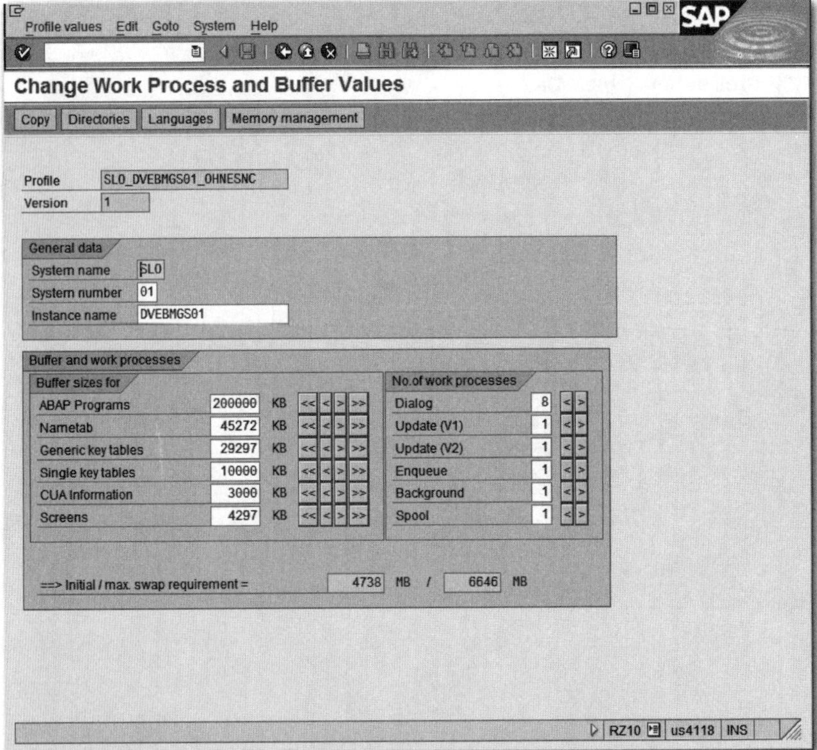


**Figure 7.4** Basic Maintenance of a Profile

- **Extended Maintenance**
  The extended maintenance mode shows the content of each profile in raw form, that is, the actual name of the parameter is shown. This mode is intended for use by experts. Besides changing parameters already present in the profile, you can use **Parameters • Create** to create new parameters at any time. The deletion of a parameter is also possible using **Parameters • Delete**.

Saving profiles

If the changes to a profile should be permanent, they must first be temporarily accepted using **Apply**. Permanent storage of the profiles in the database takes place only when they are saved. However, you shouldn't neglect to check the profile for logical correctness first using **Check**. Regarding test results, note that not all parameters — for instance, those inserted and set for error correction, specific tuning measures, or functional extension — are known to the testing program. The message

```
Unknown parameter em/reserve_mapping_window
```

in Listing 7.1 could also mean a write error or involve an undocumented parameter, which could very well be needed and queried.

After saving, however, the changes aren't yet written to the profile files at the operating system level. Only using **Profile • Activate** are the changes written to the associated files at the operating system level.

Activation

When a profile is activated, a backup file, <profile name>.BAK, is created with the contents of the last valid profile file. Only the latest version of a profile can be activated. For better tracking of the change history, all parameter changes are noted in the profile file (see Listing 7.2).

```
Directory:  /usr/sap/SLO/SYS/profile
Name:       SLO_DVEBMGS01_us4118
*************************************************************
*       Instance profile SLO_DVEBMGS01_US4118               *
*       Version               = 000011                      *
*       Date generated        = 20.05.2007 , 12:40:24       *
*************************************************************
SAPSYSTEMNAME = SLO
SAPSYSTEM = 01
INSTANCE_NAME = DVEBMGS01
PHYS_MEMSIZE = 512
exe/saposcol = $(DIR_CT_RUN)/saposcol
#old_value: 4
changed: SAP* 31.03.2006 13:30:59
rdisp/wp_no_dia = 8
rdisp/wp_no_btc = 1
exe/icmbnd = $(DIR_CT_RUN)/icmbnd
...
```

**Listing 7.2** Listing 7.2 Modified Profile File (Excerpt)

However, this means that the changes have no effect on the instance in question. The instance only takes on the new parameter values after a restart. Only a selected number of parameters in the instance profile can be applied during running operation.

Dynamic parameter changes

Using **Profile Maintenance (RZ10) • Profile • Dynamic Switching • Execute**, the instance parameters listed under **Profile Maintenance (RZ10) • Profile • Dynamic Switching • Show Parameters** can be switched on or off singly or together, without restarting the instances affected. Dynamic changes to other parameters, depending on the parameter type, can be made in different ways. You can find an overview of all dynamically switchable profile parameters in Profile Parameter Maintenance (RZ11) and then **Goto • All Dyn. Parameters** or by using function key F5 (see Figure 7.5).

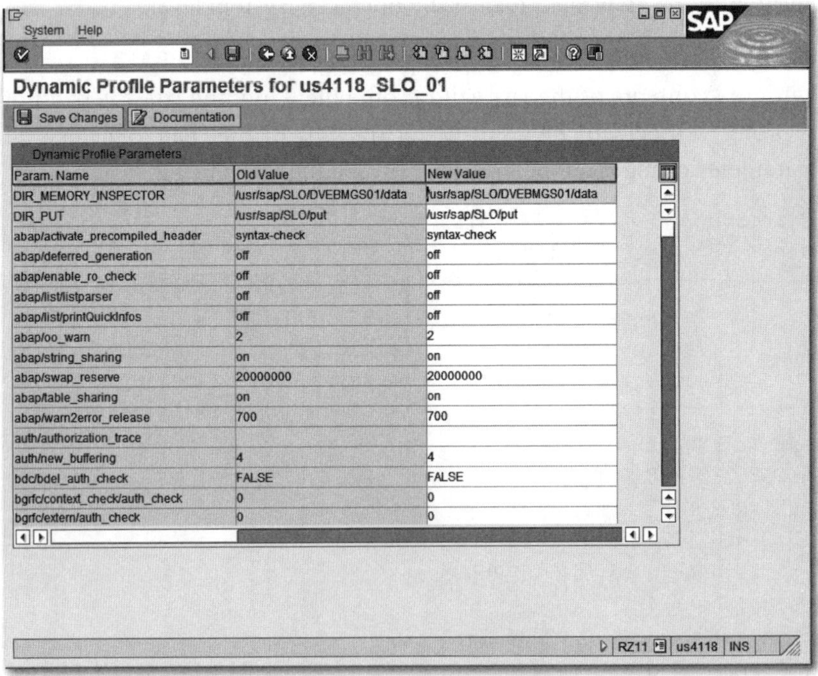


**Figure 7.5** Dynamically Changeable Profile Parameters

In Profile Parameter Maintenance (RZ11) (see Figure 7.6), all of the profile parameters are described individually and in detail. The parameter-specific

**documentation** also describes properties and usage examples. You can use **Change Value** to switch current parameter values dynamically.

The descriptions so far have involved the maintenance of profiles integrated into SAP NetWeaver AS. The parameters available for configuration of SAP NetWeaver AS for individual areas were described in the various chapters. However, a much larger number of parameters exist than this. From the point of view of the customer, a great number of parameters are irrelevant and should therefore not be changed without discussion with SAP. The most important parameters for SAP NetWeaver AS, and a short description of each, can be found in the glossary. Particularly the sizes of the main storage area of an instance are definitive for performance. You can find more detailed information in the book SAP Performance Optimization by Thomas Schneider (SAP PRESS, August 2008).

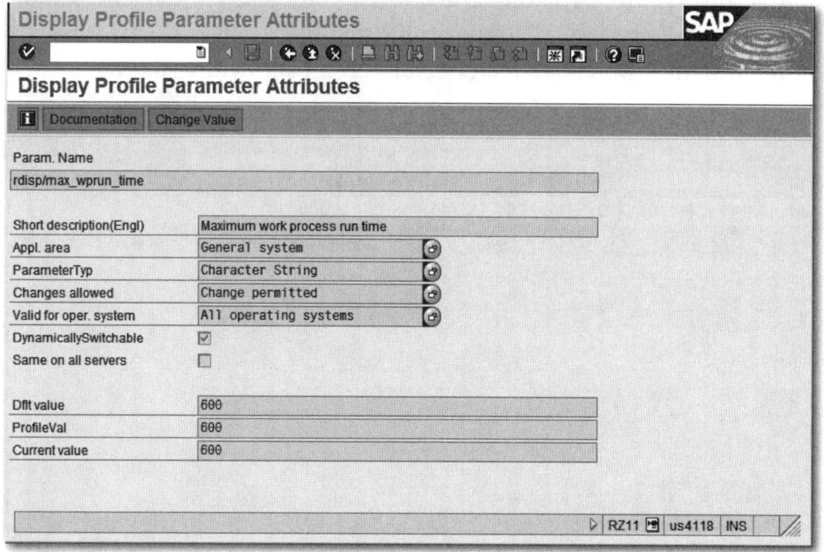


**Figure 7.6** Profile Parameter Maintenance

**Creating a new parameter**

If a parameter must be changed that you have previously used only implicitly with its default value (e.g., due to an SAP Note), then it isn't yet defined in the profiles themselves. The corresponding value is taken from the SAP source code. You can use Profile Maintenance (RZ10) to select the profile in which the parameter to be changed should be stored. Using **Extended Maintenance • Change • Parameter • Create,** you can get to the input form for the new parameter (see Figure 7.7).

After specifying the parameter name and value, the previous parameter value derived from the source code appears as a suggestion. The substitution mentioned is relative to evaluable system parameters, such as path names.

RSPARAM

The parameters currently active in your SAP NetWeaver AS ABAP can be discovered by running the report `RSPARAM`. For every SAP NetWeaver AS parameter, there is a default setting that is implemented in the kernel of the AS. Personal settings in the profiles overwrite those values. The `RSPARAM` report generates a list showing you both values for each parameter. You can also select individual parameters and view the documentation available. The dynamic switching of parameters is only valid until the next reading of the relevant profile file, that is, until the next restart of the instance; these parameter values aren't shown by `RSPARAM`.

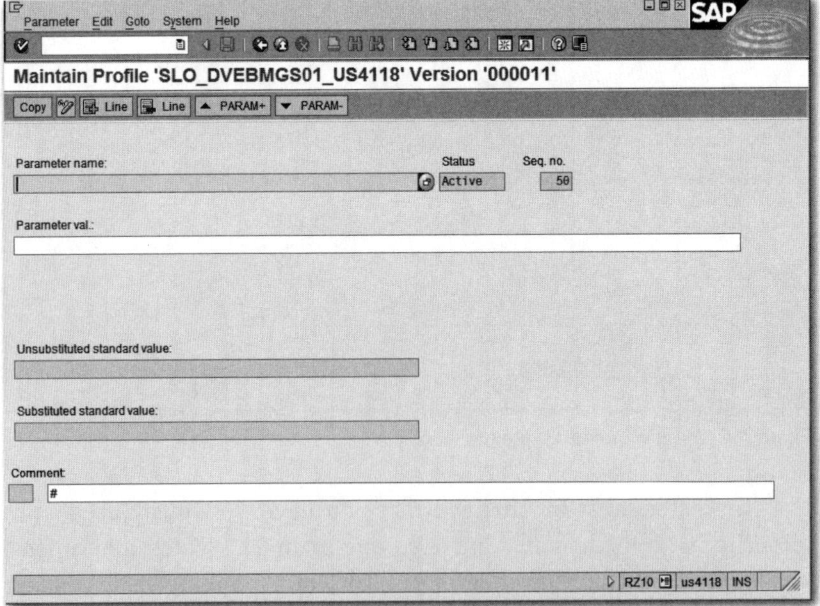


**Figure 7.7** Creating a New Parameter

sappfpar

At the operating system level, the user <sid>adm has the program `sappfpar` for obtaining information about parameter settings of an instance and main memory usage. The command `sappfpar help` returns a brief overview of the possible options for the program:

- `sappfpar <Parameter name>`
  Shows the current value of the selected parameter.
- `sappfpar all`
  Provides a list of all defined parameters.
- `sappfpar check`
  Checks the configured parameters, including the configuration of the SAP main memory areas. The resulting main memory requirements are also calculated.

If necessary, the command can be given an instance profile with `pf=<instance profile>`, an instance number with `nr=<instance number>`, or the SAP system name with `name=<SID>`.

memlimits

Also helpful is the program `memlimits` at the operating system level. The program is also available to user <sid>adm. It compares the main memory requirements of SAP NetWeaver AS ABAP resulting from the parameter settings with the defined kernel parameters of the operating system. If the SAP NetWeaver AS requirements exceed the limitations defined by the operating system, then problems can result; in some cases, the SAP system may not be able to start at all.

## 7.2 Operation Modes

The operation mode of an instance or several instances is defined by the type and number of configured work processes for a certain period of time. By using operation modes, you can adapt the configuration of your SAP NetWeaver AS to periodic variations in requirements within a day, thus using resources better. For instance, many dialog users work with the system during the day, whereas at night the background requirements increase. Thus, it's usually practical to define one operation mode for daytime operation and one for night. An operation mode is assigned a certain number and type of work process. SAP NetWeaver AS can automatically switch the operation mode depending on a defined schedule without needing to restart the instance.

Operation modes can only be created when the profiles of the instances have already been imported via the profile maintenance. Resource distribution is based on the parameters described in the profiles.

Creating operation modes

You can create operation modes as follows:

1. Select **Operation Mode Maintenance (RZ04)** and then the menu item **Operation Mode • Create** (see Figure 7.8).

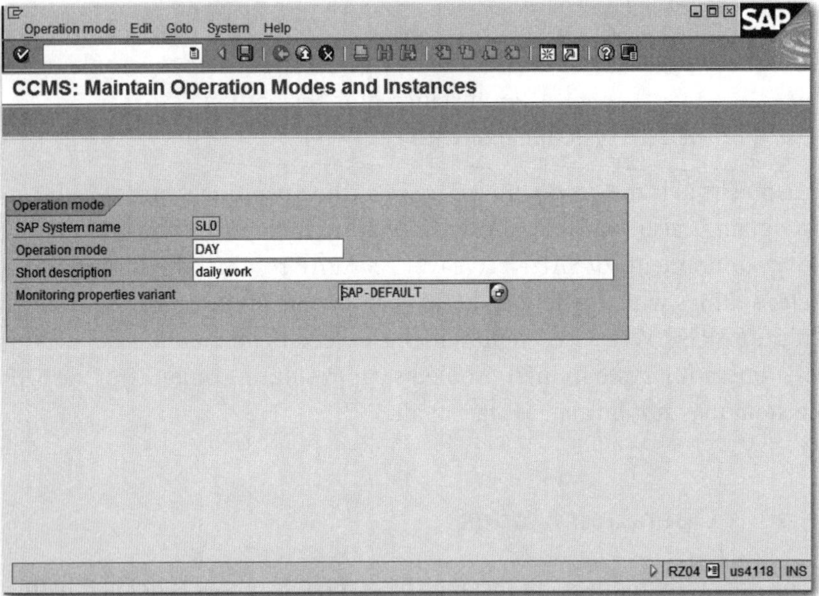


**Figure 7.8** Defining an Operation Mode

2. Give the operation mode a name, and enter a brief description.
3. Determine the monitoring properties to be activated when the operation mode switches (see Section 11.2.3, Specific Adjustment of Properties, in Chapter 11).

4. Save your entries.
5. The operation modes defined are displayed in an overview (see Figure 7.9).

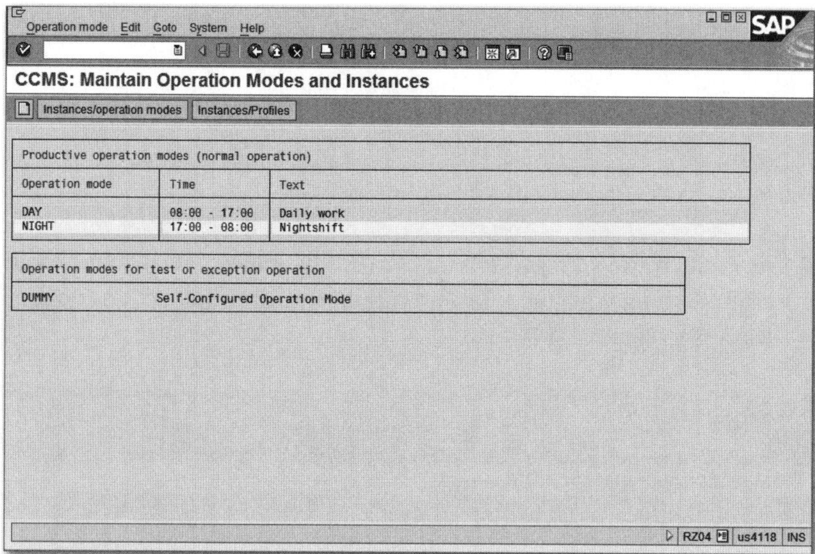


**Figure 7.9** Overview of Operation Modes

The operation mode DUMMY is always created to allow the use of system functionality such as the Control Panel and the scheduling of background jobs even when no custom operation modes have been defined. DUMMY cannot be used for operation mode switching. After you have defined your own operation modes, DUMMY can be deleted.

**Recording instance**

Now record all of the instances of your system by following these steps:

1. Select **Operation Mode Maintenance (RZ04)** again and then menu item **Operation Modes • Maintain Instances • Profile View**. The currently active default profile is displayed. In the not-yet-edited status, no application servers or instances can be found (see Figure 7.10).
2. Select **Profile • Create New Instance** from the menu.
3. Enter the name of the application server and the instance number.

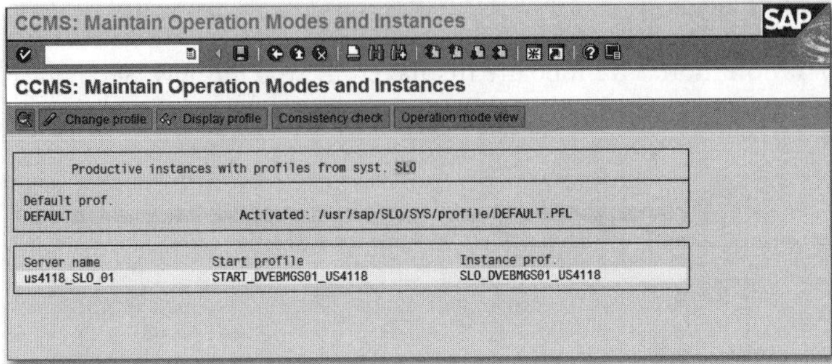


**Figure 7.10** Profile View of Operation Modes

4. Select **Current settings**. This automatically copies the current profile settings, along with the type and number of currently active configuration (see Figure 7.11).

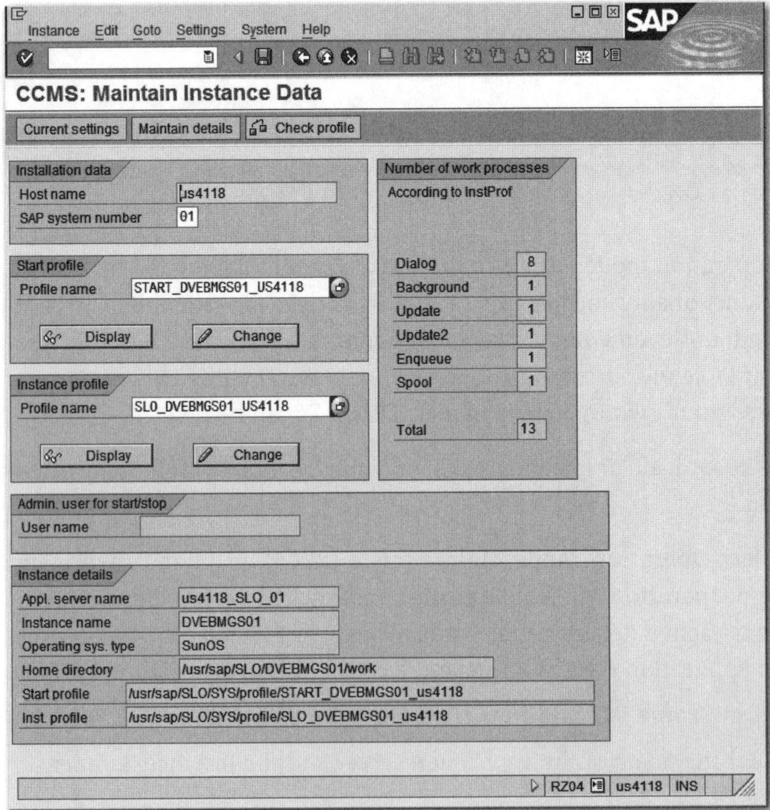


**Figure 7.11** Copying Current Settings

5. Specify a user authorized to start and stop the instance, along with a password, using **Instance • Maintain Startup User**, if you want to be able to start and stop instances through the Control Panel. By default, this is the user <sid>adm.

   Adjustments to profiles can be made by selecting the profile and clicking on **Change**. This automatically takes you to profile maintenance.

6. In a separate window, you can now define the distribution of the total number of work processes taken from the instance profile for a given operation mode (see Figure 7.12). The entries of the instance profile serve as the starting point for the number and distribution of work processes in the selected instance; the total number of configured processes remains constant. The following changes are possible in the context of a mode switch:

   - The number of enqueue work processes can be changed. Every change is reflected directly in the number of dialog work processes. If an instance was started with at least one enqueue process, then you cannot reduce the number of enqueue work processes to 0. Analogously, for instances in which the instance profile defines no enqueue work processes, no enqueue processes will be configurable using mode configuration. At least two dialog work processes must always exist.
   - For update processes and V2 update processes, the same restrictions apply.
   - The upper limit for the number of class A background processes results from the number of background processes. The number of background processes can be reduced to 0. If only class A background work processes are defined on an instance, then only class A jobs can run.
   - The number of dialog work processes cannot be changed directly but is calculated from the total number of configured processes minus the number of non-dialog work processes.
   - The number of spool work processes cannot be changed by instance maintenance.

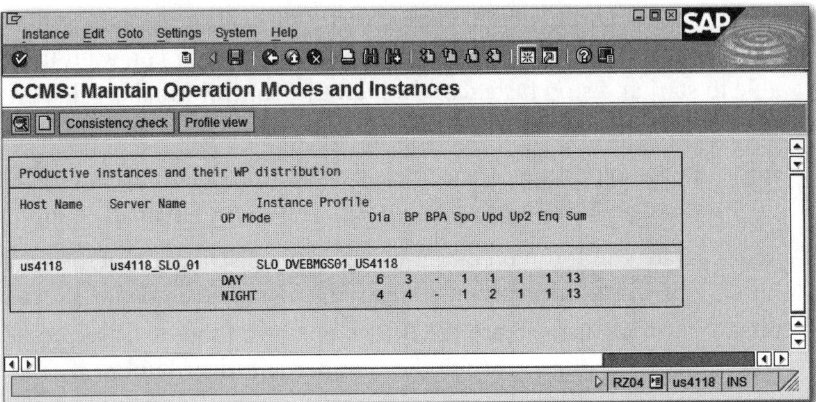


**Figure 7.12** Distribution of Work Processes

7. Save your entries.

The assignment of additional instances of an SAP NetWeaver AS to the defined instance profiles is done analogously. For an initial assignment of instances after installation, the instance definitions for all servers can collectively be created using **Operation Mode Maintenance • Settings • Based on Current Status • New Instances • Create.**

Changing assignments

> **Note**
>
> The assignments made between operation mode and instance variants can be viewed in **Operation Mode Maintenance** via **Instances/Oper.Modes**.
>
> If you want to make changes there, select the operation mode by double-clicking it. This takes you to the screen for distributing work processes. Using **Other Operation Mode**, you can change the operation mode assignment. Save your settings. You can use this menu to go to profile or instance maintenance if needed.

Time table

The last step in operation mode maintenance is the integration of the operation modes into the time table. The starting point is again Operation Mode Maintenance. Select **Operation Mode • Time Table** to integrate the operation modes into the time table (see Figure 7.13).

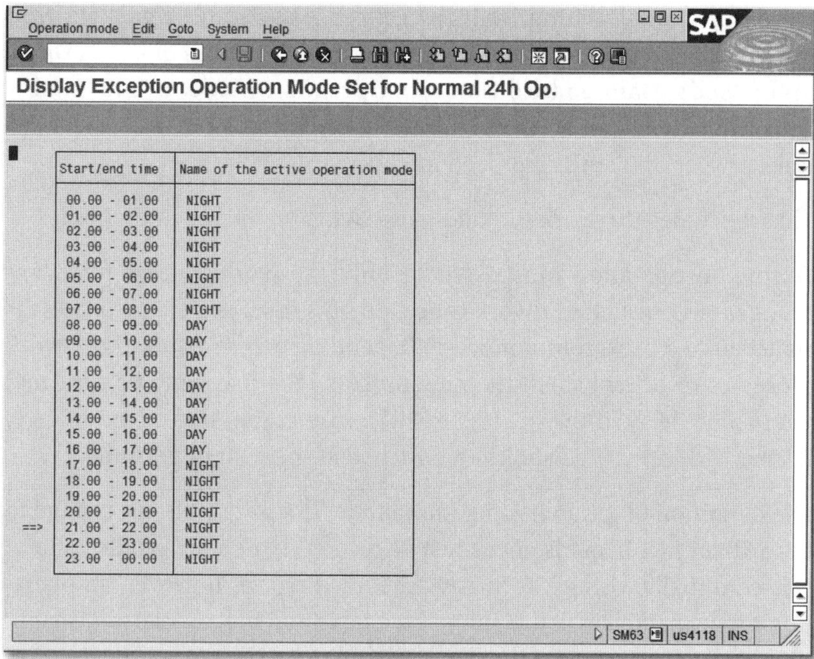


**Figure 7.13** Time Table

To activate a selected operation mode at a particular time, follow these steps:

Activating an operation mode at a certain time

1. From the time table, select **Normal Operation (24 hours) • Change**.
2. Select the level of detail of the time grid using **Edit • Time Grid**. Here, you can select from the following settings: **15 minutes, 30 minutes, and 60 minutes.**
3. Select the start and end of the desired time interval by clicking on the start of the interval, and then select **Operation Mode • Select Interval** or use the shortcut F2. Then select the end of the desired time interval in the same way.
4. Select **Assign** to assign an operation mode by entering its name.
5. Repeat steps 3 and 4 until there are no more gaps in the time table.
6. Save your entries.

You can delete the assignments made using the **Delete assignment** button. An arrow marks the current time in the time table.

Exceptions

In addition, by deviating from the generally applicable timetable, you can specify exceptional operation for individual days and times via **Operation Mode Maintenance (RZ04) • Operation Mode • Time Table • Exceptions.** This can be useful, for instance, for occasional maintenance tasks or special invoicing procedures.

This concludes the work for automatic switching of operation modes.

During an operation mode switch, only the work process types are changed. For instance, a work process that is used as a dialog process is switched to a background process. Depending on the status of the work processes to be switched, the new process type may only be activated after some delay. If the process is still in use at the time of the change, it's marked for change and then switched at the next opportunity.

The definition of different operation modes doesn't result in a change to the SAP profile. If an instance must be restarted, then the profile content is used initially. Using a regularly scheduled report, however, an operation mode marked as active in the time table and the associated distribution of the work processes is detected and set soon after startup.

## 7.3 Control Panel

The Control Panel is available for monitoring the functionality of instances and operation modes of an SAP system. Using the Control Panel (RZ03) function, you can access the initial screen of this tool (see Figure 7.14).

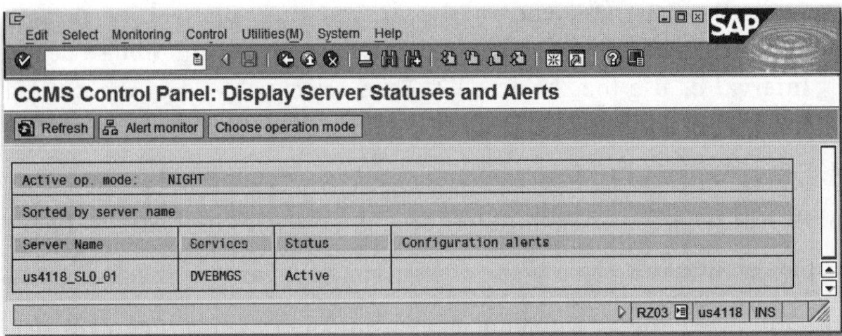


**Figure 7.14** Control Panel

Using the functions integrated into the Control Panel, you can do the following:

- Check the status of all instances of the SAP system, including operation modes.
- Start and stop instances.
- Manually change the operation mode independently of the schedule.
- Call overviews, for instance, for the type and number of work and background processes.
- Go to the alert monitors.
- Display the most important trace files.

Main function

The main function of the Control Panel is starting and stopping individual instances from a central function. Depending on the operating system on which the instances are running, some restrictions should be noted:

- **UNIX platforms**
  To execute commands on a remote UNIX computer, the `rexec` command is used. The administration user on the local system who wants to start or stop the remote instance using `rexec` must have a corresponding entry (user and password) in the *.netrc* configuration file on the target system.
- **Windows platforms**
  An SAP instance on a Windows server is stopped or started with a message to the SAP Service Manager on the remote system.
- **AS/400 platforms**
  On the AS/400 platform, an internal AS/400 mechanism is used to start and stop instances.

## 7.4 Dynamic User Distribution

Load distribution

In SAP systems with multiple application servers, it makes sense to distribute the load as evenly as possible across all of the computers or even to assign users with particularly time-critical applications to the application servers with the best performance values. To do this, so-called logon groups can be formed. A logon group is a subset of the set of all available application servers in an SAP system. The user selects the assigned logon group when logging into the SAP system. From that group, the SAP system assigns the user the application server with the smallest load from the point of view of response time. This is also referred to as load balancing or logon load balancing between the instances.

When forming logon groups, the important thing is which user groups there are with respect to application areas (e.g., FI users, SD users, CO users, etc.). Every instance has its own main memory range. In the ideal case, all of the programs and a large part of the data used by the users of an instance are already available in main memory. This ideal case can best be approached when the users of an instance have as similar a set of tasks as possible. For this user group, you can define a logon group by following these steps:

1. Select **Logon Group Maintenance (SMLG)**.
2. Select **Create entry**.
3. Enter the name of the logon group, and assign the desired instances.
4. Save the data with **Apply**.

Figure 7.15 shows the screen for definition and overview of the logon groups.

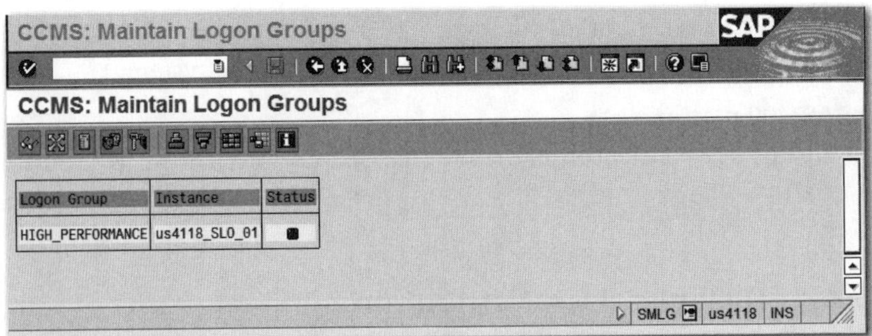


**Figure 7.15** Logon Groups

Load limits

In addition, you can specify a load limit for each instance in the form of an upper limit for the average response time, as well as a maximum number of users. These values, however, aren't absolute limits but rather threshold values used for the calculation of the current login server for this group. The load limits defined for an instance are valid in all logon groups containing that instance.

To define load limits for an instance in logon groups and the IP address assignment, follow these steps:

1. In Logon Group Maintenance (SMLG), select the desired instance.
2. Double-click to select the instance, and enter the input desired.
3. Click **Apply** to save the settings.

**IP address of the application server**

Moreover, an instance can be assigned a special IP address to log in to the frontend, which is necessary when separate local networks are used within SAP NetWeaver AS. A particularly fast network is often used between application servers and the database server because a higher transmission speed is desirable between those computers due to the quantity of data to be processed. The computers at the presentation level, on the other hand, are usually connected to the general network. In that case, the application servers have two network cards and thus two IP addresses. For the frontends, you must determine which IP address is valid.

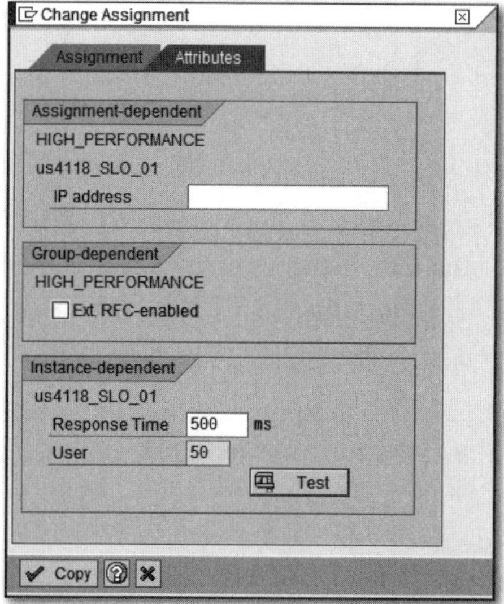


**Figure 7.16** Properties of a Logon Group

Optionally, the access through RFC queries to the logon group can be permitted or rejected (see Figure 7.15). The **Assignment** tab can be used to move the selected instance to a different logon group.

If you want an overview of the momentary system usage, in Logon Group Maintenance (SMLG), you can select **Goto • User List** to see a list of users currently logged on, or **Goto • Load Distribution** to see the selection data for distribution over instances in the logon group (see Figure 7.17).

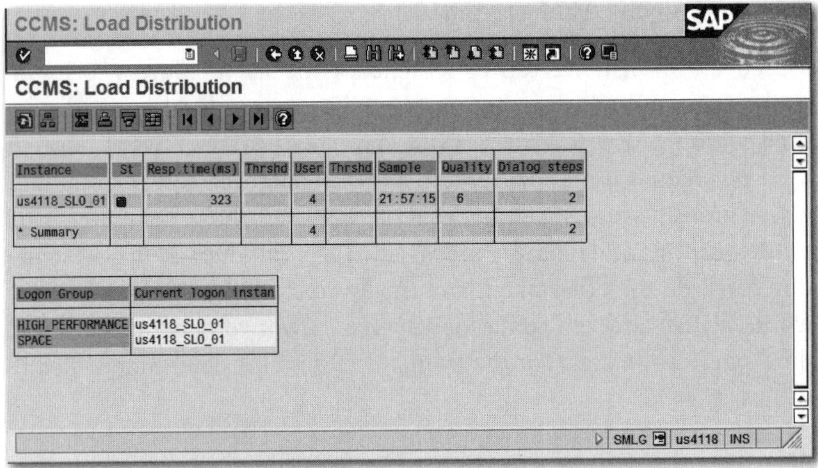


**Figure 7.17** Current Load Distribution

## 7.5 RFC Server Groups

**Load distribution of RFCs**

Similar to the load distribution of user logins with logon groups (see Section 7.4), there is a mechanism for the load distribution of RFCs. This is needed, for instance, because parallelization tools in SAP software cause data packets to be processed in a highly parallel manner to achieve optimum performance.

In this process, for instance, RFC-enabled function modules are called using the

```
CALL FUNCTION DESTINATION IN GROUP ...
```

construct. The function modules called in this way are executed by dialog work processes on each application server. To avoid overloading a dialog instance with too many simultaneous RFCs, for instance to use the resources of all existing dialog instances optimally, you can define appropriate RFC server groups.

You can access the maintenance section for RFC server groups in Transaction RZ12. Similar to the maintenance of logon groups, you must first create a name for the RFC server group, and then assign the group to the corresponding instances. If you want to assign multiple instances to an RFC server group, then simply repeat that step as many times as necessary (see Figure 7.18).

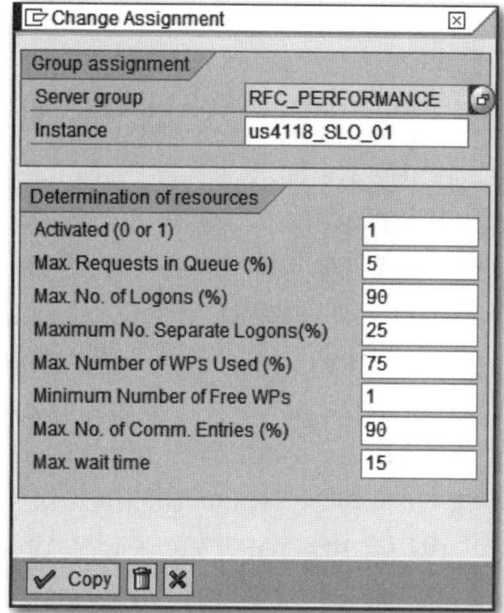


**Figure 7.18** Creating an RFC Server Group

Quotas

By clicking the **Apply** button, the default values are accepted for the parameters for resource assignment (called quotas). These default values represent a good initial configuration, but they can be customized at any time. For each parameter value, there is a detailed explanation you can view by placing the cursor in the appropriate field and pressing the F1 function key.

The quotas can be independently set for each instance in an RFC server group.

If you suspect that RFCs aren't being executed in your system due to resource limitations, you can analyze this problem using Transaction Server Resources (SARFC) (see Figure 7.19).

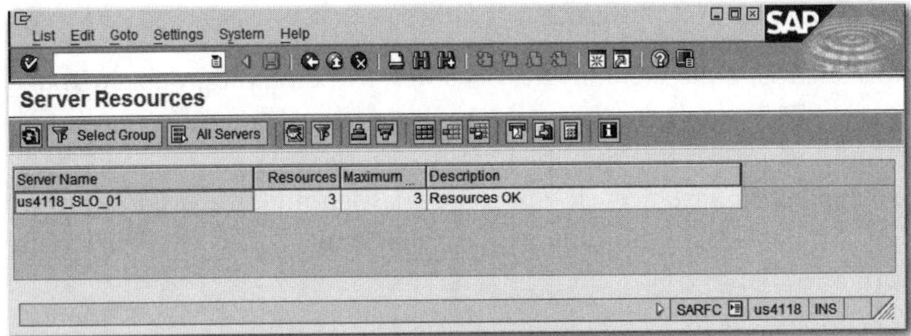


**Figure 7.19** RFC Resource Monitor

This transaction lists all of the instances configured for RFC processing:

- **Resources** shows the number of currently available server resources for asynchronous RFCs (free dialog work processes that can be used). The value is calculated from the maximum available resources (**Max. Resources**) minus the dialog work processes currently in use.
- The number in the **Max. Resources** field is the maximum available number of momentarily available server resources for asynchronous RFCs (free dialog work processes that can be used.) The number is calculated from the configured dialog work processes minus the work processes that can be kept free for dialog users (parameter `rdisp/rfc_min_wait_dia_wp`).
- In the **Description** field, if the instance is correctly configured, and there are sufficient free resources, the message **Resources OK** is displayed. Otherwise, the following error codes can be returned:
  - **1**: The resource check is disabled (parameter `rdisp/rfc_user_quotas` is set to 0).
  - **2**: The server has too few dialog work processes.
  - **3**: The quota for RFC communication channels is defined too low. Increase the parameter `rdisp/rfc_max_comm_entries`.
  - **4**: The quota for the RFC communication channels (`rdisp/rfc_max_comm_entries`) has been used up.

- **5**: The local queue for asynchronous RFC responses is full.
- **6**: The quota for the dialog work processes used by one RFC user is defined too low. Increase the parameter `rdisp/rfc_max_own_used_wp`.
- **7**: The quota for the dialog work processes used by one RFC user (`rdisp/rfc_max_own_used_wp`) has been used up.
- **8**: The quota for the share of RFC requests in the dialog queue is defined too low. Increase the parameter `rdisp/rfc_max_queue`.
- **9**: The quota for the share of RFC requests in the dialog queue (`rdisp/rfc_max_queue`) has been used up.
- **10**: An error occurred while calculating the request queue length.
- **11**: The quota for RFC logons to the server is defined too low. Increase the parameter `rdisp/rfc_max_login`.
- **12**: The quota for RFC logons to the server (`rdisp/rfc_max_login`) has been used up.
- **13**: The quota for your own RFC logons to the server is defined too low. Increase the parameter `rdisp/rfc_max_own_login`.
- **14**: The quota for your own RFC logons to the server (`rdisp/rfc_max_own_login`) has been used up.
- **15**: The server is disabled and cannot process requests.
- **16**: The server is currently being stopped.
- **17**: The server has been stopped.
- **18**: The server is currently being started.
- **19**: The server was already started and is currently in its initialization phase.
- **20**: The server is in an unknown state.

Corresponding to the error code displayed, you can adjust the resource parameters responsible directly using RFC Server Group Maintenance (RZ12). However, note that changes to parameters in the RFC server group definition take effect immediately but aren't static, which means that after the instance is restarted, the previously valid values are active again. If you want to save your parameter change permanently, then you must enter the corresponding parameter and its parameter value into the instance profile (see Section 7.1, Profile Maintenance).

## 7.6 Tips

- **Activating a special case profile**
  If you have copied a default profile as described and modified it for a particular situation (e.g., the instance profile for a one-time data migration), then when activated, the associated file at the operating system level will be overwritten with the special case values. After restarting the instance, the modified values take effect. After the action is concluded, then activation of the old instance profile and another restart of the instance can restore the normal configuration. Thus it isn't necessary to keep different profile variants at the operating system level and rename them as needed.
- **Determining manual profile changes**
  If, as recommended, profile maintenance is carried out through the SAP system, you can detect any manual modifications to the profile files using **Profile Maintenance (RZ10) • Profile • Comparisons • Profile in Database • Against Active Profile.**
- **Parameter changes**
  If it becomes necessary to change a profile parameter, then it should only be done in the suitable profile:
  - Cross-instance: `DEFAULT.PFL`
  - Instance-specific: instance profile

  If a parameter is defined in both profiles, then the entry in the instance profile "wins." If a parameter is set multiple times in the same profile, the last entry is valid.
- **Definition of logon groups**
  If there are only two application servers, then a distribution of the different user groups over these two instances doesn't make sense. For availability reasons, a logon group should always consist of at least two instances on different servers.

- **Using logon groups for servicing application servers**
  To reject logins on an application server when service work is being done, the instance can be temporarily removed from the logon group, transparently for the user, and then added back in after the work is done.

## 7.7 Transactions and Menu Paths

**Operation Mode Calendar:** SAP Menu • Tools • CCMS • Configuration • Operation Mode Calendar (SM63)

**Operation Mode Maintenance:** SAP Menu • Tools • CCMS • Configuration • Modes/Instances (RZ04)

**Control Panel:** SAP Menu • Tools • CCMS • Control/Monitoring • Control Panel (RZ03)

**Gateway Monitor:** SAP Menu • Tools • Administration • Monitor • System Monitoring • Gateway Monitor (SMGW)

**Logon Group Maintenance:** SAP Menu • Tools • CCMS • Configuration • Logon Groups (SMLG)

**Message Server Monitor:** Cannot be reached through standard SAP menu (SMMS)

**Profile Parameter Maintenance:** Cannot be reached through standard SAP menu (RZ11)

**Profile Maintenance:** SAP Menu • Tools • CCMS • Configuration • Profile Maintenance (RZ10)

**Process Overview:** SAP Menu • Tools • Administration • Monitor • System Monitoring • Process Overview (SM50)

**RFC Server Group Maintenance:** Cannot be reached through standard SAP menu (RZ12)

**Server Resources:** Cannot be reached through standard SAP menu (SARFC)

## 7.8 Additional Documentation

SAP Notes

Table 7.1 provides an overview of important SAP Notes related to profile maintenance, dynamic user distribution, and the Control Panel.

| Contents | SAP Note |
|---|---|
| Setting Up Logon Groups for Automatic Load Distribution | 26317 |
| Testing Tool for Message Servers | 64015 |
| Checking Logon Load Distribution | 27044 |

**Table 7.1** SAP Notes Concerning Instance Maintenance

## 7.9 Questions

1. **What is an operation mode?**
   a. An operation mode describes the number and type of work processes of one or more instances.
   b. An operation mode also includes all settings for the SAP main memory areas.
   c. An operation mode designates the status of the SAP system: "active" means operationally ready; "database active" means that only the SAP database is available, and the SAP system is stopped.
2. **What is a logon group?**
   a. All users assigned to the same user group form a logon group.
   b. A logon group is a logic unit of a subset of all of the application servers of an SAP system.
   c. All users with the same work tasks form a logon group.

*The SAP system environment distinguishes among various types of users: users at the operating system level, database users, and, finally, SAP users. In this chapter, the term "user" doesn't refer to individual users of the software. Like the term "client," "user" is a technical system term. This chapter deals exclusively with SAP users.*

# 8 SAP Users and Authorizations

The user concept is one of the fundamental components of the security concept of SAP. To achieve a high level of security, the system administrator must be familiar with the user concept and apply it conscientiously. This chapter first describes the management of SAP users and then covers the role and authorizations concepts of SAP. Examples are provided to clarify the procedures.

## 8.1 Basic Principles

From the view of the SAP system, a *user* is a technical system identification that executes an action. Properties are assigned to this user ID and stored in the *user master record*. Such a user can be a real user or simply a technical user that comes into play for background processing. User

Unique and unambiguous identification of a user is achieved with the user name. The user name is the character string that a real user uses to log on, and it is the ID used internally. User name

One of the most important properties of a user is the authorizations assigned to the user as roles. This chapter also covers the administration of these roles, their technical realization based on profiles, and the assignment of roles.

SAP has its own user concept. After installation of the SAP system, only super users SAP* and DDIC are available initially (see Section, 5.1, Standard Clients and Users, in Chapter 5). You can start to create additional users with either of the two super users. The previous chapters assumed that the SAP user had all rights within the SAP system — especially the rights needed to execute the activity being described. During the startup phase of an SAP system, this approach is reasonable. In production, however, it represents a security gap that we should now close.

## 8.2 User Maintenance

User master record

Specific standard clients and users are available in the SAP system right after installation (see Section 5.1, Standard Clients and Users, in Chapter 5). Users are always client-dependent: they are valid only in the client in which they were created. The password is another property of a user. It is asked for during logon and can be changed at any time — even during logon. During logon, a user can also select one of the languages available in the particular SAP installation. The user name and the properties assigned to it form the *user master record*. A user master record contains all of the data and settings required to log on a user in a client. It consists of the element groups shown in Table 8.1, which are also found in the registers of User Maintenance (SU01) (see Table 8.1).

As described in the following sections, user maintenance includes creating, changing, and deleting users as well as maintaining the user's properties as described in its user master record. You don't have to select and maintain all of the properties. For example, entering an expiration date or a time limit for the validity of a user isn't mandatory. The complexity of the settings that are possible for a user requires adjusting the SAP system to the needs of an individual user and limiting a user's authorizations to the work areas assigned to the user.

| Tab | Data Elements |
|---|---|
| **Address** | Address data |
| **SNC** | Setting for secure network communication (visible only with activated SNC) |

**Table 8.1** Register of Address Maintenance

| Tab | Data Elements |
|---|---|
| **Logon data** | Password, type, and validity period for the user |
| **Defaults** | Default settings for the Start menu, a standard printer, logon language, and so on |
| **Parameters** | User-specific values for standard fields |
| **Roles** | Role assignments |
| **Profiles** | Assigned authorization profiles |
| **Groups** | Assignment of the user to groups for mass maintenance |
| **Personalization** | Settings for individual persons, made with personalization objects |
| **License data** | Contractual classification of the user |

**Table 8.1** Register of Address Maintenance (Cont.)

### 8.2.1 Creating a User

User maintenance (SU01)

You can reach user management with User Maintenance (SU01) (see Figure 8.1). This menu displays all of the functions for creating, changing, and deleting users and for maintaining their properties.

A unique user name in the **User** field specifies the user to be maintained. You can use the **Alias** field to select users by an alternative identification, such as one created from Internet transactions in self-service, for example. You can't create an alias at this location. The following assumes that user SAMPLEUSER has been created for the first time with **User • Create** or the corresponding icon.

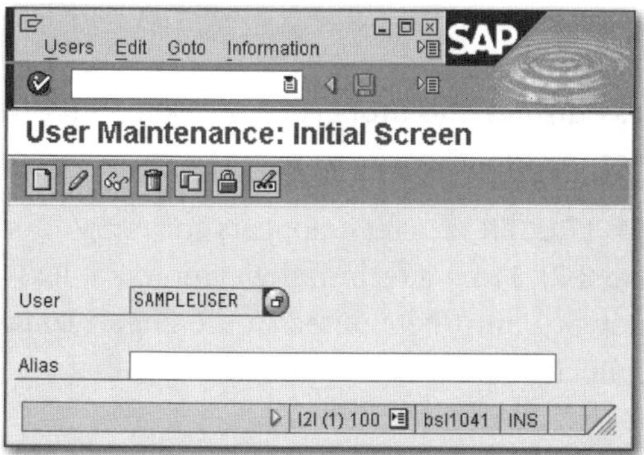


**Figure 8.1** Initial Screen of User Maintenance

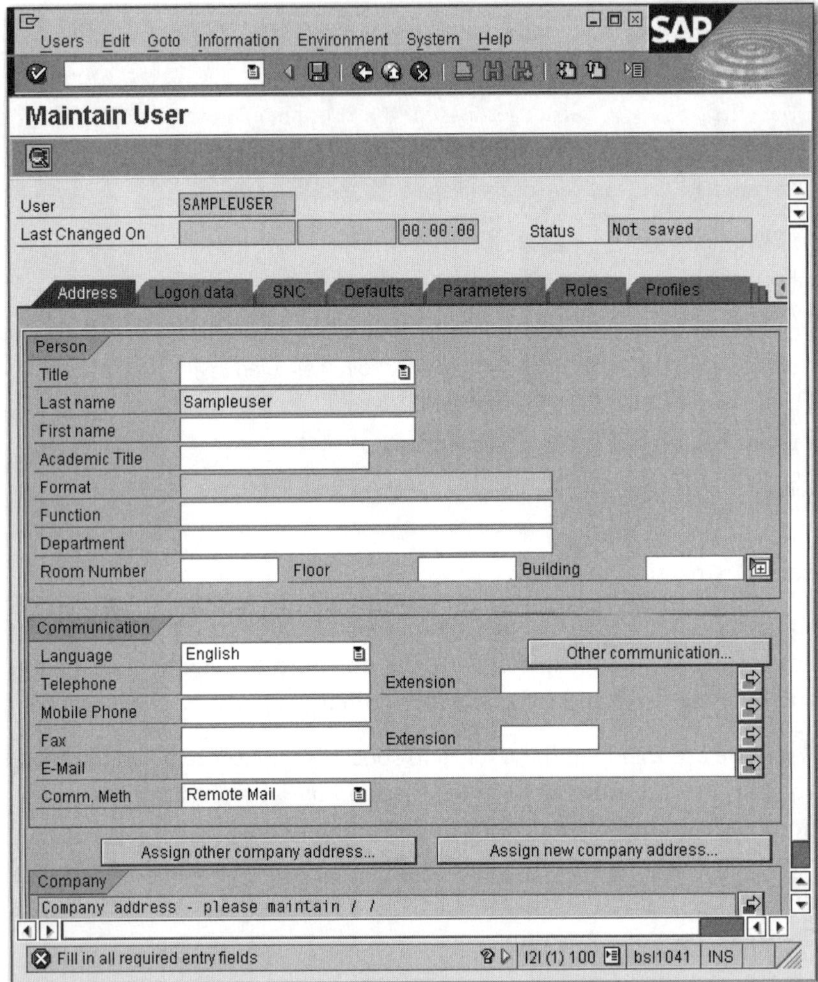


**Figure 8.2** Maintaining the Address of a User

Tabs organized by topic areas display the properties of users. Simply select a different tab to change the topic areas.

User address

During creation of user SAMPLEUSER, a screen appears for entry of a user's address data (see Figure 8.2). From a technical viewpoint, at least the family name and the password must be entered in the **Logon Data** tab. You should also enter as much address data as you know so that you can contact the user if necessary.

You don't have to enter the same address over and over for each user. You can define a *company address* and then assign it to users here.

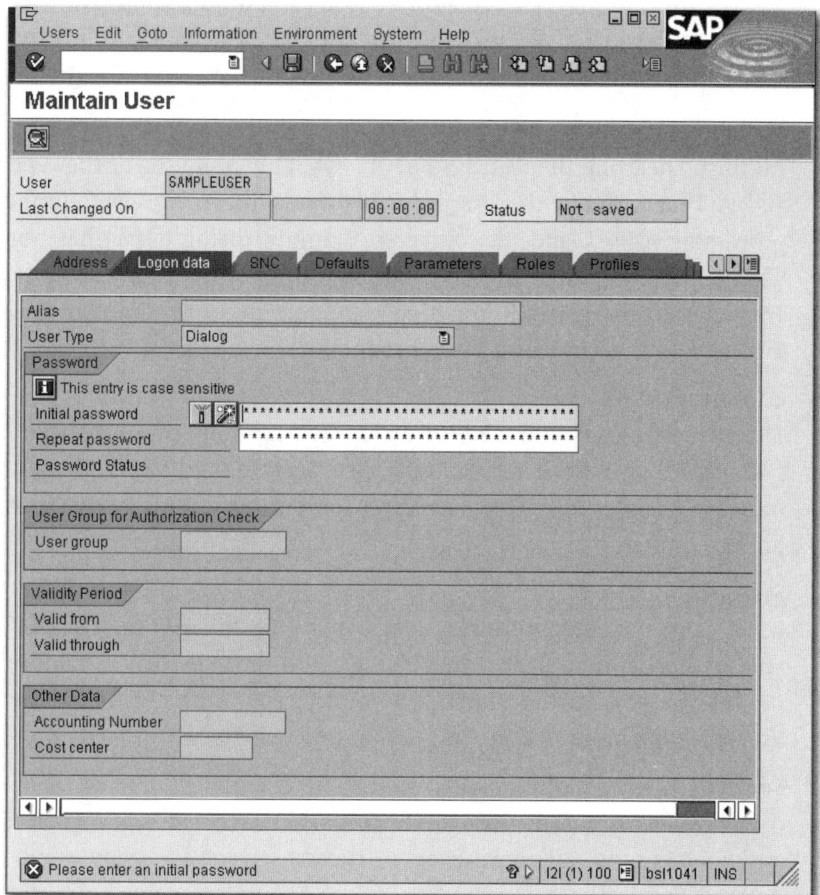


**Figure 8.3** Logon Data of a User

Logon data

You must select the password and the type for each user on the **Logon Data** tab. The default value for the user type is dialog. Figure 8.3 shows the setting for user SAMPLEUSER during the creation process.

You have several options for assigning the initial password:

- Manual entry with repetition to avoid any typos.
- Automatic generation with the **Wizard** icon.

- Deactivation of the password: login would then be possible only with single sign-on.

User types

The password is displayed in encrypted form even during entry. The user type sets the ways that the user may use the SAP system. The following options are available:

- **Dialog**
  All forms of using the SAP system are available to a user of the type *dialog*. That includes the use of background processing, batch-input processing, CPI-C, and, of course, working in dialog if that has not been explicitly limited by the assignment of specific authorizations. The SAP licensing conditions don't support multiple simultaneous logons with the same user ID in production.
- **Communication**
  This type of user is intended for dialog-free communication between systems — over RFC, for example (see Section 13.1, RFC Connections, in Chapter 13). This user can't log on to the SAP system and process in dialog.
- **System**
  Use this type of user for dialog-free communication within a system and for background processing. The general settings for the validity period of a password do not apply to this type of user. This type of user can't log on in dialog.
- **Service**
  A *service* user is a dialog user used to provide access for a large and anonymous group of actual users — those used for access over public Web Services, for example. Initial or expired passwords are not checked; multiple simultaneous logons are explicitly permitted. Security considerations obviously require that you create such user types with great caution and give them only limited authorizations.
- **Reference**
  A reference user is a general user that isn't relegated to a person. No one can log on with this user type. It serves only as a template for assigning authorization. For example, you can use it to assign identical authorizations to Internet users.

User SAMPLEUSER is created as a dialog user, which means that the user type doesn't limit the use of the SAP system.

User group

The **user group** is used for documentation and technical information and helps coordinate authorization to maintain user data. A user within a user group may maintain the data of members of another group only when that authorization has been explicitly granted to the user. Organizing users into user groups simplifies the Mass Change (SU10) of users.

User group *SUPER* is initially the only user group defined in the SAP system. It should be used for all users that have similarly extensive rights in the system. The logical assignment of a user to a user group will help you infer activity areas and rights later on. You enter and maintain user groups within user maintenance. Follow menu path **Environment • User Groups** or use User Group (SUGR). That gives you the option to define a user administrator who can maintain only the users of this user group.

The additional data (account number and cost center) can be analyzed for statistical purposes in reports. It has no effect on the functionality of the user.

User defaults

You make default settings on the **User Defaults** tab for output devices, time zones, and number and date formats. You can also set a default value for the user's logon language so that the user no longer has to enter a language at logon. All users can also adjust the defaults to their own needs by following the Own Data (SU3) menu (see Section 8.4, Personal Settings).

Parameters

On the **Parameters** tab, you can define default values for entry fields that the user will use frequently. Users can also adjust these settings with the **Own Data (SU3)** menu (see Section 8.4, Personal Settings).

SNC

If secure network communication (SNC) is used (the tab is displayed only in this case), you can use the **SNC** tab to define the SNC name that authenticates the user when you use an external security product.

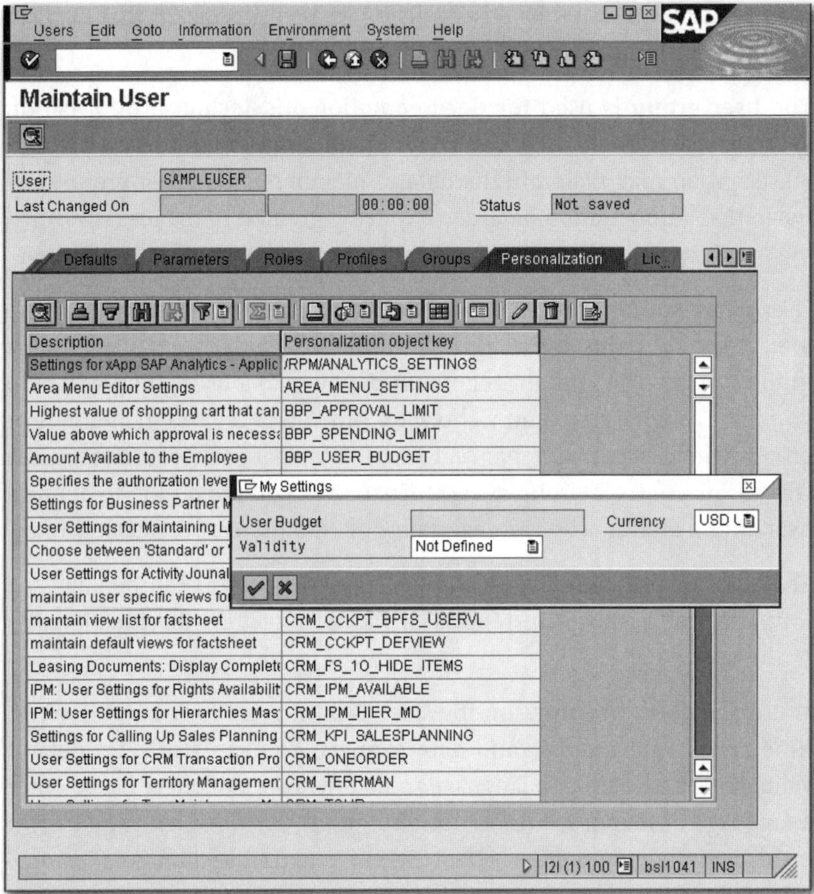


**Figure 8.4** Personalization

**Personalization**

You can use the **Personalization** tab to make individual settings for personalization objects (see Figure 8.4). The personalization objects in the application component must be defined and implemented ahead of time so that you can select them here. You can also assign them by role with Role Maintenance (PFCG).

The required authorizations are assigned to the user on the **Roles** and **Profiles** tabs. The following section describes the procedure in more detail.

### 8.2.2 License Data

SAP software contains a measurement program that is used in every system to generate information needed to calculate the license costs due for the installation. The measurement program analyzes the number and types of users as well as used components. Measurement requires classification of all users, which can be achieved with the **License data** button in User Maintenance (SU01). You should classify the user at creation to avoid follow-up work during measurement.

System measurement

The actual measurement is performed with System Measurement (USMM). You can combine the data gathered for the overall landscape in the License Administration Workbench (LICENSE_ADMIN) and transmit it to SAP with the Service Data Control Center (SDCCN).

The rules for classification and execution of the measurement depend on the SAP release and the contract. You can find a detailed description in the Guidelines for System Measurement (SAP Service Marketplace, quicklink */licenseauditing*).

### 8.2.3 Changing Users and Mass Changes

All of the data created as described in the previous sections can be changed later with the same transactions. If you want to change the data for a large set of users, things can become complicated rather quickly. In this case, you can use Mass Change (SU10) to create and execute most changes in user management for a selected set of users.

You can select the users to be changed using either the address data or the authorization data. Selection is particularly easy if you have organized the users into appropriate user groups (see Section 8.2.1, Creating a User).

You can use mass change to create, lock, and unlock users and to change logon data, parameters, roles, profiles, and groups.

Changes made to a user master record take effect only when the user logs on the next time. In particular, changes to roles and authorizations don't have an immediate effect on users who are already logged on. Such users must log off and then log on again.

### 8.2.4 Logon and Password Protection

Rules

When creating a user, the administrator can assign an initial password that users must change when they log on for the first time. Combined with the user name, this password is required to log on to the SAP system. Some rules apply to the password: some are set by default, and some can be controlled with profile parameters. The default rules include the following:

- The first three characters of the password may not appear in the same sequence in any position in the user name.
- The password can't be PASS or SAP*.
- Each user can change the password a maximum of three times on any given day.

Profile parameter

See the SAP NetWeaver Application Server ABAP Security Guide for an overview of possible profile parameters and recommendations on settings. You can download the document from the SAP support portal. The following list describes some of the most important profile parameters for protecting passwords:

- `login/min_password_lng`
  Sets the minimum length of a password (default setting: 6 characters, minimum of 3 characters, and maximum of 40 characters [but only 8 characters up to SAP NetWeaver Application Server 6.40]).
- `login/password_expiration_time`
  Sets the validity period of passwords in days.
- `login/disable_multi_gui_login`
  Controls the allowance of multiple logins by users.
- `login/password_history_size`
  Number of passwords selected by the user that the user can't reuse (default: 5).
- `login/password_change_waittime`
  Number of days that user must wait until changing the password again.

A logon with single sign-on serves as an alternative to logging on with a password. In this case, the user logs on with a user name and password only once — to a security system. The security system then delivers the logon data as a logon ticket or certificate to the system that user wants to log on to. Additional authentication isn't required. Single sign-on requires implementation of secure network communication (SNC).

### 8.2.5 Default Users

Super user

Default users SAP* and DDIC (also called *super users*) play a special role among users. By default, SAP* and DDIC are available in every client of the SAP system. SAP* has all authorizations in the SAP system. User DDIC has complete rights to manage the Repository (see Chapter 5, Client Administration). Only some components of the change and transport system (CTS) limit this user to display mode — to avoid individual development under this identification.

One of the first tasks to be performed after installation is securing these users by changing their default passwords to avoid unauthorized access to the system (see Table 8.2).

Master password

As of SAP NetWeaver 7.0 (2004s), a common default password, or master password, is assigned to the default users during installation. In this case, the default passwords given in Table 8.2 don't apply. Here, too, the uniform master password should be changed as soon as possible after the installation.

| Client | User | Default Password |
|---|---|---|
| 000 | SAP* | 06071992 |
| 000 | DDIC | 19920706 |
| 001 | SAP* | 06071992 |
| 001 | DDIC | 19920706 |
| 066 | EARLYWATCH | SUPPORT |

**Table 8.2** Default Users and Their Default Passwords

We also recommend that you change the default password (SUPPORT) of user EARLYWATCH in client 066. The EARLYWATCH user has only display rights for performance-monitoring functions, so it represents a minor security risk. The passwords of SAP* and DDIC should be guarded closely, but they must also be immediately available in an emergency.

## 8.3 Authorizations

Distribution of tasks

Creating a user is the responsibility of the SAP system administrator or a user administrator. The assignment of authorizations decides which activities a user of a given type and user group is permitted to perform. Someone other than the system administrator — the authorization administrator — should assign authorizations. Distribution of these tasks to at least two different persons is recommended to lower the security risk. If a user were to have the right to set up new users and to assign authorizations, the user could give another user all rights to the SAP system and have unlimited access to data. Distributing tasks among several persons avoids the problem. Maintaining authorizations can occur only by close collaboration with user departments or by giving the responsibility to the user departments themselves. The user departments view things from the perspective of business activities that a user should or should not be allowed to perform. An SAP system administrator, however, looks at the matter from a technical perspective when assigning and managing the authorizations. The system administrator can't decide which business authorizations a given user needs or doesn't need. The user departments must therefore decide which authorizations are assigned for specific purposes. The following tasks concentrate on the technical aspects of the authorization concept and how to work with it.

A user's authorizations are the most important properties that must be maintained for a defined user. The assignment of authorizations for any software has two purposes. First, it should limit the activities that users are permitted to perform as exactly as possible, enabling only those actions that the users need to perform. Second, users should not lack any rights needed to perform their jobs. The task of the authorization administrator is to harmonize the two purposes. The authorization concept of the SAP system provides a very complex system that consists of many individual authorizations that form units, which means that they can be fine-tuned.

### 8.3.1 Authorization Checks – Overview

Two-level check

An authorization check occurs in the SAP system whenever a transaction is called. The check occurs at two levels. The first step checks authorization for the transaction when the transaction is called. A second step occurs when an action is triggered. It checks the authorization for an activity on an authorization object (see Figure 8.5).

Role concept

Authorizations are assigned to users with *roles*. Authorizations are combined into roles and entered in the user master record. A role therefore represents a description of a work center that can be assigned to various users. In addition to authorization, roles also contain the definition of the user menu (covered in more detail in the context of role maintenance in Section 8.3.5) and workflows.

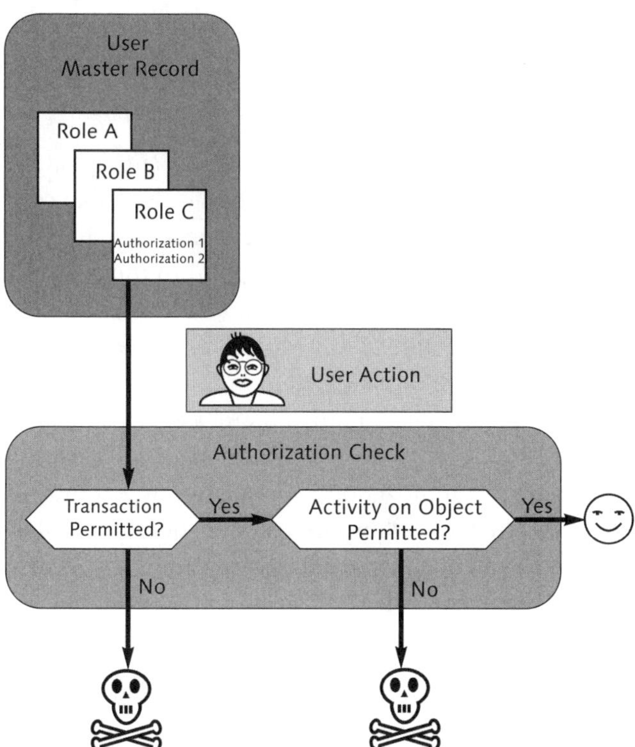


**Figure 8.5** Two-Level Authorization Check

To enable better technical handling, the authorizations of a role are grouped into profiles that are automatically generated during role maintenance. Earlier releases required manual maintenance of profiles. Roles can still be maintained manually but only in exceptional cases as of SAP NetWeaver 7.0.

User comparison

In the ideal case, the administrator managing users simply needs to select a predefined role as a template, copy it, make any required changes, and then assign the copy to a user. A user comparison (see Section 8.3.7, User Assignment and User Comparison) enters the authorization into the user context as profiles.

To explain the technical contexts, the following sections first describe the deeper layers of the authorization check: the authorization objects. They then return to the administrator's important task of assigning roles to users.

### 8.3.2 Authorizations and Authorization Objects

Every authorization in the SAP system is based on an authorization object. An *authorization object* is a module with a unique name that consists of pairs of attributes and values and of an assigned activity. The attributes are called *authorization fields* and correspond to the data elements of the ABAP Dictionary. A combination of an authorization field and a permitted value defines a dataset upon which the assigned activity may be performed. Assignment of an authorization to a specific operation (report, transaction, update, and so on) is thereby set as a default. From a technical perspective, an *authorization* is a set of values for exactly one authorization object. An authorization is permission to execute an action in the SAP system. The SAP authorization system doesn't prohibit any activities; it uses only authorizations, which also means that everything not explicitly allowed is forbidden.

Object class

Given the scope of SAP ERP, the number of authorization objects in an SAP system is considerable. To distinguish among them, they are subdivided by topic into *object classes*. You can display an overview of all of the authorization objects available in the SAP system with Object Class (SU21). Use that transaction and then select **AAAB** for cross-application authorization objects. This selection displays all of the authorization objects available for this area. A short text indicates the meaning of each authorization object. For example, authorization object S_RFC_ADM for administration of RFC connections consists of authorization field **ACTVT** (contained in every authorization object) and special fields **RFCTYPE**, **RFCDEST**, and **ICF_VALUE** (see Figure 8.6). The documentation for the object explains the meaning of individual fields and the values that they can assume.

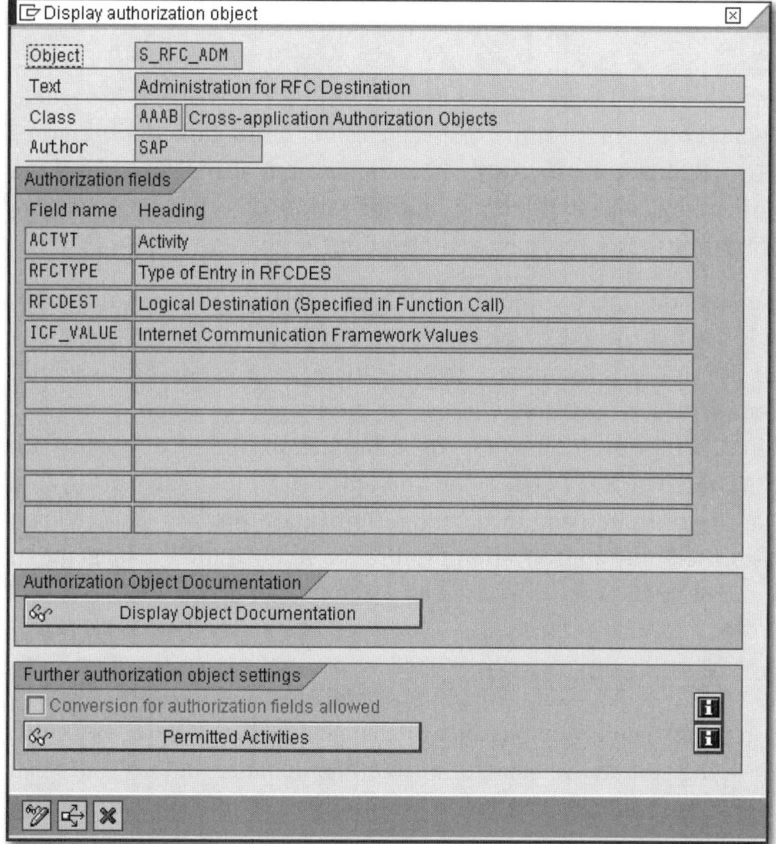


**Figure 8.6** Authorization Object S_RFC_ADM

In our example, the name or naming areas of a defined RFC connection can be assigned to field **RFCDEST**. You can use the **Permitted Activities** button to find all of the values permitted for the activity. The values in field **ACTVT** have meanings listed in Table 8.3.

| Value | Meaning |
|---|---|
| 1 | Create or generate. |
| 2 | Change. |
| 3 | Display. |
| ... | Additional values for other special activities can be defined, depending on the related authorization object. |
| * | All possible activities. |

**Table 8.3** Possible Values in Field ACTVT and Their Meaning

Most authorizations are already defined with an asterisk (*). If needed, you would only enter company-specific values. From **Role Maintenance (PFCG) • Environment • Auth. Objects**, you can also display all of the authorizations that exist for an authorization object, adjust existing authorizations, or insert new authorizations.

Role maintenance

If you consider the complexity of the SAP system, you will no doubt quickly see that although you can use this approach to define and assign all of the authorizations you require for each user, doing so would become almost impossible because of the incredible amount of effort required. Administration of a set of authorizations therefore occurs with Role Maintenance (PFCG). Here, the authorizations that belong to a role are technically combined into authorization profiles. Earlier Basis releases used only authorization profiles for authorization management; as of today, profiles are only used as a technical utility.

### 8.3.3 Authorization Profiles

Although it's technically possible to change existing profiles, you must avoid doing so because changes in role maintenance and upgrades can overwrite any changes that you make. If direct maintenance of profiles is nonetheless required, you may change only customer-specific copies of existing profiles.

Figure 8.7 shows an overview of the resulting hierarchical assignment of the authorizations.

The authorization objects (logically organized by object class) consist of standard field, **Activity**, and additional authorization fields.

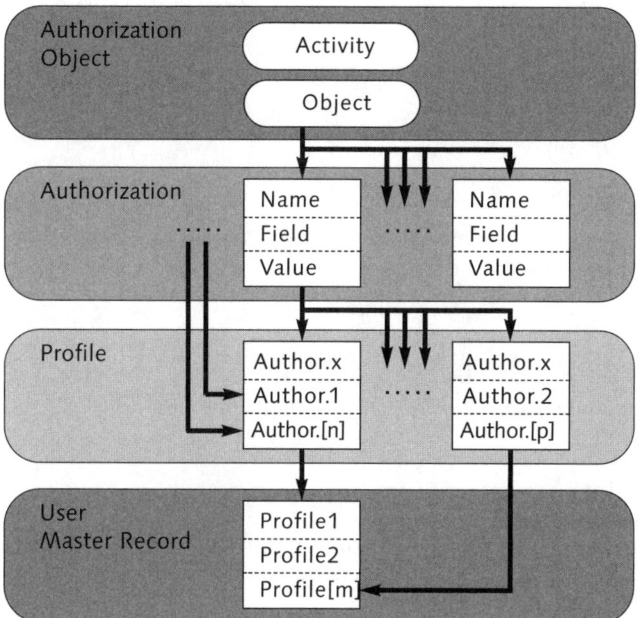


**Figure 8.7** Hierarchical Assignment of Authorizations and Profiles

An authorization is defined based on the values of the fields of an authorization object, which contain permission for an action. Setting different values can set various authorizations for an authorization object.

To simplify administration, authorizations are managed with Role Maintenance (PFCG), which combines them as it generates profiles.

The profiles are entered in the master record of users — automatically when using roles and manually in exceptional cases.

## 8.3.4 Important Profiles in the System Administration Area

Authorizations for system maintenance should also be divided by areas of responsibility and distributed using roles. The SAP system contains some profiles that have special meaning for administration: they are occasionally assigned explicitly. Table 8.4 lists such profiles.

| Profile Name | Meaning |
|---|---|
| SAP_ALL | All authorizations in the SAP system |
| SAP_NEW | Authorization profile for all of the additional authorization objects in existing functions that arise from a new release of the SAP system (upgrade) |
| S_A.ADMIN | Operator without configuration authorizations in the SAP system |
| S_A.CUSTOMIZ | Customizing (for all activities related to system setup) |
| S_A.DEVELOP | Developer with all authorizations for working with the ABAP workbench |
| S_A.SHOW | Basis: only display authorizations |
| S_A.SYSTEM | System administrator (super user) |

**Table 8.4** Important Authorization Profiles in the Administrative Area

### 8.3.5 Role Maintenance

Role

A role represents the description of a work center that can be assigned to a user. Defining roles significantly lessens the work of the user administrator. If authorizations have to be changed, only the roles need to be adjusted. After they are generated, the changes become effective for all assigned users with user comparison. A role stores the following information:

- Name of the role
- Descriptive text for the role
- Role-specific menu
- Workflow tasks of the role
- Authorization profile
- Users to whom the role is assigned
- Personalization data
- MiniApps (simple and intuitive web applications)

When users log on, they receive all of the menu entries and authorizations contained in the sum total of their profiles.

Preparations for role maintenance

To activate Role Maintenance (PFCG), you must first allow suppression of authorization checks. Set the following parameter in the instance profile:

```
auth/no_check_in_some_cases = Y
```

That is the default setting in newer Basis releases; the authorization profile generator is activated. This parameter allows suppression of the authorization check contained in individual transactions. This functionality is required for role maintenance.

Standard roles

The simplest form of role assignment is the use of standard roles that SAP has predefined. Before you create roles for your employees, you should check to see if the job descriptions in your company can be mapped to the roles delivered by SAP. To avoid any problems caused by an upgrade's change of standard roles, you should always work with copies (in the customer namespace) rather than directly with standard roles.

The information system offers an overview of the delivered roles (see Section 8.6, Information About Users and Authorizations) as does report `RSUSR070`. If these roles meet your requirements, you can copy them and perform a user assignment (see Section 8.3.7, User Assignment and User Comparison), and you need no additional role maintenance.

Role maintenance

In Role Maintenance (PFCG), you can copy, create, change, assign, compare, and transport roles. Maintenance of customer-specific roles essentially consists of two steps:

1. Assign the user menu.
2. Adjust the authorizations and authorization fields that role maintenance creates based on the user menu generated in the first step.

Let's look at the procedure based on a rather simple example. We want to create and edit a role for the SAP system administrators.

Creating or copying a role

The first step creates a role or copies an existing role:

1. Select **Role Maintenance (PFCG)** to create roles and maintain existing roles. Figure 8.8 shows the initial screen. In this example, we want to create role *ZADMIN*.

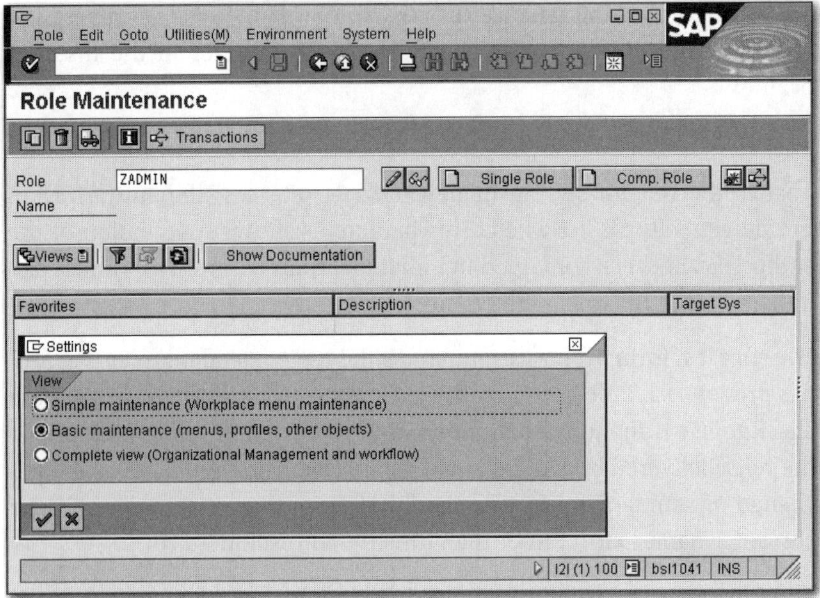


**Figure 8.8** Creating a Role

2. Enter the desired name of the role, such as *ZADMIN*; role names that begin with SAP_* are reserved for standard roles.
3. Select **Basic maintenance** as the editing view.

Basic maintenance and complete view

You can use any of three modes for editing. You use **Simple maintenance** to edit the user menu. **Basic maintenance** deals with menus, profiles, and personalization objects. The roles created here are later assigned to actual SAP users. The **Complete view** is much more complex and is directly connected to organizational management in HR. Instead of assigning actual SAP users with the names, you can assign positions, work centers, and organizational units, which gives you much more flexibility. But taking this approach makes sense only if organizational management in HR is used within the SAP system.

The example is limited to **Basic maintenance**.

4. Select **Create**.
5. Every tab in Role Maintenance (PFCG) (see Figure 8.9) has a status indicated by a color that shows the related part of role maintenance:
    - Not yet maintained (red)

- No longer current (yellow)
- Maintained and up to date (green)

In the description, you should briefly note the purpose of the role and which parts are to be copied. If you are making changes, you should document the change history.

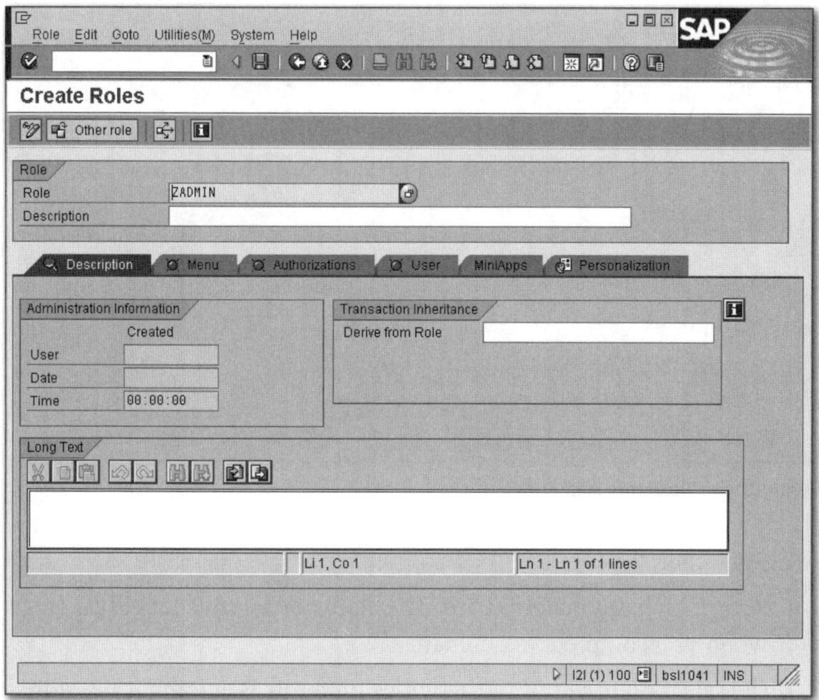


**Figure 8.9** Basic Maintenance of Roles

6. On the **Menu** tab, you can assemble the user menu. You can transfer menus from the SAP menu, from other roles, from reports, or import from a file. You can also insert individual transactions, queries, and other objects, such as web addresses. Select the options that apply to the relevant activities for the role.
7. Our example selects **CCMS Tools**, **Online System Log Analysis (SM21)**, and the web address of the SAP support portal (see Figure 8.10) from the SAP menu.

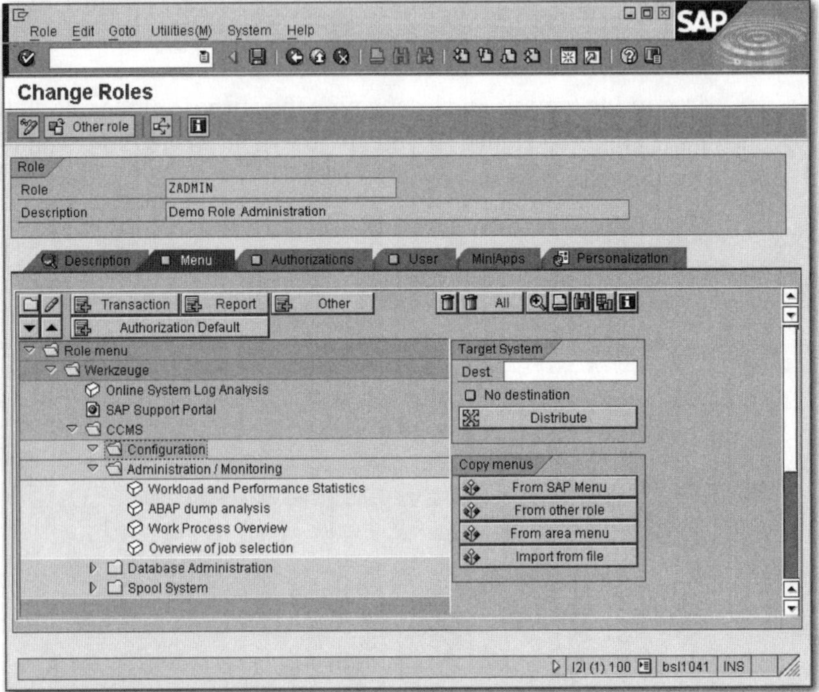


**Figure 8.10** Selecting Activities

8. Save your selections.
9. Return to basic maintenance. The status of **Menu** changes to green when you complete maintenance.

User menu

The selection of permitted activities for a role is automatically stored as a menu tree that consists of these actions. All users assigned to this role can use the menu as a *user menu*. You can use role maintenance to make further adjustments to the user menu by inserting folders to create a structure. The nodes of the menu can be moved by dragging and dropping, which makes it easy to adjust the menu hierarchy to your needs.

10. The next step maintains the authorizations and generates the authorization profiles for the selected activities. Select the **Authorizations** tab within role maintenance, and assign a name to the authorization profile you want to create. All names with an underscore (_) in the second position are reserved for SAP standard profiles. You can

have the system generate a proposal, but the proposal would not be a meaningful combination of characters and numbers. To make later analysis easier, select a name on your own or use informative short text.

Traffic lights

The required authorizations are determined from the activities you have selected and are then displayed in a hierarchy. A traffic light indicates the maintenance status for the node:

- **Green**
  The authorizations beneath this node have values that you should check.
- **Yellow**
  At least one field beneath this node could not be populated automatically with values (e.g., user or device names). The field must be populated with values.
- **Red**
  No organizational levels have been maintained yet for a field.

A role, object class, object, authorization, or field can also assume the following states (displayed as text in the overview):

- **Standard**
  All subordinate roles are unchanged from the SAP standard.
- **Changed**
  The content of at least one subordinate node was changed from the SAP standard.
- **Maintained**
  At least one subordinate field that SAP delivered empty has been filled with values.
- **Manually**
  At least one authorization was inserted manually into the subordinate node.
- **Old**
  After an upgrade, the previous objects and values are compared with the new ones. If all of the subordinate values are the same (up-to-date), the status of the node changes to old.

- **New**
  The comparison has determined that new and different values have been added.

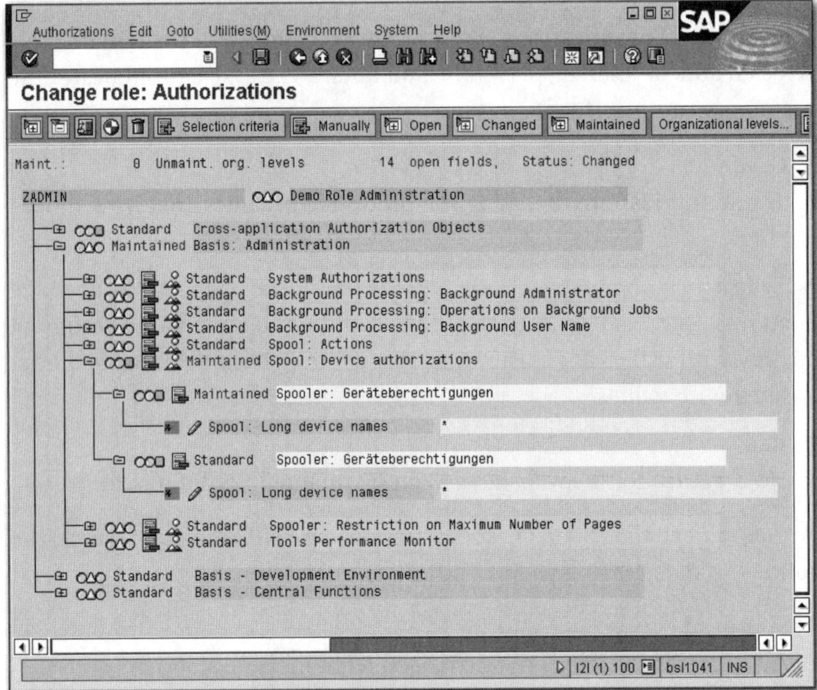


**Figure 8.11** Maintaining Authorizations

Manual change

You can now make manual changes to the selected authorizations and even assign values to them. You can also add or delete complete authorizations. Figure 8.11 shows the authorizations selected for our example. Follow these steps:

1. Select the desired node and open it.
2. You can now perform the following:
   - Deactivate unwanted subtrees or individual authorizations with the icon to the right of the status (the chart of icons gives you an overview of the many icons within this transaction).
   - Add new overall authorizations or individual authorizations with **Edit • Insert Auth**.

- Create or change the desired values for an authorization object by selecting the appropriate icons in the row. In Figure 8.11, it would make sense to create values from the SAP system for the device authorizations of the spool system. These values describe device names that would be valid for the authorization. For example, D* would permit the use of all devices whose names begin with D.
- Manually remove or insert individual transaction codes describing actions.

3. After you have made all of the desired changes, all of the traffic lights should show a status of green. Save your settings.
4. Select the **Generate authorizations** icon.
5. A profile with all of the authorizations you have selected is created and saved under the name you defined in the previous screen.
6. Return to **Basic maintenance**. After successful completion of authorization maintenance, the status changes to green.

**Composite roles**

To simplify matters, roles can be combined into *composite roles*. Creating and maintaining composite roles is largely similar to creating and maintaining individual roles.

In the initial screen of Role Maintenance (PFCG), you assign a name and create a composite role with the **Comp. Role** button. You can define the roles to be combined in the **Roles** tab, and you can import the menus of individual roles and edit them in the **Menu** tab. You can't edit authorizations.

### 8.3.6 Important Roles in the System Administration Area

In larger SAP projects, the tasks of system administration are usually split into various subdivisions and assigned to individuals or groups. User SAP* has the SAP_ALL profile, which covers all activities or application-specific tasks. That's why this user is inappropriate for general operations and is to be protected against external access. We recommend that you create special users and assign them to specific roles. Table 8.5 lists the most important roles for administrators.

| Profile Name | Meaning |
|---|---|
| SAP_BC_BASIS_ADMIN | Basis and system monitoring administrator |
| SAP_BC_SPOOL_ADMIN | Spool administrator |
| SAP_BC_BATCH_ADMIN | Background processing administrator |
| SAP_BC_CUS_ADMIN | Customizing Project administrator |
| SAP_BC_DWB_ABAPDEVELOPER | ABAP developer |
| SAP_BC_SRV_GBT_ADMIN | Communication, storage, and scheduling administrator |
| SAP_BC_SRV_COM_ADMIN | External communications administrator |
| SAP_BC_SRV_EDI_ADMIN | IDoc administrator |
| SAP_BC_MID_ALE_ADMIN | ALE administrator |
| SAP_BC_TRANSPORT_ADMIN | Change and Transport System administrator |
| SAP_BC_BMT_WFM_ADMIN | System workflow adminstrator |
| SAP_BC_BDC_ADMIN | Batch-input administrator |
| SAP_BC_USER_ADMIN | User administrator |
| SAP_BC_AUTH_DATA_ADMIN | Authorization data administrator |

**Table 8.5** Important Administrative Roles

### 8.3.7 User Assignment and User Comparison

Two options

Now that you have become familiar with the administration of users and roles in the previous sections, we can turn to the assignment of roles to users. In general, you have two options:

- Assign roles to users in **User Maintenance (SU01)**
- Assign users to roles in **Role Maintenance (PFCG)**

When you make an assignment in User Maintenance (see Section 8.2.1, Creating a User), select the **Roles** tab. You can enter the desired roles for the user directly there. The generated profiles for the roles are automatically inserted into the **Profile** tab.

You may not change generated roles directly because a manual assignment or change would mean the loss of the control and comparison functionality of role maintenance. And each change of an automatically generated profile would be lost after the next change of the role.

Assignment of a user to a role

You can assign a user to a role on the **User** tab of Role Maintenance:

1. Select the **User** tab.
2. Enter the new user in **User ID** (see Figure 8.12: SAMPLEUSER for our sample user). The user must have been created already.

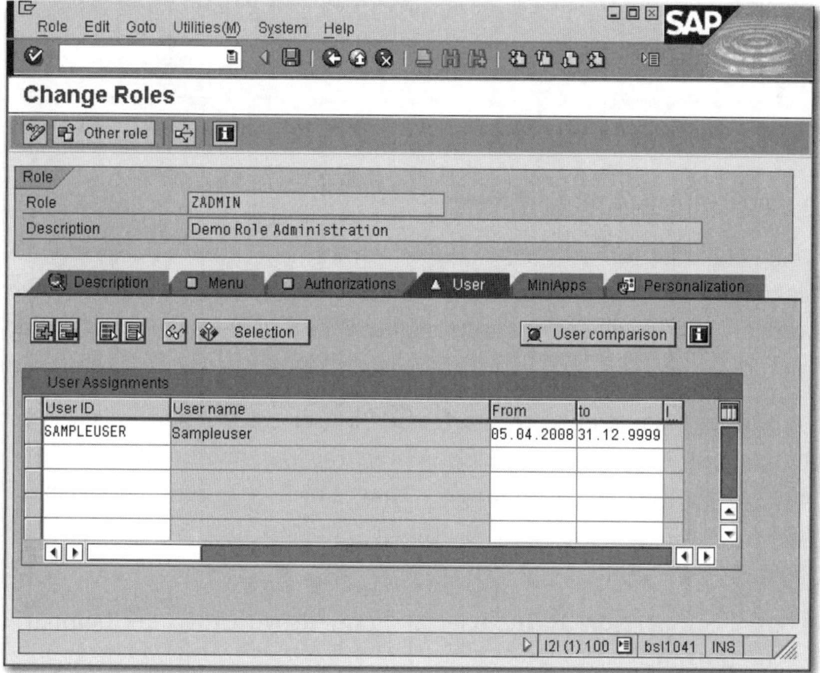


Figure 8.12 User Assignment

Validity periods

In this view of Role Maintenance, you can also define a limit for the validity period for assigning roles to users. This feature lets you schedule authorizations that will be needed in the future or authorizations that are valid only for a specific period.

3. Select **User Comparison** to assign the authorization profiles generated for the role to the selected users (see Figure 8.13). This process is also called the user master comparison.

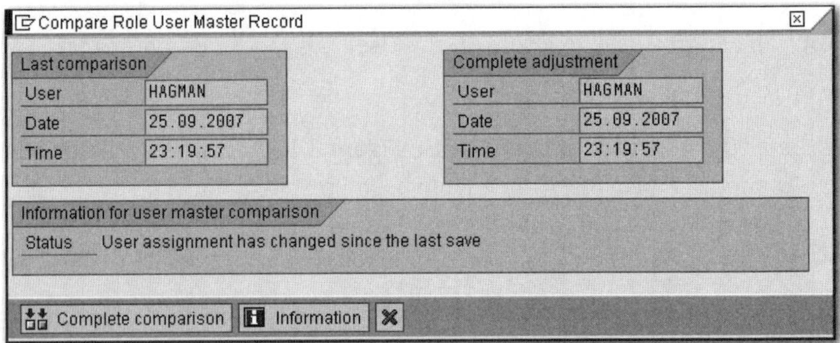


**Figure 8.13** User Master Comparison

4. End maintenance of the role.

That concludes our selected example. You can check the success of your activities with User Maintenance. The selected role and generated profile were assigned to all desired users. Figure 8.14 illustrates the situation for user SAMPLEUSER.

User comparison

As part of the example, we performed a user comparison during user assignment. Only the comparison enters the generated profile of a role into the user master. Accordingly, changes in user assignment, changes to roles, and the generation of profiles require a user comparison. You have various options for a user comparison:

- **User comparison during user assignment with the User Comparison button**
  The status display on the button indicates whether or not a new comparison is required. This method is particularly appropriate during role maintenance on the development system (see the preceding example).

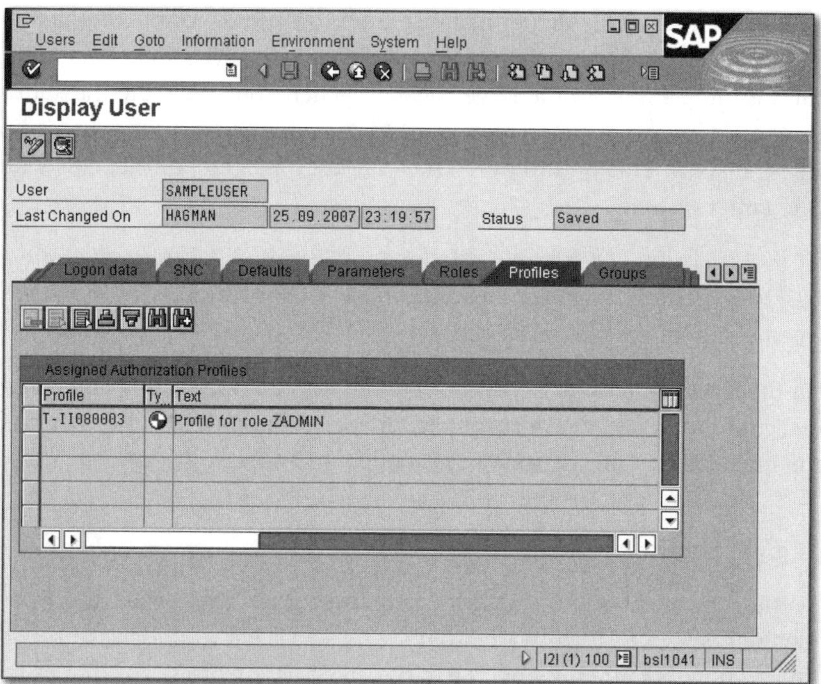


**Figure 8.14** After Comparison of the User Master

- **From role maintenance**
  Select **Automatic comparison of the user master when saving the role** from the SAP menu: **Role Maintenance (PFCG)** from **Utilities • Settings**. A comparison is then executed every time you save the role.
- **User comparison with the PFCG_TIME_DEPENDENCY report**
  Schedule this report as a background job periodically (daily at best). It's the only way to keep user authorizations up to date, especially on the consolidation and production systems, where profile changes are imported as transports. The report executes a complete user comparison and deletes any assignments that have become invalid.

### 8.3.8 Transporting Roles

You maintain roles in the development system and transport them from there to the consolidation and production system. All profiles that have been generated are also transported automatically. Accordingly, you should include a role in a transport request only after completing maintenance and generating the profiles. A follow-up generation of the profiles is unnecessary in the target system. When you create the transport request, you can decide if you want to include the user assignment in the transport. This option overwrites the user assignment that exists in the target system!

If you use central user administration (see Section 8.7.4, Administrating Users in Central User Administration), you may maintain user assignments only in the central system.

In the target system, the users receive the new authorizations only after execution of a user master comparison (see Section 8.3.7, User Assignment and User Comparison) and then log on again.

### 8.3.9 Upgrade Procedure

Authorization management has changed considerably across the various releases of SAP software. That's why you have to undertake some follow-up work after an upgrade to transfer existing profiles and roles to the current version of authorization management. You must first make a rough estimate of whether or not role maintenance was used in the initial release.

New implementation of role maintenance

If an SAP system that previously used the authorization concept without the profile generator is to be updated to a system with the profile generator, you will encounter some difficulties. In this case, SAP recommends a complete new implementation of authorization management.

For an initial release with role maintenance, you can compare existing authorizations with the newly delivered authorizations from the SAP Proposals (SU25) (by executing steps 2a to 2c of the checklist given when calling the transaction).

Time-consuming follow-up processing

Follow-up processing, which compares the existing authorizations and supplements them with new roles and profiles, can consume a great deal of time. SAP therefore delivers profile `SAP_NEW` with every update. It contains all authorizations for the new authorization checks in existing transactions. You can assign this profile temporarily to all users until the comparison of the authorization data is complete.

### 8.3.10 Troubleshooting and Traces

Particularly at the beginning of an implementation of SAP software, users often don't have all of the authorizations they need. Such users can call a list of missing authorizations right after a transaction terminates by using Authorization Data (SU53). The transaction shows the authorization required to execute the action.

System trace

With SAP System Trace (ST01) (see Section 9.5, Trace Files, in Chapter 9), you can record all authorization checks. All checked authorization objects, including the checked values, are recorded. You can select **Edit • Filter** from the menu to limit the trace to individual users, processes, or transactions. During an analysis of the trace, the administrator can then select an individual user, for example. SAP system trace is particularly helpful for checking all of the required authorizations for an action based on a successful authorization check.

## 8.4 Personal Settings

A user administrator usually maintains the data described so far for the user master record. Users from the application departments normally don't have authorization to maintain this data themselves, except for the company address. In addition to the data of the user master, users can define special settings that simplify their work with SAP software. For example, they can select their own start menus, logon language, standard printer, date format, or prepopulation for specific input fields. Users define their desired data with Own Data (SU3), which takes them to the **Maintain own user defaults** window, where they can select **Address**, **Defaults**, and **Parameters**. The tabs correspond to the tabs in User Maintenance (see Section 8.2.1, Creating a User). Figure 8.15 shows the maintenance screen for user defaults. This screen opens in a separate session so that the user doesn't have to terminate a work step that is already in process when maintaining the user defaults. The original session doesn't change.

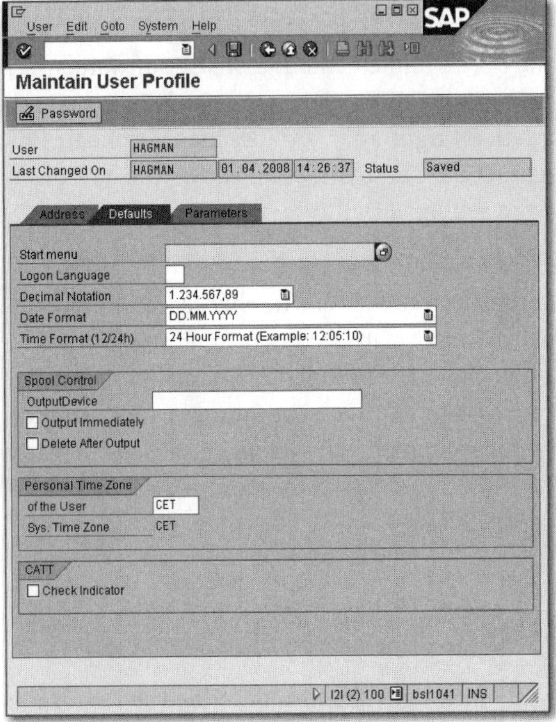


**Figure 8.15** Maintaining Defaults

Maintaining parameters

Maintaining parameters in user defaults enables all users to define individual proposed values for input fields. In other words, when they work with an application, users don't have to enter field values explicitly. The fields are populated according to their defaults. Default values can be defined for a company code, cost center, and other values. To display the required technical information for an input field, select the desired field in the screen and use F1 • **Technical information**. The **Parameter ID** field contains the parameter ID that you need for default parameters: **BUK** means company code, for example. In the personal user defaults, you can use this abbreviation to enter a value for prepopulation.

## 8.5 Internet Users

In many cases, it's possible to work anonymously on the Internet, especially when dealing only with the display of information. In the SAP system environment, however, access over the Internet usually requires an individual user name and password. That is a precondition when such access executes a transaction, such as issuing an order. Depending on the Internet application component (IAC) (see Section 1.3.2, Integrated Internet Transaction Server, in Chapter 1), setting up the normal dialog user for the activities on the Internet can be enough. Otherwise, you have to create and maintain an additional account, an *Internet user*. See the description of the IAC in use to determine which situation applies to you.

Reference user

Preparation of a normal dialog user for Internet access occurs with the familiar User Maintenance (see Section 8.2.1, Creating a User, in Chapter 1). In addition to the parameters discussed there, you can also assign an alias name to a user for logging on over the Internet. You should also assign one or more reference users to the user. You can use the reference user to enhance the authorizations of the user and give all Internet users identical authorizations.

If an IAC requires a separate Internet user, you can set one up as follows:

1. Select **Internet User (SU05)** (see Figure 8.16).

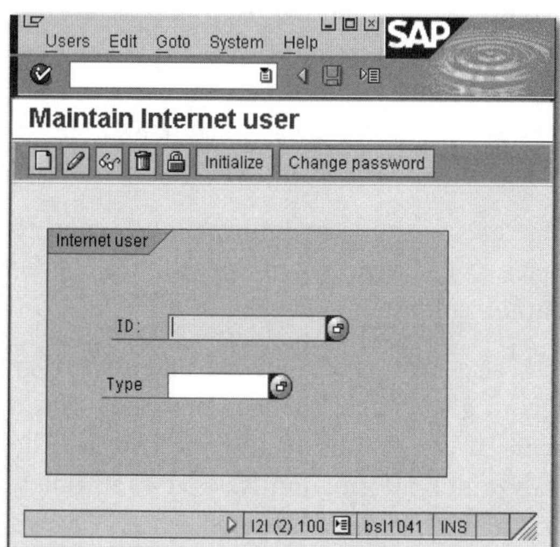


**Figure 8.16** Maintaining an Internet User

2. Enter the desired user ID.
3. Select the user type. The type essentially corresponds to a work area and limits the user's permissions. For example, **KNA1** means that the user can use only this Internet transaction. The type depends on the IACs that the user wants to execute.
4. Initialize the user.
5. The user is now active. The system automatically generates a password. You can change the password using **Change Password**.

Blocking

You can lock and unlock an Internet user. Up to now, no other data needs to be maintained for Internet users.

## 8.6 Information About Users and Authorizations

The greater the number of users working in an SAP system, the more difficult it becomes to manage the users and monitor users who are critical to security. SAP offers additional tools for these tasks.

### 8.6.1 Information System

Information System (SU01)

To give the system administrator an overview of users and authorizations, SAP offers a special **Information System (SU01) • Info • Infosystem.** It enables the administrator to analyze and compare users and the authorizations assigned by the system in many ways. Figure 8.17 shows the initial screen of the tool.

For example, administrators can use the User Information System to select all users who have been assigned a specific role or to find all of the roles that contain specific authorizations.

Analyzing change documents

The information system can also analyze change documents. Every change to a user master record generates a change document with a timestamp and the user name of the person making the change. The information system can analyze this information, so that at all times, administrators know who created, changed, or deleted a user. Change documents can't be deleted (they can be archived) and are therefore always available.

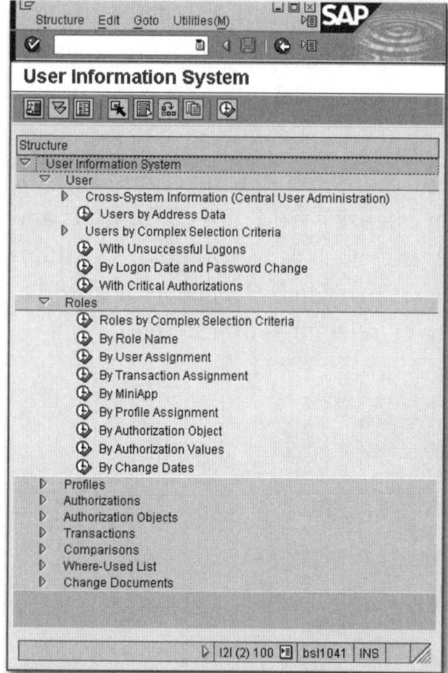


**Figure 8.17** User Information System

## 8.6.2 Security Audit Log

The security audit log offers an option for logging all of the security-related activities of users in the system. This feature is often required by auditors for users with especially critical authorizations to guarantee auditing acceptability. It's neither reasonable nor technically possible to log all actions of all users in this manner. Instead, the security audit log helps control critical users (emergency users or support users who have many authorizations) and the transparency of special, security-related events (e.g., unsuccessful logon attempts).

**Security Audit Configuration (SM19)**

To this end, the security audit log offers an option in the Security Audit Configuration (SM19) to define what types of activities to log for specific users so that the activities are permanently monitored. You analyze the audit logs according to various criteria with the Security Audit Log Analysis (SM20).

In Security Audit Configuration (SM19) (see Figure 8.18), you must first **create** a profile. All of the settings made in the following paragraphs are stored under this profile name.

Filters

You can use filters to define what events are to be logged in specific audit classes (dialog messages, transaction starts, or RFC function calls) for specific users in specific clients. You can use a wild card (*) for users and clients, but you can't use generic entries such as "SAMPLE*". The number of filters limits the number of users that can be logged with a profile. You must select each filter explicitly by selecting **Filter active**.

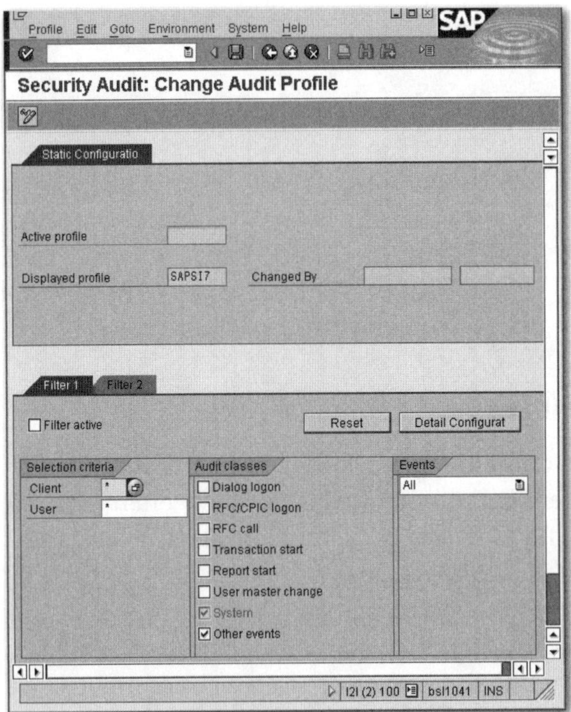


**Figure 8.18** Configuration of the Security Audit Log

Profile

After you set the filter criteria, save your profile. The icon list once again includes the additional icons for administration of the profile. To start logging according to the filter settings, you must then activate the selected profile from the menu or with the **Activate** icon. The activated profile is then used after the next system start.

As an alternative to static configuration, you can use the **Dyn. Configuration** tab to change the settings dynamically at runtime. Using filters to set parameters in dynamic configuration is identical to that of static configuration.

Files at the operating system level store the logged data. The Security Audit Analysis (SM20) enables you to select via the known filter parameters as well as by date and time or the user terminal. The selected data is formatted according to the format of the syslog (see Section 9.3 in Chapter 9).

**Profile parameters**

To use the security audit logs, the profile parameters must be activated and the number of filters that can be used must be defined. The most important parameters are the following:

- `rsau/enable`
  Activate the security audit log.
- `rsau/max_diskspace/local`
  Maximum amount of disk space that can be assigned to the audit files.
- `rsau/selection_slots`
  Number of filters permitted for the security audit log (maximum of five).

The organizational requirements for using the security audit log include consideration of local data protection laws and employee co-determination rights.

Depending on the settings for the filter criteria, the size of the analysis files can grow considerably. You should save the files at regular intervals and delete them at the operating system level.

## 8.7 Central User Administration

In a large system landscape with many users, the local form of user administration described so far can soon become very time-intensive. Maintenance of identical users in various systems and clients, the effort needed to synchronize the changes between systems, and the need for the administrator to log on to local systems make user administration tedious and error-prone. Central user administration (CUA) can help here. As of Basis Release 4.6, it has been possible to perform user maintenance in a defined client of a system and then distribute the data to additional clients in the same system or in other systems. The specially defined client is the *sender* (the central system); all other clients (child systems) are *receivers* of the data. Application link enabling (ALE) (see Section 13.2 in Chapter 13) is the technology used to exchange data. The clients among which the data is exchanged are set up and managed as logical systems.

After you set up CUA, you can create or delete users only in the central system. In CUA, you can decide if all of the attributes of the users should be managed only centrally, only locally, or in mixed operations. The required roles and authorizations must therefore be present and activated in all child systems. You need to manage each user only once — centrally — and as the administrator, you have a much better overview of all users and authorizations.

Decision-making criteria

The advantages of CUA are offset by the increased effort needed to set up the ALE scenario and to compare existing users and by the additional knowledge needed for administration. When making your decision on whether to use CUA, you can use the following points as criteria:

- Number of users per system
- Number of logical systems
- Frequency of changes to users and authorizations
- Length of time for a development (and thus the length of time during which developers are required as users in the systems)

Setting up CUA

Setting up CUA involves the following steps:

1. Set up an administration user on the central system.
2. Set up the ALE scenario:
   - Naming the logical systems
   - Assigning the logical systems to the clients
   - Creating the communication users (stored in the RFC interface) in all connected clients

- Creating the RFC interfaces
- Creating new model views of the ALE distribution model
- Maintaining and generating a partner agreement between all of the clients participating in CUA
- Distributing the model views

3. Activate CUA.
4. Set the distribution parameters for fields.
5. Distribute the company address.
6. Synchronize the users.

The following sections cover these steps in more detail.

### 8.7.1 Setting Up the ALE Scenario

Section 13.2 in Chapter 13 discusses the nature and operation of an ALE integrated scenario. This section covers only the specific settings that apply to CUA.

Required steps

All of the clients that participate in CUA must be set up as *logical systems* (see Section 13.2.3, Configuration, in Chapter 13), which are then assigned to the clients with Client Administration (SCC4). To forward the data from the central system to the child systems (or vice versa), you must create an RFC connection for each direction. RFC connections are not needed between child systems. Note that the client in which CUA occurs must also be connected to CUA as a child system. A new model view for ALE defines the data that should be exchanged between the logical systems. For CUA, that data is the predefined business objects USER and UserCompany, with distribution method `Clone`.

Finally, you generate the partner agreement and distribute it to all logical systems.

### 8.7.2 Activating and Configuring Central User Administration

Assigning the ALE model view

To activate CUA, you must assign an ALE model view to CUA. Enter the name of your model view in CUA Distribution Model (SCUA), and select **Create**. In the next screen, enter all of the child systems of your CUA and save them. After you save the distribution model of CUA again, you can distribute the model to the child systems with menu path **Distribution Model • Distribute Distribution Model**, which activates CUA.

The central configuration aspect is defining which user attributes should be maintained in specific systems — the central system or child systems. In Customizing, you can use Distribution Parameters (SCUM) for each user property to define whether or not it should be maintained (see Figure 8.19).

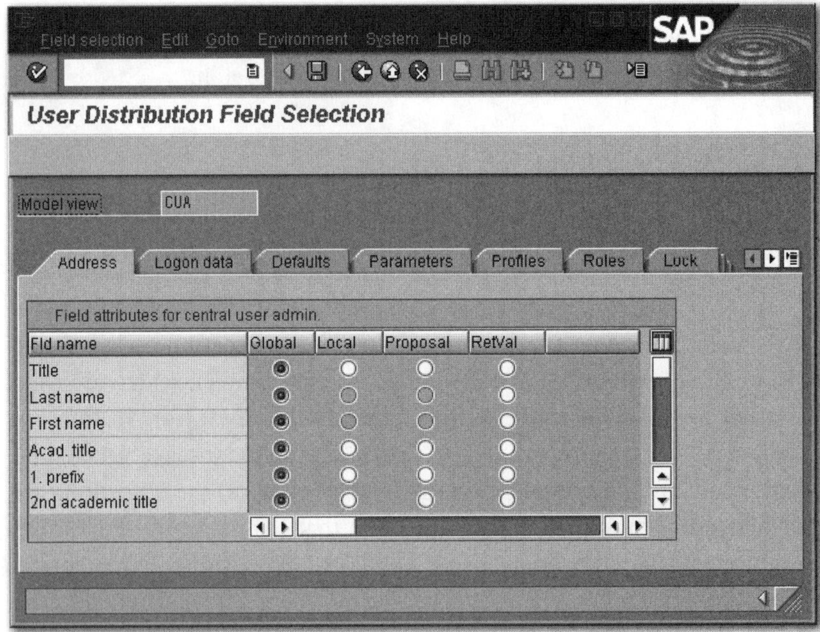


**Figure 8.19** Definition of Distribution Parameters

Table 8.6 lists the options available to the administrator.

| Option | Maintenance and Synchronization |
|---|---|
| **Global** | The field can be maintained only in the central system. Changes are then distributed automatically. |
| **Local** | Data is maintained only in the child systems and isn't distributed to other systems. |

**Table 8.6** Options for Field Selection

| Option | Maintenance and Synchronization |
|---|---|
| **Proposal** | With this option, only a proposed value is maintained and distributed when creating the user. Additional maintenance occurs in the child systems. Additional changes are not distributed. |
| **RetVal** | The value can be maintained centrally and locally. A local change can be returned to the central system and distributed to all child systems from there. |
| **Everywhere** | The value can be maintained centrally and locally. Central changes are distributed to child systems, but changes in the child systems are not distributed to the central system.<br>This option is available only for a limited number of fields. |

**Table 8.6** Options for Field Selection (Cont.)

### 8.7.3 Deleting the Central User Administration

From CUA, you can delete individual child systems and all of CUA by executing report `RSDELCUA` for the individual child system or the central system. You thereby remove the assignment of your distribution model to CUA and deactivate CUA.

Cleanup

If you delete all of CUA, you should then clean things up:

- Delete the partner agreement.
- Delete the ALE distribution model.
- Delete the RFC connections.
- Lock the communication user.

If you delete a single child system, you must limit the partner agreement, ALE model, and RFC interfaces accordingly.

### 8.7.4 Administrating Users in the Central User Administration

User Transfer (SCUG)

After you set up CUA and add new child systems, you must transfer the existing users in the child systems to the central system. You can use the Transfer Users (SCUG) function in the central system. After you select the child systems, all of the users of the child systems are displayed according to the following:

- **New user**
  This user exists only in the child system, not in CUA. All parameters are transferred to CUA during a transfer.
- **Identical user**
  A user with the same user name and real name (the real name consists of the first name and family name) exists in the CUA and the child system. The user can be transferred from the child system to CUA and distributed from there, or the user is deleted in the child system, and the definition is redistributed from CUA.
- **Different users**
  The same user name is contained in CUA and the child system but with different real names. You must decide which user to maintain further; you might have to create a new user in the central system.
- **Already a central user**
  This user is already registered identically in CUA and is managed centrally there.

You can transfer individual users or all users to CUA. The data from the central system is taken and distributed for all users who are not *new users*. If the *different users* should actually use two different users, they must be recreated in the central system, and the users with identical names must be deleted in the child system.

You maintain users in CUA with User Maintenance (SU01) (see Section 8.2.1, Creating a User). You can't create any new users in the child systems, and you can change only the fields that are ready for input that, according to your definition of the Distribution Parameters (SCUM) (see Section 8.7.2, Activating and Configuring Central User Administration), may still be maintained locally. In the central system, User Maintenance (SU01) now displays the familiar tabs and the new tab System, on which you can enter the systems to distribute the user to. User data can be defined only once; it's then identical in all child systems. For roles and profiles, the assignment for each child system can occur separately.

## 8.8 Directory Services

Redundant data

In heterogeneous system landscapes, the integration of SAP systems becomes increasingly important — and it also affects user administration. A great deal of user data is required in SAP and non-SAP systems, so it's often stored redundantly. Maintaining redundant data is cumbersome and not always synchronous.

LDAP

Directory services offer an option for various centrally managed applications within a software landscape to access data used in common. A directory service is similar to an IT address book. If a directory service works with the *standard Lightweight Directory Access Protocol* (LDAP), you can use the LDAP connector to implement data exchange with the directory service as of Basis Release 6.10. With this approach, you store central user data only once in a central directory service and can use LDAP synchronization to compare it directly with the data in an SAP system or in CUA. From the central directory service, you can distribute the data to the child systems of the CUA — even to those running lower Basis releases.

## 8.9 Tips

- **Maintenance of communications data**
  When managing communications data, especially fax numbers, in User Maintenance (SU01), you must be sure that the data corresponds to SAP conventions. Entry is required without leading zeros, with separation of the company number and the direct number, and without a country ID (which you can later select with **Additional Communication**). If you do not follow the conventions, SAPconnect (see Section 13.4, SAPconnect, in Chapter 13) can't analyze the data.
- **High memory use because of large user menus**
  Buffered tables store the user menus. Many users with large user menus can cause extremely high memory consumption. In these cases, you must reduce the size of the user menus or completely avoid user menus for individual users.

- **Client for central user administration**
  The authorization concept for CUA becomes much simpler when you set up CUA in a separate client or a separate system, such as a dedicated monitoring system, for example, the SAP Solution Manager.

## 8.10 Transactions and Menu Paths

**Authorization Data**: SAP Menu • System • Utilities • Display Authorization Check (SU53)

**Client Administration**: SAP Menu • Tools • Administration • Administration • Client Administration • Client Maintenance (SCC4)

**Company Address**: SAP Menu • Tools • Administration • User Maintenance • User • Environment • Maintain Company Address (SUCOMP)

**CUA Distribution Model**: ALE Customizing (SALE) • Configure Predefined ALE Business Processes • Set up Central User Administration • Select Model Views for Central Administration (SCUA)

**Distribution Model**: ALE Customizing (SALE) • Business Process Modeling • Maintain Distribution Model and Distribute Views (BD64)

**Distribution Parameters**: ALE Customizing (SALE) • Configure Predefined ALE Business Processes • Set up Central User Administration • Set Distribution Parameters for Fields (SCUM)

**Information System**: SAP Menu • Tools • Administration • User Maintenance • Information System (SU01 • Info • Infosystem)

**Internet User**: SAP Menu • Tools • Administration • User Maintenance • Internet User (SU05)

**License Administration Workbench (LAW)**: (LICENSE_ADMIN)

**Mass Change**: SAP Menu • Tools • Administration • User Maintenance • User • Environment • Mass Change (SU10)

**Object Classes**: SAP Menu • Tools • ABAP Workbench • Development • Other Tools • Authorization Objects • Objects (SU21)

**Own Data**: SAP Menu • System • User Defaults • Own Data (SU3)

**Partner Profile**: ALE Customizing (SALE) • Business Process Modeling • Maintain Distribution Model and Distribute Views (BD64) • Environment • Generate Partner Profile (BD82)

**Role Maintenance**: SAP Menu • Tools • Administration • User Maintenance • Role Administration • Roles (PFCG)

**SAP Implementation Guide**: SAP Menu • Tools • Customizing • IMG • Edit Project (SPRO)

**SAP System Trace:** SAP Menu • Tools • Administration • Monitor • Traces • SAP System Trace (ST01)

**SAP Proposals:** SAP Implementation Guide (SPRO) • SAP Customizing Implementation Guide • SAP NetWeaver • Application Server System Administration • Users and Authorizations • Maintain Authorizations and Profiles with Profile Generator • Edit SAP Test Status and Field Values • Copy SAP Test Status and Field Values (SU25)

**Security Audit Log A**nalysis SAP Menu • Tools • Administration • Monitor • Security Audit Log • Analysis (SM20)

**Security Audit Configuration**: SAP Menu • Tools • Administration • Monitor • Security Audit Log • Configuration (SM19)

**System Measurement**: SAP Menu • Tools • Administration • Administration • System Measurement (USMM)

**User Group**: SAP Menu • Tools • Administration • User Maintenance • User Groups (SUGR)

**User Maintenance**: SAP Menu • Tools • Administration • User Maintenance • Users (SU01)

**User Transfer:** ALE Customizing (SALE) • Modeling and Implementing Business Processes • Configure Predefined ALE Business Processes • Cross-application Business Processes • Central User Administration • Transfer Users and Company Addresses from New Systems (SCUG)

## 8.11 Additional Documentation

### Quicklinks

- SAP support portal, alias *licenseauditing*
- SAP support portal, alias *security*
- SAP support portal, alias *securityguide*

### SAP Notes

Table 8.7 provides an overview of important SAP Notes related to user administration.

| Contents | SAP Note |
|---|---|
| High Memory Consumption with Easy Access Menu | 203617 |
| CUA: Tips on Problem Analysis | 333441 |
| CUA: Minimal Authorizations for Communication Users | 492589 |
| CUA: Tips on Optimizing the Performance of ALE Distribution | 399271 |

**Table 8.7** SAP Notes Concerning User Administration

## 8.12 Questions

1. **Which statement is correct?**

   A user of type *system*

   a. can log on without a password over an RFC interface.

   b. has a password, but the settings for the validity period do not apply to it.

   c. can't log on in dialog mode.

2. **Which statement is correct?**

   a. Exactly one role can be assigned to a user.

   b. Several roles can be assigned to a user.

3. **What can be transported in a role transport?**
   a. The authorization profiles for the role
   b. The definition of the users
   c. The assignment of roles to users
4. **The authorizations of a role have been expanded. At what point can a user to whom the role was already assigned and who has already logged on work with the changed authorizations?**
   a. The user can use the changed authorizations immediately.
   b. The user can use the changed authorizations after a user comparison.
   c. The user must log on again and can then work with the changed authorizations.
   d. A user comparison must occur first. The user must then log on again to be able to work with the changed authorizations.

*The routine activities of a system administrator include monitoring and controlling individual SAP systems from a technical point of view. These tasks are as essential as the implementation of system settings because they considerably contribute to uninterrupted operation thanks to their proactive nature. In this chapter, we'll focus on the tools for system monitoring and their operation. We'll also develop a list of regularly recurring administrative tasks.*

# 9 System Monitoring

In SAP systems, you are already provided with numerous functions for monitoring and configuring the technical system status. Many of these transactions are used by the system administrators on a daily basis.

In the first sections of this chapter, we'll present the most critical transactions for system monitoring. You'll learn more about log and trace files that you can use for error analysis. We'll also discuss the specifics of ITS and ICM administration. Moreover, we'll explain some tools and utilities that will facilitate your daily administration work.

## 9.1 Server and Process Overviews

In the server overview, the process overview (which we've already briefly discussed), and the Control Panel (see Section 7.3, Control Panel, in Chapter 7) you get a detailed overview of the status of the instances in an SAP system and the functions of the SAP work processes. In this chapter, the descriptions will be supplemented by some details that are critical for the system administrator.

The Server Overview (SM51) shows all available instances of an SAP system (see Figure 9.1), including details about the computer and the Server overview type of configured work processes. The instance status is indicated as follows:

- **Initial**
  The application server has logged on to the message server but can't be accessed yet.
- **Starting**
  The configured work processes of the application server are starting up. You can't process any orders yet.
- **Active**
  The application server is in the regular status and processes its requests.
- **Passive**
  The application server is to be deactivated. It processes the current requests but doesn't accept any new requests.
- **Shutdown**
  The application server is shut down and doesn't process any requests.
- **Stop**
  The application server has no connection to the message server and can't be accessed.

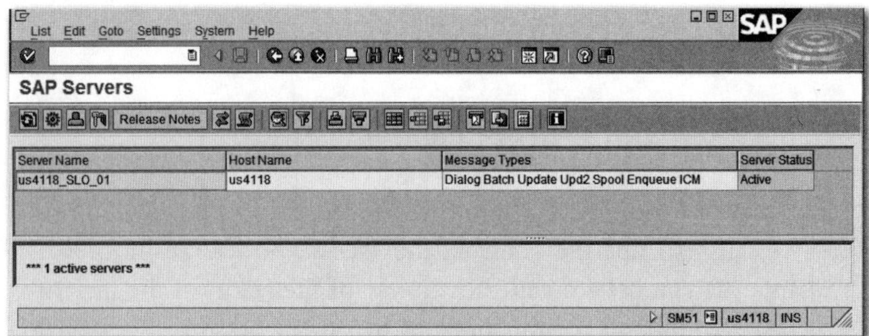


**Figure 9.1** Server Overview

You can request additional information for each list entry or start actions using the icons or the menu item **Goto**. These functions are detailed in Table 9.1.

| Menu Item Goto | Icon | Action |
|---|---|---|
| Processes | | Navigates to the process overview for the selected instance. |
| User | | Navigates to the process overview for the selected instance. |
| SNC Status | | Information about the SNC status, such as activating SNC, path to GSS library, handling of unsecure connections. |
| Release Info | Release information | Detailed release information (SAPKernel, database, operating system), as of Web AS 6.10 additional information about the message server. |
| Environment | | Environment variables of the computer, as of Web AS 6.10 integrated in the **Server Information** selection. |
| Remote Login | | Login at the selected instance (the current computer is displayed in the status bar). |
| System Log | | Navigates to the system log for the selected instance. |
| SAP Directories | | Navigates to the SAP Directory display for the selected instance. |
| OS Monitor | | Navigates to the OS Monitor (ST06, OS6) for the selected instance. |
| Communication Table | | Displays all CPI-C connections (client and server). |
| Queue Info | | Information about the request queue: Number of configure processes per request type and statistic data about the use, as of Web AS 6.10 integrated in the **Server Information** selection. |

**Table 9.1** Options in the Server Overview

| Menu Item Goto | Icon | Action |
|---|---|---|
| Host Name Buffer | | Entries in the *hosts* and *services* network configuration files can be activated without restarting the instance. |
| Gateway Monitor | | Navigates to the Gateway Monitor (SMGW) for the selected instance. |
| Server Information | | As of Web AS 6.10, the previously mentioned items **Environment**, **Queue-info**, and **Communication Table** are combined. In addition, you are provided with options to log on to the application server (**logon data**), and a connection test (**connection test**). Using the **trace search** enables you to search the developer traces for the selected instance according to the given text pattern. |

**Table 9.1** Options in the Server Overview (Cont.)

Message Server Overview

Similar to the server overview, the web application server was also provided with a Message Server Overview (SMMS). The specific functions for analyzing the message server can be found in the **Goto** menu item. In addition to the information available via the server overview, the following data is displayed and actions are enabled in the new overview:

- Display hardware key.
- Display all and change selected message server-specific system parameters.
- Display statistic data, such as number of logins, received requests, and written/read bytes.
- Display developer trace file, *dev_ms*, of the message server, and change the current trace level without restarting the instance.
- Stop application servers with or without processing the requests located in the dispatcher queue; target status: *shutdown*.

- Deactivate application servers with processing the requests located in the dispatcher queue; target status: *passive*.
- Reactivate deactivated application servers.

Process overview

You can navigate to the comprehensive process overview of an individual instance by calling the respective functions in the server overview or directly by using Process Overview (SM50). The following information is displayed in table form:

- **Internal process number**
  The system uses this number internally, for example, to assign messages to the processes. You can find the process number in the name of the associated developer trace.
- **Process Type**
  - **DIA**: Dialog work process.
  - **UPD**: Update process for time-critical changes to the database (V1 update, see Section 2.3, Update, in Chapter 2).
  - **UPD2**: Update process for non-time critical changes to the database (V2 update, see Section 2.3, Update, in Chapter 2).
  - **ENQ**: Enqueue work process for handling SAP locks.
  - **BTC**: Background work process.
  - **SPO**: Spool work process.
- **Process number at the operating system level (PID)**
  If required, you can terminate the process by entering the process number and using operating system tools.
- **Status of the process**
  - **active**: The process currently processes a request.
  - **waiting**: The process is free and is waiting for new requests.
  - **stops**: The process is currently assigned to an individual user. This is the normal status for system operation, but it can lead to performance problems if too many processes have this status.
  - **finished**: The process has been finished due to an error and hasn't restarted yet.

- **Reasons for the stop status**
  The reason is given for processes in the *stops* status. The usual stop reasons are:
  - **CPIC**: Work process waits for the CPI-C message.
  - **DEBUG**: Work process is in debugging mode.
  - **LOCK**: Work process has been exclusively assigned to a system analysis by a user.
  - **NUM**: Work process waits for a response from a number range server.
  - **OS**: Work process waits for the processing of an operating system command.
  - **PRIV**: Work process works exclusively for a user.
  - **SLEEP**: Work process waits due to resource bottleneck.
  - **VB**: Work process waits for the completion of a synchronous update request.
- **Start behavior**
  If a work process fails, the dispatcher of the instance will immediately try to replace the lost work process through restart of a corresponding process. If the work process cancels already during the startup phase due to a severe problem, the system sets the restart value to *no* to prevent futile process restarts.
- **Number of ABENDs**
  The **Error** column indicates the number of ABENDs of the work process since the last start of the instance.
- **Semaphore**
  If a work process terminates because it waits for the release of a semaphore, the number of this semaphore is indicated and highlighted in red in this column. You can use this information to analyze exceptional waiting situations. If the number of the semaphore is green, it's held by the work process. Work processes use the semaphore mechanism to reserve resources.

- **Accumulated runtime of the recently executed action in seconds**
  This is the runtime (in seconds) of the active action. If another report/program will be started or the action switches to a different work process, the runtime is set back to 0 and starts counting from the beginning.
- **Currently executing report**
  This is the name of the ABAP report/program that is processed by this work process.
- **Currently assigned user including the client**
  These two columns show the name of the user who is executing the report/program and the client in which the report is being processed.
- **Currently implemented action and processed table**
  You can use the output in the Process Overview (SM50) using **List • CPU** to extend the information of the previous CPU utilization through processes. Figure 9.2 shows an extract from a Process Overview.

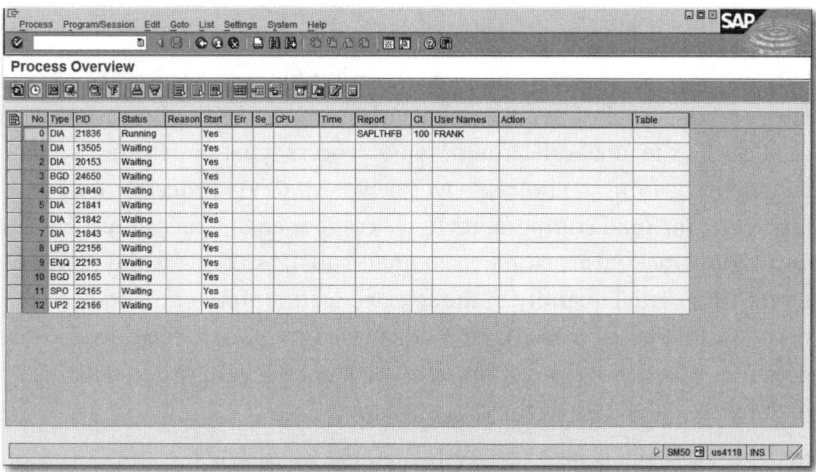


| No. | Type | PID | Status | Reason | Start | Err | Se | CPU | Time | Report | Cl. | User Names | Action | Table |
|---|---|---|---|---|---|---|---|---|---|---|---|---|---|---|
| 0 | DIA | 21836 | Running | | Yes | | | | | SAPLTHFB | 100 | FRANK | | |
| 1 | DIA | 13505 | Waiting | | Yes | | | | | | | | | |
| 2 | DIA | 20153 | Waiting | | Yes | | | | | | | | | |
| 3 | BGD | 24650 | Waiting | | Yes | | | | | | | | | |
| 4 | BGD | 21840 | Waiting | | Yes | | | | | | | | | |
| 5 | DIA | 21841 | Waiting | | Yes | | | | | | | | | |
| 6 | DIA | 21842 | Waiting | | Yes | | | | | | | | | |
| 7 | DIA | 21843 | Waiting | | Yes | | | | | | | | | |
| 8 | UPD | 22156 | Waiting | | Yes | | | | | | | | | |
| 9 | ENQ | 22163 | Waiting | | Yes | | | | | | | | | |
| 10 | BGD | 20165 | Waiting | | Yes | | | | | | | | | |
| 11 | SPO | 22165 | Waiting | | Yes | | | | | | | | | |
| 12 | UP2 | 22166 | Waiting | | Yes | | | | | | | | | |

**Figure 9.2** Process Overview

The Process Overview enables you, for example, to identify reports with exceptionally long runtimes. Additionally, using the **Process • Detail** function or double-clicking on the appropriate row gives you detailed information about the processing step. You are shown the currently processed table and the resources already consumed.

Debugging mode

For experts, the debugging mode can be very interesting and informative for executing an ABAP program. You can activate this mode for the selected process using **Program/Mode • Program • Debugging**. You navigate to the gradual execution of the instructions of the respective program. The control of running the program is passed on to the user. Executing a program in the debugging mode is very resource-intensive and may only be used in test or development systems.

For serious problems, you can cancel or restart the dialog or background work process (**Process • Cancel with Core, Process • Cancel without Core, Restart after Error • Yes**). The transaction affected is rolled back. The user generally receives a message that the process has been cancelled by the system administration. Update or enqueue processes should never be cancelled manually because otherwise logical inconsistencies might occur in the database.

Each work process writes its own error log file (see Section 9.5, Trace Files), whose level of detail can be customized according to various criteria, such as manual selection or work process type, by setting a system parameter or from the Process Overview (SM50) via **Process • Trace**. By restricting the **load components** (trace components), you can restrict the writing of trace information to defined subareas. The **display components** are a partial quantity of the selected load components and describe the trace information that is to be displayed by the collected load components. Work processes running with a trace level greater than 1 are highlighted in yellow in the process list.

Global Process Overview

In addition to the local Process Overview just described, another Process Overview is available, that is the Global Process Overview (SM66) (see Figure 9.3). Using this transaction enables you to observe the work process load of all active instances throughout the system. The display can be processed, filtered, and sorted according to different criteria.

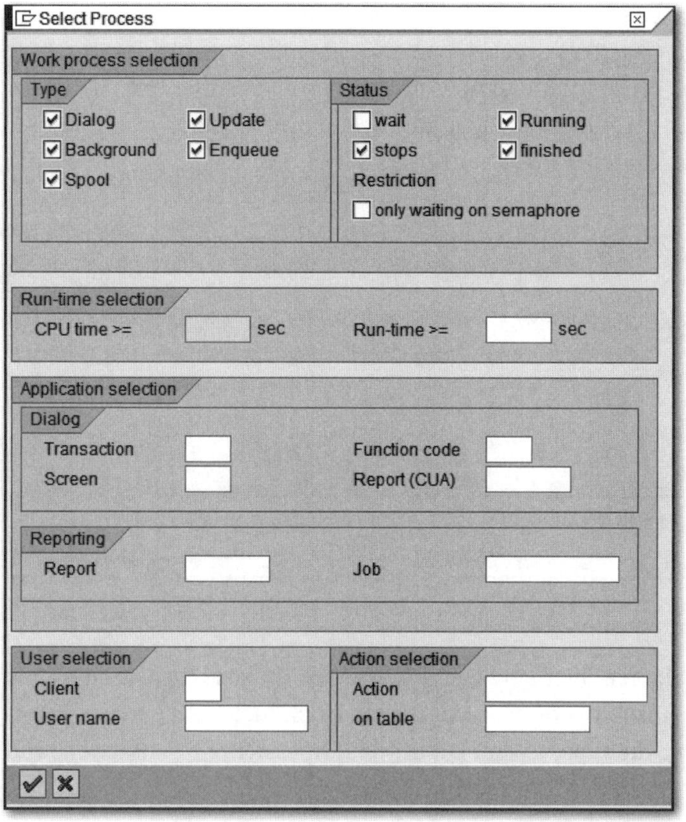

Figure 9.3 Process Selection in SM66

## 9.2 User Overviews

For additional analyses, you can navigate from the Server Overview (SM51) to User Overview (SM04) via **Goto • User** or by calling this action directly.

User activities at local instance

The overview displayed in Figure 9.4, indicates the current user activities at the local instance. For each logged-on user, the system displays at which terminal he logged on, which transaction he is currently processing, how many sessions he has opened, and when the last dialog step was implemented. For selected users, you can activate a user trace (**User**

• **Trace** • **Activate**), in which all actions of the users are logged. You can evaluate and deactivate the user trace analogously. Activating the user traces makes sense if you want to analyze problems that only occur for individual users. If required, you can delete user sessions from the user overview or compulsorily log off users.

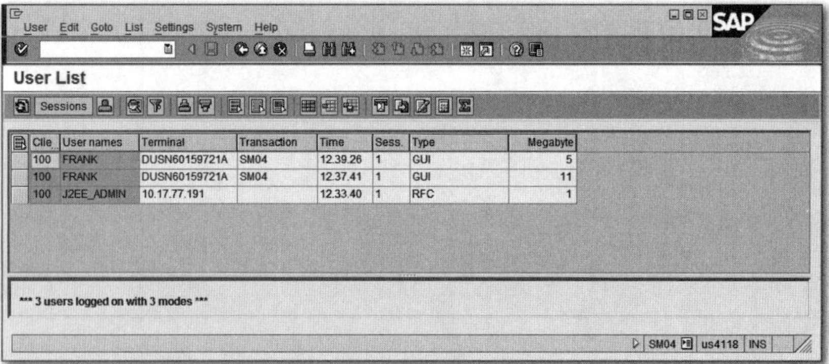


**Figure 9.4** Local User Overview

**Global User Overview**

In the Global User Overview (SM66), you see all users logged-on to one of the active instances of the respective system, including detailed information about the type, log-on client, the implemented transaction, and the time of the last dialog step (see Figure 9.5).

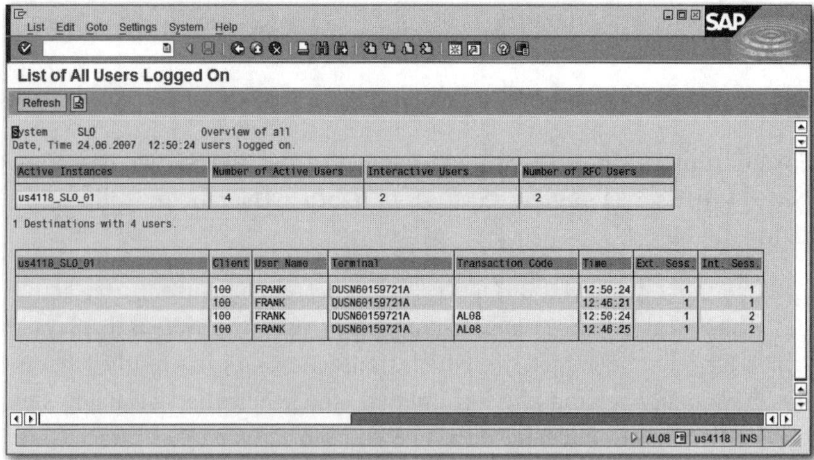


**Figure 9.5** Global User Overview

## 9.3 System Log

The most critical log

The system log is the most critical log in the normal operation of an SAP system and is the starting point for problem analysis. In the system log, messages, warnings, and errors are highlighted in different colors.

Therefore, checking the System Log (SM21) is one of the daily tasks of the system administrator. The system log is written locally for each application server, namely in the *SLOG<instance number>.log* file, in the subdirectory *log* of the instance directory, if not otherwise defined by means of a system parameter. Each log entry occupies 192 bytes, so that the standard size of 500KB corresponds to 2,065 entries. First, the log file is written initially; when a defined limit has been reached, each new entry replaces the oldest entry of the file. Or you can define a backup file to which the content of the actual log file is moved when the maximum size has been reached. Writing the log file is then started again in an empty file.

**Critical Parameters for the Local System Log**

- `rslg/max_diskspace/local`
  Size of the local *SysLog* file (bytes)
- `rslg/local/file`
  Name of the local *SysLog* file

Global system log

For UNIX systems, you are also provided with a *global system log*. The entries of all local system logs of the configured instances can be combined in this log. The respective file in the *global* subdirectory of the system directory is called *SLOGJ* by default. In contrast to the local system log, the central system log is automatically moved to a backup file, *SLOGJ0*, when the file is completely filled; the old *SLOGJ0* is overwritten. You can control the size of the global system log using the `rslg/max_diskspace/global` system parameter. This value relates to the total of *SLOGJ* and *SLOGJ0* and is set to 2MB by default.

**Critical Parameters for the Global System Log**

- `rslg/max_diskspace/central`
  Size of the global *SysLog* file (bytes)
- `rslg/central/file`
  Name of the global *SysLog* file

If you want to use a global system log, you must implement the following steps:

1. Determine the instance for which the global system log is to be held.
2. Set the necessary log parameters in the instance profiles.
3. Start a send process to all instances involved.
4. Start a collection process on the instance defined in step 1.

Selecting the system log

When starting the analysis of log entries using the System Log (SM21), you can initially select the system log that you want to view. The menu entry, **SysLog • Select**, provides the following options:

- **Local SysLog**
  Standard setting; the system log entries of the logon instance are displayed.
- **Remote SysLog**
  The system log entries of the instance selected in the instance name field are displayed.
- **All remote SysLogs**
  The system log entries of all accessible instances are displayed.
- **Central SysLog**
  The entries of the central system log are displayed. This option is only available if you set up a central system log. The entries of the local system log are always up to date; the entries of the central system log are transferred at regular intervals and might have historical statuses.

Evaluating the system log

To evaluate the System Log (SM21), you are provided with a wide range of selection criteria that can be further extended if you use the expert mode that is available at **Process • Expert Mode**. After optionally restricting the

- time frame
- user
- transaction code
- process type
- problem category
- other criteria in the expert mode

and after reading the system log, you'll see a list of all messages that fulfill your selection criteria.

Figure 9.6 shows an extract of the local system log of the SLO system. You can analyze the problems' causes by double-clicking on the entry row or via **Process • Details** from the list display. In the standard list layout, the system shows the timestamp, the affected work process, client, user, transaction code, message number, and a short text. Optionally, you can supplement this preparation by additional information, for example, the program name.

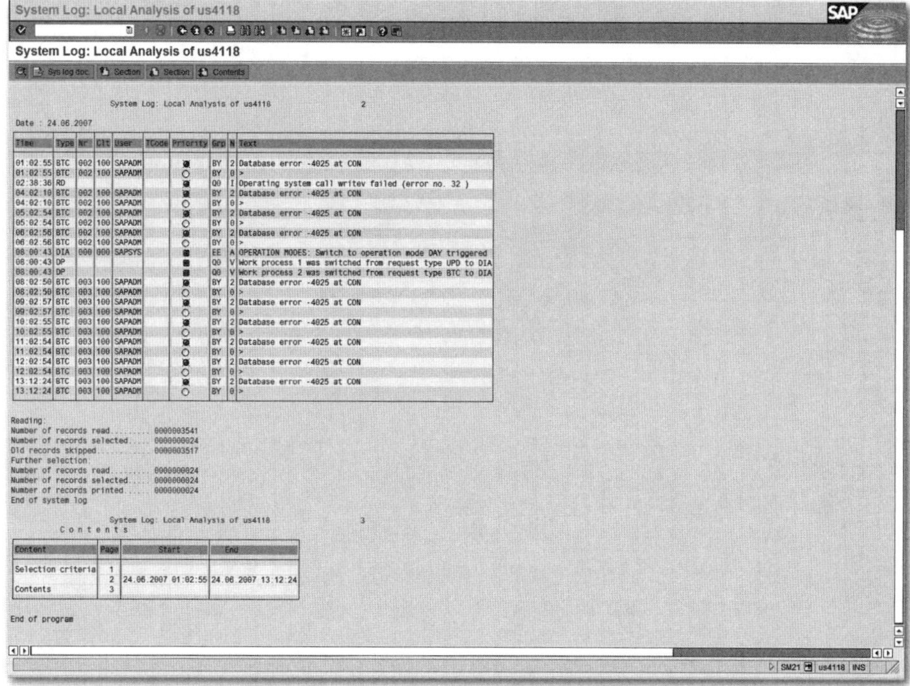


**Figure 9.6** Local System Log

## 9.4 Analysis of Runtime Errors

Short dump

If the ABAP program is terminated during the execution, a *short dump* is created and stored for the occurred error. Within a development system, a dump is a critical utility for programming; evaluating, and correcting an error, which is primarily the task of the developers.

In a short dump, the system information at the time of the program termination, the termination point in the source text, and other information that can be used for analyzing the error, is stored. In live systems, in which no development takes places, runtime errors are not supposed to occur. Therefore, the system administrator must check on a daily basis whether program terminations occurred, and if so, why. For this purpose, you can use the Dump Analysis (ST22). For each program termination, the systems stores information on the termination point, the error type, and other critical information. This includes the time of termination, and information on the SAP releases used, the relational database management system (RDBMS), operating system, and variable assignment. The users are provided with as much assistance for troubleshooting as possible (see Figure 9.7).

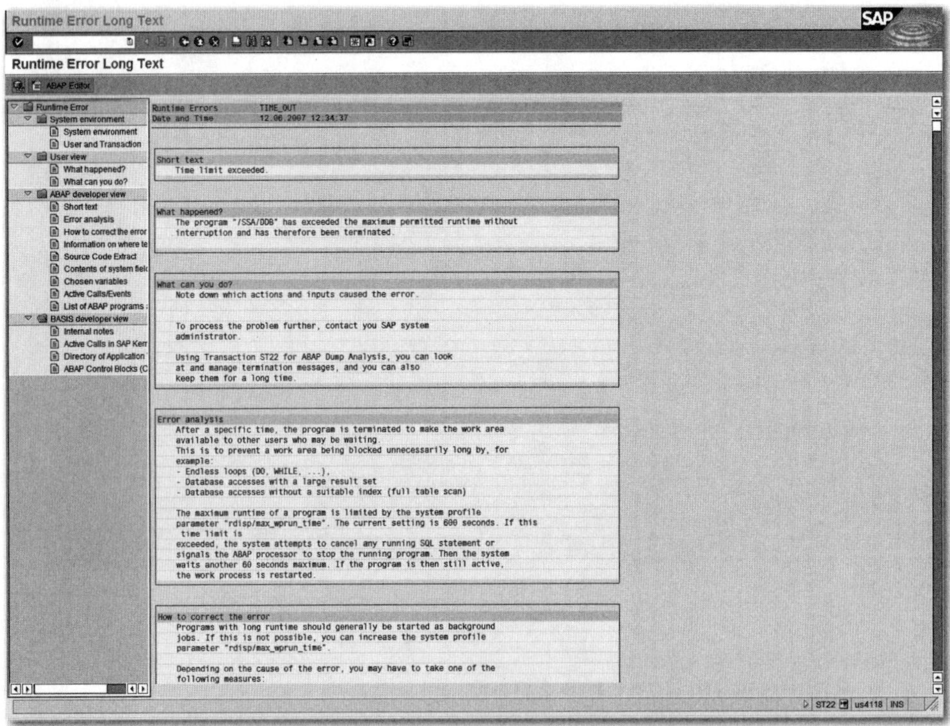


**Figure 9.7** Dump Analysis

To remove evaluated and historical runtime error records, you should implement the `RSSNAPDL` report at regular intervals. If you want to exclude short dumps from deletion because they haven't been analyzed yet, you can highlight these entries via **Short Dump • Retain/Release**.

## 9.5 Trace Files

To enable a detailed analysis of error situations, dedicated log and trace files are kept in multiple components of the runtime environment. Depending on the respective problem, the system administrator can find additional information here that can also be accessed, for example, if the database or SAP system doesn't run.

Whereas the application specialist's job is to interpret the trace content application specifically, the system administrator is responsible for managing the required system settings and resources. In particular, this means doing the following:

- Providing sufficient disk space for the output
- Cleaning up trace files in compliance with the system after the analysis has been completed
- Customizing the trace levels used, in particular, resetting the trace level or deactivating the trace after the analysis has been completed

Developer traces

For the processes of each application server, a corresponding error log file, *developer trace*, is written. This includes the *dev_<xx>* files in the *work* subdirectory of the instance directory. You can find the most essential traces in Table 9.2.

| File Name | Corresponding Process |
|---|---|
| *dev_disp* | Dispatcher |
| *dev_icm* | Internet Communication Manager |
| *dev_ms* | Message server |
| *dev_rd* | Gateway read process |
| *dev_rfc* | RFCs of external functions |
| *dev_rfc<n>* | RFC of the work process with number *n* |
| *dev_tp* | `tp` and `R3trans` |
| *dev_w<n>* | Work process with number *n* |

**Table 9.2** Developer Traces

The number of the work process is identical to the number indicated in the Process Overview (SM50).

These files are particularly essential if the instance can't be started or if processes terminate during the running operation. The logging level can be set for each instance using the `rdisp/TRACE` parameter. Additionally, you have the option of dynamically customizing individual processes from the process overview in the SAP system (see Section 9.1, Server and Process Overviews) or from the command field entry.

Trace level

Configurable levels of detail are listed here:

- **Trace level 0**
  Tracing is deactivated.
- **Trace level 1 (default setting)**
  Error messages are recorded in the trace files.
- **Trace level 2**
  Trace is full.
- **Trace level 3**
  In addition to error and action messages, the content of data blocks is recorded in the trace files.

The trace level should only be increased for a concrete error analysis because the write load for the files increases proportionally to the logging level. In a live system, the login level of normal operation isn't greater than 1.

To restart the SAP system, the *dev_<xx>* developer traces are created anew; the last version of the backup files, *dev_<xx>.old*, is stored.

You can analyze the developer traces at the operating system level or from the SAP system using the Error Log Files (ST11), Process Overview (SM50) or SAP Directories (AL11). Selecting the SAP Directories (AL11) enables you to view the files within the SAP frontend. By default, all files are accessible in the SAP directories. If you use the **Configure** icon displayed in Figure 9.8, you can provide additional directories under a logical name.

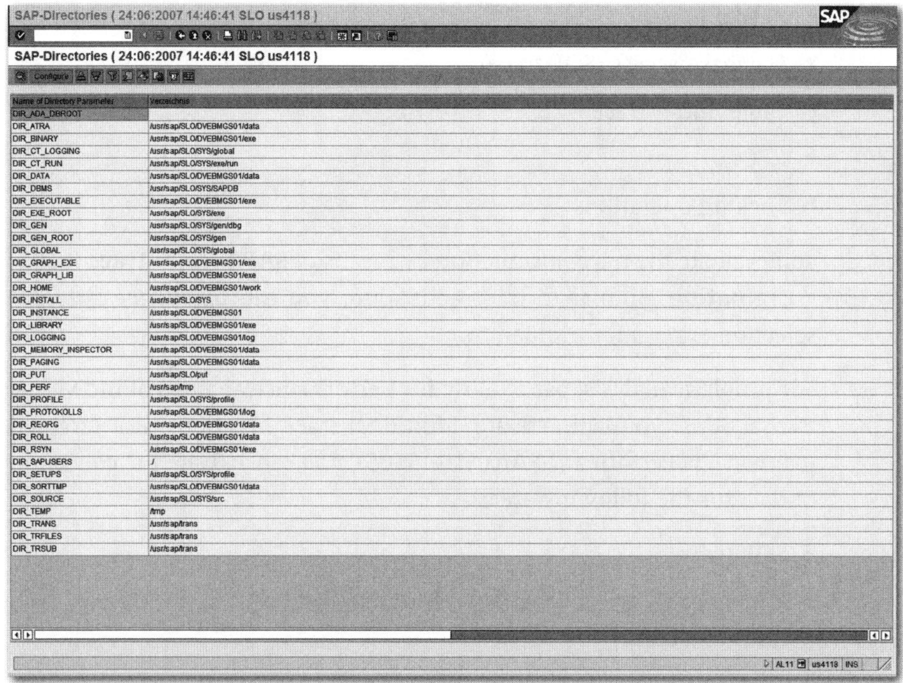

SAP-Directories ( 24:06:2007 14:46:41 SLO us4118 )

| Name of Directory Parameter | Verzeichnis |
|---|---|
| DIR_ADA_DBROOT | |
| DIR_ATRA | /usr/sap/SLO/DVEBMGS01/data |
| DIR_BINARY | /usr/sap/SLO/DVEBMGS01/exe |
| DIR_CT_LOGGING | /usr/sap/SLO/SYS/global |
| DIR_CT_RUN | /usr/sap/SLO/SYS/exe/run |
| DIR_DATA | /usr/sap/SLO/DVEBMGS01/data |
| DIR_DBMS | /usr/sap/SLO/SYS/SAPDB |
| DIR_EXECUTABLE | /usr/sap/SLO/DVEBMGS01/exe |
| DIR_EXE_ROOT | /usr/sap/SLO/SYS/exe |
| DIR_GEN | /usr/sap/SLO/SYS/gen/dbg |
| DIR_GEN_ROOT | /usr/sap/SLO/SYS/gen |
| DIR_GLOBAL | /usr/sap/SLO/SYS/global |
| DIR_GRAPH_EXE | /usr/sap/SLO/DVEBMGS01/exe |
| DIR_GRAPH_LIB | /usr/sap/SLO/DVEBMGS01/exe |
| DIR_HOME | /usr/sap/SLO/DVEBMGS01/work |
| DIR_INSTALL | /usr/sap/SLO/SYS |
| DIR_INSTANCE | /usr/sap/SLO/DVEBMGS01 |
| DIR_LIBRARY | /usr/sap/SLO/DVEBMGS01/exe |
| DIR_LOGGING | /usr/sap/SLO/DVEBMGS01/log |
| DIR_MEMORY_INSPECTOR | /usr/sap/SLO/DVEBMGS01/data |
| DIR_PAGING | /usr/sap/SLO/DVEBMGS01/data |
| DIR_PUT | /usr/sap/SLO/put |
| DIR_PERF | /usr/sap/tmp |
| DIR_PROFILE | /usr/sap/SLO/SYS/profile |
| DIR_PROTOKOLLS | /usr/sap/SLO/DVEBMGS01/log |
| DIR_REORG | /usr/sap/SLO/DVEBMGS01/data |
| DIR_ROLL | /usr/sap/SLO/DVEBMGS01/data |
| DIR_RSYN | /usr/sap/SLO/DVEBMGS01/exe |
| DIR_SAPUSERS | ./ |
| DIR_SETUPS | /usr/sap/SLO/SYS/profile |
| DIR_SORTTMP | /usr/sap/SLO/DVEBMGS01/data |
| DIR_SOURCE | /usr/sap/SLO/SYS/src |
| DIR_TEMP | /tmp |
| DIR_TRANS | /usr/sap/trans |
| DIR_TRFILES | /usr/sap/trans |
| DIR_TRSUB | /usr/sap/trans |

**Figure 9.8** Initial Screen of the SAP-Directories

**Frontend trace**

As already mentioned in Section 3.4, SAP GUI, in Chapter 3, you can activate a multilevel tracing for the frontend via the option selection in SAPLOGON. The trace files are stored in the work directory of the frontend. The current setting for this directory can be found in **SAPLOGON • Via SAPLOGON • System Information • Additional Information**. You can open and evaluate the created trace files by means of an editor.

**SAP System Trace**

Using the SAP System Trace (ST01) enables you to log process flows within the SAP system in great detail. You should use the SAP system trace in a targeted manner and in close collaboration with SAP because the logged information is very comprehensive and difficult to interpret. The SAP System Trace isn't suitable for live operations.

The available trace components are release-dependent. The following components are provided as a minimum:

- Authorization check
- Kernel functions

- Kernel in general
- Database access (SQL trace)
- Table buffer trace
- RFCs
- Locking operations

You evaluate the trace information by means of **SAP System Trace (ST01) • Evaluation**. Similar to trace activation, you can use many different selection criteria for evaluation.

Performance Trace

For problem analysis, particularly for performance analysis of individual transactions, you can activate additional trace functions in a targeted manner. Via Performance Analysis (ST05), you can activate the collection of data for the following areas:

- **SQL trace**
  Database calls of reports and transactions.
- **Enqueue trace**
  Locking procedure of the system.
- **RFC trace**
  Cross-instance RFCs of function modules.
- **Buffer trace**
  Table buffer trace.

For more details on the respective trace types, refer to Section 10.4, Performance Traces, in Chapter 10.

## 9.6 Lock Entries

The SAP system has its own lock management using the enqueue work processes. The lock entries are set by the running programs and are deleted again in regular operation without any manual intervention. If problems occur in the SAP system, for example, the dispatcher of an instance or the entire used application server fails, historical lock entries are still kept. Consequently, you must check the lock entries on a daily basis and, if required, delete them manually. Proceed as follows to check lock entries:

**Checking lock entries**

1. Via the Lock Monitor (SM12), you navigate to the selection screen of the lock entries to be displayed. You can restrict the selection with regard to the table name, the lock argument, the client, or the user.
2. Select **List**. You can view a list of all locks currently held in the system (see Figure 9.9).

   Displayed are the user and the client that holds the lock, the time of creation for the lock, and the table affected. The lock argument (*lock key*) is particularly essential. The Lock mode column gives information about the type of lock entry. Using **Process • Sort** enables you to sort the list according to different criteria.

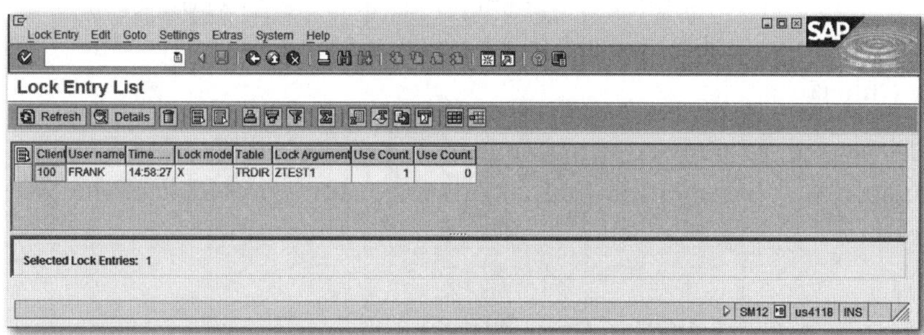


**Figure 9.9** Lock Entry List

3. Check the times of the lock entry creation. Lock entries that have been kept for a particularly long period must be analyzed. By double-clicking on the lock key of the entry, you receive more detailed information about the lock entry, for example, the transaction code that caused the lock entry.
4. If these lock entries still have open updates, you should check and clean up these update procedures first.
5. Check whether the user related to this lock entry is still logged on to the system.

**Lock mode**

As already mentioned, a lock entry can be set to different modes. The lock mode determines whether multiple users may access the datasets at the same time. The lock mode can be assigned for each table in the lock object separately. When setting the lock, you create a corresponding lock entry for each table in the lock table of the system.

A detailed description of lock management in SAP NetWeaver AS ABAP can be found in Section 2.4 of Chapter 2.

## 9.7 Performance Monitoring

Continuous monitoring of the relevant indicators, which can partly be automated, form the basis of all tuning activities to improve the performance of the SAP system. The established values can be interpreted by a system administrator and used as the basis for intervention. The integrated alert monitor is a tremendous help here, whose basic principles, usage, and configuration are explained in Chapter 11, Monitoring Architecture.

The system administrator must ensure the correct and reliable functioning of the alert monitor and all other monitors provided in the SAP system.

### 9.7.1 Administrative Principles

**Performance database**

The data collected by collectors over time forms the basis of all performance analysis in the SAP system. At the operating system level, the `saposcol` program collects all critical data about the performance of the components outside of SAP. Within the SAP system, the `RSCOLL00` ABAP program collects the data and determines the performance value for the other SAP components, such as the database and the SAP buffers. `RSCOLL00` should be planned under the default name, `SAP_COLLECTOR_FOR_PERFMONITOR`, for background execution at hourly intervals. The summarized data is written in the `MONI` table, which is also referred to as the *performance database*. You can implement the configuration of the performance database using the System Load Monitor (ST03N). Critical setting options are the following:

- Residence time of the collected statistics data
- Accumulation of the data
- Reorganization rules

The reorganization of the performance data is implemented automatically based on these settings within the background job, `SAP_COLLECTOR_FOR_PERFMONITOR`.

### 9.7.2 Monitors

For precise analysis of the performance aspects, the SAP system provides you with various monitors. These monitors comprise the following areas:

#### Workload Analysis

- **System Load Monitor (ST03N)**
  Displays the system load for each instance, work process distribution, user statistics, response time distribution, historical data, and ranking lists (see Figure 9.10).
- **Business Process Analysis (STAD)**
  Displays statistics for single record evaluation.
- **Application Monitor (ST07)**
  Displays the user distribution.

#### Buffer

- **Buffer Load(ST02)**
  Displays the quality and size of the most critical SAP buffers, and information about the memory usage
- **Table Calls (ST10)**
  Displays the table call statistics.
- **Profile Parameter Changes (TU02)**
  Displays the change history of the profile parameter.

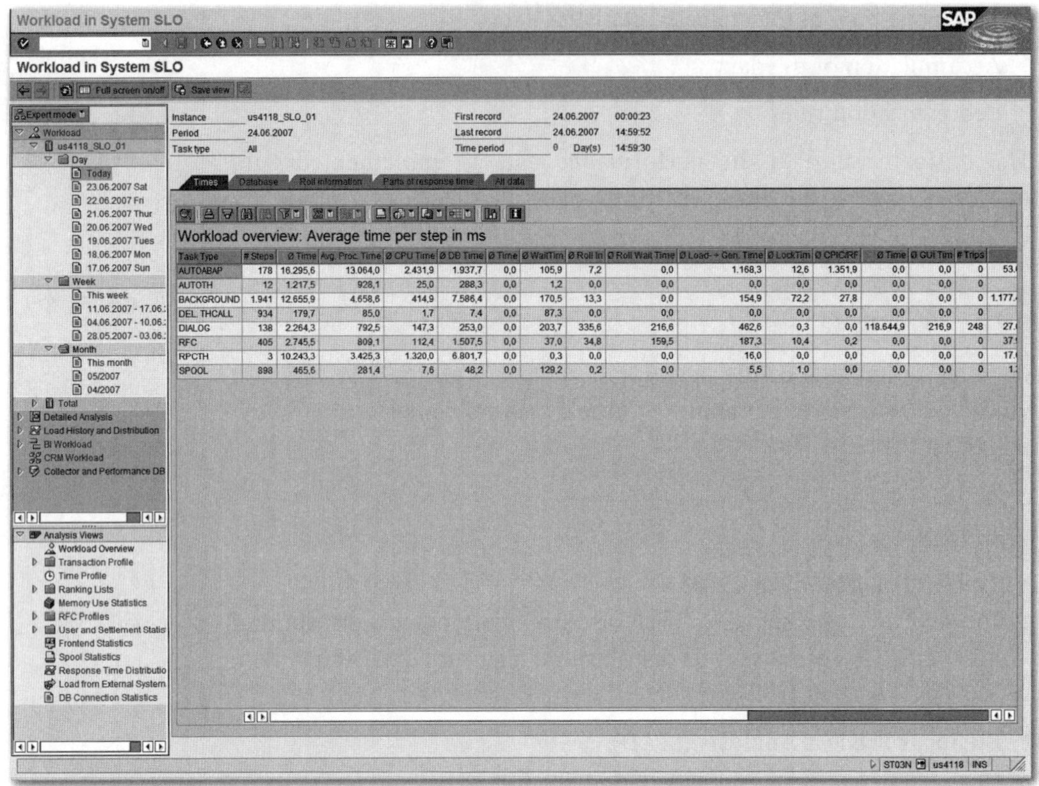


**Figure 9.10** System Load Monitor

### Operating System

- **OS Monitor (ST06)**
  Monitors the operating system resources, for example, memory, CPU, file system, and hard disk.
- **OS System Configuration (OS07)**
  Displays the current operating system parameter.
- **OS Parameter Changes (OS03)**
  Displays the change history of the operating system parameter.

### Database

- **Database Monitor (ST04)**
  Displays the most critical statistics to analyze the database activities and access to the database log.

- **Lockwaits (ST01)**
  Displays the lockwaits and escalations.
- **Tables and Indices (DB02)**
  Displays the resource statistics, tables, and indices analyses.
- **DB Parameter Changes (DB03)**
  Displays the change history of the database parameter.

## 9.8 Database Administration

The database administrator is responsible for the administration of the RDBMS and the database. The related tasks are RDBMS-specific, so we can give you only a general idea at this point.

The most essential activities

The most essential activities of the system administrator within the database monitoring and administration are the following:

- Planning, implementing, and monitoring the backup of the database
- Planning, implementing, and monitoring the backup of the transaction logs
- Planning, implementing, and monitoring the verifications of the tape content of data backup and the database consistency
- Configuring, planning, implementing, and monitoring the creation of statistics for the cost-based optimizer
- Planning the capacity and monitoring the resources (at the operating system and database levels)
- Monitoring and setting the database parameters

For each RDBMS used in an SAP system, you are provided with corresponding tools. The appearance and descriptions of the administration tools may differ.

### 9.8.1 Tasks to Be Planned at Regular Intervals

DBA planning calendar

The database plays an exceptionally significant role within the SAP system. This is the central point for data retention. Accordingly, regular backups of the dataset are indispensable for data recovery in case of an error. A DBA Planning Calendar (DB13) is integrated in the SAP system for these tasks and for other tasks to be implemented at regular intervals (see Figure 9.11).

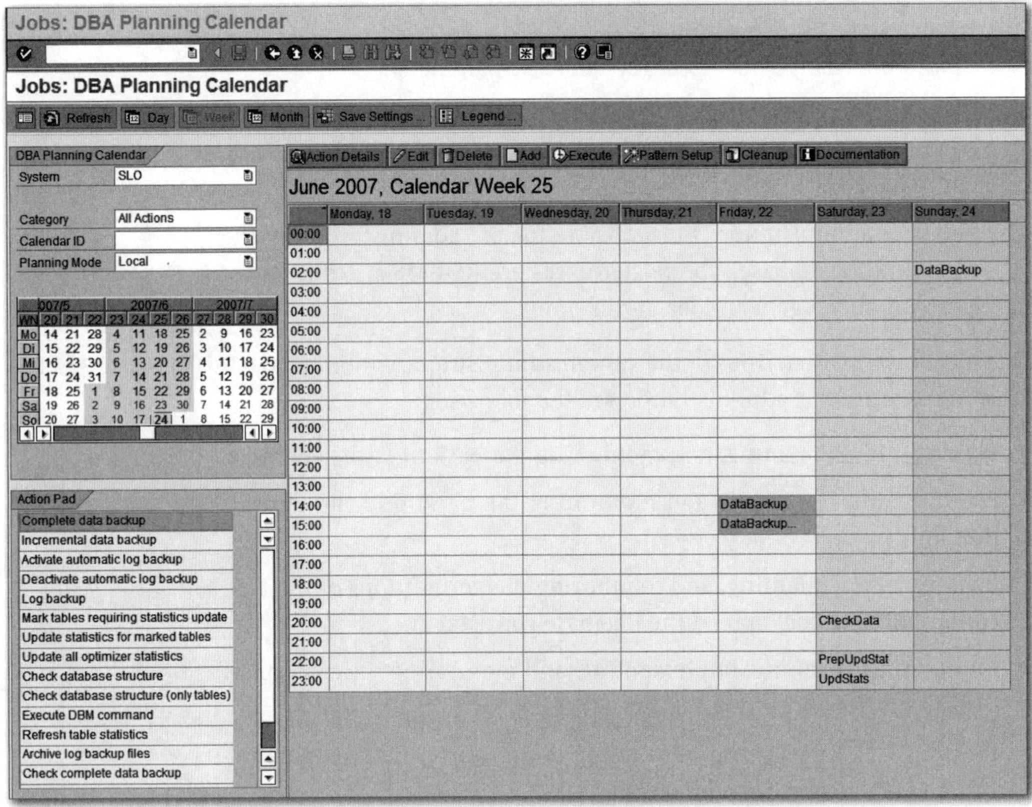


**Figure 9.11** DBA Planning Calendar MaxDB

You can plan the most critical database administration tasks in the DBA planning calendar in advance for background processing. These include the following:

- Saving the database during the running operation (online) or when stopped (offline)
- Saving the data incrementally
- Saving the log areas
- Saving the individual data areas

- Updating the optimizer statistics
- Analyzing the database structure
- Analyzing the database status

Cost-based optimizers

All RDBMSs currently used in SAP systems work using a cost-based optimizer to determine the execution strategy of the SQL commands. If you are provided with multiple execution plans, the cost-based optimizer establishes the most cost-efficient strategy. The costs are established based on the total quantity of data blocks to be processed, in other words, the datasets and the possibly used index information. The strategy determination is based on statistics about the data within the table, for example, the number of sets and the number of different values within the indexed column. The statistics used by the optimizers are not updated automatically. The database administrator must implement this depending on the dynamics of the database, but at least once per week, and after more extensive changes, such as archiving runs. Outdated statistics are worse than none at all; the impact on the access speed can be considerably high.

Verification

The analysis and verification of the entire dataset is the only defined and safe method to exclude corrupt blocks in the datasets caused by hardware errors. This procedures is very time-consuming and results in increased inbound and outbound activities of the hard disks. In SAP systems, including very large databases, you may have difficulties implementing the full analysis. A full analysis, however, is indispensable in the event of hardware problems, at least for the affected areas.

Backup

You should back up your entire database for live systems on a daily basis. You can find information on the already implemented backups in the DBA Action Logs(DB12). If an error occurs, you need additional log data to recover the datasets to catch up — based on the last full backup — all subsequent data changes. For this purpose, the data in the log areas must be consistent. Each RDBMS overwrites data in the log only when the backup has been implemented successfully. If the data backup has not been carried out, data may be lost if there is a hardware error or if the log area is completely filled. Then, the database and consequently SAP would not be available for operation any longer. For database-specific administration outside the SAP system, you can, depending on the

RDBMS used, use tools inherent to the product or provided by SAP. The best-known administration tool for Oracle databases within an SAP system installation is `brconnect`.

### 9.8.2 Database Fill Level and Objects

The database administrator needs to continuously observe the growth of the database. If there is no sufficient space for saving data, the SAP system might become inoperable. Therefore, you need to check the database fill level at regular intervals and, if required, increase the database. You can find information about the database size and the objects contained therein in the display of the Tables and Indices (DB02). This monitor provides you with information on the current database fill level and its development, as well as the size of the individual objects, for example, tablespaces or tables and indices (see Figure 9.12).

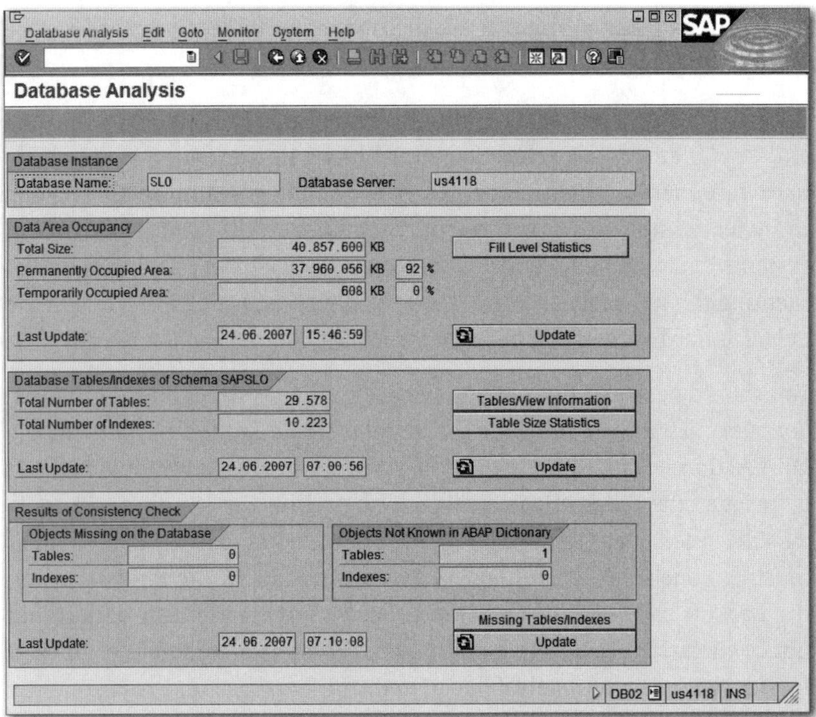


**Figure 9.12** DB02 as an Example of a MaxDB

Dictionary consistency

In addition to the space requirements of individual objects, the SAP system also continuously checks the defined objects in the SAP Data Dictionary and in the database. The system administrator must make sure that there are no deviations between SAP and the database. Missing indices can result in considerable performance losses. Particularly after upgrades, you should remember to check the consistency of the objects by using this monitor and then create the missing objects.

## 9.9 Overview of Regular Tasks

Table 9.3 comprise a summary of all regularly recurring tasks for the administration of a live SAP system. For development systems and consolidation systems, whose failure safety usually doesn't need to be high, you can customize the tasks of system monitoring accordingly.

| Activity | Path and Transaction Codes | Schedule | Details |
|---|---|---|---|
| Observe alert monitor | **Alert Monitor** | Several times a day | Chapter 11 |
| Check the system log | **System Log (SM21)** | Several times a day | Section 9.3 |
| Control runtime error | **Dump Analysis (ST22)** | Daily | Section 9.4 |
| Status of the instances and operating modes | **Control Panel (RZ03)** | Weekly | Section 7.3 |
| Status of the application server and work processes | **Server Overview (SM51)**<br>**Process Overview (SM50)** | Daily | Section 9.1 |
| Check update service | **Update Administration (SM13)** | Daily | Section 2.3 |
| Check spool service | **Output Control (SP01)** | Daily | Section 2.5 |
| Control lock entries | **Lock Monitor (SM12)** | Daily | Section 2.4 |
| Check logs of the background processing | **Job Selection (SM37)** | Daily | Section 2.2 |
| Check by means of regular maintenance jobs | **Job Selection (SM37)** | Monthly | Section 9.6 |

**Table 9.3** Regular Administrative Tasks

| Activity | Path and Transaction Codes | Schedule | Details |
|---|---|---|---|
| Maintain optimizer statistics | **DBA Planning Calendar (DB13)** | Weekly and as required | Section 9.8 |
| Implement and check updates | **DBA Planning Calendar (DB13)**<br>**Backup Logs**<br>**Database Logs** | Daily | Section 9.8 |
| Check logs of the database administration | **Database Logs** | Daily | Section 9.8 |
| Check database consistency | **DBA Planning Calendar (DB13)** | Once per update cycle | Section 9.8 |
| Check database fill level | **Tables and Indices (DB02)** | Weekly | Section 9.8 |
| Check file system fill levels | **Operating System Command** | Regularly and as required | |
| Monitor the consistency of the database objects | **Tables and Indices (DB02)** | At least after each upgrade | Section 9.8 |
| Performance analysis | **Load Analysis (ST03N)** | As required | Section 9.7 |
| Control batch input processes | **Batch Input** | Regularly if batch input procedures are used | Section 13.3 |
| Check gateway functionality | **Gateway Monitor (SMGW)** | Regularly if gateways are used | Chapter 13 |
| Check ALE processes on sending and receiving side | **ALE Status Monitor** | Regularly if ALE is used | Section 13.2 |
| RFC communication | **Transactional RFC (SM58)**<br>**qRFC Monitor Inbound (SMQ2)**<br>**qRFC Monitor Outbound (SMQ1)** | Regularly if RFC connections are used | Section 13.1 |

**Table 9.3** Regular Administrative Tasks (Cont.)

## 9.10 Administration of the Integrated Internet Transaction Server (ITS)

Status monitor

If you use integrated ITS of SAP NetWeaver AS, you must also administrate it. For this purpose, the application server provides you with the Transaction SITSPMON, the Status Monitor for Integrated ITS.

This transaction provides you with an overview of the current status of integrated ITS, of the version of the feature set, and of the settings of the current `itsp/*` profile parameters. Moreover, you are shown information about the current memory utilization, the content of the ITS-internal caches, set locks, and activated features.

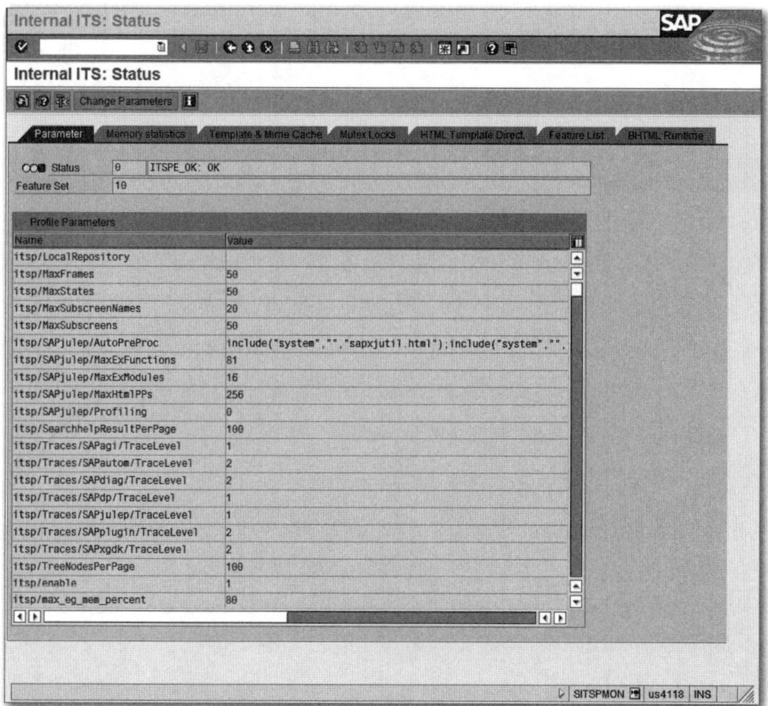


**Figure 9.13** Status Monitor of Integrated ITS

Tabstrips

This information is provided on different screens in different categories, which you can select using the corresponding tabstrips (see Figure 9.13). You can select the following categories that will be described in more detail in the following sections:

- Parameter
- Memory Statistics
- Template and Mime Cache
- Mutex Locks
- HTML Template Directory
- Feature List
- BHTML Runtime

### 9.10.1 Parameter Tabstrip

This screen gives you the current status of integrated ITS, the current feature set version, and a list of all ITS profile parameters starting with `itsp/*` and including their current values.

Table 9.4 shows the possible statuses of integrated ITS.

| Status | Description |
|---|---|
| ITSPE_OK | OK. |
| ITSPE_FAILURE | An error occurred. |
| ITSPE_DISABLED | The services is deactivated in the profile. |
| ITSPE_NOTFOUND | ITS program library was not found. |
| ITSPE_LOAD | ITS program library could not be loaded. |
| ITSPE_INIT | Initialization failed. |
| ITSPE_VERSION | ITS program library version is incorrect. |
| ITSPE_WRONG_UC | Unicode/non-Unicode combination is wrong. |
| ITSPE_MEMORY_DESTROYED | Memory overwriting was detected. |
| ITSPE_RESOURCE_FAILURE | A resource could not be assigned. |

**Table 9.4** ITS Status

As already mentioned, you are provided with an overview of the ITS profile parameter and the associated parameter values. If documentation is available for a parameter, you can view it by clicking on the parameter or by pressing the F2 function key or clicking the respective button.

Use the **Change Parameters** button to directly change the values of the parameters, `itsp/Traces/*`, `itsp/memory_check`, and `itsp/max_eg_mem_percent`.

**WARNING**

The changes made are not permanent and are lost upon restart of the server.

### 9.10.2 Memory Statistics Tabstrip

ITS Status Monitor also provides information about the memory utilization of integrated ITS for the application server on which you are currently logged on. For this purpose, the value of the `itsp/memory_check` parameter must be set to at least 1.

The memory consumption overview contains the following information:

- Number of current sessions
- Memory space of all sessions (in bytes)
- Average consumption per session (in bytes/session)
- Maximum consumption per session (in bytes)
- Memory consumption for HTML templates (in bytes)
- Total memory consumption (in bytes)

Current memory consumption

You may see negative values in the **Current memory consumption** column because the statistic is recorded at the time the `itsp/memory_check` parameter is set. If this is done during the running operation, a work process or session may release more space than requested for the period to be statistically evaluated.

### 9.10.3 Template and MIME Cache Tabstrip

The application server stores both the HTML templates, which have already been called via the ITS function (*Preparsed Templates*), and the called MIME files in different caches for fast access.

On this screen, you can observe the status of the HTML template cache, and, if required, you may also invalidate both the HTML template caches and the MIME cache. The screen consists of three parts:

- **Current status of the HTML template caches**
  - Server name
  - Valid from
  - Valid to
  - Status

  The cache remains invalid if the integrated ITS function has not (yet) been activated.
- **Functions for invalidating the HTML template caches**
  To delete the HTML template caches of all application servers assigned to this SAP system, select **Systemwide**. To delete the HTML template caches of the application server on which you are currently logged on, select **On this application server**.
- **Functions for invalidating the MIME cache**
  Select **Systemwide** to invalidate the MIME cache of the Internet Communication Manager (ICM).

WARNING

- Changes only become valid after deleting the browser cache.
- Template and MIME caches are automatically invalidated upon publishing.

### 9.10.4 Mutex Locks Tabstrip

Mutual exclusions

Mutex locks (*mutual exclusions*) prevent the competitive access to resources. The integrated ITS function uses mutex locks for the HTML template cache, which only exists once for all work processes, to prevent a work process from storing a new HTML template version in the HTML template cache while another work process still processes another HTML template.

Mutex locks are also used for the following:

- Memory statistics
- Individual HTML template cache entries
- HTML template directory

### 9.10.5 HTML Template Directory Tabstrip

This screen is used to display the HTML template cache. For each template that is already contained in the cache, you can find a separate entry consisting of the HTML template name, the IAC resource name, the number of the cache slot, and the language in which the template has been called.

Deleting cache entries

You can't change the cache directly on this screen. Cache entries don't have an expiry date but are deleted for the following reasons:

- You manually delete the cache (see **Template and Mime Cache** screen).
- The cache is full. In this case, the least recently used entries are deleted first (*least recently used algorithm*).

### 9.10.6 Feature List Tabstrip

For integrating ITS in SAP NetWeaver AS and storing the HTML templates in the SAP NetWeaver AS database, a mechanism for ensuring the compatibility had to be developed. For this purpose, a feature management has been introduced. A feature is provided if it's implemented both in the kernel and in the HTML templates. The kernel availability of a feature is ensured through the implementation in the C++ part of SAP Web AS; the availability in the templates is ensured through a table entry that is transferred via the respective support packages. Now you can query the availability in C, ABAP, and BHTML, and encode it accordingly.

The **Feature List** screen contains a list of all available features, including their name, their kernel availability (**VK**), the database availability (**VD**), and information about whether the availability of a feature is mandatory (**VZ**). If a feature is mandatory, integrated ITS is only started if this feature has been implemented in the HTML templates.

### 9.10.7 BHTML Runtime Tabstrip

This screen provides you with an overview of the number of executed BHTML functions and the total runtime.

## 9.11 Internet Communication Manager Administration

ICM Monitor

The Internet Communication Manager is administrated and monitored via the ICM Monitor (SMICM). The ICM Monitor (see Figure 9.14) is handled similar to the Process Overview and provides additional information and action options based on a list of configured worker threads, including their current statuses.

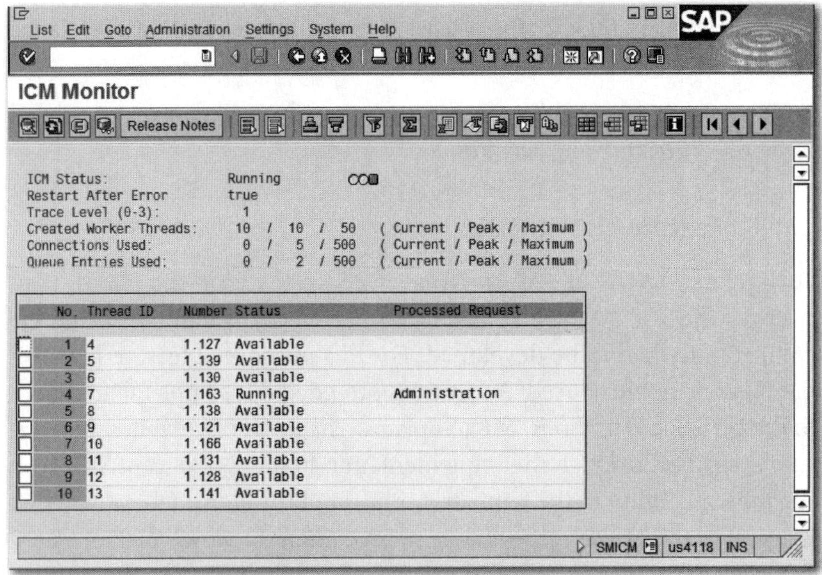


**Figure 9.14** ICM Monitor

The ICM Monitor provides you with a wide range of options to control the current status of ICM and to analyze possible errors. A short description of these options is given next. You can find all menu entries in the **Goto** menu of the ICM Monitor.

Trace files/ Trace level

Using **Goto• Trace File** or **Goto• Trace Level,** you can display or reset the *dev_icm* trace file and set the trace level (values from 0 to 3 are possible, and the default value is 1). You can also display only the first or the last part of the file (i.e., the first or last 1,000 lines), which is particularly useful for large files. For this purpose, select **Goto • Trace File • Show beginning** or **Show end**.

You can download the trace file to your local computer, which is recommended for large files, or if you want to store or forward the file. To do so, select **Goto • Trace File • Store locally**.

If you want to view the trace file of the external `icmbnd` binding program, select **Goto• Trace File • Dev_icmbnd • Display**.

Via **Goto• Parameter • Display** or **Goto • Parameter • Change**, you can display or change the ICM profile parameters. When selecting **Change**, you can view the RZ11 documentation for each listed parameter by placing the cursor on the parameter name and clicking on the **Documentation** button.

For parameters that can be changed dynamically, the value field is ready for input.

Statistic and memory pipes

Select **Goto • Statistic** to activate, deactivate, display, and reset data of the ICM statistic.

**Goto • Memory Pipes** provides additional information about the memory pipes that are used for data exchange of ICM and work process.

Host name buffer

The mapping of host names on IP addresses or of service names on port numbers is buffered in the SAP system after they have been read from the file system. If a host or service name that you want to access, is changed, you must reset the host name buffer. You can view the current buffer content and reset the buffer. Then, ICM reads the data again from the file system.

For this purpose, select **Goto • Host Name Buffer • View** or **Reset**.

Select **Goto • Services** to monitor and administrate the services (ports that the ICM uses for connections).

You can view all active ICM connections via **Goto • Connections**.

Use **Goto • Release Info** or the **Release Info** button to obtain information on the ICM version and the release and patch level of the SAP kernel.

In the HTTP server cache, you can find the functions for monitoring and administrating the ICM server cache. You can display the cache or the cache statistic, or you can invalidate the cache locally or globally.

Information on the logging of HTTP requests

Select **Goto• HTTP Log** to view the following information on the logging of HTTP requests:

- **Display entries**
  Displays the entries of the log file.
- **Information**
  Name of the log file, format of the log file, conditions for the new log file, maximum log file size, cyclical writing (yes/no), current number of characters in the log file, and current number of lines in the log file.
- **Write buffer**
  The entries in the logging file are buffered and written on the hard disk at regular intervals. Because the **Display Entries** menu item only displays entries that are already on the hard disk, you use this function to force the writing of the buffer content on the disk.

The functions are available both as a server and client for HTTP logging.

Select **Goto • HTTP Server • Display Data** to obtain information on the HTTP application server (information on the active ABAP or J2EE-Server, the URL prefix table) and to load the URL prefixes.

If no J2EE engine has been configured (`J2EE Server configured = FALSE`), all HTTP requests are passed on to the ABAP engine (to the ICF). If a J2EE engine is connected, ICM decides whether the request is forwarded to the ABAP engine or the J2EE engine based on the URL prefix table. Here, the following rules apply:

- All URL prefixes contained in the list go to the ABAP engine; all others to the J2EE engine.
- The table is determined based on the possible prefixes of the Internet Communication Framework (HTTP service tree and external aliases).
- If no J2EE engine is configured, you can't load the table. However, you can force loading by means of **Load URL Prefixes**.

Administrative activities

The **Administration** menu option of the ICM Monitor enables you to implement the necessary administrative activities. These include the following:

- **Terminate ICM**
  By selecting **Administration • ICM • Soft Shutdown** or **Hard Shutdown,** you can terminate the ICM in a soft (Signal 2) or hard (Signal 9) manner. For soft shutdown, the ICM tries to send responses to the existing clients but accepts no new connections. For hard shutdown, the process is simply canceled at the operating system level. All existing connections are lost and, consequently, all running requests.
- **Maintenance Mode**
  If ICM has the *running* status, you can set it to the maintenance mode. For this purpose select **Administration • ICM • Maintenance Mode• Activate**. You can also terminate the maintenance mode (**Deactivate**). The process runs normally again (Status: running).
- **Reload Configuration**
  During the running operation, the ICM can import configuration data that would otherwise be updated during startup or at cyclical intervals. For this purpose, select **Administration • ICM • Configuration • Reload**.

  The reload of the configuration includes the following items:
  - Invalidate the host name buffer.
  - Invalidate the server cache.
  - Update information from the message server and application server (only web dispatcher).
  - Exit the maintenance mode, if it has been activated.
  - Reload filter rules.
- **Set Start Options**
  Select **Administration • ICM • Start Options • Set** to set the trace file and trace level of ICM. By default, this is *dev_icm* and 1.
- **Restart**
  If the ICM is terminated (by the administrator or due to an error), it's automatically restarted by the dispatcher by default. You can control this option by selecting **Administration • ICM • Restart • Yes** or **No**. If you deactivate the restart and terminate ICM, it isn't restarted.
- **Administration of the J2EE engine**
  The functions available at **Administration • J2EE Instance / J2EE**

**Cluster** can be used to administrate the J2EE engine and are not included in this book.

Web administration interface of ICM

Via the URL *http(s)://host:admin_port/sap/admin*, you can access the web administration interface of ICM. Here, the *host* is the computer on which ICM runs, and *admin_port* the administration port configured by means of *icm/HTTP/admin_<xx>* and *icm/server_port_<xx>* .

The functionality and setup of the web administration interface are comparable to Transaction SMICM for ICM in AS ABAP. If you use the web administration interface, you don't require any SAP GUI, and you don't need to be logged on to the computer on which ICM runs.

For security reasons, you should use HTTPS for administration. If you use HTTP, the administrator password transfer isn't encrypted and can be eavesdropped. In the ideal case, you work with client certificates.

In the following example (see Figure 9.15), ICM runs on the bsl1041.wdf.sap.corp server and can be reached via HTTP port 8000.

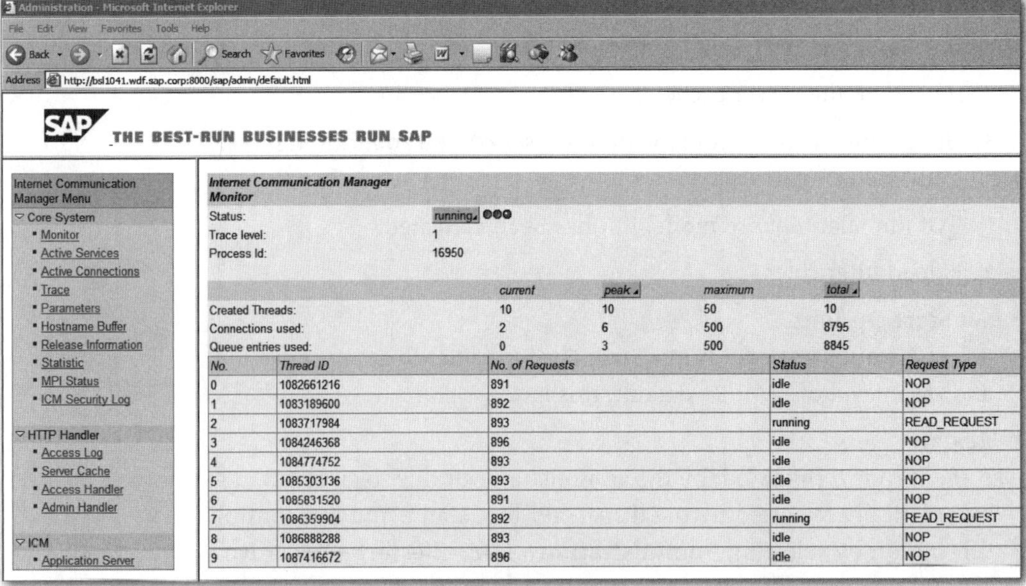


**Figure 9.15** Web Administrator Interface

## 9.12 System Administration Assistant

The tasks accumulating within the system administration can be subdivided into *recurring tasks*, which are required for system monitoring and smooth operation, and *occasional tasks*, which are implemented in exceptional cases or due to special requests. Data backup is a recurring task, and setup of a new printer is an occasional task, for example.

The System Administration Assistant (SSAA) was introduced in the context of the ready-to-run initiative to support the system administrators. The most vital subjects in system administration are listed in the System Administration Assistant in a tree structure and sorted by *daily*, *weekly*, *annually*, and *occasional* tasks. In addition to an extensive documentation for each item that can be called from the structure, you can also call the due tasks directly from there. When you complete the tasks, they are automatically marked as done.

**Adjusting the structure**

The System Administration Assistant doesn't cover all administrative tasks. The primary target was to collect the most critical or most frequently used tasks and to provide them in a compact structure. SAP provides the System Administration Assistant as a proposal of an administration concept (a concept that describes how an SAP NetWeaver system is to be operated). The structure can be customized to the customer requirements; non-relevant tasks are hidden to increase clarity and usefulness.

Figure 9.16 shows the daily administrative tasks for operating a production system using a MaxDB database; the first steps have already been done.

Figure 9.17 shows an individually customized tree structure. Here, the **Administration Tasks** node, including all subnodes, was copied from an SAP template, and the **Performance Monitoring** node, including all subnodes, was created.

As you can see in the figure, each implementation is logged with a timestamp and user name, so that you can establish easily when the corresponding task was last implemented.

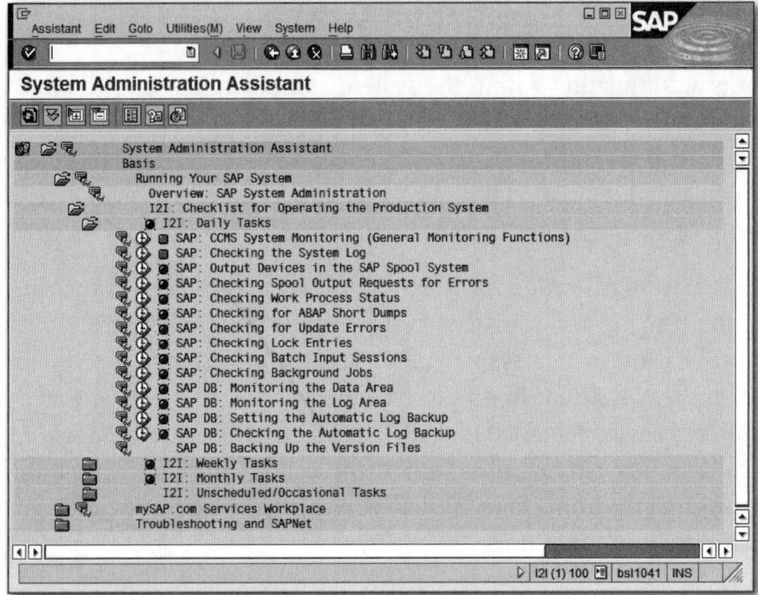


**Figure 9.16** System Administration Assistant

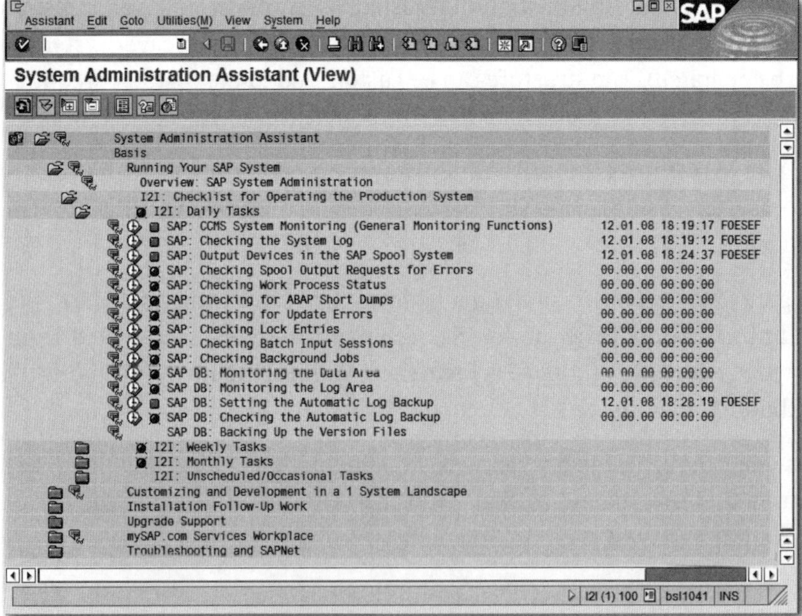


**Figure 9.17** Modified Tree Structure

## 9.13 SAP NetWeaver Administrator (NWA)

NWA combines the most critical administration and monitoring tools both for Java and ABAP systems in a new, browser-based user interface. The major advantages of NWA are the following:

Advantages

- NWA shows all data of the monitoring infrastructure, in other words, alerts, current values, and historical values.
- You don't have to switch between the different tools for administration, troubleshooting, and problem analysis of your entire SAP NetWeaver system landscape.
- For Java systems and, to an increasing extent, for ABAP systems, you are provided with landscape-wide central administration tools to start and terminate instances, to check configuration settings and logs, and to monitor problem-free functioning of the components.
- For Java, NWA represents the transition from different expert tools to one integrated, simple, and clear solution. Moreover, NWA rounds off the integration of data sources for monitoring.
- For ABAP, NWA represents the transition from many different and partly difficult-to-use expert transactions to integrated, centrally available information.
- The user interface complies with the current guidelines for interface design; it's easy to use, task-oriented, and complete. Because Web Dynpro is used, it runs as an application in the browser.

NWA has initially been delivered for SAP NetWeaver 04 SP Stack 12; an advanced version has been delivered for SAP NetWeaver 7.0. NWA and future releases will be continuously further developed and extended by additional administration and monitoring functions.

Calling NWA

To call NWA, use the following URL: *http(s):// host:port/nwa*. *host* is a computer on which a J2EE engine runs; *port* is the corresponding HTTP(S) port for accessing this instance.

Figure 9.18 shows the NWA login screen.

After you log in as a valid administration user, the **Welcome** page is displayed (see Figure 9.19).

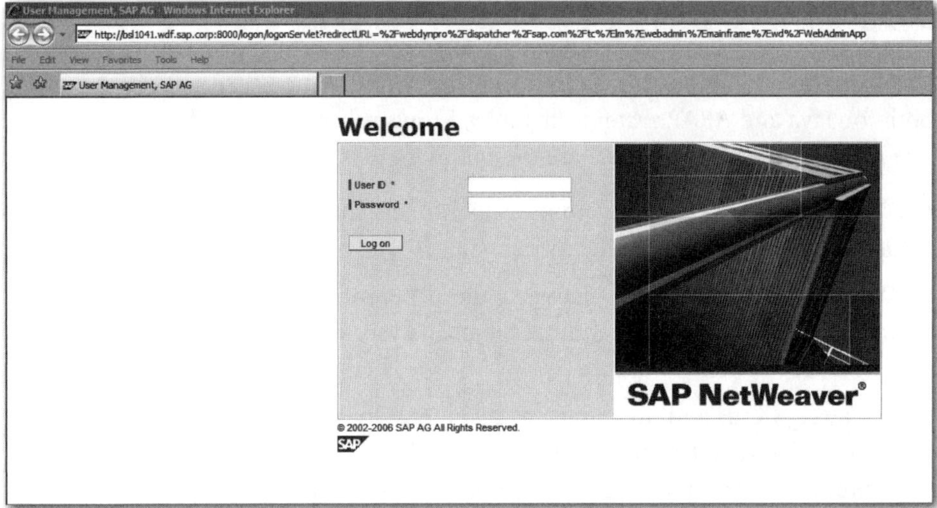


Figure 9.18 NWA Login Screen

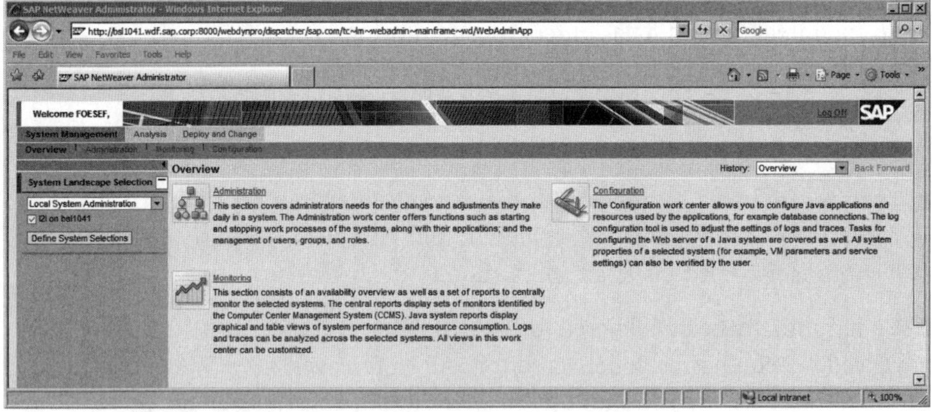


Figure 9.19 Welcome Page of NWA

To use NWA for the administration of a system landscape, you need to meet some prerequisites:

- ABAP systems must be registered in the Central Monitoring System (CEN) by means of Transaction RZ21 (see Section 11.4, Setting Up a Central Monitoring System, in Chapter 11).
- A `CCMSPING` agent (availability check) must be installed and registered for the central monitoring system (see Section 11.4).

Prerequisites

- If Java systems are to be monitored, you need to register them in CEN using the SAPCCMSR agent (see Section 11.4).
- If ABAP systems are to be monitored, you need to registered them in CEN using the SAPCCM4X agent (see Section 11.4).
- The integrated Internet Transaction Server (ITS) must be activated in the ABAP stack of CEN (see Section 1.3.2, Integrated Internet Transaction Server, in Chapter 1).

**Configuration**

If these prerequisites have been met, you need to implement some configuration steps within NWA. The template installer plug-in facilitates this process considerably. To implement the final configuration using this plug-in, you must log in as administrator in NWA and select **Implement and Change Deployment** in the top level navigation. Subsequently, implement the configuration wizards listed in Table 9.5 in the given sequence (see Figure 9.20):

| Task | Description |
|---|---|
| NWA_01 executes configuration for local SLD. | Configuring the local system landscape directory (SLD) |
| NWA_02_SLD system connects SLD to CEN (if CEN present). | Configuring the connection of the local SLD to the central monitoring system (CEN) |
| NWA_03 creates a connection to the SLD and sets required authorizations for SLD (CIM client settings). | Creating a connection to the SLD |
| NWA_04 creates a connection to the ABAP stack of CEN and starts heartbeat monitoring. | Creating a connection to ABAP stack of CEN and activating the availability check (heartbeat monitoring) |
| NWA_05_NWA system stores access data per each managed Java system (optional). | Configuring the connections to Java systems to be administrated |
| NWA_06_NWA system registers each managed ABAP system to SLD. | Registering the ABAP systems in the SLD |
| NWA_07 creates Destination for data supplier bridge. | Creating a destination for the data supplier bridge |

**Table 9.5** Configuration Wizards

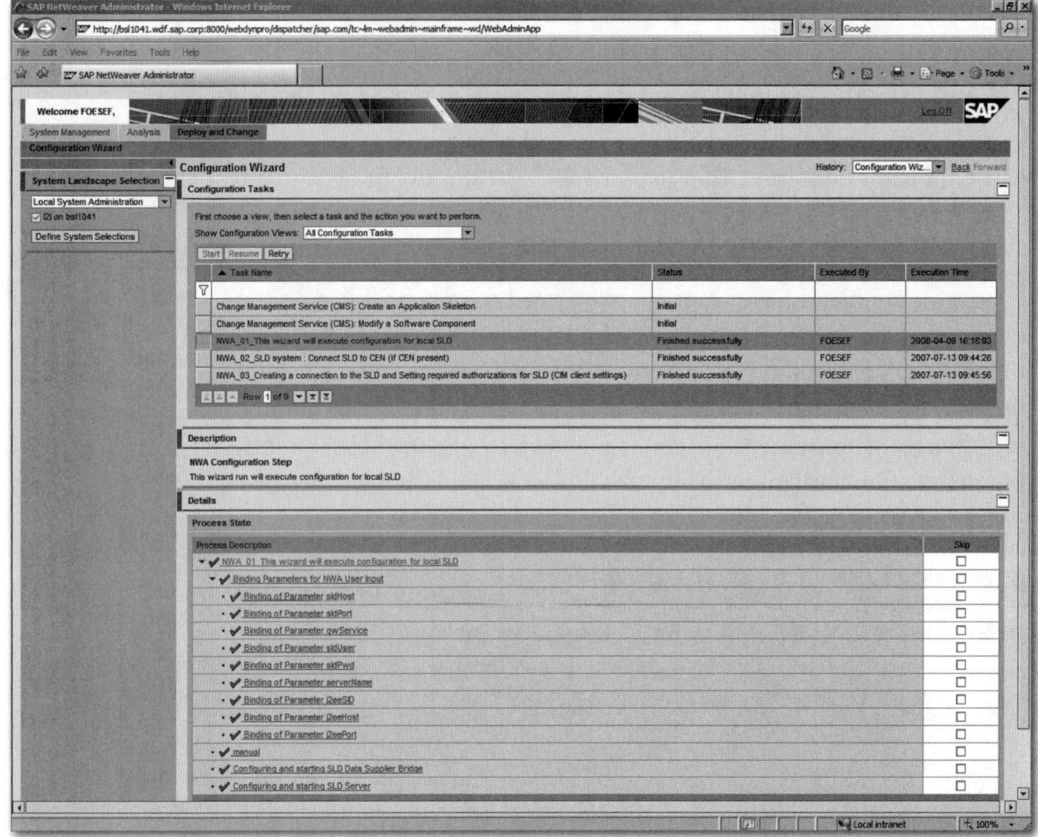

**Figure 9.20** Configuration Wizards

Wizards

Some of the wizards require input information, for example, user names, passwords, system data, or similar. If the same data is required for executing the next wizards, the input fields are preassigned with the entries already made.

You can cancel the execution of a wizard at any time. You can repeat executions that have been stopped using the same data. You can also restart each wizard several times; however, you then need to repeat your inputs.

After all configuration steps have been completed successfully, you can use the NetWeaver Administrator as a central monitoring and configuration tool.

It won't take you long to become familiar with the NWA and working with it will be intuitive and convenient. The navigation features a hierarchical system. Initially, select your work area from the top level.

Each work area is subdivided into further work subareas. For example, the **System Management** work area includes the subareas, **Overview**, **Administration**, **Monitoring**, and **Configuration**. After you have selected the required work subarea, for example, **Monitoring**, you can select the relevant functionality in the detailed navigation on the left side of the screen, for instance, **Java System Reports** (see Figure 9.21). Work subareas

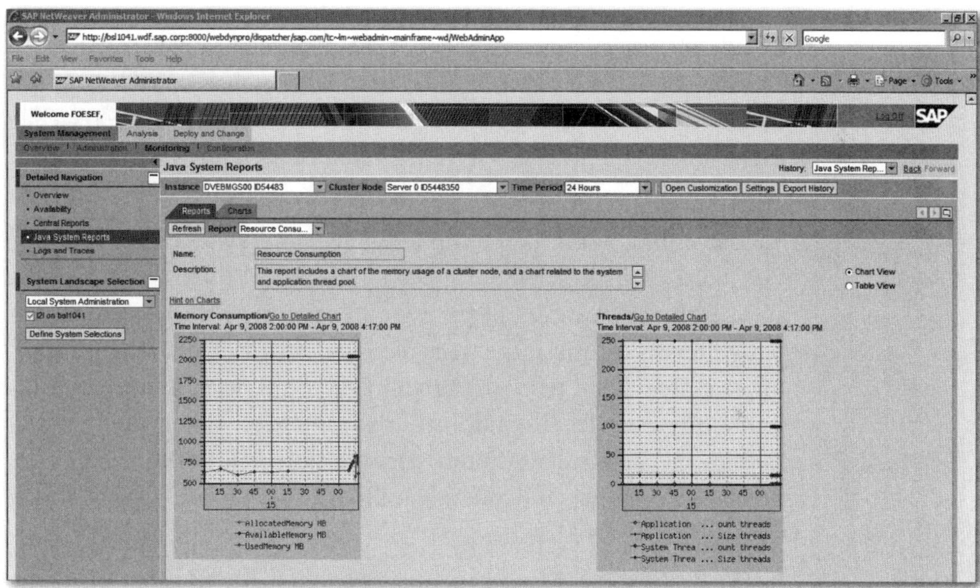


**Figure 9.21** Monitor for Displaying the Resource Consumption

The following work areas are available:

- **System Management**
  This work area comprises work subareas that enable you to administrate the system (e.g., starting and stopping services, user administration, monitoring, etc.).
- **Analysis**
  This work area contains work subareas for measuring the application performance, for detecting erroneous system configurations, and for debugging applications.

- **Deploy and Change**
  Within this work subarea, you can start the already mentioned configuration wizards to easily customize your system to your requirements.

If you select the **Overview** link in the work subareas or in the detailed navigation, a short help text appears that contains an overview of the activities available at this navigation level.

## 9.14 Tips

- **Developer trace and trace level of the dispatcher process**
  You can implement the trace level of the dispatcher by selecting **Process Overview • Process • Trace • Dispatcher** and display the trace file even though the process itself isn't listed in the Process overview.
- **Trace logging – automatic reset of the trace level**
  You have the option to determine the maximum size of the trace file (when using the SAP Web Application Server). When searching for a sporadic error, you can increase the trace level of the corresponding work process to 2 or 3; the trace file is automatically searched according to a predefined word pattern at regular intervals. If this pattern is found, the trace level is automatically reset to 1. When the trace file reaches the defined maximum size, it's stored in the *<name of trace file>.old* backup file, and a new trace file is created.
- **Repairing a local system log**
  If you accidentally deleted the local system log without deleting the associated shared memory segment SCSA as well, you can repair the system log using report `RSLG0020`.
- **Global performance analysis**
  Due to the requirement of implementing the performance analysis for the entire SAP system landscape, you need to create and evaluate trace data and statistic evaluations along the business process beyond system boundaries. In addition, you should run automated test cases and test configuration on remote systems. As of R/3 4.6C, you can use the Global Performance Analysis (ST30) for this purpose.

- **Lock table**
  The lock table isn't a table but a shared memory area. Its size can be changed by modifying the `enque/table_size` instance parameter.
- **Enqueue in a central system**
  In a central system, the dialog work processes directly access the lock table without using the enqueue process. In this Process Overview, you can't determine any activity in the enqueue process.
- **File system clean up**
  In addition to observing the fill level of the file systems that contain database and log files, it's also useful to regularly clean up the other SAP directories. A full transport or instance directory can also lead to system failures, for example, because the required logs can't be written to any longer.

## 9.15 Transactions and Menu Paths

**Alert Monitor:** SAP Menu • Tools • CCMS • Control/Monitoring • Alert Monitor (RZ20)

**ALE Status Monitor:** SAP Menu • Tools • ALE • ALE Administration • Monitoring • Status Monitor (BD87)

**Application Monitor:** SAP Menu • Tools • Administration • Monitor • Performance • Workload • Application Monitor (ST07)

**Backup Logs:** SAP Menu • Tools • CCMS • DB Administration • Backup Logs(DB12)

**Batch Input:** SAP Menu • Tools • Administration • Monitor • Batch Input (SM35)

**Buffer Load:** SAP Menu • Tools • Administration • Monitor • Performance • Setup/Buffers • Buffers (ST02)

**Business Process Analysis:** SAP Menu • Tools • Administration • Monitor • Performance • Workload • Busin. Ta. Analysis (STAD)

**Control Panel:** SAP Menu • Administration • CCMS • Control/Monitoring • Control Panel (RZ03)

**Database Monitor:** SAP Menu • Tools • Administration • Monitor • Performance • Database • Activity (ST04)

**Database Logs:** SAP Menu • Tools • CCMS • DB Administration • Operation Monitor (DB24)

**DB Parameter Changes:** SAP Menu • Tools • Administration • Monitor • Performance • Database • Parameter Changes (DB03)

**Dump Analysis:** SAP Menu • Tools • Administration • Monitor • Dump Analysis (ST22)

**DBA Planning Calendar:** SAP Menu • Tools • CCMS • DB Administration • DBA Planning Calendar (DB13)

**Error Log Files:** SAP Menu • Tools • Administration • Monitor • Traces • Developer Traces (ST11)

**Gateway Monitor:** SAP Menu • Administration • System Administration • Monitor • System Monitoring • Gateway Monitor (SMGW)

**Global User Overview:** SAP Menu • Tools • Administration • Monitor • Performance • Exceptions/Users • Active Users • Users Global (AL08)

**Global Performance Analysis:** No standard menu entry (ST30)

**Global Work Process Overview:** SAP Menu • Tools CCMS Control/Monitoring • Work Process Overview (SM66)

**ICM Monitor:** SAP Menu • Administration System Administration • Monitor • System Monitoring • ICM Monitor (SMICM)

**Job Selection:** SAP Menu • Tools • CCMS • Jobs • Maintenance (SM37)

**Load Analysis:** SAP Menu • Tools • Administration • Monitor • Performance • Workload • Analysis (ST03N)

**Lock Monitor:** SAP Menu • Tools • Administration • Monitor • Lock Entries (SM12)

**Lockwaits:** SAP Menu • Tools • Administration • Monitor • Performance • Database • Exclusive Lockwaits (DB01)

**Message Server Overview:** No standard menu entry (SMMS)

**OS Monitor:** SAP Menu • Administration • System Administration • Monitor • Performance • Operating System • Local • Activity (ST06, OS06)

**OS Parameter Changes:** SAP Menu • Tools • Administration • Monitor • Performance • Operating System • Local/Remote • Parameter Changes (OS03)

**OS System Configuration:** SAP Menu • Tools • Administration • Monitor • Performance • Operating System • Remote • Activity (OS07)

**Output Control:** SAP Menu • Tools• CCMS • Spool • Output Control (SP01)

**Performance Analysis:** SAP Menu • Tools • ABAP Workbench • Test • SQL-Trace (ST05)

**Profile Parameter Changes:** SAP Menu • Tools • Administration • Monitor • Performance • Setup/Buffers • Parameter Changes (TU02)

**Process Overview:** SAP Menu • Tools • Administration • Monitor • System Monitoring • Process Overview (SM50)

**qRFC Monitor Outbound:** Not accessible through the standard SAP menu (SMQ1)

**qRFC Monitor Inbound:** Not accessible through the standard SAP menu (SMQ2)

**SAP Directories:** SAP Menu • Administration • System Administration • Monitor • Performance • Exceptions/Users • Exceptions • SAP-Directories (AL11)

**SAP System Trace:** SAP Menu • Tools • Administration • Monitor • Traces • SAP System Trace (ST01)

**Server Overview:** SAP Menu • Tools • Administration • Monitor • System Administration • Server (SM51)

**System Administration Assistant:** SAP Menu • Tools • Administration • Monitor • System Administration Assistant (SSAA)

**System Log:** SAP Menu • Info • Syslog (SM21)

**Table Calls:** SAP Menu • Tools • Administration • Monitor • Performance • Setup/Buffers • Table Calls • Calls (ST10)

**Tables and Indices:** SAP Menu • Tools • Administration • Monitor • Performance • Database • Tables/Indices (DB02)

**Transactional RFC:** SAP Menu • Tools • Business Documents • Environment • Transactional RFC (SM58)

**User Overview:** SAP Menu • Tools • Administration • Monitor • System Monitoring • User Overview (SM04)

**Update Administration**: Not accessible through the standard SAP menu (SM14)

**Workload analysis:** SAP Menu • Administration • System Administration • Monitor • Performance • Workload • Analysis (ST03N)

## 9.16 Additional Documentation

Quick links

- SAP Service Marketplace, alias *systemmanagement*
- SAP Service Marketplace, alias *performance*

### SAP Notes

Table 9.6 provides an overview of the most important SAP Notes on SAP Service Marketplace concerning questions on system monitoring.

| Content | SAP Note |
|---|---|
| FAQ: R/3 Lock Management | 552289 |
| Multiple Enqueue Work Processes | 127773 |
| Overflow of the Lock Table | 13907 |
| Content of the TCOLL Table | 12103 |
| Getting the Latest `saposcol` | 19227 |
| `saposcol`: Monitoring Processes | 451166 |
| Description of All Available Features of Integrated ITS | 783540 |

**Table 9.5** SAP Notes Concerning System Monitoring

## 9.17 Questions

1. **Into which directory are the developer traces written?**
   a. *\users\<sid>adm*
   b. *\usr\sap\<SID>\<Instance>\work*
   c. *\usr\sap\<SID>\SYS\global*
2. **A user notifies you that his mode has been canceled with an error. Unfortunately, he can't remember any details about the cancellation. How do you ideally start the analysis?**
   a. Not at all. Without more detailed information, it's impossible to find the cause for the cancellation.
   b. Check all runtime errors in the SAP system.
   c. Check the system logs.
   d. Check the backup logs.

*In this chapter, we'll describe the basic functions of the latest ABAP Editor and the ABAP Debugger. We'll also present the most essential tools and their functionality for analyzing the performance of ABAP programs.*

# 10 Tools for Creating and Analyzing ABAP Programs

The administration of SAP NetWeaver AS is similar to the administration of any other IT system — as long as the system runs without any problems, nobody will notice the work of the administrator. But if an error occurs, the person responsible is quickly found — the admin.

This situation, with which we as the authors of this book are very well familiar, emphasizes that it's indispensable for an administrator to know the basic functions of development and analysis tools. You'll quickly be able to simulate memory consumption using a small, self-developed auxiliary program to verify system parameter settings or to provide evidence to a developer that the cause of a transaction's extremely poor response times isn't your fault but is due to a missing secondary index.

## 10.1 The New ABAP Editor

In addition to the traditional ABAP Editor, as of SAP GUI, Release 6.40, Patch Level 10 you are also provided with the new ABAP Editor. To fully integrate the new ABAP Editor into the ABAP development environment and to ensure that all related transactions can use the new editor, you must have a NetWeaver 7.0 system as the minimum technological basis.

The new ABAP Editor

The new ABAP Editor includes many practical functions for working with line-based text, which are particularly useful for handling program code. All modern editing and displaying functions for program code are combined into a single new tool. A simple modification in the **Utilities • Settings** menu item enables you to use the ABAP Editor for the following developer transactions:

- SE24 – Class Builder
- SE37 – Function Builder
- SE38 – Report Builder
- SE80 – ABAP Workbench

For this purpose, select the **Front-End Editor (New)** option in the **Editor** section (see Figure 10.1).

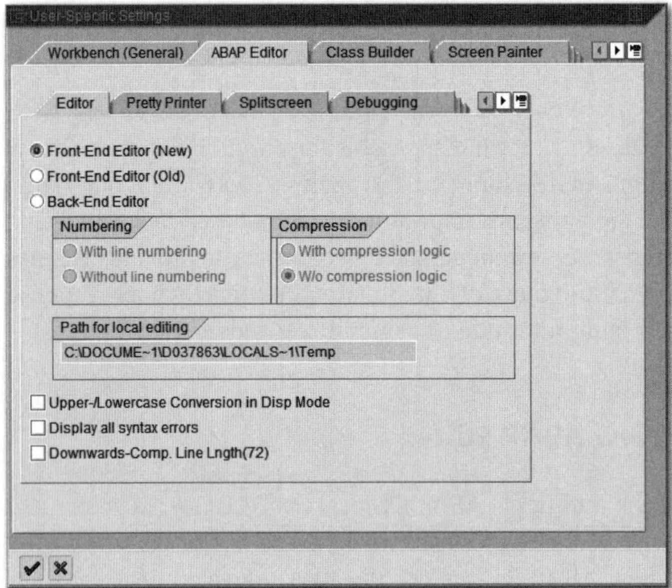


**Figure 10.1** Activating the ABAP Editor

Main screen

In addition to the numerous new options the ABAP Editor offers, for example, automatic correction or automatic completion functions, new clipboard with up to 12 levels (clipboard ring), and customizing the editor interface by means of different formatting, the ABAP Editor features a main screen with a completely new design (see Figure 10.2).

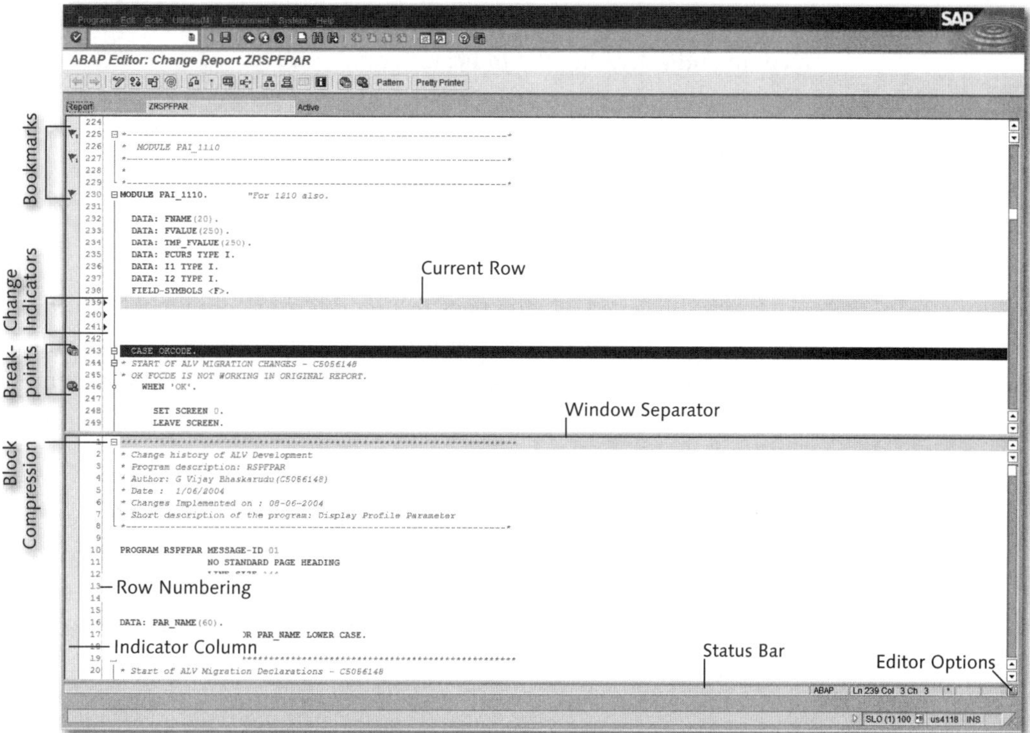


**Figure 10.2** ABAP Editor Main Screen

The main screen comprises the areas described in the following sections.

### Editor Options

Click on the folder symbol located on the right side of the status bar (lower-right corner of the Editor window) to open the options dialog of the ABAP Editor. Here, you can make the settings described in the following sections and additional configuration settings.

### Indicator Column

Setting up the main screen

The indicator column is the beige vertical bar in the left margin. In this area, you see marks, for example, breakpoints or bookmarks. You can activate and deactivate the indicator column via the editor options. We recommend activating the indicator column.

### Bookmarks

The ABAP Editor enables you to set marks (bookmarks) to facilitate the orientation in the source text. You can define up to 10 numbered bookmarks (0–9) and an unlimited number of unnumbered bookmarks. Bookmarks are displayed as blue flags in the indicator column. All functions for working with bookmarks are available by right-clicking on the indicator column and selecting the respective function in the context menu.

### Breakpoints

Session breakpoints and external breakpoints

Like bookmarks, you can define breakpoints by right-clicking on the indicator column and selecting the respective function in the context menu. You can define *session breakpoints* (stop sign with a blue screen in the foreground) or *external breakpoints* (stop sign with a person in the foreground). External breakpoints are kept also after you have completed the editor session, and in the next execution, the program flow is interrupted at this point. Session breakpoints only exist during the editor session. If you finish the editor session, the session breakpoints will be deleted.

### Row Numbers

Row numbers are displayed in a column on the left side of the program code, which considerably facilitates navigation in the source text. You can activate and deactivate the display of the row numbers in the editor options.

### Change Indicator

The change indicator indicates the rows of the source text that have been changed but not saved yet in the current editor session by means of a dark red triangle. Changed and already saved rows are indicated by means of a light red triangle in the left margin of the editor area (on the right side of the row number). You can activate and deactivate the display of the change indicators in the editor options.

### Block Compression

**Showing or hiding blocks**

Block compression lets you show or hide a block in program code. A block is a syntactically coherent source text, for example, `SELECT ... ENDSELECT`, `IF ... ENDIF`, or multirow comment texts. You can open or close blocks by clicking on the small square with the plus sign (expand) or with the minus sign (hide) on the left side of the editor area. You can activate and deactivate the block compression via the editor options.

### Status Bar

You can find the status bar at the bottom of the editor area. The status bar displays, for example, information on the status of the CapsLock key, the NumLock key, or the cursor position in the program code. You can directly navigate to the editor options via the status bar (folder symbol on the right side). You can activate and deactivate the status bar in the editor options. We recommend activating the status bar.

### Window Separator

The ABAP Editor enables you to divide the editor area (see Figure 10.3). In the individual areas, you can navigate in the source text completely independent. You can also implement other functions in one area, for example, setting a breakpoint or bookmark; the other area is then automatically updated. You can activate and deactivate the window separator by double-clicking it. If only one editor window is displayed, the window separator is located above the vertical scroll bar on the right side of the screen.

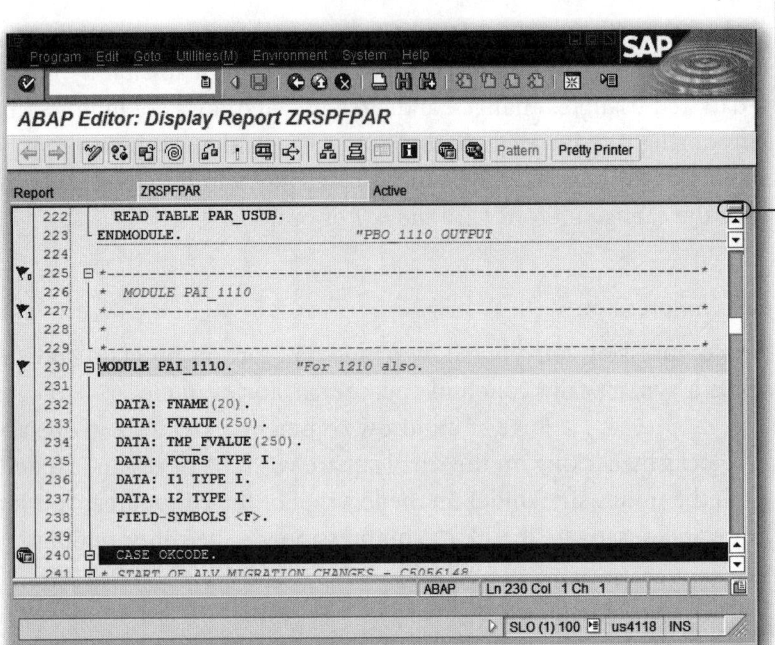


**Figure 10.3** Activating the Window Separator

## 10.2 The New ABAP Debugger

**Debugger**

Starting with SAP Web AS 6.40, a new ABAP Debugger has been included. In SAP systems with a release status older than Web AS 6.40, you can only use the classic (old) debugger, whereas in SAP systems with a release status as of SAP Web AS 6.40 both types of the debugger can be used. As of SAP NetWeaver AS 7.00, the new ABAP Debugger is used by default. In development environments, you can select which debugger is to be used. For this purpose, select one of the following transactions:

- SE24
- SE37
- SE38
- SE80

Then, in the selected transaction, select the menu item **Utilities • Settings**. Go to the **ABAP Editor** tab, and select **New Debugger** in the **Debugging** section. You can now select the required debugger.

### 10.2.1 The Technology of the New Debugger

Technology

The technology of the new ABAP Debugger differs considerably from the technology of the old debugger. The classic debugger is implemented in the same memory area or the roll area of the application to be debugged. That's why the debugger is displayed in the same window as the application. This results in some restrictions, as you can see in the following examples:

- You can't use the ABAP technology for designing the debugger interface.
- You can't analyze program parts that are directly implemented by the kernel of SAP AS, for example, conversion exits.
- Because the debugger works in the same roll area as the application, the debugger is closed when the roll area is terminated.
- When you change the roll area by means of calls, such as `SUBMIT` or `CALL TRANSACTION`, all existing settings are lost, for instance, the display of variables.

External mode

The new ABAP Debugger, in contrast, always runs in an independent external mode. This mode is kept for as long as the debugger is open. Therefore, the user changes from debugger mode to application mode during the debugger session if the application requires a user action. When the action has been completed, the user changes to the debugger mode again.

The benefit of this is that you can analyze programs without any roll area restrictions using the debugger. Although you can open a new roll area via the application, the same instance of the debugger and all settings, such as tool arrangements and displayed variables, remain active.

The startup of the new debugger is identical to the classic debugger. You should note, however, that a separate external mode is required for the debugger. In an SAP system, you can open up to six external modes per user session. If no external modes are available for starting the debugger, a message is displayed in the status bar.

To terminate the debugger and to continue the application, you must differentiate two scenarios:

1. The debugger is the active mode. You can close the debugger via the **Debugger • Terminate Debugger** menu item. The application continues in its mode. If you also want to close the application, you can select **Debugger • Terminate Application and Debugger.**
2. The application is the active mode. You can close the debugger by entering Transaction code `/hx` in the application window. The debugger connected to this application mode is terminated.

### 10.2.2 The Interface of the New Debugger

Because a separate external mode is started for the debugger, you can now use the ABAP technology for designing the debugger interface. You have the option of customizing the interfaces according to your requirements and to save this setting as the *view*. Views are available again after restarting the debugger.

Main areas

The new user interface consists of four main areas (see Figure 10.4):

1. Title bar
2. Flow control
3. Program information
4. Work areas

#### Title Bar

In the title bar of the debugger interface, you are shown which other external mode (session) is controlled by the debugger and whether the debugger is in the *exclusive mode*.

Exclusive mode means that the application to be analyzed is exclusively assigned to an SAP work process during debugging. If no other SAP work processes are available that could exclusively be used for the debugger (can be influenced via the SAP profile parameter, `rdisp/wpdbug_max_no`), the debugger changes to the *nonexclusive mode*.

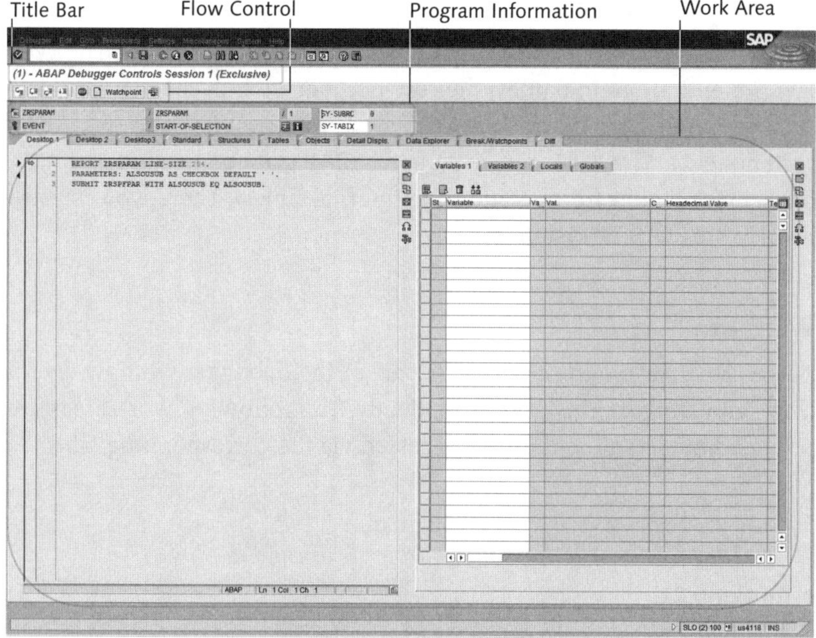


**Figure 10.4** Standard Interface of the New Debugger

**Debugging in a production system**

Because the debugger works differently and only with limited functionality in non-exclusive mode, this type of debugging isn't permitted in production systems for data security and consistency reasons. If you try to start a nonexclusive debugging session in a production system, you receive the runtime error `DEBUGGING_NOT_POSSIBLE`.

## Flow Control

The functions of flow control can be found directly below the title information and are identical to the functions of the classic debugger. These include the following:

- Single step [F5]
- Execute [F6]
- Return [F7]
- Continue [F8]

Additionally, you can also save the current layout.

Program information

### Program Information

You can find the program information below the flow control. The Web Dynpro and program names, the row numbers, the event category, and the event name are displayed. Moreover, you can view the two ABAP system fields, `SY-SUBRC` (return code of ABAP statements) and `SY-TABIX` (current row index for operations on internal tables). There, you can also display other ABAP system fields.

### Work Area

The work areas require the largest part of the debugger window. Every user can configure this area individually. The following work areas are provided by default and can be accessed via the corresponding tabs:

- Desktop 1
- Desktop 2
- Desktop 3
- Standard
- Structures
- Tables
- Objects
- Detail screen
- Data Explorer
- Breakpoints/watchpoints
- Diff

You can configure all of these work areas individually with regard to size and the tools used. The only restriction is that you can place a maximum of four tools for each work area. Moreover, you can only store the configuration of the user-specific work areas, Desktop 1, Desktop 2, and Desktop 3, via the **Store Layout** function on the database. The other work areas are reset to the basic setting when you restart the debugger.

**Critical Profile Parameters for the Debugger**

- `rdisp/wpdbug_max_number`
  Maximum number of debugging work processes in exclusive mode.
- `rdisp/max_debug_lazy_time`
  Maximum time in seconds until a debugging process is terminated that is no longer in use.

## 10.3 Runtime Analysis

Runtime analysis

The ABAP Runtime Analysis (Transaction SE30) is the tool of choice if you don't know yet which part of a program will cause a long runtime. We recommend this tool as the entry point for performance analysis of an application. If you've identified the component of an application that presumably causes the performance problem (e.g., database access), you can specifically and systematically analyze the problem using specialized traces.

Using the ABAP Runtime Analysis enables you to obtain a general overview of the execution time of your ABAP program. This measures the time required to execute the individual ABAP program units, for example, reports, function modules, subroutines, and so on. For the components listed in Table 10.1 , the runtime analysis can measure the computing time.

| Type | Component |
| --- | --- |
| Database accesses | ▸ OPEN SQL<br>▸ Native SQL<br>▸ EXPORT ... TO<br>▸ IMPORT ... FROM |
| Context application | ▸ SUPPLY<br>▸ DEMAND |

**Table 10.1** Measurable Components

| Type | Component |
|---|---|
| Modularization units | ▶ MODULE<br>▶ PERFORM<br>▶ CALL FUNCTION<br>▶ CALL SCREEN<br>▶ CALL TRANSACTION<br>▶ CALL DIALOG<br>▶ CALL METHOD<br>▶ SUBMIT |
| Internal table operations | ▶ APPEND<br>▶ COLLECT<br>▶ SORT<br>▶ INSERT<br>▶ MODIFY<br>▶ DELETE<br>▶ READ TABLE |
| Data transfer | ▶ READ DATASET<br>▶ TRANSFER |
| OO operations | ▶ CALL METHOD<br>▶ CREATE OBJECT<br>▶ RAISE EVENT |
| Other | ▶ ASSIGN<br>▶ EXPORT<br>▶ GENERATE<br>▶ IMPORT<br>▶ MESSAGE<br>▶ SET LOCALE<br>▶ SET PF-STATUS<br>▶ SET TITLEBAR |

**Table 10.1** Measurable Components (Cont.)

The analysis results are written in a performance data file. You can determine the name of the performance data file and the directory in which it's stored via the `abap/atrapath` SAP profile parameter. Using the `abap/atrasizequota` parameter, you can restrict the size of the directory. If the total of the existing performance data files exceeds the size determined in the parameter, a warning is issued. You should then delete old or no longer needed files.

**Critical Profile Parameters for the Runtime Analysis**

- `abap/atrapath`
  Directory and name mask for performance data files.
- `abap/atrasizequota`
  Maximum storage space for the *abap/atrapath* directory; a warning is issued if this value has been exceeded.

### 10.3.1 Initial Screen

Table 10.2 shows you the different options to call the runtime analysis for ABAP programs.

| Start | Transaction/Menu |
|---|---|
| Direct | SE30 |
| Via an arbitrary mode | System • Utilities • Runtime Analysis • Execute |
| ABAP Workbench | Test • Runtime Analysis |
| Initial screen of the ABAP Editor | Program • Execute • Runtime Analysis |
| ABAP Editor | Utilities • Additional Utilities • Runtime Analysis |

**Table 10.2** Options for Calling the Runtime Analysis

**Functions of the runtime analysis**

In the runtime analysis, you are provided with different functions (see Figure 10.5):

- Measurement in dialog
- Measurement in parallel session
- Scheduling a measurement
- Determining measurement restrictions
- Evaluating the performance data files

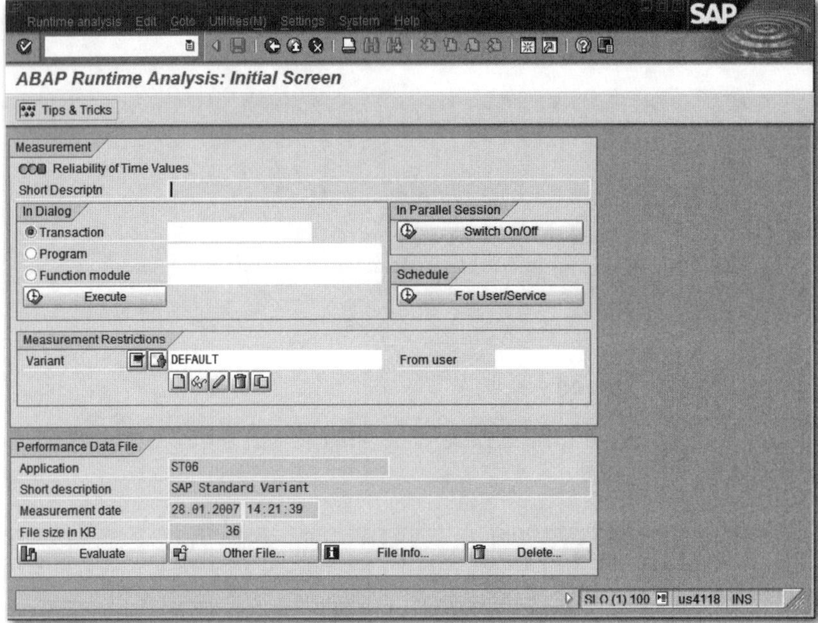


**Figure 10.5** Runtime Analysis

For measuring the dialog transaction, you can simply enter the corresponding transaction, program name, or function module in the input field and click on the **Execute** button. The measurement starts automatically. Now, the complete coding, including all possible user interactions, is run. To terminate the measurement, press the F3 function key, or select the **Back** button at the end of the transaction/program. You then return to the initial screen of the runtime analysis; the measurement is automatically terminated, and the information is stored in the performance data file.

Parallel session

If you want to analyze an already running program, select the **Switch On/Off** button in the **In Parallel Session** area. A work process list of the current instance is displayed. Select the corresponding work process, and click on the **Activate Measurement** button. The status of the runtime analysis is displayed as a symbol in the work process list. A yellow triangle means that the measurement has been marked but not yet started. A green square indicates that the measurement is active. If you want to terminate the measurement, you can mark the corresponding row in the work process list and select **Terminate Measurement**.

In older releases, some processes couldn't be measured because they couldn't be executed in dialog operation and were too short for measurement in a parallel session (e.g., HTTP requests). You can now implement this via the measurement scheduling option. The measurement starts automatically, for example, if it's scheduled for a specific user and independent of how long the user action lasts.

Selection criteria

Different selection criteria, such as user, client, process type, object type and name, expiration date, or expiration time, enable you to restrict the actions to be measured. You can also schedule a specific number of measurements with identical selection characteristics (maximum number of planned measurements) or restrict the period of time in which the measurements are to be implemented (expiration time, expiration date).

Each measurement is written in a separate performance data file. You can select a corresponding evaluation file in the **Performance Data File** area of the initial screen.

Generally, you can define measurement restrictions for all measurement types by creating or changing the variant in the **Measurement Restrictions** area of the initial screen. In a variant, you can determine for which program part you want to implement a measurement, which statements are to be measured within the program parts, the duration of the measurement, or the maximum size of the performance data file.

### 10.3.2 Single Activity Trace (SAT) – Further Development of the Runtime Analysis

As of SAP NetWeaver AS 7.0, a new transaction has been available for runtime analysis: The Single Activity Trace (SAT) extends the display and evaluation options of Transaction SE30. You can now compare two recorded measurements, which is very useful, for example, to display the impact of implemented tuning measures. Moreover, the display has been customized to the new design of the current ABAP Editor and ABAP Debugger, and offers numerous practical and very convenient functions to evaluate the content of performance data files.

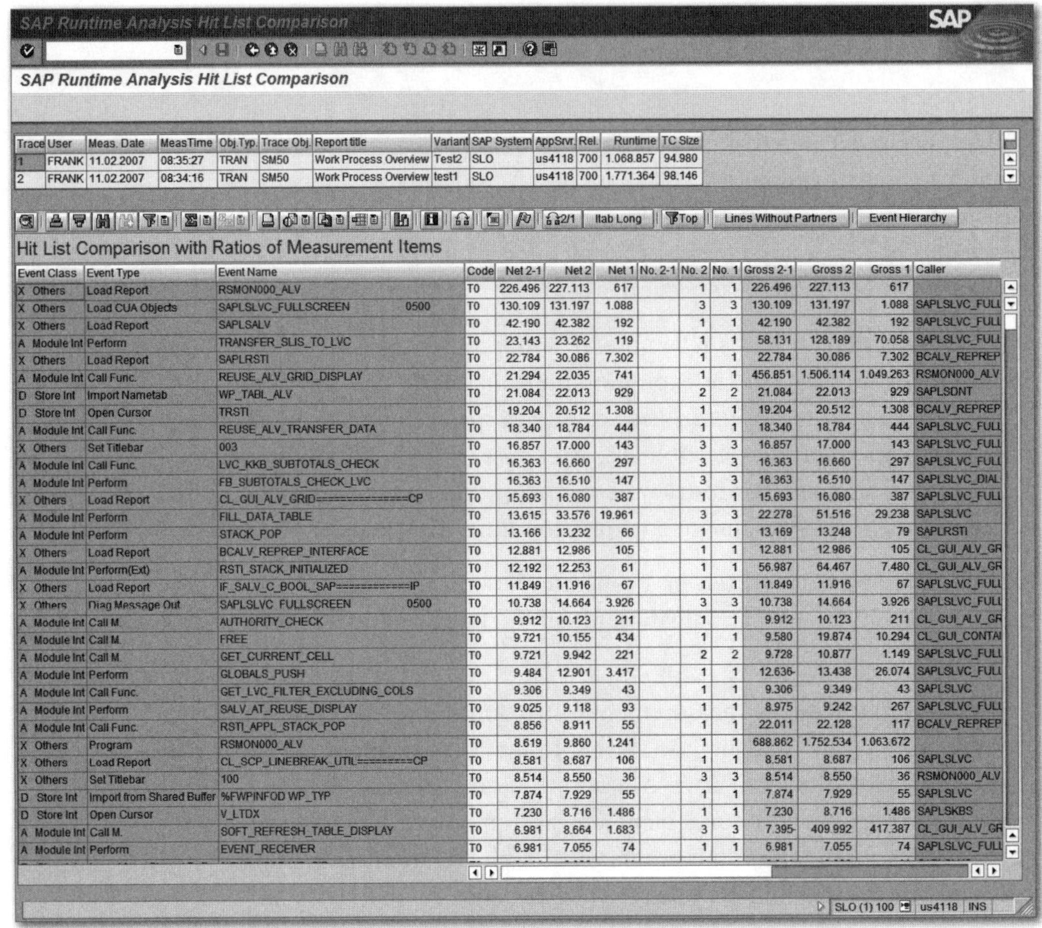

SAP Runtime Analysis Hit List Comparison

| Trace | User | Meas. Date | MeasTime | Obj.Typ. | Trace Obj. | Report title | Variant | SAP System | AppSrvr. | Rel. | Runtime | TC Size |
|---|---|---|---|---|---|---|---|---|---|---|---|---|
| 1 | FRANK | 11.02.2007 | 08:35:27 | TRAN | SM50 | Work Process Overview | Test2 | SLO | us4118 | 700 | 1.068.857 | 94.980 |
| 2 | FRANK | 11.02.2007 | 08:34:16 | TRAN | SM50 | Work Process Overview | test1 | SLO | us4118 | 700 | 1.771.364 | 98.146 |

Hit List Comparison with Ratios of Measurement Items

| Event Class | Event Type | Event Name | Code | Net 2-1 | Net 2 | Net 1 | No. 2-1 | No. 2 | No. 1 | Gross 2-1 | Gross 2 | Gross 1 | Caller |
|---|---|---|---|---|---|---|---|---|---|---|---|---|---|
| X Others | Load Report | RSMON000_ALV | T0 | 226.496 | 227.113 | 617 | | 1 | 1 | 226.496 | 227.113 | 617 | |
| X Others | Load CUA Objects | SAPLSLVC_FULLSCREEN 0500 | T0 | 130.109 | 131.197 | 1.088 | | 3 | 3 | 130.109 | 131.197 | 1.088 | SAPLSLVC_FULL |
| X Others | Load Report | SAPLSALV | T0 | 42.190 | 42.382 | 192 | | 1 | 1 | 42.190 | 42.382 | 192 | SAPLSLVC_FULL |
| A Module Int | Perform | TRANSFER_SLIS_TO_LVC | T0 | 23.143 | 23.262 | 119 | | 1 | 1 | 58.131 | 128.189 | 70.058 | SAPLSLVC_FULL |
| X Others | Load Report | SAPLRSTI | T0 | 22.784 | 30.086 | 7.302 | | 1 | 1 | 22.784 | 30.086 | 7.302 | BCALV_REPREP |
| A Module Int | Call Func. | REUSE_ALV_GRID_DISPLAY | T0 | 21.294 | 22.035 | 741 | | 1 | 1 | 456.851 | 1.506.114 | 1.049.263 | RSMON000_ALV |
| D Store Int | Import Nametab | WP_TABL_ALV | T0 | 21.084 | 22.013 | 929 | | 2 | 2 | 21.084 | 22.013 | 929 | SAPLSDNT |
| D Store Int | Open Cursor | TRSTI | T0 | 19.204 | 20.512 | 1.308 | | 1 | 1 | 19.204 | 20.512 | 1.308 | BCALV_REPREP |
| A Module Int | Call Func. | REUSE_ALV_TRANSFER_DATA | T0 | 18.340 | 18.784 | 444 | | 1 | 1 | 18.340 | 18.784 | 444 | SAPLSLVC_FULL |
| X Others | Set Titlebar | 003 | T0 | 16.857 | 17.000 | 143 | | 3 | 3 | 16.857 | 17.000 | 143 | SAPLSLVC_FULL |
| A Module Int | Call Func. | LVC_KKB_SUBTOTALS_CHECK | T0 | 16.363 | 16.660 | 297 | | 3 | 3 | 16.363 | 16.660 | 297 | SAPLSLVC_FULL |
| A Module Int | Perform | FB_SUBTOTALS_CHECK_LVC | T0 | 16.363 | 16.510 | 147 | | 3 | 3 | 16.363 | 16.510 | 147 | SAPLSLVC_DIAL |
| X Others | Load Report | CL_GUI_ALV_GRID===============CP | T0 | 15.693 | 16.080 | 387 | | 1 | 1 | 15.693 | 16.080 | 387 | SAPLSLVC_FULL |
| A Module Int | Perform | FILL_DATA_TABLE | T0 | 13.615 | 33.576 | 19.961 | | 3 | 3 | 22.278 | 51.516 | 29.238 | SAPLSLVC |
| A Module Int | Perform | STACK_POP | T0 | 13.166 | 13.232 | 66 | | 1 | 1 | 13.169 | 13.248 | 79 | SAPLRSTI |
| X Others | Load Report | BCALV_REPREP_INTERFACE | T0 | 12.881 | 12.986 | 105 | | 1 | 1 | 12.881 | 12.986 | 105 | CL_GUI_ALV_GR |
| A Module Int | Perform(Ext) | RSTI_STACK_INITIALIZED | T0 | 12.192 | 12.253 | 61 | | 1 | 1 | 56.987 | 64.467 | 7.480 | CL_GUI_ALV_GR |
| X Others | Load Report | IF_SALV_C_BOOL_SAP============IP | T0 | 11.849 | 11.916 | 67 | | 1 | 1 | 11.849 | 11.916 | 67 | SAPLSLVC_FULL |
| X Others | Diag Message Out | SAPLSLVC FULLSCREEN 0500 | T0 | 10.738 | 14.664 | 3.926 | | 3 | 3 | 10.738 | 14.664 | 3.926 | SAPLSLVC_FULL |
| A Module Int | Call M. | AUTHORITY_CHECK | T0 | 9.912 | 10.123 | 211 | | 1 | 1 | 9.912 | 10.123 | 211 | CL_GUI_ALV_GR |
| A Module Int | Call M. | FREE | T0 | 9.721 | 10.155 | 434 | | 1 | 1 | 9.580 | 19.874 | 10.294 | CL_GUI_CONTAI |
| A Module Int | Call M. | GET_CURRENT_CELL | T0 | 9.721 | 9.942 | 221 | | 2 | 2 | 9.728 | 10.877 | 1.149 | SAPLSLVC_FULL |
| A Module Int | Perform | GLOBALS_PUSH | T0 | 9.484 | 12.901 | 3.417 | | 1 | 1 | 12.636- | 13.438 | 26.074 | SAPLSLVC_FULL |
| A Module Int | Call Func. | GET_LVC_FILTER_EXCLUDING_COLS | T0 | 9.306 | 9.349 | 43 | | 1 | 1 | 9.306 | 9.349 | 43 | SAPLSLVC |
| A Module Int | Perform | SALV_AT_REUSE_DISPLAY | T0 | 9.025 | 9.118 | 93 | | 1 | 1 | 8.975 | 9.242 | 267 | SAPLSLVC_FULL |
| A Module Int | Call Func. | RSTI_APPL_STACK_POP | T0 | 8.856 | 8.911 | 55 | | 1 | 1 | 22.011 | 22.128 | 117 | BCALV_REPREP |
| X Others | Program | RSMON000_ALV | T0 | 8.619 | 9.860 | 1.241 | | 1 | 1 | 688.862 | 1.752.534 | 1.063.672 | |
| X Others | Load Report | CL_SCP_LINEBREAK_UTIL=========CP | T0 | 8.581 | 8.687 | 106 | | 1 | 1 | 8.581 | 8.687 | 106 | SAPLSLVC |
| X Others | Set Titlebar | 100 | T0 | 8.514 | 8.550 | 36 | | 3 | 3 | 8.514 | 8.550 | 36 | RSMON000_ALV |
| D Store Int | Import from Shared Buffer | %FWPINFOD WP_TYP | T0 | 7.874 | 7.929 | 55 | | 1 | 1 | 7.874 | 7.929 | 55 | SAPLSLVC |
| D Store Int | Open Cursor | V_LTDX | T0 | 7.230 | 8.716 | 1.486 | | 1 | 1 | 7.230 | 8.716 | 1.486 | SAPLSKBS |
| A Module Int | Call M. | SOFT_REFRESH_TABLE_DISPLAY | T0 | 6.981 | 8.664 | 1.683 | | 3 | 3 | 7.395- | 409.992 | 417.387 | CL_GUI_ALV_GR |
| A Module Int | Perform | EVENT_RECEIVER | T0 | 6.981 | 7.055 | 74 | | 1 | 1 | 6.981 | 7.055 | 74 | SAPLSLVC_FULL |

**Figure 10.6** Comparing Two Measurements

Process Overview

Figure 10.6 shows an example that compares two runtime analyses of a call of the Process Overview (SM50) transaction (first call = Trace 2; second call = Trace 1). In addition to displaying the gross and net run times and the number of executions of the individual components, you can also view the respective differences. In the first row of the hit list comparison, you can see the loading of the RSMON000_ALV report required 226,496 microseconds less for the second execution (Trace 1) than for the first call. The reason could be that the report had to be loaded in the program buffer for the first call, whereas the report had already been available in the buffer for the second call for direct execution.

## 10.4 Performance Trace

Performance analysis

In Performance Analysis (ST05), you are provided with different tools with which you can analyze database access, lock operations, RFCs, and accesses to the SAP table buffers. Table 10.3 gives you a more detailed description of the various trace types.

| Trace Type | Usage |
|---|---|
| SQL trace | The SQL trace writes all accesses to the RDBMS that are implemented via the database interface of the work process (SELECT, INSERT, UPDATE, DELETE, COMMIT, ROLLBACK). |
| Enqueue trace | The enqueue trace includes information about the duration of the SAP lock operations (ENQUEUE and DEQUEUE statements in ABAP programs). |
| RFC trace | The RFC trace provides information about the duration of function module calls that are executed via RFC (remote). |
| Table buffer trace | The table buffer trace writes duration of accesses to tables or table parts that are temporarily stored in SAP table buffers on the application servers. |

**Table 10.3** Trace Types

You can select each trace separately for analysis, or you can simultaneously activate the traces in any arbitrary combination.

Trace files

The trace information that is collected during analysis is stored in a file of the instance's file system. You can determine the file names via the `rstr/filename` parameter. The maximum size of the trace file is controlled via the `rstr/max_filesize_MB` parameter (default: 16MB). If the trace file reaches this size, it's renamed. For this purpose, a counter is added to the file name (00-99). Via the `rstr/max_files` parameter, you can control the number of old trace files (default: 10). If the maximum number of possible trace files has been reached, the first file is overwritten again.

**Critical Profile Parameters for the Performance Trace**

- `rstr/filename`
  Name of the trace file.
- `rstr/max_files`
  Number of possible trace files.
- `rstr/max_filesize_MB`
  Size of the trace file.

### 10.4.1 The User Interface of the Performance Trace

The user interface of Transaction ST05 generally consists of three areas (see Figure 10.7):

- Select Trace
- Select Trace Function
- Trace Status

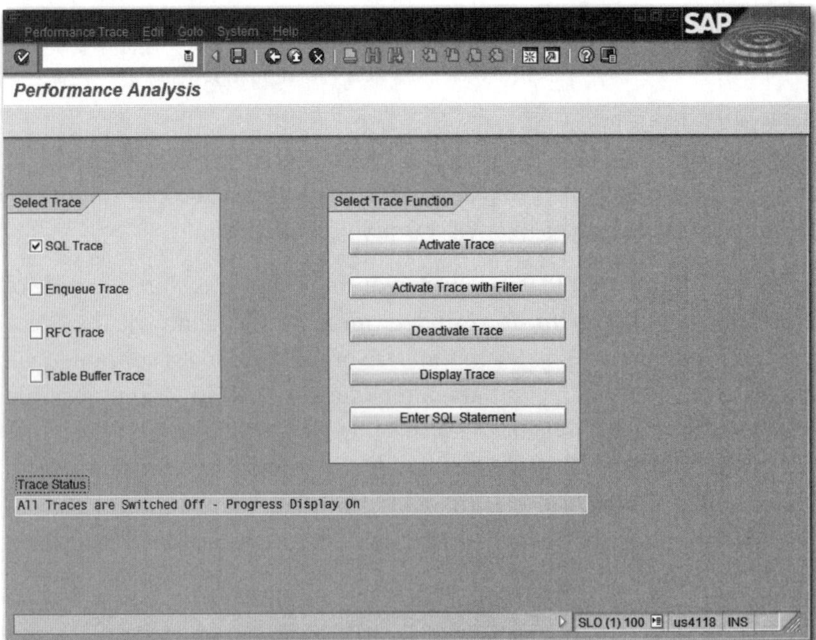


**Figure 10.7** User Interface of the Performance Trace (ST05)

In the **Select Trace** area, you can determine which type of trace is supposed to be written. Any combination of the options displayed is possible. If you select multiple options, a lot of information is written in the trace file, which results in fast growth. Therefore, we recommend selecting only one trace type for the sake of clarity. If required, you can repeat the trace using another trace type.

In the **Select Trace Function** area, you can activate the trace, activate with filter, and deactivate the trace. Moreover, you can display the trace or directly analyze an SQL statement.

Trace status

The **Trace Status** indicates whether a trace is active for the instance in which you are currently logged-on. For each instance, a trace can be activated only once. The progress bar shows the processing progress for displaying a trace file. It can be activated or deactivated in the **Edit** menu item.

### 10.4.2 Creating a Performance Trace

The performance trace is preferably used for analyzing access methods and access times to RDBMS. Its purpose is to detect particularly resource-intensive and performance-critical accesses if specific process flows are required. By default, the performance trace is deactivated. You need to activate the trace to record trace information.

Activating the trace

When activating the trace, you first determine for which type of functions it's activated (SQL, enqueue, RFC, table buffer). Then you activate the trace by clicking on the **Activate Trace** button. The trace is only active for the instance for which it was activated. You can only record the activities of the user who activated the trace.

But you can also activate the trace using the **Activate Trace with Filter** button. Here, you can determine restriction criteria. Then, only results are recorded that correspond to the criteria. Figure 10.8 shows the options for entering filter criteria.

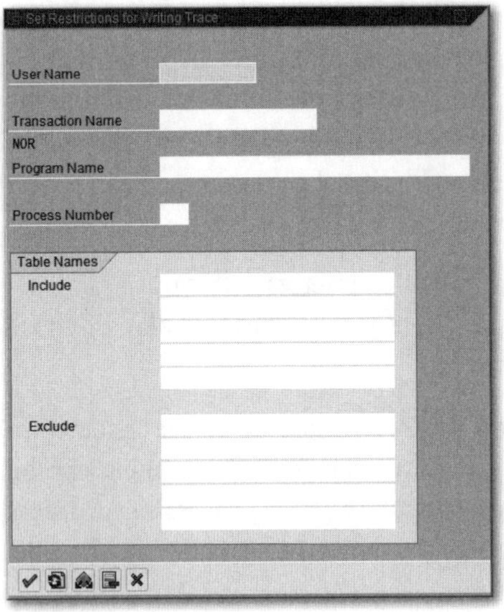

**Figure 10.8** Filter Criteria for the Performance Trace

After you have activated the trace, you can implement the action to be analyzed. It's vital that you implement the action on the same instance on which the trace is active; otherwise, no information is written. When the action to be analyzed has been completed, you need to deactivate the trace by clicking on the **Deactivate Trace** button. You can now display the content of the trace file using the **Display Trace** button. If you want to analyze the result at a later point, remember that the trace files are overwritten after a specific time.

Trace types

The output is different depending on the trace type you selected:

- **SQL trace**
  The SQL trace shows how the Open SQL commands used in the action to be analyzed are translated into standard SQL commands, and which parameters are used to execute them and transfer them to the database system. The following information can be obtained using an SQL trace:
  - Open-SQL statement of the application
  - Parameters with which the statement was implemented
  - Standard SQL statement derived from the Open SQL statement

  - Duration of a process step
  - The table that the SQL statement accesses
  - Number of result records

- **Enqueue trace**
  The enqueue trace includes all lock statements and parameters created by the analyzed action with which a lock operation was implemented. These include the following:
  - Lock statement
  - Table name of the lock object
  - Name of the program that triggered the lock
  - Lock type
  - Lock owner
  - Duration of the lock operation

- **RFC trace**
  The RFCs of the action to be analyzed are written in the RFC trace. The following information can be obtained using an RFC trace:
  - Function module called via RFC
  - Status of the RFC
  - Duration of the RFC
  - Number of sent and received bytes
  - Instance on which the RFC was implemented

- **Table buffer trace**
  The table buffer trace file comprises information about the accesses that are carried out via the SAP table buffer. The following information is recorded:
  - Duration of a buffer access
  - Buffer operation
  - Table name
  - Number of result records
  - Key value for buffer access

Trace list compressed according to SQL statements

SQL trace is the most frequently used trace type. Using this trace enables you to get an overview of the duration of the individual database accesses of an application and localize expensive database accesses, for example, statements that have been running for a long time or that have been implemented using identical selection criteria. Experience has shown that at least 50% of all performance problems can be traced back to expensive database accesses. Therefore, we'll discuss the use of the SQL traces here. The trace summarized by SQL statements is particularly helpful. This can be displayed in the SQL trace display via the menu path **Trace List • Summarize Trace by SQL Statement**, or the key combination [Shift]+ [F8].

You should pay special attention to the columns, **Executions**, **Identical**, and **Time/exec**.

The **Identical** column shows the percent value of identical `SELECT` statements (`WHERE` condition is value-identical) from the total number of statement-identical executions (**Executions** column). A high value in these columns indicates optimization potential. Here you should try to decreasse the number of identical executions of a statement, for example, through intelligent temporary storage of frequently used information or by avoiding nested `SELECT` loops.

Long-running SQL statements

A high value in the **Time/exec** column indicates long-running SQL statements. A typical SQL statement that reads table data via an appropriate index should be executed within 20ms. Again, there are also many exceptions here: If the required time per execution is considerably higher, you should carry out an in-depth analysis. To obtain more information on the tools for performance analysis and the procedure models for analyzing different performance problems, refer to the book, *SAP Performance Optimization* by Thomas Schneider (SAP PRESS, 2008).

The additional trace types available in Transaction ST05 are also very interesting; refer to the book previously mentioned for more details.

### 10.4.3 Analyzing Individual SQL Statements

Analyzing individual statements

To analyze individual SQL statements, you don't necessarily have to implement a complete SQL performance trace. You can analyze individual SQL statements via the **Enter SQL Statement** button on the ST05 initial screen. You should note that the appearance and the displayed information of the SQL traces, particularly of the `EXPLAIN` plan, depend on the database system used. You have the option of viewing the execution strategy of the SQL command that has been selected by the optimizer of the corresponding RDBMS. Here, the performance trace is the tool of choice if you assume SQL commands in a dialog program with a particularly long runtime, for which no appropriate index has been defined on a table.

## 10.5 Tips

- **Measuring variant**
  For initial measurement, the default variant is ideally suited. If you decide to activate the measurement of operations on internal tables, the performance data file will grow rapidly. Consequently, you should customize the maximum permitted file size in the variant.

  Measuring an application, particularly if you want to measure operations on internal tables, creates significant loads on the instance. In production systems, you should avoid this type of runtime analysis. If this isn't possible, you need to activate the runtime analysis only for a few minutes and only for the corresponding components.

- **Performance trace**
  By activating the performance trace, you considerably increase the write load on the respective server. Therefore, you should only use the trace production systems in emergency cases.

  To avoid redundant write load, you always need to use the performance trace in a targeted manner and only for a few selected users and actions (transaction or program name). Ideally, you can limit the trace to the affected tables, if these are known in advance.

## 10.6 Transactions and Menu Paths

**ABAP Editor**: Tools • ABAP Workbench • Development • ABAP Editor (SE38)

**Runtime Analysis:** Tools • ABAP Workbench • Test • Runtime Analysis (SE30)

**SQL Trace**: Tools • ABAP Workbench • Test • SQL Trace (ST05)

## 10.7 Additional Documentation

SAP Notes

Table 10.4 provides an overview of important SAP Notes in the SAP Service Marketplace concerning questions on tools for development support.

| Content | SAP Note |
|---|---|
| Excessive Resource Consumption of the New ABAP Editor | 952559 |
| ABAP Editor as a Part of SAP GUI 6.40 | 843289 |
| Starting the New ABAP Debugger as a Report | 966666 |

**Table 10.4** SAP Notes Concerning the ABAP Editor and ABAP Debugger

*The monitoring architecture, as an integral part of SAP NetWeaver, provides the system administrator with a central monitoring platform for the SAP system landscape.*

# 11 Monitoring Architecture

In addition to the manual monitoring and analysis options described in Chapter 9, System Monitoring, using the automatic functions of monitoring architecture enables you to increase the quality and reliability of your system administration activities.

In this chapter, we explain the structure of the monitoring architecture and the components used. We'll also show you how to adapt the monitoring architecture to meet your requirements and describe uses of CCMS agents and how specific auto-reaction methods enable you to receive email messages if certain events occur, for example.

Data collectors

In an extensible infrastructure, data and key figures for predefined objects are compiled in areas of the shared memory of SAP systems using specialized collection programs and then are cumulated and saved in database tables. You can analyze this data according to different criteria using third-party products and the alert monitor integrated into the CCMS (Computing Center Management System). In addition to the local analyses on the monitored system itself, you can also configure a central SAP Basis system (central monitoring system, CEN) where all data of monitored SAP and non-SAP systems run together. The following three layers and their interaction are displayed in Figure 11.1:

- Data collection
- Data retention
- Data administration and analysis

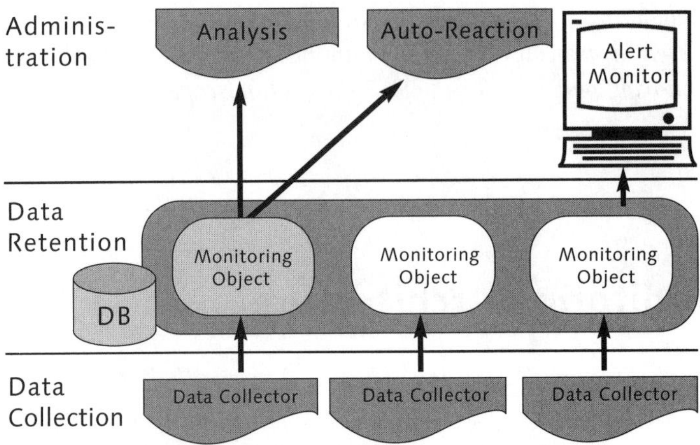


**Figure 11.1** Monitoring Architecture

## 11.1 Alert Monitor

The monitoring architecture enables you to monitor an individual SAP system locally, and in particular, several SAP systems centrally, in relation to their most important components, statistics, and performance in the system landscape. You can also connect and monitor corresponding external non-SAP systems. The alert monitor displays the collected information about the relevant systems in a tree structure.

### 11.1.1 Basic Principles

The values collected and formatted according to different criteria within the monitoring architecture are displayed in the alert monitor. As system administrator, you can set system-specific threshold values, so that if these values exceed or fall below the threshold, they will be highlighted in traffic light colors and reported as a malfunction in the alert monitor. To analyze problems in detail and notify the system administrator or introduce a troubleshooting action that can be automated, you can also define *analysis and auto-reaction methods* and assign tree elements to the monitoring architecture.

Advantage

The advantage of the alert monitor is that information can be communicated to the system administrator by being triggered in the system, without the system administrator having to make an explicit request to the relevant system or having to log on to this system. SAP systems already provide a number of specific analysis tools for the different components (see Chapter 15, Service and Support). Nevertheless, the administrator still has to initiate the analysis for these systems. As an enhancement to this, the alert monitor developed by SAP can evaluate the different areas of the system landscape itself using selected parameters, specifically set threshold values, and, if necessary, create signal warnings. If required, the system administrator can use the alert monitor information to perform a detailed analysis with the specific tools integrated into the SAP software or immediately begin solving the problem.

SAP provides alert monitors with every software product of the SAP family. These alert monitors cover all important areas of system, database, and operating system administration for operating the software components.

Monitor set

The alert monitors are grouped in *monitor sets* according to specific target groups and provided with default settings so that they can be used in their basic function immediately after a system is installed. You will find predefined monitors with minor release-dependent differences in the CCMS using Alert Monitor (RZ20):

- **SAP CCMS Monitor Templates**
  Monitors for normal SAP system administration.
- **SAP CCMS Technical Experts Monitors**
  Monitors for analyzing problems and monitoring the monitoring architecture itself.
- **SAP CCMS Monitors for Optional Components**
  Monitors for monitoring special components such as logon load distribution, selected transactions or clients, and defined log files.

Based on these monitor sets (see Figure 11.2), the customer can create his own monitors with specific views of selected areas, add more alerts by defining his own data collectors and objects (see Section 11.1.3, Technical Implementation), and change the default settings. Users can also implement external tools. The customers' requirements will determine how much the basic settings and monitor sets will need to be changed. In smaller system landscapes and in a system's implementation phase, the monitors provided by SAP are usually already sufficient with only a few customer-specific adjustments. An alert monitor analysis is relatively simple and self-explanatory. Defining your own alert monitors or implementing your own alerts, however, is considerably more difficult. The following sections can therefore lay the foundation for you. You will learn the vocabulary of the alert monitor concept that forms the basis of possible changes. We'll then show you how to customize, that is, adapt, the predefined monitors to the customer-specific characteristic of a system and landscape.

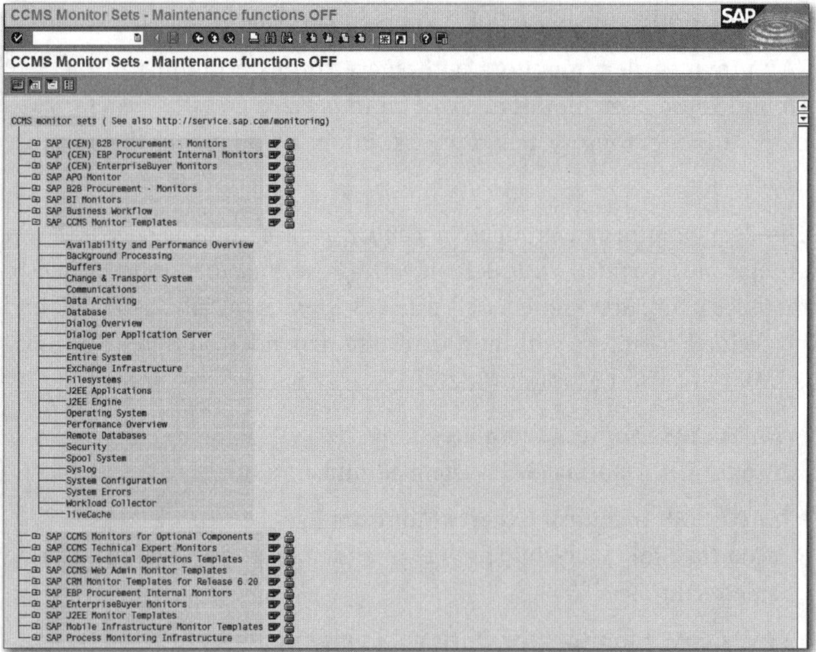


**Figure 11.2** Monitor Sets Provided by SAP

### 11.1.2 Components

A monitor set groups any number of monitors logically; the monitors themselves are each arranged in a tree structure.

**Monitoring tree elements**

The branch nodes of the monitoring tree are called *Monitoring Tree Elements* (MTE). An MTE groups lower-level leaves and other MTEs logically. This is also referred to as a *monitor summary node* or simply *node*.

Monitoring attribute

The leaves of the monitoring tree are created using *monitoring attributes*. The monitoring attribute describes the infotype of individual elements of the SAP system to be observed. It refers to an individual property of a monitoring object. The following are the types of monitoring attributes:

- **Performance attribute**
  This attribute represents a measurement of a size, or also the frequency of an event. The color changes if defined threshold values are exceeded.
- **Status attribute**
  An alert is triggered when an individual, defined message appears.
- **Log attribute**
  The messages of a log file are searched according to a predefined pattern. An alert is triggered when one of these character strings appears.
- **Heartbeat**
  This monitoring attribute is used for the watchdog monitoring of defined system elements such as SAP services, for example. An alarm is triggered if the monitored element fails.
- **Text attribute**
  Unlike the monitoring attributes just described, text attributes are only used for describing values of certain monitoring tree elements. They only provide information and do not trigger any alerts.

Monitoring object

All monitoring attributes that refer to a commonly monitored object, or to a situation, are grouped into a logical unit, the *monitoring object*, (see Figure 11.3). The merging data of a monitoring object is physically saved in a *monitoring segment* in the memory area. For example, the following are monitoring objects:

- *Dialog*, consisting of monitoring attributes such as *ResponseTime*, *ProgramErrors*, and *UsersLoggedIn*
- *R3Syslog*, which includes a *basis system*, *database*, and *applications*, among other things
- *Server configuration* with the *SAP kernel release*, *machine type*, and *host* monitoring attributes

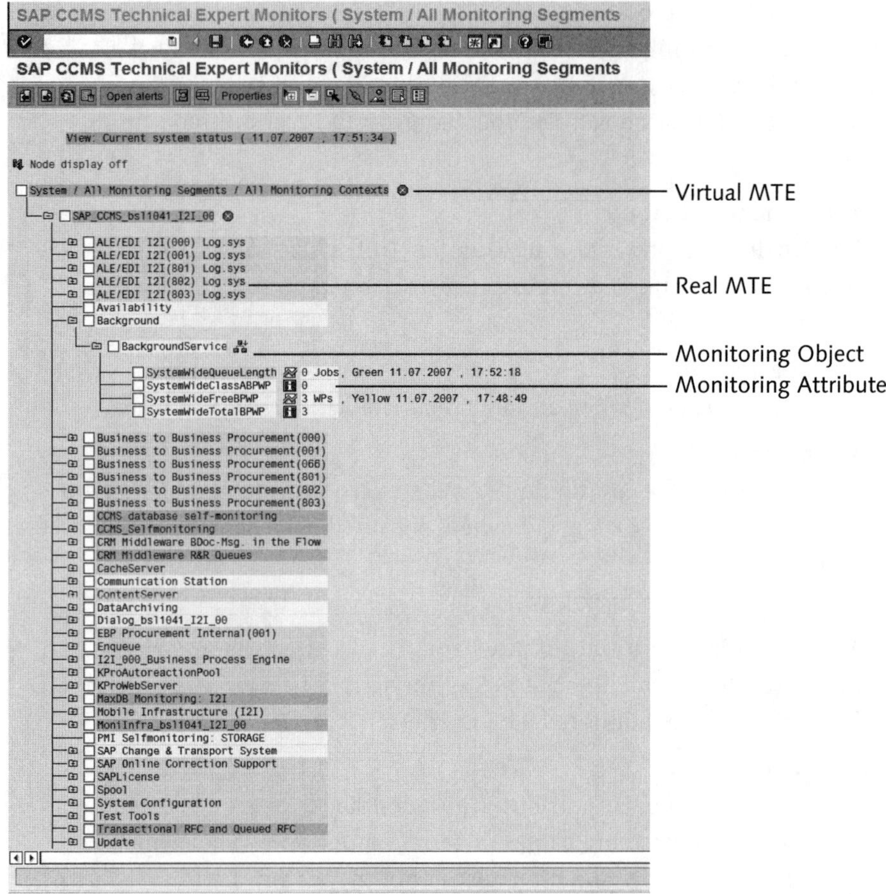


**Figure 11.3** Elements of a Monitor

A monitoring object is actually an MTE, specifically, the smallest possible monitoring summary node. Several MTEs can in turn be grouped into an MTE to improve the legibility of the data displayed. If an alarm is generated on a monitoring attribute because a value has exceeded or fallen below the set threshold, the corresponding attribute and all higher-level nodes are displayed accordingly highlighted in color, which means that the administrator will at first glance already be able to tell from the highest-level node elements whether a problem has occurred on at least one of the lower-level attributes. Red means that a problem or error has occurred, yellow indicates a warning, and green means that everything is fine (see Figure 11.4).

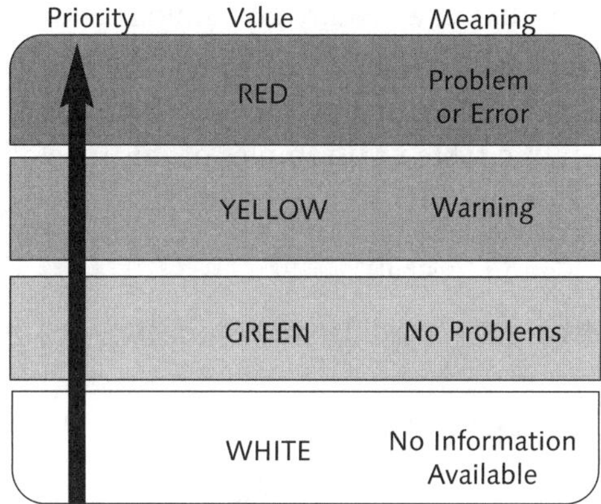


**Figure 11.4** Node Status Displayed in Traffic Light Colors

Real and virtual MTEs

If you store data for an MTE in a separate monitoring segment, the MTE is referred to as a *real* MTE. MTEs that are only used for displaying data clearly and do not have their own monitoring segment are known as *virtual* MTEs. You can use different icons to display the characteristics of monitoring nodes and attributes.

The highest monitoring summary node forms the *monitoring context*.

### 11.1.3 Technical Implementation

To ensure that current values and, if required, alerts, can be displayed at any time, the relevant statistics must be collected regularly and be available.

Data collectors

You use *data collectors* for this purpose (see Figure 11.5). These programs, based on programming languages C, ABAP, or Java, determine the required data and store it in defined memory segments (monitoring segments) of the server. In addition to the collected data, the threshold values defined by the user are stored in the memory segment, which means that by analyzing the memory, a decision can already be made as to whether threshold values are being exceeded. If you want to collect and monitor additional data, you can add data collectors. You can integrate them into the monitoring architecture using the defined program interface.

saposcol

One important collection program that you are already familiar with is the saposcol operating system collector. saposcol is a standalone program that runs once for each server, independently of an SAP instance, and collects data relating to operating systems. Examples of this type of data include the following:

- Memory consumption (virtual and physical)
- CPU load, divided into percentages according to system time, user time, and wait time
- Use of physical disk areas and of file systems
- Resource consumption of processes currently running

The data, which is collected every 10 seconds by default, is made available on the server in a defined area of the accessible shared memory. saposcol also stores statistical mean values there, calculated on an hourly basis, for many of the objects it monitors. To aggregate the data further, it's transferred from the shared memory segment into database tables.

The characteristics of saposcol are operating system-dependent, so there are negligible differences in the data collected depending on the operating system.

Examples of other data collectors include the RSDSLAN1 report, which collects data about the LAN for the CCMS_OS_LAN method, and the RSDS_BP_CLASSAWP function module, which recounts the number of batch processes reserved for Class A requests for the CCMS_BP_CLASSA_WP method.

Agents

SAP components without SAP kernels or external systems play a special role. SAP provides *agents* for these components (see Figure 11.5). You install these agents on the corresponding server, where they monitor the required component. On the server, the agents manage a separate memory segment where they store the collected data. The data can be sent from there to an assigned central monitoring instance by RFC.

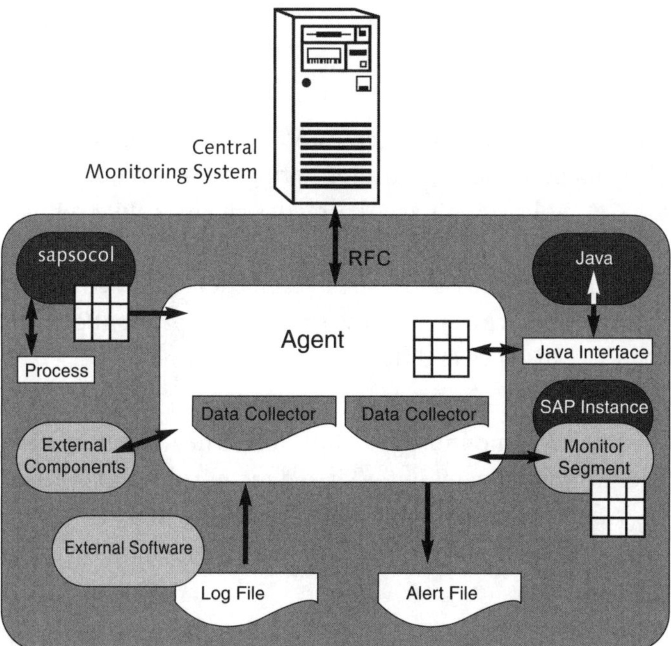


**Figure 11.5** Using Agents

SAP provides the following agents for the different systems:

- **SAPCCMSR**
  This agent monitors components, on which there is no active SAP instance (e.g., log files, TREX, independent databases, or operating system components). SAPCCMSR is closely linked to the central monitoring system that performs the monitoring. After you install the SAPCCMSR CCMS agent, it tries to link to a monitoring segment in the shared memory when it's started. If this segment isn't yet available, the agent creates it. SAPCCMSR always works in a shared memory segment that is independent of running SAP systems. The central monitoring system requires SAP Basis Release 4.6B at least.
- **SAPCCMSR -j2ee**
  The functional principle of SAPCCMSR was extended in case the SAPCCMSR CCMS agent monitors a J2EE Engine. In such a case, it must also be possible that the SAPCCMSR agent's monitoring segment doesn't belong to the central monitoring system. You can achieve this by also enhancing the system term to include Java components (e.g., J2EE

cluster). You can use the `SAPCCMSR` agent with the `-j2ee` option to do this.

- **SAPCCM4X**
  This agent improves the monitoring of ABAP instances with SAP Basis Release 4.X or higher. The central monitoring system requires SAP Basis Release 4.6C at least. This agent provides an alternative connection route to the monitoring information in the shared memory of an ABAP instance. Because this alternative connection route no longer requires a free work process, the access route is independent of error statuses of the SAP instance and therefore more robust.

  Systems as of SAP Basis Release 4.0 have their own runtime environment for the CCMS monitoring architecture. They therefore have their own monitoring segment in the shared memory area of the running system. After you install the `SAPCCM4X` agent, it tries to link to and work with this monitoring segment in the shared memory when it's started.

  If this segment isn't available (e.g., if the monitored system isn't running), the agent doesn't create it, to avoid interfering with the shared memory management in the systems that are restarting. In this case, `SAPCCM4X` works with a monitoring segment that it creates in its process memory and the content of which it compares to the content of the monitored system. `SAPCCM4X` regularly checks whether the monitored system is active again and then works with the monitoring segment in the shared memory again after it compares the contents.

  The central monitoring system initially tries to read the data of the monitored system automatically through the RFC destination of the CCMS agent. If the agent isn't active, the monitoring data of the monitored SAP instance is read using the standard RFC, as before (for more information, refer to SAP Note 322075).

- **SAPCM3X**
  This agent enables the CCMS monitoring architecture to monitor SAP instances of SAP Basis Release 3.X. These systems do not have their own runtime environment for the CCMS monitoring architecture. `SAPCM3X` therefore always works with a monitoring segment that it creates in its main memory (for more information, refer to SAP Note 308061).

In addition to executing function modules, agents can check log files and report problems in the monitoring architecture, access data collected by `saposcol`, and integrate additional data collectors using a dynamic library interface. Section 11.4, Setting Up a Central Monitoring System, contains examples for configuring agents.

**Installing and registering agents**

If you want to integrate agents into your system monitoring, follow these steps:

1. Download the current agent version from the SAP Service Marketplace (*http://service.sap.com/swdc*).
2. Copy the agent into its working directory (see Table 11.1).
3. Generate a configuration file to install the agent without dialogs. Once generated, you can reuse this file on all servers where you want the agent to run.
4. Create additional configuration files to set the parameters of specific tasks for the agent, such as the following:
   - Monitoring log files
   - Monitoring specific file systems or processes
   - Monitoring clients or transactions
5. Register the agents. In this process step, the RFC connections in the central monitoring system are automatically created for the agent.

In terms of the SAP release, all agents are downward compatible, which means that a CCMS agent can work together with an SAP system with a lower release. In reality, you should use the highest possible release of the CCMS agent. The characteristic values of agents depend on the relevant operating system. Corresponding agents are therefore stored in the SAP Service Marketplace for different operating systems and their releases. All available `SAPCCMSR`, `SAPCCM4X`, and `SAPCM3X` agents are usually archived in a shared *CCMAGENT.SAR* file. Download the relevant archive for your hardware environment from the SAP Service Marketplace. To decompress the archive, use the `SAPCAR` tool available in every SAP installation.

The agents require a working directory where configuration and log files can be stored (see Table 11.1).

| CCMS Agent | UNIX Directory | NT Directory |
|---|---|---|
| SAPCCMSR | */usr/sap/ccms/bin* | *\\<host>\saploc\prfclog* |
| SAPCCM4X | */usr/sap/<SysID>/SYS/exe/run* | *\\<host>\usr\sap\<SysID>\SYS\exe\run* |
| SAPCM3X | */usr/sap/ccms/bin* | *\\<host>\saploc\prfclog* |
| SAPCCMSR -j2ee | */usr/sap/<SysID>/SYS/exe/run* | *\\<host>\usr\sap\<SysID>\SYS\exe\run* |

**Table 11.1** Working Directories of Monitoring Agents

The *saploc* directory can also have a different name. The key factor is that it's released as a share directory under the name *saploc*. By default, this is the *<drive:>\usr\sap* directory. If the directory doesn't exist, create it during the installation.

You install and register the agents using the following:

```
sapccmsr -R [ -f <name of installation file> ]
            [ pf=<profile path> ]
sapccmsr -j2ee -R [ -f <name of installation file> ]
                  [ pf=<profile path> ]
sapccm4x -R [ -f <name of installation file> ]
              pf=<profile path>
sapcm3x -R [ -f <name of installation file> ]
            [ pf=<profile path> ]
```

If you install the agents in dialog mode, all required parameters used to describe the central monitoring system that the agent will communicate with are queried. If you want to install the agent on several servers in a bigger landscape, it's useful to create a file with the required installation data.

The significance of the profile path is different for the agents mentioned. In the case of SAPCCM4X, you need to specify the profile path; the profile is that of the monitored SAP instance. When you use the two other agents, there is either no SAP instance (SAPCCMSR), or the SAP release doesn't yet have any monitoring architecture that you can use (SAPCM3X). As an option here, you can control the following settings in a profile file:

- The size of the monitoring segment in bytes in the shared memory as *alert/MONI_SEGM_SIZE* (SAPCCMSR only)
- The *DIR_PERF* working directory of the agent and local saposcol
- The complete *exe/saposcol* path of the data collector for operating system data

Log files of agents

When you start an agent, a log file *<agent name><processID>.log* is created in the agent's working directory in each case. All initialization steps and error messages when the agent is being operated are recorded in this file. Problems with the configuration file or control file are also logged.

Agents are operated as services on Windows systems and as processes on UNIX. You therefore start and stop agents on Windows systems when you start and stop the operating system, whereas on UNIX, you use the commands

```
sapccmsr -DCCMS [ pf=<profile path> ]
sapccmsr -j2ee -DCCMS [ pf=<profile path> ]
sapccm4x -DCCMS pf=<profile path>
sapcm3x -DCCMS [ pf=<profile path> ]
```

to start an agent and, correspondingly, the -stop option to stop it.

As soon as you start the agents, the collected information is displayed in the monitor set. You can find the data of the SAPCCMSR agent from the Alert Monitor (RZ20) under **System • All Monitoring Segments • All Monitoring Contexts** in the **SAP CCMS Technical Experts Monitors** monitor set as a virtual *SAP_CCMS_<host_name> node.* Contexts called *SAP_CCMS_<host_name>_local* belong to the SAPCM3X agent. The contexts, whose data is provided by SAPCCM4X agents, are still where they were before; the only thing that changes here is the type of communication with the SAP instances already previously known. If interruptions occur in the transfer of agent information, you can get an overview of all memory segments that report on this central monitoring instance by selecting **Monitoring Properties • Tech. Infrastructure • Display Topology (RZ21)** (as of Basis Release 6.10). You'll find the segments you're looking for under the **Agent Segment Type** and can analyze their statuses in more detail by double-clicking them.

## 11.2 Customizing the Alert Monitor

The alert monitor is used to signal critical situations visually. Depending on the defined threshold values, the color changes from green to yellow to red. The definition of a critical situation in the relevant business environment differs from system to system. SAP provides monitor sets with default values that you should adjust for this reason.

### 11.2.1 Integrating Remote Systems

Defining RFC connections

To enable several components to be monitored from a central SAP system, you must register the non-local components to be monitored as a new context by selecting **Monitoring Properties**. You first need to define two RFC connections:

- **Data query**
  Read access must be possible on the data-retaining shared memory segments for querying the data collected on remote systems. You should therefore create a *communication*-type user (e.g., CSMREG) on each system involved. You can select the **Infrastructure • Configure Central System • Create • CSMREG User** menu options in Transaction RZ21 to enable the SAP system to create this user automatically. If you want to use a different user than the default CSMREG user, you should at least assign the SAP_BC_CSMREG role provided by SAP to the user.
- **Executing analysis functions**
  Because you may require further authorizations when executing analysis functions after receiving an alert, you should define the required RFC connection under your own user name (**Current User** setting, see Section 13.1, RFC Connections, in Chapter 13).

We recommend that you create the RFC connections as follows:

1. Call Transaction SM59.
2. Expand the **R/3 Connections** node in the **RFC Destinations** tree.
3. Select **Create**.
4. Enter the following details in the definition area:

- **RFC destination**: Enter a name for the RFC connection; SAP recommends <SID>_RZ20_COLLECT for the RFC destination for data collection and <SID>_RZ20_ANALYZE for the RFC destination for executing the analysis method.
- **Connection type**: Enter "3" (for R/3 system).
- **Description**: Enter a brief description for the RFC destination.
- **User** (RFC destination for data collection): Enter the CSMREG user and corresponding password.
- **User** (RFC destination for executing the analysis method): Either select the **Current User** option, or enter any user (in both cases, the user must have authorization for the alert monitor and for system administration in the destination system).

When you request data for a remote system in a monitor, you do this using the CSMREG user. Because you specified the password for the RFC destination for data collection, you do not need to log on manually.

If you start the analysis method for an MTE of the remote system, you may need to log on manually, depending on the settings of the corresponding RFC destination.

The RFC connection logs on to the remote system with these users.

You can now add another system by selecting **Technical Infrastructure • Create Entry for Remote Monitoring**.

### 11.2.2 Creating Customer-Specific Monitors and Monitor Sets

You can create your own new monitor sets and group specific monitors under them based on the monitor sets provided by SAP. The advantage of defining your own monitor is that you can focus on customer-specific requirements and particular aspects of the system landscape in question. You can use the monitors provided by SAP as templates, but you can't change them. For example, if the person responsible for interfaces wants to limit his display of the system landscape to interfaces only, he can only do this using a monitor specifically created for this purpose.

To create your own monitor with the MTEs you require, follow these steps:

1. First activate the maintenance functions from the Alert Monitor (RZ20) display by selecting **Extras • Activate Maintenance Functions**. The change functions are displayed and active in the menus.
2. Select **Monitor (set) • Create**.
3. Give the monitor set a name, and define who is allowed to maintain and display this monitor set. Note that the name must not begin with "SAP".
4. Save your entries; an empty monitor set now exists as a container for customer-specific monitors.
5. To create a static monitor within this new monitor set, select (based on your new monitor set) **Monitor (set) • Create** again; all available MTEs are displayed.
6. Select all of the required MTEs in your monitor, and save the monitor under a descriptive name.

Implementing changes

The MTEs you selected are now integrated into the new monitor. If you want to make changes, select **Monitor (set) • Change**. If, in particular, you add a new system that you also want to be displayed in central monitoring, you must explicitly add the additional system's parameters you're interested in, as described earlier. In larger dynamic system landscapes, it helps to use a rules-based enhancement of existing monitors. First, select an existing monitor that you want to update using rules, or create a new monitor. Then follow these steps:

1. Select the node in the existing structure under which you want to add the dynamic values.
2. Select **Edit • Create Node • Rule Nodes** to display the available rules, which can be used to dynamically add values to the monitor structure when the monitor is started.

Figure 11.6 shows the addition of a monitor using the CCMS_GET_MTE_BY_CLASS rule, relating to all accessible systems and the `Background` MTE class. When you call the monitor, the current data about the background processes is displayed for all registered systems accessible by RFC.

If required, you can transport monitor sets into other systems. This means that you can initially create and test your own monitor sets in a development system and then distribute them in the system landscape. To do this, use the **Alert Monitor (RZ20) • Monitor (set) • Transport Monitor Set** functions.

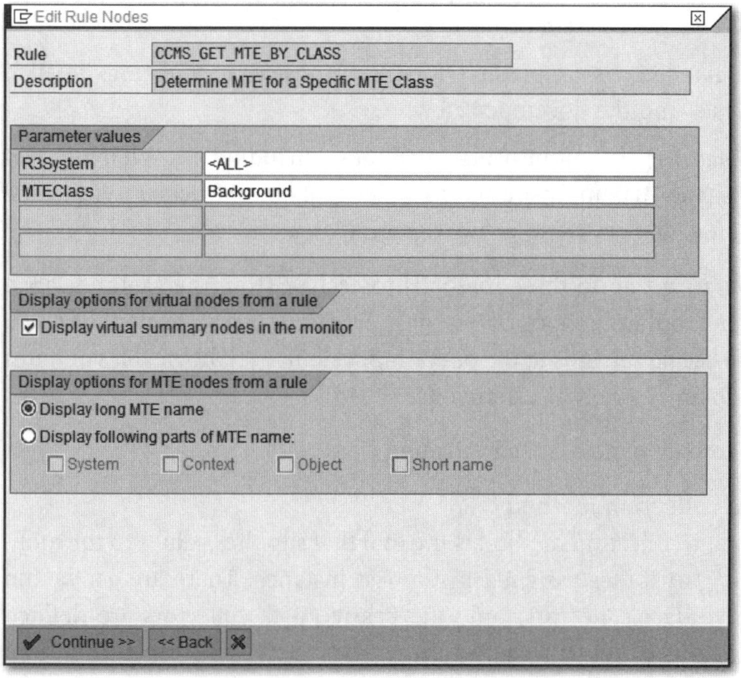

**Figure 11.6** Rules-Based Monitor

### 11.2.3 Specific Adjustment of Properties

In another Customizing step, you must adapt the predefined object and attribute properties according to specific requirements. The ideal option is to fine-tune the monitors you defined yourself. However, if you initially want to use the standard monitors provided by SAP, you can also make the customer-specific adjustments there.

Where properties are concerned, we differentiate the areas described next, which are defined depending on the type of MTE.

**General properties**

You can define the following properties in the General area:

- Description and display of the text that is to be displayed as a combination of message class and message number in the monitor if an alert is received.
- Display options for user groups, depending on a user's authorizations (up to Basis Release 4.6B).

  Graduated views are possible for the purpose of monitoring, detailed analysis, and the developer view.
- Settings for the monitoring attributes, including the weighting of alerts, the maximum number of alerts of the particular type to be retained, and restrictions for triggering an alert.

Methods

You can assign up to three methods to each MTE in the Methods area. Function modules, reports, URLs, or transactions can act as methods. You also can use commands at the operating system level, however, you must define them as external commands.

The following methods are available:

- **Data collection method**
  The data collection method is the tool that supplies values to the monitoring attributes assigned in the last instance. There are active and passive data collectors; only the passive data collectors are defined and configured in the monitoring architecture. The most important parameter here is the information about how often new values must be calculated. Active data collectors are started directly from the monitored application and are not controlled using the alert monitor. The data is delivered at intervals that you can't predict or manipulate. Data collection methods are already assigned to all MTEs by default; the `<No Method>` data collection method describes an active data collector, therefore, you can't modify it.
- **Analysis method**
  The analysis method determines which action must be executed to analyze the problem that has occurred and is displayed in the monitor in more detail. For example, for the MTE for monitoring the *R3BufferSpaceUsed* buffer quality, this would be the branch to the Buffer Load Analysis (ST02).

- **Auto-reaction method**
  These tools can react to a triggered alert, for example, by sending a message. The monitor sets provided by SAP do not contain the assignment of the auto-reaction method by default. This can and should be defined by the user.

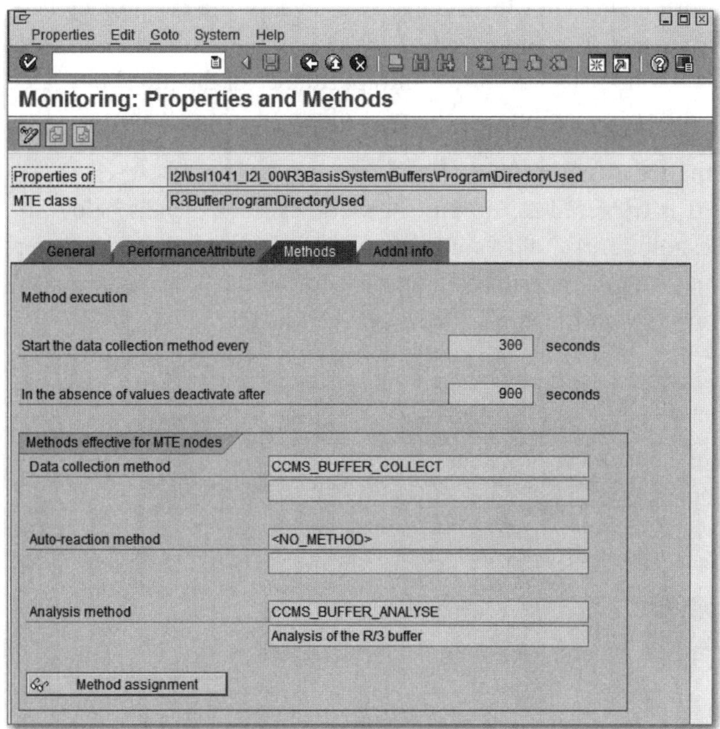


**Figure 11.7** Method Assignment

Before you can use a report, function module, URL, or transaction as a method, you must register them as methods and assign them a method name (see Figure 11.7). You use Monitoring Properties (RZ21) to do this and select **Methods • Create New Method**. When defining a method, the information you provide includes what type of method it's (data collection, analysis, auto-reaction), how you want it to be executed (manually, in dialog mode, in the background), and where you want it to be executed (local host, any server). You can also assign parameters. All of the methods available in the system are displayed in the **Methods • Definitions** overview, including predefined auto-reaction methods that you can use as you wish. Templates are already available for sending messages. As system administrator, you can also create your own new tools at any time and include them in SAP systems. For example, you can create an ABAP program that triggers a defined action in the system when a problem occurs.

Performance, status, and log attributes

The monitoring attributes form the lowest level in the monitoring tree. Under **Properties**, threshold values are also assigned in the broadest sense to the monitoring attributes. The appearance of the threshold value definition differs depending on the type of monitoring attribute:

- **Performance attribute**
  The alert is triggered as soon as the value exceeds or falls below the set threshold. Threshold values are frequently used to measure performance, such as they are here for monitoring the `R3BufferProgramDirectoryUsed` in the *Buffers* MTE (see Figure 11.8).

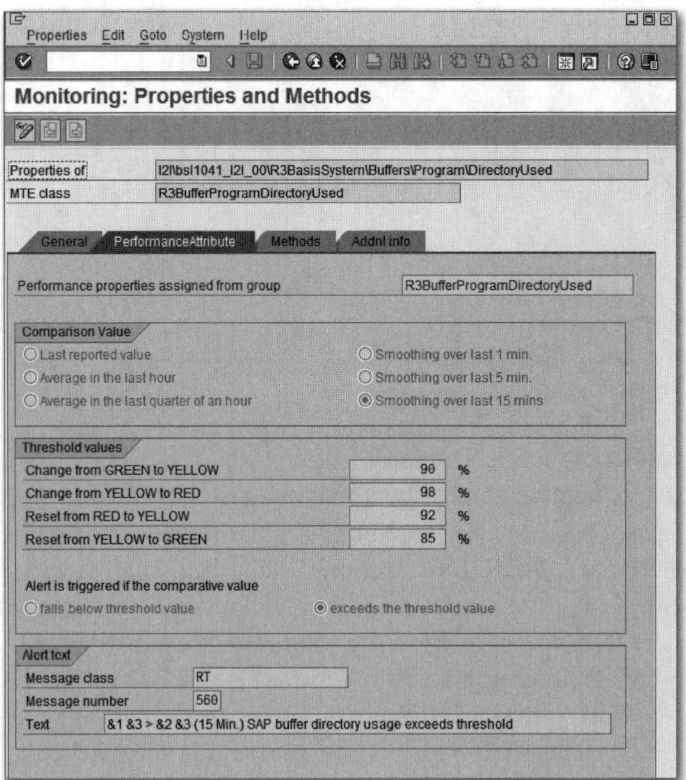


**Figure 11.8** Performance Attribute

- **Status attribute**
  One example of where you use a status attribute for generating an alert is when an error message is issued in a certain component, for example, during an update, as shown in Figure 11.9.

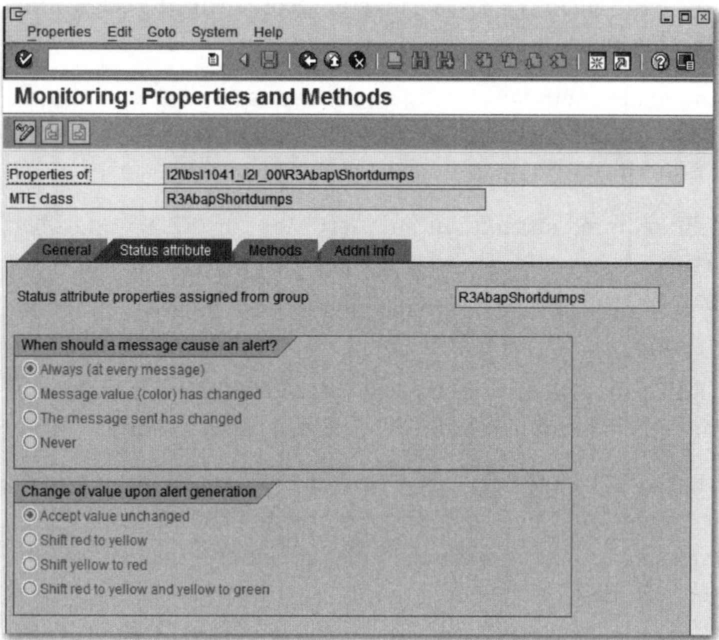


**Figure 11.9** Status Attribute

- **Log attribute**
  If the log file of a system component is searched according to a pattern, the appearance of this text can also trigger an alert. You can add other restrictions using filters.

You must pay particular attention to the setting of threshold values. Threshold values set too low, which are already exceeded in the normal operation of an SAP system, constantly cause red alerts. An alarm is therefore triggered for a status that is actually normal. Similarly, threshold values set too high, which are never exceeded, distort the alert monitor signaling. Even if the situation reached a critical point, the color would not change and thereby signal the problem to you. You need to set the threshold values in a way that all traffic lights are green in normal situations. In the implementation phase of an SAP system, it will be difficult to immediately set the relevant threshold values. You should initially use the default values provided by SAP or your own estimated values. You must then improve these values iteratively based on your own experiences.

Additional information

The person who made the last change is recorded in the **Additional Information** property.

You can implement settings directly on the corresponding attributes or, more simply, on comprehensive structures. You change the threshold values of a specific attribute as follows:

1. Select the required attribute in the Alert Monitor (RZ20), and select **Properties**.
2. Switch from display mode to change mode, and modify the required properties.
3. Select **Edit properties • Use for individual MTE**, and consequently save the redefined properties for the selected element only.

Because many MTEs have the same type of properties in terms of the number of monitoring tree elements to be considered for fine-tuning a setting, the standard setting when defining properties is the maintenance of a whole MTE class or attribute group.

MTE classes

Monitoring tree elements with the same type of physical or logical properties are grouped in *MTE classes* to simplify administration. For example, the *R3BufferHitRatio* MTE class groups all MTEs that describe the quality of a buffer. Instead of now assigning the Buffer Load (ST02) analysis method to every single MTE, you can select one attribute of this class and use it to implement the change for all MTEs.

Attribute groups

*Attribute groups* refer to the common threshold values for generating alerts for a selected object category.

Monitoring properties variants

Sometimes, it can make sense to group a combination of method assignments, threshold value definitions, and general properties in a *monitoring properties variant*. For example, the behavior of a system during an upgrade or settlement run differs from that of a normal operation; perhaps you want different auto-reactions for the automatic nightly monitoring than for during the day. You can maintain and activate different monitoring properties variants for these different situations manually or by switching operation modes. To create your own new monitoring properties variant, follow these steps:

1. Start Monitoring Properties (RZ21).
2. Select **Properties • Variants • Create.**
3. You can select an existing variant as the parent variant; properties not defined in your variant are copied from the parent variant.
4. Give the variant a name.

You can of course also copy and adapt one of the existing variants:

1. Start Monitoring Properties (RZ21) again.
2. Select **Properties • Variants • Copy.**
3. You're offered a selection of properties to transfer.
4. Give the variant a name.

Transporting monitoring properties variants

Activate the new variant by selecting **Variant • Activate**. All Customizing settings that are now made are automatically assigned to this monitoring properties variant. By switching back to the SAP-DEFAULT monitoring properties variant, you can easily access the standard SAP system. If you maintain several monitoring properties variants, you can easily adapt the monitors to special situations. You can also transport monitoring properties variants. For example, you can transport a monitoring properties variant that you created, tested, and approved in one system into every other SAP system. To do this, you use **Monitoring Properties (RZ21) • Monitoring Properties Variants• Display Overview**. Select the required variant, and select **Variant • Transport**.

You assign a monitoring properties variant to an operation mode by selecting **Operation Mode Maintenance (RZ04) • Operation Mode• Change** and entering the monitoring properties variant.

## 11.3 Analyzing Alert Monitors

Alert history

To guarantee the permanent readiness of functions of the SAP system and landscape, it's essential that you analyze the alerts. To do this, there are two views on the monitors' results. Only the currently valid alarms are displayed in the initial screen first. This view is called the **Current**

**Status**. You switch to the view of all collected alerts by clicking the **Open Alerts** button. You can display the relevant alerts in a table by double-clicking a selected MTE. These alerts are sorted according to their severity. For each monitor, you can use the properties to configure which alerts you want to be retained: all, most recent, oldest alerts, or only the alerts that correspond to the current status. You can remove alerts that you already know about from the display using **Complete Alerts** in this display or directly from the alert monitor. Although the values selected in this way are no longer used to assess the situation, they are saved in the alert database; only new values are evaluated again. You should, of course, only use this function after an analysis if you have eliminated the source of the risk or were able to establish that the cause of a message was harmless. You can display a history of all alerts that have ever occurred by selecting **Display Alert History**. This enables you to compare the current situation to previous alerts. **Display Details** displays a list with details about the selected monitoring attribute. If you need a more detailed analysis of a problem that has occurred, you can use the **Start Analysis Method** icon or double-click the MTE to go directly to the transaction assigned in each case as the analysis method.

When they have been completed, the alerts are removed from the active alerts and monitoring segment but are kept in the database. However, you should remove these entries from the database from time to time. You can do this using the analysis method for the *AlertsInDB* monitoring object in the CCMS Self-Monitoring monitor of the SAP CCMS Technical Experts Monitor collection, or you can configure an automatic reorganization, whereby alerts are deleted from the database after the monitoring segment has reached a certain fill level or after a predefined number of days. To do this, you must adapt the two `CMPL_ALERT_AFTER_DAY` and `CMPL_ALERT_IF_QUOTA` parameters for the `CCMS_Segment_Space_Collect` method by selecting **Monitoring Properties • Methods • Definitions**.

## 11.4 Setting Up a Central Monitoring-System (CEN)

The concept of monitoring architecture is based on the assumption that you declare a system in your system landscape for the central monitoring system (CEN). The monitoring information of your system landscape is collected in this system and displayed in the alert monitor.

You should only reserve this system for the purposes of monitoring and system management. Avoid using a production system in particular, to ensure that the system isn't overloaded unnecessarily. If you're using a separate SAP system, you can always keep it up to date easily in terms of the release or support package version, which means that you'll benefit from the latest developments in the areas of monitoring and system management. The system doesn't require any specific and expensive hardware but should have a release version of SAP Web AS 6.40 at least.

Configuration steps

You must implement the following steps in CEN:

- **Create the CSMREG user**
  For communication among CEN, monitored systems, and CCMS agents, you need a communication user with specific, limited authorization in all ABAP systems of your system landscape. To create the user, start the Monitoring: Properties and Methods (RZ21) transaction, select **Technical Infrastructure • Configure Central System • Create User CSMREG**, and enter any password for this user.
- **Activate the background dispatching**
  The monitoring data of the monitoring architecture is partly determined using data collection methods that are periodically executed as jobs. To ensure that these methods start correctly, you must activate the background dispatching in all ABAP systems of your system landscape.

  To activate background dispatching, start Transaction RZ21 and select **Technical Infrastructure • Local Method Execution • Activate Background Dispatching**.
- **Activate the Internet Communication Manager (ICM)**
  The monitoring architecture uses the *Generic Request and Message Generator* to monitor the availability of web components. This requires you to configure and activate the ICM in all ABAP systems of your system landscape.
- **Activate the central system dispatching**
  A part of the monitoring architecture consists of auto-reaction methods that start automatically when an alert occurs. These methods are executed by default in the system where the alert is triggered. If these methods are to be started in CEN, you must activate the central system dispatching.

To activate central system dispatching, start Transaction RZ21, and select **Technical Infrastructure • Configure Central System • Activate Central System Dispatching**.

- **Monitor remote ABAP systems**
  By default, the monitoring architecture only monitors the local ABAP system. To monitor remote systems, you must perform the following steps:
  - First define the RFC connections from CEN in the relevant monitored ABAP system (see Section 11.2.1, Integrating Remote Systems).
  - Make the RFC connections known to the monitoring architecture. To do this, start Transaction RZ21, and select **Technical Infrastructure• Configure Central System • Create Entry for Remote System**.

## 11.5 Customizing Examples

Some examples demonstrate the potential options of system monitoring using alert monitors. These descriptions will support you when dealing with similar issues.

Main tasks of an administrator

Alert monitors are available in the standard delivery for the system components provided by SAP. The system administrator's main task is therefore to adjust the threshold values and maintain the reaction methods. The provision of agents makes other monitoring options available, which you must configure.

### 11.5.1 Analyzing a Log File

You can use the `SAPCCMSR`, `SAPCCM4X`, or `SAPCM3X` agents to analyze the contents of any text files. The agent searches in these files according to predefined text patterns and displays the results in the alert monitor. You need to perform the following steps to configure the log adapter:

- **Specify the log files to be searched**
  Entries under **Logfile** in the *sapccmsr.ini* configuration file.
- **Specify the text pattern to be searched for Pattern**
  Entry in the relevant control file for searching in the log file.

- **Provide information about the appearance of the alert in the central alert monitor**
  Entries in the relevant control file for searching in the log file.

sapccmsr.ini configuration file

You must first adjust the *sapccmsr.ini* configuration file in the agent's working directory (the name of the configuration file is always *sapccmsr.ini*, regardless of the type of agent). Path specifications for controlling the agent's functions are mainly defined in this file. The path specifications refer to other specific configuration files per keyword. Table 11.2 shows the parameters you can set in the *SAPCCMSR.INI* file.

| Parameters | Description |
|---|---|
| `Plug-in <file path> [<Directory for loading additional dlls>]` | Agent's shared library to be loaded; several plug-ins are possible. The file path must not contain any spaces.<br>Some plug-ins such as *itsmon.dll*, for example, require additional shared libraries that are stored in a specific directory. Specify this directory as a second parameter; otherwise, the CCMS agent will only search for these libraries in its working directory, which is why they may not be loaded sometimes. |
| `LogFile <file path>` | Configuration file for monitoring log files (log file template); you can specify a configuration file for each log file. |
| `LogFileDir <directory path>` | You can only specify one *LogFileDir* directory in the configuration file. |
| `LogfileParam DelTree` | When you specify `Deltree`, obsolete elements that no longer have a log file are deleted from the shared memory. |
| `OsColFile <file path>` | You specify a `SAPOSCOL` filter file for filtering out subtrees of the operating system monitoring; the subtrees are not subsequently stored in the shared memory. |
| `ViewDirList <file path>` | Files, the content of which the agent can explicitly read for displaying in the alert monitor. |

**Table 11.2** Configuration Entries in sapccmsr.ini

| Parameters | Description |
|---|---|
| `AlertLog <file path>` | Full path of a log file for the detected alerts (without a suffix; the *.log* suffix is set automatically). |
| `AlertLogLevel <level>` | Scope of alert logging. |
| `PushCycleMinutes <n>` | Optional parameter that specifies how often the agent automatically reports values to the central monitoring system:<br>n=1: Default setting, values are reported every minute.<br>n=0: Values are never reported.<br>n<30: Values are reported every n minutes.<br>$n^3$30: Values are reported every 30 minutes. |
| `LongSid <target system>` | If you want to monitor several SAP systems with identical system IDs in your system landscape, enter a unique name for the agent's system here, the first three characters of which correspond to the system ID of the monitored system (for `SAPCCM4X` agent only). |
| `TrapSendFile <file path>` | Complete path of configuration file for sending the SNMP traps. |
| `TrapReceiveFile <file path>` | Complete path of configuration file for receiving the SNMP traps. |
| `GrmgDir` | You can use GRMG (Generic Request and Message Generator) to monitor the availability of technical components or steps in business processes. Both Customizing information and questions and answers about availability are exchanged as XML files here. |

**Table 11.2** Configuration Entries in sapccmsr.ini

**Syntax rules**

When creating the parameter file, you must take into consideration the following syntax rules:

- Comment lines begin with the (#) number sign.
- These lines must be entered in the format `<parameter name><space> <parameter value>`.

Listing 11.1 shows an example of a configuration file. The *c:\saploc\PRFCLOG\sapccmsr\ccmsini.ini* file was transferred as a control file for analyzing a log file.

```
### Configuration file for CCMS agents SAPCCMSR,
### SAPCM3X and SAPCCM4X
###
### Format of entries for plugins:
#   PlugIn <full path of shared library to load>
###
### Format of entries for logfile monitoring:
    LogFile c:\saploc\PRFCLOG\sapccmsr\ccmsini.ini
###
### Format of entries for the option to delete trees if
### no corresponding logfile exists:
### This Parameter is optional, if not specified the
### tree still remains
#   LogFileParam DelTree
###
### Format of entries for mechanism to filter out
### SAPOSCOL values:
#   OsColFile <full path of oscolfile template>
#
```

**Listing 11.1** Listing 11.1 Configuration File for CCMS Agents

Listing 11.2 shows the content of the transferred *ccmsini.ini* control file.

```
LOGFILE_TEMPLATE
DIRECTORY-"c:\sapdb\LVC\db"
FILENAME="knldiag"
MTE_CLASS="SAPDB_LOG"
SHOWNEWLINES=1
MONITOR_FILESIZE_KB=5
PATTERN_0="cannot"
VALUE_0=RED
SEVERITY_0=51
MESSAGEID_0="RT-013"
```

**Listing 11.2** ccmsini.ini Control File (Monitoring SAP DB Log File)

This control file initiates the automatic analysis of the *knldiag* file in the *c:\sapdb\LVC\db* directory. All monitors created by the agent for monitoring the file are assigned to the `SAPDB_LOG` monitoring tree class (`MTE_CLASS` parameter). The advantage of this is that settings and changes made to general properties or methods can refer to this MTE class overall.

`SHOWNEWLINES` causes the number of new entries added to this file in a minute to be displayed in a monitor. You must also monitor the size of the file. If the file size exceeds 5KB, for example, an alarm should be triggered (`MONITOR_FILESIZE_KB` parameter). You can use `PATTERN_<x>` to define the character strings that cause an alarm. In the preceding example, an alarm is triggered when the word "cannot" appears, specifically a red (`VALUE_<x>`). The severity of the alarm (`SEVERITY_<x>`) is set to 51. Message `013` of the `RT` (`MESSAGEID_<x>`) message class is issued. At this point, all messages created and available through Message Maintenance (SE91) can be used. `RT-013` means "No detailed description available." The control file ends with a period (.) in the last line of the file.

### 11.5.2 Auto-Reaction Method: Sending Email

An important decision when configuring a monitor is the type of auto-reaction method to use. You can basically use every function module or report as an auto-reaction method. This could also include sending an email. However, for an SAP system to send emails, you must have configured it using SAPconnect (see Section 13.4, Data Transfer, in Chapter 13).

You now still have to maintain and assign a corresponding auto-reaction method for sending emails when a red alert occurs. The standard delivery of the SAP system already contains an auto-reaction method called `CCMS_OnAlert_Email`.

1. Start Monitoring Properties (RZ21) in the system's 000 client.
2. Select **Methods • Definitions.**
3. Double-click the `CCMS_OnAlert_Email` method to select it.
4. Maintain the method's properties, in particular the # parameters. As a sender, you can use any SAP user in the *<SID>:<client>:<name>* notation. This will be used as the sender of the mails generated by the

monitor when an alert occurs. You must select a valid email address as the *recipient*. The *recipient type* parameter determines the type of address. "U" stands for Internet email. The generated emails are sent there. You can also use recipient lists.

Assigning auto-reaction methods

You assign the auto-reaction methods maintained in this way either by selecting **Monitoring Properties (RZ21) • Properties assigned to MTE classes or Properties assigned to individual MTEs** or directly using the Alert Monitor (RZ20).

If you want emails to be sent to different users depending on the alert monitor, copy the `CCMS_OnAlert_Email` method, and save it under a different name. Adjust the parameters as required.

### 11.5.3 Filtering the System Log

As another example of using alert monitors, we'll explain how to filter out and respond to specific messages in the system log of an SAP system. For example, you can send an email if a critical database error occurs. There is a separate monitor set to analyze the system log of SAP instances (see Figure 11.10). You'll find the monitors in the Alert Monitor (RZ20) under **SAP CCMS Technical Expert Monitors • System/All Monitoring Segments/All Monitoring Context**. Each instance that reports to the SAP system has a defined node, the name of which is structured as follows: *<host_name>_<SID>_<instance_number>*. Below that is the *R3Syslog* node. Depending on the subject matter, the system log is differentiated once again. All monitors in the *R3Syslog* node are supplied by active data collectors, so you can't configure them directly within the monitoring architecture.

Filtering

You can indirectly filter messages in the system log by redefining the severity level of a message. Messages in the system log are usually assigned a maximum severity level of 50 by default. However, severity levels from 0 to 250 are available.

If you only want the color of the monitor to change to red for certain selected messages, change the threshold values first for the system log monitors.

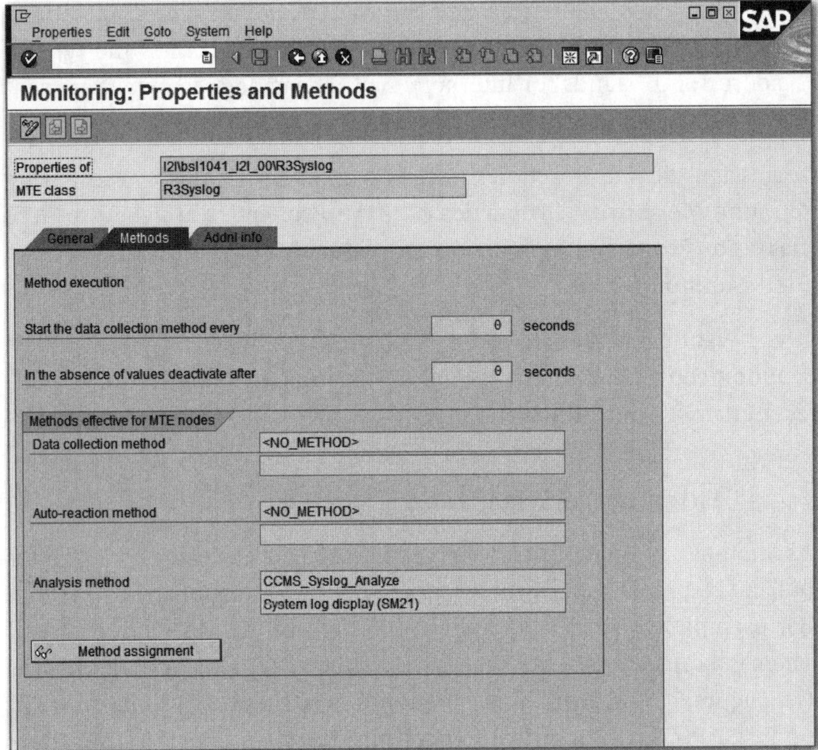


**Figure 11.10** Methods of System Log Monitors

Because all system log monitors are read by the same monitoring segment and used by the same SAP kernel data collector, changes you make to a system log monitor take effect on all system log monitors.

Select a system log monitor, for example, **Basis System**. Go to the properties, and adjust the alert settings in the **Log Attribute** area. Set the threshold value for the red coloration to greater than 50. In the next step, increase the severity level (greater than 50) of the messages you selected. This means that only these messages would exceed the threshold value for red coloration. You can use two options to change the severity level of messages:

Maintaining system log messages

1. You can use **System Log Maintenance (SE92) • Edit • List of All Numbers** to get a list of all messages available in the system in the system log. Select a required number, for example, *BY2 – Database error* &6 *occurred for* &3. You automatically go to the initial screen of **System Log Maintenance** again; the selected message number is specified by default. Select **Edit • Maintain**. In addition to defining the category in which you want the system log message to be displayed in the alert monitor tree, you can change the severity level of the message here (see Figure 11.11). By increasing the severity level of selected system log messages, you can filter these messages and initiate specific actions. In our example, by increasing the severity level in the case of message BY2, we could ensure that a red alarm is triggered when a database error occurs.

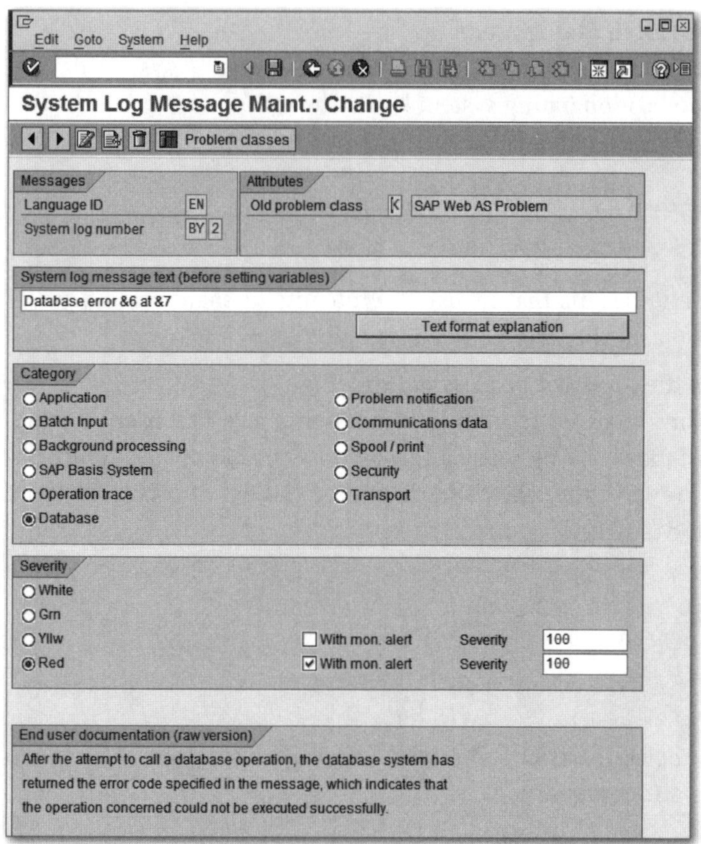


**Figure 11.11** System Log Maintenance

Adjustments in the alert monitor

2. You can also change the severity level of system log messages using the monitors' properties in the *R3Syslog* node. Again, note here that changes to one of the monitors contained in the system take effect on all monitors in the *R3Syslog* node. Changes in the alert monitor may overwrite existing definitions that were created in system log maintenance. To revaluate system log messages, select **Filter** from a monitor's properties.

This procedure enables you to get an overview of all performed message revaluations, displayed in the relevant monitor. Nevertheless, you must know the relevant message numbers.

## 11.6 Tips

- **Use saposcol in dialog mode**
  You can also use the `saposcol` collector of operating system data in dialog mode at operating system level. The call

  ```
  saposcol -d
  ```

  starts the dialog interface. By entering

  ```
  Collector> dump <parameter> <option>
  ```

  you can call the data that `saposcol` wrote into its shared memory segment. You can exit dialog mode using `quit` or `exit`.

- **Activate the saposcol process monitoring**
  If you want `saposcol` to monitor processes of a certain user or name, you must make the required information available in a *dev_proc* configuration file in the *DIR_PERF* directory. The list of processes to be monitored is structured as follows:

  ```
  $PROC
  <process_name> <user_name>
  <process_name> <user_name>
  ...
  $
  ```

  You can replace parts of names with "*". You must restart `saposcol` to evaluate the configuration.

- **Remove file systems/disk areas from the monitoring**
  You can remove disk areas and file systems from the monitoring, for example, if alerts are always reported for a situation that you know isn't critical (such as almost a 100% fill level for a static disk area). You do this in the `saposcol` working directory by configuring a *dev_filter* file with a list of the file systems and disk areas to be omitted:

  ```
  $DISK
  <disk_name>
  ...
  $FSYS
  <file_system_name>
  ...
  ```

- **Hide data in the monitoring segment**
  If you want the operating system collector to collect certain data but not transfer it to the monitoring segment of the central monitoring system, you can achieve this by making an entry in the *sapccmsr.ini* configuration file. Under the *OsColFile* key entry, specify the path name of a control file where you define the values to be hidden.

- **Sort the alerts in the alert list**
  In the alert view, the alarms are sorted within a color group according to their weighting. If you want an alarm to always appear at the very top, you can change the weighting accordingly.

- **Central auto-reaction method**
  By defining auto-reaction methods, a system can react automatically to an alert. In the standard version, this method is started on the system where the alert occurred. You can set up a central auto-reaction method; this will run centrally on the monitoring system if an alert occurs on one of the monitored systems. You perform the configuration using **Monitoring Properties • Technical Infrastructure • Assign Central Auto-Reactions**.

- **Authorizations for the SAPPCCM4X agent**
  Because `SAPCCM4X` accesses the local shared memory segments of the monitoring architecture of the monitored SAP system, it must have the necessary read access. The <sid>adm (UNIX) or SAPServiceSID (NT) authorizations are required.

- **Hold saposcol data from a remote system over 30 days**
  If you want to hold the data, which `saposcol` collected from a remote system and sent to a central monitoring system, for longer than the standard 24 hours, you must activate the **save last 30 days** option in SAPOSCOL Destination (AL15) for the destination already generated automatically.

## 11.7 Transactions and Menu Paths

**Alert Monitor:** SAP Menu • Information • Monitor (RZ20)

**Operation Mode Maintenance:** SAP Menu • Tools • CCMS • Configuration • Operation Modes/Instances (RZ04)

**Monitoring Properties:** SAP Menu • Tools • CCMS • Configuration • Alert Monitor (RZ21)

**Message Maintenance:** SAP Menu • Tools • ABAP Workbench • Development • Programming Environment • Messages (SE91)

**OS System Configuration:** SAP Menu • Tools • Administration • Monitor • Performance • Operating System • Remote • Activity (OS07)

**Buffer Load:** SAP Menu • Tools • Administration • Monitor • Performance • Setup/Buffers • Buffers (ST02)

**SAPOSCOL Destination:** SAP Menu • Tools • Administration • Monitor • Performance • Operating System • SAPOSCOL Destination (AL15)

**System Log:** SAP Menu • Information • Syslog (SM21)

**System Log Messages:** SAP Menu • Tools • ABAP Workbench • Development • Programming Environment • Syslog Messages (SE92)

## 11.8 Additional Documentation

Quick links

- SAP Service Marketplace, alias *system management*
- SAP Service Marketplace, alias *monitoring*

### SAP Notes

Table 11.3 provides an overview of important SAP Notes in the SAP Service Marketplace concerning alert monitors and agents.

| Contents | SAP Note |
|---|---|
| FAQ – CCMS Monitoring Architecture | 110368 |
| CCMS Monitoring Architecture: Meaning of Profile Parameters | 135503 |
| Central Monitoring of SAP Components | 420213 |
| Installing `saposcol` | 19227 |
| `saposcol`: Monitoring Processes | 451166 |
| `saposcol`: Disk and File System Filters | 498112 |
| Monitoring Operating System Data | 522453, 371023 |
| Installing Agents | 209834 |
| SAPCM3X | 308061 |
| CCMS Monitoring Architecture, Service Level Agreements | 308048 |
| RZ20: Monitoring Batch Jobs | 553953 |
| CCMS Agents: Monitoring Log Files | 535199 |
| qRFC and CRM Middleware, Alert Monitoring | 441269 |
| Installing the ITS Plug-In | 418285 |
| Alerts for Oracle Database Monitoring | 483856, 426781 |
| Auto-Reactions | 176492, 502959, 536535, 429265 |
| Automatically Reorganizing Alerts | 414029 |

**Table 11.3** Important SAP Notes Concerning Alert Monitoring

## 11.9 Questions

1. **Which and how many systems can you monitor using CCMS?**

   a. Only the local SAP system.

   b. Several SAP systems but not non-SAP systems.

   c. Several SAP systems, including non-SAP systems that have installed corresponding data collectors.

2. **You have discovered that an alert is triggered too often for an MTE, and you change the threshold values. Which statement is correct?**

   a. The changed threshold value definition is only valid for the currently selected MTE.

   b. The changed threshold value definition is always valid for the whole MTE class.

   c. The whole MTE class is maintained by default when you make a change; however, you can change this setting to maintain individual MTEs also.

   d. You can't change the threshold values of an MTE at all.

*This chapter focuses on archiving, which is the process of removing data from the database, and the Archive Development Kit (ADK), which is the tool required for data archiving. We'll also describe the main features of this tool and its background.*

# 12 Data Archiving

Archiving within the SAP environment can refer to one of the following three subject areas:

**Three subject areas**

- In Oracle database administration, archiving frequently concerns the process of backing up offline redo logs.
- Another form of archiving is the storage of incoming and outgoing documents such as scanned invoices and order confirmations, or the transfer of lists generated in an SAP system to external storage systems (formerly in paper form or on microfiche but now generally on optical media). In accordance with situation-specific Customizing, SAP's own *ArchiveLink* interface is used to establish a link between the archived documents and the application documents recorded in the SAP system. Original documents that have been stored externally are connected in this way to SAP business objects and are accessible from the operation or application document. As of SAP Release 4.6C, the ArchiveLink interface is based on HTTP Content Server technology; the Content Management Service (CMS) is used to store archive files on external systems.
- The main responsibility of the system administrator is to remove data belonging to business processes completed in the SAP system because this data is no longer modified or, for some reason, no longer required in the database. Therefore, this chapter focuses on the storage of data to be archived in compressed form in files at the operating system level and, if necessary, the transfer of archive files to external storage systems.

Reasons for archiving

Generally, the SAP database grows continuously in size over the years. After a certain period of time, which is specified based on legal regulations and company-specific requirements, a lot of data becomes meaningless and represents a burden because it's no longer required for daily work. The larger a table, the more time-intensive and, therefore, the more costly the search within the table. At the same time, larger volumes of data require more resources, for example, main memory, hard disks or backup media. The administration effort grows with the size of the database. For this reason, it's necessary to remove data from the database if it's no longer required in the system (but should nevertheless be retained for reading and evaluation purposes), and store it in archive files that can be accessed again.

Requirements

Frequently, data must be retained for legal reasons and, if necessary, must be readable again. Often, you also have to ensure that the data can't be modified. In these cases, you can use archives based on WORM (*Write Once, Read Multiple*), DVD, or CD-ROM.

During data archiving, data that is contained in the SAP system's database but no longer has to be immediately accessible is identified, extracted, and stored in compressed form, initially in files at the operating system level. From there, data can be forwarded, for example, to one of the aforementioned external storage systems. After the data has been successfully extracted and stored, it's deleted from the database itself. Depending on the RDBMS used, you can reuse the space that has become free in the database (if necessary, after a reorganization).

## 12.1 Archive Development Kit (ADK)

Archiving objects

*Archiving objects* are the basic building blocks for data archiving within an SAP solution. An archiving object is a logical unit of related, physical data, for example, financial accounting documents, bank master data, purchase requisitions, trip data, or payroll results, and all programs required to archive this data, such as formatting, read, write, and delete programs (see Figure 12.1). You can now fully archive the archiving object data. In this way, you ensure that the database remains logically consistent. The FI_DOCUMNT object (financial accounting documents) is an example of an archiving object from SAP Financials. It comprises data from the BKFT, BSEG, BSET, and other tables as well as SAPscript texts, change documents, and the following:

- Archiving programs (data is selected from the tables and then written to archive files)
- Delete programs (extracted data is compared with the data still in the database and then deleted if they correspond with each other)
- Reload program (in an emergency situation)
- Programs for creating and removing the index (for direct access after archiving)

In addition, there are more than 10 evaluation programs. Archived documents can also be read directly using Transaction FB03.

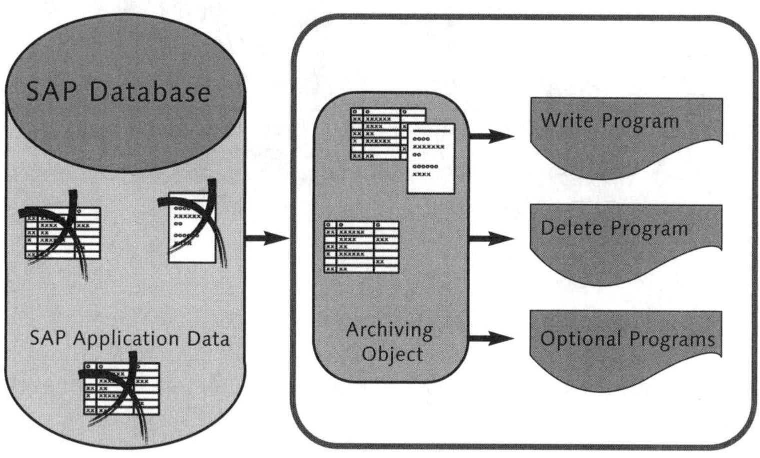


**Figure 12.1** Structure of an Archiving Object

If you want to archive data for a business object that isn't predefined in the standard SAP system, you must first determine which physical data belongs to the object, the form in which it's to be archived, as well as the necessary processing functions. Archiving objects have already been predefined for the standard SAP business processes. If necessary, you can use Transaction AOBJ (Definition of Archiving Objects) to create additional archiving objects for supplementary customer-specific processes.

Archive Development Kit (ADK)

The *Archive Development Kit* (ADK) forms the interface among the SAP application, the database, and the archive files in which the extracted application data is to be saved. The ADK provides the function modules that use the programs belonging to the archiving objects to write formatted archive data to directories outside the database (see Figure 12.2). The ADK also manages the archiving files at the operating system level and manages the archiving runs.

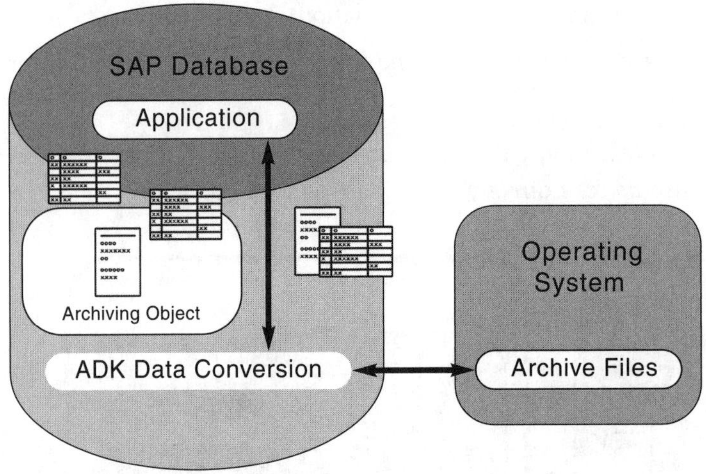


**Figure 12.2** Archive Development Kit

The archiving process is performed in three steps:

1. Data is extracted from the database, and one or more archive files are created.
2. One or more archive files are transferred to an external storage medium (optional).
3. The delete programs are started.

Phase 1

First, the user departments determine which data is to be archived. Generally, the SAP system administrator is unable to determine if and to what extent the business data is relevant. His responsibility is the technical implementation of the archiving process. The relevant archiving objects and the definition of an archiving period determine the volume of data to be archived. All of the data generated during this period is archived. The data defined in this way is formatted and then copied to a predefined directory on the hard disk outside the database in a background process started by the system administrator. Data formatting refers to the extraction of data from the database into an RDBMS-independent and hardware-independent metaformat. In addition to the actual data, information about the code pages used, the record structure, or the number formats is also saved. This information is necessary so that the archived data can be interpreted correctly during a subsequent read operation. At the same time, the data is compressed by a factor of 5 (at most); this excludes cluster tables, which are already stored in the database in compressed form. As of Release R/3 Enterprise, Unicode data can also be archived. It's possible to access archiving files that contain both Unicode and non-Unicode data. It isn't necessary to convert archiving files that already exist.

**Phase 2**

After the archive files have been created, you can choose to transfer the data to an external archive system. Here, you are provided with different variants, which can be automated to varying degrees depending on the relevant Customizing. If an external storage system is connected to the SAP system, ArchiveLink/CMS can be used after a successful write operation to forward the files that have been created. There are two possible settings: automatic data storage or manual data storage (see Figure 12.3).

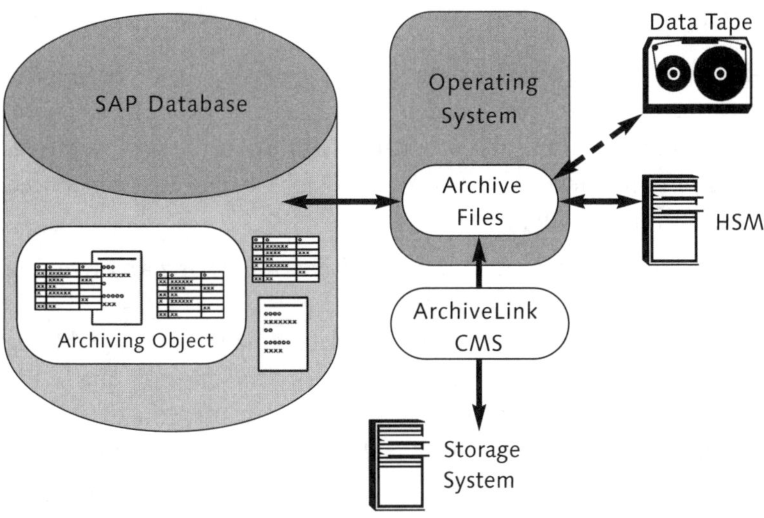


**Figure 12.3** Transferring Archive Data

To ensure regulated communication between the SAP system and the archiving system, SAP provides a certification process for archive providers. Information about certified providers is available on the Internet at *www.sap.com* under the path *partners/software/directory*.

If you use a Hierarchical Storage Management System (HSM), it's sufficient to store the archive files in a HSM directory; ArchiveLink isn't used. The HSM migrates archive files to downstream levels (disk, jukebox, tapes), controlled by access strategies. The SAP system regards the HSM as an infinitely large file system in which the archive files are always addressed using the same file names, irrespective of their actual storage location.

In addition to connecting an archiving system, the archive files created in phase 1 can also be backed up manually to another medium (e.g., data tapes).

Phase 3

If the data has been extracted successfully and stored in files, it can now be deleted from the database. In general Customizing for archiving, you can define whether the delete operation should start automatically after archiving, after the data is transferred to an external storage system, or whether it should be started manually at a later time. There are different delete operation procedures where security or performance is the most important:

- **Deletion of data from the database after closing an archiving file**
  For verification purposes, the archived data is read from the archiving file and compared with the original data in the database. Therefore, the system only deletes data from the database if it has been stored correctly in the archiving file.
- **Deletion of data from the database after transferring an archiving file to the external storage system**
  For verification purposes, the archived data is read from the archiving file in the storage system and compared with the original data in the database. Therefore, the system only deletes data from the database if it has been stored correctly in the archiving file and transferred to the storage system.

As of SAP R/3 Enterprise, the delete programs outside actual archiving can be scheduled directly as periodic background jobs.

## 12.2 Customizing

**Data selection**

Neither the SAP system administrator nor the database administrator can determine which application-specific data can be archived. This task is the responsibility of the user department; the SAP system administrator works closely with this department, especially during archiving.

First, a more application-oriented view is converted into an SAP database view. You then need to clarify which archiving object best meets your requirements. Here, you must consider that there may be some logical and time-related relationships between archiving objects.

Consider the example of the archiving object US_AUTH (*User Master Change Documents: Authorizations*). You can't archive this type of object as long as other existing objects reference this archiving object, for example, US_PASS (*User Master Change Documents: Other Data*), and have not been archived yet.

A network graphic (see Figure 12.4) can be used to illustrate the relationships between archiving objects. You can access the network graphic as follows: **Archive Administration: Initial Screen • Goto • Network Graphic (SARA)**.

The hierarchical display among archiving objects enables you to see the sequence in which data must be archived to ensure optimal data storage. Each archiving object is represented by a node within the network graphic. The colored rectangle in each node represents the archiving status of the object.

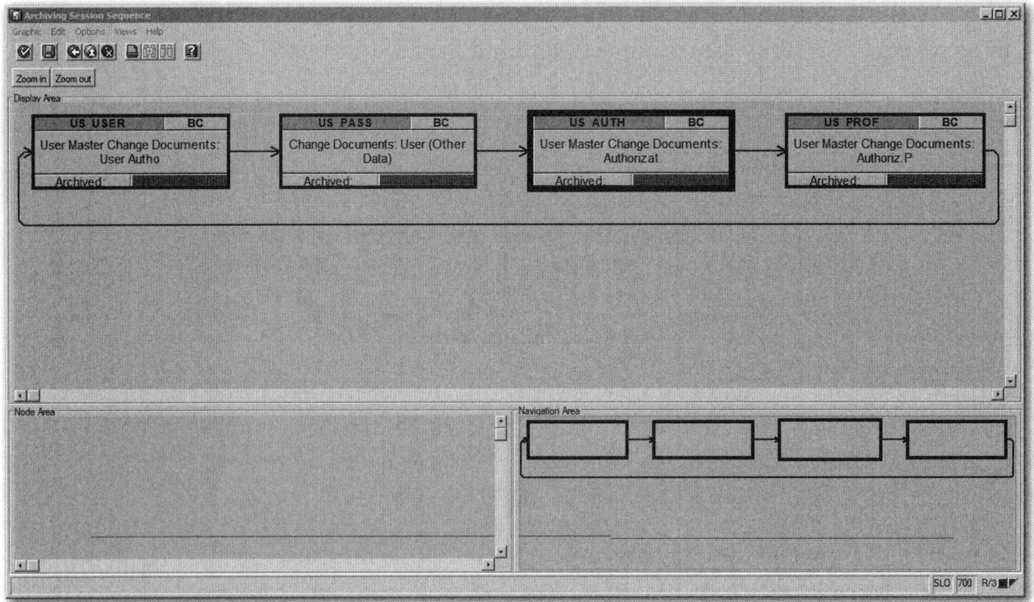


**Figure 12.4** Network Graphic for the US_AUTH Object

**Tables and archiving objects**

You can use the Tables and Archiving Objects (DB15) subcomponent of the ADK to analyze the relationship between the archiving object and the relevant tables. On one hand, it lists all of the tables from which data is contained in a selected archiving object, and, on the other hand, it displays all of the archiving objects that contain data from a selected table (see Figure 12.5).

In principle, only consistent objects can be archived.

Figure 12.5 shows all of the tables for the US_AUTH archiving object. In this case, only one table (USH12) belongs to the archiving object.

In the upper part of the screen, you can also search in the reverse sequence, that is, you can enter a table name to display the associated archiving objects.

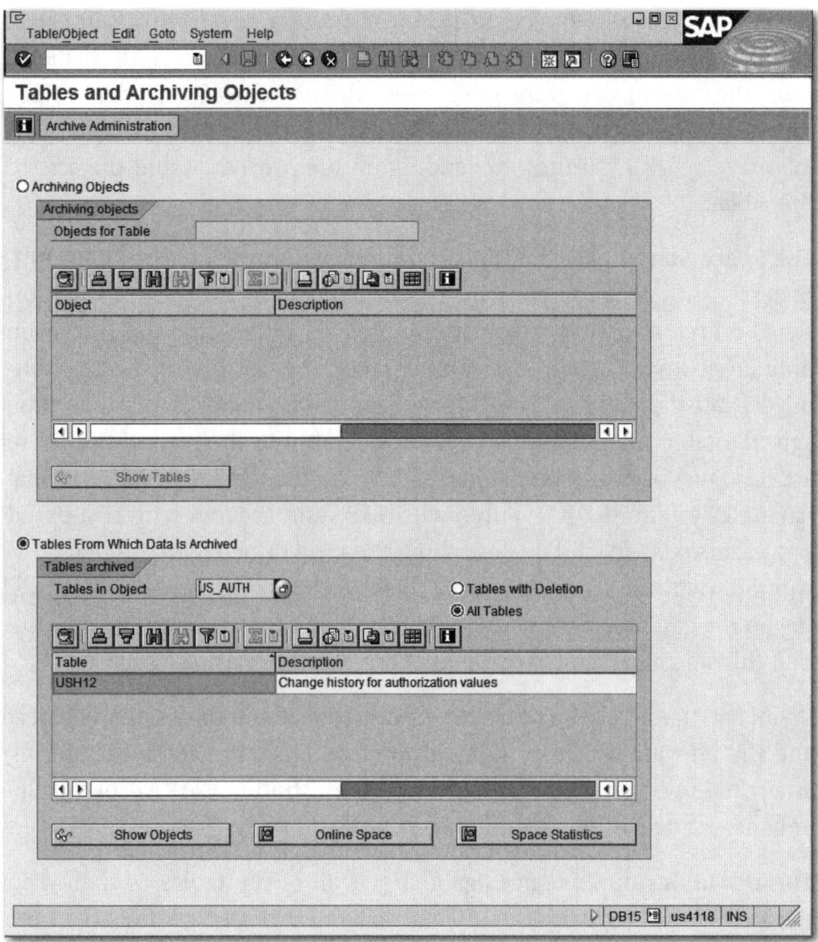


**Figure 12.5** Tables and Archiving Objects

**Data volume**

If you make a decision regarding the archiving object, you must determine the expected volume of data to be archived. To assess whether archiving is necessary, you need information about the current physical and logical size of the tables of an archiving object in the database. The physical size denotes the memory space actually occupied in the database. The logical size refers to the number of data records in the table. The size analysis has two determination variants whose availability and characteristics depend on the database used.

**Size analysis** If the database allows you to perform a size analysis, you can select **Online Space** in **Tables and Archiving Objects** (see Figure 12.5) to determine the current size of the table selected. The RDBMS used determines the actual, physical table size or a database-specific statistical value. This may take several minutes, depending on the procedure and the size of the table.

Use **Space Statistics** if the statistical information used by the SQL Optimizer is sufficient for your purposes. However, the size information based on the statistical information only ever reflects the status or even only an estimate based on a sample taken the last time the SQL Optimizer statistics were updated. If the last update took place a long time ago, the table may have changed considerably in the meantime. These aspects must be considered when estimating the table size. All relational database systems (RDBMS) used with SAP systems work with cost-based optimizers; statistical data describing the growth behavior and data distribution within the tables is used to access the table contents. Depending on the database system used, the database administrator must ensure that this statistical data is updated at regular intervals.

**Archive configuration** If you have gathered the necessary information about the archiving object and the relevant tables, you must now configure the archive. Entering an archiving object name in Archive Administration (SARA) specifically enhances the possible actions automatically.

The **DB Tables** option once again shows all of the tables contained in the archiving object. You can select **Info System** to branch directly to the Archive Information System (AIS). Here, you have to make some settings to start an archiving run for the selected object. In particular, you have to clarify the backup destination of the data to be archived. For this, you use Customizing, which comprises four areas as follows:

- Cross-archiving-object Customizing
- Archiving-object-specific Customizing
- Basis Customizing
- Application-specific Customizing

### 12.2.1 Cross-Archiving-Object Customizing

The parameters set here are cross-application parameters that apply to all archiving objects. They concern the following:

- CCMS data archiving monitor
- Access check when selecting an archive
- Verification of archive files

CCMS monitoring for data archiving (see Chapter 11, Monitoring Architecture) gives information about the archiving runs, provides an alert mechanism in the event of an error, and monitors write and delete jobs. In cross-archiving-object Customizing, you can activate or deactivate CCMS monitoring.

**Accessing archive files**

If you want to access an archive file for read, delete, reload, or evaluation purposes, you can configure whether you'll search for the required archive files either in the storage system or at the operating system level. The access check performed on stored files when selecting an archive may involve a lengthy access to the storage system.

If the archive file receives verification information while it's being written, this information can be evaluated when deleting, reading, and/or reloading the file. This prevents the deletion of data that is stored in the database but recognized as being incorrect in the storage system. However, if you set **Verification while Reading**, you may experience long response times when using an external storage system.

Since SAP R/3 Enterprise, a maximum duration (in hours) or a maximum size for archive files to be written can be agreed for the archiving run (write phase). After the first limit is reached, the archiving run stops. However, it can be restarted again (from the point where it stopped) at a more suitable time.

### 12.2.2 Archiving-Object-Specific Customizing

You can specify technical settings, such as the size of the archive files to be created, and the configuration of the process for the subsequent delete program.

Size of an archive file

Figure 12.6 shows the possible technical settings for the US_AUTH archiving object. Before you can store archive files, you must define a path name for the storage directory and also file names within the storage directory for the archive data itself. The logical file name, *ARCHIVE_DATA_FILE_WITH_ARCHIVE_LINK*, is the default setting when specifying the file name for the archive files to be created, irrespective of the operating system. The path is assigned to the logical name *ARCHIVE_GLOBAL_PATH*. A platform-specific name is determined at runtime. Some hardware conditions limit the size of the archive file. Furthermore, you may have to consider some limitations concerning the maximum file system size and the capacity of downstream media (CD-ROM, DVD, and WORM). If you don't specify a size, the size of the archive files is restricted to 2GB. If the archiving program determines that the next object to be written will exceed the maximum size defined for the archive file or the number of data objects defined here, a new archive file is started. Object-specific default settings are proposed for the following two parameters: **Maximum Size in MB** and **Maximum Number of Data Objects**.

You can select **Server Selection** to define the background servers to be used for all archiving runs or the current archiving object. If background work processes are configured on the database server, the archiving program is started on the database server; the delete runs are distributed across the other servers in the server group.

In archiving phase 1, only one copy of the data to be archived in files outside the database is created. The last phase, the deletion of data that has been copied successfully, can be configured in such a way that this phase automatically runs after phase 1. If the archive files are forwarded to an external storage system, you can configure whether the data in the database is to be deleted before or after it's stored. The archive files at the operating system level or in the storage system are used to compare data before it's deleted.

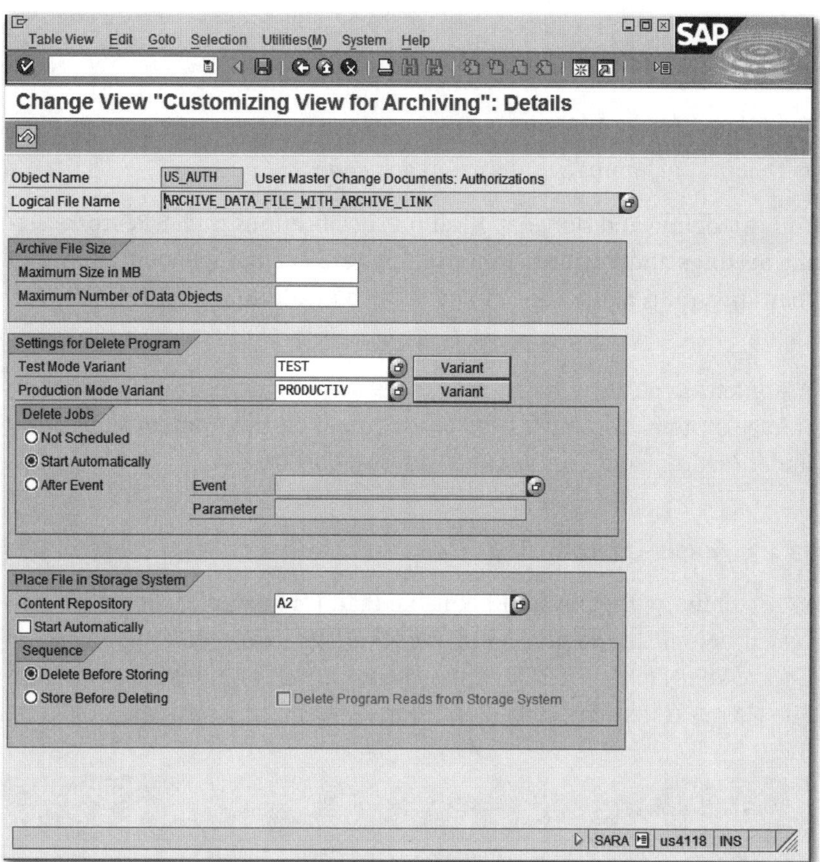


**Figure 12.6** Archiving-Object-Specific Customizing

Index

For the delete operation, you can use the **Create Index** option to create an index when selecting archiving objects. An index enables you to use the ADK to select individual data objects in the archive file. From a database perspective, data deletion (unlike data copying) is technically a change transaction that is recorded in the RDBMS log. Therefore, the database administrator must ensure that the areas that retain the before images (e.g., the Oracle rollback segment), which are required when a database transaction is rolled back, are configured with sufficient space. You can use the variants to determine the following settings for a test and production run:

- Test run
- Detail log
- Restart after termination
- Deletion of company-internal match codes

You can define additional application specifications under **Postprocessing Settings** and **Variant**. These settings are client-dependent; that is, if they are required, they have to be defined as additional settings for each client.

**Content repository**

A Content Repository must be specified to assign files to a downstream storage system. You must have already defined the Content Repository under Customizing Content Repositories (OAC0).

### 12.2.3 Basis Customizing

When defining the physical file name that, for example, should be concealed behind the logical file name *ARCHIVE_DATA_FILE*, you can use Logical File Names (FILE) for cross-client settings or, if necessary, Logical File Names (Client-Specific) (SF01) for client-specific settings.

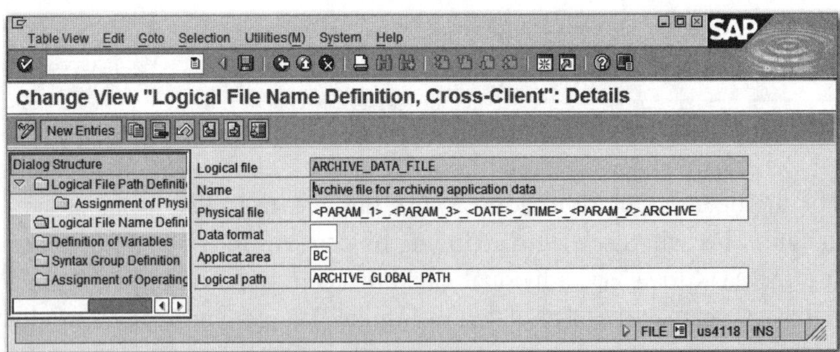


**Figure 12.7** Assigning Logical File Names

Figure 12.7 shows the client-independent definition of file names and paths. A physical, client-independent file name can be assigned to each logical file name.

### 12.2.4 Application-Specific Customizing

Depending on the archiving object you select, client-specific technical settings must also be made. However, the application manager is responsible for these settings. Only the technical settings are relevant for the system administrator.

Summary

In Customizing for an archiving run, you must also meet the following prerequisites:

- Provide sufficient disk space, preferably on locally accessible disks (for performance reasons).
- Set database parameters, especially for the deletion runs.
- Customize the archiving parameters for the application.

## 12.3 Control and Evaluation

You can use Archive Administration (SARA) to control and evaluate an archiving run. The archiving object that you select determines the specific process and the content of the actions. As a result, we can only use examples here to demonstrate the options available. You can use Definition of Archiving Objects (AOBJ) to obtain information about the object-specific characteristics.

Programs

The following list provides an overview of the programs available for controlling and evaluating archiving runs:

- **Preprocessing (optional)**
  You can use a preprocessing program to prepare the data objects to be archived for the archiving run, for example, by setting a deletion indicator. You must define the start date and output parameters. The archiving object that you select determines whether this function is provided.
- **Archive**
  You determine the start date and the possible output control parameters for the archiving run (see Figure 12.8).

In variant maintenance, you define the application-specific data selection. You can call the Job Overview (SM37) to display the background job that is automatically scheduled and executed in accordance with the settings made.

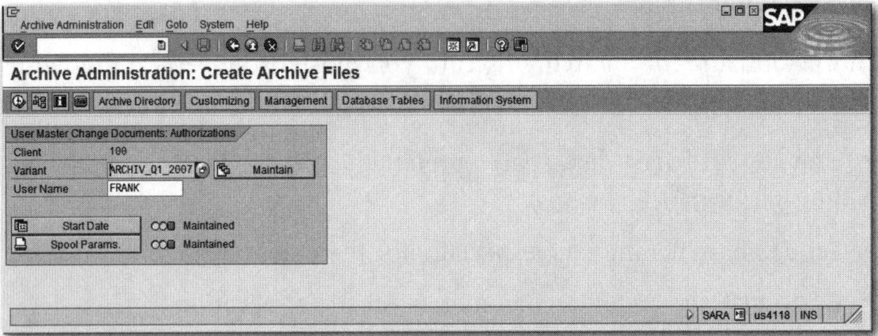


**Figure 12.8** Scheduling the Archiving Run

- **Delete**
  If you don't want the data to be automatically deleted immediately after it's archived, here you can explicitly set the start date and the output parameters for deleting the archives selected during archive selection.
- **Post-processing (optional)**
  Post-processing comprises application-specific operations that may be necessary after an archiving run. These include, for example, statistical data updates. The archiving object that you select determines whether this function is provided.
- **Evaluate**
  The archiving object that you select also determines which application-specific evaluation programs are provided. For example, the document compact journal or the line item journal is provided for the archiving object `FI_DOCUMNT`.
- **Index (optional)**
  An index can be retroactively created for archive files that already exist. Furthermore, an existing index can be removed. Depending on the application, the archive index is stored in separate application tables (e.g., in the FI Documents table) or in the cross-application archive index table.

- **Storage System**
  If, in archiving-object-specific Customizing, you did not schedule the transfer of archive files to an external storage system, the data can be transferred here if the Content Repository to be used was already maintained in Customizing for the archiving object.
- **Administration**
  Archive administration provides an overview of all archiving runs, assigned according to their status. The system provides detailed information about the runs when you double-click each run.

Any processing programs triggered by the user run in the background.

Reload

Reload means that archived data is reimported into the database. Generally, it should not be necessary to reload archived data into the database because it's possible to evaluate archived data. Furthermore, the ADK can be used to access individual data directly. The reload option is only designed for the almost immediate withdrawal of data that has just been archived if, for example, the selection criteria settings for the archiving program are incorrect. However, if you want to reload archived data after a longer period of time, you must first ensure that all data that refers to the data to be reloaded is available in the database. A reimport following a change of release is never supported. If it's possible to reload data for an archiving object, you can activate this action under **Archive Administration (SARA) - Initial Screen • Goto • Reload**.

## 12.4 Tips

Statistics

Since SAP R/3 Enterprise, you can select the **Statistics** option in Archive Administration (SARA) to view extensive information about completed archive runs. In particular, you can see the volume of data an archive run actually deleted from the database.

Restart after a termination

When an archiving or delete program terminates, we must distinguish between the following scenarios:

- **Termination During the Write Operation**
  The archive files are created sequentially. The file that is currently being processed, that is, the file that data is currently being written

to, has the status *created*. After the write operation has concluded successfully, the status is set to *active*, and the ADK can be used to evaluate or process the file that has been written. If the write program terminates, this only affects the file that is currently being written. The sequence for the procedure is as follows:

- Start the delete runs for all archive files that have been closed successfully.
- Mark the file from the terminated job as invalid in archive administration.
- Delete the incorrect archive file at the operating system level.
- Restart the archiving run after ending all other delete runs. Here, use the same selection criteria that was used for the first run.

- **Termination During the Delete Operation**
If a delete run terminates, you must first use object-specific information to analyze and solve the problem. If you can access the archive files themselves, you can restart the delete run any time after you have solved the problem. If you are unable to access the archive files themselves, you can nevertheless repair them by copying the readable part of the data to a new archive file. Up to the point of termination, only the data that is readable in the archive file itself is deleted from the database. You then use this file to restart the delete run. To repair the archive files, you require additional reports, which you can obtain from SAP Support.

Archive Information System

The SAP Archive Information System (SARI) is a tool that has been integrated into the archiving environment and used to research SAP data archives. Both the data search and data display are based on *archive information structures* that are defined by the user and filled with data from the archive.

Document Relationship Browser

You can use the Document Relationship Browser (ALO1) to display cross-application linked objects and documents that are grouped according to the process or business transaction. Objects that have already been archived are also displayed here.

For more detailed information about data archiving in SAP systems, refer to the book entitled *Archiving your SAP Data*, which was written by Helmut Stefani (SAP PRESS, 2007).

## 12.5 Transactions and Menu Paths

**Administration of Stored Documents:** SAP Menu • Tools • Business Documents • Other • Stored Documents (OAAD)

**Archive Information System:** SAP Menu • Logistics • Agency Business • Environment • Archive • Display (SARI) or as a jump from Archive Administration - Initial Screen (SARA)

**Archive Administration - Initial Screen:** SAP Menu • Tools • Administration • Administration • Data Archiving (SARA)

**ArchiveLink Monitor:** SAP Menu • Tools • Business Documents • Environment • ArchiveLink Monitor (OAM1)

**Definition of Archiving Objects:** Not accessible through the standard SAP menu (AOBJ)

**Document Relationship Browser:** Not accessible through the standard SAP menu (ALO1)

**Job Overview:** SAP Menu • Tools • CCMS • Jobs • Maintenance (SM37)

**Logical File Names:** SAP Menu • Tools • CCMS • Control/Monitoring • Performance Menu • Operating System • Local • Alerts • File System (FILE)

**Logical File Names (Client-Specific):** SAP Menu • Accounting • Company-Wide Controlling • Business Planning • Environment • Settings Menu • Basic Settings • File Names • Logical Files Names (SF01)

**Customizing Content Repositories:** SAP Menu • Tools • Business Documents • Environment • Knowledge Provider • KPro • Content Repositories (OAC0)

**Tables and Archiving Objects:** SAP Menu • Tools • CCMS • DB Administration • Data Archiving (DB15)

## 12.6 Additional Documentation

### Quick Links

- SAP Service Marketplace, alias *adk*
- SAP Service Marketplace, alias *archivelink*
- SAP Service Marketplace, alias *data-archiving*
- SAP Service Marketplace, alias *dma*

### SAP Notes

Table 12.1 provides an overview of important SAP Notes concerning archiving.

| Content | SAP Note |
|---|---|
| Unable to Read the Archive File | 79186 |
| Maintaining Logical Path and File Names | 35992 |
| Summary of Sources of Information for Archiving R/3 Data | 71930 |
| Archiving Outside SARA | 133707 |

**Table 12.1** SAP Notes Concerning Archiving

## 12.7 Questions

1. **What is an archiving object?**
    a. CD-ROM or WORM
    b. The archive files created by the archiving run
    c. A logical unit of related data and the necessary archiving programs
2. **What is data archiving?**
    a. The process of backing up archive logs
    b. The process of archiving any documents such as incoming and outgoing print lists, invoices, or application component documents
    c. The process of removing data from the database and storing it in an archive system or possibly other data media

3. **Which SAP tool is used during data archiving to transfer data to an archive?**
   a. SAP ArchiveLink
   b. HSM (Hierarchical Storage Management)
   c. ADK (Archive Development Kit)
   d. RFC
4. **Which statement is correct?**
   a. The entire archiving procedure can take place while the SAP system is running.
   b. The entire archiving procedure can only take place when the SAP system isn't running.
   c. You can't work with the SAP system while archive files are being created.

*Data distribution and transfer are essential components of the business framework in SAP. Because these two task areas strongly depend on business backgrounds, the system administrator isn't solely responsible for them. Close cooperation with user departments, developers, and technicians is absolutely necessary when implementing the scenarios. The system administrator's tasks are the technical implementation, monitoring configured processes, and coordinating problem solutions.*

# 13 Data Distribution and Transfer

You can use different solution approaches to implement cross-system business processes and transfer data. Depending on the requirements, you can choose between loose or close couplings and synchronously or asynchronously distributed processing.

*Application Link Enabling* (ALE) is the standard scenario for distributed applications. You must define data structures and communication methods for its technical introduction. As a supplement to the traditional procedure, new interfaces are implemented using BAPI technology. SAP NetWeaver Process Integration (PI) — the former SAP NetWeaver Exchange Infrastructure (XI) — is gaining importance regarding the exchange of information between different systems. In this context, SAP NetWeaver PI acts as a central integration point for all connected systems.

Standard scenario

This chapter first introduces basic technologies for data distribution. Then, it describes probably the most popular procedure, *Application Link Enabling* (ALE). The chapter deals with differences for other procedures (e.g., direct input and batch input) and provides an outlook on SAP NetWeaver PI.

## 13.1 RFC Connections

Many connections between two SAP systems or an SAP system and an external system are based on the SAP interface protocol of the *Remote Function Call* (RFC). This protocol enables additive applications to call the ABAP function within the SAP system and enables SAP systems to call external applications. External programs are provided with the RFC functions via dynamic libraries.

RFC client and server

An RFC is the call of a predefined function module in a partner system; the called program is the RFC client, and the called system is the RFC server (see Figure 13.1). In the SAP environment, RFC is based on a CPI-C interface implemented by SAP.

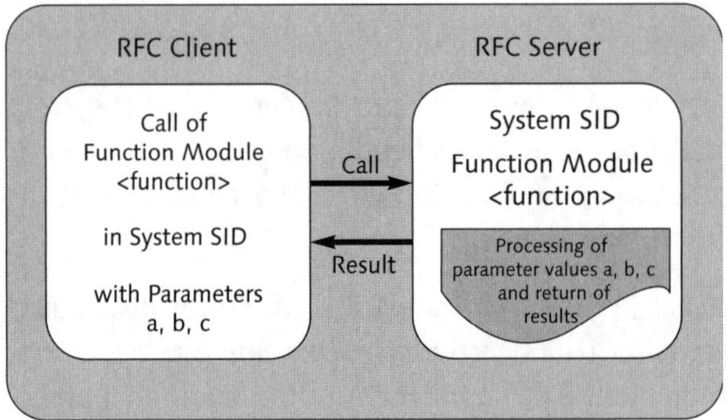


**Figure 13.1** Distribution of Tasks Across Different Systems

RFC destinations

To fully integrate an SAP system into the existing system landscape, the provided RFC connections must be defined as *RFC destinations*. Some of these definitions are already made automatically in the landscape during the configuration of an SAP system. This includes, for example, the RFC connections required for the Transport Management System, which are created during the integration of an SAP system into the transport domain. During the installation of an SAP system, RFC destinations to all corresponding application servers are generated as well. However, you must often still create additional destinations. Everyday examples from the system administration area are RFC connections for the following:

- Remote client copies (see Section 5.4, Remote Copy, in Chapter 5)
- Setting up a central user administration (see Section 13.2.3, Configuration in Chapter 11)
- Monitoring remote SAP systems using the alert monitor (see Section 11.2.1, Integration of Remote Systems, in Chapter 11)

**Definition of RFC destinations**

To define an RFC destination, all data required for the communication with the partner system are entered using a logical name. You also specify the type of the communication. Any program can use a defined RFC connection so it's neither assigned to a single function nor to a specific client. RFC connections are always unidirectional.

Each of the communication pairs named previously is implemented via a specific connection type. The parameters that are required to create a new RFC destination depend on the connection type (see Table 13.1).

| Type | Description | Necessary Information |
|---|---|---|
| I | Connection to an application server with the same database | None |
| 3 | Connection to R/3 system | Target host, system number |
| 2 | Connection to R/2 system | None |
| T | Start of an external program via TCP/IP | Depending on the activation type<br>Triggering: host name and program path<br>Registration: program ID |
| L | Reference entry (refers to another destination) | RFC destination for which an alias is created |
| S | Start of an external program via SNA or APPC | None |
| X | RFC via specific ABAP driver routines | ABAP driver |
| M | CMC connections, asynchronous connection to SAP systems | None |

**Table 13.1** Connection Types for RFC Destinations

You can create a new RFC destination via RFC Administration (SM59).

**Defining connections between two SAP systems**

Take a look at the following example of the definition of a new connection between two SAP systems:

1. RFC Administration (SM59) displays a list of all already known RFC destinations sorted by connection type (see Figure 13.2).
2. **Create** opens the input screen for a new RFC connection.

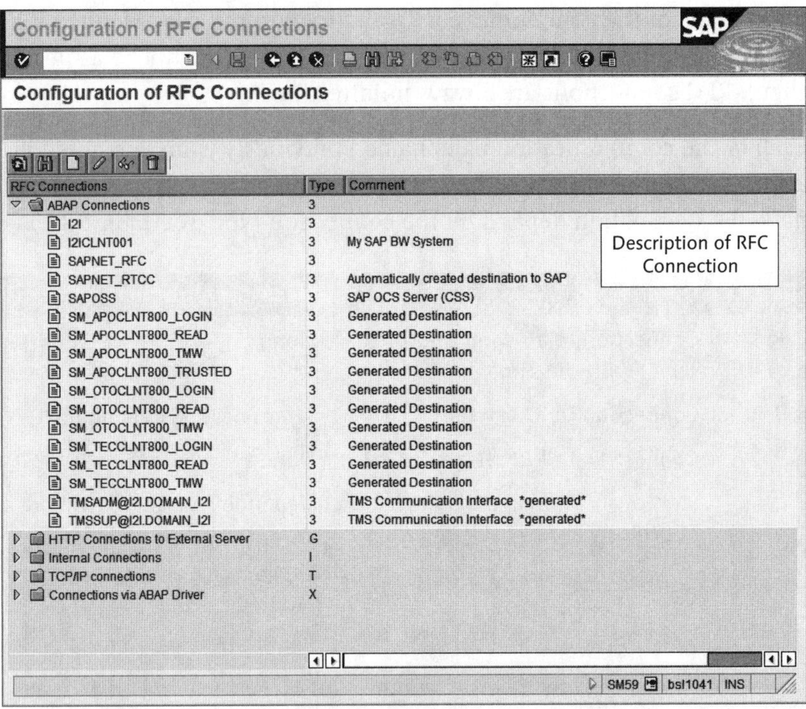


**Figure 13.2** Initial Screen of the Maintenance of RFC Destinations

3. Enter the logical name of the connection into the **RFC Destination** field. Note that the name can no longer be modified after the creation.
4. Depending on the connection type selected, the screen is automatically extended with the required input fields. Figure 13.3 shows the screen to enter the data for an RFC connection to another SAP system (Connection Type 3).

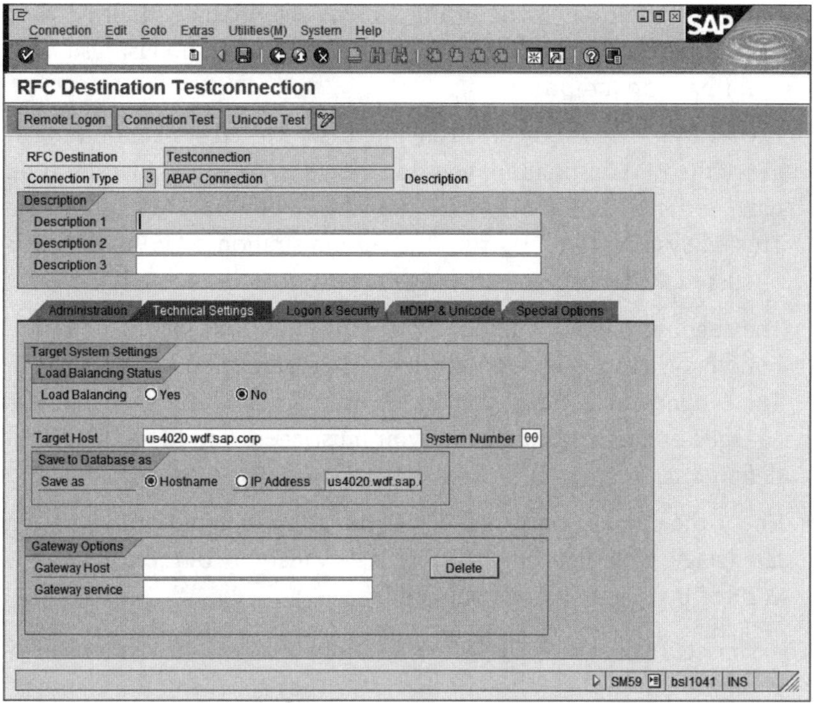


**Figure 13.3** Technical Settings of an RFC Destination

5. If you activate **Trace Option** (**Special Options** tabstrip), details of all processes that are managed using this RFC connection are logged in files at the operating system level. Both the sending and receiving system can analyze the logs using the `RSRFCTRC` report or via **RFC Administration (SM59) • RFC • Display Trace.**

   Trace option

6. Enter the **Target Host** as the host name or IP address and the **System Number** of the instance on the host.
7. Usually, you must also define the logon language, target client, user on the target system, and user's password for an RFC connection (**Logon and Security** tabstrip). Various options are possible here:
   - Explicit specification of all data in the screen. To prevent misuse, a user of the *communication* category should be used here.
   - Using the current user; this user must have the same user data in the target client.

- No specifications made in the screen; logon data is queried via a popup when the RFC connection is used. This method isn't suitable for background processing.

Trusted systems

However, if the local system is defined as a trusted system on the target of the RFC destination, you don't have to enter any identification data. You can maintain trust relationships between SAP systems via Trusted Systems (SMT1) or in RFC Administration (SM59) via **Extras • Trusted Systems** or **Trusting Systems**.

The logon data determined for a connection authorizes you to a remote system when setting up an RFC connection to this system. The assignment is static; that is, for example, if a user's password is changed at the remote system, you must check the RFC connection definitions.

8. Check the connection using **Test Connection** to avoid problems at a later stage. Note that only the physical availability of the computer is verified by issuing a *ping* command.

The overview of the defined SAP connections also lists the entries generated during the configuration of the TMS. They start with the abbreviation "TMSADM." For this RFC connection, use Connection Type 3 for connections between SAP systems.

Server groups

When defining RFC connections, you can also use the name of a group of application servers instead of entering a single target host. But first, the name must be entered via **RFC Administration (SM59) • Extras for RFC Groups** or **Server Group Maintenance (RZ12)**. The advantage of this method is that the host with the lowest load is selected from the group of application servers for establishing a connection; that is, the load is automatically distributed. This approach is used, for example, when a copy of a large client is parallelized. You can control the load behavior of the server groups by adapting the predefined resource parameters.

TCP/IP connections

The other RFC connections types are defined in the same way. Depending on the type, the specifications to be made may differ. For RFC connections for executing external programs (Connection Type T), you must first select a target host. For this purpose, an application server, a frontend workstation, and an explicit host that isn't used by the current SAP system are available. If the external program is supposed to run on an explicit host, you must specify the name or IP address of the server when you define the RFC destinations. For frontend workstations and application servers of their own SAP system, the host names are already known when logging on to the system. All computers are required to be available via the network without querying for the user name and password again. The external program that is supposed to be started is assigned to the RFC connection that is supposed to be defined.

Instead of starting the external RFC server program explicitly, you can also register the program at an SAP gateway. The registered program then waits for requests from different SAP systems that are directed to the gateway stating the registration.

**Logical connections**

It's also advisable to use entries of Connection Type L, which are *logical entries* that refer to another RFC destination. In this case, an RFC destination is first defined that only determines the physical target, that is, the required host. Then, the L connections are created that reference the entry. The RFC connection of the L type copies the target host and connection type of the RFC destination it refers to. A logical RFC connection is complemented only by logon data if required. Therefore, you obtain a greater independence when defining RFC destinations. For example, if an SAP system is transferred from one host to another, only the RFC destinations, which serve as the reference point for L connection definitions, must be adapted.

**RFC communication types**

There are several RFC communication types for which you can use specific additional configuration parameters:

- **Synchronous RFC**
  In a synchronous function call, the called system waits until the requested processing step is completed on the remote system and then continues to work locally.
- **Asynchronous RFC**
  In asynchronous RFCs, the called program forwards the request to the remote system and immediately continues to work locally. The remote system executes the requested processing step in a decoupled

way. Asynchronous calls of the RFC client get lost if the remote system isn't available when it's called.

- **Transactional RFC**
  The transactional RFC is also asynchronous. By assigning a *transaction ID*, it ensures that even requests that are sent several times (due to network problems, for example) are only processed once. In contrast to asynchronous RFC, the remote system doesn't have to be available when the RFC client program starts its call. The data is held in the source system until the target system can be reached again. The RSARFCSE report runs periodically in the background. It identifies calls that have not run yet by their transaction IDs and tries to schedule them again.
- **Queued RFC (qRFC)**
  The qRFC is an enhancement of the transactional RFC. Here, requests are collected in queues and not processed via transactional RFCs until all previous requests have been correctly handled. This procedure ensures that the requests are processed in the sequence in which they are received.

You can customize the properties of the defined RFC destinations from the detail screen of the connection definition via **Edit • TRFC Options** or **ARFC Options**.

A communication partner can't always reach all application servers or the message server of the RFC client system. Particularly for connected external programs, you often have to specify only one application server in the connection description. If more than this application server is supposed to communicate with the external program, you can define the application server that is known to the external program as the gateway for the RFC connection. Consequently, the entire communication between the RFC client and the external system is processed via this application server.

Monitoring RFC calls

The monitoring of the transactional RFC is performed by tRFC Monitor (SM58), and for queued RFCs by qRFC Monitor Inbound (SMQ2), qRFC Monitor Outbound (SMQ1), and qRFC Monitor (SMQR).

## 13.2 Application Link Enabling

The business processes of an enterprise can often not be mapped by a single, central system. Main reasons for this are distributed information flows, for example, between relatively independent branch offices of an enterprise. Another reason may be the technical bottlenecks caused by the size of a single central system. Security aspects may also be of relevance. Furthermore, it may be required to communicate with external program systems (e.g., warehouse management systems). If one or more of these reason make it impossible to use a central system configuration, but continuous data synchronization or message flow is nevertheless required, you can solve this problem by coupling the systems using Application Link Enabling mechanisms. The following sections can only describe the basic principles of this technology due to its complexity with regard to business and technical aspects. They will explain the most important issues of ALE processing from the system administrator's point of view.

### 13.2.1 Technical Basics

*Application Link Enabling* (ALE) is a method and technology provided by SAP to support business-controlled message exchange between loosely coupled systems. ALE comprises business scenarios and function modules that enable you to transfer and synchronize data from or to an SAP system without customer-specific developments.

**Questions on the concept**

The analysis of the business requirements on the application side and the transfer to appropriate technical tools are the starting points for considering an ALE scenario. Typical questions that may be asked in this regard include the following:

- Which processes are supposed to be mapped on a cross-system basis?
- Which objects are involved in which processes?
- Which data has to be considered in various systems?
- What is the format in which the data should be provided and which information must therefore be transferred?

- Which transfer techniques are suited to map the requirements in an appropriate way? Criteria are frequency, necessity for a return message, timeliness, and so on.
- What is the data flow between the systems involved?

The ALE technology is integrated in the applications and customizing, and it provides a wide range of distribution services. It enables you to transmit information on the processing status to the sender. However, it doesn't only transfer data but also triggers follow-up actions in the target system.

Exchanged data

From the point of view of the SAP system, the data that is supposed to be exchanged may include the following:

- **Transaction data**
  Data from applications and flow data.
- **Master data**
  Customer or material master data, for example.
- **Customizing data**
  Data that is required to ensure a standardized ALE complete view.

Data can be exchanged between SAP systems and R/3 systems as well as between SAP and external systems. The focus of the implemented scenarios lies on the distribution between SAP systems. The data distribution between SAP systems is largely independent of the corresponding release status of the systems; that is, upgrades of the SAP systems in the system landscape don't have to be performed simultaneously. The systems are loosely coupled either via synchronous (reading) or asynchronous (editing) communication. The technical properties of the coupling are defined in *port descriptions*. The port types correspond to the communication methods selected; file interface, RFC, CPI-C, and Internet interface are currently used.

Message type

The *message type* describes the semantics of a message that is supposed to be transferred into a remote system. A sample message type is material master data that is supposed to be stored in a central master system and distributed to downstream systems, for example, if changes have been made.

IDoc types

The information itself can be sent via an *Intermediate Document (IDoc)*. An IDoc type, which describes the structure of the data that is supposed to be sent, is assigned to a message type as the container for the data to be exchanged. A specific IDoc type is available for every application area that is supposed to provide data for exchanges. You must define the data, including tables and fields, that is supposed to be sent on the basis of IDoc types. When an IDoc type is filled with detailed data according to the structure specifications, it's called an IDoc.

Creating IDocss

Depending on the application, one out of three methods can be used to create IDocs (see Figure 13.4).

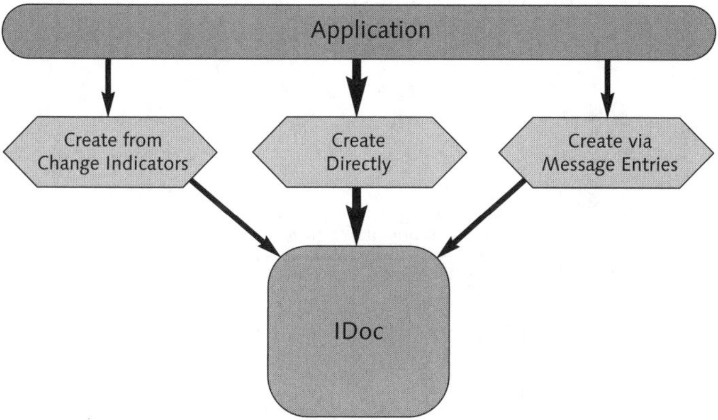


**Figure 13.4** Methods for Creating IDocs

IDocs are often created directly from the application. The application program either fills an internal table in the IDoc format and transfers it to an ALE service or uses a BAPI with an ALE interface.

The second method is to create IDocs from *change pointers*. The business background for this method is the automated synchronization of systems with regard to defined master data. Each time a selected object is changed — for example, the material master record — a change pointer for that record is recorded in a database table. You can generate IDocs from these change pointers and replicate them into one or more target system either manually or using scheduled ALE reports.

In the third method, SAP's *message control* is used to create the respective IDocs. In many applications, for example, when creating an order, sending messages is one of the standard scenarios. The generic service of the message control enables you to print a message or send it in electronic form. For this purpose, the respective application makes *message entries* of the ALE type in the NAST table. Depending on the configuration, the entries can be analyzed immediately by the SAP message control or at regular intervals using the `RSNAST00` report to create IDocs.

You can't select one of the methods freely because they depend on the respective application.

**IDoc structure**

An IDoc is composed of several segments. Each segment has a structure description and documentation. Several tables are used to store this data at the database level. IDocs have a hierarchical organization (see Figure 13.5).

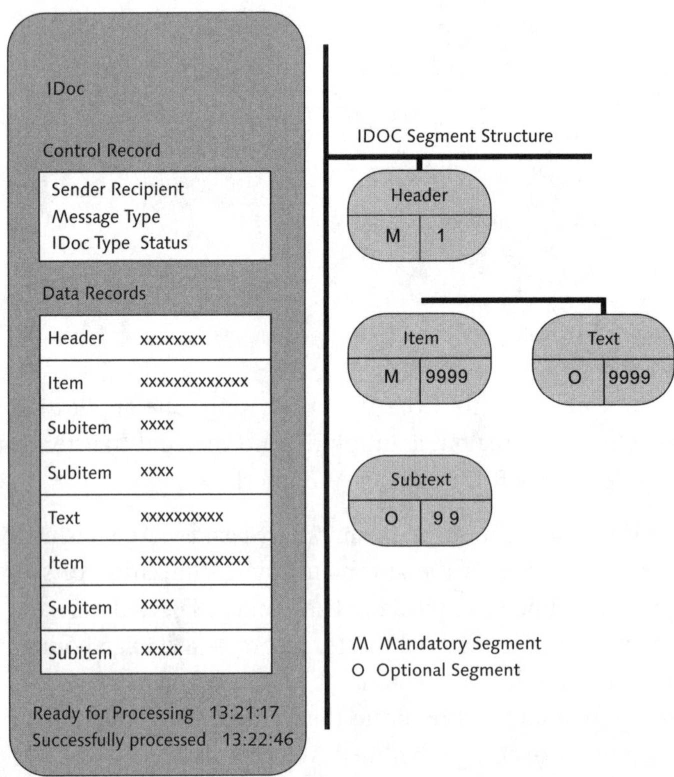


**Figure 13.5** IDoc Structure

Each IDoc contains only one control record that consists of technical information for the transfer, for example, sender, receiver, and message type. The control record already defines which processing steps are required for the transmitted data. The control record is followed by the actual data of the ALE message. They are stored in different segments according to the hierarchy. A cluster table describes the structure of the segments and contains a field with the data that is supposed to be distributed. However, the structure and name of the table depend on the respective SAP release. The status information is the third component of the IDoc structure.

The Customizing is responsible for defining the data exchange. The SAP system administrator, however, has the task to technically define the ALE connections. He must again closely collaborate with the application manager or consultant that is responsible for the application side.

### 13.2.2 Close and Loose Coupling Using BAPIs

You can also use the ALE mechanisms if a distributed business process is supposed to be implemented via a remote call of BAPIs.

**Close coupling**

Instead of sending a message in IDoc format that has been generated by the application, the name of a business object type and a method are sent. This method is synchronously processed on the target system. Synchronously started methods should only execute reading or analyzing functions.

**Loose coupling**

To asynchronously start a BAPI on the target system, you can send the interface parameters required as an IDoc. When the information is received, this triggers the processing of the required method with the transferred parameters in the target system.

### 13.2.3 Configuration

The following text describes the basic principles of configuring an ALE connection between two SAP systems. The focus is on the technical aspects and tasks of the system administrator instead of the application's point of view.

The procedure consists of the following steps:

1. Defining the partners in an ALE landscape
2. Creating a model view for the ALE distribution model
3. Generating partner profiles

**Setting up logical systems**

The communication partners within an ALE scenario are called *logical systems*. You must define them first. In an SAP landscape, logical systems are implemented by clients. It's therefore not relevant whether the partners are physically located on identical or separated SAP systems when setting up an ALE communication. You should follow the following naming convention when assigning a name to the logical system: <SID>CLNT<client>. Then, the naming convention can be used to identify partners. Figure 13.6 illustrates the input of the logical systems. From the Customizing tree, you can directly navigate to this overview using the Execute icon.

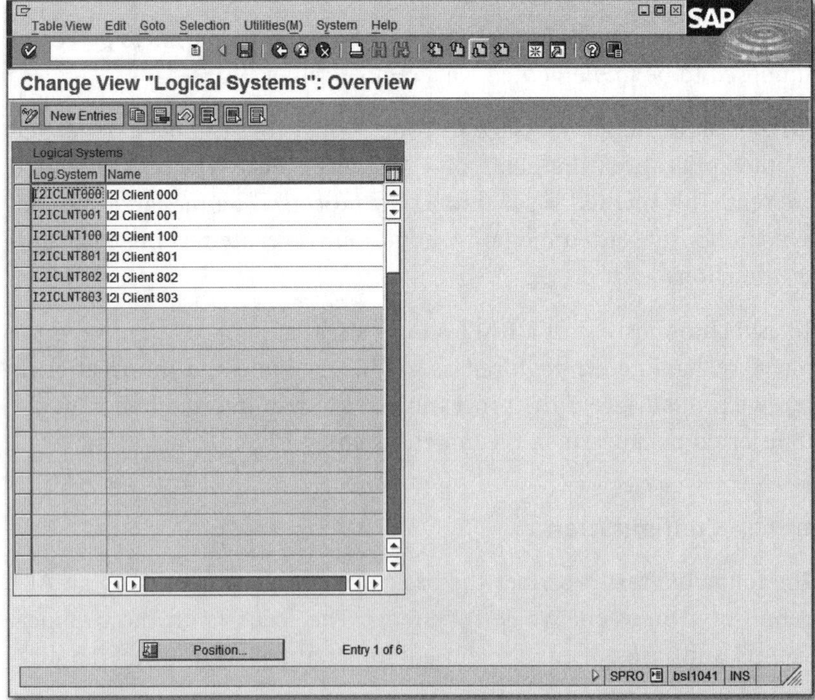


**Figure 13.6** Maintaining Logical Systems

The changes made are recorded in a Customizing request that has to be assigned by the user if the respective client had been configured using the option **Automatic recording of changes**. This request enables you to transfer tested basic settings into other systems. The settings are stored in a cross-client table, that is, they must be created only once for each SAP system.

Assigning to clients

In the next step, the logical system names are assigned to the selected clients of the respective SAP system. For this purpose, go to the Assign Logical System to a Client activity in the ALE Customizing or use Client Maintenance (SCC4) as described in Section 5.2, Creating New Clients, in Chapter 5 (see Figure 13.7).

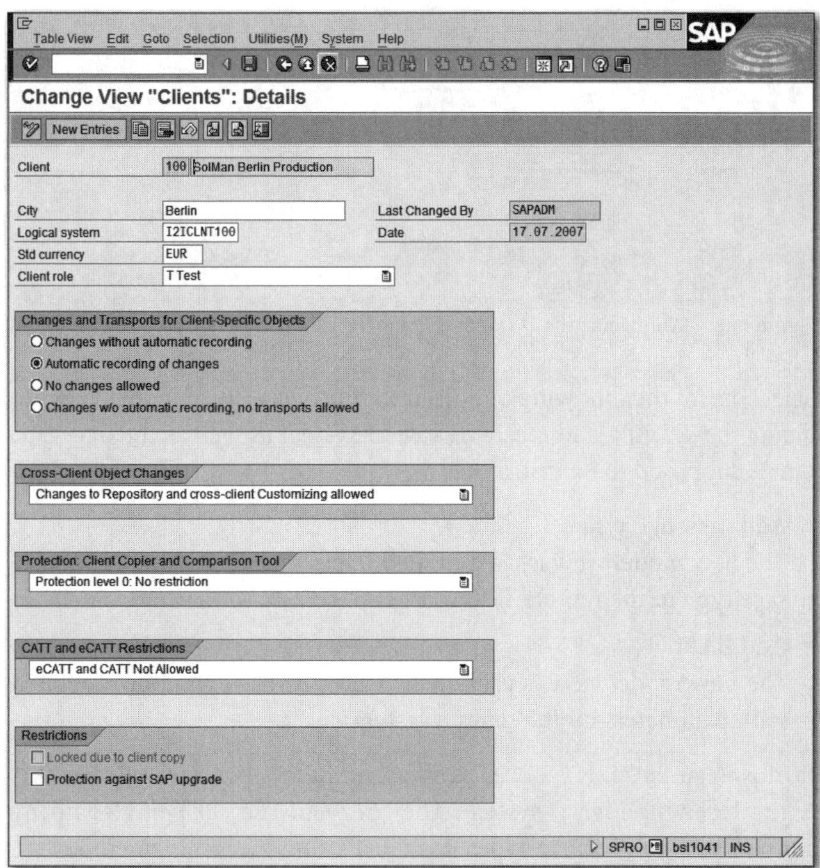


**Figure 13.7** Client Maintenance

You determine the possible end points of the ALE data distribution when defining the logical systems. Next, define the data flow in the system landscape.

**Maintaining the distribution model**

By using the logical system names, the *distribution model* specifies the communication partners and data that are supposed to be sent. The model is entered and maintained in one system so that it only exists in one active version in all systems involved. For this purpose, use the direct way to Create Model View (BD64). Enter the respective short text and a technical name for the planned model view (see Figure 13.8).

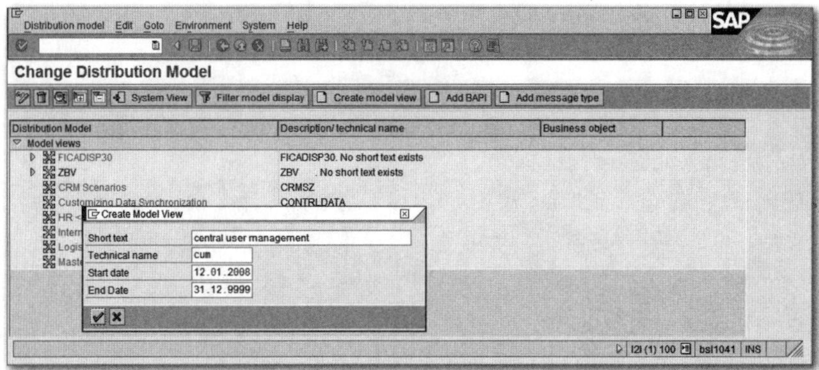


**Figure 13.8** Maintaining the Distribution Model

**BAPI/ message type**

Select one of the following options from the overview of model views to define the sending and receiving logical system as well as the data type that is supposed to be distributed:

- **Add message type**
  The new model view is used to send IDocs that are assigned to a message type to the remote system.
- **Add BAPI**
  The new model view is used to activate a BAPI method or provide it with parameters on the remote system.

In this example, I2ICLNT100 is the sending system, and I2ICLNT001 is the receiving logical system. The *User* and *UserCompany* (company address) business object types are filled using the `Clone` method (see Figure 13.9).

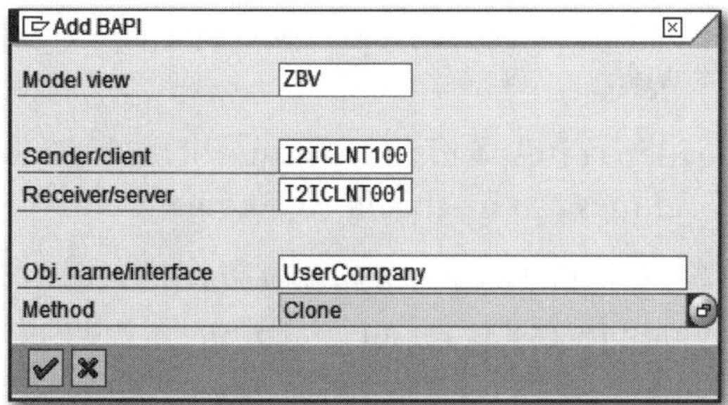


**Figure 13.9** Add BAPI

Filter

The amount of send data can be reduced by defining *filters*. When message types are filtered, IDoc segments and their subsegments aren't forwarded if an object type value pair is specified, and the segments have a field of this object type that doesn't contain the value defined. The filtering of BAPIs checks parameter value pairs. If a parameter corresponds to the set value, an IDoc is generated and distributed via the BAPI.

Special settings

Additional selection options for business process modeling and implementation of the ALE Customizing are listed here:

- Configure predefined ALE business processes
- Configure the distribution of master data
- Configure the synchronization of Customizing data

This enables you to exactly differentiate the data to be distributed and the usage of additional ALE functions. For example, you can distribute material master data in the branch for master data distribution; for this purpose, the generation of change pointers is activated. A change pointer indicates changes made to master records and thus enables you to generate a respective IDoc manually or by means of a report.

Communication

In all clients involved, you must create a specific user for the communication between the systems. For security reasons, this user should be of the *communication* type and not a dialog user.

For the communication between the partners of the ALE group, an RFC connection of Connection Type 3 (connection to an SAP system) must be created in each system. In the example of the central user administration, RFC destinations have to be created from the central system to all child systems and — depending on the setting of the parameter changeability — in the reverse direction as well.

If the name of the RFC destination corresponds to the name of the logical receiver systems, additional settings can be generated automatically.

Partner profiles

The Partner Profiles (BD82) of the ALE Customizing describe the parameters for inbound and outbound processing for all systems involved (see Figure 13.10). During the generation of the partner profiles, the profile is distributed to all **Partner Systems** selected or to all partners of the model view if only the **Model View** is defined without explicitly stating partners. In the example, the child systems are thus the partners for the definition of the partner profiles from the central system.

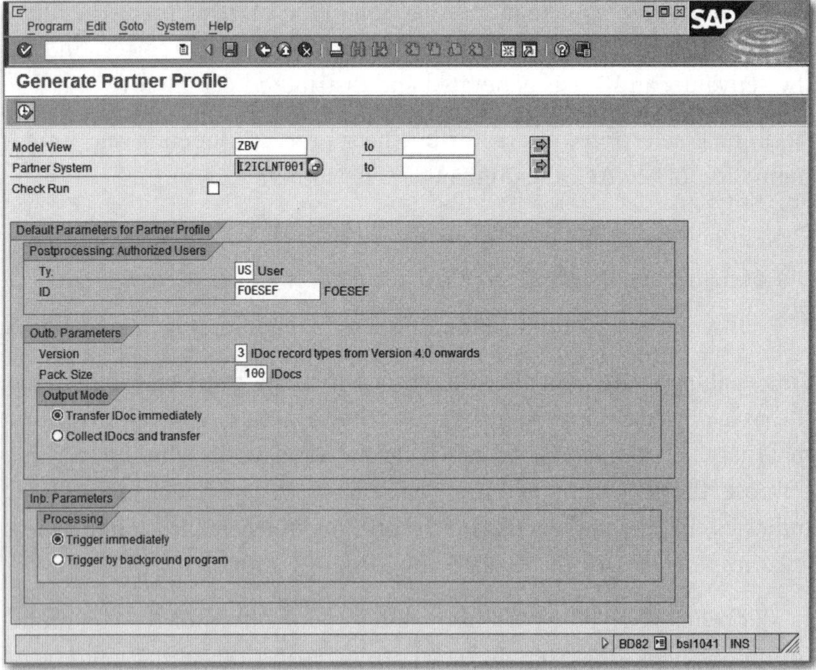


**Figure 13.10** Generating Partner Profiles

In the outbound parameters, you define the package size and output mode. You can transfer every generated IDoc immediately to the receiver or collect several IDocs and then transfer them. Many small packages have the disadvantage that the connection to the target system must be set up and the logon procedure performed for each package. This considerably decreases the performance. If you collect IDocs and transfer them later, there are temporary differences in the dataset of the sending and the receiving system. Additionally, peak loads occur in the receiving system when large number of IDocs are transferred. Because of these issues, a compromise must be found. SAP generally recommends collecting several IDocs and sending them as a package.

The receiver's inbound parameters that are supposed to be maintained affect the control of the receiver's side of the IDocs. IDocs can be processed immediately or in the background. For performance reasons, inbound IDocs shouldn't be processed immediately. Instead, they should be processed during periods of low load. This also enables you to parallelize the processing of inbound IDoc packages. After the definition of the partner profiles has been completed, you must save and generate them. During the generation, the port and the resulting details of the IDoc processing are also generated. The port must be made known manually by means of the port definition only if a file interface is used. The partner profiles determine how messages of the ALE processing are managed. The partner profiles depend on the partner type and the message type that is supposed to be sent. Figure 13.11 illustrates the communication data flow between the logical systems.

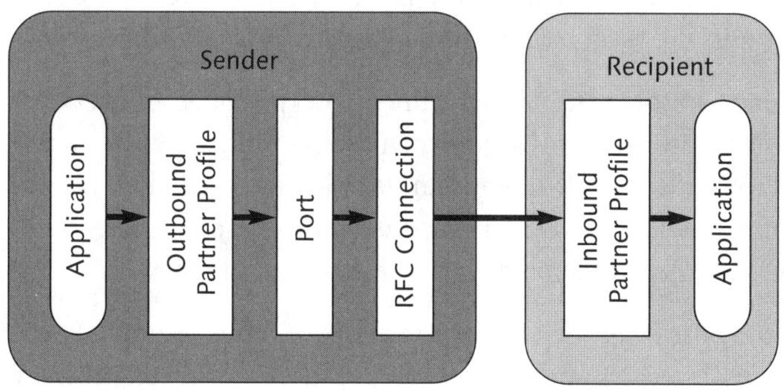


**Figure 13.11** Message Flow

**Port**

A *port* defines the type of the connection with the partner. The data can be transferred via tRFC, sequential files, or the Internet. A unique port number is assigned to each port.

The partner profiles can only be generated successfully if the names of the RFC connections correspond to the names of the logical systems. Otherwise, you must maintain the partner profiles manually.

To ensure that the settings that have been made and generated are fully functional, you can run the Check all Partner Profiles for Consistency function in the IDoc Check (IDOC).

Distributing model settings

The settings for the distribution have to be known by all partner systems, so, in the last step, the model settings are distributed via **Distribution Model Maintenance (BD64) • Edit• Distribute Model View**.

### 13.2.4 Monitoring and Analysis

Auditing

If the ALE connection was configured so that the receiver sends a message to the sender providing information on the execution, the sender can quickly check the success of the transfer. The advantage of this procedure is that the messages are directly sent to the responsible party when errors occur. There, the messages are resolved and can then be reprocessed. This procedure is called *auditing*. For this purpose, ALEAUD is provided, which enables you to send the sender messages with information on the IDocs received on the opposite side and their processing. As a prerequisite to use this return message, you must define a message flow for this message type in the distribution model and schedule a periodical background job in the receiver system that returns the audit files.

The ALE Status Monitor (BD87) (see Figure 13.12) provides an overview of the processing status of the IDocs, which can be filtered using numerous criteria. From this overview, you can navigate to detailed views and trigger the reprocessing of IDocs that had been processed incorrectly or incompletely after the problem has been determined and solved.

You can sort the entries in the status monitor by various criteria to support different analyses. Double-click to obtain more details and display the IDoc definition.

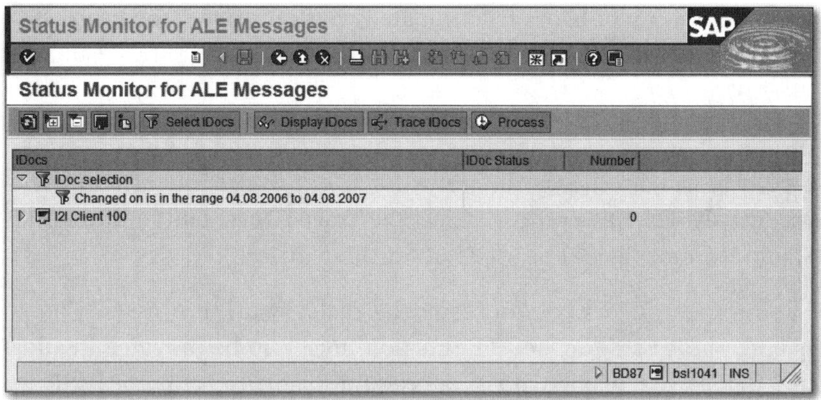


**Figure 13.12** Status Monitor

The IDoc List (WE05) provides a detailed view of the IDocs but doesn't enable you to resend them.

The status monitor described and additional analysis functions are integrated in the monitors of the ALE administration. From the SAP menu, you can navigate to the ALE administration via **Tools • ALE • ALE Administration.**

Checking the processing of the IDocs also includes controlling the work of the scheduled background jobs to process the IDocs. Table 13.2 lists the corresponding programs.

| Program | Meaning |
|---|---|
| RSEOUT00 | ALE outbound processing |
| RBDAPP01 | ALE inbound processing |
| RSNAST00 | Creating IDocs from the message control |
| RBDMIDOC | Creating IDocs from change pointers |
| RBDMOIND | Status conversion after successful tRFC transfer |
| RBDCPCLR | Reorganizing the change pointer table |
| RSARFCEX | Processing canceled IDoc send processes |

**Table 13.2** Background Jobs for the Distribution

If the processing of IDocs is terminated, you can trigger the processing manually after the problems have been solved using IDoc Error Handling (BD73).

In addition to the configurable return message via the ALEAUD message type, you can also query the status for IDocs you're interested in synchronously. For this purpose, select the **Trace IDocs** button in the ALE Status Monitor (BD87) or use IDoc Tracking (BDM2).

Parallel and sequential processing

The receiving IDocs are processed by dialog work processes. Consequently, processes for the ALE function must also be provided in addition to the usual dialog work processes for dialog users to process IDocs at the target system. Receiving IDocs can be processed in parallel or sequentially. When IDocs are processed in parallel, approximately as many dialog work processes must be added as the average amount of IDocs received in parallel. Sequential processing requires less dialog work processes, but only one IDoc can be processed at a time. This may cause bottlenecks and thus decreases the performance on the receiver's side. However, IDocs are processed one after the other. The technical team must discuss the advantages and disadvantages of the processing methods in collaboration with the user departments and implement the respective measures technically.

Separate SAP instance

In addition to the already mentioned advantage of a load distribution between SAP instances by means of forming groups when the RFC connections are defined, it may also be useful to operate a separate SAP instance for processing IDocs in particular. Of course, you must perform a cost/benefit analysis because additional hardware may be required if you want to implement this solution.

## 13.3 Data Transfer

If, for example, data that has been available in legacy systems is to be migrated to a new business solution, you need flexible, high-performance support for the following tasks:

- Converting many different data formats that were extracted by tools of the legacy systems into a format that can be read by SAP tools

- Transporting the converted legacy data to the new SAP system and clarifying which data is to be mapped in which table fields and which different data structures in the legacy and new system require customizing
- Guaranteeing complete transfer

The type of external data transfer to the SAP system depends on the receiving application. Because every application component requires different data, most applications have their own data transfer program that you must operate. For selecting the right transfer technique, these characteristics, the data volumes to be considered and the frequency of transfer (one-off or regularly), play a significant role.

**Data transfer techniques**

In the SAP system, different data transfer techniques are supported: batch input, call transaction, direct input, and transfer via BAPIs. If, in exceptional cases, the application has no suitable standard interface for transferring external data, you can use the transaction recorder to create data that has to be processed via batch input or call transaction.

### 13.3.1 Batch input

The batch input procedure has been used as a standard technique in the SAP environment to transfer data to the SAP system by simulating a user dialog for a long time. The data consistency is guaranteed because all transaction checks are implemented.

The data transfer is carried out in two steps:

1. Create a batch input session that contains all relevant data (transactions, dynpros, fields, field values).
2. Process this session in the system so that all data is imported into the SAP system.

**Batch input sessions**

To prepare external data and transfer it to a batch input session, you can usually use predefined programs. In exceptional cases, you need to develop a separate batch input program. The batch input program reads the data that must be available in SAP-compliant format, prepares it, and transfers it to the batch input session. A batch input session simulates the dialog input of transaction codes and the corresponding data entry. In fact, the read values are assigned to the screen fields of the corresponding transaction that needs to be filled. The structure of the batch input session determines the fields involved. It results from the transactions assigned and the SAP structures used.

The technique of the batch input procedure enables the data transfer for each SAP dialog screen, including the related integrity security. This is valid both for SAP standard programs and for customer-specific developments within the SAP system.

**Automatic recording**

The automatic recording of transactions is particularly useful, which, in turn, can be used to automatically create the associated batch input session structures and a batch input program. You can start automatic recording using the Transaction Recorder (SHDB). You can then implement all transactions for which data is supposed to be transferred by means of the batch input procedure. Based on these recordings you can generate the sessions and customize them as required. In the next step, you can generate the corresponding ABAP program and, if necessary, customize it. Manual programming that used to be necessary is therefore reduced to a minimum.

When the screen fields of the assigned transactions in a batch input session have been filled with values, the batch input session is transferred to the batch input queue. Based on this, you can process the session; the transactions contained are executed in the background, and the data is processed. From the database perspective, the APQD table is used to store the sessions while simultaneously implementing the batch input queue.

**Processing the batch input session**

For processing the batch input session, you have two options:

- Manual start using the e-batch input; implementation in the dialog or in the background
- Automatic start by scheduling the ABAP program, `RSDBCSUB`

Figure 13.13 shows the basic principles of the batch input procedure.

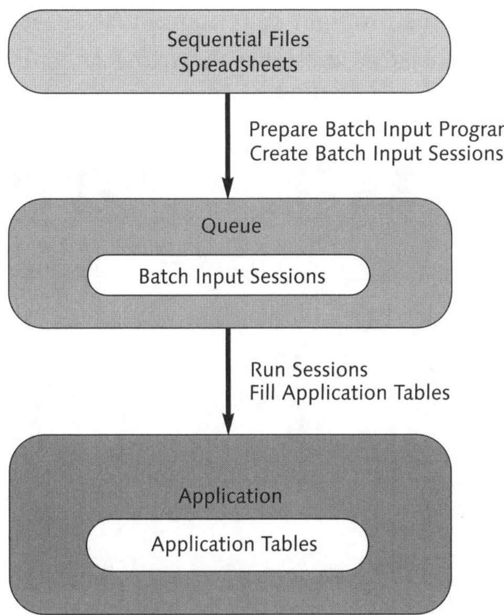


**Figure 13.13** Basic Principles of the Batch Input Procedure

**Monitoring by the system administrator**

From the system administrator's point of view, monitoring the batch input processes is relevant. For the batch input procedure, larger data volumes are imported into the SAP database within a relatively short period of time. The system administrator needs to consider the space requirement in the database, the increased write quantity, and the increased data volume in the database logs. So if you plan a data transfer using batch input, you should include the system administrator for planning.

During the development of a batch input program, you must consider the length of the transactions. Because a batch input program runs in the background, no screen change takes place, which means that no `Commit` is set from the database perspective. You must control the length of a transaction by means of explicit `Commits`.

You can access the analysis of the batch input processes and manually start a run via Batch Input (SM35) (see Figure 13.14). For evaluation, you're provided with different views regarding different aspects. You can only solve problems relating to the program or content in close collaboration with the system administrator, specialist departments, and developers.

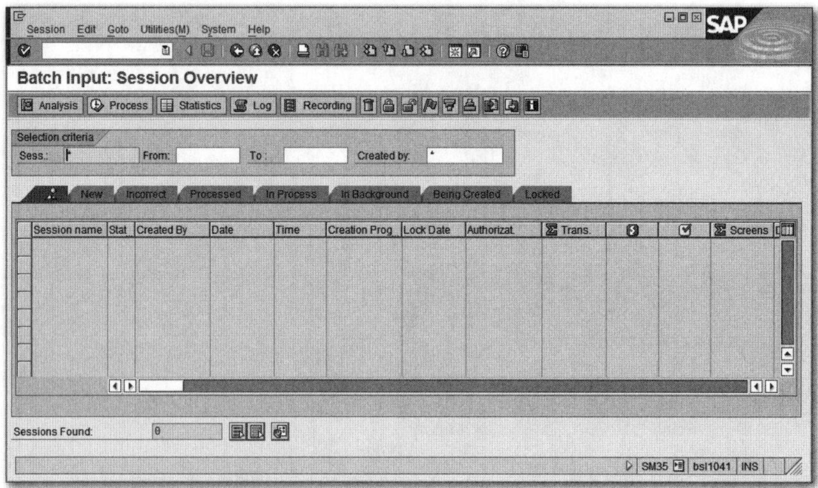


Figure 13.14 Batch Input: Session Overview

Deleting processed sessions

You should occasionally delete successfully processed sessions from the database for space reasons. For this purpose, you're provided with the RSBDCREO report for background processing. This report is intended to be scheduled daily for standard basis jobs.

### 13.3.2 Direct Input

For direct input, the data of the data transfer file is subject to all checks that would also be implemented in dialog mode. However, they are then directly transferred to the SAP system.

Strictly speaking, the direct input method is a further development of the batch input procedure. Whereas in batch input, the data is transferred to a session, in other words, the data is assigned to the corresponding dynpro fields, this step is omitted for direct input. Instead, the function modules available in the system are used for data transfer. The developer must call the appropriate function modules. Whereas in the batch input method, all consistency checks of the data are implemented automatically using the dynpro technique, the corresponding function module implements them for the direct input procedure.

Direct input programs can be directly started for test purposes. In this case, no log is created; a restart in not possible if problems occur. For the use in a production system, the data transfer via direct input should be controlled in the background by means of Direct Input Management (BMVO).

Although direct input is much faster, it doesn't have the automatic restart capabilities that batch input has, and it's more difficult to correct errors.

### 13.3.3 Fast Input/Call Transaction

For the fast input method, the step of initially transferring data to a session is replaced by another technique. First, the data to be transferred is written in an internal table where it's processed by calling the requested transaction with the `CALL TRANSACTION` ABAP statement. The internal table must have the necessary data structure for the transaction. For fast input, the developer is again responsible for logging the process flows. Fast input is faster than batch input (because fast input doesn't have batch input logging features) but generally slower than direct input.

### 13.3.4 BAPI

Another option to transfer data is the use of BAPIs (*Business Application Programming Interfaces*). The data is imported via an ALE model by calling a BAPI of the receiving application. For this purpose, the source data must be in IDoc format.

Here, as well, the same checks are performed as in dialog mode.

**BAPI**

A BAPI enables internal and, in particular, external access to data and business processes defined in SAP systems. The basic component of the object-oriented approach is *business object types* that map real-world objects from a software point of view. Predefined examples are charts of accounts, a sales order, or a purchasing organization. The access to these object types is only possible via standardized, platform-independent, release-independent, and open methods — BAPIs.

All business object types and the corresponding BAPIs are maintained in the *Business Object Repository* (BOR) of an SAP system. The BAPI Explorer (BAPI) enables you to obtain an overview of the defined object types, their methods, and their characteristics, and to make changes. Objects are the incarnations of an object type.

In addition to object-specific methods, there are some BAPIs for all object types, for example:

| | |
|---|---|
| `<Object>.Display` | Display an object |
| `<Object>.Delete` | Delete an object |
| `<Object>.GetDetail` | Display detailed data of an object |

In the technical sense, these methods have been implemented as function modules. Via BAPIs, you can connect external programs and business processes beyond system boundaries using an ALE distribution.

### 13.3.5 Legacy System Migration Workbench

Migration steps

For one-off or regular migration of data from non-SAP systems, you can use the Legacy System Migration Workbench (LSMW). The migration comprises the following steps:

1. Read structured data from one or multiple files that are stored on an application or presentation server.
2. Convert data in compliance with conversion rules. Many of the common conversion rules have already been predefined. Based on the rules customized to the specific situations, you can create conversion programs that migrate business data objects and that don't work at the table or field level.
3. Import data into the target system by means of standard interfaces (batch input, direct input, BAPI, IDoc). During the migration, the same checks are performed as for the dialog mode.

The Legacy System Migration Workbench is fully integrated into the SAP system; however, it's not contained as a standard component up to Basis Release 6.10. You can download the necessary transports at the *lsmw* quick link from SAP Service Marketplace; as of Basis Release 6.10, you need Version 3. The LSMW Version 4.0 is an integral component of SAP NetWeaver AS ABAP.

### 13.3.6 Data Transfer Workbench

Transferreing large data volumes

By means of the Data Transfer Workbench (SXDA), you can transfer large data volumes to your SAP system. The data transfer is project-controlled; the management of the project, which comprises extraction, cleanup, conversion, loading, and checking, is performed by the Workbench.

The Data Transfer Workbench analyzes the necessary structure description depending on the target application, integrates the data transfer programs, and, if required, uses additional self-developed tools.

The transfer involves data in SAP format; here, we recommend integrating the LSMW for reading the data in the external format and converting it. For subsequent loading of data, batch input, direct input, and the BAPI mechanism are supported.

## 13.4 SAPconnect

SAPconnect is a standardized interface for external communication that supports sending by telecommunication services, such as fax, text messages (pager/SMS), Internetmail, and X.400, as well as sending to printers and sending between different SAP systems. SAPconnect facilitates the connection of external communication components to the SAP system.

The former interface, SAPcomm, has been replaced by SAPconnect.

External providers are connected via the certifiable interfaces, BC-CON (fax) and BC-PAG (paging). In the Basis releases up to 4.6D, the email connection is implemented using RFC, depending on the opposite end via SAP Exchange Connector, Lotus Domino MTA, or SAP Internet Mail Gateway (`sendmail`). As of Basis Release 6.10, the Simple Mail Transfer Protocol (SMTP) is the standard protocol for email connection; an SMTP server can be directly accessed using an SMTP plug-in. SMS and fax services can be addressed via SMTP as of Basis Release 6.20. The documents are attached to emails, and forwarded to internal fax servers or an external provider.

SMTP functionality

For using the SMTP functionality, you need to customize the profile parameter of the SAP instance to enable the loading of the dynamic library by which the SMTP plug-in is implemented. Additionally, the user type, *System*, with the `S_A.SCON` authorization profile, is required for every client in which emails or status messages are received.

Each external communication system to which messages are supposed to be transferred must be created as a *node*. The connection parameters are set depending on the connection type (SMTP, RFC). The SMTP plug-in is part of the Internet Communication Manager (ICM).

Connection to the Alert Monitor

For monitoring external components, the communication environment of SAPconnect is connected to the alert monitor (CCMS). If nodes are to be displayed in the alert monitor, you need to activate the **Node is to be monitored by the Alert Monitor** flag in the node definition. You can access the administration interface (see Figure 13.15) of SAPconnect via SAPconnect Administration (SCOT).

Daily administration tasks

Table 13.3 provides an overview of the daily administration tasks that accrue when using SAPconnect. Here, you're provided with the previously presented SAPconnect Administrator (SCOT) and Transaction SOST (Overview Send Requests), which will be described next.

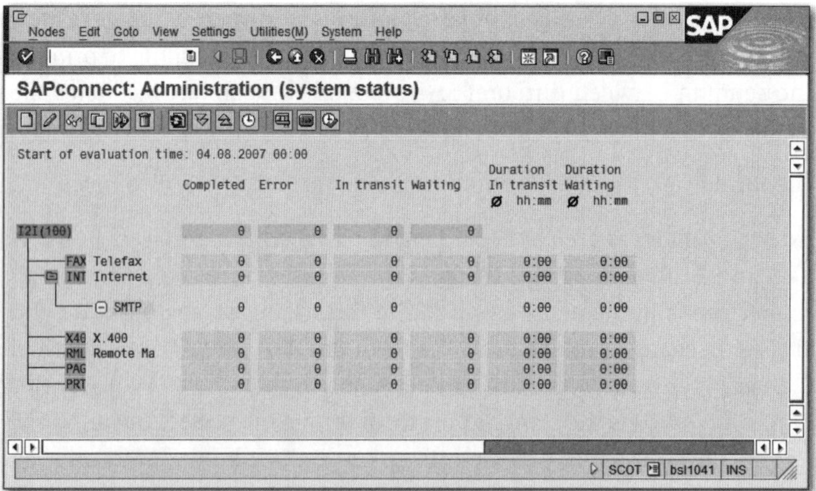


**Figure 13.15** SAPconnect Administration Interface

| Task | Description |
|---|---|
| Displaying and managing sent messages | Using the Overview Send Requests (Transaction SOST), you can display and manage all messages sent via SAPconnect. |
| Checking routing | Using the routing test enables you to check whether the routing is performed correctly for outbound messages in the communication environment. You're shown how the appropriate node is determined based on the given recipient address, and whether fax and paging numbers are converted according to the rules for the recipient number conversion. |
| Managing the confirmation of receipt for Internet messages | For specific recipients, you define that no confirmation of receipt is expected. |
| Maintaining the inbound distribution | The inbound distribution enables you to distribute external inbound documents (e.g., via the Internet or fax) according to specific rules. |
| Parallelizing the sending process for performance optimization | To optimize the performance in case of increased message occurrence, you can parallelize the SAPconnect send process. As a result, you can process send requests in multiple work processes that can run on different application servers. Here, only a background job is implemented that starts multiple work processes, which distribute the send requests to packages and send them in parallel via different servers. |
| Monitoring the send operation and error analysis | For monitoring the running send operation, you're provided with different views on the communication environment. An overview of the current operation statuses of your external components is available in the alert monitor. Additionally, the SAPconnect administration provides different tools for analyzing errors. |

**Table 13.3** Overview – Administration Tasks

SAPconnect Send Request (SOST) provides an overview of the send processes. You can set filters for the **period** to be considered, the **Address type**, the **Sender**, and the **Status** (see Figure 13.16).

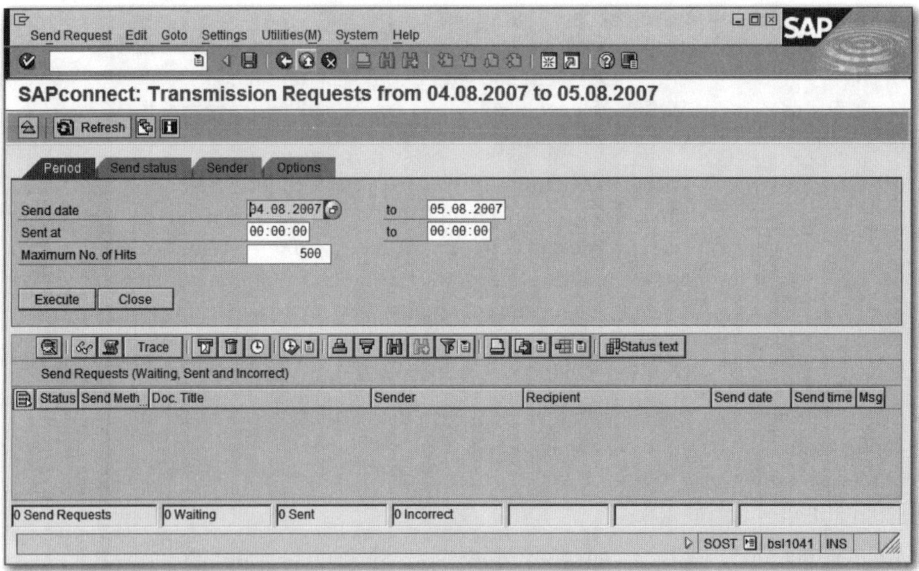


Figure 13.16 Overview – Send Request

## 13.5 SAP NetWeaver Process Integration

**Integrating different systems**

By means of SAP NetWeaver Process Integration (SAP NetWeaver PI, formerly SAP NetWeaver Exchange Infrastructure or SAP NetWeaver XI), you can implement cross-system business processes. You can connect systems from different manufacturers (non-SAP and SAP systems), systems that are based on different versions, and systems that are implemented in different programming languages (Java, ABAP, etc.). SAP NetWeaver PI is based on an open architecture, primarily uses open standards (especially from the XML and Java world), and offers services that are indispensable in a heterogeneous and complex system landscape (see Figure 13.17):

- Modeling and designing messages, transformations, and cross-system integration processes
- Configuration for controlling collaborative processes and the underlying message flow

- Runtime for message and process control
- Adapter Engine for integrating heterogeneous system components
- Central monitoring of message flows and processes

SAP NetWeaver PI supports both enterprise-internal and cross-enterprise scenarios.

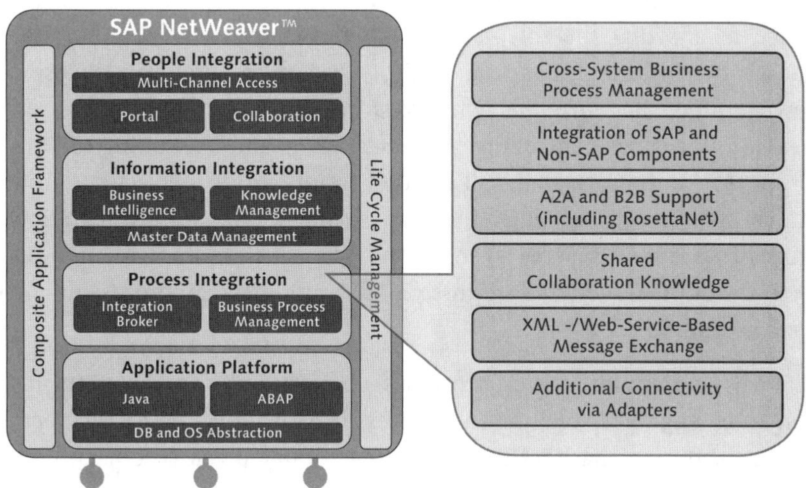


**Figure 13.17** Overview – PI

SAP NetWeaver PI is customized to generally accepted standards to enable the integration of external systems. Therefore, the central concept is an XML-based communication via HTTP (*Hypertext Transfer Protocol*): Application-specific content is transferred via messages to a freely definable XML (*eXtensible Markup Language*) schema from the sender to the recipient through the *integration server*.

**Decoupling**

Sender and recipient that exchange messages via the integration server are decoupled from each other. This decoupling makes it easy to combine systems that are technologically different. Every system that can exchange messages with the integration server can also exchange messages with all other systems connected to the integration server. SAP XI supports the following approaches for communicating with the integration server:

- Direct communication via *proxies*, which are generated into the application system based on a description in WSDL (*Web Services Description Language*).
- Communication via *adapters*. In this case, you create interfaces for the message exchange in the application system, if they aren't available yet.

The simple message processing on the integration server is stateless, which means that the integration server isn't aware of any correlations between different messages. Cross-system integration processes, however, describe correlated processes that can use already processed messages for other controlling processes, for example, waiting for the response to a message that will be used to initiate further actions. You can centrally model, change, and manage the cross-system integration processes using SAP NetWeaver PI. The processes are implemented on the integration server and are integrated in the message processing via the configuration.

Shared collaboration knowledge

Like cross-system integration processes, you can store the entire integration knowledge of a collaborative process in SAP NetWeaver PI. Objects during the design phase reside in the Integration Repository; objects during the configuration phase are located in the Integration Directory. The principle of the exchange infrastructure is based on *shared collaboration knowledge*: You don't need to collect information about a collaborative process from the systems involved, but you can retrieve it centrally. This procedure significantly reduces the costs of developing and maintaining distributed applications.

## 13.6 Tips

- **Renaming logical systems**
  Avoid renaming logical systems because the name of a logical system must be unique in an ALE landscape. If this is necessary, for example, after a client or system has been copied and the copied components have been integrated into the ALE group, you can use the Convert Logical System Names (BDLS) transaction for implementation.

- **Deleting IDocs**
  IDocs that are no longer used can be deleted via the standard archiving procedure for the IDOC object type (see Section 12.2, Customizing, in Chapter 12).

## 13.7 Transactions and Menu Paths

**ALE Management**: SAP Menu • Administration • System Administration • User Maintenance • Central User Maintenance • ALE-Customizing (SALE)

**BAPI Explorer**: SAP Menu • Tools • Business Framework • BAPI Explorer (BAPI)

**Batch Input**: SAP Menu • Administration • System Administration • Monitor • Batch Input (SM35)

**Client Maintenance:** SAP Menu • Tools • Administration • Administration • Client Administration • Client Maintenance (SCC4)

**Data Transfer Workbench:** SAP Menu • Tools • Data Transfer Workbench (SXDA)

**Direct Input Management:** No standard menu entry (BMV0)

**Distribution Model Maintenance**: No standard menu entry (BD64)

**IDoc Error Handling**: No standard menu entry (BD73)

**IDoc List**: No standard menu entry (WE05)

**IDoc Check**: No standard menu entry (IDOC)

**IDoc Tracking**: No standard menu entry (BDM2)

**Partner Profile**: ALE Administration (SALE) • Model Business Processes • Maintain Distribution Model and Distribute Views (BD64) • Generate Partner Profiles (BD82)

**Port Definition**: No standard menu entry (WE21)

**qRFC-Monitor Inbound**: No standard menu entry (SMQ1)

**qRFC Monitor Outbound**: No standard menu entry (SMQ2)

**qRFC Monitor**: No standard menu entry (SMQR)

**RFC Administration**: SAP Menu • Administration • RFC Destinations (SM59)

**SAPconnect Administration:** SAP Menu • Tools • Business Communication • Communication • SAPconnect (SCOT)

**SAPconnect Send Requests:** No standard menu entry (SOST)

**Server Group Maintenance:** No standard menu entry (RZ12)

**tRFC Monitor**: SAP Menu • Administration • System Administration • Monitor • Transactional RFC (SM58)

**Transaction Recorder**: No standard menu entry (SHDB)

**Trusted Systems**: No standard menu entry (SMT1)

## 13.8 Additional Documentation

Quick Links

- SAP Service Marketplace, alias *ale*
- SAP Service Marketplace, alias *bapi*
- SAP Service Marketplace, alias *communication*
- SAP Service Marketplace, alias *connectors*
- SAP Service Marketplace, alias *dta*
- SAP Service Marketplace, alias *ibf*
- SAP Service Marketplace, alias *lsmw*

### SAP Notes

Table 13.4 provides an overview of important SAP Notes concerning data transfer and data distribution.

| Contents | SAP Note |
|---|---|
| $$$ Meaning of Entry Types in SMQS | 484753 |
| ALE: Sending IDocs and QOUT Schedulers | 580869 |
| Resource Management for tRFC and aRFC | 74141 |
| Problems with Logical System Names | 423184 |
| Conversion of Logical System Names | 121163 |
| CUA: Tips for Performance Optimization | 399271 |
| SXC: Version Overview and History | 122657 |

**Table 13.4** SAP Notes Concerning Data Transfer and Data Distribution

## 13.9 Questions

1. **Which statement is correct?**

   For data distribution based on ALE,

   a. you create a fixed connection between the partner systems.

   b. you loosely couple partner systems during data transfer.

   c. you use functions of the respective RDBMS for data exchange, for example, SAPDBA.

2. **Which techniques can you use for data exchange?**

   a. CPI-C

   b. Sequential files

   c. tRFC

   d. Internet

   e. Telnet

3. **How can you reprocess tRFCs that were cancelled due to communication errors?**

   a. Automatically by activating the option of automatic retry for the definition of the tRFC connection

   b. Scheduling the job, `RSARFCE`

   c. Scheduling the job, `RSEOUT00`

d. Correcting the error and re-implementing the application transaction

4. **What is the purpose of the batch input procedure?**

   a. Transferring data from sequential files into the SAP database

   b. Processing mass data in the background

   c. Importing files using the transport control program, `tp`

*The architecture of SAP NetWeaver is reflected in the individual installation phases. The RDBMS and the database are created first, then the individual instances, starting with the central instance, and lastly the frontends.*

# 14 Installation Concepts

This chapter describes both the prerequisites and the basic procedure for installing an SAP NetWeaver system. However, this not only concerns the operating information provided in the manuals but also the background to understanding the processes. In this chapter, we'll introduce the `SAPinst` installation tool. We'll also discuss the installation options provided by this tool and explain where you can find troubleshooting information in the event of an error. Lastly, we'll outline the post-installation work, that is, the actions that must be performed after the SAP system has been installed so that it's ready for production.

## 14.1 Preparations

**Sizing**

Before you can start the actual installation, you must make some decisions regarding the hardware and software to be used. The main influencing factors are summarized next. The most important points include estimating the initial expected size and the growth behavior of the future SAP system as well as mapping these requirements to a suitable system landscape (*sizing*). Essentially, the following parameters influence the size of an SAP system:

- Total number of users and number of users active concurrently
- Solutions used and number of users for each solution
- Volume of data to be recorded and the retention periods

- Requirements for batch processing
- Data exchange via interfaces
- Number and scope of output requests

On our company website at *http://service.sap.com/sizing*, we provide a *Quick Sizing Tool* for estimating the system size based on the customer's specifications. Here, it's particularly crucial to know the planned number of users for each application module and to estimate the activities in the SAP system (low, medium, high). This is known as *user-based sizing*.

Another option is *throughput-based sizing*. Here, the planned number of subsequent users is less significant than the volume of documents to be processed using the future solution.

User-based sizing requires less time and effort than throughput-based sizing. However, the former produces less accurate results. Throughput-based sizing requires considerably more time and effort to determine the volume of documents, but the sizing results are accordingly more accurate.

**Hardware requirements**

The next few steps involve choosing suitable hardware (the operating system, the RDBMS software, the peripherals, etc.). The planning phase should never be rushed because failure to make correct decisions at this stage will result in increased time and effort later as well as higher costs.

**Hardware combinations**

The operating system/database combinations permitted for operating an SAP NetWeaver system landscape are listed on SAP Service Marketplace under *http://service.sap.com/pam* (**p**roduct **a**vailability **m**atrix). In addition to the hardware homogenous installations, whose physical components use the same operating system, heterogeneous installations are also possible:

- Use of different UNIX derivatives for database servers and application servers
- Use of a UNIX server for the database and use of Windows servers for the application instances

In terms of planning and operation, it requires more time and effort to install and manage heterogeneous environments than homogeneous installations. For licensing reasons, mixed homogeneous installations are not supported (e.g., the development system in a Windows environment and the consolidation and production system on UNIX systems).

**Checklist**

The first pre-installation step should be to use the checklist associated with the installation package to check the system prerequisites. It lists the most important requirements for each RDBMS and operating system.

## 14.2 Installation with SAPinst

`SAPinst` is the basic program for installing every SAP NetWeaver system. The program is available on the SAP installation master DVD contained in the delivery of SAP software or as a download from the SAP Support Portal.

**Components**

In the first step of an SAP NetWeaver installation, you install the `SAPinst` tool. `SAPinst` comprises the actual `SAPinst` program itself, the `SAPinst` GUI, and the GUI server. This division enables `SAPinst` to separate the operation of the `SAPinst` GUI and the remaining components from each other (e.g., the `SAPinst` GUI on a local administrator PC and the remaining components on the relevant server).

In the following example, we assume that all of the `SAPinst` components are installed on one host.

When you start `SAPinst`, a *sapinst_instdir* directory is created in the *%ProgramFiles%* folder. If this isn't possible, the system tries to create this directory in a temporary directory (e.g., *TMP*, *TEMP*, etc.).

Below the *sapinst_instdir* directory, an additional directory containing log files is created for each installation.

After you have successfully started the `SAPinst` program, the initial screen is displayed (see Figure 14.1). Here, you must decide which software components you want to install. These are also known as *usage types*.

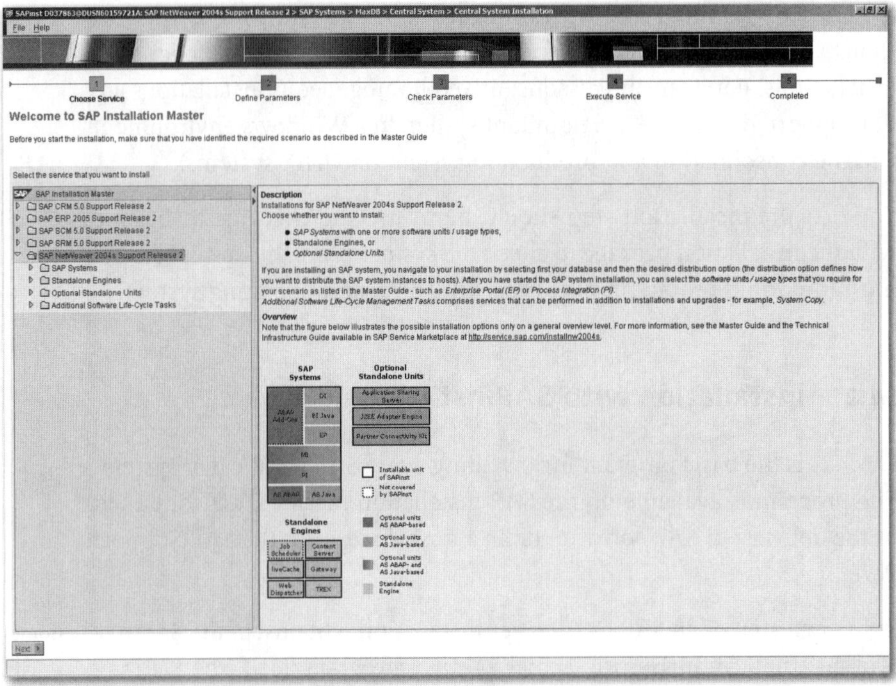


**Figure 14.1** SAPinst – Initial Screen

`SAPinst` then queries numerous parameters and saves them to the directory that has been created. If this step is completed without any errors, the system now starts to install the software components selected previously.

If an error occurs during installation, `SAPinst` doesn't terminate but simply stops. The system displays a dialog box containing a brief error description as well as the path for the log file (see Figure 14.2). You can then choose between one of the following options for continuing the installation:

- **Retry**

  `SAPinst` retries the installation from the point where the error occurred. This is possible because the installation progress is continuously recorded in the *keydb.xml* file.

  If an error occurs, analyze the log files, try to solve the problem, and then choose **Retry** to retry the installation. If the error occurs again, the system will display the same dialog box again.

- **Stop**
  SAPinst stops the installation at the point where the error occurred, closes the dialog box, and stops the SAPinst GUI and the SAPinst server. The installation progress up to this point is recorded in the *keydb.xml* file. Therefore, you can continue the installation later from the point where the error occurred without having to repeat any of the preceding installation steps.
- **Continue**
  SAPinst continues the installation from the point where the error occurred. The error is ignored.

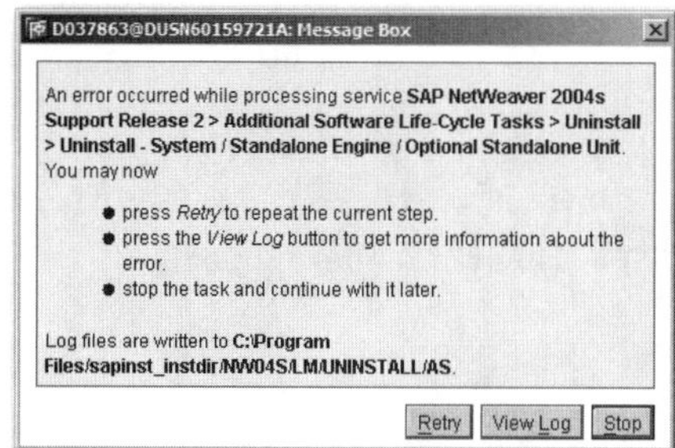

**Figure 14.2** Dialog Box in the Event of an Error

XML descriptions

XML description files (see Table 14.1) are used to control the installation process; the log output is stored centrally in the *sapinst.log* file.

| File | Contents |
|---|---|
| CONTROL.XML | Instructions for installing SAP components |
| KEYDB.XML | Description of the process and status of the current installation |
| MESSAGES.XML | Catalog of message texts and assignment between the message and the message number |
| DIALOG.XML | Description of the dialogs with the user |
| PACKAGES.XML | List of CD-ROM labels |
| SAPINST.LOG | Log file of the installation run |
| SAPINST_DEV.LOG | Detailed log file of the installation run |

**Table 14.1** List of the Most Important Control and Log Files for SAPinst

The SAPinst installation process comprises two phases:

1. **Input Phase**
   The input information required (e.g., the installation type, SID, instance number, host name, and so on) is queried by the user and recorded in the *KEYDB.XML* description file (see Listing 14.1).
2. **Processing Phase**
   All of the steps necessary for the current installation (controlled by the configured description files) are processed without any additional input information.

```
  - <strval>
      <![CDATA[ WAS  ]]>
    </strval>
  </fld>
- <fld name="WapsInstanceNumber">
  - <properties>
      <property name="GUIENG_USER_INPUT" value="GUIENG_
      TRUE" />
    <properties>
  - <strval>
     <![CDATA[ 00  ]]>
    </strval>
  </fld>
- <fld name="WapsInstanceName">
  - <strval>
     <![CDATA[ DVEBMGS00  ]]>
   </strval>
  </fld>
- <fld name="WapsInstanceHost">
  - <properties>
     <property name="CHANGEABLE" value="YES" />
     <property name="CONTEXT_PARAM_CHANGEABLE"
     value="YES" />
     <property name="GUIENG_USER_INPUT" value="GUIENG_
     TRUE" />
    </properties>
  - <strval>
     <![CDATA[ P6020792  ]]>
    </strval>
  </fld>
```

**Listing 14.1** Excerpt from *KEYDB.XML*

R3setup

If, as a result of earlier installations, you're already familiar with the `R3setup` tool for installing an SAP system, you'll now notice some fundamental differences between `R3setup` and `SAPinst`:

- Unlike `R3setup`, `SAPinst` doesn't terminate when an error occurs but instead proposes the Retry option in its error dialog box after the problem has been solved (refer to Figure 14.2).
- During the input phase, you can return to any stage of the process, if necessary.
- Each substep performed is recorded in the *sapinst.log* file (see Listing 14.2).

```
TRACE
showing dialog with index 33
TRACE
The controller is about to execute the dialog step
WebAs|ind|ind|ora|WebAs|620|0|SAPComponent|ind|ind|ind|ind|ind|
0|DatabaseSystem|ind|ind|ora|ind|ind|0|DatabaseCommonParameters
|ind|ind|ora|ind|ind|0|dialogGetCommonParamsPostprocess
TRACE
CALLING
COraCommonParameters::computeDependantParametersAfterDialog
***** Transaction begin ********************************
TRACE
CDomainObjectCache::readFromKeyDb: Reading from
tGlobalDbParameters WHERE dbSid = 'WAS'
ERROR 2002-11-05 12:49:22
MDB-06169  The Oracle Home name '' is not the name of
an Oracle Home directory registered on this host.
***** Transaction end **********************************
TRACE
JS Callback has thrown exception
ERROR 2002-11-05 12:49:23
FJS-00012  Error when executing script.
```

**Listing 14.2** Listing 14.2 Error Recording in the sapinst.log Log File

**Multiple Components in one Database (MCOD)**

It's possible to install several SAP systems on one shared database (fully supported as of Web Application Server 6.20). This procedure facilitates easier database administration, but it barely conserves any system resources because all of the requirements of the individual components determine the sizing-relevant requirements for equipping the server. A further disadvantage is the fact that any maintenance work performed on the database impacts all of the systems installed on that database.

SIDs

Installing an SAP system within a Multiple Components in One Database (MCOD) configuration is the same as installing a system with a dedicated database, the only difference being the naming convention for the SAP system and the shared database. The database name is the same for all SAP systems used within the MCOD installation, but the SIDs of the SAP components differ. The MCOD installation is integrated into `SAPinst`.

## 14.3 Post-Installation Actions

After you have completed the actual software installation with `SAPinst`, numerous settings must be made in both the SAP system and the relevant RDBMS for the SAP system to work. This phase is known as *post-installation*.

SAP license key

It's particularly important to request an SAP license key for the new system. The license key is a 24-digit ID number that is retained in the database of the SAP system. The number is created from system-specific and server-specific data and, therefore, can only be used for the current installation. Consequently, several licenses must be installed in parallel for installations within a hardware cluster or for the use of a standby system that remains up to date through log shipping and is activated under the identity of the source system in the event of a serious problem. To determine the system hardware key required by SAP AG to generate the license key, you use the command

```
saplicense -get
```

on the host of the message server at the operating system level. You must provide SAP with this ID along with some other data, so that an SAP license ID can be generated for you. The easiest way to request a license key is to log on to SAP Service Marketplace.

License administration

The SAP license is activated using `saplicense -install`; the necessary parameters are queried in dialog mode. Since SAP R/3 4.6C, you can use

License Administration (SLICENSE) to execute the following actions in the SAP system (see Figure 14.3):

- Display the licenses that have been imported.
- Import another license (a temporary license, if necessary).
- Delete a license.
- Determine the hardware key.

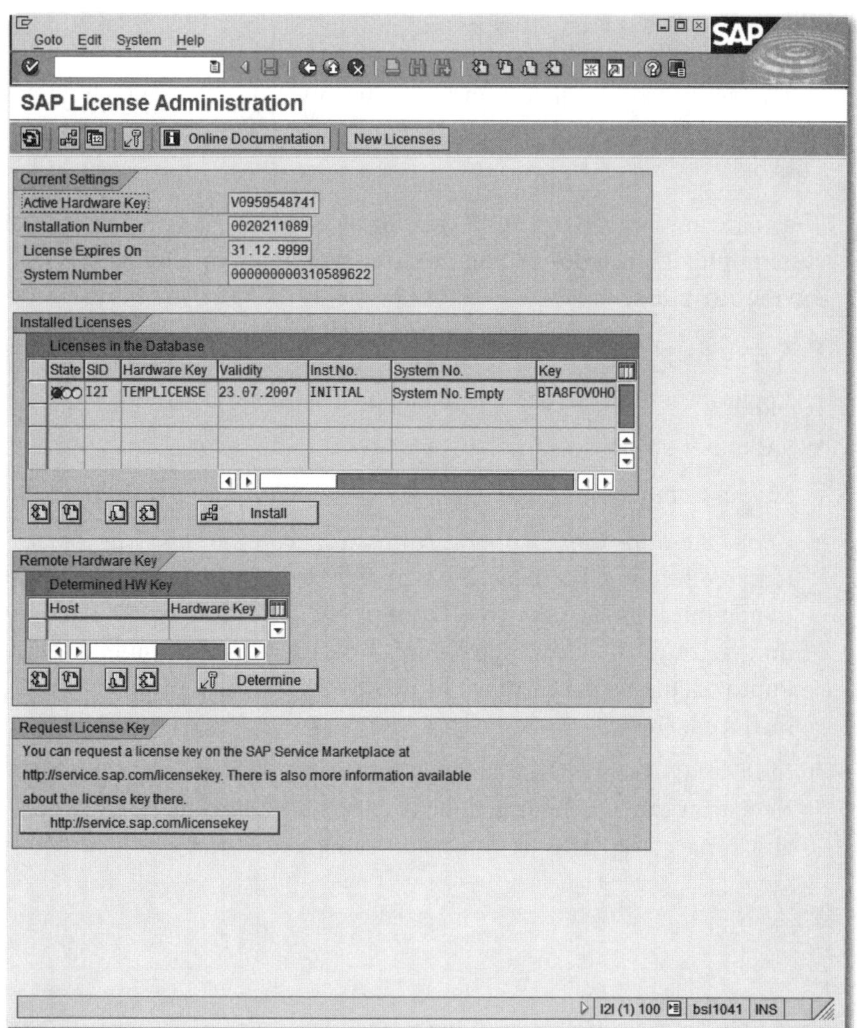


**Figure 14.3** Transaction SLICENSE

The license is immediately active after you import it. Furthermore, you do not have to restart the SAP system.

**Frontend installation**

You can already install frontend software irrespective of the SAP NetWeaver system installation. The following variants are possible:

- SAP GUI for Windows
- SAP GUI for Java
- SAP GUI for HTML

They determine the different procedures that you must apply. Both local and server-based installation methods are offered for the widely used frontend installation on Windows PCs. Software distribution is also possible.

**SAPLOGON frontend configuration**

The configuration of SAPLOGON as part of the post-installation work for a system initially includes adding the new systems by specifying the following attributes:

- Any description of your choice.
- Application server as the host name or IP address.
- SAProuter string.
- System number.
- Under the **Additional...** option, you can specify the code page or the required frontend language as well as the settings for Secure Network Communication and the connection speed. The "low speed connection" setting influences the volume of data sent to the frontend. This improves the response times in the WAN, but ease of operation is sacrificed.
- In SAPLOGON, the SAPLOGON language settings are defined under Options. Here, you can also branch directly to the *sap*.ini* configuration files and, if necessary, activate frontend tracing (see Figure 14.4).

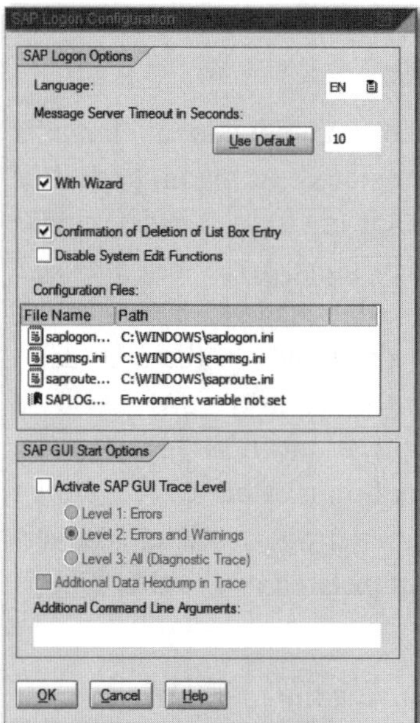


**Figure 14.4** SAP Logon Options

Installation check

After you have successfully installed the system, you should check the system's basic functions by stopping the entire SAP NetWeaver system, including the database, and then restarting it. You can use the Installation Check (SM28) to check that the software you have installed is complete and version-compatible (e.g., compatibility between the SAP release and the operating system release). The accessibility of the message server is also tested. Furthermore, the check determines whether all work process types (dialog, background, update, spool, and enqueue) are available in the SAP NetWeaver system that you have installed. The check also verifies whether the information generated for the enqueue server and update service corresponds with the actual conditions, and whether critical structure definitions are consistent.

Another important point to consider is that the passwords of the default users (see Section 8.2.5, Default Users, in Chapter 8) must be changed to protect the new SAP NetWeaver system from unauthorized access. Users can change their passwords immediately at logon. One of the first post-installation actions of the system administrator is to create a separate administrator user under whose ID any other administration work is performed.

Language import

In the standard SAP installation, all of the language-dependent elements in English and German are already fully integrated. At logon, each user can choose between the English and German user guide. If users require additional languages in an SAP system, they must perform a *language import*. Here, both the required and existing language elements of the new language required are imported into the tables in the SAP database. Consequently, there must be sufficient space in the SAP database for each new language. Each of the 28 languages available is assigned a translation degree that describes the extent of translation. Only German and English are complete. In the case of other supported language versions, not all screen and menu entries are translated or the (F1) help is incomplete.

Client copy

Another post-installation action involves copying the clients required for production operation from standard client 000 or 001.

Backup

After the installation and the post-installation actions are complete, you must perform a complete offline backup of the system that you have just installed. In Windows NT systems, you should also back up the entries in the Registry. You can also use the `rdisk` command. To ensure high availability of a Windows NT system, it makes sense to install a second Windows NT operating system on a separate hard disk. If the operating system hard disk fails, a second operating system installation can be used to start the machine. Depending on the data backup software used, an operating system containing SAP entries and database entries can be backed up in this way. At the very least, you should create an *emergency repair disk* from which the host can be started in an emergency without the operating system on the hard disk. You can also use the `rdisk` command here.

For performance and security reasons, neither the SAP database server nor the SAP application server should act as the Primary Domain Controller or Backup Domain Controller in Windows NT environments. However, as a result of implementing the user and group definitions required for SAP operation at the operating system level with fewer permissions, this point is less controversial.

Installing online documentation

The online documentation is available in HTML format and can be displayed using a Web browser. To access the online documentation directly from the SAP NetWeaver system, you must make some settings in the SAP system in addition to actually storing the documentation in the required format (Standard HTML or Compiled HTML). You no longer have to define system parameters; the settings are made by calling Setting Variants for Help (SR13). Entries in the *sapdoccd.ini* configuration files for accessing the online documentation can override the system settings locally.

The post-installation phase, which is only briefly outlined here, comprises considerably more steps. The most important steps are described in the installation guide. Even though the SAP system is already fully functional after these post-installation actions have been performed, the role of the system within the system landscape must still be defined, the Correction and Transport system must be initialized, users must be set up, and so on.

## 14.4 Tips

- **License key**
  A hardware key is used to determine the license key. Therefore, if an SAP system copy is installed on other hardware, you always have to request and import a new license key. Until this key is implemented, you only have limited use of the system (only SAP* users can log on).
- **Changes to the R3setup control files**
  Any editor can be used to make the necessary changes to the `R3setup` control files. On Windows systems, the `R3Sedit` tool is also available.
- **Changes to the SAPinst control files**
  Once again, any editor can be used to make the necessary changes to the `SAPinst` control files. It's easier to use XML editors. Some useful links for downloading test versions are available on SAP Service Marketplace under the quick link */sapinstfeedback*.

- **SAPinst Templates for other purposes**
  In addition to the standard installation activities, numerous other related tasks are also completed using `SAPinst`. For example, there are templates for system copies, NT cluster configurations, database exports, or the integration of SAP systems into the Active Directory.
- **Installing multiple instances on one server**
  Both Windows and UNIX platforms permit the installation of several instances of an SAP system, several components of SAP systems, or even several SAP systems on one server. However, you must note the restrictions associated with database release compatibility: 32-bit kernels and 64-bit kernels must not be operated together.
- **Enhanced language management functions**
  Following the basic changes in language management for R/3 4.6C, additional functional enhancements have been provided:
  - As of Basis Release 4.6D, you can execute the language installation and language supplementation runs in parallel.
  - As of Web Application Server 6.10, you can use Language Management (SMLT) to process the language-relevant changes within the Support Packages.
  - As of Web Application Server 6.20, you can also forward language-relevant data to clients other than client 000 (`RSREFILL` report) in Language Management (SMLT).
  - As of SAP NetWeaver Application Server 7.0, you can load language packages directly from the frontend.

## 14.5 Transactions and Menu Paths

**Setting Variants for Help (SAP Library)**: SAP Menu • Tools • Customizing • IMG • SAP Reference IMG Edit Project • General Settings • Setting Variants for Help (SR13)

**Installation Check**: SAP Menu • Tools • Administration • Administration • Installation Check (SM28)

**License Administration**: Not accessible from the SAP standard menu (SLICENSE)

**Language Management**: SAP Menu • Tools • Administration • Administration • Language Management (SMLT)

## 14.6 Additional Documentation

### Quick Links

- SAP Service Marketplace, alias *installation*
- SAP Service Marketplace, alias *platforms*
- SAP Service Marketplace, alias *instguides*
- SAP Service Marketplace, alias *sizing*
- SAP Service Marketplace, alias *quicksizing*
- SAP Service Marketplace, alias *network*
- SAP Service Marketplace, alias *sapinstfeedback*
- SAP Service Marketplace, alias *ti*
- SAP Service Marketplace, alias *licensekey*
- SAP Service Marketplace, alias *mcod*
- SAP Service Marketplace, alias *languages*

### SAP Notes

Table 14.2 provides an overview of important SAP Notes concerning the installation of an SAP landscape.

| Contents | SAP Note |
|---|---|
| Useful Log Files for Installation Problems | 331082 |
| Configuring the LDAP Connector | 188371 |
| Directory Integration | 448360 |
| Windows Language Versions and SAP Server Products | 427452 |
| How Many Work Processes Must Be Configured? | 39412 |
| Improving SAPLOGON Performance | 559711 |

**Table 14.2** Installation Notes

| Contents | SAP Note |
|---|---|
| Multiple Components in one Database (MCOD) Installation | 388866 |
| Several Instances/Systems on One UNIX Host | 21960 |
| Two R/3 Systems on one Windows NT Host | 28392 |
| SAP GUI 6.10/6.20 | 402189 |
| Notes About Additional Resource Requirements | 89305, 113795, 323263, 517085 |
| Requesting License Keys | 94998 |

**Table 14.2** Installation Notes (Cont.)

## 14.7 Questions

1. **Which statement is true?**

For a basic SAP installation,

   a. only the RDBMS must be installed.
   b. one database instance and one central instance must be installed.
   c. the database instance and the central instance can be on one system.
   d. one database instance, one central instance, and at least one application server must be installed.

2. **Which statement is true?**
   a. SAP supports mixed homogeneous system landscapes.
   b. SAP doesn't support mixed homogeneous system landscapes.
   c. SAP only supports mixed homogeneous system landscapes if they are maintained by a certified system administrator.

3. **Which statement is correct?**
   a. In the case of an MCOD installation, each system to be installed requires an independent database name that differs from other installations.

b. In the case of an MCOD installation, the database name is determined during the first installation. All other systems must use the same database name.

c. In the case of an MCOD installation, you can select any database name for each system to be installed. However, we recommend that you use the same name for all systems.

*SAP provides a wide range of tools, services, and support for users and operators of SAP software.*

# 15 Service and Support

In addition to the comprehensive information available on the SAP website, *www.sap.com*, SAP provides the SAP Service Marketplace with all kinds of services for customers — from problem handling, to software download, to consultation services (see Figure 15.1). This chapter describes how you can meet the prerequisites for the remote support provided by SAP or its partners.

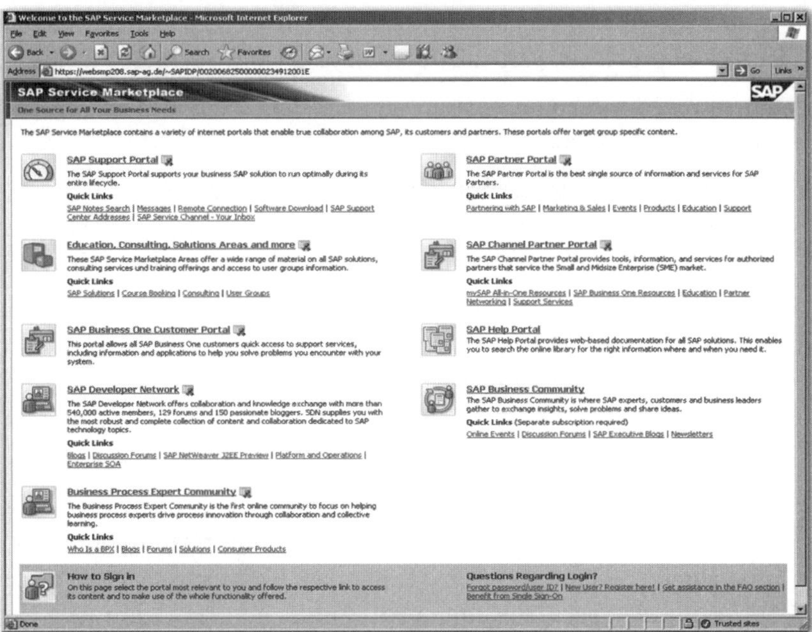


**Figure 15.1** Start Screen of the SAP Service Marketplace

## 15.1 Overview of the SAP Service Marketplace

The SAP Service Marketplace breaks down into the following areas:

- **SAP Support Portal**
  This area is geared to service and support teams. If problems occur during the operation and use of SAP software, you can create a message in the SAP Support Portal stating central system indicators, such as application, release, and installation number. SAP then processes this message. You define the weighting of the problem message, which should be related to the scope of interference to your business. This weighting influences the response time of the SAP support team. The priority "very high" indicates a system downtime of a production solution.

  All customers can access the SAP solution database via **SAP Notes Search**. SAP employees enter and maintain SAP Notes for customers. These notes not only deal with aspects of how you can eliminate or work around problems, but they also describe procedures of how you can avoid problems, particularly when using new software elements.

  **Software Download** provides *support packages* and is available for the continuous maintenance of SAP software.

- **Education, Consulting, Solution Areas, and more**
  This area provides information on all trainings and expert workshops offered by SAP. You can book the trainings online. Moreover, this area provides short descriptions of the solutions provided by SAP and corresponding consulting services.

- **SAP Business One Customer Portal**
  This specific portal for customers of the Business One solution is under construction.

- **SAP Developer Network**
  The SAP Developer Network provides useful information on typical programming requirements and supports the exchange of experience between developers. This forum will gain more importance with the increasing prevalence of Enterprise SOA. The new architecture allows for a flexible, customer-specific expansion of a solution. Because this

approach is rather new compared to widespread ABAP-based solutions, practical experience and recommendations are particularly needed.

- **Business Process Expert Community**
  SAP provides numerous comprehensive business processes that are included in the software by default and only have to be adapted to specific customer requirements via Customizing. Considering the wide range of services, the greatest challenge is to select the options that meet the business requirements in the best way. However, customer-specific developments may still be necessary. The Business Process Expert Community enables you to exchange experience with other experts.
- **SAP Partner Portal**
  In many areas, SAP collaborates with partners, such as hardware or software vendors, that supplement or expand existing SAP solutions. **SAP Partner Portal** is solely provided for these partners.
- **SAP Channel Partner Portal**
  This area is the platform that focuses on the support of small and midsize enterprises that use the Business ByDesign solution.
- **SAP Help Portal**
  You can access the online help for SAP systems also from within the SAP Help Portal. This is useful, for example, if you want to compare different versions and therefore changes in solutions that you no longer use or do not yet use. Via the SAP Help Portal, you can access help documents of all solutions and versions.
- **SAP Business Community**
  The SAP Business Community serves to exchange experience and knowledge between SAP customers and with SAP. Customers are informed about future information meetings and trade shows here. Customers that are interested in exchanging experience with others can search for customers with similar requirements according to their profile and contact each other.

Quick links

You can also access the main services provided by the SAP Service Marketplace directly using quick links. Table 15.1 lists essential quick links.

| Service | Quick Link in SAP Service Marketplace |
|---|---|
| Problem management | message |
| Solution database | notes |
| Addresses of the global support centers | supportcenters |
| Support packages and plug-ins for SAP Solution Manager | supporttools |
| Administration of service connections | serviceconnection |
| Maintenance of system data | system-data |
| Registration of developers and objects (SSCR) | sscr |
| Registration of namespaces | namespaces |
| Application for license keys | licensekeys |
| Application for migration keys | migration-keys |
| Download of support packages | patches |
| User administration | user-admin |
| Service catalog | servicecat |

**Table 15.1** Main Services and the Respective Quick Links in the SAP Service Marketplace

## 15.2 SAP Solution Manager as a Collaboration Platform

SAP Solution Manager has been supplied as a self-contained SAP solution for some years now. It serves as the central system and service management platform for one or more SAP system landscapes. In recent years, and particularly due to the increasing popularity of Enterprise SOA technologies, business processes are represented by means of an interaction between services. Previously, business processes were strictly assigned to one technical system. This has been superseded by complex system landscapes in which business processes are embedded. Consequently, the operation and administration of *one* system has emerged as an increased system and solution landscape-oriented operation. The necessity of cross-system, end-to-end-oriented system administration increases to the same extent as the fixed, and for the end user, the obvious assignment between business process steps and technical systems loses importance. Therefore, SAP Solution Manager is the integrated SAP platform for all challenges in IT service and application management.

Functional areas

Figure 15.2 illustrates the functional areas that SAP Solution Manager currently provides. SAP Solution Manager supports the best practices for IT operation that have been developed in the IT Infrastructure Library (ITIL).

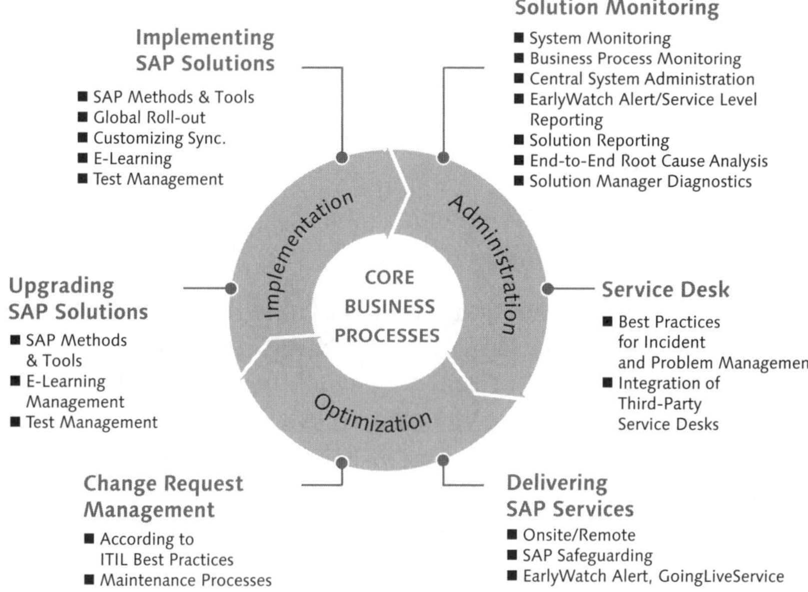


**Figure 15.2** Overview of SAP Solution Manager

For a detailed description of the functions in SAP Solution Manager and their areas of use, refer to *SAP Solution Manager* by Marc O. Schäfer and Matthias Melich (SAP PRESS 2008). This book concentrates exclusively on the descriptions of the tasks that are regularly required from technical system administrators.

SAP Solution Manager Starter Pack

Most of the administrative activities described in this book can be executed locally in the respective systems or remotely from SAP Solution Manager. For this purpose, direct connections are maintained on the basis of RFC. These interfaces enable you to collect all required information from the systems connected or to distribute it across these systems. You have to define all connections in SAP Solution Manager so that the

SAP Solution Manager system can assume a central role. In addition, you must also customize the integrated service tools. Because this work is usually done only once, it's advisable to use the SAP Solution Manager Starter Pack, where experienced consultants configure SAP Solution Manager according to your specifications. The easiest way to order this service is from the service catalog of SAP Service Marketplace (alias: *servicecat*).

Use the solution_manager transaction in the respective system to access SAP Solution Manager. The start screen then lists the solution landscapes defined. Select a solution landscape to navigate to the details.

### 15.2.1 Services

As the standard support, the SAP Solution Manager service area provides a wide range of services for every customer.

EarlyWatch Alert

The *EarlyWatch Alert* (EWA) is a service that runs automatically. It analyzes and evaluates technical values that have been measured in systems based on empirical SAP values. If possible, it then provides recommendations for optimization. The EWA enables you to uncover critical developments or effects in the areas of resource use and distribution, performance (average and related to transactions), data management and backup, as well as change and release management that deviate considerably from average customer values. Therefore, EWA is an excellent tool for system operation. Due to the close relationship between the technical values measured in the systems and their actual initiators, namely, the business processes, you as a system administrator should provide the technical information in a comprehensible way to the user departments. SAP strongly recommends to run EWA once a week for each system, that is, for SAP NetWeaver AS ABAP and the Java area.

GoingLive service

Whereas EWA serves particularly to ensure the running operations of production systems, the *GoingLive service* supports the production startup of a new solution and/or a new system. The standard support usually includes an annual GoingLive service or a similar service free of charge.

In general, the GoingLive service for production startup consists of three components. The first service session is the *GoingLive analysis session* and should be executed approximately eight weeks prior to the production startup. The analysis session mainly focuses on aligning the workload expected to the hardware resources planned. If the planned hardware isn't sufficient for the workload expected, the system informs you. For an optimal configuration, you're provided with information on parameter settings. The second part of the GoingLive service is the *optimization session*. The core business processes are analyzed and optimized with regard to performance. The system runs the third session, which is called the *verification session*, some time after the production startup has been completed. During this session, the continuous technical measurements in the system reveal particularly weak points of the running operation, and fine-tuning recommendations are provided.

SMO

In addition to these services that are provided by default, SAP offers additional remote or local services and so-called self services within the scope of the premium engagement. This includes in particular *Solution Management Optimization Services* (SMO), which focus on the optimization of specific subareas of the solution operation.

### 15.2.2 Monitoring

Unlike other products for the monitoring of software operation, the SAP Solution Manager monitoring area uses a business process-oriented approach. Individual technical values are assigned to the systems and the business processes running in the systems. Chapter 11, Monitoring Architecture, describes how you can set up technical monitoring within CCMS. Based on this, you should use SAP Solution Manager as the central monitoring platform. to more easily determine the effects of problems in the system operation on system-wide business processes. SAP Solution Manager supports various views of the system landscape.

System Monitoring

The technically oriented view (*System Monitoring*) lists all systems and their connections. The start screen indicates the general condition of a system as a red, yellow, or green icon. If you select a system, you automatically navigate to the defined monitor architecture of the respective system. The alert monitors that are defined in the respective system form the basis of these monitors (see Chapter 11, Monitoring Architecture). In principle, the monitoring in SAP Solution Manager represents a defined view of the system monitors that are specified in alert monitoring.

**Service Level Reporting** The *Solution Management and Reporting* area should be of particular interest for operators of software solutions. Based on the EarlyWatch Alert service that runs on a regular basis automatically, you can define *Service Level Reporting* for a system landscape. Using the system data collected, a report is then created that provides information on relevant key figures. These key figures include, for example, data growth, historical development of response times, workload, hardware use, or availability. In this way, you can easily provide regular reporting in the system landscape.

**Business Process Monitoring** The business-oriented view (*Business Process Monitoring*) illustrates the cross-system flow and processing steps within the business processes (see Figure 15.3).

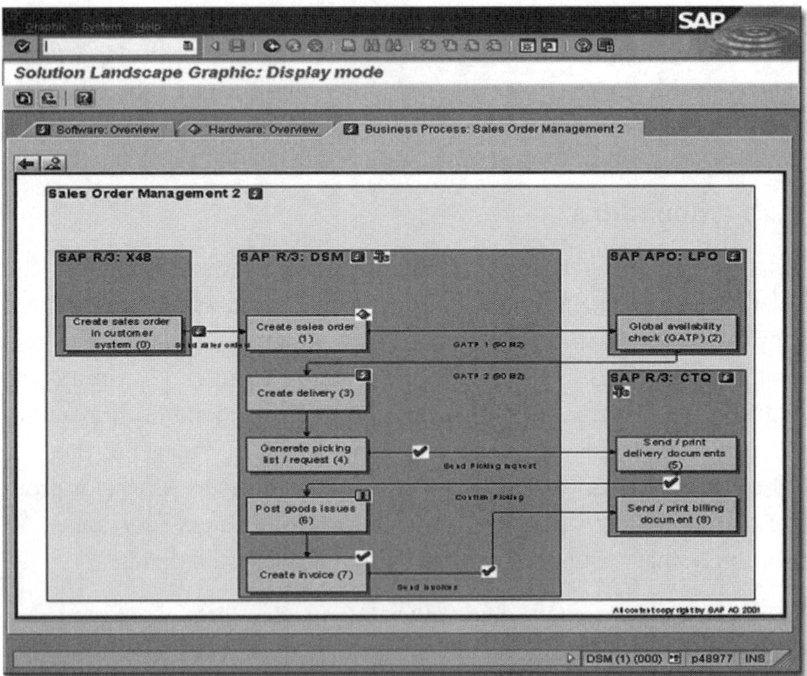


**Figure 15.3** View of the Steps in the Core Business Process

Interruptions of the business process are indicated by red marks. The respective alert monitors and analysis functions are assigned to each business process. By double-clicking on a business step to select it, you automatically navigate to the alert monitors and then to the analysis functions. Thanks to the representation of the business processes as well as the assignment of alert monitors and analysis functions, it's considerably easier to keep an overview of the core business processes. You can manage the problems according to their effects on the business.

End to End

Due to the continuing implementation of Enterprise SOA technologies, for example, based on SAP NetWeaver, the business process-oriented approach gains even more importance. If users determine an incident on their frontend PC while they perform a business process step, the first challenge for the support is to allocate the incident to a technical component or service. Only after the allocation can the tools available for the respective technical component be used to analyze and solve the problem. The term *End to End* (E2E) defines this approach of a holistic consideration of business processes; it's an overall analysis from frontend, to different elements, to backend. Currently, SAP Solution Manager provides E2E tools for the following purposes:

System landscape-wide recording of actions

- **E2E Trace**
  *E2E Trace* allows for a system landscape-wide recording of actions, such as transactions, users, or all activities in a period. Therefore, for the first time, it's possible to create and analyze traces for cross-system activities (i.e., across ABAP, Java, C/C++, or .NET, including SQL statements). Graphical displays of the response time distribution across the different technical components considerably simplify the localization of performance bottlenecks, for example. In addition to the SAP tools, Wily Introscope and BMC AppSight are also integrated.

  Figure 15.4 shows an example of a proportional distribution of the response times of the different components on the basis of E2E Trace. In this case, the processes run on the application server most of the time. Therefore, you should start a detailed analysis there. Based on that graphical presentation, you can navigate to the individual processing steps.

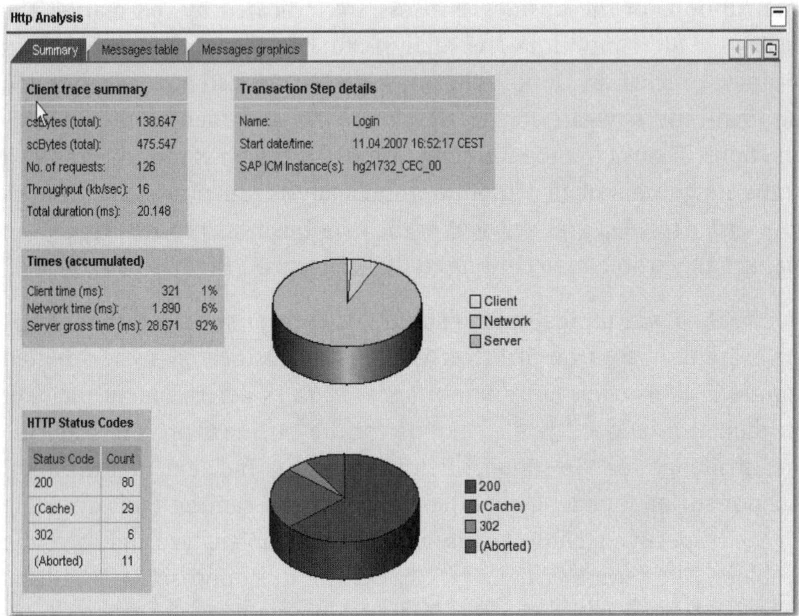


**Figure 15.4** Accumulated E2E Trace

Surveying and analyzing exceptional situations

- **E2E Exception Analysis**
  In the ABAP world, short dumps that occurred were analyzed for each system and assigned to the business processes. The E2E Root Cause Analysis now enables you to survey and analyze all exceptional situations of the entire system landscape that occurred in a specific period. This includes messages in the system log as well as short dumps of the individual systems on the basis of ABAP and error messages, including out-of-memory exceptions from the Java world. For system administrators, this tool is thus the ideal point of entry to search for terminations in cross-system and cross-technology business processes.

- **E2E Workload Analysis**
  This tool answers the question as to which of the technical components involved has to manage the highest workload. This is particularly useful for performance analyses and optimization.

The E2E root cause analysis tools play a central role for the processes of the incident and problem management as well as for the activities of the proactive system operation in general. The change management process faces a similar challenge. This process is supposed to be mapped in a consistent and harmonized way, independently of the technologies and systems used. Here, necessary changes are more closely connected to business processes than to technical systems.

- **One Transport Order**
  *One Transport Order* (OTO) enables you to control Java objects via the CTS that you already know from the ABAP world. For this purpose, you can use this tool alone or together with the CTS.

- **Change Control Management**
  Monitoring changes
  *Change Control Management* (CCM) is an additional component of SAP Solution Manager. It monitors changes to the technical configuration, business configuration, or coding, and the implementation of patches, support packages, or releases centrally. You can define a period and analyze the changes made in this period. Moreover, you can compare various systems with each other as well as the status of one system at different times. This tool thus enables you to determine whether any changes made may have caused a sudden incident.

## 15.3 Configuration of the Support Connections

If you require the assistance of SAP and its partners, the employees usually need to log on to your systems via remote connections. You should create the prerequisites at an early stage before incidents occur to set up the connections without problems in emergency situations.

### 15.3.1 Remote Connections to Customer Systems

If SAP is supposed to process incidents, it may be required to enable SAP employees to access customer systems. For this purpose, you must maintain the data of your SAP systems in SAP Service Marketplace, such as the IP addresses of the hosts and the ports of the application servers. If required, the SAP employees prompt you to open specific connections. In this case, you must release the respective connections via SAP Service Marketplace using the corresponding software. Depending on the service requested, different connections are available:

- Access to SAP solution using a frontend
- Access to operating systems, for example, using Telnet or pcAnywhere, or servers, such as Citrix or Windows Terminal Server
- Connection to administration tools of different RDBMS

Maximum security

No matter what access type is used, the access must meet maximum security requirements and ensure full access control by the customer. To implement this, a combination of organizational and technical measures is required.

### 15.3.2 SAProuter Program

SAProuter

Connecting the local network to the outside world involves some security risks. Only authorized persons and applications may access the local network and the computers available there. Usually, firewalls are used to protect the access. As an extension at the application level, SAP provides the `SAProuter` program. It's an application level gateway to secure the communication between remote SAP systems or between an SAP system and the outside world. `SAProuter` enables you to control and log all incoming and outgoing connections to local SAP systems. Consequently, it's sufficient that only the computer on which `SAProuter` runs is connected to the WAN. All other computers, particularly application servers and database servers, do not need separate accesses. The administrative networking tasks required center at one point. `SAProuter` is installed on the computer that is the interface between the local network and the outside world.

The computer on which `SAProuter` runs must be available via an officially assigned IP address. In colloquial language, *SAProuter* refers also to the computer on which `SAProuter` runs although it's usually only one of the many functions of this computer. The connection type of the local network to remote systems depends on the customer's preferences concerning costs and benefits. Possible solutions may be based on the following:

- ISDN
- Leased lines
- Internet

The type and scope of the planned use should be the decisive criteria for selecting and dimensioning the connection.

The connection from SAP to the customer is structured in a similar way (see Figure 15.5). The SAP firewall systems and `SAProuter` run on defined computers. Altogether, they are usually called SAProuter, which, strictly speaking, refers only to the computer on which `SAProuter` is installed. Every customer that wants to set up such a connection to the SAP service must first apply for a registration of the respective SAP system at SAP. For this purpose, you must state the IP addresses of the SAP servers and the `SAProuter` computer. SAP stores the customer's IP addresses and releases the access. In return, SAP also operates `SAProuter` computers that are used to create connections to SAP. The `SAProuters` listed in Table 15.2 are currently available at SAP.

| Computer | Location |
|---|---|
| sapserv1 | Connection via the Internet (VPN) |
| sapserv2 | Connection via the Internet (SNC) |
| sapserv3 | Walldorf (Germany) |
| sapserv4 | Philadelphia (USA) |
| sapserv5 | Tokyo (Japan) |
| sapserv6 | Sydney (Australia) |
| sapserv7 | Singapore (Singapore) |

**Table 15.2** Available `SAProuters`

Due to the continuous growth in the number of SAP installations, the range of `SAProuters` is extended on an ongoing basis. Figure 15.5 illustrates the basic process for establishing a connection between the customer system and SAP.

As a prerequisite for a connection, you must ensure that the connection between the `SAProuter` of the customer and the assigned `SAProuter` of SAP, sapservx, can be physically set up. For this purpose, use the operating system command, `ping`.

**Installing SAProuter**

Because it's a part of the standard version, the executable `SAProuter` program is stored in the kernel directory during system installation. You can find the current SAProuter version in SAP Service Marketplace via the quick link, */patches*. You should create a specific directory for SAProuter and the related log and configuration files on the server selected and copy the respective programs into this directory. For faster identification, this directory is often given the name*/usr/sap/saprouter* or *<LW>:\usr\sap\saprouter*.

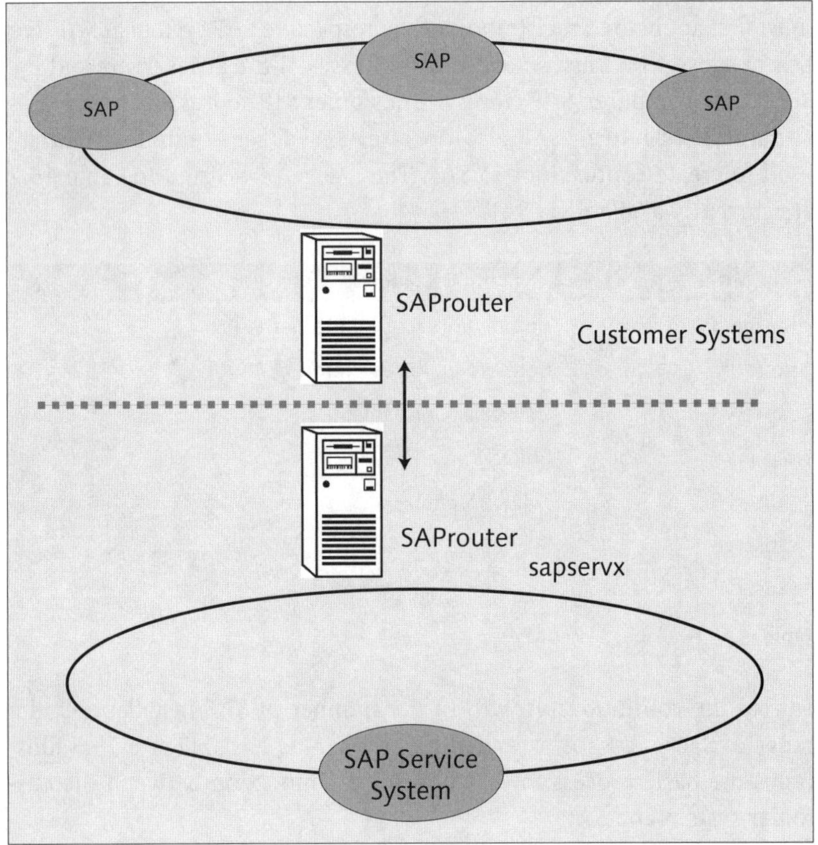


**Figure 15.5** Basic Connection via SAProuter

**Route permission table** To define which connections are permitted or denied, SAProuter analyzes a *route permission table* as the basis for the access control. This table has the standard name *saprouttab* and is more of a text file than a table in the actual sense. It's usually stored in the directory that also contains SAProuter. The entries in the saprouttab table have the following syntax:

```
[P|S|D] <source_system> <target_system> [<service> <password>]
```

The buttons, P, S, and D, stand for the following functions:

- **Permit**
  The connection that follows is explicitly permitted.
- **Secure**
  Only connections via the SAP protocol are permitted. The SAP protocol is an add-on for the TCP/IP protocol; it's only used by SAP components.
- **Deny**
  The connection that follows is explicitely denied.

In addition, you can secure the access by specifying a password. You can use wildcards (*) as placeholders.

For example, possible entries in saprouttab may be:

```
D   194.3.*.* host1
```

In this case, the access to the local computer, host1, were denied for all computers from the 194.3.*.* network, independent of the service requested.

The following entry permits access to ServiceX on host2 for the computer with the IP address 195.7.8.102 by entering the password, Schrat:

```
P   195.7.8.102 host2ServiceX   Schrat
```

If several entries are made for a connection in the routing table, the first suitable entry is used. You may have several routing tables and start SAProuter by entering the saprouttab table that is supposed to be analyzed as required.

Start SAProuter using the saprouter -r command, and stop it using saprouter -s.

Table 15.3 lists the essential options to control the program.

| Option | Meaning |
|---|---|
| -r | Starts SAProuter using the standard route permission table, saprouttab. |
| -s | Stops SAProuter. |
| -n | Reads the route permission table again without restarting SAProuter. Possible changes only affect new connections. |
| -l/-L | Provides output routing information in less/more detail. |
| -t | Changes the trace level 1 -> 2 -> 3 -> 1. |
| -d | Writes detailed connection information to the *dev_rout* file. New information is attached to an already existing file. |
| -T <file> | Changes the name of the log file to <file>. |
| -p | Performs soft shutdown of SAProuter. SAProuter shuts down when all connections are closed. |
| -R <saprouttab> | Assigns any routing table that deviates from the standard |
| -c <id> | Cancels a specific connection with the <id> ID. However, you must first determine the ID using the -l option. |
| -K | Starts SAProuter in an SNC configuration. The argument of the option is the SNC name of the SAProuter server. |
| -G | Starts the option to specify a log file. |
| -V | Starts the option to specify a trace level. |
| -S | Starts the option to specify a deviating port (3299 is the standard port). |

**Table 15.3** Options of the SAProuter Program

From a technical point of view, you can also implement several SAProuters consecutively. However, you then also have to enter all of them.

**Router string**

The SAProuter connection between two communication end points is defined via a *router string*. The router string consists of substrings of the following form:

```
/H/<host/IP_address>/S/<service/port_number>/W/password
```

You must release the route between the local system and SAP's `SAProuter` in *saprouttab*.

### 15.3.3 Configure Users

S user

The users that can access the services in SAP Service Marketplace must be configured specifically. One SAP Service Marketplace user with full administration rights is defined per customer number. This user can then create additional users for the customer number and assign the required rights. You can find this function in SAP Service Marketplace using the */user-admin* quick link. If you enter the customer number, you can also directly request users at the start page of SAP Service Marketplace. The users are then created without authorizations; that is, the SAP Service Marketplace administrator must customize the users on the customer side.

The created IDs always have the S<10-digit_number> form so that they are also referred to as *S users*.

### 15.3.4 Maintenance of Customer Data

To enable the SAP support employees to connect to your systems in emergency situations, you must maintain the access data of the different systems. For this purpose, use the *system-data* quick link provided by SAP Service Marketplace. You must enter the data of the local customer `SAProuter`, a password if required, the system ID, the installation number, and the local IP addresses of the system servers.

## 15.4 Tips

- **Online documentation on the Internet**
  You can find the entire online documentation for SAP solutions and the industry solutions via *help.sap.com*. No ID is required.
- **SAP trainings**
  You can find the entire SAP training catalog via */education* in SAP Service Marketplace. You can also book courses online.

- **Installation and upgrade guides**
  The installation and upgrade guides for all components under maintenance are stored under the */instguides* quick link in the SAP Service Marketplace.
- **SSCR: Requesting developer and object keys**
  A valid license must have been imported to request these keys. A temporary license isn't sufficient.
- **Email notification when the status of customer messages changes**
  Use the message wizard in the SAP Service Marketplace to create customer messages and maintain the email address in your profile. You'll then receive an email when one of your messages has been solved or set to customer action.

## 15.5 Transactions and Menu Paths

**Note Assistant**: No standard menu entry (SNOTE)

**OSS**: System • Services • SAP Service (OSS1)

## 15.6 Additional Documentation

Quick Links

- SAP Service Marketplace, alias *saprouter*
- SAP Service Marketplace, alias *remoteconnection*
- SAP Service Marketplace, alias *internetconnection*
- SAP Service Marketplace, alias *supporttools*
- SAP Service Marketplace, alias *solutionmanager*
- SAP Service Marketplace, alias *dbosmigration*

### SAP Notes

Table 15.4 provides an overview of important SAP Notes concerning service and support topics.

| Content | SAP Note |
| --- | --- |
| Network Provider for Connections to the SAPnet R/3 Frontend | 33953 |
| Schedule Connection to SAP Extranet, OSS, and SAPnet | 137342 |
| Service Connections, Composite Note | 35010 |
| SAProuter Documentation | 30289 |
| Schedule for VPN Connection to the SAP Network | 486688 |
| SAP Support Services – Central Preparation Note | 91488 |
| Service Tools ST-A/PI Applications | 69455 |
| Access to SAP Service Marketplace | 422409 |
| Registration of Developers/Objects | 86161 |

**Table 15.4** SAP Notes Concerning Service and Support Topics

## 15.7 Questions

1. **What is the purpose of the SAProuter program?**
   a. To replace a firewall
   b. To establish remote connections to application servers of an SAP system in a controlled manner
   c. To establish connections between the frontends and application servers of an SAP system in the local network
2. **In which file do you have to maintain the routing data of SAProuter by default?**
   a. saprouttab
   b. DEFAULT.PFL
   c. autoexec.bat
3. **Which prerequisites must be met to enable SAP to establish a service connection to the SAP customer system?**
   a. The SAP system must be registered in the OSS.
   b. The connection data of the application servers of the SAP system and SAProuter must be maintained on the customer side.
   c. The connection must have been opened by the customer.

# Appendices

# A Control Questions and Answers

## Chapter 1: Architecture of SAP NetWeaver Application Server ABAP

1. **Which services are provided by the application layer?**

   a. Communication service

   b. Dialog service

   c. Spool service

   d. Update service

   e. Message service

   f. Transport service

   g. Gateway service

   h. Network service

   i. Enqueue service

   j. Background service

   k. Change service

   Answer: b, c, d, e, g, i, j

2. **Which of the following recommendations is correct?**

   a. The dispatcher and dialog processes should not run together in one instance.

   b. The enqueue server and message server work closely together and, therefore, should be operated in one instance.

   c. The background service and update work closely together and, therefore, should never be operated on different instances.

   Answer: b

3. **What is the purpose of the gateway service?**

   a. Communication between SAP processes

   b. Communication between SAP systems and instances of another SAP system

c. Communication with the spooler of the operating system

d. Connection of external programs such as MAPI, EDI, and telex services

e. Communication with SAP systems

Answer: b, d, e

4. **How many message servers are active in an SAP system?**

 a. 0

 b. 1

 c. 2

 Answer: b

5. **How many update tasks can be active for each instance?**

 a. 1

 b. 2

 c. The SAP system automatically regulates the number, according to requirements.

 d. Any number, depending on the resources available. The administrator must define the number in advance.

 Answer: d

## Chapter 2: Process Concept of SAP NetWeaver Application Server ABAP

### 2.2: Background Processing

1. **Which transaction can you use to analyze job logs?**

 a. SE38

 b. SM37

 c. S000

 Answer: b

2. **Which external programs can you use to trigger events in the SAP system?**

 a. sapevt

 b. sapxpg

   c. sapstart
   d. spmon

   Answer: a

3. **What does the Ready status mean for a background job?**
   a. The job scheduling was completed and saved.
   b. The job was run and is ready for printing the log.
   c. The job is waiting for system resources so that it can begin running.

   Answer: c

### 2.3: Updating

1. **The update was deactivated because of a tablespace overflow. Which actions are required after you extend the tablespace?**
   a. No actions are required; the update is automatically activated again.
   b. The update must be activated.
   c. All update records must be manually updated again.

   Answer: b
2. **What status does an update record have when it's waiting to be updated?**
   a. Active
   b. Released
   c. init
   d. Start

   Answer: c
3. **Which SAP profile parameters can you use to control whether an SAP user is sent a message when his update is canceled?**
   a. rdisp/vbmail
   b. A message is always sent to the user.
   c. rdisp/rbdelete

   Answer: a

### 2.4: Lock Management

1. **Where is the lock table stored?**
   a. In the database
   b. In the enqueue server's main memory
   c. In each application server's main memory

   Answer: b

2. **Are the locks in the lock table also set on the database?**
   a. No
   b. Yes
   c. Only if the locks are unique table locks

   Answer: a

3. **Can you avoid the ENQ work process in a central system?**
   a. Never; it is absolutely essential.
   b. Yes, because the work processes of a central instance communicate directly with the lock table; however, we don't recommend this approach.

   Answer: b

4. **Can the lock table already contain lock entries directly after you start the system?**
   a. Yes, the locks inherited by the update task and saved in a backup file are reloaded into the lock table directly after you start the system.
   b. No, this isn't possible because you did not execute any transactions in the system.

   Answer: a

5. **Is there only a lock table on the enqueue server if there is also an ENQ work process?**
   a. Yes, because the ENQ work process creates the lock table.
   b. This depends on the operating system you're using.
   c. No, there is always a lock table, completely irrespective of whether an ENQ work process exists.

   Answer: c

### 2.5: Output Processing

1. **Which types of access methods are there?**
   a. Local access methods
   b. Remote access methods
   c. Special access methods
   d. Access methods with formatting
   e. Access methods without formatting
   f. Internal access methods
   g. External access methods

   Answer: a, b, c

2. **For which authorizations does SAP provide authorization objects?**
   a. Device authorizations
   b. Display authorizations for spool requests
   c. TemSe administration authorization
   d. Authorizations for operations with spool requests

   Answer: a, b, c, d

3. **Which of the following statements is correct?**

   An output request
   a. is generated by the spool work process from a spool request.
   b. can be printed out several times.
   c. can be output on any printer.

   Answer: a, b

4. **Which access methods are recommended for mass printing?**
   a. Local access method L for transferring data to the host spooler using the corresponding command interface
   b. Local access method C for directly transferring data to the print manager of the host spooler using the corresponding command interface
   c. Local access method F for frontend printing

   d. Remote access method S for the work center printer via SAPLPD
   e. Remote access method U based on the Berkeley protocol

   Answer: a, b

5. **What is a dedicated spool server?**
   a. A selected application server of the SAP system used for managing spools centrally.
   b. The application server assigned to an output device defined in the SAP system. The spool service of the dedicated spool server takes over the formatting and management of the spool requests sent to this device.
   c. The frontend host (desktop) that is currently managing a frontend printing action.
   d. The application server of the SAP system explicitly assigned to a user as a spool server for his spool requests.

   Answer: b

### Chapter 3: Getting Started

1. **Which profile is used to configure the SAP system?**
   a. SAP profile
   b. Instance profile
   c. Application server profile
   d. DEFAULT.PFL
   e. Start profile
   f. Stop profile

   Answer: b, d, e

2. **You're unable to start your SAP system. Where do you find information about the cause of the problem?**
   a. startdb.log
   b. startsap_<host_name>_<instance_number>.log
   c. startsap.log
   d. Developer traces

e. System log

f. SQL trace

Answer: a, b, d

3. **Which of the following statements is correct?**

   a. The SAPLOGON program allows you to define receipts for different SAP systems.

   b. When you use the SAPLOGON program, you no longer have to use the SAP GUI.

   c. The names entered in SAPLOGON must be identical to the SID of the SAP system.

   Answer: a

### Chapter 4: Setting Up the System Landscape

1. **Which of the following statements applies to TMS configuration?**

   a. A transport domain can contain several transport groups.

   b. All systems that access a shared transport directory */usr/sap/trans* are assigned to a transport group.

   c. In a system, only one transport layer can be defined at a specific point in time.

   d. The transport layer indirectly determines the route to the target system.

   Answer: a, b, d

2. **Which statement is applicable?**

   In a multisystem landscape, the transport:

   a. Is only controlled by the system into which data is to be imported or from which data is to be exported.

   b. Is controlled centrally by the Domain Controller of the transport domain.

   c. Is only controlled at the operating system level when you use the `tp` program.

d. Is verified in a transport domain by each SAP system in the domain.

Answer: b, d

3. **Which of the following transport routes do we distinguish between?**

   a. Direct transport route

   b. Indirect transport route

   c. Consolidation route

   d. Delivery route

   e. Alternative route

   Answer: c, d

4. **Which program at the operating system level is responsible for executing transports?**

   a. R3load

   b. SAPinst

   c. tp

   d. dpmon

   e. sapdba

   Answer: c

### Chapter 5: Client Administration

1. **Which of the following statements on the client concept in SAP NetWeaver AS are correct?**

   a. Customizing settings are always client-independent.

   b. A client is a unit within an SAP system that is independent in terms of business accounting.

   c. Each client has its own application data.

   d. Each client has its own technical data independent of the other clients.

   e. Each client has its own application tables.

   Answer: b, c

2. **Which methods of copying clients are offered by SAP NetWeaver AS?**
   a. Local copy
   b. Remote copy
   c. Data exchange procedures
   d. Client export
   e. Data backup

   Answer: a, b, d

3. **Which data can be transmitted in a remote client copy?**
   a. Client-dependent application data
   b. Client-dependent table definitions
   c. Client-independent data
   d. All data in the SAP system

   Answer: a, c

### Chapter 6: Software Logistics

1. **Which statement is correct?**
   a. The transport system for an SAP system is equivalent to copying clients.
   b. The transport system for an SAP system is used for exchanging development and Customizing data between different SAP systems.
   c. The transport system for an SAP system is used for exchanging data between different clients on a single SAP system.

   Answer: b

2. **Which statement is correct?**

   A development class is
   a. a defined group of developers.
   b. client-independent.
   c. assigned to the object when changing an SAP original object.

d. assigned to a transport layer.

Answer: b, d

3. **Which statement is correct?**

   Modifications to SAP-specific objects

   a. must be registered in the OSS.

   b. aren't allowed.

   c. are urgently recommended for the implementation of company-specific processes.

   Answer: a

4. **Which statement is correct?**

   A Repository object in an SAP system

   a. is automatically blocked when a developer makes changes to the object. When the changes are saved, the block is automatically removed.

   b. can only be changed when a corresponding change request is assigned. Thus, the object is automatically locked against changes from all other users until the assigned task and the change request are released by the developer.

   c. can only be changed when a corresponding change request is assigned. Changes to the object can then only be made by the users involved in the change request.

   Answer: c

**Chapter 7: Maintaining Instances**

1. **What is an operation mode?**

   a. An operation mode describes the number and type of work processes of one or more instances.

   b. An operation mode also includes all settings for the SAP main memory areas.

   c. An operation mode designates the status of the SAP system: "active" means operationally ready; "database active" means that only the SAP database is available, and the SAP system is stopped.

   Answer: a

2. **What is a logon group?**
   a. All users assigned to the same user group form a logon group.
   b. A logon group is a logic unit of a subset of all of the application servers of an SAP system.
   c. All users with the same work tasks form a logon group.
   Answer: b

### Chapter 8: SAP Users and Authorizations

1. **Which statement is correct?**
   A user of type *system*
   a. can log on without a password over an RFC interface.
   b. has a password, but the settings for the validity period do not apply to it.
   c. can't log on in dialog mode.
   Answer: b,c
2. **Which statement is correct?**
   a. Exactly one role can be assigned to a user.
   b. Several roles can be assigned to a user.
3. **What can be transported in a role transport?**
   a. The authorization profiles for the role
   b. The definition of the users
   c. The assignment of roles to users
   Answer: b
4. **The authorizations of a role have been expanded. At what point can a user to whom the role was already assigned and who has already logged on work with the changed authorizations?**
   a. The user can use the changed authorizations immediately.
   b. The user can use the changed authorizations after a user comparison.
   c. The user must log on again and can then work with the changed authorizations.

d. A user comparison must occur first. The user must then log on again to be able to work with the changed authorizations.

Answer: d

### Chapter 9: System Monitoring

1. **Into which directory are the developer traces written?**

   a. \users\<sid>adm

   b. \usr\sap\<SID>\<Instance>\work

   c. \usr\sap\<SID>\SYS\global

   Answer: b

2. **A user notifies you that his mode has been canceled with an error. Unfortunately, he can't remember any details about the cancellation. How do you ideally start the analysis?**

   a. Not at all. Without any more detailed information, it's impossible to find the cause for the cancellation.

   b. Check all occurred runtime errors in the SAP system.

   c. Check the system logs.

   d. Check the backup logs.

   Answer: c

### Chapter 11: Architecture Monitoring

1. **Which and how many systems can you monitor using CCMS?**

   a. Only the local SAP system

   b. Several SAP systems but not non-SAP systems

   c. Several SAP systems, including non-SAP systems that have installed corresponding data collectors

   Answer: c

2. **You have discovered that an alert is triggered too often for an MTE, and you change the threshold values. Which statement is correct?**

   a. The changed threshold value definition is only valid for the currently selected MTE.

b. The changed threshold value definition is always valid for the whole MTE class.

c. The whole MTE class is maintained by default when you make a change; however, you can change this setting to maintain individual MTEs also.

d. You can't change the threshold values of an MTE at all.

Answer: c

### Chapter 12: Data Archiving

1. **What is an archiving object?**

   a. CD-ROM or WORM

   b. The archive files created by the archiving run

   c. A logical unit of related data and the necessary archiving programs

   Answer: c

2. **What is data archiving?**

   a. The process of backing up archive logs

   b. The process of archiving any documents such as incoming and outgoing print lists, invoices, or application component documents

   c. The process of removing data from the database and storing it in an archive system or possibly other data media

   Answer: c

3. **Which SAP tool is used during data archiving to transfer data to an archive?**

   a. SAP ArchiveLink

   b. HSM (Hierarchical Storage Management)

   c. ADK (Archive Development Kit)

   d. RFC

   Answer: c

4. **Which statement is correct?**
   a. The entire archiving procedure can take place while the SAP system is running.
   b. The entire archiving procedure can only take place when the SAP system isn't running.
   c. You can't work with the SAP system while archive files are being created.

   Answer: a

### Chapter 13: Data Distribution and Transfer

1. **Which statement is correct?**

   For data distribution based on ALE,
   a. you create a fixed connection between the partner systems.
   b. you loosely couple partner systems during data transfer.
   c. you use functions of the respective RDBMS for data exchange, for example, SAPDBA.

   Answer: b

2. **Which techniques can you use for data exchange?**
   a. CPI-C
   b. Sequential files
   c. tRFC
   d. Internet
   e. Telnet

   Answer: a, b, c, d

3. **How can you re-process tRFCs that were cancelled due to communication errors?**
   a. Automatically by activating the option of automatic retry for the definition of the tRFC connection
   b. Scheduling the job, RSARFCE
   c. Scheduling the job, RSEOUT00

d. Correcting the error and re-implementing the application transaction

Answer: a, b

4. **What is the purpose of the batch input procedure?**

   a. Transferring data from sequential files into the SAP database

   b. Processing mass data in the background

   c. Importing files using the transport control program, `tp`

   Answer: a

## Chapter 14: Installation Concepts

1. **Which statement is true?**

   For a basic SAP installation,

   a. Only the RDBMS must be installed.

   b. One database instance and one central instance must be installed.

   c. The database instance and the central instance can be on one system.

   d. One database instance, one central instance, and at least one application server must be installed.

   Answer: b, c

2. **Which statement is true?**

   a. SAP supports mixed homogeneous system landscapes.

   b. SAP doesn't support mixed homogeneous system landscapes.

   c. SAP only supports mixed homogeneous system landscapes if they are maintained by a certified system administrator.

   Answer: a

3. **Which statement is correct?**

   a. In the case of an MCOD installation, each system to be installed requires an independent database name that differs from other installations.

   b. In the case of an MCOD installation, the database name is determined during the first installation. All other systems must use the same database name.

   c. In the case of an MCOD installation, you can choose any database name for each system to be installed. However, we recommend that you use the same name for all systems.

   Answer: b

**Chapter 15: Service and Support**

1. **What is the purpose of the SAProuter program?**

   a. To replace a firewall.

   b. To establish remote connections to application servers of an SAP system in a controlled manner.

   c. To establish connections between the frontends and application servers of an SAP system in the local network.

   Answer: b

2. **In which file do you have to maintain the routing data of SAProuter by default?**

   a. saprouttab

   b. `DEFAULT.PFL`

   c. *autoexec.bat*

   Answer: a

3. **Which prerequisites must be met to enable SAP to establish a service connection to the SAP customer system?**

   a. The SAP system must be registered in the OSS.

   b. The connection data of the application servers of the SAP system and `SAProuter` must be maintained on the customer side.

   c. The connection must have been opened by the customer.

   Answer: a, b, c

# B Important Transaction Codes

Table B.1 lists the essential transaction codes for SAP NetWeaver system administration. You can enter the SAP transaction codes in the command field of the SAP GUI using the following options:

- **/n<transaction code>**
  The currently active transaction is terminated, and the requested new transaction is started in the same session.
- **/o<transaction code>**
  The new transaction is started in a new session.
- **/h<transaction code>**
  The new transaction is started in the debugging mode of the current session.

In the command field, only enter `/h` without a transaction code, and confirm by pressing [Enter]. From then on, the current transaction runs in debugging mode.

| Transaction Code | Description |
|---|---|
| AL08 | Global User Overview |
| AL11 | Display CCMS Operating System Files |
| AL12 | Buffer Monitoring Tool |
| DB02 | Missing Database Objects and Space Requirement |
| DB12 | SAPDBA Logs |
| DB13 | Weekly Planning |
| FILE | Archiving: Assignment Between Logical and Physical File Name – Cross-Client |
| PFCG | Role Maintenance |
| RZ01 | Graphical Background Job Scheduling Monitor |

**Table B.2** Essential Transaction Codes for SAP NetWeaver System Administration

| Transaction Code | Description |
|---|---|
| RZ03 | Control Panel: Operation Mode and Server Status |
| RZ04 | Instance Maintenance |
| RZ10 | Profile Parameter Maintenance |
| RZ12 | Maintenance of RFC Server Groups |
| RZ20 | Alert Monitor |
| RZ21 | Customizing of the Alert Monitor |
| SA38 | ABAP Reporting |
| SALE | IMG Application Link Enabling |
| SARA | Archive Administration |
| SARI | Archive Information System |
| SC38 | Start Report Remote |
| SC80 | CATT Utilities |
| SCAT | Computer Aided Test Tool |
| SCC1 | Client Copy Using a Transport Request |
| SCC3 | Client Copy Log |
| SCC4 | Client Administration |
| SCC5 | Delete Client |
| SCC6 | Client Import |
| SCC7 | Post-Process Client Import |
| SCC8 | Client Export |
| SCC9 | Remote Client Copy |
| SCCL | Local Client Copy |
| SCMP | View/Table Comparison |
| SCU0 | Customizing Comparison |
| SDBE | Explain an SQL Statement |
| SE01 | Transport Organizer |
| SE03 | Workbench Organizer: Tools |
| SE06 | Set Up Workbench Organizer |

**Table B.1** Essential Transaction Codes for SAP NetWeaver System Administration (Cont.)

| Transaction Code | Description |
|---|---|
| SE07 | CTS Status Display |
| SE09 | Workbench Organizer |
| SE10 | Customizing Organizer |
| SE11 | SAP Data Dictionary Maintenance |
| SE12 | SAP Data Dictionary Display |
| SE14 | Tools for Creating Data Dictionary Tables at the Database Level |
| SE15 | Repository Information System |
| SE16 | Display Table Contents |
| SE17 | General Table Display |
| SE80 | ABAP Development Workbench |
| SE93 | Transaction Code Maintenance |
| SF01 | Archiving: Assignment Between Logical and Physical File Name – Client-Specific |
| SFT2 | Public Holiday Calendar Maintenance |
| SFT3 | Factory Calendar Maintenance |
| SHDB | Record Batch Input |
| SICK | Installation Check |
| SLICENSE | SAP License Administration |
| SM01 | Lock Transactions |
| SM02 | System Messages |
| SM04 | Local User List |
| SM12 | Display and Delete Locks |
| SM13 | Display Update Records |
| SM21 | System Log |
| SM28 | Installation Check |
| SM30 | Call View Maintenance |
| SM31 | Table Maintenance |
| SM35 | Batch Input Monitoring |

**Table B.1** Essential Transaction Codes for SAP NetWeaver System Administration (Cont.)

| Transaction Code | Description |
|---|---|
| SM36 | Schedule Background Jobs |
| SM37 | Overview of Background Jobs |
| SM49 | Execution of External Commands |
| SM50 | Work Process Overview |
| SM51 | Instance Overview |
| SM56 | Number Range Buffer |
| SM58 | Asynchronous RFC Error Log |
| SM59 | RFC Connections (Display and Maintenance) |
| SM63 | Display/Maintain Operating Modes |
| SM64 | Trigger an Event |
| SM65 | Background Processing Analysis Tool |
| SM66 | Global Work Process Overview |
| SM69 | Maintenance of External Operating System Commands |
| SMLG | Maintenance Assignment of Logon Group to Instance |
| SMLI | Language Import |
| SMLT | Language Administration |
| SO00 | SAPoffice: Short Message |
| SO01 | SAPoffice: Inbox |
| SO02 | SAPoffice: Outbox |
| SO03 | SAPoffice: Private Folders |
| SO04 | SAPoffice: Shared Folders |
| SO21 | Maintain PC Work Directory |
| SO99 | Upgrade Information System |
| SP01 | Spool Control |
| SP02 | Display Spool Requests |
| SP11 | TemSe Directory |
| SP12 | TemSe Administration |
| SPAD | Spool Administration |

**Table B.1** Essential Transaction Codes for SAP NetWeaver System Administration (Cont.)

| Transaction Code | Description |
| --- | --- |
| SPAM | SAP Patch Manager (SPAM) |
| SPAU | Display Modified Runtime Environment Objects |
| SPDD | Display Modified DDIC Objects |
| SPRO | Access to Customizing |
| ST01 | SAP System Trace |
| ST02 | Statistics of SAP Buffers |
| ST03 | Workload Analysis |
| ST04 | Statistics on Activities of the Respective RDBMS |
| ST05 | SQL Trace |
| ST06 | Operating System Monitor |
| ST07 | Application Monitor |
| ST10 | Table Call Statistic |
| ST11 | Display Developer Traces |
| ST14 | Application Analysis |
| ST22 | ABAP Runtime Error Analysis |
| STAD | Transaction Statistics (Single Record Statistics) |
| STMS | Transport Management System |
| SU01 | User Maintenance |
| SU01D | User Display |
| SU02 | Maintain Authorization Profiles |
| SU03 | Maintain Authorizations |
| SU05 | Maintain Internet Users |
| SU10 | Mass Changes to User Masters |
| SU12 | Mass Changes to User Masters – Delete All Users |
| SU2 | Maintain Own User Parameters |
| SU20 | Maintain Authorization Fields |
| SU21 | Maintain Authorization Objects |
| SU22 | Authorization Object Usage in Transactions |

**Table B.1** Essential Transaction Codes for SAP NetWeaver System Administration (Cont.)

| Transaction Code | Description |
|---|---|
| SU24 | Adjust SAP Check Indicators |
| SU25 | Profile Generator Upgrade and Initial Installation |
| SU26 | Compare Authorization Checks |
| SU3 | Maintain User's Own Data |
| SU53 | Display Check Values |
| SU56 | Analyze User Buffer |
| SUPC | Mass Generation of Profiles |
| SWDC | Workflow Definition: Administration |
| SWUE | Trigger an Event |
| TU02 | Display Active Parameters |

**Table B.1** Essential Transaction Codes for SAP NetWeaver System Administration (Cont.)

# C Profile Parameters

SAP offers numerous profile parameters. For all profile parameters, SAP already implements fixed default settings upon delivery. Customers may change all parameters but should not change them arbitrarily. Of the wide range of parameters, customers have to customize relatively few parameters; all other parameters may only be customized in consultation with or upon recommendation of SAP. The specific settings made by the customer overwrite the default settings.

The following tables summarize and introduce the essential parameters of SAP NetWeaver.

Table C.1 lists parameters that are only set in SAP's default profile, `DEFAULT.PFL`, and thus affect the entire system.

| Parameter | Meaning |
|---|---|
| `SAPSYSTEMNAME` | Three-digit ID (SID) of the SAP system |
| `SAPDBHOST` | Name of the database server |
| `sna_gateway` | Name of the host on which the SNA gateway runs |
| `sna_gwservice` | Port of the SNA gateway |
| `rdisp/mshost` | Name of the host on which the message server runs |
| `rdisp/vbname` | Instance whose update service serves as the dispatcher of the updates |
| `rdisp/enqname` | Instance that provides enqueue services |
| `rdisp/btcname` | Instance that provides event schedulers |
| `rdisp/bufrefmode` | Parameter for buffer synchronization in distributed systems<br>For central instances: `sendoff/exeauto`<br>For distributed systems: `sendon/exeauto` |

**Table C.1** Parameters in the Default Profile

| Parameter | Meaning |
|---|---|
| rdisp/<br>bufreftime | Time interval between two buffer synchronization processes in<br>seconds<br>Default: 60 |
| auth/no_check_<br>in_some_cases | Activation of the profile generator<br>N inactive<br>Y active (default) |
| dbs/ora/<br>tnsname | Logical name of an Oracle database<br>Identifies the Oracle database if you use Oracle SQL*Net V2; you must store the corresponding name in the *tnsname.ora* configuration file<br>Default: $(SAPSYSTEMNAME) |

**Table C.1** Parameters in the Default Profile (Cont.)

The parameters in Table C.2 are typical parameters in the instance profile. However, you can also use them in the DEFAULT.PFL default profile. The parameter values entered in the default profile apply to the entire system if no other values have been entered in the respective instance profile.

| Area | Parameter | Meaning |
|---|---|---|
| Dialog | rdisp/wp_no_dia | Number of dialog work processes. |
| Spool | rdisp/wp_no_spo | Number of spool work processes. |
| | rspo/store_location | TemSe location.<br>db in the database.<br>G in the global directory of SAP, */usr/sap/<SID>/SYS/global.*<br>L in the local file of the instance, */usr/sap/<SID>/<instance>/data.*<br>T local in the directories, */tmp* (UNIX) or<br>*TEMP* (Windows NT). |

**Table C.2** Parameters and Their Default Values in the Instance Profiles – Part 1

| Area | Parameter | Meaning |
| --- | --- | --- |
| Spool (cont.) | rspo/host_spool/print | Operating system command for printing, including options. |
| | rspo/tcp/retries | Number of tries to connect to a remote output device (access method U).<br>Default: 3 |
| | rspo/tcp/retrytime | Time in seconds between two tries to connect to a remote output device.<br>Default: 300 |
| | rspo/tcp/timeout/connect | Permitted wait time in seconds for connecting to a remote printer.<br>Default: 10 |
| Update | rdisp/wp_no_vb | Number of update work processes. |
| | rdisp/wp_no_vb2 | Number of update work processes for V2 updates. |
| | rdisp/vbreorg | Delete incomplete update requests at a restart of an instance.<br>1 default: active<br>0 inactive |
| | rdisp/vbmail | Notify a user when an update is canceled.<br>1 default: active<br>0 inactive |
| | rdisp/vbdelete | Number of days after which canceled update requests are supposed to be deleted.<br>Default: 50 |
| Background | rdisp/wp_no_btc | Number of background work processes. |

**Table C.2** Parameters and Their Default Values in the Instance Profiles – Part 1 (Cont.)

| Area | Parameter | Meaning |
|---|---|---|
| Background (cont.) | rdisp/btctime | Time interval in seconds between two batch scheduler runs.<br>Default: 60 |
| Enqueue | rdisp/wp_no_enq | Number of enqueue work processes. |
| SAP memory | rsdb/ntab/entrycount | Maximum number of buffer entries in the TTAB buffer.<br>Recommendation: 30,000 |
| | rsdb/ntab/ftabsize | Size of the FTAB buffer (in kilobytes).<br>Recommendation: 30,000 |
| | rsdb/ntab/irbdsize | Size of the IRDB buffer (in kilobytes).<br>Recommendation: 4,000 |
| | rsdb/ntab/sntabsize | Size of the STAB buffer (in kilobytes).<br>Recommendation: 2,500 |
| | rsdb/cua/buffersize | Size of the FTAB buffer (in kilobytes).<br>Recommendation: 5,000 |
| | zcsa/presentation_buffer_area | Size of the Dynpro buffer * 2 (in bytes).<br>Recommendation: 20,000,000 |
| | sap/bufdir_entries | Maximum number of buffer entries in the Dynpro buffer.<br>Recommendation: 4,500 |
| | zcsa/table_buffer_area | Size of the generic buffer (in bytes). |
| | zcsa/db_max_buftab | Maximum number of entries in the generic table buffer. |
| | rtbb/buffer_length | Size of the single record table buffer (in kilobytes). |

**Table C.2** Parameters and Their Default Values in the Instance Profiles – Part 1 (Cont.)

| Area | Parameter | Meaning |
|---|---|---|
| SAP memory (cont.) | rtbb/max_tables | Maximum number of entries in the single record table buffer. |
| | abap/buffersize | Size of the ABAP program buffer. |
| | rsdb/obj/buffersize | Size of the import/export buffer (in kilobytes). |
| | rsdb/obj/max_objects | Maximum number of entries in the import/export buffer. |
| | rsdb/obj/large_object_size | Estimated size of the largest object in the import/export buffer (in bytes). |
| | rdisp/ROLL_MAXFS | Size of the roll area, that is, roll buffer plus roll file (in blocks of 8KB).<br>Recommendation:<br>optimum: 32,000<br>minimum: 16,000 |
| | rdisp/PG_MAXFS | Size of the SAP paging area, that is, paging buffer plus paging file (in blocks of 8KB).<br>Recommendation:<br>optimum: 32,000<br>minimum: 16,000 |
| | rdisp/ROLL_SHM* | Size of the roll buffer (in blocks of 8KB). |
| | rdisp/PG_SHM* | Size of the SAP paging buffer (in blocks of 8KB). |
| | em/initial_size_MB* | Initial size of the extended memory (in megabytes). |
| | em/max_size_MB* | Maximum size of the extended memory (in megabytes; only for Windows NT). |

**Table C.2** Parameters and Their Default Values in the Instance Profiles – Part 1 (Cont.)

| Area | Parameter | Meaning |
|---|---|---|
| SAP memory (cont.) | em/address_space_MB* | The address space reserved for the extended memory (in megabytes; only for Windows NT). |
| | ztta/roll_first* | Size of the first allocated memory area from the roll area in bytes.<br>Recommendation: 1 |
| | ztta/roll_area* | Size of the roll area in bytes<br>Recommendation: 2,000,000 (Windows NT).<br>6,500,000 (other) |
| | ztta/roll_extension* | Amount of memory that can be requested by the work process in the extended memory, in bytes.<br>Recommendation: 2,000,000,000 (Windows NT)<br>1/3 size of the extended memory < (others) |
| | abap/heap_area_dia* | Size of the heap memory in bytes that a dialog process may occupy.<br>Recommendation: Default: 2,000,000,000 |
| | abap/heap_area_nondia* | Size of the heap memory in bytes that nondialog processes may occupy.<br>Default: 400,000,000 |
| | abap/heap_area_total* | Maximum heap memory for all work processes (in bytes). |

**Table C.2** Parameters and Their Default Values in the Instance Profiles – Part 1 (Cont.)

| Area | Parameter | Meaning |
|---|---|---|
| SAP memory (cont.) | abap/heaplimit* | If a work process occupies more memory space than this value specifies in bytes, the work process is automatically restarted after the processing step has been completed in order to release the annexed memory space.<br>Recommendation: 20,000,000 |

**Table C.2** Parameters and Their Default Values in the Instance Profiles – Part 1 (Cont.)

The parameters marked with * are automatically set by the Zero Administration Memory Management for SAP in Windows operating systems (see SAP Note 88416 in the OSS). They should be deleted from the profiles if SAP is used with Windows operating systems. The preceding recommendations apply only to SAP operation in UNIX environments. Table C.3 lists fixed default settings provided by SAP upon delivery.

All recommendations apply only to hosts with a main memory size of at least 500MB for an SAP instance or 750MB for a central SAP system. Refer to *SAP-Performance Optimization Guide* (SAP PRESS, 2008) by Thomas Schneider for additional recommendations.

| Area | Parameter | Meaning |
|---|---|---|
| Alert monitor | alert/ALERTS | File name under which the alerts of the CCMS monitor architecture are stored. |
| Login | login/fails_to_session_end | Number of allowed incorrect logon attempts before SAP GUI will be closed.<br>Default: 3 |
| | login/fails_to_user_lock | Number of allowed incorrect logon attempts before the user will be locked.<br>Default: 12 |

**Table C.3** Parameters and Their Default Values in the Instance Profiles – Part 2

| Area | Parameter | Meaning |
|---|---|---|
| Login (cont.) | login/failed_user_auto_unlock | Unlock locked users on the following day.<br>1 will be unlocked<br>0 remain locked |
| | login/min_password_lng | Required minimum length of passwords.<br>Default: 3 |
| | login/password_expiration_time | Maximum validity period of a password.<br>Default: 0 no restrictions |
| | login/no_automatic_user_sapstar | 0 If the SAP* user is deleted, the automatic user, SAP*, with password PASS is available.<br>1 No automatic user, SAP*. |
| | login/system_client | Default login client. |
| | rdisp/gui_auto_logout | Automatic logout when the user is inactive for a time interval that has been specified in seconds.<br>0 inactive |
| System log | rslg/max_diskspace/local | Maximum size of the file for the local system log. |
| | rslg/max_diskspace/central | Maximum size of the file for the global system log (only UNIX). |
| Trace | rdisp/TRACE | Logging level in developer traces.<br>0 Trace off<br>1 Default: only errors<br>2,3 Extended trace |
| Batch input | bdc/altlogfile | Directory for the reorganization of the batch input log file (RSBDCREO). |

**Table C.3** Parameters and Their Default Values in the Instance Profiles – Part 2 (Cont.)

# D Menu Structures

The following menu trees illustrate the structure of the essential menu entries from the administrator's point of view:

- **Tools • ABAP Workbench**
- **Tools • Administration**
- **Tools • CCMS**

## Tools • ABAP Workbench

**Overview**

Application Hierarchy

  - SAP
  - Customer

Object Navigator

Business Object Browser

Modification Browser

Reuse Library

Info System

Data Browser

Workbench Organizer

BAPI Explorer

**Development**

Dictionary

Data Modeler

Finish

  - Menu Painter
  - Screen Painter

ABAP Editor

Function Builder

Class Builder

Context Builder

Shared Objects Area Management

Shared Objects Monitor

Programming Environment

- Text Elements
- Logical Databases
- Messages
- Syslog Messages
- Split-Screen Editor
- Dialog Modules
- OLE
    - OLE2 Configuration
    - OLE Demo

Business Object Builder

SAP Business Workflow

- ......
- More Tools
- Authorization Objects
    - Fields
    - Objects
    - Field Selection
    - Number Ranges
    - Change Documents
    - Application Log
    - Gen. Tab Maintenance Dialog
    - NLS: Character Sets, Languages, Locales
    - Transactions
    - Area Menus

**Test**

- Runtime Analysis
- SQL Trace

Test Workbench

- Test Repository
- Test Organizer
  - Test Catalog Management
  - Test Plan Management
  - Info System
  - Central Settings
- Test Tools
  - Extended CATT
  - CATT
- Executing the Test

Coverage Analyzer

Code Inspector

Runtime Monitor

System Log

Dump Analysis

Setups/Tune Buffers

Extended Analysis

QA Worklist

Current Setting for Checkpoint Groups

Memory Inspector

**Utilities**

Documentation

Key Word Documentation

Demos

Sample Library

Internationalization

Translation

- Short and Long Texts
- ABAP Query

Maintenance

- Support Package Manager
- Correct Workbench
- Upgrade Utilities
    - Compare Dictionary
    - Compare Programs
    - Quick Viewer
- SAP Query
    - Queries
    - InfoSets
    - User Groups
- Business Add-Ins
    - Definition
    - Implementation
- Enhancements
    - Definition
    - Project Management

**Tools • Administration**

**Administration**

System Messages

SAP Licenses

Transaction Administration

Installation Check

Network

- Maintenance of the HTTP Service Tree
- RFC Destinations
- TXCOM Maintenance
- THOST Maintenance

Client Administration

- Client Maintenance
- Client Copy
    - Local Copy
    - Remote Copy
- Special Functions
    - Copy Transport Request
    - Delete Client
- Client Transport
    - Client Export
    - Import Follow Up
- Copy Logs
- Customizing Objects
    - Cross-System Viewer
    - Object Comparison

Language Administration

System Measurement

Consolidate System Measurement

Data Archiving

NLS: Character Sets, Languages, Locales

**Monitor**

System Monitoring

- Process Overview
- Server
- User Overview
- Gateway Monitor
- Message Server Monitor
- ICM Monitor
- ICF Display of Recorded Objects

Updating

Batch Input

Transactional RFC

Performance

- System Load
    - Aggregated Statistical Records – Local
    - Aggregated Statistical Records – Global
    - Individual Statistical Records (only ABAP)
    - Individual Statistical Records (all) and Traces
    - User Distribution
- Settings/Buffer
    - Buffer
    - Table Accesses
    - Parameter Changes
- Operating System
    - Local
        - Activity
        - System Configuration
        - Parameter Changes
    - Remote
        - Activity
        - System Configuration
        - Parameter Changes
    - Network
        - LAN Check via PING
    - SAPOSCOL Destination
- Database
        - Activity
        - Exclusive Locks
        - Tables/Indices
        - Parameter Changes
- Exceptions/Users
    - Exceptions
        - System Log

        - ABAP Runtime Error
        - SAP Directory Paths
    - Active Users
        - Process Overview
        - Global Process Overview
        - SAP Instances
        - Local Users
        - Global Users
        - Traces
        - Performance Trace
        - SAP System Trace
        - Developer Traces
        - Activate ST05 Context Trace
    - Search Engine
        - TREX Administration
        - SES Index Monitor
    - System Log
    - Security Audit Log
        - Configuration
        - Analysis
        - Reorganization
- Dump Analysis
- Lock Entries
- Number Range Buffer
- User Buffer
- System Administration Assistant

User Maintenance

- Users
- Display Users
- User Mass Maintenance
- User Groups
- Enterprise Address

- Info System
  - .......
- Central User Administration
  - ALE Customizing
  - Distribution Model
  - Field Selection
  - User Transfer
  - Log Display
- Role Administration
  - Roles
  - Compare User Master
  - Generate Profiles for Roles
  - Authorizations and Profiles (Manual Maintenance)
  - Edit Authorizations Manually
  - Edit Profiles Manually

Transports

- Transport Organizer
- Transport Management System

**Tools • CCMS**

**Control/Monitoring**

- CCMS Monitor Collections

Central Performance History (CPH)

Control Panel

Global Process Overview

Execute External Commands

Performance

- System Load
  - Aggregated Statistical Records – Local
  - Aggregated Statistical Records – Global

    - Individual Statistical Records (only ABAP)
    - Individual Statistical Records (all) and Traces
    - User Distribution
- Settings/Buffer
    - Buffer
    - Table Accesses
    - Parameter Changes
- Operating System
    - Local
        - Activity
        - System Configuration
        - Parameter Changes
    - Remote
        - Activity
        - System Configuration
        - Parameter Changes
    - Network
        - LAN Check via PING
    - SAPOSCOL Destination
- Database
    - Activity
    - Exclusive Locks
    - Tables/Indices
    - Parameter Changes
- Exceptions/Users
    - Exceptions
        - System Log
        - ABAP Runtime Error
        - SAP Directory Paths

        - Active Users
            - Process Overview
            - Global Process Overview
            - SAP Instances
            - Local Users
            - Global Users

**Configuration**

Properties and Methods

Operation Modes/Instances

Operation Mode Calendar

System Profiles

Logon Groups

Display/Change External Commands

**DB Administration**

Backup Logs

DBA Planning Calendar

- Local
- Central

Operation Monitor

Cost Optimization

- Statistics Creation
- Configuration

Check

- Monitor
- Configuration

DB Connection Maintenance

DB Parameters

Data Archiving

**Print**

- Output Control

Printing Assistant for Landscape

Spool Administration

Font Maintenance

TemSe Content

TemSe Administration

**Background Processing**

- Define Job

Jobs – Overview and Management

Job Planning Monitor

Maintain Events

Trigger Event

Check Settings

Background Objects

Execute External Commands

**Data Transfer Workbench**

**Easy Enhancement Workbench**

# E Glossary

**ABAP** Advanced Business Application Programming. Programming language of the SAP system to develop applications programs.

**ABAP dictionary** Central metadata of all objects in the SAP system.

**ACID** Describes the basic properties of transaction management in the area of databases as well as SAP: Atomic, Consistent, Isolated, Durable.

**ADK** Archive Development Kit. Comprises tools for defining business-related data to form a logical archiving unit (archiving object), methods for transferring data to be archived as function modules to an archive file, sample programs, documentation, archive management to start the programs, data transfer control, and network graphics to map dependencies between archivable data.

**ADO** Active Data Object. Application-defined object.

**ALE** Application Link Enabling. ALE is a technology to create and operate distributed applications. The basic concept of ALE is to guarantee a distributed but integrated SAP installation. This involves business-controlled message exchange using consistent data stored across loosely coupled SAP applications.

Applications are integrated using synchronous and asynchronous communication, not by using a central database.

You can use the ALE distribution model to distribute business objects across the systems of an SAP landscape.

ALE consists of three layers: application services, distribution services, and communication services.

**Alert monitor** Graphical monitor to analyze system states and events.

**ANSI** American National Standards Institute.

**API** Application Programming Interface. An API is a logically related record of interfaces (functions or services) that can be used by an application of predefined functions.

**APPC** Advanced Program to Program Communication. Program-to-program communication within the IBM world, based on the LU6.2 protocol.

**Application server** Computer on which at least one SAP instance is located.

**ArchiveLink** Communication interface between SAP components and external components that is integrated into the Basis component of the SAP system. SAP ArchiveLink includes the following interfaces:

User interface: interface to the SAP applications

Interface to external components: archive systems, viewer systems, scan systems

**Archiving object** Logical object of business-related data in a database. The data is read from the database by an archiving program and deleted from the database by the respective delete program after the data has been successfully archived.

**ASAP** Accelerated SAP. Standardized procedure model to implement SAP solutions.

**BAPI** Business Application Programming Interface. A standardized programming interface that facilitates external access to business processes and data in the SAP system.

**Batch input** Methods and tools to quickly import data from sequential files or spreadsheets into the SAP database.

**Operation mode** Defined number and types of work processes of one or more instances in a specified period. Operation modes can be switched automatically.

**CCMS** Computing Center Management System. Tool to monitor, control, and configure the SAP system. The Computing Center Management System supports 24/7 system administration functions. You can analyze and distribute the system load as well as monitor the resource requirements of the different system components.

**Control Panel** Central tool to monitor the SAP system and its instances.

**CPI-C** Common Programming Interface Communication. Basic programming interface for synchronous, cross-system program-to-program communication.

**CTS** Change and Transport System. The Change and Transport System provides the tools to organize development projects in Customizing and in the ABAP Workbench and transport the changes between SAP systems and their clients. The CTS consists of the following three blocks: Transport Organizer, Transport Management System, and Transport Tools.

**Customizing** Adjusting an SAP component to customer-specific requirements by selecting variants, parameter settings, and so on.

**Data archiving** Relocating data that is currently no longer used from the relational database into archives (see also archiving object).

**Database** A database comprises files that are required for permanent data storage on a hard disk and one or more database instances. There's only one database in each SAP system.

**Database instance** Administrative unit that enables database access. A database instance consists of database processes with a shared record of database buffers in the shared memory. Usually, there's only one database instance in each database. DB2/390 is an example of a database system where one database may comprise several database instances.

In an SAP system, a database instance may be located alone or together with one (or several) SAP instance(s) on one computer.

**Database server** Computer on which (at least) one database instance is located.

**DBA** Database administrator.

**DCL** Data Control Language. Language elements to control user transactions.

**DDL** Data Definition Language. Language elements to define relations.

**Deadlock** Several transactions keep locking themselves while each waits for the other to release blocked objects.

**DIAG protocol** Communication protocol between SAP GUI and dialog work processes of the SAP application level.

**Dialog work process** SAP work process to process user requests that run in dialog mode.

**Dispatcher** Coordinated process of the work processes of an instance.

**DML** Data Manipulation Language. Language elements to request and change data.

**Button** Element of the graphical user interface. Clicking on the button once executes the function that is assigned to this button. You can use the mouse to trigger the button and also the keys on your keyboard. For this purpose, position the cursor on the respective button and press the Enter key, or use the Enter button. Buttons may contain text and/or graphical icons.

**Dynpro** DYNamic PROgram that consists of a screen image and the underlying flow logic.

**EDI** Electronic Data Interchange. Cross-enterprise electronic exchange of structured data (e.g., business documents) between domestic and international business partners that use different hardware, software, and communication services. For this purpose, the data is formatted according to defined standards.

**eCATT** extended Computer Aided Test Tool. You can use this tool to generate test data as well as automate and test business processes.

**FDDI** Fiber Distributed Data Interchange.

**Firewall** Software to protect a local network against unauthorized access from outside.

**Frontend computer** "Generally, a computer or processing unit that produces and manipulates data before another processor receives it." (Computer Fachlexikon, Microsoft Press).

**GUI** Graphical User Interface. Medium that allows users to exchange information with the computer. On the user interface, you can choose commands, start programs, display files, and perform other functions by using function keys or buttons, selecting menu options, and clicking on icons.

**Background processing** Processing that doesn't take place on the screen. Background processing enables you to process data in the background while other functions are executed on the screen at the same time. Background processes have the same priority as online processes, although they aren't visible to users and run without immediate user interactions (i.e., there's no dialog).

**High availability** Property of a service or a system to remain in productive operation for a large proportion of the time. High availability for an SAP system means that unplanned and planned downtime are kept to a minimum. Well managed system administration plays a key role in this. Reduction of unplanned downtime can be achieved by preventive hardware and software solutions whose goal is to reduce single points of failure in the services that support the SAP system. Reduction of planned downtime can be achieved by optimal scheduling of necessary maintenance activities.

**HSM** Hierarchical Storage Management. Software and hardware to archive data. An HSM system manages data internally, based on the access frequency in a hierarchical structure, and represents itself as an unlimited file system to the application.

**HTML** Hypertext Markup Language. Platform-independent language to create text and graphics pages in the Internet.

**HTTP** Hypertext Transfer Protocol. Protocol to transfer data between a Web server and the Web client.

**IAC** Internet Application Component. Complete business solutions to link the SAP system to the Internet. Internet application components (IACs) allow Internet users to process business processes via the Internet or intranet by executing transactions, functions, and reports via the interface of a web browser.

**ICM** Internet Connection Manager. Infrastructure that allows you to access an SAP NetWeaver system via the Web (HTML access).

**IDES** International Demo and Education System. IDES contains several sample enterprises that provide a model for mapping the relevant business processes in the SAP system. Its simple user guides and variety of master and transaction data enable you to run through complex scenarios. IDES is an excellent training tool for the project team.

**IDoc** Intermediate Document. IDoc type that is filled with specific data.

**IDoc type** SAP format for transferring the data of a business process. An IDoc is a concrete business process formatted in the IDoc type. An IDoc type is described using the following components:

A control record
Whose format is identical for all IDoc types.

One or more data records
A data record consists of a fixed administrative part and a data part (segment).

The number and format of the segments can be different for each IDoc type.

Status records
They describe the processing stages through which an IDoc can pass. Status records have an identical format for all IDoc types.

**IMG** Implementation Guide. A tool for configuring the SAP System to meet customer-specific requirements. The implementation guide contains the following elements for each application component:

All steps for implementing the SAP system.

All default settings and activities for configuring the SAP system.

The hierarchical structure of the IMG maps the structure of the SAP application component and lists all of the documentation that is relevant for implementing the SAP system.

**Instance** SAP instance. Administrative unit that groups processes of an SAP system that provide one or more services.

An SAP instance can provide the following services:

D: Dialog

V: Updating

E: SAP lock management (enqueue)

B: Background processing

S: Print formatting (spool)

G: SAP gateway

An SAP instance consists of a dispatcher and one or more work processes for each of the services as well as a shared record of SAP buffers in the shared memory.

The dispatcher manages processing requests, and work processes execute these requests. Each instance provides at least one dialog service and one gateway. Optionally, the dispatcher can provide additional services. However, there must be only one instance that provides the SAP lock management service.

**IPC** Inter Process Communication.

**ITS** Internet Transaction Server. Interface between the SAP system and a Web server to generate dynamic HTML pages.

**LAN** Local Area Network. Network within a location that usually provides higher data transfer rates compared to the WAN environment.

**LDAP** Lightweight Directory Access Protocol. Protocol for accessing information directories. LDAP enables every application on any platform to access directory information, such as email addresses and public keys. LDAP is an open protocol; consequently, it's not relevant for the user on which server type the directory is located.

**LUW** Logical Unit of Work. From the point of view of business logic, an inseparable sequence of database operations that meets the ACID principles. From the point of view of a database system, this sequence constitutes a unit that ensures data integrity.

**Client** In commercial, organizational, and technical terms, a self-contained unit in an SAP system with separate master records within a table.

**MAPI** Messaging Application Programming Interface. Interface that enables you to read SAPoffice emails from other applications (MAPI clients), such as Microsoft Outlook.

**MCOD** Multiple Components in One Database. Combined installation of OLTP and OLAP components of an SAP system landscape in a database. This reduces the database administration costs.

**Session** User session in an SAP GUI window.

**OLE** Object Linking and Embedding.

**OLTP** Online Transaction Processing. Processing related to data updating.

**OMS** Output Management System.

**OS** Operating system.

**OSS** Online Service System. The OSS is one of SAP's central service and support systems. It can be used by all SAP customers and partners. New service offers, however, are exclusively provided via SAP Service Marketplace.

**PAI** Process After Input. Programming processes after data has been entered into a screen template (for applications developed in ABAP).

**PBO** Process Before Output. Programming processes before a screen template is displayed (for applications developed in ABAP).

**Performance** System throughput; throughput measures the efficiency of an IT system.

**Popup** A window that is called by and inserted into a primary window.

**Port** Description of the channel used by the SAP system for exchanging electronic data with an external system.

**Profile** 1. Technical collection of authorizations that is automatically generated by the profile generator during role maintenance.

2. File at the operating system level that is used to parameterize the SAP system at the start (e.g., instance profile).

**Profile generator** Tool for generating profiles in role maintenance. The authorization profiles are generated automatically based on the activities in a role.

**Q-API** The queue application programming interface facilitates buffered asynchronous data transfer between remote applications and SAP systems based on CPI-C.

**RAID** Redundant Array of Independent Disks. RAID is a hardware-based technology that supports disk redundancy by using disk mirroring and similar methods.

**RDBMS** Relational Database Management System.

**RFC** Remote Function Call. RFC is an SAP interface protocol based on CPI-C that considerably simplifies the programming of communication processes between systems. RFCs enable you to call and execute predefined functions in a remote system or in the same system. RFCs manage the communication process, parameter transfer, and error handling.

**Role** The collection of activities that a person performs to participate in one or more business scenarios of an organization. A roles is defined by authorizations, reports, and user menus.

**SAP GUI** SAP Graphical User Interface (see GUI).

**SAProuter** Software module that acts as a part of a firewall system and controls the network connections between your SAP network and external networks (e.g., SAPNet connection).

**Server** The term "server" has several meanings in the SAP world and should thus only be used when it refers to a logical unit, such as an SAP instance, or a physical unit, such as a computer.

**Shared memory** Main memory area that can be accessed by several operating system processes, for example, by all work processes of an instance. Also used in the area of RDBMS. In this context, it also refers to the main memory area shared by the RDBMS processes.

**SID** SAP System Identifier. Placeholder for a name of an SAP system with three characters.

**SNC** Secure Network Communication. Interface that allows SAP to communicate with an external security product to protect the communication links between the components of an SAP system.

**SQL** Structured Query Language.

**SSCR** SAP Software Change Registration. Procedure that registers all manual modifications to SAP sources and SAP Repository objects.

**Support package** Set of corrections for errors provided by SAP for a defined release status of an SAP component (previously, hot package).

**System landscape** Specific combination of systems installed at a customer site. The system landscape describes the systems and clients required and their significance, as well as the transport routes for the implementation and maintenance processes. Methods and technologies in the foreground are particularly the process of copying clients and the transport system. The system landscape may, for example, consist of a development system, a test system, a consolidation system, and a production system.

**TCP/IP** Transmission Control Protocol/Internet Protocol.

**TDC** Transport domain controller. Application server of an SAP system of the transport domain, in which the transport route configuration between the SAP systems of the transport domain is controlled.

**TemSe** Temporary Sequential objects. Data storage of the output management.

**TMS** Transport Management System. Tools to manage transport requests between SAP systems.

**TO** Transport Organizer. Comprehensive tool for managing and organizing all change and transport request.

**Transaction code** Sequence of alphanumeric characters that identifies a transaction in the SAP system.

**Transaction** Database transaction: Operational unit on a database that meets the ACID principles.

**SAP transaction (=SAP LUW)** Logical process in the SAP system that is a self-contained unit from the user's point of view. An SAP transaction ensures that ACID principles are met across several database transaction steps. Short form for transaction code that can be used to call an ABAP program.

**Transport** A concept of SAP's software logistics: Exporting and importing SAP objects between SAP systems.

**Transport domain** Logical group of SAP systems to which defined rules apply for transport. The transport domain controller controls the transport domain.

**tRFC** Transactional RFC. RFC to which the ACID principles apply.

**URL** Uniform Resource Locator. Internet address.

**WAN** Wide Area Network. Network that covers rather long geographical distances. WANs usually consist of at least two LANs (Local Area Networks). Computers connected to such a network are usually linked via public networks, such as the telephone network. They can also be linked via rented lines or satellites. The largest WAN is the Internet.

**WORM** Write Once, Read Many. Memory medium that can be written once but can be read as many times as required. WORM ensures that data stored on this medium can't be changed for several years. It's mainly used for data archiving.

**WP** Work process. The application services of the SAP system process-specific processes, for example, for dialog management, change documents updates, background processing, spooling, and lock management. Work processes are assigned to dedicated application servers.

**XML** eXtensible Markup Language. A specification of the W3C. XML is a lean version of SGML, which has been especially developed for web documents. It enables you to generate specific tags to provide functions that can't be implemented using HTML. For example, XML supports links to several documents. HTML links, in contrast, can only refer to one document. XML has been accepted as the standard for data exchange. In the SAP world, XML is used for data exchange with external system as well as the markup language in the configuration files of the installation (from Basis Release 6.10).

# F References

Rajeev, Kasturi, *SAP R/3 ALE & EDI Technologies* (McGraw Hill, 1999).

Armin Kösegi, and Rainer, Nerding, *SAP Change and Transport Management*. (Bonn, Germany: SAP PRESS, 2006).

SAP AG, *Online Documentation Release SAP NetWeaver 2004s. http://help.sap.com*.

SAP AG, *SAP NetWeaver 2004s Installation Guide. http://service.sap.com/instguides*.

SAP AG, *SAPinst Troubleshooting Guide V1.20. http://service.sap.com/sapinst*.

SAP AG, *Language Import Guide. http://service.sap.com/instguides*.

SAP AG, *Online Help Installation Guides. http://service.sap.com/instguides*.

SAP AG, *Security Guides Volumes I-III. http://service.sap.com/securityguides*.

SAP Labs, *SAP Guide to System Administration* (Bonn, Germany: SAP PRESS, 2002).

Thomas Schneider, *SAP Performance Optimization Guide*. (Bonn, Germany: SAP PRESS, 2008).

Helmut Stefani, *Archiving Your SAP Data*. (Bonn, Germany: SAP PRESS, 2007).

# G The Authors

**Frank Föse** has worked as a Technology and Performance Consultant at SAP Systems Integration AG in Ratingen, Germany since 2001. His support work focuses on the areas of system analysis and system tuning, sizing for SAP landscapes, and performance optimization in complex applications. Even before finishing his degree in industrial engineering, Frank worked with SAP technology. After completing his studies, he worked as an SAP system administrator in a medium-sized pharmaceutical company, where he supported the SAP implementation project and the system go-live.

**Sigrid Hagemann** joined SAP Systems Integration AG in Bensheim, Germany in 2001, where she works in Business Consulting Technology in the IT management and technology consulting areas. The main focus of her work is consulting for SAP customers to optimize the operation of their system landscapes. The Mathematics graduate began working with SAP technology in 1993 when she took on a role in the Fujitsu Siemens Competence Center in Walldorf, Germany.

**Liane Will** has been working in the Active Global Support department at SAP AG since 1998. She supports customers with the implementation and optimization of their system operations and with managing their SAP solutions. Based on her extensive support experience, she is already the author of a number of books (published by SAP PRESS) on best practices in system administration. Before she joined SAP, Liane developed SAP support tools for databases.

# Index

## A

## B



## C

## D

## E



## F



## G



## H

## M



## N

## O



## P

## Q



## R

## S

## T

## X



## Z

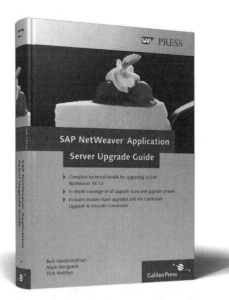

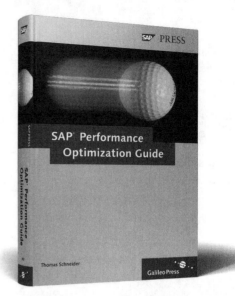